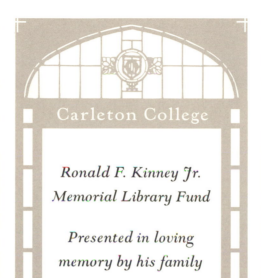

THE FURIES

ARNO J. MAYER

The Furies

*Violence and Terror in
the French and
Russian Revolutions*

* * *

PRINCETON UNIVERSITY PRESS

PRINCETON, NEW JERSEY

Library of Congress Cataloging-in-Publication Data
Mayer, Arno J.
The furies : violence and terror in the French and Russian
Revolutions / Arno J. Mayer.
p.   cm.
Includes bibliographical references and index.
ISBN 0-691-04897-5 (cl : alk. paper)
1. France—History—Revolution, 1789–1799—Influence
2. Soviet Union—History—Revolution, 1917–1921—
Influence. 3. Political violence—France. 4. Political violence—
Soviet Union. 5. France—History—Reign of
Terror, 1793–1794. 6. Terror—Soviet Union. I. Title.
DC183.5 .M35 2000
944.04—dc21   99-059145

ALSO BY ARNO J. MAYER

Why Did the Heavens Not Darken? The "Final Solution"
in History

The Persistence of the Old Regime:
Europe to the Great War

Dynamics of Counterrevolution in Europe, 1870–1956

Politics and Diplomacy of Peacemaking:
Containment and Counterrevolution at Versailles,
1918–1919

Political Origins of the New Diplomacy,
1917–1918

To Ruth

Of all the passions, hatred of the *ancien régime* was paramount. No matter how much people suffered and trembled, they always considered the hazards of a return to the old order worse than all the pains and vicissitudes of their day and age.

Alexis de Tocqueville

The task to be accomplished is not the conservation of the past, but the redemption of the hopes of the past.

Max Horkheimer and
Theodor W. Adorno

CONTENTS

✳ ✳ ✳

CONTENTS

PART FOUR
THE SACRED CONTESTED

PART FIVE
A WORLD UNHINGED

PREFACE

* * *

THIS BOOK, like any historical work, has a history, and it was crafted in a specific political and historiographic context. In 1987, I finished *Why Did the Heavens Not Darken?* and resumed work on the sequel to *The Persistence of the Old Regime*, which I had put aside to ponder and search into the Judeocide. But a turbulence in the surrounding political and intellectual atmosphere distracted me.

I spent much time in France in 1987–90, the years of the rites of the bicentennial of the French Revolution, in which historians were prominent officiants. There was nothing exceptional about French historians, particularly the public intellectuals among them, playing their self-assigned roles. They had been doing so practically ever since 1789, taking three distinct positions: abjure and excoriate the Revolution, root and branch; redeem the "revolution without a revolution" over against the radical revolution of the Terror; exalt and justify the Revolution, *en bloc*. There is something archetypal about these three positions: since 1917 they have defined the debates about the Russian Revolution, except that the third position eventually split in two over the question of the continuity or break between Lenin and Stalin.

The "crescendo of violence" (Jules Michelet) has been the single most important defining issue of the indomitable debate about the Great Revolution. For the bicentennial, French historians reenacted the tried and true battle between the prosecutors who blame one or more ideologically driven political leaders for the spiraling Furies, including the Terror, and the defenders who attribute them to the force of circumstance. Indeed, it seemed as if old polemical wine was being poured into new historiographic bottles.

Presently, however, the bicentennial debate became singularly polemical and impassioned. In part this was so because as may be expected, it served as a screen for heated arguments about France's unmastered recent past. Had Vichy been the last stand of the counterrevolution dating from 1789, shielded by Nazi Germany? Had the French Communists, since the 1930s, been nothing but latter-day Jacobins, subservient to Soviet Russia? Not unrelated, the great historical ventilation was marked by the changing Zeitgeist which, in turn, it helped to shape. Because or in spite of the return of the tempered "left" to power in France in 1981, there was a vigorous resurgence of the far "right" and of traditional conservatism. This political and intellectual mutation coincided with the ascendancy of Ronald Reagan and Margaret Thatcher, along with their neoconservative clerks, in the United States and Great Britain, as well as with the breakthrough of *glasnost* and *perestroika* in East Central Europe and Russia. Simultaneously, academic Marxism was going out with the tide.

This was the context in which ultraconservative historians resurfaced to revive and update their position: they argued that in addition to being an inexpiable sin, the French Revolution was the ultimate source of all the purgatorial fires of the twentieth century. No doubt these latter-day "counterrevolutionaries" would have remained inconsequential had they not found soul mates, not to say fellow travelers, among moderate conservatives and new-model liberal democrats. Among them in particular the ex-Communist renegades, who by European standards carried disproportionate weight in the Parisian intelligentsia, became vital intermediaries: even if unintentionally, they legitimated the resurgent die-hard position and its champions, and made them *salonfähig* in the 6th and 7th arrondissements. Georg Simmel, founder of "formal" sociology, incisively conceived renegades to be sworn to a "distinctive loyalty" because rather than "naively grow . . . into a new political, religious, or other party," they join it after having broken with a previous one, which never ceases to "repel" and incense them.

The inverted true-believers took two successive steps to concretize the charge of the right-wing resurgence, in the process emerging as its chief and emblematic voice. First, they postulated the essential sameness of the ultimate causes and inner workings of the crescendo of violence of the French and Russian revolutions: Robespierre, Rousseau, and the Great Terror were said to be all but analogous with Lenin/Stalin, Marx, and the Gulag. They read the Jacobin Terror by the light of the Bolshevik Terror at the same time that they asserted that the rule of fear and blood of 1793–94 had been the dress rehearsal and portent for that of 1917–89.

Their second step was to stretch the analogic fabric to comprise the Third Reich. The Soviet and Nazi regimes were deemed to be fundamentally if not wholly identical: both were variants of the same totalitarianism, whose philosophic roots reached back to the Jacobin moment. Whatever the dissimilarities between the two regimes—there was no Soviet equivalent for Nazism's genocidal racism—they were outweighed not only by the likenesses of their structures and methods of domination but also by the purpose of their murderous Furies. Compared to the line of descent from the Jacobin to the Bolshevik terror, that between the Bolshevik and Nazi terrors was not only immediate but material: by virtue of their chronological head start the Cheka/KGB and the Gulag presumably served as models for the SS state and concentration camps which Hitler set up to better fight Bolshevism at home and abroad. The ground was being seeded for the rehabilitation and justification of the anti-Communist warrant of Fascism and National Socialism, including of Vichy France's "national revolution."

There were important family resemblances between the *querelle des historiens* in France and the concurrent *Historikerstreit* in Germany, particularly the style of intellection and political purpose of the "assailants." Oblivious to space and time, and making no effort to curb their "virus of present-mindedness" (Marc Bloch), they forced the similarities between the Soviet and Nazi systems, leaving little room for basic differences and contrasts, notably concerning the reason and role of terror and war. Profoundly troubled, I considered turning to a comparative and interactive study of the Soviet and Nazi Furies which would not be a portrait in black and white. But the prospect of plunging, once more, into the Judeocide gave me pause.

At this point, in late 1989, my good friend Maurice Agulhon extended an invitation for me to lecture at the Collège de France on Europe's *ancien régime* between the two world wars. I refused, insisting that the bicentennial debate had thrown me off course. In conversation, over wine, I complained at some length about the transparent insufficiencies of the ongoing comparisons of the crescendos of violence in revolutionary France and Russia. Having vented my spleen, I facetiously suggested that I speak on this topic, about which I was in total ignorance. Instead of sending me packing, Maurice Agulhon reached for pen and paper and wrote down the title for a lecture series: *Violence et Terreur aux Temps de la Révolution Française et de la Révolution Russe*. These *leçons*, delivered in Spring 1991, became the foundation for this book.

An objective and value-free study of the most harrowing and controversial aspects of the revolutionary phenomenon is, of course, a logical impossibility. Paul Ricoeur rightly insists that there is no greater pretense than to allege that "ideology is the thinking of my adversary, that it is the thinking of the *other*." In dealing with the crescendo of violence it is difficult to strike a reasonable balance between explanation and condemnation, understanding and justification, detachment and proximity. No doubt by overreacting to historians who blithely assume the role of the prosecutor, judge, and moralizer, I lay myself open to the charge of assuming that of the cynic or apologist. Such is the risk—but also the intellectual challenge and responsibility—of "brushing history against the grain" (Walter Benjamin) and of striving for empathetic understanding of the Furies.

This work does not cover all aspects of the French and Russian revolutions. Instead, it is, specifically, a conceptually informed probe of their upward spirals of violence and terror. Based primarily on secondary sources, it intends to open new perspectives rather than present new facts. Because of the distinctly more thorough and sophisticated scholarship on the Jacobin than on the Bolshevik Furies, the former is of considerable heuristic importance for the study of the latter. At the same time, and paradoxically, there is a need to recover greater empathetic nearness to the French Revolution, which is over-studied and over-objectified, and to seek greater critical distance from the Russian Revolution, whose historiography is only beginning to be extricated from deafening and blinding polemics.

By choosing *The Furies* as the main title of this book, I mean to suggest that much of the revolutionary violence and terror, by virtue of being fear-inspired, vengeance-driven, and "religiously" sanctioned, was singularly fierce and merciless. Not unlike in the time of Aeschylus' Greece, intense foreign and civil war, fear and disorder, were entwined with an endless cycle of spiraling violence in defense of the old order and in support of the new, characteristic of moments of rupture and (re)foundation. The transmutation of the "raging" female divinities Erinyes into the kindly Eumenides marked the termination of a difficult transition from a crescendo to a diminuendo of violence. This mutation was symbolized by the establishment of the Council of the Areopagus, which concluded the struggle between chaos and cosmos. Unlike the ancient Furies, which were one-sided, those of the French and Russian revolutions were manifold and dialectical.

I am indebted to Richard Wortman for his close critical reading, for Princeton University Press, of the penultimate version of my manuscript. Time and again I used Maurice Agulhon and Philip Nord as sounding boards on questions of French history, and Moshe Lewin and Stephen Kotkin on questions of Russian history. At different stages of my research and writing I had the thoughtful help of Kristin Gager, Guillaume Garreta, Gavin Lewis, and Moshe Sluhovsky. I owe a particular debt of gratitude to Pamela Long, who typed and retyped successive drafts with altogether uncommon accuracy, speed, and, above all, infectious good cheer and understanding. Brigitta van Rheinberg, my editor at Princeton University Press, wielded the scepter with a firm hand and disarming wit, and so did Jodi Beder, my copy editor. At the insistence of Régine Azria, my sprightly and reflective neighbor, an early version of chapter 13 was published in the *Archives de Sciences Sociales des Religions*, number 90 (April–June 1995).

Despite growing disagreements which eventually undermined a steadfast personal and intellectual *complicité*, François Furet accompanied me in my quest. Still and always Carl Schorske, Pierre Vidal-Naquet, and Sheldon Wolin, besides spoiling me with their unconditional friendship, have been my essential scholarly and intellectual lifeline. This book is written with and for them.

Arno J. Mayer

Princeton and Chérence
Summer 1999

THE FURIES

INTRODUCTION

❋ ❋ ❋

IN THIS early dawn of the twenty-first century, following one of humanity's darkest seasons, revolution is seen as offering little promise and posing little threat. But only yesteryear, during the discontinuous yet not unrelated epochs of the French and Russian revolutions, promise and threat were vigorous and inextricably entwined. Indeed, revolution presents two contrasting faces: the one glorious and appealing; the other violent and terrifying.[1] Today utopia is completely eclipsed by dystopia. In much of the First and Second World there is a consensus, articulated by Hannah Arendt, that "freedom has been better preserved in countries where no revolution ever broke out, no matter how outrageous the circumstances of the powers that be, and that more civil liberties exist even in countries where the revolution was defeated than in those where revolutions have been victorious."[2] Revolution is seen as unnecessary, and its human and material costs morally and historically indefensible. The grand romance and the great fear of the French and Russian revolutions have given way to the celebration of essentially bloodless revolutions for human rights, private property, and market capitalism. This perspective, rooted in liberal and conservative values, precludes the revolutionary premise, and is as prejudicial to the critical study of revolution as the revolutionary premise itself.

It may be wise to bear in mind that in this season of globalism, this viewpoint is open to question in the still heavily peasant societies of the developing countries, with their run-away, overcrowded, and uneasy urban centers. Four of the 6 billion people dwell in these unprovidential lands, and untold millions of them live at or below the level of poverty. The costs of this unjust and oppressive social order, over the long run, are "at least as atrocious as those of revolution, perhaps a great deal more."[3] Indeed, historical inertia exacts a chronic price, intermittently heightened by famine and epidemic, war and civil war. Among the reasons "for the absence of revolt in [this] context of exploitation and misery" figure, above all, the "deadly risks" that

3

governing and ruling classes "can impose on would-be rebels" with their enormous coercive and daunting force and violence, both physical and symbolic.[4]

Be that as it may, in this study of the Furies of the French and Russian revolutions I postulate that there is no revolution without violence and terror; without civil and foreign war; without iconoclasm and religious conflict; and without collision between city and country. The Furies of revolution are fueled primarily by the inevitable and unexceptional resistance of the forces and ideas opposed to it, at home and abroad. This polarization becomes singularly fierce once revolution, confronted with this resistance, promises as well as threatens a radical refoundation of both polity and society. Hannah Arendt quite rightly emphasized that revolution "confront[s] us directly and inevitably with the problem of beginning," since it entails more than mere "change."[5] Jules Michelet even suggested that it might be wiser "to speak of Foundation than Revolution."[6]

This problem of foundation or refoundation has engaged political and social theorists through the ages, and few if any of them entertained the theoretical or historical possibility of a radically fresh start without recourse to uncommon violence and reversion to barbarism. Prototypically, Machiavelli emphasized that "there is nothing more difficult to carry out, more doubtful of success, nor more dangerous to handle, than to initiate a new order of things."[7] He argued that no thoroughgoing foundation or refoundation could survive in the face of intense disorder and resistance without an absolute ruler resorting to swift, extraordinary, and, if need be, cruel violence.

✳ ✳ ✳

In rethinking the role of violence in revolution, I bear in mind not only the Furies inherent in the notion of a new foundation but also the reality and urgency of collective violence since time immemorial.[8] This grim and stubborn fact challenges the widespread presumption that violence is as rare as revolution. Foreign war, perhaps the most common and essential form of deadly collective violence, is one of revolution's chief radicalizing agents: war decisively revolutionized the French Revolution in 1792–94; and war and the imminence of war revolutionized the Russian Revolution in 1917–21 and in the 1930s. Civil war is the other common form of collective violence which fires the Furies of revolution, all the more so if it should inter-lock with quasi-religious foreign war. There is no better guide for the study of the lethal fusion of foreign and civil war in a time of general convulsion than Thucydides' discussion of the furious and raw savagery on Corcyra (Corfu) during the Peloponnesian War.[9] In any case, the violence accompanying revolution runs to extremes, or ap-pears to do so, precisely because revolution entails *both* foreign and civil war.

As a rule, the analysis and explanation of the revolutionary Furies is biased by the age-old assumption that "a foreign war [is] a much milder evil than a civil war," and that there is nothing wrong with deflecting dangerously "heated passions . . . among us . . . into some war with our neighbors."[10] It is difficult to understand why revolution should not be "permissible because of its violence and bloodshed," while war is "wholly permissible and morally justifiable." Although both are "sinful" and "evidence of sin," to "accept history" is to ac-cept the one and the other, and neither of them can be "judged solely from the perspective of individual morality."[11] The hecatombs of the foreign wars of the French and Russian revolutions exceed those of their civil wars, and yet the former are glorified and mythologized, the latter execrated. In the wake of the slaughter of the two world wars of the twentieth century, Maurice Merleau-Ponty had good reason to wonder whether "after so much exhortation to 'Make the Supreme Sacrifice' for the Fatherland" one ought perhaps to show more under-standing for the "rallying cry to 'Make the Supreme Sacrifice' for the Revolution."[12]

It was Chateaubriand who first questioned the axiom that foreign war is morally superior to civil war. He noted that frequently "a people has reinvigorated and regenerated itself by means of internecine dis-cord." To be sure, it is horrible when close neighbors of a community "lay waste each other's property and stain each other's home with blood." Chateaubriand wondered, however, whether it is "really that much more humane to massacre a German peasant whom you do not know and with whom you never exchanged a word, whom you rob and kill without remorse, and whose wives and daughters you dis-honor with a clear conscience simply because *c'est la guerre?*" In his alternative vision, "civil wars are less unjust and revolting as well as more natural than foreign wars." They have the merit of turning on personal injuries and animosities, and at least or at worst the adversaries know "why they draw their swords." By contrast, nations tend to go to war because "a king is bored, an ambitious placeman means to advance himself, or a minister is out to supplant a rival."[13]

✳ ✳ ✳

Revolution at once springs from and feeds on the collapse of the state's undivided and centralizing sovereignty and its dissolution into several centers of competing power or impotence.[14] During the French and Russian revolutions each of several centers eventually turned to violence in an effort to reclaim or secure a monopoly on the legitimate use of coercion in its own favor at the national, regional, or local level. The attendant spiral of violence was amplified by the simultaneous breakdown of the judiciary and law enforcement generally, opening a breach for the return of repressed vengeance, particularly in zones of rampant civil war and terror, such as in the Vendée and Tambov, and in the cities of the Midi and Ukraine.

As Jacob Burckhardt suggested, whereas "intrinsic resistance paralyzes spurious crises [or revolutions], it fiercely inflames genuine ones."[15] For certain, "it takes two to make a revolution," and counterrevolution is revolution's other half.[16] Revolution and counterrevolution are bound to each other "as reaction is bound to action," making for a "historical motion, which . . . is at once dialectical and driven by necessity."[17] It is another central postulate of this study that revolution and counterrevolution ask to be conceived and examined in terms of each other. The inveterate governing and ruling classes of France and Russia could hardly have been expected to freely abandon their vested interests and prerogatives, especially since these were tied into a religious, cultural, and mental universe which was being sharply challenged. Before long the political field was polarized across what Carl Schmitt conceives as a "friend-enemy" divide or dissociation,[18] with each side fighting savagely for its "holy of holies."[19]

In any case, counterrevolution was real and tangible. It was not, in the main, a phantasm: an aristocratic or capitalist plot invented by Jacobin and Bolshevik zealots or strongmen to enliven their Manichaean ideology and rhetoric with a view to justifying and legitimating revolutionary terror. Besides, conspiracy mongering was common on both sides of the friend-enemy divide. And much of it was nonideological and wild, conspiratorial "reasoning" being second nature above all in "primitive" peasant societies such as France and Russia in 1789 and 1917. Needless to say, counterrevolution is as complex, plastic, and factious as revolution. At the top of the resistance there is both the discord and synergy of conservatives, reactionaries, and counterrevolutionaries.[20] There is, in addition, a basic distinction and tension between this composite and organized *counter*-revolution from the top and the spontaneous and irregular *anti*-revolution from the ground up.[21] This anti-revolution, primarily in the form of peasant resistance, was the epicenter of the civil wars in the French and Russian revolutions in which the incidence and ferocity of violence and terror, even by the standard of Corcyra, were beyond compare. The mindset and reason of the counterrevolution from above being elitist, it failed to connect with the popular anti-revolution from below, with the result that counterrevolutionary fortunes became heavily contingent on foreign aid and military intervention promoted by émigrés.

Counterrevolution is at least as deeply anchored and durable in the political tradition and culture of France and Russia as revolution. Its core ideas were first formulated as negations to the ideas of the *philosophes* in eighteenth-century France, and with accretions and variants have stayed the course ever since. Indeed, the controversion of the central ideas of the Enlightenment "is as old as the [Enlightenment] itself,"[22] and through its history the Enlightenment has been "inseparable from a Counter-Enlightenment shadow." Moreover, to the extent that ideas make history, "the putative dangers of . . . rationalistic, secular Enlightenment thought are more than matched by the dangers inherent in anything the Counter-Enlightenment would offer in its place." If the Enlightenment must assume some of the blame for "the Great Terrors of the left-wing totalitarian regimes" of the recent past, then the Counter-Enlightenment must assume an equally heavy responsibility for those of Nazi Germany.[23] In any case, in exploring and judging the violence and terror of the French and Russian revolutions, in their domestic as well as international aspects, it is important to remember that the counterrevolution was not innocent; that without it there would have been no Furies; and that at key junctures the forces of resistance came close to winning the day.

✳ ✳ ✳

Another premise of this study is that religious conflict was a significant revolutionizing force. With France of 1789 and Russia of 1917 85 percent rural, peasant, and illiterate, church and religion were omnipresent. In both countries the organic unity of "the political" and "the sacred" was intact at the apex of political society.[24] Moreover, bolstered by their vast and awe-inspiring institutional endowments, the Gallican Catholic Church and Russian Orthodox Church wielded enormous influence in everyday life. For their part, the reformists and revolutionists were swayed by the progressive reason of the Enlightenment, which was primarily turned against the dogma and hegemony of the established churches. Confirmed cosmopolitans, and concentrated in a few cities, reformists and revolutionists disdained the world of the peasants which they were determined to liberate from the blight of ignorance and superstition nurtured by the priesthood. While the countryside was a distant backdrop for the platforms of the guillotine and the courtrooms of the show trials, its villages were the principal theater of the deadly peasant wars, which were intensified by antithetical cosmologies.

There could be no transfiguring political and civil society without substantially modifying the relationship of state and church, and without considerably loosening organized religion's grip on critical spheres of social and cultural life. Clearly, nothing could have been more divisive than the instant desacralization of high politics; disestablishment of the state church; dispossession of ecclesiastic property; and emancipation of religious minorities. Nearly all the bishops and most of the lower clergy eventually resisted institutional reform. Moreover, Pope Pius VI and Supreme Patriarch Tikhon anathematized and excommunicated Jacobins and Bolsheviks, thereby contributing to the escalation of a temporal conflict into a religious one. Probably more in France than in Russia, country priests played a considerable role in the peasant resistance to revolution.

Even as the two revolutions disestablished and reined in the official church, they launched alternative religions as part of their search for a sanctification of their new foundation. Half mimetic and half invented, these quasi-religions spawned their own dogma and catechism, as well as their own high priests, rituals, holy places, and martyrs. The all but simultaneous disestablishment of the dominant church and emergence of a parallel faith and cult were products of the friend-enemy dissociation, which they greatly exacerbated.

＊ ＊ ＊

The force and indeterminacy of the revolutionary maelstrom is such that it gives rise to a headlong rush into an exigent but indeterminate future led by mostly inexperienced political leaders. These neophytes come face to face with what Edmund Burke decried as "the enormous evils of . . . dreadful innovation" and Hannah Arendt considered the "strange pathos of novelty . . . inherent in all revolutions."[25] This study will emphasize that, pressed by unsuspected and perplexing events, would-be leaders of the French and Russian revolutions had no choice but to make grave and perilous decisions without the benefit of a "science of the future"[26]—decisions for which there were no rational criteria. Following 1789 and 1917 the emerging disorders in the surrounding environment, both domestic and international, were too sweeping and intense for decision makers to be able to control and channel them according to preconceived and preordained ideological blueprints. To be sure, the Jacobin and Bolshevik ideologies played a crucial role. But they were fluid and flexible, not rigid, and they limited or facilitated rather than determined the actors' choices.

The concept of ideology is at once too vague, charged, and mechanical to provide an explanatory frame. Revolutionary actors resort to ideology to legitimate and justify actions and policies as well as to criticize and invalidate those of their adversaries. In moments of vanishing sovereignty and failing hegemony, ideology also fosters social and political solidarity by spawning reassuring myths, slogans, and prophecies. It is not to "deny the crucial importance of ideologies and public programs in revolutionary situations" to insist that they are "a poor guide" to a revolution's genesis, course, and outcome.[27]

Besides, in 1788 France knew no ready-made revolutionary designs: at best "a dozen . . . obscure writers professed to be true republicans and revolutionaries."[28] The bulk of the deputies and of the new-model political class did not discover and embrace the Enlightenment until after the fall of the Bastille,[29] when they harnessed the writings of the *philosophes* "to root their legitimacy as well as to justify their actions and give them a lineage."[30] This is not to say that the "regime of 1793 was the legitimate consequence or necessary and inescapable instrument" of these founding texts.[31] As late as December 1793 Robespierre held that "the theory of revolutionary government was as new as the Revolution which had brought it about," insisting that it was "pointless to look for this theory in the books of political writers, who in no way had foreseen this Revolution."[32]

In 1917, compared to 1789, the leading revolutionary actors were, of course, by far better armed with ideology and program which, to boot, were bolstered by political organizations and disseminated by periodicals. Even so, the case for ideological determinism is no stronger for the Russian than for the French Revolution. None of the three major revolutionary parties— Menshevik, Socialist Revolutionary, Bolshevik—were prepared for the chaos that confronted them in 1917, with the result that their guiding principles and party platforms were untimely. To be sure, the Bolsheviks acclimatized Marx and Marxism to Russian conditions, and canonized them. But the Soviet leaders were driven, above all, by the force of circumstance, not Marxist-inspired precepts, when, after calling for "peace, bread, and land," they signed a peace at Brest-Litovsk and ratified the distribution of the land to the peasants. The adoption of War Communism in 1918 and the New Economic Policy in 1921 was a vast improvisation all but shorn of Marxist principle, and so was the Great Turn to forced-draft industrialization and collectivization. As for the iron organization and rule of the party, it was deeply conditioned by the authoritarian politics and culture of late imperial Russia. It was also favored, strengthened, and justified by the emergency rule of 1917–21 and, thereafter, by unrelenting external pressures, including war, both hot and cold.

* * *

Revolution and international politics are intimately interrelated, the outside world's reaction being as consequential as the revolution's impact on other countries and on the concert of powers. From the beginning the appeal of the French and Russian revolutions could not be confined to their countries of origin. Almost overnight both acquired a world-historical resonance and reach by virtue of the universal(izing) nature of their core messianic ideas and projects, which kept their luster untarnished and their enchantment seductive longer abroad than at home. Indeed, great revolutions are epidemic and cosmic, unlike revolts, which are endemic and territorial.[33] While the true-believers expected and prophesied that the revolution would triumph far and wide, the governors of other states were fearful of contagion. With the brazen revolutionary regime and the hostile great powers misreading each other's capabilities and suspecting each other's intentions, international politics grew more and more permeated with ideology, increasing the risk and incidence of war. Beginning in 1792 the Girondins, for essentially domestic political reasons, pressured the French Assembly and government to rush into war. In turn, unexpected military setbacks demanded the steeling of the regime, now run by the Committee of Public Safety. The Soviet government, for its part, was largely a product of war, in which it remained trapped until 1921. Unlike the Jacobins, the Bolsheviks assumed, or were forced to assume, an essentially defensive posture in the face of hostile foreign intervention, invited by Russia's raging civil war and imperial breakup. But no matter how different their running starts on the world scene, the two revolutions were, as noted, revolutionized by foreign war: the Committee of Public Safety and the Council of People's Commissars used terror to enforce conscription, price and wage controls, food requisitions, and the confiscation of church valuables. There was as close a connection between the decree on the *levée en masse* (mass mobilization), the proclamation of the Terror, and the adoption of the Law of Suspects in 1793 as there was between the decree on the "Socialist Fatherland in Danger" and the official declaration of "the Red Terror" in 1918. Likewise, the solemn regicide of Louis XVI and the secretive and unceremonious execution of Nicholas II were hastened by rising suspicions of these rulers' encouragement of domestic resistance and foreign military intervention.

For nearly a quarter century, almost unintentionally, successive French governments carried the internal struggles attending their nation's new beginning to the four corners of Europe and beyond. By fixing the ideas of 1789 to the top of their bayonets, the Napoleonic armies may be said to have *externalized* the French Revolution's founding violence in the form of a "war of liberation." In the words of Karl Marx and Friedrich Engels, the post-Thermidorean regimes

11

"perfected the terror by substituting permanent war for permanent revolution."[34] Of course, this would-be crusade for human rights turned into a bid for the mastery of Europe which consumed several million lives, among them those of one million French soldiers. Ultimately, the armies of the victorious coalition of European powers, not internal resistance or counterrevolution, restored the Bourbons to their contested throne, but without reinstating an immaculate status quo ante. The triumphant but costly wars of 1795 to 1814 had facilitated the reestablishment of an undivided sovereignty, the appeasement of "heated passions," and the consolidation of some of the chief revolutionary gains, extended to include the *Code Napoléon*.

* * *

In foreign policy, diplomacy, and war, the trajectory of the Russian Revolution was wholly different from the French. In 1918–21 the foreign intervention in support of the counterrevolution remained limited: the Allies were worn out from the Very Great War; (unlike in 1792) there was popular opposition to intervention; and the task seemed forbidding, given the geography and complexity of Russia. Following the glorious but brutal and exhausting early founding years, the Bolsheviks turned inward to pursue an increasingly autarkic course—economic, political, and cultural. With the cordon sanitaire, the first "containment policy," firmly in place, this forced and improbable self-isolation favored the growth of a defiant siege mentality and justified the continuation of the ironbound political culture forged during the civil war.

Soviet Russia, unlike post-Thermidorean France, was quarantined and lacked the military capability and missionary zeal to send forth revolutionary armies far and wide. To be sure, eventually, during the Second World War, Moscow broke through the cordon sanitaire, reclaimed most of imperial Russia's pre-1917 borders, and prepared the ground for its primacy in eastern Europe. But this "expansion" was the by-product of unintended and unforeseen diplomatic and military developments. Certainly the near-fatal but ultimately victorious Great Patriotic War was not a preconceived war of either Communist liberation or territorial conquest. And after 1945, with the Second Cold War, the Western powers resumed the quarantine, now termed containment. Except warily during the makeshift Grand Alliance of

1941–45, the Soviet Union was never accepted in the council of nations on a basis of equality, and kept being treated as an outsider.

By quarantining and isolating the revolutionary regime diplomatically, economically, and financially, the outside world helped create the preconditions for Stalin's "Socialism in One Country." This marginalization provided much of the rationale and justification for the furious pace of the industrialization and collectivization of the Second Revolution of the 1930s. In particular, the military imperative warped the breakneck drive for modernization and compounded the risks in braving the "strange pathos of novelty." Meanwhile, Stalin exploited foreign perils to further his project and power. In the process he fiercely spurred on the construction of "Socialism in One Country," brutally perverting it into "Terror in One Country." Indeed, the quarantine and gathering war clouds provided the reason not only for the soaring priority of military-related heavy industry in successive Five-Year Plans but also the escalating domestic Furies culminating in the Great Purge Trials, the court-martial of General Tukhachevsky, and the *Stalinshchina*.

There was, of course, a world of difference between the first terror of 1917–22 and the second terror of the 1930s. The first terror was inseparable from the civil war with the Whites, the intervention of the European powers, and the struggles against the *jacqueries*, or peasant revolts. Its flux and reflux were closely though not perfectly correlated with military operations, making it difficult, if not impossible, to separate the casualties of military engagements from the victims of the enforcement terror. In the heat of foreign and civil war the Bolsheviks easily convinced themselves that the antirevolutionary peasant rebellions were part and parcel of the counterrevolutionary resistance with ties to the hostile outside world. In this respect they proceeded very much like the Jacobins in the Vendée.

In the 1930s, in contrast, the Bolshevik regime was involved in neither civil war nor foreign war, and the internal resistance was of less consequence than the international peril. Accordingly the second terror may be said to stand apart from what Chateaubriand conceived as civil war. And yet, it clearly belongs to internal, not external war. The *Stalinshchina* claimed few military casualties, and the bulk of the victims were Soviet citizens, whereas the casualties and victims of France's "externalized terror" under Napoleon were not, in the main,

French. Indeed, even considering the increasingly pressing foreign and military dangers, the Furies of the 1930s were essentially domestic and fratricidal, which largely accounts for their remaining singularly unfathomable.

* * *

This is a deliberately comparative study of violence and terror in the French and Russian revolutions. It points up a web of significant similarities which are explored and refined by analogic analysis. Of course, any comparative probe risks turning into a "chase for resemblances" instead of a "recognition and appreciation of differences."[35] To postulate resemblance is merely to posit that central aspects of the two revolutionary moments separated in time and space were neither totally unique nor totally alike, thereby forcing attention to telling dissimilarities and contrasts between them.

The comparative perspective helps to broach new questions, such as the role of vengeance; to bring to light and challenge unspoken scholarly assumptions, such as the anomaly and monstrosity of violence; and to identify singularities, such as the import of the precedent of the French for the Russian Revolution. Comparative analysis facilitates identifying the importance of historical legacies and memories, such as of the great religious massacres in France and the Siberian Exile System in Russia, for the contours and dynamics of the two terrors respectively. It also sparks a reassessment of the relative place of church and religion as well as of international politics and war in the hierarchy of radicalizing spheres and causes.

A comparative reading requires relating the similarities of the dynamics of the two revolutions to the dissimilarities in the environment in which they unfolded.[36] The long-run preconditions and immediate causes of the French and Russian revolutions were, of course, radically different. France, in 1789, with a population of 28 million, was the most populous and largest power of the European system, except for Russia. Its military was second to none, and so was its economy. France was also considered the most advanced country of the "civilized" world. Its cultural position and reach were beyond compare. French was the lingua franca of the finest of Europe's ruling and governing classes, of the diplomatic world, and of the nascent transnational Enlightenment. Immediately following the radiant days of 1789 French became the language of liberty, equality, and fraternity. The strength and grandeur of France was carried by a population that was, like that of most of Europe, 85 percent peasant, rural, illiterate, and "primitive" Catholic.

France stood tall and strong when, after the fall of the Bastille, the National Assembly abolished feudalism and adopted the Declaration of the Rights of Man and the Citizen. Notwithstanding the unsettling fiscal pinch on the eve of the Revolution, successive provisional governments were economically and financially relatively secure as they adopted increasingly radical policies. Following the frontier defeats of 1792, France's new governors managed to rally the "nation-in-arms" for nearly a quarter century of expansionist warfare without straining the economy and exchequer until after the retreat from Moscow in 1812.

Russia in 1917 bore no resemblance to France in 1789. To be sure, it, too, had a population that was 85 percent peasant, rural, illiterate, and "primitive" Orthodox. But more than a century after 1789 this social and cultural profile was out of season in the concert of great powers. Forty times the size of France, the Romanov empire had a population estimated at between 140 and 160 million, only less than one-half "great" Russian. In nearly every major respect the overwhelmingly agrarian economy was of another time, and so was the world of artisans and craftsmen. The industrial sector was small and, like the railways, concentrated in the western regions, dependent on foreign loans, and distorted by military imperatives. Russian never was, nor became, a world language.

Although the Renaissance and Reformation barely touched Russia, in their time the ideas of the Enlightenment exercised "a full and powerful influence." For sectors of Russia's ruling and governing elites, however, these ideas were less a "promise to liberate man from superstition and oppression and unite him with Reason and Nature" than a "recipe for modernizing and strengthening the state" for the purpose of "catching up" with the West.[37] Eventually, between 1848 and 1917 Marxism entered Russia as a form of Second Enlightenment, with an updated prescription for rapid Western-style development to prepare the ground for the socialist transformation of society. Unlike the public intellectuals and sympathizers of the first Enlightenment, who had access to the court and the *salons*, the champions of the second Enlightenment in Russia were political dissidents, rebels, and revolutionaries, most of whom went underground or into exile, or were jailed and sent to Siberia.

Whereas in 1789 France was strong, prosperous, at peace, and a hub of Europe's high culture, in 1917 Russia was not only backward and on the margins of European civilization but also caught up in a draining and all-devouring war. Indeed, when first the reformists and then the Bolsheviks assumed power, the country faced military defeat, economic collapse, and famine along with the breakdown of political authority, jeopardizing the very survival of the state. These were the extreme circumstances which brought the Bolsheviks to power and, at the same time, weighed on their rule from the creation. The fact that the revolution in "backward" Russia at once failed to spread to central Europe and was locked in by the "advanced" Western powers and Japan substantially complicated the Bolsheviks' gargantuan task.

❋ ❋ ❋

Just as there is no historical explanation without comparison, explicit or implicit, there is none without theory. History may well be "the least scientific of all the sciences," and by virtue of its flux and indetermination historical analysis balks "conceptual rigor."[38] Even so, historians formulate their questions and explanations with the help of theoretics and concepts, whether they do so out loud or *sotto voce*.[39] In this study of the revolutionary or founding Furies I willfully and explicitly look to political and social theorists for help in framing questions, analytic constructs, and arguments: Machiavelli and Hobbes; Montaigne and Montesquieu; Burke and Maistre; Tocqueville and Marx; Weber and Schmitt; Arendt and Ricoeur.

Of course, this theoretical borrowing is not innocent. It is informed by the same subjective valuations which inform every other aspect of the historical quest. There is, above all, the risk of perverting the inner logic of a unified theoretical construct by appropriating one of its subtheorems to bolster a historical exploration or argument. It is of small comfort that as "users of history . . . fabricated . . . and valorized . . .

by others," theorists are equally predatory and risk perverting historical constructions when marshaling discrete historical facts and events to support their reasoning.[40] Above all, theorists tend to slight chronology, while historians never lose from sight that historical time is "the plasma in which events are immersed, and the environment from which they derive their meaning."[41]

It is as difficult to reasonably and effectively blend fact and theory as it is to blend narrative and thematics. In his magisterial "critical history of the French Revolution," Edgar Quinet consciously combined thematics and theoretics, but without ignoring diachronics.[42] Breaking new ground, Quinet devoted a separate and long chapter, entitled "Theory of the Terror," to a probing conceptual and comparative discussion of what he considered the most problematic and contested aspect of the French Revolution.[43] But he also emphasized, strongly, that any attempt to explain the Terror called for a "careful reconstruction of dates." According to Quinet, not to pay close attention to the chronology of the clashes between the old and the new France is to "isolate the French Revolution in time . . . and suspend it in a vacuum." And to tell its story without taking account of the forces of opposition, which as often as not were on the offensive, is like "telling the story of a military battle without taking account of the enemy army."[44] Indeed, to interpret the French and Russian revolutions, particularly their Furies, undialectically is to risk rendering them either as infamous chapters in the history of human madness and crime or as dreadful and fatal calamities—as inevitable real-life tragedies. Usually the past masters of such constructions ascribe the crescendo of violence to a convergence of the irresistible force of a messianic and Manichaean belief system with the iron will of an all-powerful and demonic leader. Ultimately such over-ideologized and over-personalized explanations are obsessively monocausal. In historical discourse, "all too often the fixation on a single cause is merely the insidious form of a search for a responsible person premised on a value judgment." Unlike the lawyer, who pleads a case, and the judge, who holds the scales, the critical historian "asks 'why,' and realizes that the answer will not be simple."[45]

* * *

17

NOTES

1. Alain Rey, *Révolution: Histoire d'un mot* (Paris: Gallimard, 1989), pp. 17–18; and John Dunn, *Modern Revolutions: An Introduction to the Analysis of a Political Phenomenon* (Cambridge: Cambridge University Press, 1972), p. 12.

2. Hannah Arendt, *On Revolution* (New York: Viking, 1965), p. 41.

3. Barrington Moore, Jr., *Social Origins of Dictatorship and Democracy: Lord and Peasant in the Making of the Modern World* (Boston: Beacon, 1966), pp. 103–4, 485–86, 491, and 505. See also E. H. Carr, *What Is History?* (New York: Vintage, 1961), p. 102.

4. James C. Scott, *The Moral Economy of the Peasant: Rebellion and Subsistence in Southeast Asia* (New Haven: Yale University Press, 1976), pp. 193–94 and pp. 226–27.

5. Arendt, *On Revolution*, p. 13. See also Dana R. Villa, *Arendt and Heidegger: The Fate of the Political* (Princeton: Princeton University Press, 1996), p. 156 and p. 171.

6. See his opening lecture of 1845 in Jules Michelet, *Cours au Collège de France, 1838–1851*, 2 vols. (Paris: Gallimard, 1995), vol. 2, p. 17.

7. Machiavelli, *The Prince and the Discourses* (New York: Modern Library, 1940), p. 21 (*The Prince*, ch. VI).

8. Wolfgang Sofsky, *Traktat über die Gewalt* (Frankfurt/Main: S. Fischer, 1996).

9. Thucydides, *The Peloponnesian War*, trans. Thomas Hobbes, vol. 1 (London, 1812), bk. 3, pp. 183–87; trans. Rex Warner (London: Penguin, 1954), bk. 3, pp. 207–12; trans. Steven Lattimore (Indianapolis: Hackett Publishing, 1998), bk. 3, chs. 80–84.

10. Michel de Montaigne, *Essais*, bk. 2, ch. 23.

11. Nicolas Berdyaev, *The Origin of Russian Communism* (London: Geoffrey Bles, 1948), pp. 131–32.

12. Maurice Merleau-Ponty, *Humanism and Terror: An Essay on the Communist Problem* (Boston: Beacon, 1947/1969), p. xxxiv.

13. Chateaubriand, *Mémoires d'Outre-tombe*, vol. III, 12:4.

14. Rod Aya, "Theories of Revolution Reconsidered: Contrasting Methods of Collective Violence," in *Theory and Society* 8:1 (July 1979): pp. 40–45.

15. Jacob Burckhardt, *Weltgeschichtliche Betrachtungen* (Stuttgart: Kröner, 1978), p. 174.

16. Chalmers Johnson, *Revolution and the Social System* (Stanford: Hoover Institution of War, Revolution, and Peace, 1964), pp. 6–7.

17. Arendt, *On Revolution*, p. 8 and pp. 47–48.

18. See Heinrich Meier, *Carl Schmitt and Leo Strauss: The Hidden Dialogue* (Chicago: University of Chicago Press, 1995).

19. Burckhardt, *Weltgeschichtliche Betrachtungen*, p. 177.

20. Arno J. Mayer, *Dynamics of Counterrevolution in Europe, 1870–1956: An Analytic Framework* (New York: Harper and Row, 1971), chs. 2–3.

21. See Claude Mazauric, "Autopsie d'un échec: La résistance à *l'anti*-révolution et la défaite de la *contre*-révolution," in François Lebrun and Roger Dupuy, eds., *Les résistances à la Révolution: Actes du Colloque de Rennes, 17–21 Septembre 1985* (Paris: Imago, 1987), pp. 237–44.

22. Isaiah Berlin, cited in Raymond Tallis, *Enemies of Hope: A Critique of Contemporary Pessimism* (London: Macmillan, 1997), p. 1.

23. Tallis, *Enemies*, p. 2, p. 61, and p. 55.

24. Peter Berger, *The Sacred Canopy: Elements of a Sociological Theory of Religion* (New York: Doubleday, 1967); and Roger Caillois, *L'homme et le sacré*, 3rd ed. (Paris: Gallimard, 1950).

25. Paul Langford, ed., *The Writings and Speeches of Edmund Burke*, vol. 9 (Oxford: Clarendon, 1991), p. 156; and Arendt, *On Revolution*, p. 19, p. 27, and p. 39.

26. Merleau-Ponty, *Humanism and Terror*, p. xxxiii.

27. Aya, "Theories," pp. 46–48.

28. Daniel Mornet, *Les origines intellectuelles de la Révolution française, 1715–1878*, 6th ed. (Paris: Colin, 1967), p. 217.

29. See Timothy Tackett, *Becoming a Revolutionary: The Deputies of the French National Assembly and the Emergence of a Revolutionary Culture, 1789–1790* (Princeton: Princeton University Press, 1996).

30. Roger Chartier, *Les origines culturelles de la Révolution française* (Paris: Seuil, 1990), pp. 14–15.

31. Edgar Quinet, *La Révolution* (Paris: Belin, 1987), p. 45.

32. Robespierre, *Discours et rapports à la convention* (Paris: 10/18, 1965), p. 190.

33. Eugen Rosenstock, *Die europäischen Revolutionen: Volkscharaktere und Staatenbildung* (Jena: Eugen Diederichs, 1931), ch. 1; and Jacques Ellul, *Autopsie de la révolution* (Paris: Calmann-Lévy, 1969), ch. 1.

34. *The Holy Family*, in Marx and Engels, *Collected Works*, vol. 4 (London: Lawrence and Wishart, 1975), p. 23 (italics in text).

35. Marc Bloch, "Pour une histoire comparée des sociétés européennes," in Bloch, *Mélanges historiques*, vol. 1 (Paris: S.E.V.P.E.N., 1963), pp. 16–40, esp. p. 17 and p. 38.

36. Bloch, "Pour une histoire comparée," p. 17.

37. Ernest Gellner, *Times Literary Supplement*, December 9, 1994. See also Isaac Deutscher, *The Prophet Armed: Trotsky, 1879–1921* (New York: Oxford University Press, 1954), pp. 187–89.

38. Burckhardt, *Weltgeschichtliche Betrachtungen*, p. 83.

39. See Paul Veyne, *Comment on écrit l'histoire* (Paris: Seuil, 1971), esp. pp. 174–82.

40. Michel Foucault in *Quinzaine littéraire*, March 1 and 15, 1986, and Foucault, *Dits et écrits, 1954–1988*, vol. 4 (Paris: Gallimard, 1994), pp. 73–75. For the problematic relationship between history and sociology, see Rudolf Hamann, *Revolution und Evolution: Zur Bedeutung einer historischen akzentuierten Soziologie* (Berlin: Duncker & Humblot, 1981), pp. 11–17.

41. Marc Bloch, *Apologie pour l'histoire ou métier d'historien* (Paris: Colin, 1974), p. 36.

42. Quinet, *La Révolution*, p. 61.

43. Ibid., ch. 17.

44. Ibid., p. 55 and pp. 70–71.

45. Bloch, *Apologie*, p. 156; A. J. P. Taylor, *The Origins of the Second World War* (New York: Atheneum, 1962), p. 13; Carr, *What Is History?*, pp. 99–100 and p. 113. See also Carlo Ginzburg, *Le juge et l'histoire* (Paris: Verdier, 1997), passim.

PART ONE

Conceptual Signposts

Francisco Goya: *The Sleep of Reason Produces Monsters* (preparatory drawing for the *Caprichos*), 1797

Revolution

REVOLUTION is a word-concept of multiple meanings. It evokes dialectically linked oppositions: light and darkness; rupture and continuity; disorder and order; liberation and oppression; salvation and damnation; hope and disillusion.[1] Precisely because it is Janus-faced, revolution is intrinsically tempestuous and savage. The Furies of revolution are fueled above all by the resistance of the forces and ideas opposed to it. This confrontation turns singularly fierce once it becomes clear that revolution entails and promises—or threatens—a thoroughly new beginning or foundation of polity and society. Hannah Arendt rightly insists that "revolutions are the only political events which confront us directly and inevitably with the problem of beginning."[2] Comprehensive and forced, as well as rapid, such an uncommon fresh start involves not only the radical mutation of the established governing and ruling elites but also the simultaneous desacralization of the old order and the consecration of the new in the urgent quest for legitimacy.

Revolution provokes enormous resistance in part because it entails far-reaching changes not only in politics but also in society and culture, including church and religion. In 1789 in France and in 1917 in Russia state and church were firmly joined, and there was no reforming the one without reforming the other, and without redefining their relationship, precipitating a struggle occasioning an escalation from liberal to illiberal secularism. Indeed, society being largely "built and cemented on a foundation of religion . . . it is impossible to loosen the cement and shake the foundation without endangering the superstructure."[3] Since the ideologically fired presumption to recast political and civil society, including its sacred core, transcends national borders, it also arouses strong resistance abroad. By reason of its ideology, which disturbs the international system, revolution is an intrinsically world-historical phenomenon. It becomes a potent siren for sympathizers and converts far and wide; at the same time, it looms as a ubiquitous specter for foreign powers, which then provide the lifeblood for resistance in the world arena and in the epicenter of the revolutionary eruption as well.

✳ ✳ ✳

Shortly after the first anniversary of the French Revolution, before the Great Terror, Count de Mirabeau, without losing faith, avowed that he "never believed in a great revolution without bloodshed" and that he considered civil war "a necessary evil."[4] Over a century later, before 1914, Jean Jaurès, while reflecting critically on the French Revolution and forewarning of an Armageddon pregnant with another revolution, still considered revolution a necessary and fruitful, even if barbarous "means of progress."[5] But after 1945, following Europe's harrowing Second Thirty Years War, marked by extreme revolution and counterrevolution, Hannah Arendt concluded, as noted, that "no matter how outrageous the circumstances of the powers that be . . . freedom had been better served in countries where no revolution had ever broken out."[6]

Except in some precincts of the Third World, where political freedoms cannot take first or absolute priority, the principle of revolution is either utterly disvalued or so redefined as to fit revolutions that are found acceptable, even extolled, this side of paradise: the "revolutions without revolution" of 1789 to 1792 in France and of February–March 1917 in Russia, or the recent "velvet" revolutions in eastern and east-central Europe. In this day and age the only genuine and virtuous revolution is said to be one in which at best limited violence, well short of terror, is used to force the establishment of a *Rechtsstaat* to guarantee individual rights, political freedoms, private property, and free-market capitalism. At the same time, by reason of its promiscuous use, the word *revolution* is being trivialized. Every single aspect of contemporary society, economy, and culture is said to be in perpetual revolution: business, finance, telecommunications, life sciences, medicine, health services, work, and leisure. What were once conceived as gradual mutations have been reconceived as revolutions, most of them represented in essentially positive terms, and this despite the reigning disbelief in the idea of progress. Of course, the political fate of the word *revolution* has been extraordinary. In France, Marc Bloch noted, "whereas the *ultras* of 1815 shuddered at the very word revolution, those of 1940 used it to dissemble their coup d'etat."[7] Since then, as if in extension of Vichy's practice, it has become increasingly fashionable to characterize the National Socialist takeover and regime in Germany a revolution rather than a counterrevolution.

Meanwhile the inherently polarizing duality of the blinding promise and panic fear of revolution continues to perplex historians and social theorists as much as it confounded contemporaries of the French and Russian revolutions. Precisely because of the built-in tension between its light and dark sides, revolution continues to be one of the most vexed historical and political questions. Indeed, it is a topic about which it is "neither possible nor proper to be neutral . . . [and] value-free."[8] There are good reasons to distrust scholars and public intellectuals who allege that "ideology is the thinking of my adversary"[9] while claiming the high ground of objectivity for themselves even as they brace it with pluralistic liberalism or conservatism which "excludes the revolutionary hypothesis."[10] Ultimately the study of revolution bears out Benedetto Croce's aphorism that "all genuine history is contemporary history."[11]

✳ ✳ ✳

The word-concept of revolution has a history, its changing meanings being defined in arguments advanced in specific contexts and expressed in contemporaneous language and rhetoric.[12] Intellectuals and scholars contribute to this periodic redefinition, probing current understandings which, by virtue of the apparent contradictions, they consider to be inadequately conceived and theorized.[13] In any case, the components, structures, dynamics, and contours of the word-concept of revolution are periodically revised in the light of changing circumstances, and so are its correlations with other concepts, which are equally subject to revision. But at all times revolution "has many meanings" in that "whatever the context, the word seems to overflow the precise and definite meaning assigned to it."[14] Whoever uses the word-concept of revolution freights it with his or her particular idea of its nature and dynamics. This is as true of splitters and nominalists as it is of lumpers and holists. Whereas the former presumably foreswear totalizing and dialectical reason, the latter implicitly embrace it.

But whatever their methodological premises, students of revolution tend to seek unifying explanations in part to master their own unease in face of a perplexing and disquieting problem which tests the limits of understanding and justification.

Prior to the seventeenth century, with kings and princes ruling by divine right, willful rebellions were unthinkable for being profane and sinful. It was a time when "revolution went by the name of civil war," which was considered a "subspecies of war" fueled by feudal, seignorial, or confessional conflicts.[15] Montesquieu noted that there were "plenty of civil wars without revolutions"; and not unlike Voltaire after him, he envisaged the overturn of despotic government without civil war.[16] Impressed by the Glorious Revolution of 1688, which marked the establishment of a constitutional monarchy without bloodshed and terror, Voltaire and his fellow dissidents began to conceive of revolution as a "counter-concept" opposite civil war, which they considered a "legacy of the fanatical religious parties which would be left behind by the advance of civilization."[17] Ultimately the intention and outcome of the revolution in England was a restoration of monarchic power. This was in keeping with the cyclical connotations of the term revolution which politics appropriated from astronomy. Besides, in England the "final moment of 1688 was called revolution," not the Puritan rebellion and the civil wars of mid-century. This was in contrast to France a century later, where it was "precisely the first moment" that went by that name.[18]

The revolution in America, like that in England, was actually a restoration. The secessionists of the Thirteen Colonies fought a war of liberation against the British government for having violated England's own political principles which the rebels claimed for themselves. No wonder the colonists represented this founding act as their War of Independence, and it was not until a decade after 1776, and especially after 1789, that it began to go by the name of American Revolution. Like the Glorious Revolution, it was driven by tradition. The rebels never intended to bring about major changes in the colonies' moral, social, or economic values or institutions. The political and civil freedoms which were reclaimed were not extended to Blacks and Native Americans, who easily accounted for one-fifth of a total population of 2.5 million. To be sure, numerous Loyalists fought on the side of the British against the insurgents, but there was nothing counterrevolutionary about this resistance, whose core values were not at war with those of their adversaries. Nor was there a civil war following the establishment of the new and independent American government, at any rate not until 1861. Although within a generation or two there were considerable changes in the political practices, social relationships, and cultural tastes of the ex-colonial society, none of them had been imagined or projected by the secessionists and they evolved gradually, without brutal ruptures with the past.[19]

By contrast, the French and Russian revolutions were anything but "cyclical" and restorative. Both were made by self-conscious revolutionaries open or sworn to new ideas. Admittedly, in 1788 ready-made ideological canons or blueprints were nonexistent in France: at best "a dozen writers professed to be true republicans and revolutionaries, and they were very obscure."[20] The advocates of disestablishment of the Gallican Church were equally scarce. The ideas, agents, and agencies of the *lumières* (Enlightenment) had, however, fostered an atmosphere favorable to questioning, but not defying, the reign of privilege, feudalism, and absolutism. When the Estates-General met in the spring of 1789, enlightened and progressive factions of the ruling and governing classes looked for constitutional, fiscal, and legal reforms respectful of the person and office of Louis XVI, as well as of the spirit of the monarchist regime. In the summer and fall of that same year, however, when the National Assembly abolished seignorial rights and feudal privileges and adopted the Declaration of the Rights of Man and the Citizen, this not only represented a drastic acceleration of the revolutionary process, but was also associated with a decisive change in the very meaning of the word-concept revolution. These spectacular measures were voted under the pressure of events, and carried the imprint of the critical ideas and principles of the unstructured dissidence of the eighteenth century. But this was also the moment of the sudden emergence of political actors who represented themselves to be revolutionaries as they plunged into the emergent debates and struggles over the direction and defense of what they here and now proclaimed to be the Great Revolution. It was these self-proclaimed and self-conscious revolutionaries who may be said to have "invented the Enlightenment," in that they harnessed the writings of the *philosophes* to ground their legitimacy and philosophic genealogy as well as to justify their actions.[21]

In Edgar Quinet's insightful reading, once the champions of reformist revolt turned into architects of revolutionary change, "they needed a foundation that had nothing in common with tradition." This invention of a new foundation was not only the "grandeur . . . [but also] the most vulnerable side of the French Revolution," all the more so since this ideological warrant "had to be defined in opposition to [the reigning Catholic] religion." Quinet held that "everything was new" in this praxis: "for the first time in history philosophy had to serve as institution, belief system, and archive at the same time that it had to descend into the streets."[22] This reading is consonant with Robespierre's assertion that neither the "books of political writers who did not foresee this Revolution nor the laws of tyrants expert in the abuse of power" provided guidance for a "theory of revolutionary government that was as new as the revolution which spawned it."[23]

* * *

The level of revolutionary self-consciousness was, of course, considerably greater a century later. By then discussions about the glories, missteps, and betrayals of the French Revolution, as well as controversies about its lessons, were central to the political debates, theoretical and tactical, of Russian liberals and socialists. The upheaval of 1905 seemed to validate this concern by confirming, *pace* the Slavophiles, that Russia's development would be similar to central and western Europe's. The reformists were split between constitutional monarchists who urged timely reforms from above as the best antidote to revolution, and republicans, both liberal and socialist, who advocated a bourgeois revolution which would short-circuit a Jacobin onset. The Bolsheviks and Socialist Revolutionaries also embraced this Europeanist vision, except that they stressed two peculiarities of contemporary Russia's potentially explosive condition: the former looked to the new if still sparse industrial proletariat to become the chief political carrier and beneficiary of revolution; the latter meant to rally and serve the timeless and weighty peasantry.

No wonder the mimetic element, with the French Revolution as its main referent, was present from the very creation of the Russian Revolution of 1917. Both the old and new elites, not the subaltern underclass of workers and peasants, superimposed the fever chart of the Russian Revolution on what they assumed to have been the fever chart of the French Revolution with a view to determining the degree to which the temperature curves of the two revolutions diverged from each other. The question was not whether the two revolutions were similar, but the extent to which they were. Being more self-conscious about their role in the unfolding drama than their predecessors of 1788–89 had been, the formative revolutionary elite acted with "less naiveté and originality." While the Mensheviks and Bolsheviks saw themselves and each other as Girondins and Jacobins, the Octobrists and Constitutional-Democrats (Kadets) had every appearance of being the *monarchiens* or *feuillants*—the moderates—of their day. All except the far left and the far right worked and hoped to bring the revolution to a close without either yielding to the rule of terror or falling back into the ancien regime. In fact, before being caught up in the revolutionary tempest, the actors of all camps, including the counterrevolutionaries, thought they "knew what a revolution was all about and the course it was likely to take."[24]

The Russian Revolution "was the first to rely intellectually on a predecessor and . . . to recognize a connection between revolutions." Far from being mere mimesis, this self-awareness also involved setting the Russian Revolution off from its elder, the *Grande Révolution*, by proclaiming itself to be "the last, the true, and the genuine" revolution destined to be both permanent and global. Certainly the Bolsheviks intended 1917 to be the "antithesis" of 1789, the revolution of the fourth estate—the proletariat—superseding that of the third—the bourgeoisie. They proposed to close the gap between the abstract rights and freedoms of 1789 and the continuing wretchedness of the human condition by marrying political with social renewal.[25]

In Russia first in 1905 and then in 1917 revolution involved "a conscious modeling" after both "the men and . . . the experience" of the French Revolution.[26] Indeed, for the Bolsheviks this mimesis may have been as important an orienting factor as ideology. To the extent that Lenin and Trotsky "set out to accomplish and direct a revolution" according to an ideological and strategic blueprint, it was predeliberated in critical awareness of the French Revolution and its aftershocks, notably the European upheavals of 1848 and the Paris Commune of 1871.[27] Many of the Bolsheviks' great prescripts of the first hours were dictated less by ideology than by circumstances they read in the light of 1789–94. They did, of course, invoke, expound, and eventually exalt the works of Marx and Engels, much as the Jacobins had extolled those of Voltaire and Rousseau. But the terrors of the Russian Revolution no more rose out of the ideas of the "fathers" of Socialism than those of the French Revolution had risen out of ideas of the "fathers" of the Enlightenment. Besides, Marx and Engels were no more champions of violence and terror than the *philosophes*.[28]

Perhaps the distinctiveness of revolution, in its post-1789 sense, can be made to stand out clearer by contrasting it with the related phenomenon of revolt. Visceral and instantaneous, revolt is inhospitable to the ways of theory and ideology. Its agents mean to preserve or reclaim established rights and institutions rather than radically recast or overturn them. Although both revolution and revolt are turned against established elites and authorities, the former is driven by ideology and hope, whereas the latter is moved by tradition and despair or disillusionment. Rebels, unlike revolutionaries, have a tendency to set upon local and tangible enemies who are readily vilified and turned into scapegoats. Ultimately a revolt has a limited horizon, is ill-organized, and is short-lived, its leaders being unwilling or unable to merge or coordinate their objectives and operations with those of other insurgencies beyond their locality or region. The Vendée and the Federalist rebellion during the French Revolution have many of the characteristics and deficits of revolts against constituted authority, and so do the *jacqueries* of Makhno in Ukraine and Antonov in Tambov during the Russian Revolution. Conceiving their project as national in scope and transnational in implication, revolutionaries, for their part, resolve to institutionalize their own revolt at the expense of crushing all others in their drive to establish or impose their monopoly of centralized state power.

✳ ✳ ✳

The word-concept of revolution, on the other hand, has since 1789 denoted a set of characteristics peculiar to a particular historical moment and process. One of the chief defining circumstances is the breakdown of the state's undivided and centralizing sovereignty into several centers of competing power or impotence, with each center resorting to violence to reestablish a monopoly on the use of force—legitimate violence—for itself, either nationally or regionally.[29] This collapse and fragmentation of political authority, which breeds both domestic and foreign violence, is accompanied by the breakdown of the judicial system, entailing the wreck of the sluice gates holding back the return of repressed vengeance. A reign of upward spiraling chaos and violence provides the enabling context for a radically new beginning not only in political regime but also in society, law, church, and culture. This founding moment is one of intense and sudden ruptures which provide impassioned but confounded revolutionary leaders with the opportunity to articulate an unsteady synthesis of millenarian, eschatological, and Manichaean precepts. They rush to do so unmindful of what Edmund Burke decried as "the enormous evils of . . . dreadful innovation"[30] and Hannah Arendt considered "the strange pathos of novelty,"[31] but also in the heat of circumstances which call for pressing decisions for which there are no rational criteria. The members of this nascent and untried governing and ruling class "speak a new language" with fresh words, or old words which assume new meanings, along with a new logic, style, and syntax. This emergent language expresses new ideas and principles which in time crystallize into a Weltanschauung whose idioms have transnational reverberations, both friendly and hostile.

There may well be no more telling defining characteristic of revolution than its international temper. Compared to revolts, which are endemic and territorial, revolutions are epidemic and cosmic. Indeed, "any genuine revolution is a world revolution," its principles being "universal."[32] Although the two great revolutions started as Franco-French and Russo-Russian affairs, they never spoke only or primarily for one people or country. Characteristically, when championing the text of the Declaration of the Rights of Man which the Constituent Assembly adopted in August 1789, Jérôme Pétion, a radical, commended it for speaking "for man in general," and Adrien J.-F. Duport, a moderate, for seeking to promote "the great truths of all times and countries."[33] Burke instantly recognized and denounced "the Declaration of a new species of Government on new principle . . . [as] a real crisis in the politicks [not of France but] in all countries," in character with an "epidemic."[34] For his part Hegel hailed the French Revolution as a "world-historical" event precisely because of its engagement on behalf of man, regardless of religion or nation.[35] Needless to say, in their time Marx and Engels fully shared this view.

The Russian Revolution had this same universalizing immanence and reason. Of course, given the circumstances of their rise to power, the Bolsheviks were acutely conscious of the crucial importance of the course of international politics for their fortunes. This consciousness was evident in the Decree on Peace of November 8, 1917, which, along with the Decree on Land, was their first official act. There followed the Declaration of the Rights of the Toiling and Exploited People of January 8, 1918, adopted by the Third Congress of Soviets. A clear echo of the great charter of 1789, it was certain to be heard around the world. Compared to the time of the French Revolution, foreign supporters and sympathizers were potentially more numerous, plebeian, and diverse. And particularly the workers and intellectuals among them were better and more easily organized. With an eye to the restless proletariat and disillusioned intelligentsia of the First World, the Bolsheviks convened the founding congress of the Third International (Comintern) in Moscow in March 1919. As for the Congress of the Peoples of the East, which met in Baku in September 1920, it signaled that the Russian Revolution, from its Eurasian base, looked to set astir the semi-colonial and colonial world as well. In point of fact, even the founding declaration of January 8, 1918 included a condemnation of bourgeois civilization for "barbarically enslaving many millions of working people in Asia and in the colonies generally."

Of course, as at home, so in the world at large, the two revolutions were at once a dream and a specter, a calling and an illusion. While they rallied converts and sympathizers in some quarters, they made sworn enemies and skeptics in others. There is no studying and understanding the former apart from the latter, since they were each other's Nemesis. No less striking, and paradoxically, in no time the inherent universalism of the French and Russian revolutions, confronted with a hostile outside world, became coupled with nationalism, creating an intense and inevitable contradiction between their ecumenicalism and particularism: in France the sacralization of *la nation*; in Russia the embrace of "Socialism in One Country."

✳ ✳ ✳

The French and Russian revolutions grew into revolutions of world-historical importance to a large extent because they had their origin and infancy in the lands of great powers. Except as a satellite, a small country has difficulty spawning or sustaining a viable revolution, since one or another great power is likely to intervene to crush it. Upon taking root in a major country, a revolution unsettles the international system in two ways: the initial chaos and weakness of the host country invite other states to advance their rival interests at its expense, thereby disturbing the balance of power and increasing the risk of war; the fear of contagion provokes the powers into joining forces to resolutely contain or fight the revolutionary power, in the process permeating world politics with ideology and unsteadying international order by banishing a major player from it. The failure of early intervention—direct and indirect, military and diplomatic, economic and cultural—to smother the revolution is due as much to the conflicting interests and lack of diplomatic cohesion among the intervening states as it is to the military and spatial sinews of the country in which the revolution occurs.

In any case, there is no denying the "close interrelatedness . . . [and] mutual dependence" of revolution and foreign war, which have violence as their "common denominator." Indeed, revolution and war are inconceivable "outside the domain of violence," which sets them off "from all other political phenomena."[36] Just as revolution breeds war, so war, particularly defeat in war, begets revolution. And ultimately foreign war does more than civil war to revolutionize revolution.

The chronology of the interplay of revolution and war was strikingly different in the French and Russian revolutions, even if war decisively radicalized both: in 1789, "first revolution and then war"; in 1917, "first war and then revolution." Born in peacetime, the French Revolution had three years to take form without foreign war, and in the main without civil war as well. It was only as of 1792 that it became "more and more a European event, . . . [its] signpost pointing outward from Paris to the world." Three years of peace were followed by twenty-three years of European war in which the Great Revolution and the *Grande Nation* were inseparable. To the contrary, the Russian Revolution was born and had its infancy in war so that Russia "steered from three years of war with the world into an internal revolution" whose signpost pointed increasingly inward.[37] Moreover, some of the essential characteristics of the Russian Revolution took shape in four years of inseparable foreign and civil conflict. Thereafter, starting with the Treaty of Riga of October 1920 and until 1939, the revolution was all but contained within Russia's amputated borders.

There were, then, two radically different paths. Following a few years of peace, for nearly a quarter century France engaged in successful foreign war which significantly influenced the course of the revolution at home, including the course of its terror. By contrast, the Russian Revolution barely survived the early years of what was a devastating civil and foreign war aggravated and prolonged by outside intervention. This trial was followed by two decades of unrelenting quarantine which deeply affected the life of the Soviet regime and project. From 1792 to 1815 and 1920 to 1939, domestic and foreign affairs were intensely intertwined. Sometimes the domestic repercussions of international politics outweighed the impact of internal on external developments, though at other times the roles were reversed. Overall there is, however, no denying or disputing that the interrelationship of foreign war and revolution was of vital importance, particularly as it bore on the flux and reflux of civil violence.

❋ ❋ ❋

The bayonets of revolution and counterrevolution need ideology as much as ideology needs them. Ideology is the lifeblood of revolution, and like revolution it is a highly charged word-concept. In politics as well as in intellection, to be ideological is to be biased and unobjective. Ideologies are said to dissemble and misrepresent, if not falsify reality.[38] Just as one person's religion is another's obscurantism or fanaticism, so one individual's ideology is another's partisanship or prevarication.

Ideology is a collectively held worldview consisting of a body of ideas, tenets, and principles expressed not only through written or spoken words but also with symbols, gestures, attitudes, and rituals. It advocates a project of change—or opposition to change—at the same time that it explains, justifies, and legitimates the actions of those seeking to further and implement it. Being action-oriented, ideology, to be effective, is "expressed in normative maxims, slogans, and rhetorical formulas" designed to persuade, reassure, and inspire partisans and supporters. Accordingly ideology is the "mutation of a system of thought into a belief system" whose tenets become "impermeable and inaccessible to argument."[39] These tenets are intended to be "believed

. . . [rather than] explored, tested, and held under the searchlight of consciousness,"[40] with the result that their proponents move in a closed system "impregnated with orthodoxy . . . [and] intolerance,"[41] disposing them to face their adversaries and critics in a "friend-enemy" logic and spirit.[42]

Although the belief system's major articles of faith are closely inter-linked, their position within the system as well as their relation to each other change with changing circumstances. Ideology is inherently flexible and adaptable, not rigid and immutable. Its exponents and executors constantly attune principle and reality, theory and practice. Ideology "evolves and plays different roles in different phases of revolution."[43] Rather than fix iron parameters for action, it "sets limits on possible policy choices," particularly in moments of great peril and bewilderment.[44]

In revolutionary moments ideology also, or above all, serves a founding function. It is "tied to the need of a [new] social group to project an image of itself, to present itself in the theoretical sense, as if going and acting on stage."[45] No less important, in the quest for legitimacy ideology celebrates the tempest and spirit, as well as heroes, of the founding act with a view to project its "shockwaves" well beyond the generation of the "founding fathers."[46]

※ ※ ※

As previously noted, the breakdown of sovereignty is the essential pre-condition for the escalation of revolt into revolution. This collapse of legitimate authority goes hand in hand with the dislocation of the legal and social order as well as of cultural and intellectual life. Meanwhile, the intractable political dislocation is fueled by economic and financial difficulties which, in turn, are aggravated by the general disorder. But above all, the disintegration of the central state results in the creation of two or more fragile and competing centers of sovereignty with ample space for local and regional disorder and self-affirmation, as well as for personal and communitarian self-expression and liberation.

Indeed chaos is the hallmark of the indeterminate revolutionary situation. This chaos is not only a spring of hope and resolve. It is also a source of fear and uncertainty. Michelet noted that in revolutionary France there was widespread fear of "universal disorganization," with "growing paralysis of the cities [and] . . . agitation in the country-side."[47] In the face of this social decomposition, which probably was greatest in rural France, "the body politic was [as if] dead." The center, in Paris, was "unable and unwilling to act": the armies went without arms and provisions and the laws of the Assembly "were not dispatched to the provinces," leaving not a few of them "to their own devices."[48]

Even if Michelet overstated the fear and the reality of France's disintegration and lawlessness by 1792, it must have been considerable, all the more so since it coincided with the start of war, the frontier defeats, the declaration of a national emergency, the Brunswick Manifesto, the drive against refractory priests, the reversal of the throne, and the prison massacres. Ironically, the nascent revolutionary regime was often seen as a "reign of anarchy," with the Assembly helpless by virtue of having no administrative organs, law courts, and enforcement agencies of its own. The vacuum of effective power all but invited an "access of fury" by Jacobins "rallying the [political] clubs and appealing to violence." Their purpose was to save France by reuniting unruly elements and stray provinces in a new political and social edifice, with a "vigorous negation of the old order as its cornerstone."[49]

What was true of France was also true of Russia. In fact, the chaos in France in 1792 was child's play compared with Russia's in 1917, let alone in 1918 to 1921. At the onset of the revolution in the late tsarist empire, some of the major cities as well as much of the countryside were in upheaval, and in no time there were serious food shortages, the economy was spent, and rail transport was paralyzed. This social and economic disorder was both cause and effect of the disintegration of the army, the fall of the monarchy, the collapse of political and legal authority, and the breakup of the empire, compounded by the strains of foreign and civil war. Russia's time of troubles at once paved the Bolsheviks' way to power and weighed them down with an impossible burden. With them as with the Jacobins, to control the situation, in the words of Michelet, "fury took the place of force, which was wanting."

* * *

The virtual breakdown of authority in an environment of swelling social disorder aggravated by foreign and civil war demands resolute action in which innovation is dictated as much by critical circumstances as by the rage to remake the world. In the conservative perspective, the chaos of revolution is no excuse or license for radical change. Burke, indeed, was blind to this contingency when he condemned "the enormous evils of this dreadful innovation" due to "[t]he revolution harpies of France, sprung from night and hell, or from that chaotick anarchy, which generates unequivocally 'all monstrous, all prodigious things,' cuckoo-like, adulterously lay their eggs, and brood over, and hatch them in the nest of every neighboring State." Although these "obscene harpies" affected "divine attributes," they were "foul and ravenous birds of prey . . . [who] leave nothing unrent, unrifled, unravaged, or unpolluted with the slime of their filthy offal."[50] In retrospect, and soberly, Tocqueville saw France's predicament in the first flush of revolution as "the tumultuous spasms of a disjointed society . . . [defying] the old regime [that was] nearly uprooted and holding out at only a few points and the new one [that was] not yet established."[51]

Indeed, a chief defining characteristic of the revolutionary moment may well be this "hiatus between the no-longer and the not-yet" in which "the relationship between foundation and innovation" is inseparable from the "unpredictability of emergences."[52] Merleau-Ponty considered this moment one in which "history is suspended and institutions verging on extinction demand that men make fundamental decisions which are fraught with enormous risk by virtue of their final outcome being contingent on a largely unforeseeable conjuncture," latent with "tragedy."[53] Hannah Arendt was equally alive to the hazards of innovation in historical moments located somewhere between an extinct past and an unfathomable future. Rather than embrace Burke's "hatred to innovation"[54] she discerned a certain "pathos of novelty," or a mixture of wonderment and apprehension, that takes hold of historical actors in the face of painful and destructive decisions bearing on a perilous tomorrow. Indeed, for Arendt "the element of novelty" is as "intimately associated" with revolution as the elements of "[new] beginning and violence." In the eye of the revolutionary storm, bewildered and inexperienced politicians improvise and innovate without the benefit of well-grounded theoretical and programmatic precepts, as they opt for a *fuite en avant*, a necessary but perilous rush forward, meant to restore a single sovereignty.[55]

This headlong "march into the unknown,"[56] intended to reconstitute state authority as an essential step to a new beginning, is bound to be violent, terrifying, and savage, there being no prior laws, national or international, to put it under constraint. A revolution has a protracted life. It entails rebellions, mutinies, and protests whose control or suppression involves the new regime's use of repressive violence which, with time, becomes legitimate force. The revolutionary leaders perceive and denounce these resistances as counter-revolts belonging to the counterrevolution, not unlike the military resistance of the outside world. The regime represents its own violence on the one hand, and that of counterrevolution on the other, in terms of the belief system which explains and justifies the revolutionary project as a whole. Before long the violence of the beginning is sacralized and assigned a central place in the founding myth.

❋ ❋ ❋

According to Tocqueville, compared to the goals of the upheavals of the seventeenth century, the "real object of the [French] Revolution was less a new form of government than a new form of society; less the achievement of political rights than the destruction of privileges." The Revolution was uniquely comprehensive, in that it at one and the same time "assailed political and social beliefs, aspired to reform the individual and the State, tried to change old customs, established opinions, and fixed habits on every subject simultaneously."[57] Jacob Burckhardt considered this broad-gauged revolution the expression and carrier of a radical crisis whose "fanaticisms" were in the nature of a "fever" and which served to "sweep away a mass of social and cultural forms that had long since lost all vitality" but would have been impossible to "remove from the world" in times of normalcy.[58] Ultimately Burckhardt, like Tocqueville, prized above all historical continuity and preservation.[59] Even so, he, contemporaneously with Tocqueville, developed an ever more burning interest in the dynamics and lessons of revolutionary moments, with their "ruptures and reactions," which were at once terrifying and salutary.[60]

Although revolution accelerates history, it is not a sprint but a marathon—it "lasts a long time." It takes at least one generation for its radical transformations to take root, entailing a "melt-down bringing popular opinions, impulses, and habits to a boil" along with the release of the "underworld of madness and hatred" which intensify the "barbarization, mutilation, and goring" of society.[61] This de-civilization is the downside of the crisis which secretes decisive changes in the governing and ruling class; in the economic, social, and legal order; in the code of speech and dress; in the style of architecture and monuments; in the ways of thinking and argumentation. In some spheres changes take longer than in others, but in none do they happen overnight.[62]

Still, precisely because of its Janus-faced and far-reaching nature, as well as its relatively long life, a revolutionary crisis can be considered an historical epoch with a precise beginning but an ill-defined and problematic end. Indeed, compared to a historical period, which has an uncertain opening as well as closing, an epoch starts with "a beginning event which gives rise to the new (*das Neue*) by reason of a 'revolution' of things meant to be irreversible."[63] There is no analogous terminal event to set off the end of the revolutionary epoch from the start of the post-revolutionary era.

With a spectacular turning point as its threshold, an epoch has a physiognomy, a form and structure, a chronology, a tempo, and a *Zeitgeist*. But the whole is more than the sum of its parts. Of course, Burke instantly had the intuition that 1789 marked a radical discontinuity and challenge in the history of Christian Europe. After a while Joseph de Maistre, having read Burke, conceded his own "error" of initially having considered the revolution an "event" when, in fact, it was an "epoch." Confident that the "chaos," which was providential, would end in unpredictable ways, Maistre nevertheless "expressed compassion for generations condemned to experience . . . the adversities of epochs of world history."[64] For him the revolution was not simply a disorder but a new order with an ideological consistency: by defying Christianity in France the enemy, in the form of "the goddess of Reason," was "attacking the citadel." It was this moral or religious struggle which led Maistre to "consider the French Revolution a great epoch whose untold consequences will be felt well beyond the time and land in which it exploded."[65]

Hegel celebrated what Maistre deplored and dreaded. For Hegel the French Revolution was an "agitated time of hoping and fearing" for the advance of the idea of the freedom to be human. The year 1789 marked the start of a "new epoch" which he hailed for being a "rosy . . . [and] glorious mental dawn." From his perspective "in its substantial import . . . the revolution is World-Historical," and as such a "turning point" into an "epoch of the world's history" whose political resolution remained uncertain.[66]

Actually, Lenin developed a perceptive idea of epoch as he reflected about the complexity and pace of the transformation of Russia. In 1923, in one of his last writings, he held that it would take at least "an entire historical epoch . . . of one or two decades" to win over the peasantry for the modernization of agriculture under the New Economic Policy. Overall he expected the near future to "be a special historical epoch, and without this epoch, without universal literacy, without a sufficient degree of explaining, of teaching the population how to use books, and without a material basis for all this, without a certain guarantee, if only, let us say, against crop failure, against famine, and so on—without that we shall not attain our goal."[67]

A quarter of a century later Merleau-Ponty, as if following in Maistre's footsteps, distinguished between normal and epic historical moments. Having experienced the chaos, violence, and intellectual bewilderment of the Second World War through the defeat and occupation of France, and sympathetic to the flawed promise of the Russian Revolution, he undertook to rethink the explosive contradictions of his time. Merleau-Ponty propounded that when living in what Charles Péguy called "a historical *period*, when political man can afford to confine himself to administering the established regime and law, humanity can hope for a history without violence." But when individuals "have the misfortune or good luck to live in an *epoch*, or in a moment in which a nation's or society's traditional ground crumbles, and willy-nilly man has to reconstruct human relations himself, then each man's liberty is a mortal threat to all other men, and violence reappears." Merleau-Ponty followed Machiavelli in conceiving an epoch as a time of (re)foundation freighted with primal violence.[68]

For Hannah Arendt, the French Revolution inaugurated an "epoch of world history" in which "politics became a matter of foreign affairs" and in which the "pathos of novelty" combined with the "two-edged compulsion of ideology and terror" to produce the "chaos of violence." Even more strongly than Merleau-Ponty, though also guided by Machiavelli, she focused, as noted before, on the quintessential linkage of revolution and new foundation. Of course Arendt, like Merleau-Ponty, was intensely concerned with the colossal difficulties of preserving the spirit and intention of the founding act during the institutionalization of the new regime.[69]

✳ ✳ ✳

NOTES

1. Alain Rey, *Révolution: Histoire d'un mot* (Paris: Gallimard, 1989), pp. 17–18; and John Dunn, *Modern Revolutions: An Introduction to the Analysis of a Political Phenomenon* (Cambridge: Cambridge University Press, 1972), p. 12.

2. Hannah Arendt, *On Revolution* (New York: Viking, 1965), p. 13. See also Dana R. Villa, *Arendt and Heidegger: The Fate of the Political* (Princeton: Princeton University Press, 1996), p. 156 and p. 171.

3. J. G. Frazer, *The Belief in Immortality and the Worship of the Dead*, vol. 1 (London: Macmillan, 1913), p. 4.

4. Mirabeau, cited in Antoine Vallentin, *Mirabeau*, vol. 2 (Paris: Grasset, 1947), pp. 345–46.

5. Cited in Boris Souvarine, *Stalin: A Critical Study of Bolshevism* (New York: Longmans, Green, 1939), p. 253.

6. Arendt, *On Revolution*, p. 111.

7. Bloch, *Apologie pour l'histoire ou metier d'historien* (Paris: Colin, 1993), p. 144.

8. Dunn, *Modern Revolutions*, pp. 1–2.

9. See Paul Ricoeur, *Du texte à l'action: Essais d'herméneutique*, vol. 2 (Paris: Seuil, 1986), pp. 303–31, esp. p. 305 and p. 314.

10. Maurice Merleau-Ponty, *Humanism and Terror: An Essay on the Communist Problem* (Boston: Beacon, 1969), p. xvii.

11. Benedetto Croce, *Teoria e storia della storiografia*, 2nd ed. (Bari: Laterza, 1920), p. 4.

12. See Quentin Skinner, "Meaning and Understanding in the History of Ideas," in *History and Theory* 8:1 (1969): pp. 3–53.

13. See Gilles Deleuze and Felix Guattari, *Qu'est-ce que la philosophie?* (Paris: Editions de Minuit, 1991). See also Paul Veyne, *Comment on écrit l'histoire* (Paris: Seuil, 1971), pp. 174–90, 379–82.

14. Jules Monnerot, *Sociology and Psychology of Communism* (Boston: Beacon Press, 1953), p. 295.

15. Eugen Rosenstock, *Die europäischen Revolutionen* (Jena: Eugen Diederichs, 1931), p. 3. See also Reinhart Koselleck, *Critique and Crisis: Enlightenment and the Pathogenesis of Modern Society* (Oxford: Berg, 1988).

16. Koselleck, *Critique*, p. 160, n. 6.

17. Koselleck, "Der neuzeitliche Revolutionsbegriff als geschichtliche Kategorie," in Helmut Reinalter, ed., *Revolution und Gesellschaft: Zur Entwicklung des neuzeitlichen Revolutionsbegriffs* (Innsbruck: Inn-Verlag, 1980), pp. 23–34, esp. 26–27. See also Karl-Heinz Bender, "Der politische Revolutionsbegriff in Frankreich zwischen Mittelalter und gloreicher Revolution," in Reinalter, ed., *Revolution und Gesellschaft*, pp. 35–52, esp. pp. 47–49; and Rosenstock, *Die europäischen Revolutionen*, pp. 7–8.

18. Rosenstock, *Die europäischen Revolutionen*, pp. 9–10. See also Karl Griewank, *Der neuzeitliche Revolutionsbegriff* (Weimar: Böhlaus, 1955); and Arendt, *On Revolution*, p. 36.

19. See Theodor Draper, *A Struggle for Power* (New York: Times Books, 1996); Gordon Wood, *The Radicalism of the American Revolution* (New York: Knopf, 1992); and Barbara Clark Smith, "The Adequate Revolution," in *William and Mary Quarterly*, vol. 51 (October 1994): pp. 684–92.

20. Daniel Mornet, *Les origines intellectuelles de la Révolution française, 1715–1878*, 6th ed. (Paris: Armand Colin, 1967), p. 217.

21. Roger Chartier, *Les origines culturelles de la Révolution française* (Paris: Seuil, 1990), pp. 14–15, 30.

22. Edgar Quinet, *La Révolution* (Paris: Belin, 1987), pp. 150–51.

23. "Sur les principes du gouvernement révolutionnaire" (December 25, 1793), in Robespierre, *Discours et rapports à la convention* (Paris: 10/18, 1965), pp. 187–206, esp. p. 190.

24. Rosenstock, *Die europäischen Revolutionen*, p. 14.

25. Ibid., pp. 14–15. See also Walter Benjamin, *Zur Kritik der Gewalt und andere Aufsätze* (Frankfurt/Main: Suhrkamp, 1965), p. 41; and Maurice Merleau-Ponty, *Sens et non-sens* (Paris: Nagel, 1966), p. 180.

26. Arendt, *On Revolution*, pp. 50–51.

27. Mornet, *Les origines*, p. 471.

28. See Shlomo Avineri, *The Social and Political Thought of Karl Marx* (Cambridge: Cambridge University Press, 1970), esp. ch. 7.

29. Rod Aya, "Theories of Revolution Reconsidered: Contrasting Methods of Collective Violence," in *Theory and Society* 8:1 (July 1979): pp. 39–99, esp. pp. 40–45; and Charles Tilly, *European Revolutions, 1492–1992* (Oxford: Blackwell, 1993), pp. 8–14.

30. "Letter to a Noble Lord" (1796), in Paul Langford, ed., *The Writings and Speeches of Edmund Burke*, vol. 9 (Oxford: Clarendon, 1991), pp. 145–87, esp. p. 156. As early as 1790 Burke averred that "the very idea of the fabrication of a new government is enough to fill us with disgust and horror." *Reflections on the Revolution in France*, in *Writings and Speeches of Edmund Burke*, vol. 8 (Oxford: Clarendon, 1989), pp. 53–293, esp. p. 81.

31. Arendt, *On Revolution*, p. 39.

32. Rosenstock, *Die europäischen Revolutionen*, p. 5; and Nicolas Berdyaev, *The Origins of Russian Communism* (London: Geoffrey Bles, 1948), p. 114.

33. Cited in Frank Attar, *La Révolution déclare la guerre à l'Europe* (Paris: Editions Complexe, 1992), p. 16.

34. Burke, "Thoughts on French Affairs" (1791), in Langford, ed., *Writings and Speeches*, vol. 8, pp. 338–86, esp. p. 340.

35. Hegel cited in Joachim Ritter, *Hegel and the French Revolution: Essays on the Philosophy of Right* (Cambridge, Mass.: MIT Press, 1982), p. 51.

36. Arendt, *On Revolution*, p. 7 and p. 9.

37. Rosenstock, *Die europäischen Revolutionen*, p. 22.

38. See Anthony Arblaster, "Ideology and Intellectuals," in Robert Benewick, R. N. Berki, and Blikhu Parekh, eds., *Knowledge and Belief in Politics: the Problem of Ideology* (London: Allen & Unwin, 1973), pp. 115–29, esp. p. 115. See also Clifford Geertz, "Ideology as a Cultural System," in Geertz, *The Interpretation of Culture* (New York: Basic Books, 1973), p. 199.

39. Jacques Ellul cited and commented by Ricoeur, *Du texte*, pp. 307–8.

40. Giovanni Sartori, "Politics, Ideology, and Belief System," in *The American Political Science Review* 63:2 (1969): pp. 398–411.

41. Ricoeur, *Du texte*, p. 309.

42. Robert Putnam, "Studying Elite Political Culture: The Case of Ideology," in *The American Political Science Review* 65:3 (1971): p. 655.

43. Jack Goldstone, *Revolution and Rebellion in the Early Modern World* (Berkeley: University of California Press, 1991), p. 417.

44. Rosemary O'Kane, *The Revolutionary Reign of Terror: The Role of Violence in Political Change* (Brockfield, Vt.: Edward Elgar, 1991), p. 53 and p. 83.

45. Ricoeur, *Du texte*, p. 306.

46. Ibid., p. 307 and p. 309.

47. Michelet, *Histoire de la Révolution française*, 2 vols. (Paris: Laffont, 1979), vol. 2, pp. 135–36.

48. Michelet, *Histoire*, vol. 1, p. 738.

49. Ibid., vol. 2, pp. 149–72.

50. Burke, "Letter to a Noble Lord," in Langford, ed., *Writings and Speeches*, vol. 9, p. 156.

51. Alexis de Tocqueville, *"The European Revolution" and Correspondence with Gobineau*, trans. John Lukacs (Garden City, N.Y.: Doubleday, 1953), p. 105.

52. Miriam Revault D'Allonnes, *Ce que l'homme fait à l'homme* (Paris: Seuil, 1995), p. 15.

53. Merleau-Ponty, *Humanism and Terror*, p. 43 and p. 62.

54. Burke, "Letter to a Noble Lord," p. 157.

55. Arendt, *On Revolution*, p. 19, p. 40, and p. 43.

56. Vladimir Mayakovsky cited in Roy Medvedev, *Let History Judge: The Origins and Consequences of Stalinism* (New York: Knopf, 1972), p. 234.

57. Tocqueville, *"The European Revolution,"* p. 160 and p. 125.

58. Jacob Burckhardt, *Weltgeschichtliche Betrachtungen* (Stuttgart: Kröner, 1978), pp. 188–89.

59. See Karl Löwith, *Meaning in History* (Chicago: University of Chicago Press, 1949), pp. 21–24.

60. Burckhardt, *Betrachtungen*, passim.

61. Rosenstock, *Die europäischen Revolutionen*, pp. 21–22.

62. See Koselleck, "Das achtzehnte Jahrhundert als Beginn der Neuzeit," in Reinhart Herzog and Reinhart Koselleck, eds., *Epochenschwelle und Epochenbewusstsein* (Munich: Wilhelm Fink, 1987), pp. 269–82.

63. Hans Robert Jauss, "Il faut commencer par le commencement," in Herzog and Koselleck, eds., *Epochenschwelle*, pp. 563–70, esp. p.568; and Koselleck, "Das achtzehnte Jahrhundert," p. 269.

64. "Discours à la Marquise de Costa" (1794), cited in Robert Triomphe, *Joseph de Maistre: Etude sur la vie et sur la doctrine d'un matérialiste mystique* (Geneva: Droz, 1968), p. 163.

65. Maistre, *Considérations sur la France*, in Maistre, *Ecrits sur la Révolution* (Paris: Presses Universitaires, 1989), p. 112.

66. Cited in Ritter, *Hegel*, p. 43, p. 47, and p. 51.

67. Cited in Medvedev, *Let History Judge*, p. 74.

68. Merleau-Ponty, *Humanism and Terror*, p. xvii (italics in text), and *Sens et non-sens* (Paris: Gallimard, 1996), p. 125.

69. Arendt, *On Revolution*, introduction, ch. 1, and pp. 140–41.

Counterrevolution

THERE CAN BE no revolution without counterrevolution; both as phenomenon and process, they are inseparable, like truth and falsehood. They are bound to each other "as reaction is bound to action," making for a "historical motion, which is at once dialectical and driven by necessity."[1] The struggle between the ideas and forces of revolution and counterrevolution was a prime mover of the spiraling violence inherent to the French and Russian revolutions.

Although counterrevolution is the other half of revolution, it tends not to be recognized and theorized as such. This relative neglect of the necessary antithesis of revolution is reflected in the catalogues of major research libraries. The subject index of the on-line catalogue of Firestone Library at Princeton University, which follows that of the Library of Congress, can be taken as characteristic. In 1990, this catalogue had several thousand entries, since its inception in 1980, under the heading "revolution." It also had over six hundred entries under the heading "conservatism." But the fewer than two hundred titles listed under "reaction" referred, without exception, to books and articles in the natural sciences. As for the heading of "counterrevolution," it was absent altogether. That same year, the on-line bibliography of the Bibliothèque Nationale in Paris was similarly skewed.

This disregard recently was reinforced by the argument that counterrevolution was a myth or phantasm with little, if any, basis in reality. In this reading, the revolutionaries of 1789 and 1917 eventually reified counterrevolution in an invented polymorphous "aristocratic" (1789) or "capitalist" (1917) conspiracy. The idea of this plot presumably was implanted or emerged as the organizing principle of the Manichaean ideology and rhetoric with which Jacobins and Bolsheviks justified the use of rampant violence and terror against their real and imagined enemies.[2]

In any case, counterrevolution is essential, not accessory, and it has as much of a place in the French and Russian—nay, European—political tradition and culture as revolution. In eighteenth-century France its ideas broke forth as negations of the ideas of the dissenting *philosophes*. In his seminal study of the intellectual origins of the French Revolution, Daniel Mornet devotes a powerful chapter to "the resistances of religious and political traditions," setting forth the major beliefs and tempers which after 1789 framed the counterrevolutionary persuasion.[3] Characteristically, Mornet's classic kept inspiring the study of the unfolding and diffusion of the Enlightenment without commensurate attention to the incipient anti- or counter-Enlightenment.[4] Perforce the central ideas of the *lumières* from the outset, and the ideas of the counter-Enlightenment were *semper et ubique* engaged in battle with those of the Enlightenment. If there is a filiation of thought from the "rationalistic secular Enlightenment" of the eighteenth and nineteenth centuries to the terrors of the French and Russian revolutions, then there is an equally weighty line from the "irrational[ism] and anti-universal[ism] of the Counter-Enlightenment to the rise and terrifying rule of Fascism, especially National Socialism."[5] With the necessary adaptations, perhaps Tocqueville's judgment of the 1850s should serve as a starting point for sober reflection by both champions and critics of ideological determinism: "our times are as blind and as stupid in their systematic and absolute denigration of what is called the thought of the eighteenth century as were the men of that century in their blind infatuation with it."[6]

* * *

The word-concept *counterrevolution* has a much shorter history than the word-concept *revolution*. For all intents and purposes, it was a child of the epoch of the French Revolution. Of course, there were oppositions to the Enlightenment during the eighteenth century, and challenges to the radical changes which broke forth in 1788. At first the nascent revolutionaries had to confront and gauge this credal and political resistance without the benefit of an organizing construct or defining name. They tended to conceive it as being carried by the privileged orders of the *ancien régime*, notably the high aristocracy, nobility, and clergy. Before long, however, the new men of power thought and argued more in political than social terms, opposition to the government of the day becoming the critical touchstone. The master-concept of counterrevolution took form during this shift from a social to a political perception and representation of resistance to revolution.[7]

Presently the Jacobin practice of conflating all resistances, without distinction, and tying them to an all-embracing conspiracy, gave the word-concept counterrevolution a distinct politico-ideological coloration. But its polemic uses and abuses do not justify questioning either the construct as such or the historical particulars it was meant to reckon in. Indeed, it is difficult to decry the word-concept counterrevolution without bringing into question the word-concept revolution, both word-concepts being equally problematic and yet indispensable.[8] A recent proposal to replace the word counterrevolution with the word resistance because it lends itself to being rendered in the plural invites skepticism.[9] It comes at a time when the word resistance has a certain aura for calling to mind the heroic struggle against Fascism in Nazi-dominated Europe. It is worth noting, in passing, that in bygone days Jules Michelet ingenuously used resistance interchangeably with counterrevolution for reasons of literary grace.[10]

※ ※ ※

Old regimes are not easily destabilized and brought down, above all because the privileged orders fight back rather than vacate the stage, negotiate their demise, or lie down to die. To be sure, cleavages in the governing and ruling classes are an essential if not sufficient precondition for successful revolt or revolution. But these internal divisions ought not to be exaggerated: in the face of growing perils the old elites tend to mend their fences even if they fail to agree on a common strategy to restabilize the situation in their own favor. They are driven to do so by an elementary sense of self-preservation braced by material concerns, tested loyalties, wounded pride, and fear of chaos. Just as the upper ten thousand do not fade away willingly and overnight, neither do the established order's inveterate institutions, which are only marginally less resilient than the mentalities, worldviews, and traditions which sustain them. Both civil society and polity are wired for preservation, not sudden death, and their agents will give battle for their survival. A serious crisis comes to a revolutionary boil with the "material resistance . . . of counteracting forces consisting of all long-established institutions and laws, . . . including those individuals who are tied to [this complex] by duty and advantage." Given the stakes, the "ferocity and pathos" of engagement on both sides is hardly surprising: "on the one side an abstract sense of loyalty and a religion, on the other a new universal principle," without regard for the means and costs of the showdown on either side.[11] According to Burckhardt, only such castes as "the Church hierarchy and the old French aristocracy were absolutely incorrigible, although individual members realized that an abyss was opening before them."[12] But Tocqueville, for his part, judged that what "inflamed, embittered, and exasperated the people's . . . hatred of the aristocracy" was less the extent of "class hatreds . . . [due to] social abuses . . . than the duration and sharpness of the struggle over them."[13] Marx similarly stressed the explosive nature of the violent resistance of incumbent social classes to "legal" reform, which he characterized as "the war cry of the violent counter-revolution against an evolution that is, in fact, 'pacific'."[14]

It goes without saying that the radical recasting of the Estates General and the fall of the Bastille in 1789, and the replay of the revolution of 1905 compounded by the abdication of Nicholas II in 1917 could not help but arouse and intensify resistance. In France the Queen, the Comte d'Artois, and the Marquis de Favras were among the first and foremost diehards; in Russia senior army officers, the courtiers of the last Romanov, and the Union of the Russian People. Following further setbacks for the old order, these deep-dyed reactionaries and incipient counterrevolutionaries of the first hour lost their monopoly on resistance when such stalwart conservatives of preventive reform as Charles Alexander de Calonne and Paul Miliukov went over to the opposition not only at home but also among the émigrés who were rallying foreign support for the counterrevolution.

Following the breakdown of sovereignty in 1789 and 1917, the opponents of radical reform and revolution lost little time seeking or making occasions to make a stand. In France, unlike in Russia, for almost three years the monarch was central to these efforts, most of which were more of an "offensive" than "defensive" nature, all the more so in the perception of ascendant and naturally suspicious revolutionaries. Indeed, this battle for sovereignty radicalized the situation, each confrontation fostering militancy, fear, distrust, and blindness in the opposing camps, soon to be locked into the friend-enemy dissociation. In 1789 as in 1917, the forces of the old order were at least as aggressive as those of the new.[15]

Between 1789 and 1794 in France and 1917 and 1921 in Russia resistance was the rule, not the exception, although it was disjointed and inconstant. Even so, the inchoate central governments of the formative new regimes were hard put to extend their sovereign authority over large parts of the country at a time when their capital cities were intermittently at a boil.

In mid-1793 some sixty of France's eighty-three departments were more or less out of control and a majority of the population in various degrees balked the republican authorities, raising serious apprehensions about a runaway national disintegration. By then France may well have counted as many counterrevolutionaries as revolutionaries, and two years later the number of counterrevolutionaries is likely to have been even greater. Armed resistance, making for severe centrifugal pulls, was most potent in the west and the south, where no lesser cities than Lyons, Marseilles, and Toulon were in open rebellion. Seen from Paris, in particular from the vantage point of the Committee of Public Safety, this reformist-federative insurgency risked being usurped by counterrevolutionary forces with ties to the émigrés and their European patrons.

Russia's crisis of disorganization was even more far-reaching and severe than France's, which accounts for the discomfiture of the reformist provisional governments of Prince Georgy Lvov and Alexander Kerensky. Of necessity Bolshevik rule was imperiled by resistance and decomposition from the outset, and increasingly so starting in early 1918. The fledgling regime had but a narrow base of support in both city and country, which explains the potential strength of its foes. Indeed, the "objective" facts of its imperilment, both domestic and international, were so formidable that there was little need for the Bolsheviks to overestimate and overdramatize them (although they certainly represented them in keeping with their unsteady ideological reason). For four years Russia's civil and peasant wars were intertwined with, and aggravated by, insurgencies for secession or autonomy, especially along the western marshes of the crumbling ex-empire, and most of these armed risings enjoyed foreign support.

In both crisis-torn France and Russia there were times and places in which it was easier to "opt for" and "live inside" the counterrevolution than the revolution.[16] In some respects the elements of counter-revolution, both passive and active, were as strong and defining as the revolutionary ones. *Prima facie* counterrevolution was the great loser of 1789 to 1795 in France and 1917 to 1921 in Russia. But this outcome was by no means inevitable. In France the victory of the forces of resistance, including the sworn counterrevolutionaries among them, came within the range of historical possibility at the time of the royal family's flight to Varennes in June 1791; the revolt of the Vendée and the "Federalist" uprisings in 1793; and the royalist insurrection of the 13 Vendémiaire (October 5, 1795). In Russia the opposition stood fair to prevail with the challenge of General Kornilov in August 1917; the uprisings in Yaroslavl and the assassination of Bolshevik leaders, including the attempt on Lenin's life, in the summer of 1918; the uphill civil war in mid-1919; and the convulsions of the first half of the 1930s. Subsequently, in the fall of 1941 the armies of the Axis powers came within an ace of eradicating the Bolshevik regime and dismembering the Soviet Union. The fact that the opponents of revolution were the losers, and partly the victims, of the struggle for the reestablishment of a single sovereignty is no reason to ignore or minimize their weight, nor should they be either exalted or vilified.

✳ ✳ ✳

In their symbiotic relationship, counterrevolution is more ideologically reactive and contrived, as well as less creative and organic, than revolution.[17] It emerges as a praxis rather than a theory. Not unlike revolution it is, of course, multifaceted. Above all, counterrevolution is inextricably bound up with reaction and conservatism, all the more so in times of trouble. During the revolutionary tempest it also rallies those individuals and groups who sooner or later feel disappointed, affronted, or betrayed by the revolution. Although inherently reactive, in both word and deed, counterrevolution is as likely to be militant and aggressive as passive and defensive.

Reaction is one of the major components of the counterrevolutionary complex. Even in times of normalcy, reactionaries consider civil and political society to be corrupt and decaying. Pessimistic about both the present and future, they are daunted by change and long for a return to the world of a mythical and romanticized past. Opposed to the leveling of society, reactionaries cling to the hierarchic, prescriptive, and deferential ways of monarchy, church, estate, and community. By and large reaction is in the nature of a reflexive traditionalism which, as an un- or pre-political conservatism, is anchored in the "unconscious" psychological predisposition of "isolated" individuals. Although this latent or "dormant" reactionist temper becomes manifest and active in a time of troubles, it remains essentially un- or "pretheoretical."[18]

Conservatism is another vital element of the counterrevolutionary amalgam. Rather than make a fetish of the past or the future, it is firmly fixed upon the present, even though its core ideas and values are ageless and enduring. Conservatives take a pessimistic view of what they consider an unchanging human nature and, like reactionaries, they gainsay the equality or advancement of humanity. They take the individual to be defined by society, whose organic growth and structure frame a system of authority which is historically, if not divinely, consecrated. At once natural and necessary, this stratified authority is validated and perpetuated by the primary and interwoven institutions of family, property, and minimal state. Until recently, natural conservatism was deeply embedded in agrarian and religious custom, and its character was determined by this anchorage. But with time it has adjusted to the modernizing world, becoming increasingly secular, urban, and tolerant of the interventionist state. In any case, whatever the makeup of civil and political society, conservatism's core value and objective is the preservation of the established order. Eschewing abstract ideals and principles, conservatives are supreme pragmatists and empiricists. To the extent that they do have a theoretical posture, it consists of challenging and refuting the orientations of their adversaries rather than formulating new ones of their own. In the face of society's inevitable and constant if creeping mutation, they favor gradual change and amelioration over immobility and intransigence.

The shift from natural or traditional to political conservatism took place in the wake of the Enlightenment. In "conscious and reflective . . . opposition to the . . . 'progressive' movement" conservatism developed into a "counter-system" with a distinct "theoretical nucleus . . . and a new form of thought" eminently adaptable to changing historical circumstances.[19] As may be expected, times of real or imagined crisis challenge political conservatives to articulate and defend their values, institutions, and practices. Compared to reactionaries, whose essential values and whose aversion for populist politics they share, committed conservatives become distinctly more theoretical and programmatic.

As for counterrevolution, it is, above all, more doctrinal, principled, and impassioned than reaction and conservatism. Sworn to a Weltanschauung, counterrevolutionaries are guided by an ideology and a program. Many of their political, social, and cultural values overlap with those of their indispensable even if reluctant reactionary and conservative collaborators. But their political formula is altogether more extremist in its assault on subversive and corrupting agents, its call for regeneration and purification, and its incitement of hatred of alleged domestic conspirators and their foreign accomplices. Counterrevolutionaries tend to be more "revolutionary" in style and *modus operandi* than in substance.

After 1870 counterrevolutionary ideologues and politicians began to be drawn less from the traditional elites of wealth, privilege, and culture than from the middle classes. Unlike the notables of reaction and conservatism who continued to disdain and distrust the demos, the new-model counterrevolutionary tribunes took to mass politics. Rather than rely on deference and prescription, they appealed to the lower orders of city and country, inflaming and manipulating their resentment of those above them, their fear of those below them, and their estrangement from the real world about them. They may be said to have raised the popular anti-revolution from below to vitalize and collaborate with the counterrevolution from above.

As noted before, when times are out of joint there are significant family resemblances between, on the one hand, reaction and conservatism and, on the other, counterrevolution. These resemblances pertain to ideas, values, attitudes, and objectives, as well as to social carriers. Despite certain dissonances there is a shared appreciation, not to say celebration, of order, tradition, hierarchy, authority, discipline, and loyalty. The three branches of the counterrevolutionary constellation also converge in their distrust of human nature, derogation of reason, and suspicion of modernity. Of course, their strategies and end-purposes diverge, but not to the point of serious divisions during the escalating friend-enemy dissociation, which is greatly influenced by the ebb and flow of foreign intervention, the counterrevolution's essential, if not ultimate, recourse.

While historians dissect the counterrevolutionary world and categorize its major components, the actors of the time are driven to see it as a single whole, blind to their internecine discords concerning intentions, ends, and means. Not only are revolution(aries) and counterrevolution(aries) interlocked, but so are their reciprocal misperceptions, which are fired by mutual suspicion and hostility. Revolutionaries quite naturally overperceive and conflate all resistances, making them out to be omnipresent, all-powerful, and cunning beyond compare. Their fiery excoriations of their enemies, which are amply reciprocated, merely feed the frenzy of distortion and misjudgment. During revolutionary moments decision makers on all sides act less according to how things stand than according to how they perceive and define them. Indeed, such moments are hothouses for the social deformation of reality which predisposes actors to foster and practice the politics of wish fulfillment.

✻ ✻ ✻

Any discussion of conservatism in relation to counterrevolution in the two great revolutions of modern times must, of course, begin with Edmund Burke. An Anglo-Irishman, not a Frenchman, he formulated the first major and unrivaled statement of conservative principles of the epoch of the French Revolution. Even though he propounded his credo in the heat of events, to this day it has lost none of its authority. It continues to reign supreme partly because there is no counterpart of Burke's classic *Reflections on the Revolution in France* for the epoch of the Russian Revolution. In hindsight Burke tends to be seen as a natural and pragmatic conservative thinker, particularly compared to Maistre, his contemporary, who is portrayed as a thoroughbred counterrevolutionary theorist.[20] In the context of his time, however, Burke's position was anything but sober and moderate. He was very much the ideological conservative with close counterrevolutionary affinities, his rhetoric and tone of argumentation being intensely aggressive, censoring, and categorical.[21] Convinced that the French Revolution was an absolute sin, Burke precluded compromise and mercy. Besides, he had a conspiratorial view of the trailblazers and protagonists of revolution, who he insisted had to be faced down with force and violence. With a touch of zealotry, Burke commended England's political system, with its presumed genius for peaceful reform, as the shining example for all humanity. This moralizing went hand in hand with his extenuation of the despotism of the *ancien régime* and his uncharacteristic blindness to the weight of historical continuities in the French Revolution.

Somewhat like Marx and Engels around the middle of the next century, who claimed that Europe was haunted by the specter of communism, Burke saw it haunted by the specter of a cabal of millenarian literati and their agents bent on establishing an earthbound heavenly city destructive of Christian values and traditions. As early as late summer and fall 1789, he took fierce exception not only to the premise of the Declaration of the Rights of Man but also to the revocation of the King's absolute veto and the move of Louis XVI and the National Assembly from Versailles to Paris under pressure of the street. Probably these three events, followed by the nationalization of church property, prompted Burke to write his *Reflections*. In any case, his prescient if militant book was published in November 1790, well over two years before the execution of the King and the reign of the Terror. He castigated every untried initiative for being informed by abstract and speculative reasoning about the perfectibility of man and society, with emphasis on individual freedom and popular sovereignty. By way of opposition Burke argued for practical reason rooted in the life and history of society in which concrete custom, tradition, and experience are of commanding importance. In his brief for historical over natural rights, he assigned as high a place to prejudice, ignorance, and prescription as he did to rationality, enlightenment, and self-direction. All in all, Burke considered humanity to be driven by raw passions, instincts, and interests that needed to be tamed and channeled by the master institutions of property, family, government, and religion.

With the abolition of seignorial rights and the nationalization of ecclesiastical properties, the revolution in France violated real property which, inseparable from family, was the bedrock of a stable society. This transgression was all the more baneful for undermining in particular large landed property, an essential fount of immemorial rights, and for defying the ways of the free market and the night-watchman state, at any rate in the economic sphere. In Burke's vision, along with property and family, the Christian religion was a vital "basis of civil society" and the lifeblood of custom and tradition, the key to the historical continuity and steadiness he prized above all else.[22]

Ultimately, and notwithstanding his cautious and reluctant acceptance of the modern world, Burke championed a society of traditional hierarchies and wholesome values built around crown, church, and nobility whose decline and corrosion he lamented. The revolution in France was emblematic of the wages of this regression which Burke charged to "the new monied interest" and its attorneys, acting in concert with the Parisian men of letters.[23] With distinct counter-revolutionary overtones he denounced the big city's parasitic economic interests and advocates of novelty. Ahead of his time, Burke even came close to political Jew-baiting: "Jew-jobbers [having] been made bishops" in France, England should send its excess of "house-breakers, receivers of stolen goods, and forgers of paper currency" across the Channel "to fill new episcopal thrones: men well versed in swearing; and who will scruple no oath which the fertile genius of any of your reformers can devise."[24] Burke also lashed out at an insidious "set of literary men, converted into a gang of robbers and assassins, . . . a den of bravoes and banditti [who] assume the garb and tone of an academy of philosophers."[25] Declaring Rousseau to embody the perversion of the *lumières*, he defamed him as "a sort of offal and excrement, [who sends] the spawn of his disgustful amours . . . to the hospital of foundlings."[26]

With the revolution bound to spill over France's borders to create a turbulent epoch comparable to that of the Reformation, Burke urged military intervention by the European powers which, as a counter-crusade, would have to disregard the rules of traditional warfare. The émigrés hailed Burke not only for this call for intervention but also for his probing censure of the revolution which they had embraced for providing them with principles and legitimating arguments. Even those émigrés who rejected his vaunted model of English parliamentarism in favor of a pure and simple restoration claimed Burke as their own. By and large he was a critical influence for the three major branches of the extended counterrevolutionary family.

✳ ✳ ✳

In early 1791 Maistre claimed that Burke's *Reflections* had "reinforced his own anti-democratic and anti-Gallican ideas" as his "aversion for everything that was happening in France was turning to horror," all the more so because "the evil . . . was contagious."[27] There is no denying the Burkean elements in Maistre's position. Both were unqualified and uncompromising in their condemnation of the revolution in France, which they considered a deliberate anti-Christian campaign animated by a set of wicked though consistent abstract principles. Maistre even wondered whether "in the eyes of God Voltaire was not more at fault than Marat, because Voltaire may well have created Marat and certainly did more harm than him."[28] But above all Protestantism, by way of its subversive "sect, . . . gave birth to anarchy and served as universal dissolvent." Characteristically, not a single Protestant writer in France "took pen in hand for the right side."[29] Maistre, like Burke, felt called upon to put forward a well-founded alternative to the false reason of man and of the Enlightenment. The chief tenets of their respective counter-catechisms were essentially analogous, except that Maistre predicated rather than argued his fundamental beliefs or principles, which were, to boot, religiously founded. Indeed, as a staunch Catholic Maistre not only prized religion for its political and social utility, as did Burke, but held it to be the ultimate foundation of state and society. He sought to reconcile the customs, traditions, and prejudices prized by Burke with an absolutist and theocratic monarchy answerable to God and the Pope, whose infallibility he upheld. In a world infested with sin and retribution, suffering and conflict, war and bloodshed, there was need for strict authority, hierarchy, and obedience in state, church, and society.[30]

Glorifying the *ancien régime*, Maistre located the good polity and society in the past, not the future, and he would have it restored by way of a counterrevolution, which he professed "would not be a revolution, but the opposite of a revolution," save in method.[31] This counterrevolution called for armed intervention by a coalition of Christian powers to excise the revolutionary cancer as well as mend and reinforce the fabric of historical continuity.

To repeat, the family resemblances between Burke and Maistre were considerable, especially considering the context in which their texts were written and read. Despite radically different premises and rhetorical idioms, they agreed that the revolution in France was an absolute evil and a single bloc; that it marked an absolute discontinuity with the past; that it was fathered by subversive sects and ideas; that it was an inherently contagious pestilence; and that it needed to be undone, *coûte que coûte*.

Conservative and counterrevolutionary theorists tend to preach to the converted, their primary audience being members of the *ancien régime*'s ruling and governing classes, whom they provide with rationales for their oppositional stands. As mentioned before, time-honored elites quite naturally stand their ground and give battle. Counterrevolution is quintessentially a vocation of the upper ten thousand determined not to yield their privileged positions in civil and political society. Not that all of them hold fast, especially in the beginning; under a mounting popular pressure not a few of them urged or supported reform in 1788–89 and in 1916–17. But this discord, which was momentary, was no more than an "inharmonious harmony" in face of the ominous breakdown of sovereignty. Indeed, there was something chaotic about the early resistance of the notables of the court, church, land, army, civil service, and academy. Rather than vanish or dissolve, this composite power, social, and intellectual elite was disoriented and in disarray, all the more so with the headlong defiance of the sacred authority and dazzling aura of monarchy and court, which culminated in the regicide of King Louis XVI and Tsar Nicholas II. This collapse of the monarchy, one of the chief centripetal and cementing institutions, did even more to blunt the counterrevolutionary forces than their internecine ideological and strategic disagreements and personal rivalries.

* * *

Counterrevolution, which originates with the classes, remains lame and ineffectual unless it connects with the anti-revolution, which is a matter of the masses.[32] Evidently counterrevolution, not unlike revolution, can be made only *with* the masses, which is not to say that either the one or the other is made *for* them.

In both 1789 and 1917 the struggle between revolution and counterrevolution was structurally conditioned: "men do not make . . . their own history under circumstances chosen by themselves, but under circumstances directly found, given, and transmitted from the past, . . . [with] the tradition of all the dead generations weigh[ing] like a nightmare on the brain of the living."[33] The commanding heights of revolution were in urban France and Russia, notably in the capital cities, and its chief actors, whatever their social and geographic origins, were thoroughly citified and cosmopolitan. But the lands they proposed to revolutionize were 85 percent rural and agrarian, with the peasantry mired in "the muck of ages, . . . [or] interests and relationships left over from earlier periods."[34] As if setting the peasants at defiance, the emerging revolutionists meant to emancipate them by conquering their piety, superstition, and illiteracy. Actually in the short run the directors and commissioners of this liberating drive deepened the abyss of distrust and suspicion between city and country, as well as between center and periphery, by virtue of being sworn to the moral credo of Enlightenment and progress which ran counter to the time-honored catechism of Providence, tradition, and prejudice. This antithesis was as central to the theoretics of Voltaire and Marx as it was to the *idées-forces* of Robespierre and Lenin, even if the force of circumstance prompted the latter two to temper them in practice. The Jacobins and Bolsheviks, inspired respectively by Voltaire and Marx, looked upon the peasantry and rural artisanate with metropolitan condescension and contempt coupled with anxiety about their becoming the mainstay of a potential "reaction of the countryside against the town."[35]

In any case, the bottom-up anti-revolution was primarily a matter of the countryside and village. This was so despite the fact that in 1789 and 1917 the incipient revolutionary regimes defused the seething rural unrest with land reforms intended to relieve the peasantry's chronic land hunger and stored-up resentments. But in both France and Russia this conciliation was relatively short-lived: the mobilization for war and civil war forced unsteady governments to accelerate and intensify their drive to restore a single sovereignty with a view to raising taxes, requisitioning food, and conscripting soldiers. Especially in certain isolated and "backward" rural provinces, some of them in would-be secessionist peripheries, this intrusion triggered anti-revolutionary risings, being perceived as not only exploitive and repressive but also overweening, alien, and impious. The habitual and deep-rooted provincial distrust of the outside world was fired, in particular, by the new regime's attack on church and religion as well as its special emissaries' imperious disregard of supposedly benighted regional languages and folkways. The territorial elites which prized local cultures and used them to advantage felt threatened or were displaced, with the result that they became potential leaders of the spontaneous and irregular anti-revolution from below.[36] Not surprisingly, the rank and file of this anti-revolution aimed to curb the centralizing, modernizing, and secularizing reach of the revolution rather than restore the *ancien régime* of feudal or seignorial servitude.

Just as the urban *journées* quickened the revolution, so the rural *jacqueries* energized the anti-revolution. At the onset the non-urban furors were reactive and spontaneous, and no less fearsome than city tempests. Their carriers were "primitive rebels" seeking to remedy rampant injustices and reclaim ancient rights rather than press for the implementation of blueprints for a new Land of Promise.[37] The anti-revolution from below remained impulsive, ill-organized, and parochial despite certain efforts by the counterrevolution from above and abroad to harness, discipline, and politicize it for its cause. The gulf between them was too large: the émigrés of the French Revolution and the Whites of the Russian Revolution, including their respective foreign backers, had at best limited understanding and sympathy for the mind-sets, motives, and objectives of the anti-revolution which was too popular and populist for their taste, as well as too raw. Needless to say, they also feared for their material interests, notably their lands. Even so, the anti-revolution and counterrevolution were linked. Whereas the partisans of the former acted for the most part intuitively, the agents of the latter acted with studied conviction reinforced by rhetorical justification. Both were moved by the beliefs, values, and settled dispositions discerned and commended by Burke and Maistre, as well as by their epigones in times to come. Of course, the revolutionaries perceived and berated this resistance as a pervasive enemy whose coherence, strength, and cunning they relentlessly exaggerated.

✳ ✳ ✳

The counterrevolutionaries in France defined themselves in opposition to the *lumières*. In their reading, anticlericalism was the pivot of the Enlightenment's attack on the established order, and this reading was accurate: its main target was not the social and political system as such, but the religious and ecclesiastic order that buttressed it. To be sure, monarchy and church were inseparable, and with politics and religion closely identified, an assault on the one was an assault on the other. They were not, however, one and the same, there being a division of labor between them. While crown and court provided a vital integument for political society, church and religion cemented civil society. But the *philosophes*, for their part, were far more probing and caustic in their criticism of the latter than of the former: the church was charged with being not only the fountainhead of superstition, obscurantism, and prejudice but also the chief bulwark against reason, progress, and freedom. By virtue of its institutional autonomy and density as well as its wealth, the church was more pervasive than the state, its agents reaching into every village and hearth. In addition to the clergy administering the sacraments and running the educational and welfare systems, the primates of the First Estate held the prerogative of performing the *sacre* of the king.

The aim of the prophets of Enlightenment was not to overthrow or destabilize the throne but to desacralize it by attacking the metaphysics and pretensions of the church. Voltaire and Diderot fully realized that church and religion were not only "the most formidable and respected obstacle" to the advance toward their earthly paradise but also the undisputed nerve center of the anti-Enlightenment.[38] This realization, never absent from the thought of the *philosophes*, became a central preoccupation with the Calas Affair of 1761. Not unlike the Dreyfus Affair over a century later, it crystallized philosophical debates and political conflicts over the fundamental beliefs and institutional structures of its time; and the rift that it opened between the opposing camps was never really healed.

In 1761 Jean Calas, a Protestant, was accused of having murdered his son Marc-Antoine, allegedly to keep him from converting to Rome. After being summarily found guilty and condemned to death, Calas was savagely tortured and then strangled before his body was finally burnt. The destiny of Calas was paradigmatic of what Voltaire excoriated as the hydra-headed and "cruelly oppressive" *infâme* emblematic of the superstition and intolerance which informed France's civil and political society. It pointed up the close association of unenlightened monarchic despotism and unreconstructed church in which the latter was the senior partner. Charging that religious prejudice had swayed Calas's judges to "rack the most innocent of men," Voltaire summoned one and all to "cry out" against this "worst injury to human nature since Saint Bartholomew's Day."[39] To be sure, Voltaire's injunction to *écraser l'infâme* was directed against established religion in general. But above all Voltaire aimed his fire at the Gallican Church for being the very embodiment of the intolerance, arbitrariness, and torture that he urged be eradicated so as to pave the way for a better world.

If the critics of the Enlightenment fixed upon Voltaire as the foremost and most dangerous gadfly, it was partly because of all the *philosophes* he was sharpest in his understanding and censure of the interconnection of religion and politics. They realized only too well that he shared their premise that the political struggles of their time were inherently religious, and they had good reason to engage him. But the battle was uphill. Without the backing of a state censor and grand inquisitor, the crude and sardonic broadsides of the latter-day apologists did not carry beyond the faithful. Elie Fréron and Jean-Marie-Bernard Clément, Abbé Augustin Barruel and Antoine Rivarol, Sabarier de Castre and Simon-Nicolas-Henri Linguet were no match for Voltaire and Rousseau, Diderot and Montesquieu. Free-floating men of letters, both clerical and lay, they were short of a clear-cut vision, and their critique of the ideas and leading lights of the Enlightenment carried less by its discursive reason than its sectarian temper.

Be that as it may, the *anti-philosophes* anticipated some of the major arguments of Burke and Maistre, commonly buttressed by a glorification of Christianity and Catholicism, along with a high regard for the authority, hierarchy, and mission of the established church. At the same time that they denounced the lay heretics for the pretense of their philosophic and individual reason, they charged them with being new-model barbarians and fanatics posing as anti-fanatics.

These postulations were advanced as part of a sweeping assault on the general direction of European developments since the Reformation, which presumably had burst the floodgates holding back moral decay and material corruption, most notably in the cities. The counter-Enlightenment's "prophets of despair" set the twin notions of pessimism and decadence, whose touchstone was a chimerical past, against the opposing twins of optimism and progress, which tempted the ever-hazardous future.

Although the *anti-philosophes* foretold society's fate in apocalyptic terms, not uncommonly they blamed it on an earthly conspiracy, determined to sap the foundations of throne and altar. The conspiracy was said to consist of *philosophes* and encyclopedists, Illuminati and Freemasons, Protestants and Jansenists. These coadjutors, sworn to erroneous ideas, were responsible for the corruption of religious and moral life. Their task was facilitated by those members of the church who were lax in the practice and defense of the true faith. In Victor Hugo's trenchant telling of the *anti-philosophes'* position, France would never have fallen on evil days "had Voltaire been hanged by the neck and Rousseau sent to the galleys." Ultimately it was "all the fault of the writers and rhymesters, the Encyclopedists, Diderot, d'Alembert, and all those wicked rascals!"[40] Clearly the proponents of the *anti-lumières* excelled at instrumentalizing the artifice and demonology of the plot well before it became the stock-in-trade of revolutionary and counterrevolutionary politics.

The champions of the anti-Enlightenment did not speak to the winds, not the least because their discourse was graced by a defense of church and religion. Their ideas, and not those of the *philosophes*, were mainstream throughout the land. In France's villages and small towns the "*gens du peuple* continued to practice their religion," which permeated all aspects of everyday life.[41] But they were not alone in being impervious or "passively hostile" to the Enlightenment. Even if less consistent, the countryside's elites, including the provincial bourgeoisie, were essential carriers and pacesetters of "the formidable resistance of powerful and tenacious traditions." Nor were the large cities so seething with dissent that they were closed to the appeals of the *anti-philosophes*.[42]

There was, of course, formidable institutional support for "adherence to the old and tried, against the new and untried." The Catholic religion and church were a vital part of an aggressive defense against the Enlightenment. Starting around the middle of the eighteenth century, "the partisans of the church developed the [principal] themes of the polemic against the *philosophes* . . . [and] the high clergy fought pitilessly against dangerous books." This campaign against "pen and courage" was backed by "the law . . . , the Sorbonne . . . , the *parlement* . . . , the prison . . . , and even the hulks and the gallows."[43]

Clearly, although the counterrevolution and anti-Enlightenment were the great losers of the revolutionary epoch, they were neither destroyed nor delegitimated. Throughout Europe their political and intellectual proponents took comfort from the restoration regime in France between 1815 and 1830 as well as from the Holy Alliance of the European powers. Just as the revolution kept marching on, so did the counterrevolution.

✳ ✳ ✳

In 1917 counterrevolutionary ideas were even less unforeseen than in 1789. Actually in both cases they were forged in antithesis to the Enlightenment. What conservatives and reactionaries considered the unspeakable presumption and fury of the French Revolution left its mark on the anti-Enlightenment of the nineteenth century. Although its publicists adapted and devised idioms to suit the new age, there was a striking persistence in postulates, themes, arguments, and articulations. Like the *anti-philosophes* of the eighteenth century, those of the nineteenth were, for the most part, unattached literati. And, like them, they were eristic dystopians and Cassandras rather than sober philosophical and social theorists. In books and pamphlets, as well as in articles in the blossoming periodical and daily press, they continued the critique of the *lumières*, now said to be the fountainhead of runaway science and materialism. Skeptical of all progress, they saw nothing but decadence and decline in their own time and in times to come.

In the conservative imagination the big city and industry became a central cause and symptom of decay: the death of community, the miscegenation of high culture, the corruption of morals, and the contumacy of workers. Whereas heretofore the ideas of a sect of *philosophes* were said to have provided the stuff of subversion, now it was the ideas of Marx, championed and propagated by Socialists. Meanwhile, Jews replaced Protestants and Freemasons as the nerve center of the ever latent conspiracy poised to undermine and threaten the established order.

One of the most striking changes is that with the advancing nineteenth century the new conservatives ceased to set great store by religion and church, and the theocratic temptations of the Maistreian variety were wearing thin. The mystique emanating from the conjoined throne and altar was ebbing; they meant to preserve and revitalize it by investing it in nation, Volk, or race. During the epoch of the French Revolution counterrevolution had largely been a matter for the classes, not the masses. By convention and interest the émigrés and their foreign sponsors had proudly ignored the lower orders, and in the Vendée the local notables initially had fought shy of the peasant rebellion. By the fin de siècle more and more public intellectuals and politicians of the second anti-Enlightenment appealed to the losers, victims, and apostates of modernity thought to be open to the new secular creeds.

Ironically the new conservatism was less developed in Russia than in central and western Europe, no doubt because the challenges and problems of modernity seemed more remote. Politically the Romanov monarchy was the most unreconstructed old regime of the major powers, the Tsar's authority remaining sacred and undivided. Russia also lagged far behind economically, industrial capitalism having made only limited inroads. The revolution of 1905 neither belied nor changed these realities. Its primary cause was military defeat in the Russo-Japanese War, not the uprising of workers and peasants that was made possible by the momentary dislocation of the regime. To be sure, pressed by a loyal opposition Nicholas II issued the October Manifesto establishing a Duma and granting certain civil rights. But almost immediately he reneged. He circumvented the judiciary and manipulated the franchise with a view to reclaim much if not most of the power he had reluctantly and provisionally yielded in 1905.[44] During this would-be "aristocratic reaction," Nicholas II as well as many senior officials and churchmen condoned or supported Russia's fledgling new conservatives, who exerted their influence through the ultranationalist Union of the Russian People, which in the conservative camp stood apart for its effort to mobilize the wayward masses of the city, not the country. As was to be expected, these populist but antidemocratic rightists—or protofascists—exaggerated the revolutionary threat to the Romanov autocracy, the Orthodox Church, and the Russian empire. Their intellectual mentors were even less notable than the *anti-philosophes* of eighteenth-century France, except for Dostoyevsky, whose integral antimodernism and chauvinism, though dated, were seasonable and influential.[45]

Characteristically the new conservatives fixed the responsibility for this comprehensive imperilment primarily on the Jews, whose allegedly all-embracing conspiracy was set forth in the spurious *Protocols of the Elders of Zion*. There followed the Russian equivalent of the Calas Affair. In 1913 Mendel Beilis, a Jewish clerk, was charged with the ritual murder of a Christian schoolboy, Andrei Yustshinsky, who had in fact been killed by a band of robbers.[46] Nevertheless, in a prolonged public trial in Kiev legal and police authorities, in concert with the minister of justice, made every effort to get a conviction. Unlike the elder Calas, Beilis finally was acquitted. His case did not become a *cause célèbre* comparable to the Calas and Dreyfus affairs, in part because no writer of Voltaire's or Zola's aggressive tolerance and rhetorical genius stepped forward to dramatize the vital issues it raised, which went well beyond the blood libel. Even so, it vividly demonstrated the perseverance of *l'infâme* in Russia after the reforms of 1905. Particularly leaders of the disloyal opposition, including the Bolsheviks, denounced the regime's exploitation of anti-Judaism, in the form of political anti-Semitism, as evidence of the ascendancy of the new conservatism; the opposition to anti-Judaism was the more vehement because both the throne and the altar encouraged it.

The new counterrevolutionary credo and tactics never gained much ground in Russia after 1917. During the founding years down to 1922 the counterrevolution in the Russian Revolution was cut from the same cloth as its forerunner in the French Revolution from 1789 to 1795. As the "other half" of the revolution, it contributed its proportional share to the violence and terror of the incipient Soviet regime's civil, foreign, peasant, and religious wars. The Cheka and concentration camps were as emblematic of the Bolshevik terror as the guillotine was of the Jacobin terror. Notwithstanding their respective singularities, at bottom the two Furies were homologous. Both were fired by the dialectic of revolution and counterrevolution, and in 1789–95 as in 1917–22 the battles and reprisals of civil war claimed far more lives than the executions and torments of political terror per se.

But whereas the dialectical correlations between revolution and counterrevolution followed similar courses in France and Russia during the critical founding years, they diverged radically thereafter. After Thermidor, and until 1815, France's new if changing revolutionary regime was constantly at war, with the Directory, Consulate, and Empire exploiting the glories and benefits of military campaigns to deflect and reduce unresolved political, social, and cultural conflicts at home. And following 1815 the restoration regime was reintegrated into the European system rather than ostracized or saddled with the political burdens of a Carthaginian peace. Between 1795 and 1814 the resounding triumphs of French arms, despite the enormous sacrifice of French and enemy lives, facilitated the reestablishment of a unitary sovereignty and the consolidation of the chief gains of the founding years, with embers still very much burning in the revolutionary and counterrevolutionary ashes. This recomposition continued during the following fifteen years, with the chancelleries of the major powers welcoming old-new France into the Europe of the Holy Alliance as part of a prophylaxis against renewed disorders fraught with danger for the surrounding world.

The Bolshevik regime faced an altogether different situation. The Treaty of Riga, of March 1921, foreshadowed by the Treaty of Brest-Litovsk, of March 1918, not only forced the Soviets to yield millions of square miles, people, and economic assets as well as vital strategic outposts, but also and above all confirmed the quarantine and containment of their regime. Indeed, Soviet Russia was locked out of the world concert and economy, except for a limited and tenuous opening to defeated Germany, the other great power that was intermittently excluded from the Versailles system. In other words, following the formative founding years, unlike the new regime in Paris, which continued to move out into the world, the new regime in Moscow was virtually compelled to turn inward and pursue an autarkic course. This forced and improbable isolation at once vindicated the brazen political culture of the civil war, fostered a defiant siege mentality, and justified continuing emergency rule. The evolution of the Soviet regime—its hardening or relaxation—would depend in no small measure on external relations, notably on its ability to relax or end the quarantine in favor of peaceful coexistence.

By 1921–22 the counterrevolution was crushed and shut out of Russia. Unlike after 1795 in France, the internal exiles did not resurface, the émigrés did not return, and the new-wrought political regime went essentially unchallenged from the right within Russia. Indeed, the counterrevolution took root abroad. It developed and came of age throughout Europe in the form of Fascism. Not that anti-Communism was the ultimate source and reason of Fascism; but it most certainly was a necessary determinant and bold watchword of every variety of Fascism, including National Socialism, its most extreme and paradigmatic form. Moreover, reactionaries and conservatives conjured up anti-Communist spirits to explain and justify their forbearance of or collaboration with counterrevolutionaries sworn to "friend-enemy" politics with violence at its core. In line with the logic of the situation, with time Communism and Fascism—the Soviet and National Socialist regimes—became fatally bound to each other "as action is bound to reaction." In fact, in the final analysis the issue is not whether they interacted but why and how they did. During the 1930s this interaction deeply affected not only the domestic politics but also the foreign policy and diplomacy of most European countries. Without close attention to this manifold and complex interplay, there is no explaining the twisted diplomacy of appeasement, the cunning Nazi-Soviet Pact, and the *unholy* Grand Alliance. Through most of its life the Soviet regime, unlike post-revolutionary France, was kept at bay.[47]

To be sure, in 1943–45 Moscow managed to seize the offensive and break through the *cordon sanitaire* to the Elbe. But this improbable and narrow success came after an even narrower brush with defeat and collapse, in 1941, raising the counterfactual question of what the costs and consequences of the counterrevolution's victory that year would have been for Russia and the world. In any case, with the resumption of the Cold War in 1944–45 the Soviet Union was again forced on the defensive and cordoned off until 1989–91, when the cumulative weight of external economic and military pressures contributed significantly, if not decisively, to its implosion.

✱ ✱ ✱

67

NOTES

1. Hannah Arendt, *On Revolution* (New York: Viking, 1965), p. 8 and pp. 47–48. See Jean Starobinski, *Action et réaction: Vie et aventures d'un couple* (Paris: Seuil, 1999). The page proofs of this probing genealogical study of these two interactive terms reached me after my book went to press.

2. François Furet, *Penser la Révolution française*, rev. ed. (Paris: Gallimard, 1983); and Furet, *Le passé d'une illusion: Essai sur l'idée communiste au XXe siècle* (Paris: Calmann-Lévy, 1995).

3. Daniel Mornet, *Les origines intellectuelles de la Révolution française, 1715–1878*, 6th ed. (Paris: Armand Colin, 1967), pt. 3, ch. 1, pp. 205–24.

4. For two notable exceptions, see Paul H. Beik, *The French Revolution Seen from the Right: Social Theories in Motion, 1789–1799*, repr. of 1956 ed. (New York: Howard Fertig, 1970); and Klaus Epstein, *The Genesis of German Conservatism* (Princeton: Princeton University Press, 1966).

5. Raymond Tallis, *Enemies of Hope: A Critique of Contemporary Pessimism* (London: Macmillan, 1997), pp. 1–2, 55, 61.

6. Alexis de Tocqueville, *"The European Revolution" and Correspondence with Gobineau* (Garden City, N.Y.: Doubleday, 1959), p. 171.

7. See Matthias Middell, "Konterrevolution während der französischen Revolution, 1789 bis 1795: Zeitgenössischer Begriff und aktuelle Forschung," in Manfred Kossok and Editha Kross, eds., *1789: Weltwirkung einer grossen Revolution*, vol. 1 (Liechtenstein: Topos Verlag, 1989), pp. 99–109.

8. See Norman Hampson, "La contre-révolution a-t-elle existé?" in François Lebrun and Roger Dupuy, eds., *Les résistances à la Révolution* (Paris: Imago, 1987), pp. 462–68, esp. p. 467.

9. See Lebrun and Dupuy, eds., *Les résistances*, passim, esp. pp. 11–19.

10. Michelet, *Histoire de la Révolution française*, 2 vols. (Paris: Laffont, 1979), passim. In vol. 1, bk. 3, two chapters (4 and 5) are entitled "Résistances."

11. Jacob Burckhardt, *Weltgeschichtliche Betrachtungen* (Stuttgart: Kröner, 1978), p. 174 and p. 177.

12. Burckhardt, *Betrachtungen*, p. 169.

13. Tocqueville, *"The European Revolution,"* p. 161.

14. Cited in Maximilien Rubel, ed., *Pages de Karl Marx: Pour une éthique socialiste*, vol. 2 (Paris: Payot, 1970), p. 79.

15. See Quinet, *La Révolution* (Paris: Belin, 1987), p. 497; and Michelet, *Histoire*, e.g., vol. 2, p. 275.

16. See Richard Cobb, *Reactions to the French Revolution* (London: Oxford University Press, 1972), pp. 31–32, 35.

17. The following discussion of counterrevolution draws on my *Dynamics of Counterrevolution in Europe, 1870–1956: An Analytic Framework* (New York: Harper, 1971), chs. 2 and 3.

18. Karl Mannheim, *Essays on Sociology and Social Psychology* (New York: Oxford University Press, 1953), ch. 2, esp. pp. 95–98, 116.

19. Mannheim, *Essays*, p. 99 and p. 116.

20. See Isaiah Berlin, *The Crooked Timber of Humanity: Chapters in the History of Ideas* (London: John Murray, 1990), pp. 91–174 ("Joseph de Maistre and the Origins of Fascism").

21. Isaac Kramnick, *The Rage of Edmund Burke: Portrait of an Ambivalent Conservative* (New York: Basic Books, 1977), esp. pp. 20–51, and chs. 7 and 8.

22. Burke, *Reflections on the Revolution in France* (1790), in Paul Langford, ed., *The Writings and Speeches of Edmund Burke*, vol. 8 (Oxford: Clarendon, 1989), p. 141.

23. Ibid., pp. 160–62 and 344–46.

24. Burke, "A Letter to a Member of the National Assembly" (1791), in Langford, ed, *Writings and Speeches*, vol. 8, p. 304. See also Burke, "Reflections," p. 99, p. 105, p. 135, and p. 154.

25. Burke, "Letter to a Noble Lord" (1796), in Langford, ed., *Writings and Speeches*, vol. 9, p. 174.

26. Burke, "Letter to a Member of the National Assembly," pp. 314–15.

27. Cited in Robert Triomphe, *Joseph de Maistre: Étude sur la vie et sur la doctrine d'un matérialiste mystique* (Geneva: Droz, 1968), pp. 138–40.

28. Maistre, *Considérations sur la France* (1797), in Maistre, *Écrits sur la Révolution* (Paris: Presses Universitaires, 1989), pp. 91–217, esp. p. 100. Maistre struck this observation from the original published version of the *Considérations*.

29. "Réflexions sur le Protestantisme dans ses rapports avec la souveraineté" (1798), in Maistre, *Écrits*, pp. 219–39, esp. p. 219 and p. 232.

30. See Richard A. Lebrun, *Joseph de Maistre: An Intellectual Militant* (Montreal: McGill-Queen's University Press, 1988), pp. 93–94 and 102–3; and Isaiah Berlin, *The Crooked Timber of Humanity*, passim.

31. Maistre, *Considérations*, in *Écrits*, p. 201.

32. Claude Mazauric, "Autopsie d'un échec: La résistance à l'anti-révolution et la défaite de la contre-révolution," in Lebrun and Dupuy, eds., *Résistances*, pp. 237–44.

33. Karl Marx, *The Eighteenth Brumaire of Louis Bonaparte* (New York: International Publishers, n.d.), p. 13.

34. Marx and Engels, *The German Ideology* (New York: International Publishers, 1947), p. 69 and p. 73.

35. Marx, *Eighteenth Brumaire*, p. 31.

36. See Bärbel Plötner, "Regionalsprachen in der Revolution," in Kossok and Kross, eds., *1789: Weltwirkung*, vol. 1, pp. 142 ff.; and David Bell, "Lingua Populi, Lingua Dei: Language, Religion, and the Origins of French Revolutionary Nationalism," in *American Historical Review* 100:5 (December 1995): pp. 1403–37.

37. See E. J. Hobsbawm, *Primitive Rebels: Studies in Archaic Forms of Social Movement in the 19th and 20th Centuries* (New York: Norton, 1959).

38. Diderot cited in Reinhart Koselleck, *Critique and Crisis: Enlightenment and the Pathogenesis of Modern Society* (Oxford: Berg, 1988), pp. 171–72.

39. Voltaire cited in Gilbert Collard, *Voltaire, l'affaire Calas et nous* (Paris: Belles Lettres, 1994), p. 157. See also David D. Bien, *The Calas Affair: Persecution, Tolerance, and Heresy in Eighteenth-Century Toulouse* (Princeton: Princeton University Press, 1960), esp. chs. 5 and 6.

40. Victor Hugo, *Quatre-vingt treize* (Paris: Gallimard, 1979), p. 447.

41. Mornet, *Les origines*, pp. 214–15.

42. Ibid., p. 205 and p. 211.

43. Ibid., pp. 207–8, 212.

44. Rogger, *Russia in the Age of Modernization and Revolution, 1881–1917* (New York: Longman, 1983), chs. 10 and 11.

45. Rogger, "The Formation of the Russian Right, 1900–1906," in *California Slavic Studies*, vol. 3 (1964): pp. 66–94; and Rogger, "Was There a Russian Fascism?" in *Journal of Modern History* 36:4 (December 1964): pp. 398–415.

46. Rogger, "The Beilis Case: Anti-Semitism and Politics in the Reign of Nicholas II," in *American Slavic and East European Review* 25:4 (December 1964): pp. 615–29.

47. See chapter 15 below.

Violence

VIOLENCE is as inseparable from revolution and counterrevolution as these are from each other. Violence has, of course, many faces and purposes. Certainly not all violence in revolution is ideologically driven and, by that token, excessive and boundless. Although violence is inherent to revolution, it is not unique to it. Nor is it as rare as revolution itself. Violence is basic to society and polity, especially to their foundation and consolidation. At the creation there is often recourse to war, which, like revolution, is "inconceivable outside the domain of violence."[1] The founding myth of nearly every society or state romanticizes and celebrates its primal bloodshed. In general, violence is endemic and kaleidoscopic, by turns explosive and suspended, the relatively short "peaceable intervals" being due less to "pangs of humanitarianism and moral moderation" than to man's inability "to live with uninterrupted and perpetual violence."[2]

In a distant and not so distant past, violence "was part of a natural and God-given order," an unquestioned and anonymous "social practice," not in need of "justification." Even the "revolts in premodern societies were part of the endemic violence of their time," the idea of "a society without violence" being unthinkable. It was only in early modern times, and particularly in the eighteenth century, that violence was summoned to justify itself at the "bar of reason," along with the "divine right of kings and religion." The idea that violence, both domestic and international, was barbaric and unenlightened, and the faith that it was destined to vanish, continued to gain ground during the nineteenth century. Although the exorbitant and senseless violence of the First World War "broke this dream," first formulated by Immanuel Kant in 1795, it persisted, until the Second World War shattered many remaining illusions.[3]

71

With these two monstrous conflicts the twentieth century very likely became the most violent century in recorded history. Its wars were so uniquely bloody and savage because they were an amalgam of conventional war, civil war, and *Glaubenskrieg*. Culminating in Auschwitz, Dresden, and Hiroshima, they punctured what remained of the pretense that the advance of civilization was measured by man's progressive mastery of violence. Simultaneously they exploded the Eurocentric myth that overseas colonialism was bringing the blessings of "civilization" to the "uncivilized."[4] There are certain affinities between, on the one hand, the Furies of religious crusades, confessional wars, revolutionary terrors, and overseas civilizing missions, and, on the other, the Furies of the killing fields, firebombings, and atomic discharges of the two world wars. The ultimate genius behind these ordeals of twentieth-century war was less the deadliness of modern weapons than their sacralization along with the causes they were made to serve.[5]

Although today faith in human reason and progress is widely foresworn, the attendant belief in the end of violence, both within and between states, dies hard. It is ironic that at the very time that war caused unprecedented floodtides of blood, in part by bearing ever more heavily on noncombatants than on soldiers, the concert of powers put in place equally unprecedented rules and institutions designed to make war less bloody, savage, and uncivilized: the Geneva Conventions of 1929 and 1949, the League of Nations, the United Nations, the Nuremberg and Tokyo Tribunals, the Genocide Convention. In this same spirit the "world community" recently established ad hoc International War Crimes Tribunals for the Balkans and Rwanda to punish genocide, war crimes, and crimes against humanity in a postatomic era which is as likely to see ethnic, religious, and intercultural civil conflicts as traditional cross-border wars between sovereign states.[6] Some of these conflicts assume the mask or form of a war of secession or state formation which invites intervention by the concert of powers, as in the case of Kosovo in 1999. Clearly, violence is not about to recede or disappear. It "merely keeps changing its face," as ploughshares continue to be beaten into swords in the form of the latest weaponry.[7]

But these recent miseries and disasters of war have deflected "attention from . . . the chronic persistence of violence *within* all extant civil

societies [and] the (not unrelated) permanent possibility that civil societies can and do regress into uncivil societies."[8] In the First World a
heightened consciousness and abhorrence of the horrors of unbounded war between states go hand in hand with a fierce excoriation
of political violence particularly within nondemocratic states, which,
to boot, are portrayed as singularly warlike and aggressive. This holier-
than-thou perspective ignores or minimizes the culture of violence in
democratic states, fostered by the celebration and mass marketing of
a violence that is at once immaculate and lethal.

Since violence has played such an enormous role in human affairs
through the ages, and exceptionally so in the twentieth century, it is
surprising that contemporary political and social theorists have rarely
"singled it out for special consideration."[9] This avoidance can be attributed, in part, to the ethical and epistemic difficulty of conceptual-
izing and theorizing violence without justifying, absolving, or condemning it. Indeed, since 1789, and certainly since 1917, violence
has severely challenged the ideal (or pretense) of scholarly objectivity.
The political and social theorists who have pondered the vexed problem of violence have done so in times not of normalcy but of grave
unsettlement, in which their position is anything but detached or neutral. Indeed, for them it is a matter of method to combine theoretical
reflection and political *engagement*.[10] But to say that the most penetrating reflections on violence have a singular and urgent polemical
context and purpose is not to dismiss them for being mere works of
circumstance, since they transcend the political reasons and contingent events of their inception and construction. In any case, in early
modern times Machiavelli and Hobbes fit this pattern; and in the
more recent past, Weber, Schmitt, Arendt, and Ricoeur.

✳ ✳ ✳

No doubt the one-line dictionary definition which makes physical coercion the quintessence of violence is unduly restrictive. Given its protean nature, there is something to be said for the premise that violence
is a political, legal, and cultural construction. Of course, such a premise merely forces attention to the identity of those engaged in this
construction and to their reasons, procedures, and intentions. The net
effect is a return to the time-honored concern with the why and how

of the distinction between, on the one hand, authorized or legitimate force and, on the other, unauthorized or illegitimate violence.

Both conceptually and in practice, force and violence are construed as opposites, though the boundaries between them are forever being tested, contested, and adjusted. Force is conceived as organized, controlled, and limited, in accordance with legal norms and conventions. The chief symbolic representation of this authorized violence which is public and collective, is the disciplined body of police or soldiers engaging in either a passive show of force or a limited use of it. By contrast, unlawful violence is widely perceived to be frenzied, shapeless, and disorderly, its agents being moved by undisciplined impulses and passions. Typically, unauthorized violence is pictured as an ugly peasant horde or urban rabble rushing to slay, mutilate, or massacre innocent and helpless victims.[11] Clearly both force and violence are very much a matter of position and perception, particularly concerning the source and degree of their respective lawfulness. The advocates and apologists of violence contest the legitimacy of the force used against them, and in so doing challenge the existing legal or constitutional order, or are accused of doing so.[12]

All in all, the advantage is on the side of force, which benefits from the sacred aura of the state. As the "most flagrant manifestation" and "ultimate" expression of power, violence assumes legitimacy and virtue by reason of being exercised by a state that monopolizes and projects it as the only pure— nonpartisan or neutral—force.[13] Authorized violence also benefits from being organized, planned, and measured, thereby appearing rational and pondered. By contrast, whatever its intention, unauthorized counter-violence is widely perceived as impulsive, random, and erratic, as if moved by blind fury, hatred, and vengeance.[14]

Clearly, there is no sovereign, not to say legitimate power, without the sword, the *ultima ratio regnorum*. Machiavelli noted that in his own time Savonarola "failed entirely in his new rules once the multitude began to disbelieve in him, and he had no means of holding fast those who had believed nor of compelling the unbelievers to believe."[15] No less direct, Hobbes argued that "covenants, without the sword, are but words."[16] A few centuries later, in the wake of 1848, while wrestling critically with the terror of the French Revolution, Quinet held that in its time it would have been futile to "attack the

[old] system by moral preaching alone" and to "keep reciting the litany that to spill blood is contrary to the commandments of God and Church."[17] Similarly, when Max Weber, confounded by the Russian and German revolutions of 1917–19, set to rethinking politics and power, he maintained that under extreme conditions the "absolute ethic" of the Sermon on the Mount or the Gospel was not relevant when deciding "which ends should sanctify which means."[18]

Since ancient times war against foreign enemies has been judged far less severely than civil war opposing members of the same community or country. In the sixteenth century Montaigne gave voice to this view, which is held to this day. He deemed "foreign war . . . a much milder evil than civil war" and considered that by and large to have recourse to the former to avoid the latter was a "bad means for a good purpose."[19] Among the reasons for this understanding and teaching, three stand out: compared to foreign war, civil war is much more cruel and savage; it involves and indiscriminately visits violence on innocent noncombatants; and it lacerates the fabric of civility. The third of these traits was of greatest concern to Burke, who considered civil wars to "strike deepest of all into the manners of the people," in that "[t]hey vitiate their politics; they corrupt their morals; they pervert even the natural taste and relish of equity and justice."[20] Needless to say, decivilizing violence is at its worst when civil and foreign war become intertwined and ideologically fired, as they did during the Peloponnesian War as well as the Thirty Years Wars of the seventeenth and twentieth centuries. In Corcyra, the first Greek city to "display the passions of civil war" during the Peloponnesian War, this convergence resulted in "death in every shape and form," in people going "to any extreme and beyond it," and in "unheard of atrocities of revenge" as the "ordinary conventions of civilized life [were] thrown into confusion."[21]

* * *

New beginnings entail two types of violence: the violence of foundation, which sets up and anchors a new order of legitimacy; and the violence of conservation, which maintains and enforces it.[22] Not many states have been founded by peaceful convention, and revolutionary refoundations confirm Merleau-Ponty's postulate that violence is "the common origin of all regimes."[23] In a time of new beginnings, rank coercion is used to establish and entrench a new legal or constitutional order which spells the transformation of illegal violence into legitimate force. Eventually even the worst of this founding violence is half forgotten and half transfigured by reason of being glorified consistent with a narrative of symbolic justification.[24]

The problem of new and, therefore, violent foundations is central to the theoretics of Machiavelli.[25] As noted, in his sober judgment "nothing [is] more difficult to carry out, nor more doubtful of success, nor more dangerous to handle than to initiate a new order of things." Precisely because such a turn affects not only political but civil society, the "reformer has enemies in all those who profit by the old order, and only lukewarm defenders in all those who would profit by the new order, . . . partly from fear of their adversaries, . . . and partly from the incredulity of mankind."[26]

In any case, since the moment of new foundation, which entails radical rupture, is marked by great instability and resistance, there is, according to Machiavelli, no alternative to violence. He posits that with the situation balanced on a razor's edge, it calls for a single political leader from among the founders to use "extraordinary measures, such as violence and arms," to expedite the change in regime.[27] Unconcerned with morality and metaphysics, Machiavelli urges that rather than incur the risk of a protracted campaign of violence, the ruler should "commit all his cruelties at once," even if these are "neither Christian nor human . . . [and are] destructive of all civilized life."[28]

If, however, the new prince is to found a lasting state and be more than a mere tyrant, he must know how "to use both the beast and the man," which involves making himself widely feared and loved, with religion and law fostering the consensual basis for his rule.[29] Ultimately perhaps the best measure of the proper mix of fear and love is "whether cruelties increase or decrease over time."[30]

In some important respects Hobbes consciously follows in Machiavelli's footsteps.[31] He, too, means to theorize the creation of a new political order without anchorage in revealed religion. He has, of course, a realistically pessimistic view of human nature conditioned by a perpetual war of all against all. But if Hobbes rethinks the problem of new beginnings with even greater urgency than Machiavelli it is because he does so in a time of religious war freighted with execrable civil strife. Indeed, he made a special point of stressing that the *Levia-*

than was a "Discourse of Civil and Ecclesiastical Government occasioned by the disorders of the Present Time," and that it had no "other design than to set before men's eyes the mutual relation between protection and obedience."[32] Hobbes postulates a conflictual and ferocious natural world, modeled on decivilizing civil war, as the ultimate source of the rampant disorder which the state is to curb by the exercise of undivided sovereignty. Just as Machiavelli assigns an indispensable and paramount role to the prince during the fiercely contested founding moment, Hobbes looks to the absolute monarch, responsible before God, to claim and establish a monopoly of power with minimal regard for moral limits, there being as yet no legal checks. On this score Hobbes merely gives voice to the reigning conventional wisdom that "it is more dangerous to be tolerant than to be severe and cruel, the consequences of even the slightest tolerance being more deadly and devastating than momentary harshness."[33] This reasoning eventually provoked Rousseau's plaint about "the strong armed with the formidable power of the law," in league with "a handful of oppressors," lording over "a famished mob, crushed by suffering and famine."[34]

Marx and Engels stress the inherent weight of violence in history and its role in major transitions, particularly in tomorrow's uphill passage to socialism, which presumed a new foundation. Marx notes that through the ages "conquest, enslavement, murder-cum-robbery, in short *Gewalt* (force, violence) play[ed] a preeminent role."[35] Indeed Marx and Engels hold that *Gewalt* has been recognized and "accepted as the driving force of history."[36] Taking the long view, they considered violence to be most evident in primitive economic accumulation and the colonial system, though Marx also deemed it "the midwife of every old society which is pregnant with a new one."[37] In the Marxist perspective, "the course of social development was historically accompanied by a change in the forms of coercion."[38] The emergence of the state saw the growth of special institutions charged with forcible coercion, in the form of army, bureaucracy, and law courts which are disproportionately responsive to the elite—in Marx's time, increasingly to the bourgeoisie.[39] In the wake of the fierce repression of the revolts of 1848 and 1870–71 Marx and Engels considered these agencies, particularly the military and police forces, formidable obstacles to a radical transformation in civil and political society, the "era of barricades and street fighting being gone for good."[40] In the event this assessment kept strengthening their predisposition for a peaceful and legal transition to socialism. Marx and Engels envisaged such a transition a serious historical possibility in the parliamentary democracies with popular suffrage, notably in England, the United States, the Netherlands, and, after 1880, in France. Needless to say, they did not preclude the old elites resorting to violence to block the legal road to power, and precipitating civil war, particularly in semi-parliamentary imperial Germany and autocratic imperial Russia.[41]

＊ ＊ ＊

Especially in Germany after the First World War and in the United States after the Second World War, the discussion of power and violence was significantly shaped by the writings of Max Weber. In particular Weber's construction of three pure or ideal-typical forms of domination or authority—traditional, rational-legal, and charismatic—assumed considerable heuristic force in the analysis of existing power structures and, above all, of their collapse and refoundation.

In dealing with revolutionary violence, Weber's theoretics are very much marked by the furious events of his time, notably the revolution in Russia and the not unrelated end-of-war crisis in Germany and throughout much of central and eastern Europe. Caught up in this historical turbulence, he clearly defined himself as a liberal democrat and became an early adept of the new Democratic Party in the nascent Weimar Republic. He cautiously sympathized with the moderate Socialists and for prudential reasons advocated cooperation with them. But as a reasoned and outspoken critic of revolution, Weber was resolutely hostile to the Russian Bolsheviks and German Spartacists. He decried their absolute ethic and utopian project, which he expected to precipitate a severe reactionary backlash, all the more so since in both Russia and Germany military defeat, not a broad-based social revolt, had brought about the "enormous breakdown, which tends to be called a revolution."[42] Indeed, Weber viewed Russian and German developments through the quasi-Marxist prism of his earlier writings on the Russian upheaval of 1905–6, emphasizing the deficiency of social and cultural preconditions for bourgeois liberalism, let alone social democracy or communism. In any case, he was at once confounded and disquieted by the Bolshevik takeover and Spartacist defiance, fearful that Friedrich Ebert and Philipp Scheidemann, the first President and Chancellor of the Weimar Republic, were condemned to share Kerensky's fate.

More than likely the inadequacy of Weber's social or sociological concepts for the analysis of the improbable turn of events in eastern and central Europe prompted him to become his own political theorist. To be sure, in his seminal lecture "Politics as a Vocation," delivered to uneasy university students in Munich some two months after the revolution from above of November 1918, Weber still claimed to speak "sociologically" when he insisted that ultimately there was no defining the modern state other than in terms of the "specific means" intrinsic to any political association: "physical *Gewaltsamkeit*," that is, violence or force.[43] His position was informed, however, by the same pessimistic understanding of human nature and sociability, and of the workings of the state system, as Machiavelli and Hobbes. In Weber's reading, also, "the prince" forged the modern state by "expropriating" the "administrative, military, and financial" powers of "neighboring and autonomous 'private' authorities."[44] Indeed, "nearly all community formations (*Vergemeinschaftungen*)," including those of political associations, "have their origin in violence,"[45] which they subsequently also use for consolidation and defense.[46] Significantly, in support of this Machiavellian-Hobbesian position Weber alluded to Trotsky's dictum at the Brest-Litovsk peace negotiations in early 1918 that "every state is founded on *Gewalt*." Not that violence is "the normal or the one and only instrument of the state," but it is "specific" to it. After stressing that "the relation between the state and violence is particularly close these days," Weber put forth a novel and arresting postulate: "the state is that human community which . . . (successfully) claims or exercises the *monopoly of the legitimate use of physical violence or force* within a given territory."[47]

During the great convulsion of 1917–19 Weber considered it unexceptional that the provisional governments of Russia and Germany, respectively, should go to all lengths to secure exclusive control over the use of violence, if need be by turning to violence themselves, so as to demonstrate that the state is the "sole source of the 'law' " that can authorize its use.[48] Violence being the "decisive means" in this high-stake political struggle, "whoever has recourse to it, no matter for what end—and every politician does so—exposes himself to its specific consequences." Weber invoked the assassination of Karl Lieb-knecht and Rosa Luxemburg, the two most prominent Spartacists, to insist that such a fate was likely, not to say fitting, for "fighting zealots, be they of the religious or revolutionary genus."[49]

This, then, was the context in which Weber put forth his typology of three ideal-typical forms of domination or authority. The third type, or charismatic rule, is conceived and relevant for understanding "enormous breakdowns" and new foundations. In Weber's construction, this form of authority is rooted in the "out of the ordinary personal qualities of an individual leader," as exercised by the religious "prophet" or, in the political domain, by "the elect warlord, the plebiscitary ruler, the great demagogue, or the party leader."[50] Unlike legal and traditional rule, the other two types of authority, charismatic leadership is unrestrained by timeless rules and traditions. It is also, or above all, an exceptional and intermittent historical phenomenon. Indeed, Max Weber attributes "revolutionary violence" to charismatic rule and repeatedly characterized it as "a uniquely 'creative' revolutionary force of history."[51]

✳ ✳ ✳

Methodologically Carl Schmitt was a soul mate and disciple of Max Weber and, like him, one of the great social theorists of his time. But notwithstanding their shared critical engagement with historical materialism, Weber and Schmitt were worlds apart ideologically. Schmitt wrestled with the problem of violence starting with the First World War and increasingly and controversially so through the Weimar Republic and the Third Reich, into the Cold War. Confronted with the general crisis of his time he, too, came up against the limits of the sociological imagination, abandoning the sociology of law for conceptually informed political theory. But Schmitt, contrary to Weber, stood against Weimar's pluralistic liberalism and parliamentary democracy, as well as the Versailles Treaty. His opposition to the new republican order was basically reactionary. Even so, spurning the idea of a pure and simple restoration, he proposed to modernize the antidemocratic creed and rhetoric. Indeed, notwithstanding his radical skepticism about human equality and mass society, Schmitt gravitated, both ideationally and politically, toward the populist counterrevolution. Shortly after joining the National Socialist Party in May 1933 he was appointed to the Prussian State Council. Although he eventually ceased to have official ties with the Nazi regime, like Martin Heidegger he never forswore his new faith, not even during or following the high tide of horror, when he could no longer plead "blind and naked Ignorance."[52]

Inspired by Hobbes, even if with a different vision, Schmitt embraces the premise of a chaotic state of nature in which sinful men are locked in mutual enmity and conflict.[53] He differs from Hobbes in two respects: sensitive to Germany's geopolitically conditioned security dilemma, Schmitt construed the dismal state of nature to be shaped and aggravated by the war of all against all between and among the states; and skeptical of the sovereign's ability to tame the state of nature, he postulates it to be immutable and perpetual. Schmitt considers this intrinsically permanent and all-pervasive enmity—manifest or latent—the motor of the "friend-enemy" opposition or dissociation which he postulates to be the defining characteristic, not to say essence, of the political phenomenon. Not surprisingly, from his all but counterrevolutionary perspective, he conceives the enemy "other" as the universal aggressor in a zero-sum political struggle that brooks no compromise.

Schmitt locates the source and dynamics of violence in the fluctuating heat and momentum of the ultimately polarizing friend-enemy opposition. In the 1920s, hearkening to the *Dolchstoss* legend about Germany's recent military defeat, he focuses on the domestic side of this opposition only as it affects the state's war-making capacity. But as of the early 1930s, in face of the intensifying cleavages in civil and political society, he discusses domestic and foreign politics, civil war, and war "in the same breath."[54] By erasing the boundaries between the endogenous and exogenous spheres of violence, as well as denying primacy to either one, Schmitt posits a single political field in which war, civil war, and revolution are inseparable.[55]

During the 1930s, with the rising tide of dictatorship and violence, both national and international, Schmitt keeps radicalizing and hardening his thesis. He moves toward conceiving the domestic and foreign enemy as a dangerous "heretic," all the more so with conventional international war becoming a "holy war and crusade" in which the enemy must be "annihilated" rather than merely defeated.[56] Presently he considered the National Socialist takeover and consolidation of power confirmation for his postulate, formulated in 1922, that "[s]overeign is he who decides on the exception [state of emergency] in the face of grave political and social disorder."[57] By 1937, in his article "Total Enemy, Total War, and Total State," Schmitt seems to shift and narrow the focus to international politics: he insists that "[w]ar is at the heart of the matter" and that just as "total war determines the nature and development of a state's *Totalität*," so the nature of the "total enemy" gives total war its "particular bent."[58] In actual fact, given his political position and fund of ideas, in declaring "war" to be "the heart of the matter" Schmitt took war to comprise civil war and revolution, all the more so since in his reading the defining mortal enemy was, in essential respects, similar in all three. In any case, Schmitt's conceptualization of the nature and dynamics of the seamless friend-enemy dissociation lying at the core of politics *in extremis* is of considerable heuristic value for the study of revolutionary moments.

✳ ✳ ✳

Hannah Arendt recognized herself in Karl Jaspers's injunction not to "succumb either to the past or the future . . . [since] what matters is to be entirely present."[59] An assimilated Jew, Arendt left the Third Reich and eventually settled in the United States, where she became an exemplary émigré scholar and public intellectual sworn to keep "examining and bearing consciously the burden" which her century had "placed on us."[60] While the ferocities of German Fascism and the Second World War are the essential background for her historically informed conceptual and phenomenological analysis of totalitarianism, the black liberation and anti-Vietnam movements in America, as well as the world-circling rebellion of 1968, marked her theoretical reflections on violence, "the common denominator [of her] century of wars and revolutions."[61]

Along Weberian lines, Hannah Arendt constructs an ideal-typical opposition between power and violence, all the time conceding that "though they are distinct phenomena they usually appear together." She conceptualizes power as "the essence of all government." Being "an end in itself" power requires not "justification . . . [but] legitimacy," a substantive point on which she follows Weber. A collective phenomenon, power "belongs to a group" as long as that group acts and speaks "in concert." When the legitimacy of the incumbent power holders is challenged, these seek to bolster their position by appealing to the past, notably to the "initial getting together" in which, paradoxically, violence had played a role.[62] In sum, violence recedes as power grows.

Inversely, the greater the breakdown of sovereign power, the greater the scope for the rule of pure violence. Above all, Arendt claims that although violence "can destroy power, it is utterly incapable of creating it."[63] Nor can it promote such great causes as "revolution, progress, or reaction." Against the background of the civil disorders of the 1960s in America and Europe, she sees violence serving the "short-term goal" of dramatizing and publicizing grievances, making it "more a weapon of reform than of revolution."[64]

Inasmuch as violence, in contrast to power, is inherently "instrumental," it requires "implements" to be effective. Governed "by the means-end category," the rationality of violence is measured by the extent to which "it is effective in reaching the end that must justify it."[65] Arendt makes a special point of insisting that by virtue of being instrumental, violence needs "justification," leaving political theorists to deal with the "speech and articulation" used to spell out the grounds for its application.[66] Needless to say, the more comprehensive the end-purposes to be served, the greater the delusion of violence, as when revolutions thrust beyond the establishment of political freedoms to attack "the social question."[67]

This radicalization of purpose is a function, in part, of willful actors facing unprecedented and unanticipated crossroads in moments of severe rupture which, according to Arendt, leads to their being gripped by "a strange pathos of novelty," or an uneasy mixture of astonishment and awe.[68] Under the circumstances, and lacking conceptual understanding and agency, theirs is less a march into a scripted future than a *fuite en avant*. This leap in the dark entails a betrayal of the revolutionary activists' starting intentions as they transform their movement into a regime. There is forever a tension between this perversion and the founding legend which celebrates and purifies the emergence of radical novelty, including its characteristically violent side. Indeed, the founding moment is at once a source of violence and a crucible for the conversion of violence into power. Hannah Arendt, following Machiavelli, considers it "obvious" that the "problem of beginning," freighted with violence, is relevant "to the phenomenon of revolution." Invoking the "legendary" narratives of "our" beginnings in biblical and classical antiquity—"Cain slew Abel, and Romulus slew Remus"—Hannah Arendt postulates that "violence was the beginning and . . . [that] no beginning could be made without using violence, without violating."[69]

Paul Ricoeur—like Weber, Schmitt, and Arendt—looks to the decomposition of sovereign (state) power as the conjuncture most likely to reveal the essence of the relationship of politics and violence. He sees the revolutionary situation as the "crossroad of two violences with the one defending the established order, the other forcing the access to power of new social strata." Ricoeur sees "the problem of political evil" posed in this struggle between "defending" and "founding" forces fraught with imperative decision making, in which "violence becomes the motor of history." He posits, furthermore, that "power provides the greatest occasion for man to demonstrate his capability for evil" under extreme conditions in which "violence generates new institutions by redistributing power among states and among classes."[70] Following Arendt, he invokes Machiavelli for having seen that the "real problem of political violence is not that of useless, arbitrary, and frenetic violence but that of violence calculated and limited to promote the establishment of a durable state." Although this lawless foundation is legitimated after the fact, its origin is forever "marked by the successful use of violence." Indeed, since "all new nations, powers, and regimes are born in this fashion," this "founding crime" should serve as a reminder that there is "something contingent and singularly historical" about the "new legitimacy" which "absolves" it.[71]

* * *

In a worsening climate of discomposure, the growing incidence of violence in France in mid-1789 and in Russia in February 1917 was essentially spontaneous and popular. This violence of the first hour was, in Hannah Arendt's terms, the violence of revolt, not revolution. In both instances its success was, of course, as much a function of the irresolution of the royal courts and the disarray of the security forces as of the strength and resolve of the rebels. This first violence was neither accidental nor artless, nor was it the inevitable embryo of the subsequent terror.

In France, notably in Paris, socially and economically fueled popular disorders preceded the storming of the Bastille, a towering symbol of law and order. The crowd that charged this fortress-prison on July 14, 1789, ran into heavy fire, which claimed about 100 dead and seventy-five wounded. In turn, once the assailants had carried the day, in retaliation for their own casualties and in open defiance of legitimate and customary force, they seized the Marquis de Launay, the governor of the Bastille, as well as Jacques de Flesselles, the capital's chief magistrate. With raging passion the crowd paraded these hapless but not entirely innocent old-regime officials through the streets, beating and stabbing them, until they were finally decapitated and their severed heads fixed and exhibited on top of pitchforks. A week later, on July 22, L.-B.-F. Bertier de Sauvigny, the intendant of Paris, and Joseph-François Foullon de Doué, his father-in-law, suffered a similar fate. Meanwhile, a *grande peur* spread through much of the countryside. There the violence took the form of the physical manhandling and defamation of landed nobles as well as the burning of tax records, vandalism, and pillage.

These urban *émeutes* and rural *jacqueries* were without ideology and organization, and they were not related, except in the perception of the upper ten thousand. Needless to say, the collective disobedience and lawlessness horrified and frightened prominent members of the ruling and governing classes, some to the point of fleeing abroad post-haste. But at the time the reactions to this violence of the first hour among reformist politicians and public intellectuals were not altogether negative, even if there were only few voices of outright approval or justification. Ever so many seasoned and overnight reformers silently condoned the violence of popular remonstrance at the same time that they harnessed its moral energy and made the most of its specter to advance their emergent political agenda. Indeed, it is most unlikely that without the force of this violence the feudal regime and privileges would have been abolished and the Declaration of the Rights of Man and the Citizen would have been issued. Even so, realizing "that they were playing the role of sorcerer's apprentice," not a few of the reformers began to disavow popular violence as it found political champions, even instigators.[72] In like manner, with time the intelligentsia's "enthusiastic approbation of the glorious [if violent] dawn of 1789 metamorphosed into a mortifying rejection of the horrors of 1793–1794."[73]

In all major respects the first violence developed along similar lines in Russia in 1917, except that its scale, intensity, and speed were much greater, as was the decomposition of power, law, and security. In the twin capitals, but especially in Petrograd, war-induced food and fuel shortages compounded by runaway inflation and ill-seasoned unemployment fomented mass demonstrations, industrial strikes, and looting. These disorders, carried by swelling crowds, became increasingly difficult to control once Petrograd's military garrison mutinied to protest a police regiment's firing into a throng, killing forty and wounding another forty. Oblivious to the erosion of his monopoly of legitimate force, the tsar issued orders to continue the repression. But not unlike in 1905, his generals had difficulties mustering reliable troops for this crackdown while the loyal opposition, pressed by liberal democratic and socialist reformers, urged a radical change in policy. All this time mutinous soldiers and junior officers assaulted their superiors. Alone in Petrograd, where crowds attacked police stations, prisons, and court houses, at least 1,500 people were killed or wounded, including not a few public officials. In nearby Kronstadt and Helsingfors sailors savagely murdered scores of officers of the Black Sea Fleet.[74] After nearly a month of wild and violent lawlessness, on March 4 Nicholas II abdicated and Grand Duke Michael renounced the throne, leaving authority in the hands of an embattled Provisional Government beholden to a revived Duma and a new-born Congress of Soviets. Compared to the early violence of protest in the French Revolution, its equivalent in the Russian Revolution may have had fewer gory and "archaic" sides, although in the aggregate it took many more lives, even without the peasant revolt, which exploded somewhat later.

Ironically the overthrow of tsarism also involved "more physical assaults and rhetorical aggressions . . . on servants of the old regime" than the Bolshevik seizure of power. At the time only "hypocrites or politicians with failing memories" sought to hide this cold fact with an eye to representing the allegedly "bloodless" February revolution as "morally superior" to the October revolution. Besides, except among the apologists of the old order, this "violence from below" was widely considered "inevitable," and editorialists never really "denounced it, nor did they warn that it might be fraught with catastrophe."[75]

* * *

As noted, in both mid-1789 and in February 1917 violence triumphed over force largely because of the irresolution and faintheartedness on the part of the sovereigns and some of their chief counselors. This failure of nerve enraged and activated the last-ditchers of the old regime at the same time that it encouraged the militants among the rebels, low and high. Gradually the advocates of reform were outflanked and intimidated by extremists who embodied and fostered the friend-enemy dissociation. The contraction of the center then weakened the floodgates restraining the rising tides of violence, which threatened to sweep them away and feed into large-scale reciprocal terror warranted by civil and foreign war.

This quantum jump of violence is both cause and effect of the breakup of a state's single sovereignty into multiple and rival power centers, which is accompanied by a radical dislocation of the security and judicial system. As a consequence, the positive legal standards for judging and circumscribing acts of political violence give way to moral and ethical criteria. In other words, in the calculus of means and ends, the principles of "law" are superseded by those of "justice."[76] Increasingly, on the opposing sides, the ends justify the means—in rhetoric and practice, if not in theory. It is in this conjuncture that the boundaries between violence and terror become indistinct, controversial, and divisive. Needless to say, in their absolute friend-enemy dissociation, and deaf to the vexed ends-means question, fervid revolutionaries and counterrevolutionaries charge each other with resorting to aggressive, willful, and indiscriminate terror at the same time that they claim their own violence to be defensive, incidental, and circumscribed. But most of the other actors keep agonizing and debating about when and how to draw a credible line between the two.

One of the actors, Isaac Steinberg, Lenin's first deputy minister of justice, sought to counterpose violence and terror conceptually after his abortive effort to do so in practice, which led to his early resignation. According to Steinberg, revolutionary violence is "defensive, unavoidable, and necessary," while revolutionary terror is "aggressive and provocative." The one is moved by "righteous anger against the old order and passion for the new world," the other by "rage, hatred, and vengeance." Compared to violence, which targets only "proven enemies," terror is indiscriminate and unscrupulous. Whereas the agents of violence have compassion for their victims, the agents of terror are cold-hearted. An unreconstructed advocate of the right to rebel, Steinberg, a Left Socialist Revolutionary, rather too simply set the "barricade" of voluntary freedom fighters over against the "torture chamber" of a state-run enforcement terror.[77]

He was very much aware of the difficulty of drawing an "objective" line between the terror he "fully rejected" and the violence he "tolerated." Steinberg "called for struggle" without which there was no overcoming the counterrevolutionary "resistances" whose scale and intensity largely defined the scale and intensity of revolutionary violence. He summed up his position with the defiant motto: "Struggle—always; violence—within limits; terror—never."[78]

Steinberg's revolutionary profession echoes that of Dominique Garat, who was France's minister of justice in 1791–92 and minister of the interior during the Great Terror. Originally backed by Brissot, Condorcet, and Rabaut Saint-Etienne, he, too, reflected critically on the violence-terror conundrum after having confronted it as a member of an embattled provisional government seeking to (re)establish an undivided sovereignty. Garat, like Steinberg, remained faithful to the right to rebel, which after 1789 was widely hailed as "*une chose sainte*." The right to "raise the sword against the people's oppressors" ensued from this "sacred right of insurrection," but only on condition that hard-core principles not be violated in the process.[79] Along with nearly the entire political class, Garat was shaken, in particular, by the prison massacres of September 1792 in Paris in which wild crowds brutally murdered hundreds of innocent men and women. Rather than probe the excessive excesses of these terrifying *journées*, Garat simply and conveniently blamed them on Marat, this "monstrous creature . . . and evil spirit." At the same time he was scandalized that responsible leaders who agreed on "the need to break despotism and the aristocracy . . . but abhorred bloodshed" were unwilling or powerless to stop the slaughter.[80]

Even so, Garat did not swear off the right of people to rise against established but oppressive powers to either get redress or "destroy them in order to get change." This type of insurrection lasts from "the time the old powers begin to be challenged to the time the insurgents terminate it and swear allegiance and do homage to the new powers." Whereas the "*ends* of a legitimate insurrection are sacred, its *means* are seldom very pure," all the less so if "it goes on too long, usually by way of crimes." In any event, Garat concluded that "epochs of insurrection which are destined to punish great crimes are also epochs in which great crimes are perpetrated," making the French Revolution "at once the most glorious and infamous epoch."[81]

✳ ✳ ✳

NOTES

1. Hannah Arendt, *On Revolution* (New York: Viking, 1968), p. 9.

2. Wolfgang Sofsky, *Traktat über die Gewalt* (Frankfurt/Main: Fischer, 1993), p. 217 and pp. 224–25.

3. Bernd Huppauf, "Krieg, Gewalt, und Moderne," in Frauke Meyer-Gosau and Wolfgang Emmerich, eds., *Gewalt, Faszination und Furcht: Jahrbuch für Literatur und Politik in Deutschland*, vol. 1 (Leipzig: Reclam, 1994), pp. 12–40, esp. pp. 18–19. See also Norbert Elias, *Über den Prozess der Zivilisation: Soziogenetische und psychogenetische Untersuchungen*, vol. 2 (Frankfurt/Main: Suhrkamp, 1978), esp. pp. 312–35.

4. Sofsky, *Traktat*, p. 224. See also John Keane, *Reflections on Violence* (London: Verso, 1996), pp. 30–31.

5. See Arno J. Mayer, *Why Did the Heavens Not Darken? The "Final Solution" in History* (New York: Pantheon, 1988), passim.

6. In 1998 a United Nations conference forged a draft treaty establishing a permanent International Criminal Court to bring individuals to justice for war crimes, crimes against humanity, and genocide. The Convention Against Torture dates from 1984.

7. Sofsky, *Traktat*, p. 13.

8. Keane, *Reflections*, p. 22.

9. Arendt, *On Violence* (New York: Harcourt Brace, 1970), p. 8; and Keane, *Reflections*, pp. 6–7.

10. See Sheldon Wolin, *Politics and Vision: Continuity and Innovation in Western Political Thought* (Boston: Little, Brown, 1960), passim, esp. ch. 8. See also Vladimir Jankélévitch, *Le pur et l'impur* (Paris: Flammarion, 1960), p. 187.

11. Julien Freund, *L'essence du politique* (Paris: Sirey, 1965), pp. 513–15.

12. David Riches, ed., *The Anthropology of Violence* (Oxford: Basil Blackwell, 1986), p. 3 and pp. 8–9.

13. Arendt, *On Violence*, p. 35; and Paul Ricoeur, *Histoire et Vérité*, 3rd ed. (Paris: Seuil, 1955), p. 246.

14. See Sofsky, *Traktat*, pp. 22–23, 44, 56.

15. Niccolò Machiavelli, *The Prince and the Discourses* (New York: Modern Library, 1940), ch. VI, p. 22.

16. Hobbes cited in Arendt, *On Violence*, p. 5.

17. Edgar Quinet, *La Révolution* (Paris: Belin, 1987), p. 46.

18. Weber, "Der Beruf zur Politik," in Johannes Winckelmann, ed., *Max Weber* (Stuttgart: Alfred Kröner, 1973), pp. 167–85, esp. pp. 173–74, 177, 180–81.

19. Michel de Montaigne, *Essais*, bk.2, ch. 23.

20. Burke cited in Keane, *Reflections*, p. 157.

21. Thucydides, *The Peloponnesian War* (London: Penguin, 1954), bk. 3, ch. 5 ("Revolution in Corcyra"), pp. 208–11.

22. Walter Benjamin, *Zur Kritik der Gewalt und andere Aufsätze* (Frankfurt/Main: Suhrkamp, 1965), p. 45. See also Jacques Derrida, *Force de loi: Le fondement mystique de l'autorité* (Paris: Galilée, 1994), esp. pp. 79–80, 86, 89, 98, 112–13.

23. Maurice Merleau-Ponty, *Humanism and Terror: An Essay on the Communist Problem* (Boston: Beacon, 1969), p. 109.

24. See Thomas Paine, *The Rights of Man* (London: J.M. Dent, 1915), pt. 2, ch. 2, p. 163.

25. My discussion of Machiavelli's reflections on new foundations or beginnings is very much inspired by Louis Althusser, *Écrits philosophiques et politiques*, vol. 2, (Paris: Stock/IMEC, 1994), pp. 42–161. See also Wolin, *Politics and Vision*, ch. 7. All quotations from Machiavelli are cited from Machiavelli, *The Prince and the Discourses* (New York: Modern Library, 1940).

26. Machiavelli, *The Prince*, ch. 6, p. 21.

27. Machiavelli, *The Discourses*, bk. 1, ch. 18, p. 171.

28. Machiavelli, *The Prince*, ch. 8, p. 35, and *The Discourses*, bk. 1, ch. 26, p. 184.

29. Machiavelli, *The Prince*, ch. 18, p. 64.

30. Wolin, *Politics and Vision*, p. 222.

31. My treatment of Hobbes follows Reinhart Koselleck, *Critique and Crisis: Enlightenment and the Pathogenesis of Modern Society* (Oxford: Berg, 1988), pp. 23–41; and Wolin, *Politics and Vision*, ch. 8. For the latest analysis of the filiation from Machiavelli to Hobbes, see Noel B. Reynolds and Arlene W. Saxenhouse, *Thomas Hobbes: Three Discourses* (Chicago: University of Chicago Press, 1995).

32. Thomas Hobbes, *Leviathan* (London: J.M. Dent, 1914), p. 391.

33. Koselleck, *Critique*, p. 16.

34. Cited in Charles E. Vaughan, ed., *The Political Writings of Jean Jacques Rousseau*, vol. 1 (Cambridge: Cambridge University Press, 1915), p. 302.

35. Marx, *Das Kapital*, in Karl Marx and Friedrich Engels, *Gesamtausgabe* (MEGA), vol. 6 (Berlin: Dietz, 1987), p. 644.

36. Marx and Engels, *The German Ideology* (New York: International Publishers, 1947), p. 10.

37. Marx, *Kapital*, p. 644 and p. 674.

38. Hal Draper, *Karl Marx's Theory of Revolution*, vol. 1 (New York: Monthly Review Press, 1977), p. 241 and p. 251.

39. Richard Hunt, *The Political Ideas of Marx and Engels*, vol. 2 (Pittsburgh: University of Pittsburgh Press, 1984), pp. 342 ff.

40. Engels cited in Hunt, *Political Ideas*, p. 357.

41. A. Schaff, "Marxist Theory on Revolution and Violence," in Bob Jessop and Charlie Malcolm-Brown, eds., vol. 3, *Karl Marx's Social and Political Thought: Criti-*

cal Assessments (London: Routledge, 1990), pp. 217–24, esp. 220–21; Maurice Barbier, *La pensée politique de Karl Marx* (Paris: L'Harmattan, 1992), pp. 159–63; Hunt, *Political Ideas*, pp. 349 ff.

42. Weber, "Politik als Beruf," in Weber, *Gesammelte politische Schriften* (Munich: Drei Masken, 1921), p. 433.

43. Weber, *Schriften*, pp. 396–97.

44. Ibid., p. 401.

45. Weber, *Gesammelte Aufsätze zur Wissenschaftslehre* (Tübingen: Mohr, 1922), p. 440.

46. Weber, "Richtungen und Stufen religiöser Weltablehnung," in Weber, *Soziologie-Politik: Universalgeschichtliche Analysen* (Stuttgart: Kröner, 1973), pp. 441–83, esp. pp. 453–54.

47. Weber, *Schriften*, p. 397 (italics in text).

48. Ibid., p. 397.

49. Ibid., p. 446.

50. Ibid., p. 398.

51. Cited in Wolfgang Mommsen, *Max Weber: Gesellschaft, Politik und Geschichte* (Frankfurt/Main: Suhrkamp, 1974), p. 122.

52. Joseph W. Bendersky, *Carl Schmitt: Theorist for the Reich* (Princeton: Princeton University Press, 1983); Helmut Quaritsch, ed., *Complexio Oppositorum: über Carl Schmitt* (Berlin: Dunker & Humblot, 1988), pt. 1; Brend Ruthers, *Carl Schmitt im Dritten Reich: Wissenschaft als Zeitgeistverstärkung*, 2nd ed. (Munich: Beck, 1990).

53. This paragraph is largely based on Heinrich Meier, *Carl Schmitt and Leo Strauss: The Hidden Dialogue* (Chicago: University of Chicago Press, 1995), esp. pp. 12–13, 18–19, 33.

54. Meier, *Schmitt and Strauss*, p. 25.

55. Ibid., pp. 22–24.

56. Cited in ibid., pp. 25–26.

57. Schmitt, *Political Theology: Four Chapters on the Concept of Sovereignty* (Cambridge, Mass.: MIT Press, 1985), ch. 1, esp. p. 5.

58. For this article see Schmitt, *Positionen und Begriffe im Kampf mit Weimar-Genf-Versailles, 1923–1939* (Hamburg: Hanseatische Verlagsanstalt, 1940), pp. 235–39.

59. Arendt chose this axiom as the epigraph for her *The Burden of Our Time* (London: Seker and Warburg, 1951), the title of the original English edition of *The Origins of Totalitarianism*.

60. Arendt, *Burden*, p. viii.

61. Arendt, *On Violence*, p. 3.

62. Arendt, *On Violence*, p. 44 and p. 52.

63. Ibid., p. 56.

64. Ibid., p. 79.

65. Ibid., pp 51–52.

66. Ibid., pp. 9–10.

67. Ibid., ch. 2. See also Jacob Burckhardt, *Weltgeschichtliche Betrachtungen* (Stuttgart: Kröner, 1978), p. 176.

68. Arendt, *On Revolution*, p. 39.

69. Ibid., p. 10.

70. Ricoeur, *Histoire et vérité*, pp. 253–54.

71. Ibid., pp. 271–72.

72. Georges Gusdorf, *La conscience révolutionnaire: Les idéologues* (Paris: Payot, 1978), p. 268.

73. Ibid., p. 281.

74. Orlando Figes, *A People's Tragedy: The Russian Revolution, 1891–1924* (London: Cape, 1996), pp. 312–20.

75. Isaac Steinberg, *Gewalt und Terror in der Revolution: Oktoberrevolution oder Bolschewismus* (Berlin: Rowohlt, 1931), pp. 30–31. See also Figes, *Tragedy,* p. 321.

76. See Benjamin, *Kritik der Gewalt,* p. 29.

77. Steinberg, *Gewalt und Terror,* pp. 144–46.

78. Ibid., p. 31, p. 300, p. 310.

79. Dominique Joseph Garat, *Mémoires sur la Révolution: Exposé de ma conduite dans les affaires et dans les fonctions publiques an III* (Paris, 1795), p. 23.

80. Ibid., pp. 21–22.

81. Ibid., p. 19 and p. 24.

Terror

THE PROBLEM of terror is even more complex and perplexing than that of violence. Since 1789 it has challenged and humbled social theorists and historians who strain to strike an equitable balance between engaged and distanced explanation. In the wake of Auschwitz, the Gulag, and Hiroshima, terror has become an even more disconcerting and controversial issue than it was during the century following the Furies of the French Revolution. Indeed, scholarly and popular debates about the reasons, functions, and effects of generic terror have been both enriched and complicated by the questions raised by students of the singularities of the Furies in the French and Russian revolutions respectively.

One can either muse about the tantalizing historical possibility of revolution without terror or declare the relationship of revolution and terror to be so inscrutable as to defy analysis. In the meantime there is no denying, however, that historically terror has been an essential property of revolution, and inherent to its dynamics. Terror, like violence, is interactive, and it is safe to say that following the revolts of 1789 and 1917 there would have been no terror had there been no tenacious and uncompromising domestic and foreign resistance. Besides, terror is not the exclusive preserve of revolutionary regimes, judging by its role in the life of a great variety of other autocratic authority systems, as explored by Machiavelli, Bodin, and Montesquieu.

The point at issue is not terror as such but its changing variety, scale, and intensity, notably its excesses, or "excessive excesses."[1] Infant and labile revolutionary regimes invariably are caught between the Scylla of becoming cold-blooded in order to win the life-and-death struggle of foundation and the Charybdis of exercising moderation at the risk of prematurely coming to a "lame and impotent conclusion." As noted, although a broad range of sober if idealistic politicians and public intellectuals are reluctant to forfeit the benefits of founding violence, they do worry about its spiraling out of control. In January 1793, halfway between the prison massacres and the Great Terror, Thomas Jefferson articulated this position (of which he was later disabused): "My own affections have been deeply wounded by some of the martyrs to this cause, but rather than it should have failed, I would have seen half the earth desolated." He insisted that he "deplored . . . [and mourned] as much as anybody" and until "my death . . . the many guilty persons [who] fell without the forms of trial," as well as the innocents. For Jefferson, although "blind to a certain degree, . . . the arm of the people . . . [was] a machine not quite so blind as balls and bombs." But at that moment he continued to judge its use to have been "necessary," all the more so because "the liberty of the whole earth was depending on the issue of the contest." Jefferson even wondered whether a "prize" of the magnitude of liberty "was ever . . . won with so little innocent blood."[2]

Five years later Kant still took a similar position. To be sure, he wondered whether the costs of the revolution in France might be too horrible and high for "a right-thinking person" to "decide . . . to go through with the experiment . . . a second time." Ultimately Kant concluded, however, that despite these costs "this revolution finds a wishful sympathy in the hearts of its spectators (who themselves are not involved in the game) which borders on enthusiasm, and whose open expression is fraught with danger—proof that this sympathy can have nothing less than a basic moral disposition in the human race as its cause."[3] Considering the terror a moral phenomenon driven by "the rage against evil [*das Böse*],"[4] Hegel kept the faith in the "glorious dawn" with even less hesitation than Kant. He saw the reign of terror as a necessary price for the transition to a constitution "established in harmony with the concept of right" which would serve as the "foundation [for] all future legislation."[5]

But Kant and Hegel were the exception. More commonly members of the intelligentsia who had cheered the fall of the Bastille and the Declaration of the Rights of Man became disaffected. In the manner of Schiller and Goethe, they viewed the revolutionary Furies as a "return to barbarism" rather than a midwife for the birth of freedom and justice, all the more so since they saw the terror answering the "cries of the rabble," whom they scorned and feared.[6] Michelet also was troubled by the terror—the "crescendo of murders"—associated with the Revolution's fight for survival. But with his benign view of *le peuple*, he wondered what the saviors of the French nation could have done "had the people answered: 'we would rather perish than become unjust.' "[7]

This same concern was voiced concerning the revolution in Russia. Within a year of the Bolshevik takeover and shortly before being assassinated by proto-Fascists in Berlin, Rosa Luxemburg considered that "it would be demanding something superhuman . . . [or] a miracle from Lenin and his comrades" to expect them to "conjure forth the finest democracy . . . as well as a model and faultless proletarian revolution in an isolated land, exhausted by world war, strangled by imperialism, [and] betrayed by the international proletariat." She went on to forewarn, however, that even in these "devilishly hard conditions . . . the danger begins when [revolutionaries] make a virtue of necessity and want to freeze into a complete theoretical system all the tactics forced upon them by these fatal circumstances."[8] In a similar vein Boris Kagarlitsky, a non-Leninist Marxist Soviet dissident, pondering the fortunes of the Russian Revolution in the mid-1980s, conceded that "humane" revolutions which foreswear terror are either "crushed by counterrevolution [or] fall under the blows of reaction." Even so, such abortive revolutions score "a moral victory," in that future generations will be able to once more embrace their ideas and try again. Kagarlitsky contended that rather than accept the logic of "the stark choice of either-or," the "Lefts" needed "to find a middle . . . [or] democratic way in order to be politically strong and morally pure."[9]

Indeed, the issue of violence and terror has divided reformers and revolutionaries, as well as historians, ever since 1789. Almost instantly the polemical and scholarly battle lines were drawn, and they hold to this day: on the one hand, those who consider the terror as a necessary evil, if the revolution was to survive; on the other, those who ignore or, *à la rigueur*, approve the initial founding violence but hold the terror to have been needless, barbaric, and counterproductive. With time, especially in the twentieth century, the issue of the filiation and escalation from mere violence to full-scale terror has become intensely controversial. But otherwise, insofar as the basic terms of the debate are concerned, they remain essentially constant.

Terror invites interpretations that are variously overdetermined, monocausal, demonizing, and didactic. Perhaps no other subject makes it quite so difficult to resist the temptation to read first beginnings in terms of subsequent developments and outcomes, usually with a view to giving lessons for the present and future.

Three major hypotheses frame the discussion of revolutionary terror. The first thesis posits contingent circumstances to be its primary cause and engine. In this interpretation, terror is driven at least as much by real and practical concerns as by ideological prepossessions or utopian professions. At bottom terror is an instrument designed to deal with circumstances perceived to endanger the survival of the fledgling revolution or revolutionary regime. It is forged in the heat of refractory domestic and international problems and pressures. These are all the more difficult to master because of the breakdown of the state apparatus and judicial system. According to this *thèse des circonstances*, the would-be revolutionary rulers face civil war fueled by not only pressing material problems but also sharp political, social, and cultural discords. Most of the leaders are inexperienced in national politics, and all of them are confounded by the "pathos of novelty." In addition to an intractable domestic situation, they face a hostile world environment which they aggravate with their own politically driven foreign policy, diplomacy, and warfare.

The second thesis postulates ideology as the essential prerequisite as well as the necessary (if not altogether sufficient) cause and engine of terror. It presumes the actions and decisions of revolutionary actors to be moved by ideas and beliefs which instantly freeze into dogma. Driven by preconceived and unchanging intentions, these actors become the chief agents for the realization of the ideological imperative to exorcise the *ancien régime* and destroy the counterrevolutionary resistances, with the ultimate objective of radically regenerating man and society. In this construct there is a tight coupling between ideological preconceptions and policy effects and outcomes.

The third thesis assigns a central, not to say exclusive place to the mind-set and psychological drives of supreme revolutionary actors who embrace a categorical ideological creed to further their arrogation of power. This interpretation presumes that the mental structures of key actor-agents predispose them not only to vastly exaggerate, if not wholly invent the counterrevolutionary resistances facing them, but also and above all to conceive that these resistances are orchestrated by the masterminds of an all-embracing and cunning plot. For such actors, obsessed by conspiracy and prone to scapegoating, terror ceases to be instrumental to become essential, or an end in and for itself.

Needless to say, in practice neither of these three interpretive frameworks is ironbound. The open-minded proponents of each of them adjust their explanatory paradigms to accommodate elements of the other two. For the champions of the first two positions it is never, really, a matter of all contingency or all ideology, but a mixture of the two, with a decisive weighting in favor of either the one or the other. Moreover, elements of the third thesis—the personality-mentality thesis, which subsumes the "great-man" logic—surface in both the first and the second, especially when these deal with the "excessive excesses" of terror and with the adoption and operation of terror as a governing instrument. Ultimately neither the thesis of "environmental circumstances" nor that of "genetic ideas" can do without "conceptual individuals" who are assigned a pivotal role in the establishment and direction of the reign of terror which they come to embody.[10]

The underlying issue may be said to be that of genetic versus environmental factors in the inception and escalation of revolutionary terror. The notorious difficulty of determining the respective weight of these two sets of factors in biogenetics is surpassed only by that of fixing their respective weight in "social inheritance." In any case, historians and social theorists will forever debate the proportion of the "environment" of historical circumstances and the "genes" of ideology in the terrors of the French and Russian revolutions.[11]

By and large "environmentalists" consider revolutionary terror to be a legitimate child born of extreme necessity. They are far more attentive to historical contingency than to ideology, which they presume plays an instrumental and subordinate role. Besides slighting ideology, environmentalists have difficulties establishing, with precision, the connections between, on the one hand, particular contingent events and, on the other, the application of specific terrorist policies. In addition, they face the impossible challenge of ranking the disparate factors in some reasoned order of importance and to explore their interactions.

Whereas the environmentalists are inclined to approach terror with sympathetic if critical understanding, which is often disvalued as apologia, the "geneticists" tend to do so with a turn of mind predisposed to unqualified condemnation. Paying scant attention to the flux and reflux of events, they wrench the terror out of the complex historical environment, apart from which it is reduced to a fragmented and isolated phenomenon. Moreover, rather than problematize and explore the postulated primacy of ideology paired with a congruent mind-set, they simply keep reaffirming it, with little if any regard for the tangled correlation of ideas and circumstances. For the geneticists, terror is the unwanted and illegitimate offspring of a revolution that runs amuck for not being terminated in good time—for not being, in Robespierre's phrase, "a revolution without a revolution."

Critical engagement with and between these two theses—circumstantial primacy and ideological determinism—both qualified by the axiom of the emergence of conceptual personae, ought not to preclude taking account of other mainsprings of terror: the spiraling stress between city and country; between the profane and the sacred; between innovation and tradition. As Marx and Engels suggested, in 1793 as in 1871, when political developments outstripped the social and economic readiness for radical change, the exercise of political will and terror with a view to forcing history was less a function of the strength and self-confidence of the bourgeoisie and its supporters than of their weakness and fright.[12] These disparities precondition the terror that surfaces in a revolutionary moment characterized by multiple sovereignty, defaulting institutions, and conceptual aporia. Such a conjunction is like a reversion to a political state of nature, which fosters what Schmitt defines as the friend-enemy dissociation and invites what Arendt considers the crime or violence of new foundation. In this indeterminate swirl of events, both friend and enemy are tempted by metapolitics, the one dizzy with hope for a fresh start, the other consumed by fear of an untimely end. Terror may be said to break in upon politics when politics becomes quasi-religious or when a utopia beckons or demands to be realized. Undaunted by the perplexities of radical novelty and the wages of violence, bewildered revolutionaries accelerate their lunge into an imperative but uncontrollable and hazardous future. But anti- and counterrevolutionaries are no less fiery in pursuit of their millennium, which is to reclaim an idealized but imperiled past and present.

＊ ＊ ＊

Not unlike the concept of revolution, the concept of political terror has a history. Machiavelli considered terror the essential stratagem for rulers seeking to establish a new political regime.[13] Not only the would-be despot of an embryonic tyranny but also the would-be rulers of a nascent republic must resort to terror in order to secure the survival of the new form of government. If need be, they have to physically annihilate their internal political enemies, particularly those tied to the old regime. Not to do so is to sign the death warrant of a nascent political foundation. Besides, the primal terror leaves a residue of latent fear which is an essential principle and instrument of everyday rule. Of course, for Machiavelli terrorizing violence is essentially a pragmatic agency: its success is measured by criteria of political efficiency, informed by *virtù*, and not by ideological standards.

Jean Bodin, following Machiavelli, set out to call in question the divine or religious foundations of state power, insisting that not even the *sacre* of the king could affect the secular essence of sovereignty.[14] Though rooted in profane history, the state is based on "force and violence." As a contemporary of the Saint Bartholomew's Day Massacre, Bodin was much concerned with removing religion as a source of civil discord. His argument for royal absolutism was framed in response to Huguenots who advanced constitutional arguments for resistance. At any rate, Bodin conceives terror as the chosen tool not of ruling and governing elites bent on founding or defending a regime, but of disfavored strata seeking to challenge them. The stratagem of violence belongs to the *estat populaire*—the masses—looking to supplant the noble and the wealthy—the classes. In other words, in Bodin's conception terror is used by the underclass of the poor and the weak—*les méchants et vicieux*—to "preserve or restore the equality of all citizens," not by incumbent elites—*les plus vertueux*—to protect or foster their own liberties and positions.

Machiavelli and Bodin considered political violence an instrument for the repression, even extermination, of political enemies, without specifically calling or defining it as terror. Also, in their scheme of things this as yet unnamed variant of political violence was not regime-specific. Montesquieu changed the terms of the discussion by "introducing the term terror into the political vocabulary and giving it a precise meaning": he made terror, which for him is a synonym for fear, "the defining characteristic of the governing principle of despotism."[15] To be sure, the aristocratic and republican forms of government, informed, respectively, by the principles of honor and virtue, resort to limited and exemplary violence or force against threatening domestic foes. But precisely because they stop short of terror, or rule by fear, both are chronically in danger of degenerating into despotism. In Montesquieu's analysis this deteriorated form of government, which he abhors, is said to be ruled by active terror, all the more so in a time of troubles when rising disquiet about real and imagined perils yields to fear, with individuals "frightened and tormented" by the prospect of being overwhelmed by these perils.[16]

While Montesquieu is troubled by the political costs of the degeneration of both monarchy and republic, he is particularly alert to the hazards attending the fight for survival of failing and embattled republics. To be sure, he condones their right to "destroy" those seeking to "subvert" them. But in so doing he does not lose sight of the danger that "there is no inflicting great punishment nor, for that matter, carrying through great political changes, without putting exorbitant powers in the hands of a few citizens." Indeed, there is the danger of the "avengers establishing a tyranny under the pretext of avenging the republic."[17]

✴ ✴ ✴

The *idée maîtresse*, or defining idea, that terror is the essential armature of despotism made its way among the *philosophes*, who brought it to bear on the rule of the Bourbon dynasty. They applied it to France's Catholic Church as well: "the imposture prevails by way of terror, which is how papalism maintains itself and keeps its hold on a frightened people."[18] It was only a short step from conceiving of terror as an autocratic ruling instrument to envisaging it as a tool of opposition, or counter-terror, to be wielded by either a rebel faction of the governing class or the *estat populaire*, as implicitly presaged by Montesquieu and dreaded by Bodin.

This oppositional conception of terror began to take shape early in the French Revolution and kept being changed in the rush of events. There was, to begin with, a phase of spontaneous and wild terror from below. It started, as noted, in July 1789, with the original explosion of popular violence in Paris and the *grande peur* in the countryside, and it continued through the prison massacres of September 1792. In fact, these massacres were at once the culmination of this first phase of a bottom-up terror and the embryo and precipitant of a would-be legitimate and quasi-legal terror from above, which was formally adopted and proclaimed in September 1793. Until Thermidor this top-down terror, which was conceptualized by revolutionary leaders, functioned as a principle, system, and instrument of government designed to punish, avenge, and educate as part of a quest to reestablish a single political and legal sovereignty. It is worth stressing, following Michelet and Quinet, that this enforcement terror, though a radically new departure, had certain traditional overtones by virtue of its quasi-religious ardor and righteousness reminiscent of the religious terrors of the past. Both in the old days and the new, the powers that be instrumentalized a fear that was both real and imagined, holy and profane.

Marat and Robespierre were the emblematic figures of the terror, the former for the first phase, the latter for the second. Marat was among the first and chief logicians and champions of violence-charged popular furies. By early fall 1789 he declared that it was these furies that had "bent the aristocratic faction of the Estates-General . . . by using terror to remind them of their duty." Before long Marat commended this "salutary terror" for being "indispensable for the consummation of the great purpose of the constitution." By late 1792, though discomfited by the brutality of the September massacres, Marat maintained that ever so many "enemies of the revolution" would refuse to take the right path "unless pushed by fear of popular vengeance . . . and [then] kept on it by terror."[19]

Although Robespierre eventually became one of the principal advocates and agents of terror from the summit of power, such was not his initial position. At the start he seriously doubted that "liberty could be secured by using the same means despotism had used to destroy it," and he held to this belief for over two years.[20] Though he meanwhile supported political terror against the enemies of the revolution,

Robespierre did not shift from a "negative" to a "positive" construction of revolutionary terror until the trial of Louis XVI in December 1792. Thereafter he, unlike Marat, conceived and projected it as a governing principle and policy directed from the top down and intended to further a broad range of domestic and foreign objectives.[21]

With Thermidor this official terror was discredited and denounced, and some of its chief directors and operatives were executed or jailed. But other forms of terror persisted, in particular the unofficial and retributive White terror of resurgent and rehabilitated anti- and counterrevolutionaries, which went essentially unpunished. During the civil war of the French Revolution the various resistances condoned or encouraged spontaneous terror and exercised enforcement terror on a scale and with an intensity commensurate with their engagement. Indeed, overall the terror practiced by all sides in this civil strife, not unlike that practiced during the civil wars of the Russian Revolution, took many more lives and was far more savage than the more dramatic political terror of the guillotine and the Cheka.

✳ ✳ ✳

Edgar Quinet deserves a special place in the history of the history of the French Revolution. He intended his unconventional *La Révolution*, first published in 1865, to be not merely what he himself called "a critical history of the French Revolution" but "a political and philosophical reflection on the revolutionary phenomenon in Europe's past."[22] Significantly, Quinet presented the core of his discussion of the terror in a seminal chapter which, uncharacteristically for a historian of his generation, he titled a "theory of the terror."[23] Though appalled by the Terror of 1793–94, he made every effort to "penetrate its spirit and system,"[24] even to the point of speculating why, unlike past terrors, this one had "failed."

Quinet judged the mainsprings and dynamics of the terror to "spring from the inexorable shock of the old and the new France" which generated "opposing electric currents making for perpetual thunder and lightning." With neither side about "to capitulate," the confrontation turned into a vicious circle of "terrible reprisals" freighted with the "spirit of extermination," but "with the old France almost always provoking the new." According to Quinet, beginning with the royal session in the Estates-General of June 23, 1789, and through the Brunswick Manifesto of July 1792 and beyond, "each attack by the court incited a new attack by the people, [and] each reaction a new counteraction." In his view, ineluctably a succession and accumulation of provocations and threats called forth retaliations that only with time were perceived and shaped "to constitute a system."[25]

Quinet was among the first inveterate republicans to criticize historians for invoking the imperilment of the fledgling regime to justify the establishment of the Terror. For one thing, just as he stresses that usually the counterrevolution was on the offensive, he maintains that "nearly everywhere . . . most of the [Jacobin] terror was perpetrated not before but after victory." He notes, in particular, that Jean-Baptiste Carrier's notorious drowning of prisoners in the Loire river reached a peak fully five months after the successful republican defense of Nantes against the Vendeans; and that it was only after the recapture of Lyons that the Committee of Public Safety ordered France's second city to be leveled and politically cleansed. Clearly, notwithstanding his pioneering turn to conceptually informed thematic history, Quinet continued to pay close attention to chronology. No doubt his approach to time was overly narrow: he overlooked that the civil war left a legacy of raw mutual hatred, suspicion, and fear; and he neglected that when the Vendée and southern cities were finally overpowered, Paris was still fighting a difficult foreign war. Be that as it may, the chronology of the Furies in Nantes and Lyons bolsters Quinet's thesis that ultimately the savage enforcement terror was gratuitous rather than "necessary."[26]

In addition Quinet underscores that by virtue of being increasingly consumed by a spirit of "suspicion," the Jacobins failed to realize that "as a rule what they considered a conspiracy was merely a concatenation of circumstances." Sworn to the Rousseauist view that man was fundamentally good and craving to break his chains, when they met with widespread resistance Robespierre and Saint-Just attributed it to "deception and betrayal, . . . even by their own friends."[27] But rather than emphasize the blinding effect of Jacobin ideas on emblematic revolutionary leaders, Quinet stressed that an unchanging logic and instrumentalization of the *complot* was ingrained in French history.

Characteristically, only yesterday the country's rulers had invoked the specter of conspiracy to justify the Saint Bartholomew's Day Massacre (1572) and the revocation of the Edict of Nantes (1685). Indeed, judging by the frequent recourse to this "ancient fable," conspiratorial thinking ran deep among both the classes and masses. Admittedly, Quinet considered it "absurd" but hardly surprising that in mid-1792 Paris should have been swept by the rumor that "a few thousand priests and courtiers were about to break out of their jails, seize control of the capital, and decimate its inhabitants."[28] Even so, he wondered about the extent to which the ensuing prison massacres were due to a mixture of "genuine popular fear and [political] calculation"[29] by champions of revolutionary terror who exploited the conspiratorial fever for their own ends.[30]

Just as the fear-inspiring arguments of the pseudo-syllogism of the *complot* were not invented by the revolutionaries, neither was the Great Terror. Quinet saw it as a "time-honored weapon" inherited from yesteryear, not unlike Tocqueville, who also considered it "very typically French."[31] According to Quinet, the new men of power reshaped this tested weapon for their purposes with elements taken from an "arsenal" comprising "the iron cages and bravos of Louis XI, the scaffolds of Richelieu, and the mass proscriptions of Louis XIV,"[32] as well as from the fiery rhetoric of the seventeenth century.[33] There was no denying that revolutionary France was heir to a past heavy-laden with "blind furor and fanaticism" for which, to boot, no one ever spoke words of "remorse."[34]

Although he dwelled on the long reach and heavy hand of the fear and violence of times past, Quinet was careful not to conflate them with those of the French Revolution. As if to dramatize the break between the old and the new, he counterposed, in particular, "the terrorists of the Middle Ages to those of 93." The former "were driven exclusively by a barbarian temperament," untouched by any "theory." By contrast, rather than driven by "natural impulses," the men of '93 were animated by a "cruel idea" and held to a "system," which for them was all important.[35]

As mentioned above, Quinet considered this system to have grown out of the upward spiral of reciprocal violence between the new and the old France. It was only with time that Robespierre, Saint-Just, and Jean Nicolas Billaud-Varenne converted what initially were "outbursts" of frenzied anger, indignation, and fear "into a principle and instrument of ruthless government . . . and salvation." By freezing and disciplining the spontaneous "furies of the people . . . [and] passions of the crowds" they choked off all sources of "pity and repentance."[36]

Once the Jacobins carried this old-new terror into execution, why did it misfire? At first sight the terrorists of 1793–94 should have succeeded in crushing the "old spiritual order," much as militant Christians and Muslems, using "similar methods," had done in the distant past. As we shall see, Quinet was neither the first nor the last historian and social theorist to ponder the quasi-religious sides of revolution.[37] Moreover, as a student of the history of Christianity, including its reigns of terror, he challenged the view that violence is ineffective against allegedly invincible ideas and religious beliefs. To support his case, Quinet claimed that quite easily "the Moslems had converted or reduced the Christians of the East; Count of Montfort the Albigensians; Sigismund and the [papal] legate the Taborites and the Calixtines; and the Duke of Alba the Protestants of the [Spanish Netherlands]."[38]

Although the Jacobins had ways and means of coercion comparable to those of their precursors, they lacked the coherence and intemperance of their convictions. The Jacobins were "terrified by new ideas" and scared of "making innovations in the moral order." To be sure, they introduced new republican holidays and reined in the clergy. But they flinched at abrogating the holy days and rites of the Catholic religion and church. In Quinet's judgment, to "tyrannize priests without deconsecrating their cult was like striking the body without touching the soul."[39]

The new terror was, above all, incoherent. At the same time that Robespierre and Saint-Just "put new life into the ancient principle of terror," they espoused political liberty and religious freedom. Quinet claimed that they could not have it both ways: "if they wanted terror, they should have forsworn toleration; but if they wanted toleration, they should have renounced terror."[40] There was the additional difficulty that the Jacobin executive thundered forth its terror and "set limits" to its field agents, unlike the old rulers who, with their "iron temperament," were discreet and gave a free hand to their deputies, who were never "disavowed . . . or punished" for letting their "passions and hatreds" run wild.[41]

Indeed, a well-founded terror has "neither breaks nor limits" and needs to impress one and all that it is "everlasting, inconstant, and unseen." In almost every respect the Terror of 1793–94 was deficient, above all because its champions, by speech and tract, kept proclaiming and justifying it *urbi et orbi*. Since the world abhors "lurid killings and permanent new-wrought scaffolds" and is sickened by the sight of "blood spilled in broad daylight," a steady terror calls for victims to perish "in the dark of night, far from the living, anonymous, forgotten, without echo, without witness, and without a last will."[42]

In one respect the ways of punishing and killing were significantly different in 1793 than in 1685. At the time of the revocation of the Edict of Nantes, and until past the mid-eighteenth century, physical and psychological torture was normal. The assault on the Protestants had witnessed unspeakable horrors which, though out of the ordinary, were of a piece with the existing penal culture. The Great Terror of 1793–94, on the other hand, "neither practiced torture, nor dismembered or burned its victims, nor broke the bones of the condemned before throwing them into the flames" for their ultimate agony.[43]

The old penal system died away very slowly. This was driven home by the interminable and glaring torment of Damiens in 1757, which came straight out of the conventional theater of hell, intended to instill fear and reinforce subservience, among the masses rather than classes.[44] But starting in the second half of the eighteenth century, a growing number of public intellectuals joined an abolition campaign against "the publicity and the conscious infliction of physical suffering,"[45] which contributed to the abrogation of torture along with the decline of "somber . . . and primitive festivals and spectacles" of punishment.[46] No doubt Quinet agreed with Michelet that whereas the Church of the Middle Ages "had exhausted itself inventing ways to intensify the suffering" of the damned, the Revolution proposed to "alleviate" it by resorting to the guillotine, designed to kill "rapidly and discreetly."[47] Firmly planted in the Enlightenment and democratic-republican tradition, Quinet was insensitive to "the simultaneity of the unsimultaneous" in the world of the terror. He was blind to the ways in which the Revolution invested the guillotine with a theatrical ritual of its own, which suggests that the break with the past was anything but total.[48] Not only the prison massacres of September 1792 and the atrocities of the opposing sides in the Vendée but also the Thermidorean counter-terror marked an even greater resurgence of the old sacrificial ways of punishment than the hastily improvised rites around the new-wrought scaffold. Evidently the common people were less touched by the new sobriety than the elites—a fact that Quinet likewise passed over.

While Quinet reimagined and reconstructed the resurgent archetypal mental and behavioral traits of the elites and counter-elites, he all but ignored those of the common people of town and country, whom he tended to consider objects rather than subjects and agents of history. From his top-down vantage point, he saw little if anything of the spontaneous violence of the conspiratorially minded lower orders in Paris, the cities of the Midi, and the Vendée. Probably Quinet did not deepen his vision because he considered the social question to have been of distinctly secondary importance in the confrontation between the new and the old France.[49] He was convinced that "alone religious and political questions, notably the question of liberty, set off the thunderstorms" of the Revolution, and that it was for "them, and them alone, that men spilled blood and endured more than flesh and blood can bear."[50]

There remains the question whether by reason of the immanence of the friend-enemy disjunction in revolution a stratagem of fear other than cold-blooded terror was available. Quinet thought so, and sympathetically weighed Bertrand Barère's tentative proposal that the Committee of Public Safety "substitute exile for the guillotine." In Quinet's judgment—colored, no doubt, by his own exile under the Second Empire—deportation abroad "produces the same effects as death."[51] Or, in the words of Burckhardt, who had read Quinet, in France an exile is "deader" than a victim of the guillotine: whereas the latter's family "seeks his vengeance," the former is abandoned and "not remembered until after his death."[52] Quinet conjectured that although the Girondins "could have avoided the scaffold by taking refuge abroad," they decided against exile for "fear of being mistaken for émigrés . . . and leaving the impression . . . that they had become untrue to themselves."[53] But for Quinet the fate of Louis XVI is particularly instructive. He credits Billaud-Varenne, "this genius of the terror," with having urged, during the king's trial, that instead of executing him the police should simply "escort him to the border." Quinet presumed that Louis would have been "infinitely less dangerous" had he been allowed or forced "to wander about Europe, under an assumed name, . . . without court, estates, and army, and subsidized by an indulgent Convention."[54] Denied martyrdom, he might never have returned to be (re)consecrated in the guise of his brothers.

* * *

During the French Revolution legal torture was ended, and the public spectacle of the last gasp was phased out as well.[55] But this abolition of the rack and its attendant dramatics, which were among the most hateful symbols of the *ancien régime*, did not spell the end of collective punishment. To be sure, the novel ways of disciplining and punishing were less brutal and were practiced hidden from view. This is not to say, however, that collective violence was on the wane in the public realm. Rather, the transformation of the penal system was perfectly compatible with a transformation in the venue of massacre: facing allegedly ever more dangerous city crowds, the French state reconceived the popular and largely spontaneous massacre of revolt from below, making it into an instrument of terrifying law and order from above.

Just as the torture of Damiens in 1757 was prototypical of the domineering genius of the waning *ancien régime*, so the crushing of urban rebels in Paris during the June Days of 1848 and the Commune of March–May 1871 was emblematic of the rising new order. Both times the repression took the form of mass killings and summary executions which were contingent on the adaptation of the military order of battle for policing purposes. Although these massacres were not impulsive, gratuitously brutal, and religiously fired, they were anything but rational and restrained. In June 1848 between 1,700 and 3,000 insurgents were killed in the capital, and the number of seriously wounded was of the same order of magnitude. In addition, several thousand were captured during the showdown and several thousand suspects were arrested following the repression, and many of them were transported to Algeria for imprisonment there.[56] The government's ironhanded fury was even fiercer at the time of the Commune, notably during the "bloody week" of May 21–28, 1871, when some 10,000 people were killed and some 40,000 were arrested. Many of these prisoners were summarily executed by way of reprisal after the fighting was over. Of the many thousands tried by emergency tribunals about 5,000, presumably the most threatening among them, were banished to New Caledonia.[57]

Both outsized repressions were meant to restore order, to exorcise the elite's unholy fear of the dangerous underclasses, and to serve as a warning to would-be rebels in years to come. To be sure, the communards of 1871 in particular were not innocents, having seized and lynched some 50 prisoners, including several clerics, among them one of the capital's archbishops. Still, their violence, including their scorching and sacking of several public and religious buildings, in what was largely a defensive move, paled in comparison to the avenging fury unleashed by the *Versaillais* in accord with the anti-communard Assembly. Indeed, the military overkill and the inordinate retribution in Paris took more lives than any previous massacre in French history and stands out as the harshest conservative top-down enforcement terror in Europe between 1815 and 1917.

Even if one of the prime objectives of this avenging rage was to dash hope and instill fear, it was neither celebrated nor memorialized as the founding violence of the contested Third Republic. No great avenue or public square in the French capital was named for Adolphe Thiers, the *spiritus rector* of the head-on assault by the so-called "honest people," and while the radical left defiantly turned the *mur des Fédérés* into a sectarian counter-monument, the far right sought to have the Sacré-Coeur incarnate the righteousness of the anti-republican cause. Although most makers of democratic France did not hesitate to call in the army to advance their project, they felt uncomfortable about periodically renewing their founding blood sacrifice, a sacrifice which they at once justified and denied, not to say repressed. In any case, it was not until the epoch of the Russian Revolution that, in the Soviet Union and the Third German Reich, terror and counterterror bent toward the invisibility which Quinet postulated as one of the defining characteristics of absolute terror.

✳ ✳ ✳

Merleau-Ponty stands out for having made one of the first and most searching efforts to think and theorize the revolutionary terror of the epoch of the Russian Revolution. He wrote *Humanism and Terror: An Essay on the Communist Problem* in 1946, when, as mentioned, he felt betrayed by the Liberation and apprehensive about the looming Cold War. In this disquieting twilight of postwar Europe Merleau-Ponty, not unlike Sartre, fearlessly contended that it was as "impossible to be an anti-Communist as it was to be a Communist and to sacrifice liberty to Soviet society." He meant to translate his "freedom of thought into the freedom to understand," the essential precondition for responsible political action.[58]

Two critical postulates upheld Merleau-Ponty's exploration of violence and terror. First, that Communist dogma at once fostered and disguised the degradation of Marxism and the Soviet regime, which not only managed but deserved to survive. This premise was rooted in his rejection of polemical anti-Communism, with its disregard for the multiple contingencies which weighed heavily on the Russian Revolution from the start. Second, that by unequivocally condemning the violence of the Soviet regime, the liberal humanism of the Western countries at least implicitly denies the founding violence of their own beginnings. In sum, Merleau-Ponty was equally skeptical of the Communist profession of faith and the liberal "mystification."[59]

These, then, are the heterodox assumptions underlying Merleau-Ponty's forceful postulate that the "Terror of History culminates in Revolution, and History is Terror because there is contingency." Following Lenin and Trotsky, Stalin forged policies, including terrorist ones, "as a function of the circumstances peculiar to our time: socialism in one country, fascism, and the stabilization of Western capitalism." Lenin, Trotsky, and Stalin all were agreed that to "repudiate," in principle, terrorist measures designed to suppress and intimidate "determined and armed counterrevolution" was to "repudiate the Socialist revolution." Of course it was "difficult to delimit permissible terror." Although there are "all kinds of gradations between a Trotskyist and Stalinist dictatorship, and between Lenin's and Stalin's line," according to Merleau-Ponty there "is no difference that is an *absolute* difference" and there is no saying, with precision, where "Marxist politics ends and counterrevolution begins." In the 1930s Stalin, Trotsky, and Bukharin were at one in rejecting "the liberal ethics because it presupposed a given humanity, whereas their aim was to make humanity." Having abandoned "the principle of unconditional respect for others" it was "difficult to mark the limits of legitimate violence," and concerning violence there were no fundamental differences "between the various Marxist policies."[60]

Sensitized to the "ambiguity and contingency" of history by the resistance in wartime France, Merleau-Ponty claimed "history to be terror" precisely because rather than move into the future "along a straight line," human actors do so by "taking their bearings, at every turn, in a general situation which is changing" and indeterminate.[61] Indeed, men "are actors in an open, not closed history" of a world which is "not simply an object of contemplation but something to be transformed." This unfinished and unclosed condition is all the more tempting for revolutionaries whose "dictatorship of the truth" can do no more than embrace and foster a future that "will only be a probabilistic calculation and not absolute knowledge." Such being the case, "a revolution, even when founded on a philosophy of history, is a forced revolution and it is violence; correlatively, opposition in the name of humanism can be counterrevolutionary."[62]

In the 1920s and 1930s the debates by Soviet decision makers over generally problematic policy alternatives were not informed by the perspective or hindsight of an "end of history" which might have provided them with an "absolute truth" with which to evaluate rival options and protagonists.[63] Merleau-Ponty posited that they shared the "assumption that the contingency of the future and the role of human decisions in history makes political divergencies irreducible and cunning, deceit and violence inevitable." As if following in Quinet's footsteps, he made every effort to penetrate "the unfinished world of the revolutionaries" who, though locked in internecine struggles, had "no differences in principle" concerning terror. In Merleau-Ponty's reading, while "neither Bukharin, nor Trotsky, nor Stalin, as Marxists, regarded Terror as intrinsically valuable, [they] imagined . . . using it to realize a genuinely human history which had not yet started," thereby justifying "revolutionary violence." Marxism propounds neither a dogmatic philosophy and vision of the "future of mankind [to be imposed] by fire and sword [nor] a terrorism lacking all perspective." Rather, to the extent that Marxism "is a theory of violence and a justification of terror, it brings reason out of unreason, and the violence it legitimates should bear a sign distinguishing it from regressive forms of violence." But ultimately Merleau-Ponty, in keeping with his existentialist disquiet, wondered whether from the perspective of the "ambiguity and contingency" of the crisis and infighting in the Bolshevik party and Soviet government, "violence is the infantile disorder of a new history or merely an episode in an unchanging history."[64]

✳ ✳ ✳

Merleau-Ponty probed the problem of terror in the unsettled aftermath of what he conceived to have been the epochal confrontation of Communism and Fascism, in which he clearly sympathized with the former. Hannah Arendt, for her part, did so in the dawn of the Cold War, when the two isms began to be conflated. Indeed, she was among the pioneers of public intellectuals who postulated the essential similarity, if not identity, of Communism and Fascism, notably National Socialism, which they conceptualized as belonging to a distinct and indifferentiated totalitarianism. After 1945, with the resumption of the "capitalist world's" struggle against the Russian Revolution in the form of the Cold War, this new-wrought political society called for extrinsic diagnosis rather than empathetic understanding. In essential respects Arendt supplements or displaces Merleau-Ponty's existential perspective, which blends critical *Einfühlung* and alertness to contingency, on the one hand, with a phenomenological point of view that combines objectification and ideological determinism, on the other.

Hannah Arendt makes a "decisive difference between . . . tyrannies and dictatorships established by violence and . . . totalitarian domination based on terror."[65] By the same token she distinguishes between two species of terror, the one essentially instrumental, the other an end in and of itself, or intrinsically totalitarian.

The first of the two types of terror is "enacted in good faith" and directed against "real, [i.e.] known or suspected enemies" during a revolutionary regime's early beginnings. In particular "Robespierre's 'terror of virtue' " was of this type: although his terror was, in its own right, "terrible enough" and "boundless," it was "directed against a . . . hidden enemy," so that the real enemy had to have "the mask of the disguised traitor . . . stripped off."[66] As for the circumstances

"justifying" the terror of the French Revolution, they included counterrevolutionary resistances, popular revolts for social justice, and the
perils of foreign intervention.

The second type of terror is of another nature altogether. Arendt
discerns a "totalitarian" terror specific to the twentieth century: that
of the Russian Revolution and Nazi Counterrevolution, intended to
achieve ideological rather than political goals. All in all Arendt, compared to Merleau-Ponty, considered terror to be driven more by fixed
ideology than contingent circumstance. In her reading, successive
purges in the Bolshevik party were "motivated chiefly by ideological
differences," so that the "interconnection between terror and ideology was manifest from the very beginning."[67] As further evidence of
the enormous if not primary importance of ideology, Arendt stresses
that judging by developments in both Soviet Russia and Nazi Germany, terror does not become, in Quinet's sense, a system or a form
of government until "after the extermination of real enemies has been
completed and the hunt for 'objective enemies' [has] begun." In sum,
and paradoxically, credible resistance is "the last impediment to [the]
full fury" of terror, not its urgent justification or "pretext."[68]

The Russian Revolution was, Arendt argues, the first to "consciously" use "terror as an institutional device to accelerate the momentum of the revolution," and it did so "guided by the concept of
historical necessity whose course was determined by movement and
counter-movement, by revolution and counterrevolution." In her
construction this "concept of historical necessity" and the attendant
"concept of 'objective enemies' " were "entirely absent from the
French Revolution."[69]

Despite her emphasis on the immanence and primacy of ideology
in the terror of the Russian Revolution, Arendt allows for a distinct
break in it, in that she sets apart the terror of the first founding years
of 1917 to 1921. In terms reminiscent of her reading of the terror of
the Committee of Public Safety, she notes that during this initial phase
the Soviet regime faced real domestic and foreign enemies which
"might ally themselves." Arendt contrasts this "dictatorial" terror
under Lenin to the "totalitarian" terror under Stalin during the
1930s. Contrary to Merleau-Ponty, she holds that by then the Soviet
regime "was no longer in danger" from within or from abroad.[70] In

keeping with her thesis, Arendt argues that once past all danger the Bolsheviks set to punishing "possible or even necessary enemies," which involved "putting the mask of the traitor on arbitrarily selected people," including former "friends and supporters."[71] Indeed, terror became "total" and the "essence of totalitarian domination" once it was "independent of all opposition . . . and nobody any longer stood in the way."[72]

The radicalizing force of the "social question" very much engaged Arendt's attention. Tocqueville had preceded her with this concern, and she seems to have taken her cue from him. In Tocqueville's view, the objective of the English and American revolutions was political freedom, while that of the French Revolution was "principally [social] equality." In particular, contrary to the leaders of the thirteen American colonies, who sought to secure or reclaim free government, the leaders of revolutionary France aimed at "the destruction of privilege," which involved a "total subversion of society." Above all, the role of "the multitude" was much greater in France than it had been in either England or America. Tocqueville postulated that the "top of society, [which] was civilized . . . and gentle, . . . endured the Revolution [while] the bottom, [which] was barbarian . . . [and] uncivilized, actually made it." As for the relationship between the two tiers, Tocqueville hypothesized that to advance their project "the disinterested enthusiasm of the upper [classes] made good use of the needs and passions of the lower [classes]."[73]

In contraposing the "success" of the American Revolution to the "failure" of the French, Arendt stresses that since the former was not burdened with the "predicament of poverty," it could afford to confine itself to the pursuit of political freedom.[74] To be sure, there was "poverty" in America, as in most of the rest of the world since "time immemorial." But the colonists "were not driven by want" and there were no *miséreux* in the streets or fields to "overwhelm" the Founding Fathers.[75] As a result theirs was a struggle against political tyranny rather than economic and social injustice, or for a new form of government rather than a new social order.[76] Of course, for Arendt—and the colonists—to pass over the "social question" was to be blind to the violence and cruelty of slavery, not to be confronted until nearly a century after the foundation of the American republic, in a violent and deadly civil war.

In the French Revolution, to the contrary, the political sphere was invaded by the needy of Paris whose suffering became so unbearable as to "explode into rage," thereby "releasing overwhelming forces." In Arendt's reading, "the masses of the suffering people . . . [took] to the streets unbidden and uninvited by those who then became their organizers and spokesmen." Indeed, the wretches of the French capital did not become active agents until sworn revolutionaries "began to glorify [their] suffering . . . [and] set out to emancipate the people not *qua* prospective citizens but *qua malheureux*." Thereafter the quest for political freedom was perverted by reason of soaring pressure to meet the furious demands of economic and social necessity.[77]

Although "no revolution has ever solved the 'social question' and liberated men from the predicament of want," all revolutionaries inspired by 1789 have continued to "use and misuse the mighty forces of misery and destitution in the struggle against tyranny or oppression." Dismayed by the monstrous costs of the economic and social project of the Russian Revolution, Arendt expounds the view that "every attempt to solve the social question with political means leads into terror, and that it is terror which sends revolutions to their doom." By taking a social turn, revolutionaries make a "fatal" if not entirely avoidable "mistake," since by doing so they tempt violence and corrupt the foundation of a steadfast democratic order which Arendt posits to be the supreme vocation of modern revolution.[78]

✳ ✳ ✳

These theoretical reflections running from Machiavelli through Quinet to Arendt at once inspire and confound historians of revolutionary terror. Were the terrors of 1789 to 1795 and 1917 to 1922, respectively, a seamless web or were they internally differentiated and disjointed? What were the connections between the spontaneous insurgent violence from below and the subsequent enforcement terror from above? In the escalation from the one to the other, what was the mixture of temporality and ideology? To what extent was the organized and centralizing terror of mutually reinforcing civil and foreign war designed to bring convulsive and erratic popular violence under control? To what degree was the praxis of revolutionary actors informed by their propensity to conjure up conspiracies, to brave conceptual aporia, to tempt Providence, and to vindicate founding violence?

The defining and confining conditions for terror include the ebb and flow of popular violence, of civil and foreign war, of economic and social stresses, of anti- and counterrevolutionary resistances, and of internecine political feuds. All these pressures and cross-pressures unfold in a context of ruptured political and judicial sovereignty as well as of centrifugal gravity.

Any discussion of the mainsprings and dynamics of the escalation of violence needs to examine the balance and interconnection of bottom-up and top-down violence, with close attention to chronology. Just as there is no revolution without violence and terror, so there is none without popular furies on both sides of the growing friend-enemy divide. To be sure, defecting elites excel at exploiting the physical and moral force of the initial violence of protest in the interest of prophylactic reforms. But they find it difficult to consolidate such reforms without enlisting or condoning further outbursts of popular violence in the face of unexceptional resistances.

Indeed, essentially spontaneous popular interventions played a critical role in 1789 and in 1917. Both times elites of the loyal opposition took advantage of urban and rural upheavals to press their drive for limited if indeterminate political, social, and cultural reform. In 1789 the verbal, symbolic, and physical violence attending the Réveillon riots of April 27–28, the storming of the Bastille on July 14, and the Great Fear of late July contributed to the establishment of the National Assembly on June 17, 1789, the renunciation of seignorial rights between August 4 and 11, the adoption of the Declaration of the Rights of Man and the Citizen on August 26, and the transfer of King Louis XVI and the Assembly from Versailles to Paris on October 5–6. In 1917 the violence accompanying the mass demonstrations and strikes for peace, bread, and higher wages in Petrograd on February 13–14 and 23–24, the concurrent desertion of soldiers and mutiny of sailors, and the storming of the Peter-Paul Fortress, followed by the burning of the Palace of Justice on February 27, helped bring about the establishment of the Provisional Government on March 2 and the abdication of Tsar Nicholas II on March 4.

As previously noted, the circumscribed popular furies in 1789 and in 1917 were disproportionately effective because the incumbent governments lacked the political will or military capability to repress them. Besides, to follow Arendt, while this violence of the first hour dramatized and publicized grievances, it was not driven by a coherent leadership or project. Even assuming that ideologically the initial *enragés* of the cities, rebels of the countryside, or mutineers of the armed forces were not completely artless, probably only few of them were impregnated with the ideas or tenets of the Enlightenment of the eighteenth or nineteenth century.

In point of fact, the first explosions of popular violence in 1789 and 1917 assumed some of the features of former times, before the state had imposed its monopoly on the legitimate use of violence and administration of justice. The Furies of the July days in France and the February days in Russia were marked by a savagery and vengeance running counter to the reputed civilizing process.

Michelet insists that *le peuple*, not the Legislature, the Commune, or the Jacobin club, deserves credit for the great remonstrances of July 14 and October 6, 1789, as well as of August 10, 1792. Not since the crusades had France seen a comparable élan among people of all stations, in town and country.[79] Characteristically, from the outset the new worldly elite of wealth, education, and the professions at once hailed and feared this paroxysm of popular self-affirmation fraught with dark dangers. While some notables, *à contrecoeur*, applauded the lower orders for their heroic contribution to the struggle for freedom, others almost instantly fretted about the risk of unbinding them. The ghastly murder and dismemberment of several notables following the fall of the Bastille merely confirmed the upper ten thousand in their profound disquiet about the coarseness, savagery, and irrationality of the rabble, for which they disclaimed all responsibility. Indeed, in 1789 and in 1917 the reformists' flirtation with the ordinary people, including their crowds, was short-lived.

In both revolutions popular violence assumed many forms and was moved by diverse motives and purposes on all sides of the friend-enemy divide. Acts of collective popular violence ranged from spontaneous to organized, irregular to paramilitary, urban to rural, local to regional. Its agents were variously driven by a sense of injustice, rancor, frustrated expectation, fear, principle, and fanaticism. Their objectives were to seek redress, claim a voice, preserve threatened gains, pressure hesitant governments, reclaim violated traditions, crush real and imagined enemies, and wreak vengeance.

In the sweep of European history perhaps the chief peculiarity of the explosions of spontaneous violence early in the French and Russian revolutions was their intended victims and targets. Quinet suggestively notes that whereas in the Middle Ages such explosions "were above all directed against *les petits*," in the French Revolution they were significantly aimed at "*les grands*" as well. As a rule, outrages against ordinary people neither "arouse indignation" nor "produce an echo," so that "centuries go by without anyone hearing about them." Conversely, assaults on notables instantly cause a "terrible uproar" and are denounced for "going against the course of nature." Besides, through the ages nearly all the world held with those "shedding blood in the name of Heaven" but accursed whoever did so "on behalf of men on Earth," which with 1789 became the order of the day.[80]

The prison massacres of September 2–6, 1792, were at once the closing climax of the agitational terror from below—which the Girondins approved as much as the Montagnards—and the beginnings of the enforcement terror from above. In mentality and practice this popular violence, a heritage from the abyss of time, was unpremeditated, fitful, and primitive. By contrast, the untried terror of the embryonic revolutionary regime was deliberate, centralized, organized, and codified. Rather than fasten upon victims for their presumed individual responsibility, the new terror fixed them for their alleged association with a social or political group targeted for intimidation or exclusion. As part of their effort to reestablish an undivided political and judicial sovereignty, the embattled revolutionary authorities set up tribunals intended to legitimate and institutionalize the terror. Hereafter, instead of being instantly savaged and pilloried, suspects and prisoners were hauled before summary courts. While the politically reliable judges of these courts returned not a few verdicts of not guilty, they pronounced the death sentence for the majority of the accused before they were unceremoniously executed and buried. This shift in venue from the streets and squares, with their spontaneous, anarchic, and glaring terror, to the prisons and emergency tribunals, with their willful, streamlined, and muted terror, brought a quantum jump in the number of victims.[81]

Fear was a common denominator of the popular and official terrors. Their connecting link was less ideology than the uncertainties and perils of fractured sovereignty and civil war which fired the conspiratorial turn of mind and the attendant propensity to strike at scapegoats. Of course, with the civil war heating up and exacerbated by foreign war, terror became increasingly ideologized and polemicized. The opposing sides exploited its uses and abuses for political ends: on one side, a swelling and instrumentalized fear of manifold dangers, heightened by the conspiratorial stratagems of domestic and foreign enemies; on the other, a similar fear of the perils of the consolidation and unfolding of an intrinsically murderous regime.

Clearly, by 1792, in the wake of the royal family's flight to Varennes and with the prospect of worsening food shortages, the revolutionary camp was gripped by panic in the face of an imminent foreign invasion and a fast-spreading aristocratic conspiracy, seemingly orchestrated by the royal court and the émigrés. With self-appointed tribunes justifying and inflaming the popular furor, this fear lost some of its earlier ingenuous spontaneity of action and purpose. Even if, as in the case of the prison massacres, most of the killings were barbaric and the bulk of the *victims* were, politically, "blameless in life and pure of crime," the designated *targets* were of a different order altogether. By the agency of the tribunes, popular pressures were deliberately directed at the political arena in which critical decisions were being made in both domestic and foreign affairs. The subsequent drive to make the terror official government policy—to transform bottom-up agitational terror into top-down enforcement terror—sought to make the means of terror as modern and rational as its intended aims. While the revolutionary tribunal, the law of suspects, and the guillotine may be said to have symbolized the new ways and means of the cold terror, the warrant to create a new man and society encapsulates its extravagant pretense and purpose. It is this quasi-religious zeal which in revolutions makes for the sudden return and intensification of traditional impulses and practices, alongside contemporary ones.

The establishment and operation of the reign of terror was inseparable from the tangled contingencies of civil war, foreign hostility, economic disorganization, and social dislocation, which called for quick, centralizing, and coercive action. The ensuing forced-draft political, military, and economic mobilization and deployment were backed by an enforcement terror, complete with rhetorical intimidation, arbitrary arrests, quasi-legal summary justice, and mass execution. To be effective, the regime of revolutionary terror had to rule by patent fear, which often escaped control.

There were, then, two overlapping but not preordered or consistent phases of terror.[82] The first phase was the one in which a diffuse and upturning "process of violence" worked against the newly incumbent, unsteady, and hesitant authority system. Deliberate "acts or threats of violence" against things and persons were represented and perceived as generating an atmosphere of fear intended to affect the behavior of embattled and wavering decision makers.

The second phase of terror "coincide[d] and coact[ed] with . . . [the] system of authority and . . . [was] directed" by those who had only yesterday assumed or seized power. These new men of power put in place a "system of terror" to further their improvised policies. Even if they used violence and fear primarily, if not exclusively, to establish and extend their own precarious control, they claimed to do so in the interest of eventually implementing radical structural changes. The embryonic revolutionary regime appointed a "directorate of violence" to run the system of terror, which quickly acquired its own "agents of violence" in the form of executioners and men-at-arms. Although the aim was to have a centralized and orderly system of terror as part of the effort to reestablish a single sovereignty, entire "zones" spun out of control. In these "zones of terror" the process of violence had many of the archaic features of the "hot terror," with little or no semblance of legality.

By virtue of never managing to establish a single seat of authority and coordinated battle plan, the anti- and counterrevolution remained confined to outlying zones in which the processes of violence were distinctly archaic and erratic. By necessity rather than choice, there was nothing comparable to the "cold terror" of the revolution in the zones of resistance, whose counter-terror was heavily local, communal, and personal.

It is hardly beyond reason to suggest that violence and terror were both cause and effect of the dialectic of revolution and counterrevolution. Almost from the outset, and well before the establishment of the Reign of Terror, the foes of the French Revolution viewed and portrayed it in the darkest of colors. Typically, Edmund Burke had nothing but contempt even for the constitutional monarchists who thought they could "deceive without fraud, rob without injustice, and overturn everything without violence," as they presumed to usurp France's government "with decency and moderation." Needless to say, the censure of these champions of compromise, who were "ineffectual and unsystematic in their iniquity," was mild compared to the one Burke leveled, well before Varennes, against the as yet inchoate Jacobins of the revolutionary left.[83] Without naming names, he castigated them for being usurping "madmen" whose so-called state "was a college of armed fanatics for the propagation of the principles of assassination, robbery, rebellion, fraud, faction, oppression, and impiety." Burke charged France's new "despots," who were governing "by terror," to be inspired by an "infamous gang" of *philosophes* who, determined to undermine the fear of God, left "no awe, but that of their committee of research, and of their lanterne." If these "tyrants" and their "hired blood-thirsty mob without doors" would not disavow their murderous and barbarous practices, which threaten the Continent, the European monarchies might have to intervene, their armies entering France "as a country of assassins" which was not "entitled to expect" the benefits of "civilized" warfare, one of the Christian world's noblest achievements.[84]

This general outlook was, of course, congenial to many of the émigrés. Once they realized that they "could not convert the revolutionaries they thought only of annihilating them." In July 1792 the Count Armand Marc de Montmorin, the king's foreign minister who perished in the September massacres, proposed to "strike the Parisians with terror," since "only fear pushes the Assembly in one direction until another terror pushes it in another." In sum, these people understood no language "other than that of fear," which was that of the Brunswick Manifesto. Indeed, at Koblenz the émigrés were reported to speak only "of hanging, of exterminating, of subjugating" their enemy brothers. They assumed that the population inside France was more terrified of the vengeance of the émigrés than of either counter-revolution or invading armies.[85]

This conceptual excursion was meant to raise and reformulate questions, not to provide answers, let alone a theoretic construct or *idée maîtresse*. A reading of theorists from Machiavelli to Arendt suggests that terror has a long history, is interactive, and bears upon radical regime changes or refoundations in times of fractured political and legal sovereignty. On the one hand this reading serves as a reminder that conspiratorial thinking and discourse, rule by fear, and use of terror are not unique to revolution. On the other it forces critical attention to the singularities of the Great Terrors of the French and Russian revolutions, the one postulated to be systemic, the other totalitarian. But above all, to take note of Machiavelli on cruelty, Bodin on bottom-up violence, Montesquieu on fear, Quinet on conspiracy, Merleau-Ponty on the "terror of history," and Arendt on the "social question" is to seek help in an effort to find a path beyond "the often explored and marked-out old map"[86] which restricts discussion to the force, weighting, and interaction of circumstance, ideology, and leader.

✱ ✱ ✱

NOTES

1. For the notion of "excessive excesses," see Alec Nove, "Stalin and Stalinism," in Nove, ed., *The Stalin Phenomenon* (London: Weidenfeld and Nicolson, 1993), p. 28 and p. 201. See also Wolfgang Sofsky, *Die Ordnung des Terrors: Das Konzentrationslager* (Frankfurt/Main: Fischer, 1993), ch. 20.

2. Jefferson to William Short, January 3, 1793, cited in *The Papers of Thomas Jefferson*, vol. 25 (Princeton: Princeton University Press, 1992), pp. 14–17, esp. p. 14.

3. Cited in Ernst Bloch, "A Jubilee for Renegades," in *New German Critique* 4 (Winter 1975): pp. 24–25. See also André Tosel, *Kant révolutionnaire: Droit et politique* (Paris: Presses Universitaires, 1990).

4. Cited in Hermann Lübbe, *Praxis der Philosophie, praktische Philosophie, Geschichtstheorie* (Stuttgart: Philipp Reclam, 1978), pp. 78–96, esp. p. 89.

5. Cited in Bloch, "Jubilee," p. 25.

6. Ibid., pp. 21–22; and Lübbe, *Praxis*, p. 79.

7. Jules Michelet, *Histoire de la Révolution française*, 2 vols. (Paris: Robert Laffont, 1979), vol. 1, pp. 435–36.

8. Cited in Mary-Alice Waters, ed., *Rosa Luxemburg Speaks* (New York: Pathfinder Press, 1970), pp. 394–95.

9. Kagarlitsky, *The Thinking Reed: Intellectuals and the Soviet State, 1917 to the Present* (London: Verso, 1988), p. 72, n. 54. For Kagarlitsky the deaths of the *communards* in Paris in 1871 and of Salvador Allende in Santiago in 1973 were "glorious," the death of Bukharin "shameful."

10. For a discussion of the "conceptual individual," see Gilles Deleuze and Felix Guattari, *Qu'est-ce que la philosophie?* (Paris: Éditions de Minuit, 1991), esp. pp. 61–63.

11. Leszek Kolakowski uses this genetic language in his discussion of the terror in the Russian Revolution in Robert C. Tucker, ed., *Stalinism: Essays in Historical Perspective* (New York: Norton, 1977), p. 297.

12. Shlomo Avineri, *The Social and Political Thought of Karl Marx* (Cambridge: Cambridge University Press, 1970), pp. 187–93; Richard Hunt, *The Political Ideas of Marx and Engels*, vol. 2 (Pittsburgh: University of Pittsburgh Press, 1984), esp. p. 206; Joseph L. Walsh, "Marx and Sartre on Violence in the French Revolution," in Yeager Hudson and Creighton Peden, eds., *Revolution, Violence and Equality* (*Studies in Social and Political Theory: Social Philosophy Today*) 10:3 (1990): pp. 204–21, esp. pp. 213–14.

13. This discussion of Machiavelli on terror follows Helmut Kessler, *Terreur: Ideologie und Nomenklatur der revolutionären Gewaltanwendung in Frankreich von 1770 bis 1794* (Munich: Wilhelm Fink, 1973), pp. 124–26, 159.

14. For this discussion of Bodin, see Julian Franklin, *Jean Bodin and the Rise of Absolutist Theory* (Cambridge: Cambridge University Press, 1973); and Kessler, *Terreur*, pp. 126–27.

15. Kessler, *Terreur*, p. 159. For Montesquieu on terror, see ibid., pp. 128–29, 159–60; Gerd Van den Heuvel, "Terreur, Terroriste, Terrorisme," in Rolf Reichardt and Eberhard Schmitt, eds., *Handbuch politisch-sozialer Grundbegriffe in Frankreich, 1680–1820*, vol. 3 (Munich: R. Oldenbourg, 1985), p. 94; Julien Freund, *L'essence du politique* (Paris: Sirey, 1965), pp. 529–30.

16. President Franklin D. Roosevelt may be said to have spoken in the spirit of Montesquieu's *Spirit of the Laws* when in 1933 he proclaimed that "we have nothing to fear but fear itself."

17. Montesquieu, *De l'esprit des lois*, bk. 12, ch. 18.

18. Baron Holbach cited by Van den Heuvel, "Terreur," p. 96. See also John Hope Mason and Robert Wokler, eds., *Denis Diderot: Political Writings* (Cambridge: Cambridge University Press, 1992).

19. Marat cited by Van den Heuvel, "Terreur," pp. 99–100.

20. Robespierre cited in Kessler, *Terreur*, p. 161.

21. Ibid., pp. 162–63.

22. Edgar Quinet, *La Révolution* (Paris: Belin, 1987), p. 61.

23. Ibid., bk. 17. Quinet discusses the terror in other chapters as well.

24. Ibid., p. 44.

25. Ibid., pp. 497–98.

26. Ibid., p. 55 and p. 43.

27. Ibid., pp. 500–501.

28. Ibid., p. 316.

29. Ibid., p. 375.

30. Ibid., p. 531.

31. Alexis de Tocqueville, *"The European Revolution" and Correspondence with Gobineau* (Garden City, NY: Doubleday, 1959), p. 108.

32. Quinet, *La Révolution*, p. 505.

33. Ibid., pp. 502–3.

34. Ibid., p. 505.

35. Ibid., p. 513.

36. Ibid., p. 498. For the contemporary criticisms of Quinet's reading of the terror by Alphonse Peyrat and Louis Blanc, see François Furet, *La gauche et la Révolution au milieu du XIXe siècle* (Paris: Hachette, 1986).

37. See chapter 6 below.

38. Quinet, *La Révolution*, p. 492.

39. Ibid., p. 493.

40. Ibid., pp. 493–94.

41. Ibid., pp. 515–16.

42. Ibid., pp. 516–17.

43. Ibid., p. 504.

44. See Michel Foucault, *Surveiller et punir: Naissance de la prison* (Paris: Gallimard, 1975), chs. 1 and 2; and Dale K. Van Kley, *The Damiens Affair and the Unraveling of the Ancien Regime, 1750–1770* (Princeton: Princeton University Press, 1984).

45. See Petrus Cornelis Spierenburg, *The Spectacle of Suffering: Executions and the Evolution of Repression* (Cambridge: Cambridge University Press, 1984), esp. p. viii and p. 200.

46. Foucault, *Surveiller*, p. 14.

47. Michelet, *Histoire*, vol. 1, p. 62; and Foucault, *Surveiller*, p. 20.

48. Daniel Arasse, *La guillotine et l'imaginaire de la terreur* (Paris: Flammarion, 1987), esp. pt. 3.

49. Quinet, *La Révolution*, p. 131.

50. Ibid., p. 146.

51. Ibid., pp. 529–30.

52. Jacob Burckhardt, *Vorlesungen über die Geschichte des Revolutionszeitalters* (Basel/Stuttgart: Schwabe, 1974), p. 266, and *Weltgeschichtliche Betrachtungen* (Stuttgart: Kröner, 1978), p. 187.

53. Quinet, *La Révolution*, p. 427.

54. Ibid., pp. 350–51.

55. The next three paragraphs lean on Alain Corbin, *Le village des cannibales* (Paris: Aubier, 1990).

56. See Charles Tilly and Lynn Lees, "Le peuple de Juin 1848," in *Annales: E.S.C.* 29:5 (September–October 1974): pp. 1061–91, esp. pp. 1069–70.

57. Jacques Rougerie, *Procès des communards* (Paris: Julliard, 1964); Georges Bourgin, *La guerre de 1870–1871 et la Commune* (Paris: Flammarion, 1971); Stewart Edwards, *The Paris Commune, 1871* (New York: Quadrangle, 1973).

58. Maurice Merleau-Ponty, *Humanism and Terror: An Essay on the Communist Problem* (Boston: Beacon Press, 1969), p. 49 and p. 76.

59. See the introduction of Claude Lefort to Merleau-Ponty, *Humanisme et terreur* (Paris: Gallimard, 1980), pp. 11–32. See also Barry Cooper, *Merleau-Ponty and Marxism: From Terror to Reform* (Toronto: University of Toronto Press, 1979).

60. Merleau-Ponty, *Humanism and Terror*, pp. 96–97 (italics in text).

61. Ibid., p. 94.

62. Ibid., pp. 92–93.

63. Ibid., p. 92.

64. Ibid., pp. 97–98.

65. Hannah Arendt, *On Violence* (New York: Harcourt, Brace, 1970), p. 55.

66. Arendt, *On Revolution* (New York: Viking, 1965), pp. 95–96.

67. Ibid., p. 95.

68. Arendt, *On Violence*, p. 55, and *The Origins of Totalitarianism*, 2nd enlarged ed. (New York: Meridian, 1958), p. 393 and p. 422.

69. Arendt, *On Revolution*, pp. 95–96.

70. Arendt, *Origins*, p. 322.

71. Arendt, *On Revolution*, p. 96, and *On Violence*, p. 55.

72. Arendt, *Origins*, p. 464.

73. Alexis de Tocqueville, *Oeuvres Complètes*, vol. 2 (Paris: Gallimard, 1953), pp. 334–37.

74. Arendt, *On Revolution*, p. 62.

75. Ibid., p. 108 and p. 63.

76. Gordon Wood challenges this view. He insists that the American colonists' project was not confined to securing a democratic-republican form of government, but ought to be seen as having had a significant social objective as well. Wood, *The Radicalism of the American Revolution* (New York: Knopf, 1992), passim. See chapter 1 above.

77. Arendt, *On Revolution*, p. 107.

78. Ibid., p. 108.

79. Michelet, *Histoire*, vol. 2, p. 264, p. 747, and p. 766.

80. Quinet, *Révolution*, p. 484.

81. See Brian Singer, "Violence in the French Revolution: Forms of Ingestion/ Forms of Expulsion," in Ferenc Fehér, ed., *The French Revolution and the Birth of Modernity* (Berkeley: University of California Press, 1990), pp. 150–73. For a detailed discussion of the September prison massacres, see chapter 7 below.

82. This paragraph and the next draw heavily on Eugene Victor Walter, *Terror and Resistance: A Study of Political Violence* (New York: Oxford University Press, 1969), chs. 1–2.

83. Burke, "A Letter to a Member of the National Assembly" (1791), in Paul Langford, ed., *The Writings and Speeches of Edmund Burke*, vol. 8 (Oxford: Clarendon, 1989), p. 333.

84. Ibid., pp. 305–6 and 319–20.

85. Albert Soboul, *La Révolution française*, 2 vols. (Paris: Gallimard, 1972), vol. 1, p. 527.

86. Mona Ozouf, "The Terror after the Terror: An Immediate History," in Keith Michael Baker, ed., *The Terror* (Oxford: Elsevier/Pergamon, 1994), pp. 3–18, esp. p. 17.

Vengeance

VENGEANCE is an integral part of both the Red and the White terror in revolution. There is, of course, vengeance without terror, just as there is violence without terror. But for there to be terror there must be vengeance and violence. While vengeance, fired by quasi-religious fervor, belongs to the inner recesses of terror, violence pertains to its instrumentation. With the breakdown of sovereignty and the rule of law, revolutionary moments see a reversal in the vector of vengeance: from being directed outward in order to foster in-group solidarity it turns inward, with the result that it fosters discord and internecine strife. Indeed, revolution is open season for vengeance in vital precincts of political and civil society on both sides of the friend-enemy divide. It is wrought in the name of master and slave, God and World Reason, hearth and nation, idealized past and millenarian future. During the climacteric of the revolutionary moment, the terrorists embody the avenging gods: historical revenge for the injustices of a refractory past and divine revenge for the impieties "upon this bank and shoal of time."

Like terror, vengeance is complex, multiform, polyvalent, and opaque, and it, too, belongs to the domain of violence. Especially in the First World, in this *début de siècle*, the word-concept of vengeance, again like that of terror, has negative connotations and resists sympathetic understanding.

While terror defies the ideological equipoise of historians, vengeance tests their teleological innocence. In the progressive imagination—as well as in the liberal persuasion—it is disvalued for being uncivilized, heathen, and archaic. This construction is largely a function of vengeance being implicitly measured against the legal system of the

modern state, to the clear advantage of the latter: on one side benighted vengeance, on the other enlightened justice. In particular,
the constitutional state's judiciary is valued for being the province of
independent and rational judges sworn to apply codified laws and to
publicly pass sentences subject to review and redress. By contrast, vengeance is depreciated for being irrational, uncontrolled, without end,
and beyond appeal. Besides, it is frowned on for being "turned toward
the past, not the future" by virtue of putting retribution or retaliation
ahead of deterrence and rehabilitation. Whereas legal punishment is
viewed as "mediated, measured, and personalized," vengeance is portrayed as "instant, unbound, and willful."[1]

This antithesis is, of course, overdrawn. On the eve of 1789 and
1917, apart from the coexistence of overlapping legal and vengeful
spheres in France and Russia, state justice was not entirely free of the
avenging logic, nor was revenge pure savagery. Even in a linear perspective, which tacitly celebrates the advance from vengeance to the
rule of law, it is worth noting that "vengeance is possible 'only in
society, not in nature,' . . . and that it is socially determined behavior."[2] In primitive, tribal, and peasant societies vengeance is anything
but unwitting, blind, and dark: the selection of victims is not haphaz-
ard, nor is the place, time, and method of revenge and re-revenge. No
doubt, "vengeance can be just, but it is not justice."[3] The reparation of
injured life, honor, property, or power is guided by punitive principles
compatible with bolstering the solidarity of the in-group without,
however, severing relations of reciprocity with the out-group.

Still, when all is said and done, and notwithstanding rules and rituals, avenging violence, even when contained, has many of the brutal
features of the justice system in an advanced *ancien régime*. As the
unifying and centralizing state tightened its monopoly on the legitimate use of violence and administration of criminal justice, it not only
proscribed but also appropriated and adapted some of the ways of
traditional vengeance. In the new theater of punishment, with its
staged rack, stake, and scaffold, spectators were prone to view torturers
and executioners as "symbol[s] of forbidden vengeance." Indeed, initially public penal retribution "served to seal the transfer of vengeance
from private persons to the state." The state's judicial system "rationalized" vengeance by breaking the "vicious circle" of deliberate re-

venge and re-revenge, thereby also eliminating the danger of escalation. At the same time, by virtue of the consecration of the state's political and legal authority, this rationalized vengeance was invested with a religious sanction. In due time, to "take the law into one's own hands" was to invite not only legal sanction but moral, social, and religious reprobation. Far and wide vengeance came to be represented and perceived as the blind and naked justice of the "prehistory" of the modernizing Western world as well as of all "uncivilized" and "decivilized" societies far and wide.[4]

In revolutionary moments, however, vengeance ceases to be a system for the ritualized regulation and control of violence governed by precepts of social solidarity and reciprocity, to become a powerful force for disorder as well as a ferocious agency in the struggle for sovereignty and domination. Broadly speaking, "the traditional system of regulated vengeance runs amuck when it becomes swept up in a social or historical context . . . which bursts the bounds of its retributive universe and practice."[5] It was in the logic of the situation that in 1789 and 1917 vengeance should have become problematic, inasmuch as the collapse of the state, including the judiciary, gave free rein to individual drives as well as folkways which were thought to have been tamed by the "civilizing" process.

❋ ❋ ❋

Whether one condemns, justifies, or simply excuses the eruption of avenging furies in revolutionary seasons, one can find arguments to back each position embedded in the age-old, highly ambiguous Western tradition concerning vengeance in general. This tradition comprises three different attitudes to vengeance: glorification as a deserved punishment of offenders; condemnation for its brutality and attendant unending cycle of willful violence; and appropriation and mastery of it for purposes of social control.

Certainly vengeance is not proscribed by the Decalogue, nor does it figure among the Seven Deadly Sins. Indeed, the idea and precept of vengeance occupy a notable place in the Hebrew Bible: the proverbial avenging principle—eye for eye, tooth for tooth, foot for foot, life for life—is set down in Exodus (21:23–25), Leviticus (24:19–20), and Deuteronomy (19:21). These Jewish Scriptures expound a religion of vengeance centered round a vengeful God at the same time that they set rigid limits rather than give a free course to violence. In refinement of the ancient *lex talionis*, and aiming for symmetrical reprisals, the Hebrew Bible distinguishes between proper or wise vengeance and improper or sinful revenge. While the injunction against private vengeance for personal motives is categorical, there is some latitude when it comes to avenging injury to the immediate family and the people of Israel. Indeed, by history and tradition, Jews entreat God to punish the foes of His children by wreaking a messianic vengeance. The faithful, with "a two-edged sword in their hand," praise the Lord for their victory over Israel's enemies: "To execute vengeance upon the heathen, and punishments upon the people/To bind their kings with chains, and their nobles with fetters of iron" (Psalm 149: 6–8). But ultimately the Jewish Scriptures declare the right of unqualified and incontestable vengeance to be a divine prerogative, reserved to the almighty and wrathful Hebrew God.[6]

Although the New Testament has its own share of ferocious preachings, on this point the two Scriptures converge. The Lord's enunciation in both the Romans (12:9) and the Hebrews (10:30) that "vengeance is mine, I will repay" is at once a pledge of intervention by God in heaven and a ban on retribution or retaliation by Man on earth. There is certainly no gainsaying the severe restrictions on personal vengeance in the Christian Scriptures: "You have heard how it was said: Eye for eye and tooth for tooth. But I say this to you . . . if anyone hits you on your right cheek, offer him the other as well" (Matthew 5:38–39). But with time, while the Church was lenient with individual sinners whose vengeance it reined in, it became distinctly avenging in dealing with the sinful collectively. The Book of Revelation, probably one of the more influential books of the Holy Bible, is permeated with a wrathful and vengeful spirit, its savageries directed against one and all, except the small number of the elect. And the Church was unremittingly harsh toward misbelievers and heretics, such as Jews, Muslims, and Protestants. The sempiternal cry for revenge against the Jews, blamed for the death of Jesus, perhaps best illustrates the force of the avenging tradition in the Christian worlds, all the more so since the apostles of the Protestant Reformation never even considered repudiating it.

In any case, in the Sacred Writings—in the Judeo-Christian tradition—vengeance is an urgent and perplexing rather than adventitious theme. The Scriptures seek to set limits to a socially and psychologically conditioned avenging impulse or drive which is only too human but also paradoxical and freighted with inhumanity.

✳ ✳ ✳

Of course, the idea of vengeance was very much alive in classical Greece. Aristotle was not out of season when he held that "to take vengeance on one's enemies is nobler than to come to terms with them; for to retaliate is just, and that which is just is noble."[7] Thucydides was of a more critical mind. In *The Peloponnesian War* he was troubled by the pernicious fallout of vengeance. In his chapter on the "revolution" in Corcyra he highlights the escalation of dehumanizing violence which found its consummation in revenge and re-revenge. For Thucydides the defining characteristic of the war between the city-states, at its apogee, was its close interpenetration with civil strife, with the two opposing factions in each city-state appealing for help from outside. This two-tiered friend-enemy dissociation, typical of revolutionary moments, fostered the politics of suspicion along with preventive violence in both camps. A first-hand observer, Thucydides claimed that having aligned their commonwealth with Athens against Sparta, the Corcyreans massacred "those of their own citizens" whom they charged, often disingenuously, with "conspiring to overthrow . . . democracy." With time, "in city after city . . . the passions of civil war" fueled a "violent fanaticism," with the result that in the "struggles for ascendancy nothing was barred." In Thucydides' telling, the political leaders of the time eventually carried revenge to such extremes that it became even "more important than self-preservation." He distinguished between those driven to vengeance by material "misfortune" or "ungovernable passions" and those who, in "their hour of triumph," thirsted for revenge for having "been arrogantly oppressed instead of wisely governed . . . in the past." In terms of governance, this disparate rush to vengeance at once reflected and fostered "the breakdown of law and order" to the point of undermining "those general laws of humanity which are there to give a hope of salvation to all who are in distress."[8]

In addition to figuring prominently, since days of old, in theology and history—though history soon tended to lose it from sight—vengeance has also been a "central preoccupation of European literature and drama."[9] Homer, then Aeschylus, Sophocles, and Euripides in ancient Greece; Seneca in early imperial Rome; Dante in the late Middle Ages; Shakespeare and Racine in the dawn of modern Europe—all at one and the same time capture, dramatize, and influence the ethical and social debates surrounding the issue of vengeance, which in their constructions become prisms dispersing light on the trials and tempers of their times and homelands. But given the pervasiveness and variability of vengeance, most of these writers found it "impossible to discuss [vengeance] without ambiguity and internal contradictions." At all times tragedy in particular is without a "coherent attitude to vengeance." Indeed, to press it for "either a positive or negative theory of vengeance is to misapprehend the essence of the tragic." On the stage the different protagonists "espouse or condemn vengeance with equal passion, depending on their changing positions on the chessboard of violence."[10]

Nevertheless, in the sixteenth and seventeenth centuries some of the greatest dramatic tragedies squarely confronted the mounting strain between personal and public vengeance as the centralizing state sought to establish its monopoly on the prescription, administration, and enforcement of justice. Evidently, the long-term objective was to supersede the code of vengeance with the rule of law. With the fusion of throne and altar in both Catholic and Protestant lands, the theater of the time portrayed and validated the divine presumption of the nascent legal authority, ultimately vested in the anointed kings. Shakespeare's *Hamlet* is emblematic of this preoccupation with the moral and psychological aspects of the tension between, on the one hand, profane, wrongful, and illegal private revenge and, on the other, sacralized, just, and justiciable public vengeance. *Hamlet* is a morality play, with a distinctly unresolved moral: "to revenge or not to revenge."[11] It is a mirror of Elizabethan England, where quite understandably the precept of revenge "retained an attraction for a considerable portion of the population" at the same time that it was denounced for being unlawful, immoral, and irrational.[12]

❋ ❋ ❋

131

At the same time and for the same reasons, philosophers and political thinkers began to be even more forthright in their censure of personal vengeance. They looked to earthly vengeance becoming the province of political and legal authorities that were recognized for being at once legitimate and anointed. Francis Bacon, Shakespeare's contemporary, characterized "[r]evenge . . . [as] a kind of wild justice" and urged that "the more man's nature runs to [it], the more ought the law to weed it out." While he allowed for revenge "for those wrongs which there is no law to remedy," he claimed that it was the measure of "superior" man to forbear vengeance, not least because it is without end. Unlike "public revenges," which Bacon viewed with indulgence, "private revenges" were pernicious by virtue of being the doing of "man that studieth revenge," thereby keeping "his own wounds green, which otherwise would heal." Indeed, men of vengeance are as "vindictive . . . as they are mischievous" and not uncommonly they delight "not so much in doing the hurt, as in making the party repent."[13]

This drive for forced repentance was equally abhorrent to Montaigne. His faith in Christianity shattered by the wanton cruelties of the wars of religion and the Spanish conquest of the Americas, as well as the clergy's inability or unwillingness to intercede on behalf of the natives, he ascribed them to the conceit of cultural supremacy and the spiritual maiming of blind faith which caused aborigines to be demonized as the inferior "other."[14]

Not unlike Hannah Arendt in the wake of the Second Thirty Years War, Montaigne looked to the Europeans' unseemly conduct overseas for clues to their conduct at home. He stressed that judging by what he "had been told," there was "nothing barbarous and savage" about the indigenous peoples of South America. They were barbarians only in the sense that "each man calls barbarism whatever is not his own practice," all the more if he has lived a cloistered life. At first sight the other's ways and rites of war seem uncivilized, in particular in his treatment of prisoners whom they eventually kill in the presence of a "great assembly" and then "roast and eat in common and send small pieces to their absent friends" as an act of "extreme revenge." But the vengeance wrought by the Portuguese, partners in the war of conquest, was no less extreme: they buried their prisoners up to "the waist" and shot "the rest of their body full of arrows" before finally

hanging them. Of course, Montaigne deemed it more savage to torture and eat a man "still full of feeling . . . than to roast and eat him
after he is dead." In all conscience Montaigne noted that only yesterday the French had blinked at terrible outrages "not among ancient
enemies but among neighbors and fellow citizens, and, to make matters worse, on the pretext of piety and religion."[15]

Convinced of humanity's predisposition to extreme violence, Montaigne was deeply troubled by an apparent reversion from mere killing
to the willful infliction of moral and physical cruelty. He was less concerned with soldiers killing in battle to "avoid an injury to come, not
to avenge one already done," than with victors perpetrating extreme
atrocities after the end of hostilities to satisfy "their appetite for vengeance." For Montaigne, "all that [was] beyond plain death" was
"pure cruelty" and emblematic of a refusal to forego vengeance for
clemency, even at the expense of the victor's reputation.[16]

Montaigne's profound disquiet about Christianity's share of responsibility for the rampant crimes against humanity of the recent
religiously charged conflicts and colonial conquests was shared a century and a half later by Montesquieu. He contended that since vengeance was a source of political immoderation and despotism in the
commonweal, it was important to "put an early end to . . . [it] after a
republic has successfully destroyed those who sought to subvert it."
In Montesquieu's judgment, clemency and moderation were preferable to unforgivingness and severity, all the more so since there was no
inflicting great punishments or, for that matter, carrying through
great political changes, "without putting exorbitant powers in the
hands of a few citizens." Indeed, there was the danger of the "avengers
establishing a tyranny under the pretext of avenging the republic."[17]

✻ ✻ ✻

Both the Enlightenment faith in human nature, reason, and progress,
and the conservative reaction against the avenging Furies of the
French Revolution, led nineteenth-century thinkers increasingly to
condemn vengeance. In particular, Hegel, Schopenhauer, and
Nietzsche conceded its universality and persistence at the same time
that they looked for its decline and ultimately its extinction, above all
in what they took to be the civilized—European—world, in which
vengeance was being driven back by morality and the law.

It is "wondrous strange" that Nietzsche, one of modern Europe's most influential if enigmatic philosophers and cultural critics, should have pondered the phenomenon of vengeance with such uncharacteristically visionary overtones.[18] He judged the "avenging instinct" to have had such a "strong grip on humanity . . . [that it] left its mark on metaphysics, psychology, historical representation, and, above all, morality."[19]

For Nietzsche, the basic root of vengeance is memory, which he set to probing concurrently with Freud, though in a different key.[20] He at once appreciated and deplored man's phenomenal capacity to remember, or not to forget. In fact, Nietzsche considered this innermost memory a "festering sore" which he allegorized as a "tarantula," or a poisonous spider, and equated with the spirit of vengeance.[21]

In Nietzsche's reading, the ideal-typical and primary carriers and executors—individual and collective—of this spirit of vengeance are persons of resentment (*ressentiment*). They, above all, store up feelings of injury, weakness, inferiority, degradation, inadequacy, and envy stemming from defeats or slights which they claim to have suffered unjustly at the hands of those stronger and of higher status than themselves. Normally the instinct of avenging resentment sustained by this feeling of repressed and latent insufficiency functions as "an instinct of self-preservation."[22] But the pervasively anguished men of resentment clamor to quench their grinding thirst for vengeance. And when they do have the opportunity to do so, they pass all bounds. Nietzsche's summary formulation is striking, all the more so because it takes account of the weight of memory: "Disappointed arrogance, suppressed envy, perchance the arrogance and envy of your fathers: in you they break forth as a flame and frenzy of revenge."[23]

At the same time that he empathetically discerned the mainsprings of the warrant for vengeance, Nietzsche voiced his forebodings about its built-in dangers. Ever the caustic critic of the Enlightenment, he was, above all, troubled by the speciousness of the avengers' high-principled self-representation which, to boot, ran counter to his own values. Convinced that "men are not equal . . . [and] shall [never] become so," Nietzsche warned against the "preachers of equality." He saw "vengefulness . . . leap forth from behind . . . [the] talk of justice" and cautioned that those who "call themselves 'The Good and the

Righteous' . . . lack naught but power to become Pharisees" in their own right. Nietzsche was particularly wary of "folks of all kindred and descent" who are driven by a strong "impulse to punish," inasmuch as "[f]rom their faces peer the hangman and the bloodhound."[24]

Strange to say, and perhaps inadvertently revealing himself, Nietzsche allowed himself to muse upon freeing humankind from the miasma of vengeance: "For *to deliver man from vengeance*: that I consider to be the bridge to the highest hope and a rainbow after long and violent storms." It is worth noting that Nietzsche himself italicized his meditated vision.[25] The words chosen to express it are no less telling in that he looked to deliver humankind from vengeance, which was a profane aspiration, rather than to redeem him, which would have implied "the way of repentance" so antithetical to his contempt for the Christian ethos.[26] In any case, his imagined bridge was to lead from a world enslaved to vengeance to a world in which there would be neither space nor time for avenging persecution.

Max Scheler, in reaction to Nietzsche, held with the Christian ethos relating to the weak, the sick, and the poor. In addition, Scheler broached the problem of *ressentiment* less as a social-cultural than a social-psychological critic. But whatever their ethical and methodological differences, Scheler, like Nietzsche, fixed on the link between *ressentiment* and vengeance. For Scheler, *ressentiment* was "a lasting mental attitude caused by the systematic repression of certain emotions and affects." In and of themselves the feelings in question "are normal components of human nature." But when repressed, they veer toward "revenge, hatred, malice, envy, the impulse to detract, and spite." Nonetheless such malignant emotions, even when inflamed, turn into *ressentiment* only if they are "suppressed" as a consequence of being "coupled with the feeling that one is unable to act them out—either because of weakness, physical or mental, or because of fear." Evidently Scheler, like Nietzsche, made a special point of fixing on what Ernst Bloch later called *gestaute Wut*, or pent-up rage or fury.[27] Scheler insists, however, that this rage is inherently "re-active" by virtue of being induced by others, rather than self-actuating and open to a new future. In particular, among the weak and impotent "the desire for revenge," which is coupled with anger and rage, is not a self-actuating "emotional reaction" but is precipitated or triggered by a prior "attack or injury." For the individual, "vengeance" restores "damaged feeling[s] of personal value, . . . injured 'honor,' or . . . 'satisfaction' for . . . endured . . . wrongs."[28]

But, of course, even when personal, vengeance is rarely either a purely individual or a terminal affair. In fact, it is distinctly group-based and self-perpetuating, each retribution calling forth another reprisal. As previously noted, unless domesticated and regulated, vengeance, even when ritualized, is a vicious circle of reciprocal and interminable violence. With time the judicial system seeks to "rationalize" this peculiar violence by reducing if not eliminating it altogether. To be successful, this system requires a strong political authority. Indeed, any major breakdown of this authority necessarily entails a decline and collapse of the rationalization of vengeance.[29]

✳ ✳ ✳

In spite of all its ambiguity and the disapproval of leading thinkers, vengeance still had some fine moments during the long nineteenth century in Europe and its overseas colonies: at the same time that the practice of "an eye for an eye" persisted in the pre-modern provinces of the United Kingdom and the Continent, Britain took revenge for the Indian Mutiny of 1857 and France clamored for *revanche* after its defeat by Prussia in 1870–71. Nor is there any denying that the avenging temper left a considerable imprint on the international conflicts and civil wars as well as the revolutions and counterrevolutions of the General Crisis and Thirty Years War of the twentieth century. Vengeance animated not a few of the bayonet charges on the killing fields of the Very Great War, and during the Second World War vindictive retribution informed the fire bombing of Dresden as well as the atomic bombing of Hiroshima and Nagasaki. From the outset Hitler left no doubt that National Socialist Germany meant to take revenge for the defeat of 1918 and the shame of Versailles. In July 1941 Churchill vowed that Hitler having begun the indiscriminate bombing of cities, the British could "mete out to the Germans the measure, and more than the measure, that they have meted out to us";[30] after December 7 of that same year Americans rallied to the avenging call to "Remember Pearl Harbor";[31] and in 1944 Moscow's chief propagandist encouraged the sorely tried soldiers of the Red Army to exact "not an eye for an eye, but two eyes for one."[32] This epoch's tempestuous vindictive rage culminated in the Judeocide, which was triggered and largely driven by the vengeful fury of the Third Reich's failing military fortunes.[33] Since 1945 the murderous cycle of revenge and re-revenge has helped to poison and draw out the wars of decolonization; the Anglo-Irish and Arab-Israeli conflicts; the racial strife in South Africa; and the ethnically, religiously, and culturally freighted violence in Russia, ex-Yugoslavia, Turkey, Algeria, Rwanda, Sierra Leone, Somalia, Sudan, Zaire/Congo, Kashmir, and Timor. Meanwhile in certain precincts of the First World there is a recrudescence of the ever-latent retributive passion and reason, increasingly "acted out" both inside and outside courtrooms, and before television cameras.

There is something universal and persevering about vengeance, with due allowance for enormous socially and culturally defined variations and politically conditioned fluctuations. Of course, some historical situations are more conducive to the discharge of vengeance than others. In Europe since early modern times, in particular revolutionary moments have favored the return of "repressed" vengeance, the breakdown of the state's monopoly of legitimate violence and justice creating an expansive space as well as a fertile soil for the eruption of avenging furies. Such times of trouble are choice forcing houses for the resurgence of retributive and vindictive vengeance for historic wrongs, for setbacks in foreign and civil war, and, especially in the countryside, for hateful intrusions of the peremptory state and the corrupting city. Vengeance is wrought for reasons—real or imagined—of religion, culture, politics, and ideology, as well as in the name of family, community, class, and nation. In some instances it is governed by time-tested rules and rituals, in others it is wild and blind, and in still others it is organized and militarized.

On this score the revolutionary moments of 1789 and 1917 were prototypical. The paralysis of centralizing sovereignty entailed the disintegration of the legitimate and independent administration of justice. This dual breakup was all the more fatal because the return of traditional vengeance coincided with the surge of founding violence mixed with wild vengefulness. In turn, government sought to reclaim the monopoly of all violence by reestablishing an effective judicial system: in the words of Michelet, "a revolution which wants to endure must, above all, wrest the sword of justice from its enemies."[34] Since the agents of this "violence to end violence" were self-styled avengers driven by a burning belief system and missionary zeal, it was both fierce and unconditional.

In this guise vengeance was a "natural" rather than "social" phenomenon, driven by a broad range of aggressive and destructive impulses charged with unreason and unrestraint. Although conditions of fractured sovereignty were also open season for individual vengeance, they fostered, above all, a vengeance whose agents and reasons were collective. Even more than traditional vengeance in normal times, this out-of-the-ordinary vengeance was careless about the responsibilities and intentions of its victims, overconfident in the achievement of symmetry in the retributive exchange of "a tooth for a tooth," and specious in charging others with taking the first step. Michelet was sensitive to this complexity in his treatment of the Vendée. After noting the explosion of hatreds and avenging Furies in the opposing camps in which there was less reason "to fear death than torture," Michelet frowned upon the "sorry debate about which side initiated this cycle of cruelties and committed the most horrible crimes."[35]

✳ ✳ ✳

NOTES

1. Raymond Verdier in Verdier and Jean-Pierre Poly, eds., *La vengeance: Études d'ethnologie, d'histoire, et de philosophie*, vol. 3 (Paris: Cujas, 1984), pp. 151–52; and Gérard Courtois in Courtois, ed., *La vengeance*, vol. 4 (Paris: Cujas, 1984), pp. 9–11, 29.

2. Hans Kelsen cited in Verdier and Poly, eds., *La vengeance*, vol. 1, p. 37, n. 4. See also Courtois, ed., *La vengeance*, vol. 4, pp. 11–12, 23–24.

3. Hegel cited in Jean-Philippe Guinle, "Hegel et la vengeance," in Courtois, ed., *La vengeance*, vol. 4, p. 212.

4. René Girard, *La violence et le sacré* (Paris: Grasset, 1972), ch. 1; and Verdier and Poly, eds., *La vengeance*. vol. 3. The questionable religious "ontology" underlying René Girard's thesis about the central and sacralizing role of the *victime émissaire* does not negate the heuristic value of his discussion of the violence of foundation.

5. Courtois in Courtois, ed., *La vengeance*, vol. 4, p. 27.

6. See André Lemaire, "Vengeance et justice dans l'ancien Israel," in Verdier and Poly, eds., *La vengeance*, vol. 3, pp. 13–33; and Israel Jacob Yuval, " 'Extra Synagogam nulla salus': Le sort des chrétiens dans l'eschatologie juive," in Florence Heyman, ed., *Lettre d'information du Centre de Recherche Français de Jerusalem* 12 (December 1995): pp. 33–39.

7. Cited in John Kerrigan, *Revenge Tragedy: Aeschylus to Armageddon* (Oxford: Clarendon, 1996), p. 22.

8. Thucydides, *The Peloponnesian War*, trans. Rex Warner (New York: Penguin Classics, 1954), bk. 3, ch. 5: "Revolution in Corcyra."

9. Kerrigan, *Revenge Tragedy*, passim.

10. Girard, *Violence*, p. 29.

11. Peter Mercer, *Hamlet and the Acting of Revenge* (London: Macmillan, 1987), p. 4.

12. Linda Anderson, *A Kind of Wild Justice: Revenge in Shakespeare's Comedies* (Newark, Del.: University of Delaware Press, 1987), p. 17. See also Pietro Marongiu and Graeme Newman, *Vengeance: The Fight against Injustice* (Totowa, N.J.: Rowman and Littlefield, 1987), ch. 5.

13. Bacon, *The Essays* (New York: Penguin, 1985), pp. 72–73 ("Of Revenge").

14. See Judith N. Shklar, *Ordinary Vices* (Cambridge, Mass.: Harvard University Press, 1984), ch. 1.

15. Montaigne, "Of Cannibals," in *The Complete Works of Montaigne: Essays, Travel Journal, Letters*, trans. Donald M. Frame (London: Hamish Hamilton, 1957), pp. 146–59, esp. p. 152 and p. 155.

16. Montaigne, "Cowardice, Mother of Cruelty," in Montaigne, *Complete Works*, pp. 523–30, esp. pp. 524–25, 530.

17. Montesquieu, *Esprit des lois*, bk. 12, chs. 4 and 18.

18. Heidegger claims, extravagantly, that Nietzsche's reflections on vengeance may well provide the key to "his way of thinking, and hence to the inner core of his metaphysics." Martin Heidegger, *Was heisst Denken?* (Tübingen: M. Niemeyer, 1954), esp. p. 38.

19. Giorgio Colli and Mazzino Montinari, *Nietzsche Werke: Gesamtausgabe*, VIII, 15 (30) 2 (Berlin: de Gruyter, 1972), p. 219.

20. See Paul-Laurent Assoun, *Freud et Nietzsche* (Paris: Presses Universitaires, 1980), esp. pp. 212–20; and Gilles Deleuze, *Nietzsche et la philosophie* (Paris: Presses Universitaires, 1962), p. 131, n. 2.

21. Friedrich Wilhelm Nietzsche, *Ecce Homo*, bk. 1, ch. 6, in Walter Kaufmann, trans./ed., *Basic Writings of Nietzsche* (New York: Modern Library, 1968), pp. 685–87; and Nietzsche, *"Thus Spake Zarathustra"* (London: J. M. Dent, 1933), pp. 90–92. See Gilles Deleuze, *Nietzsche*, pp. 131–34, esp. p. 133; and Arno J. Mayer, "Memory and History: On the Poverty of Remembering and Forgetting the Judeocide," in *Radical History Review* 56 (Spring 1993): pp. 14–15, 20.

22. Cited in Gerd-Günther Grau, *Ideologie und Wille zur Macht: Zeitgemässe Betrachtungen über Nietzsche* (Berlin: de Gruyter, 1984), p. 245.

23. Nietzsche, *Zarathustra*, p. 90.

24. Ibid., pp. 90–91.

25. Ibid., p. 90.

26. Cf. Heidegger, *Was heisst Denken?* p. 44.

27. Max Scheler, *Ressentiment* (New York: Schocken Books, 1972), pp. 45–46, 48; and Ernst Bloch, *Erbschaft dieser Zeit* (Frankfurt/Main: Suhrkamp, 1962), p. 116.

28. Scheler, *Ressentiment*, p. 46 and pp. 48–49.

29. Girard, *La violence*, pp. 28–29, 39.

30. Cited in Robert Rhodes James, ed., *Winston S. Churchill: His Complete Speeches, 1897–1963*, vol. II (New York: Chelsea House, 1974), pp. 6448–52.

31. John D. Dower, *War without Mercy: Peace and Power in the Pacific War* (New York: Pantheon, 1986).

32. Cited in Mayer, *Why Did the Heavens Not Darken? The "Final Solution" in History* (New York: Pantheon, 1988), p. 422.

33. Ibid., ch. VIII and pt. 3.

34. Jules Michelet, *Histoire de la Révolution française*, 2 vols. (Paris: Robert Laffont, 1979), vol. 1, p. 262.

35. Ibid., vol. 2, p. 489.

Religion

THE FRENCH and Russian revolutions originated and unfolded in countries in which a monopolistic official religion and church permeated every aspect of civil and political society. There was no carrying through consequential reforms, let alone revolutionary transformations, without significantly changing the relationship between, on the one hand, the political, social, and cultural spheres and, on the other, the ecclesiastic sphere. Since criticism of church and, to a lesser degree, religion was central to the enlightenments of the eighteenth and nineteenth centuries, it is hardly surprising that after 1789 and 1917 there should have been a drive for disestablishment, followed by willful secularization, even in the absence of a grand plan. In the face of stubborn but unexceptional resistance, the separation of church and state became increasingly confrontational. It spilled over into an assault on religion, intensely radicalizing the opposing camps. In its uphill battle to desacralize the hegemony of throne and altar, the revolution eventually spawned a secular or political religion of its own. This bid for a substitute religion intensified the founding violence attending the drive to restore a single political sovereignty, which involved mastering the dominant church's schism over its place in tomorrow's world.

It is difficult to delineate the defining characteristics of the religious phenomenon. In the present context religion may be taken as "the human enterprise" of establishing and administering "a sacred cosmos." This self-enclosed system entails or implies the "dichotomization of reality into sacred and profane spheres": the one is pure and noble, inspiring respect, love, and gratitude; the other impure and ignoble, arousing contempt, hatred, and horror. This antinomy of the "sacred" and the "profane" is coupled with that of "chaos." Indeed, the sacred cosmos, which "emerges out of chaos," aims at allaying humanity's fear of being "swallowed up" by the forces of anomie. In its "world-maintaining" guise, religion legitimates political, social, and cultural relations and institutions. Revolutionary epochs are forcing houses for the subversion of this religious legitimation.[1]

Starting with the Enlightenment, and until recently, by and large, the terms "religion" and "religious" assumed ever more negative connotations in modern political and historical discourse. To be religious was to be reasonless, dogmatic, intolerant, superstitious, and fanatical. And not unlike the peasantry and petite bourgeoisie, religion was expected to languish before collapsing into the dustbin of history. In turn, as a politicizing and socializing agency, the church tended to be seen "as a monolithic entity invariably championing the interests of stability, social integration, and the status quo." In actual fact, religion is a vast mansion with ever so many rooms. There are, to be sure, religions of the status quo. But there are also "religions of resistance, revolution, and counterrevolution,"[2] and all three play an important role in times of foundation.

In the struggle for foundation the French and Russian revolutions developed a secular religion, the Russian Revolution using the French as its model. They meant to endow their respective Enlightenment and Socialist projects with a religious aura by forging a belief system and liturgy; designing and staging public ceremonies, including cults of martyrs; and adopting new calendars and fixing new holy days. This invention and instrumentalization of a new prophecy was intended to "religionize" the foundation of a heavenly city on earth much as the old regime had "politicized" church and religion to bolster its temporal power. In both revolutions, a would-be religion emerged "to close the gap, in favor of human hopes, between what men are and what they would like to be, at least in [their] youthful, fresh, and active phase."[3] But no doubt there was a prosaic reason for this studied emergence as well. As Machiavelli argued, religion is an indispensable governing agency, to be valued for its political effectiveness rather than theological and clerical correctness. Indeed, especially the rulers of a new regime have to enlist the "fear of the gods" along with military force if they are to secure ascendancy—and legitimacy—over both the people at large and political adversaries.[4]

✶ ✶ ✶

On the eve of 1789 and 1917 the practice of the Gallican Catholic and Russian Orthodox religions, respectively, was an integral part of the everyday life of the vast majority of men and women in France and Russia. In both countries, in major respects, villages and small towns vastly outweighed cities, as attested by the bulk of the population living and laboring in rural areas. Particularly the mostly illiterate peasants and muzhiks were pious and under the influence of official churches, which winked at magic and superstition. Even in the allegedly impious cities, religious faith and practice was steady among not only the masses but the classes, and the established churches had enormous political, cultural, and social sway, with repressive consequences for religious and ethnic minorities. To reform or revolutionize French and Russian political and civil society meant challenging what were, in effect, religions and churches of the status quo. There was no breaking the cake of custom, for which they provided the lifeblood, without curbing religious leaders, institutions, and rituals. Quinet rightly emphasized that "alone among modern nations France made a political and social revolution before having consummated its religious revolution," and added that it was this peculiar sequence in the reordering of state-church relations which accounts for the Great Revolution's "originality and monstrosity, immensity and implacability." To a degree this insight is valid for Russia as well, as is Quinet's axiom that it is difficult, if not impossible, to "revolutionize society without revolutionizing the church."[5] In any event, the separation of state and religion was "*the* great problem" of modern Europe, and it was the "logical consequence of the idea of religious toleration, one of the strongest convictions of our time."[6]

This separation was a formidable and forbidding undertaking, and, except in very vague terms, it had been unthinkable even for the *philosophes* of the eighteenth century. Their successors of the nineteenth century were barely better prepared, although their critical reflections on church and religion were at once more radical and studied. For Feuerbach and Marx, as well as for Nietzsche and Freud, religious doctrine and practice was a conduit for the expression and evacuation of illusions, fantasies, and obsessions fired by the agonies of everyday life. With understanding for the functions of religion, Marx considered it at once an expression and a defiance of "real distress." But he conceived religion, above all, as the "sigh of the oppressed creature" in a "heartless world," as well as "the opium of the people."[7]

Whereas Marx, like Voltaire, banked on reason and the rational mind, Freud focused on the subconscious. But not unlike for Marx, for Freud, the last great *philosophe* of the European Enlightenment, religion enabled human beings, collectively, to "secure a certain happiness and protection against suffering through a delusional re-moulding of reality." He postulated that religion "depress[es] the value of life and distort[s] the picture of the real world in a delusional manner—which presupposes an intimidation of the intelligence." By forcing individuals into "a state of infantilism and drawing them into a mass-delusion, religion succeeds in sparing many people an individual neurosis."[8]

In any case, the revolutionists of 1789 and 1917 gradually assumed the heavy task of organizing the removal of critical spheres of polity, society, and culture "from the domination of religious institutions and symbols."[9] Having decoupled state and church and desacralized political power, they proceeded to extricate education, the civic register, and social welfare from clerical control.

It is difficult to imagine a more intractable and divisive issue than the abrupt desacralization and laicization of political and civil society. Eventually it engages opposing true believers as it turns into a main battleground between, on the one hand, the religion of revolution and, on the other, first the religion of the status quo and then the religions of counterrevolution and resistance. Whereas in the time of the Reformation the struggle was between two "revealed" religions, in the time of the French and Russian revolutions it was between time-less revealed religion and embryonic political or secular religion. The French Revolution pioneered in "laicising the religious passion and transferring it from the ecclesiastical to the political arena." Its counter-religion forswore intervention by superhuman and supernatural agencies as well as preoccupation with "matters of ultimate concern," such as the nature and fate of humankind. But the alternative religion was no less religious for that. Jacobins and Bolsheviks "religionized" politics by way of doctrine, myth, and ritual, at the same time that they generated a millenarian ambience charged with a mixture of faith, intolerance, and fanaticism pregnant with violence and terror. They secularized and politicized millenarianism, determined "to change *things*, not just to convert *people*."[10]

Both revolutions took root in and fired "an age of faith as well as reason." In retrospect it is hard to understand and explain what "sustain[ed] this childlike faith, what unexamined prepossessions en-able[d] the Philosophers to see the tangled wilderness of the world in this symmetrical, this obvious and uncomplicated pattern." This incongruence may have been due, in part, to their having been "not professional philosophers sitting in cool ivory towers but crusaders" with a dual mission: to destroy "false doctrines" that had "corrupted and betrayed" humankind; and to put forward "another interpreta-tion of the past, the present, and the future." In challenging "the doctrines of Christian philosophy," the *philosophes* "substituted the love of humanity for the love of God . . . [and] the self-perfectibility of man for vicarious atonement." This alternative teaching, which was soon perceived and represented as having "culminated in the great Revolution, . . . gave an emotional and even a religious quality to the conviction that the future . . . would be infinitely better than the pres-ent or the past."[11]

Much the same can be said about the *démarche* of the Socialists who before and after 1917 replaced "the love of God" with the love of humanity's underclass. Indeed, Marxism, not unlike the Enlighten-ment, had its millenarian, Promethean, and redemptive cogency. While in *The Heavenly City of the Eighteenth-Century Philosophers* Carl Becker explored the blinding faith of the French Enlightenment, in *The Origin of Russian Communism* Nicolas Berdyaev discussed the faith of Russian Marxism. In Berdyaev's view, Marxism was "a doc-trine not only of historical and economic materialism . . . but of deliv-erance, of the messianic vocation of the proletariat, of the future per-fect society." Indeed, in addition to being "a science and a politics" Marxism was "a faith, a religion." It fitted conditions in the tsarist empire all the better because Russian Marxists took revolution to en-tail "not merely a conflict concerned with the social and political side of life, but a religion and a philosophy" bearing on "totality, en-tireness, in relation to every act of life."[12]

Berdyaev held that by giving prominence to its "messianic myth-creating religious side" Lenin Russified Marxism, incarnating it in a particular social carrier. Bolshevism transformed the failing "myth of the peasant people into the myth of the proletariat," so that despite the shift from an organic to a class-conflict postulate, the myth of the Russian people "arose in a new form."[13]

The secular millenarianism of the French and Russian revolutions rallied true believers, whose "spiritual intensity . . . [and] militance" were of the order of "the Crusades or the Wars of Religion."[14] Unlike soldiers, who are drafted and "ordered to launch an attack," revolutionaries are "volunteers who answer an inner calling."[15] This also means that their adversary is not a foe but an enemy of infidels or traitors.

Although strongly marked by national (and nationalist) singularities, the secular millenarianisms of 1789 and 1917 had, as noted before, a universal vocation and reach. In particular Marxism won countless partisans far and wide whose conduct was very much that of religious disciples or converts, not a few of them ready to make sacrifices of conscience and person. But there is also one striking difference between the believers of secular and revealed religion: the former are much more readily and rapidly disabused and disenchanted than the latter. Everyday experience shows doctrine and cause to be flawed and compromised, with the result that disenchanted revolutionaries defect or rebel. Charging the apostles of their chosen religion with cunning and hypocrisy, they make a pretense of having been duped as they forswear *The God That Failed*, some of them to become heretics, others renegades.[16]

✻ ✻ ✻

Both the French and Russian revolutions secularized the religious passion once their drive to disestablish the official church ran into predictably stiff resistance. This showdown over the church question unwittingly but also inevitably escalated into a religious contest, both domestic and international, thereby intensifying and polarizing the larger struggle into which it was grafted.

Burke was among the first to speak of the events in France as a "total . . . [or] compleat revolution" giving rise to a "*new species* of Government" based on "new principles." In his view, formulated well before the crescendo of violence, this incipient new regime, whose chief actors, with "Condorcet . . . at their head," were "sworn enemies to King, Nobility, and Priesthood," foreshadowed "a real crisis in the Politicks of Europe." Burke likened this crisis to that of the Reformation and the wars of religion, Europe's "last Revolution of doctrine and theory." Neither narrowly political nor territorial, the affairs in France were like the heresy which had given rise to the great schism in Western Christianity: it was "*a Revolution of doctrine and theoretick dogma,*" involving changes "made upon religious grounds, in which a spirit of proselytism makes an essential part." Both then and now the "effect was to *introduce other interests into all countries, than those which arose from their locality and natural circumstances.*" Similar to the doctrine of "Justification by Faith and Works," the republican doctrine had a universal compass, with its "theoretick truth and falsehood governed by [neither] circumstances . . . [nor] places." Due to "a system of French conspiracy," everywhere Europe "was divided into two great [doctrinally informed] factions," so that states were no longer simply "alienated" from each other but also "divided" internally, within themselves.[17]

Troubled that the longer the "present system exists, the greater . . . its strength" and contagion, Burke proposed to rally international support to contain or crush the French Revolution, convinced that there could be "no counterrevolution from internal causes solely."[18] He conceived the upcoming struggle with an impious and fanatical France as "a religious war" in which religious factors would outweigh "every other interest of society."[19] Convinced that Christianity was the bedrock of Europe's civil societies and a major fount of its civilization, Burke reproved any diminution of the Catholic Church and religion in France.

Whatever their philosophic differences, Maistre shared Burke's preoccupation with the Revolution's religious kernel, making its success contingent on "the scope and energy of its spirit, or of what might more appropriately be considered its faith." Viewing the Jacobins as the chief apostles and carriers of an unprecedented and unique secular providence, Maistre grudgingly admired them for their "infernal genius" at the same time that he cursed them for their "satanic character." Like Burke he considered the Revolution a divine punishment or vengeance for the transgressions of the Enlightenment, destined to end with the restoration of a regenerate Catholic monarchy.[20]

The religious homology, however, is not the monopoly of fiery conservative and counterrevolutionary thinkers and public intellectuals. Tocqueville, paragon of mid-nineteenth century liberal conservatism, wove it into his contemplation of the logic of revolution. There is no missing the heuristic force of the title of the third chapter of his *The Old Regime and the French Revolution*: "How and Why the French Revolution Was a Political Revolution Which Proceeded in the Manner of a Religious Revolution." Tocqueville, inspired by Burke and Maistre, suggests that a study of the practices of religious revolutions of the past might help throw light on those of the French Revolution.[21] Like them the French Revolution, contrary to all previous "civil and political revolutions," was without "a land of its own" and virtually "wiped all the old borders off the map." Wherever there were insurrections against the old world, the zeal for liberty was quickened by impatience with the heavy hand of church and religion. As in the time of the Thirty Years War, after 1789 foreign and civil war became inseparable, and so did issues of "principle" and "interest." In Tocqueville's construction, one of the important defining characteristics of religious revolutions is that by virtue of considering humanity "in the abstract, independent of place and time, . . . they rarely confine themselves to the territory of a single people or even to a single race." The French Revolution offered the new spectacle of a political revolution seeking to regenerate not France but humankind, using "preachment and propaganda . . . to inflame passions and inspire conversions." It eventually "assumed those features of a religious revolution which so frightened contemporaries" even though it was an "imperfect religion without ritual, without God, and without promise of an afterlife." Despite these deficits this peculiar religion, "like Islam, flooded the world with its soldiers, apostles, and martyrs."[22]

Even if Tocqueville judged the French Revolution to have been futile and hence pointlessly destructive, like Burke he saw it as a "compleat" revolution, seeking to both change the old form of government and abolish the old form of society. The attack on the Catholic Church was part of this expansive project, which did not, however, include an assault on religion as such. In line with the writings of the *philosophes*, the Revolution turned its furor less against Catholicism's "religious doctrine" than against its "political institution" whose dignitaries were strategic members of the economic and social establishment.[23]

As it turned out, with the consolidation of the Revolution in major spheres of political and civil society, the profane reasons for battling the church vanished. Ever attentive to the overlap of continuity and change, Tocqueville contraposed the permanence of certain radical political and social changes to the transience of "irreligious" passions and actions. As the old religion renewed its ascendance and unbelief receded, the church recovered lost ground "wherever men [of property] felt threatened by popular disorder and feared lurking revolutionary perils." In Tocqueville's estimate, "the most irreligious class before 1789, the old nobility" was in the vanguard of the return to religion after 1793, followed by the bourgeoisie.[24] Evidently, he meant to make a distinction between, on the one hand, the religious characteristics and dynamics of revolution and, on the other, the interpenetration of declericalization and dechristianization.

*　*　*

Contemporaries of Tocqueville, Michelet and Quinet, both sworn republican freethinkers, also placed religion at the center of their reflections on the French Revolution. Of course, the two historians disagreed about its inner nature.[25] Michelet saw the Revolution as Christianity's "heir as well as adversary,"[26] although it spelled a radical incompatibility between the religion of divine grace and the promise of justice and law grounded in human values. Quinet, for his part, drew a sharp distinction between Christianity and Catholicism, between the Gospel and the Church. In his view, 1789 opened a breach for the reclamation of such great Christian virtues as equality, fraternity, and universality, forever violated and perverted by the Catholic Church, in league with the sanctified monarchy. Here was an opportunity to renew the "golden age" or the "first hours" of primitive Christianity by way of radical reform in both state and church, "political and religious revolution . . . being inseparable." But presently, with the nation becoming "more and more democratic," the Gallican Church, backed by the Apostolic See, became uncompromising. According to Quinet, despite the best efforts of the "lawmakers, Girondins, and Montagnards the hostility between the old and the new spiritual power went from bad to worse," with the opposing sides increasingly "hating, lacerating, and lifting the sword against each other."[27]

Despite their differences as to the weight or purchase of France's long-lived religious past, as "brothers in heart and thought," Michelet and Quinet converged in their analysis of the role of church and religion in the revolutionary process. Michelet was mainly concerned with explaining the bearing of religion on the crescendo of the terror. For him the Revolution was both a religion and a church. Sacred and redemptive, it had its own deities, articles of faith, rituals, and sacraments. Indeed, in Michelet's view, whereas the counterrevolution, swearing by the "old faith," remained "discordant" and never jelled as a religion, the Revolution became "more and more concordant" and increasingly "revealed itself to be the religion that it really was."[28]

Although Michelet, following others, stressed that the French Revolution, like Christianity, "disregarded space and time" to the point of "eliminating geography," unlike Tocqueville he explored the domestic rather than international dynamics and consequences of this impetus. Like Quinet, he saw a continuity in the struggle between the principle of violence and the precept of charity, with the former almost invariably stealing the march.[29] Michelet singled out the Inquisition for being most revealing of Christianity's ingrained violence, which left such a deep and fatal mark on Europe and now resurfaced in the guise of the revolutionary terror. The spirit of the Spanish Inquisition's torture, auto-da-fé, and death by fire was the same as that of the Committee of Public Safety's revolutionary tribunal. As for the scale of victims, there was no common measure between their respective hecatombs: the Great Terror of 1793–94 claimed "sixteen thousand victims" in all of France compared to the "20,000 victims burned at the stake in just sixteen years in a single province of Spain." To be sure, as a historian of his time, as well as a fervent anticlerical, Michelet uncritically embraced the tendentious nineteenth-century conception that the Inquisition had disastrously savaged and terrorized Spain. But he fastened on the Inquisition also because the war against misbelievers on the Iberian peninsula was of a piece with the war against "the Albigensians, the Vaudois of the Alps, the *beggards* [pseudo-mystical beggars] of Flanders, the Protestants of France, . . . the Hussites, and so many other peoples the Pope had agreed to have put to death." Taking the long view, for over six centuries the old system of linked religious and political power "had strangled, strung up, and dismembered millions of men and women whose flesh was pyramided for burning to glorify the kingdom of heaven." Convinced that ordinary killing and death were too profane and clement, the medieval Church had "exhausted itself inventing" tortures to heighten the suffering of the victims and the cathexis of the spectators.[30]

Michelet anticipated Marc Bloch's and Walter Benjamin's concern about historians writing from the perspective of the victors, half-deaf to the humanity and agony of the victims. He was troubled by the difficulty of "chronicling the atrocities . . . of our enemies" who made a point of covering their tracks, "throwing away the ashes" of their burned victims, including their "calcinated bones."[31] This unmastered past, by crying out for vengeance, may have contributed to disposing the Jacobins to issue and execute their warrant for terror.

Michelet invoked religious attributes in accounting for the Revolution's exceptional and unexpected material and spiritual force. He noted that the melting away of class, social, and party differences quickened the birth of a well-defined community of new believers rallied around the *idée patrie*. Erstwhile enemies, including members of opposing sects and faiths, became reconciled, with Catholic priests and Protestant pastors showing the way by attending each other's church services. This coming together was reflected in the nationwide but Paris-bent Federation movement which was the first crystallization of the new religion of the *patrie* and of humanity. To bolster this incipient faith, in the provinces as in the capital "the rituals of the old and artificial church . . . were adapted and enlisted for the purpose of consecrating the festivals" of the new: traditional processions were refitted, while oaths and baptisms were administered at ageless altars on which the "Holy Sacrament" was embodied and displayed in the form of the "decrees of the Assembly."[32]

Nonetheless, Michelet considered it one of the French Revolution's great shortcomings that it failed to realize that "it carried the embryo of a religion and . . . was itself a church."[33] Even Robespierre and Saint-Just never "dared touch religion and education" and—unlike Marat—were circumspect on "the subject of property." Indeed, "the Revolution was vacuous without a religious revolution," and without a "social revolution" it lacked "support, strength, and depth."[34] Al-

though it was "fertile" in forging new institutions and laws, it remained "sterile" in the matter of infusing them with a distinct ethos.
To prosper, the Revolution needed to nourish the "national soul"
by showing the political and social project of the Enlightenment, as
well as its religion, to be for the benefit of all, regardless of social
station. As it turned out, the Revolution faltered in two vital respects:
"it . . . closed churches without establishing [new] temples; it cleared
the way for property to change hands without . . . breaking the rules
of property."[35]

Quinet shared Michelet's interest in the religious lineaments and
vectors of the Revolution, as well as his concern with the way in which
these influenced the Terror. He held that during the Terror the Jacobins, whom he likened to latter-day Jesuits, resorted to practices reminiscent of the Inquisition of the late Middle Ages and of the absolute
monarchies of early modern Europe, guided by the reason of state.
Starting with Pope Gregory VII, the Holy Fathers developed the principles and practices of proscription, excommunication, and liquidation which by way of the Crusades were applied in distant lands before
being adapted for use inside Europe, with the throne gradually gaining ascendancy over the altar.[36] According to this reading, the Jacobins
did not pioneer a new theory and practice of enforcement terror but
inherited and modernized an old one, capped by a "rhetoric of fire."[37]

The Revolution "fell back on the violent methods of the sixteenth
century," including the fiery "temperament of Catholicism," to create
a new world "in less than seven days."[38] There was something ironic
about "the sword of Saint Bartholomew's Day becoming the chosen
instrument" of Rousseau's sentimental logic, with the masses resorting "to the violence of the Middle Ages with an eye to rushing
headlong into the future."[39] Indeed, the stake and the guillotine bore
resemblance, and so did Saint Bartholomew's Day and September 2.

The "revolutions" in England, the American colonies, and the
Dutch Netherlands were spared the Furies because they were
grounded in, respectively, "the Anglican Church, . . . the Presbyterian
traditions, and . . . the new Calvinist faith." By contrast, Quinet argued, the Reformation having bypassed France and the absolutist
royal power having crushed the Protestants, the Revolution had "neither crown nor church" to build on, facilitating philosophy's emergence as an essential founding stone. Whereas heretofore the ideas of

the Enlightenment had "fertilized and stirred the minds of individuals," they now "set in motion the streets . . . either to transform the old religion or to crystallize into the religion of a new people."[40] Not surprisingly, France having missed the Reformation's religious quarrels which elsewhere had encouraged a "spirit of analysis and discussion," even mild dissent was perceived and represented as heresy. Presently the "intolerance" of Saint-Just resembled that of any Pope, and the Convention bade fair to turn "Paris into a new Rome with a spiritual authority on the order of the Vatican."[41]

While Michelet faulted the Jacobins for not realizing that the Revolution was a political religion and church, Quinet scorned them for not being fit to carry out their religious mission. In his judgment they naively assumed that debate and persuasion could dissolve an age-old church and belief system. The revolutionaries continued to hesitate between toleration and proscription until well after it was clear that, in the words of Saint-Just, the "two opposing cities" were irreconcilable. Even the ultra-Jacobins kept trying to win over the priests without making a concerted effort to "emancipate" their parishioners, who were their lifeblood and *raison d'être*.[42] But above all, with the possible exception of Robespierre and Saint-Just, they lacked the "fiery . . . and icy temperament" and the "carnivorous instinct" of the religious fanatic and executioner, perhaps because they fell short of the "mystical exaltation . . . and creative audacity" of the Reformers of the sixteenth century.[43] Not even the most impassioned revolutionary tribunes had any of the "thunder and fury" characteristic of Huss, Luther, or Zwingli.[44] By and large the Jacobins "trembled at what would have made Luther laugh," so that unlike their counterparts of the sixteenth century, who "emancipated half of Europe from its medieval religious institutions, they . . . failed to extricate a single village from them." The Jacobins might have been more forceful in deracinating the old belief system had they known how to create "a nation without a religion, without a cult, and without a God."[45]

* * *

It is striking that several of the incumbents and close associates of France's distinctive Chair of the History of the French Revolution, established at the Sorbonne to coincide with the Revolution's first centennial, took a keen interest in the ecclesiastical and religious question. But each of them did so from a different perspective, making for considerable discordance. Although Alphonse Aulard, Albert Mathiez, Marcel Reinhard, and Albert Soboul were confirmed republicans and secularists, they were not only at variance about the nature of the Revolution's would-be secular religion. They also differed about the respective weight, in its gestation and practice, of intention and contingency, authenticity and imitation, profanity and sacrality, spontaneity and organization. Even so, all four postulated that this religion had many of the defining characteristics of religion in general: belief system, catechism, martyr, priest, altar, cult, rite, and hymn. Alone Reinhard wondered whether the sacred ever crystallized sufficiently for the Revolution's would-be religious cults to be considered genuine religions.

The interpretation of Aulard, the first holder of the chair from 1891 to 1923, is ingenuously functionalist. In his reading—as in that of Michelet and Quinet before him and Mathiez and Soboul after him—in 1789 no one had called for an assault on either the Gallican Church or Catholicism. Until late 1792 the members of the major political factions in the legislative assemblies were at once tempted by an indeterminate Enlightenment and respectful of the old faith. All this time the mass of the people, particularly the peasants, "instinctively continued to practice their hereditary habits."[46] In his day Aulard still needed to insist that the attempt to de-Christianize France and establish first the Cult of Reason and then the Cult of the Supreme Being "originated neither in a preconceived philosophic idea nor a reasoned . . . or fanatical belief system."[47] To be sure, select circles entertained certain theoretical constructs, such as Rousseau's idea of civil religion. But ultimately, according to Aulard, the Revolution's new-model religion was a "necessary and essentially political consequence of the state of war into which the resistance of the *ancien régime* . . . had plunged the Revolution." Specifically, "the enthronement of the Goddess of Reason in Notre-Dame [in November 1793] or the glorification of the God of Rousseau on the Champ de Mars [in June 1794]" had, above all, a political rationale. For the zealots of 1793–94 such moves, along with other expressions of symbolic and verbal violence, were essentially "defensive."[48]

Aulard considered the Revolution to have "made the mistake" of forcing refractory priests to swear an oath to the secular republic with a view to "nationalizing Catholicism." This oath became both the "reason and pretext" for the clergy's unholy alliance "with the enemies of the *patrie*," as expressed in its incitement of opposition to the military draft in early 1793. Indeed, the shift from fighting the Church to attacking the Catholic religion did not get under way until the second half of 1793, when the Revolution had to do battle in the Vendée and against Europe. It was in this moment of peril that a few fiery spirits, in their iron "resolve" to save the nation, wildly imagined that they "could overnight destroy an age-old religion and improvise a new and powerful" ersatz belief system.[49] This entailed "substituting new dates and festivals for Catholic ones, abolishing the Christian Sunday in favor of a Republican sabbath, replacing the names of saints by those of 'objects which are truly representative of the essence of the nation.' "[50]

In Aulard's analysis the two major would-be secular religions—the Cult of Reason and the Cult of the Supreme Being—made few converts in the provinces and countryside, where "the popular masses ignored or scorned" them, their hearts being unmoved by "cerebral ceremonies."[51] Although he loathed Robespierre, Aulard all but endorsed his charge that the rabid de-Christianizers damaged the revolutionary regime by offending not only the silent majority in France but also "popular sentiments and governments" throughout Europe. In his self-possessed speech of November 21, 1793, Robespierre denounced fanaticism for being "both ferocious and capricious," and warned against fomenting "a new fanaticism to fight the old." He was particularly troubled by those making "the battle against superstition a pretext for turning atheism into a religion" and the Convention into the fountainhead of a "metaphysical system," at odds with popular religion.[52]

Mathiez, like his teacher Aulard, treated the religious phenomenon in essentially political and social terms. For both historians the search for an alternative religion was a matter of political expediency in the face of mounting resistance at home and abroad. Mathiez saw the creed of the Revolution's embryonic cult generating love and reverence for France's new political institutions and principles with a view to "regenerating not only the French people but all humanity." In contrast to Catholicism's mystique and promise of salvation in the hereafter, this cult held out the hope of progress in this world. For

Mathiez the clash between these two precepts for redemption fired an inherently religious struggle.[53]

On one point Mathiez marked himself off from Aulard. Inspired by Emile Durkheim's sociology of religion, he held that the "specifically religious characteristics" of the inchoate revolutionary cults were defined more by their rites and symbols than their doctrines.[54] There was, to be sure, the Declaration of the Rights of Man, which emerged as the virtually unspoken "national catechism."[55] But especially in the cities, the faith of the converts was stoked above all by secular ceremonies and festivals which effectively imitated and rivaled those of the Venerable Church. Mathiez meant to demonstrate, over against Quinet, that "in religious sincerity, mystical exaltation, and creative audacity the men of the Revolution barely lagged behind the men of the Reformation."[56]

To summarize, in Mathiez's own words: the Revolution's religion had "its binding dogmas (the Declaration of Right, the Constitution); its symbols wrapped in a venerable mystique (the national colors, the liberty trees, the altars of the *patrie*, etc.); its ceremonies (the civic festivals); its prayers and chants." In late 1792, in order to "change into a genuine religion," it still needed to "become conscious of itself, by breaking with Catholicism, from which it was not yet completely extricated."[57] The defiant opposition to the civil constitution of the clergy triggered this rupture, which was pressed for and instrumentalized by true believers, some of whom were "frenzied and fanatical" in their war against the "beliefs, symbols, and institutions" of the old religion "they meant to suppress and replace."[58]

Soboul went beyond Aulard and Mathiez by exploring the "specificity" as well as the "ensemble" of the religious phenomenon in the revolutionary process. He shifted the focus from the Faustian cults of Reason and of the Supreme Being, which were the "official and . . . artificial productions" of revolutionary leaders, to major "popular cults," which were "expressions of the religious spontaneity of the revolutionary masses," the bulk of participants in public ceremonials. In addition, instead of pointing up the "break between the traditional and new religion," Soboul explored their interpenetration. As he saw it, the new popular cults were intrinsically syncretic, although in form and practice they remained "very close to Catholicism."[59]

The cults of Lepelletier, Marat, and Chalier, the three most prominent "martyrs of liberty," best reflected this skewed syncretism. Many of the ceremonies took place on Sundays and not a few were held in churches. Soboul also notes the "ambiguity" of words like martyr, saint, and deity "taken over from Christianity's religious vocabulary" and likely to foster mental contagion in favor of national or revolutionary rather than personal salvation. Funeral processions were "modeled on the Catholic processions which were now forbidden." In the untried ritual observances "the draperies, candelabra, and sarcophagi were taken from traditional religious ceremonials, while the national colors replaced the black color of mourning." Altars were adapted for patriotic rites, "the statue of Liberty supplanted that of the Virgin," and "wreaths of cypress leaves and inscriptions" evoked memories of the birth of freedom in the ancient world. A distinct ceremonial symbolism gradually crystallized, composed of "elements borrowed from the Catholic cult and Antiquity," and syncretized with revolutionary ingredients.[60]

Soboul, like Aulard, was attentive to social variants: whereas "militants of petty bourgeois and middle class background who had a modicum of classical culture . . . and disbelief hearkened to memories of antiquity, the sansculottes, . . . doubtless immersed in the traditional religious environment, borrowed elements from the Catholicism in which they were raised."[61] But whatever the "lineaments" of the new cult, its manifestations and intentions were "essentially political," and Soboul's fundamental question remains unanswered: "to what extent did a [deep-seated but not immutable] religious sentiment . . . [and] fervor heighten the exaltation of the civic spirit?"[62]

＊　＊　＊

The works of Aulard, Mathiez, and Soboul prompted Marcel Reinhard to raise some fundamental issues of interpretation in his courses at the Sorbonne. His starting premise was twofold: the inherent difficulty of "creating a religion, ab origine and out of thin air"; and the "failure of this effort" in 1789–94.[63] To be sure, Reinhard mapped the advance from spontaneous practice to deliberate construction. All along he wondered, however, whether this religion-cum-church-building was ever driven by a genuine "desire to found a religion," or whether at bottom it was simply a matter of "political tactics."[64] At the outset there were, to be sure, deputies who "considered themselves priests" of the Revolution, among them Barnave, who actually proposed that the Declaration of the Rights of Man be proclaimed France's "national catechism." There were, in addition, hymns to martyrs as well as to *patrie*, liberty, reason, and nature. Eventually elements of these paeans were integrated into the Cult of Reason and the Cult of the Supreme Being, which had their altars, vows, and rites. But Reinhard stopped to ask whether their principal "traits" were not "more of the domain of ritual than religion"[65]—in other words, that they may have been more in the nature of civic and patriotic "festivals which in the final analysis were not a religion [capable of] replacing" the established but contested church and faith.[66]

Reinhard also dismissed the Cult of Reason as an eclectic syncretism trapped in "memories of Christianity" even as it embodied the resolve to "substitute something new for them."[67] A confluence of "popular and sansculotte currents" combined with a current that was "bourgeois, enlightened, and deist," the Cult of Reason was an amalgam of a "cult of great men, of the *Patrie*, and of Liberty."[68] As for the Cult of the Supreme Being, which "oscillated between atheism and theism," it was every bit as syncretic as the Cult of Reason. Both had multiple components, but those of the latter had a more "human" inflection than those of the Cult of the Supreme Being, which was more "transcendent."[69]

Among historians of the French Revolution, Reinhard stands out for postulating the sacred as an essential defining characteristic of religion. For him, the revolutionary cults lacked a distinctive and authentic sacred attribute or core. Reinhard ascribed this deficit to the religion-makers' "astonishing ignorance" of the religious phenomenon and of essential "psychological and sociological factors" which he traced to the "revolutionary personnel being cut off from the people at large."[70] With commendable caution Reinhard concluded that on the whole, there "were very few genuinely religious elements," certainly as compared to "pride," which was profane: "pride in being a revolutionary, pride in serving a new ideal, and pride in fighting for it . . . at the risk of one's life." As for God, he was "called to witness rather than invoked or implored." There being no signs of "humility, even among those of humble station," there was "neither supplication, nor fear of the sacred." To the contrary, the call(ing) was "for confidence, courage, and bravery to the point of fearlessness."[71] Evidently Reinhard—not unlike the revolutionaries— took the Christian religion as his archetype, probably excessively but also instructively so.

✻ ✻ ✻

In Russia, as in France, public intellectuals and political objectors could not avoid addressing and debating the role of religion in state and society. Of course, in the late eighteenth century the link between the Bourbon absolute monarchy and the Catholic Church had been perfectly normal. A century later, however, the symbiosis between the Romanov autocracy and the Orthodox Church made Russia old-fashioned in comparison with most other European nations. But this very backwardness made preoccupation with the question of church, state, and society all the more acute for Russia's reformers and revolutionaries. Especially after 1905–6, not only did several idealists among the intelligentsia delve into "God-building" or "God-seek-ing," but so did prominent Marxist Socialists, much to the dismay of their fiercely godless colleagues.[72] To be sure, during this same period in France, Jean Jaurès suggested that the socialist movement was a "religious revolution."[73] But this train of thought was rare to the west of Russia.

In any case, the discussion in Russia was marked by Marx, whose thought and political *engagement*, like Voltaire's, transcended na-tional borders and was distinctly pan-European, indeed universal.[74] To be sure, Voltaire had been glaringly French while Marx was any-thing but Russian. Also, whereas Voltaire had sought to influence and advise Europe's crowned heads, Marx proposed to dethrone them. Still, they were analytically at one in stressing that church and religion were essential bulwarks of the established order: without reducing or transforming them it would be difficult, if not impossible, to improve the human condition. Marx might as well have been speaking of Rus-sia when he held, intemperately, that because religion "was one of the chief pillars of the Prussian state . . . it had to be knocked away before any political change could be thought of."

For Marx religion was not pure and indeterminate irrationalism. Like politics and culture, it was conditioned significantly by exploitative social and economic relations. As noted above, Marx conceived religion as a consequence, symptom, or reflection of a wrongful society or world. It was "an expression of the reality of poverty" as well as a "protest against it." Central to the culture of the masses, not the classes, religion was at once a "sigh of the oppressed" and an "opium" intended to help them compensate for or sublimate their misery. Unlike Ludwig Feuerbach and the left Hegelians, Marx could not conceive challenging religion without probing its social foundations. In his view "religion does not make man . . . [but] man makes religion," and man does so as member of a specific "state [and] society."

Clearly, Marx considered the critique of religion and the battle against it an integral part of the critical analysis of the existing world and the struggle to change it. In a particularly striking formulation Marx called for " criticism of heaven to turn into criticism of the earth, criticism of religion into criticism of law, and criticism of theology into criticism of politics." Ultimately he believed, of course, that scientific progress would dissolve the fallacies of religion, to be replaced by enlightened secular attitudes, values, and moral principles consistent with the class struggle and the construction of a new order. Meanwhile, however, critical intellection and politics would hasten this process of unmasking the religious pretense.

Marx's view of religion was particularly telling for a broad range of Russian Socialists embattled in a country of great oppression whose official church was deeply anchored in the worldview and beliefs of the masses, yet also closely linked with the political and social order of tsarism. Georgi Valentinovich Plekhanov, perhaps the leading Menshevik intellectual, treated religion, in the Marxist manner, as a web of superstitions, prejudices, and misconceptions correlated with grinding socioeconomic conditions. Although he agreed with Marx that in the long run religion would vanish with the march toward socialist modernity, Plekhanov made a point of asking how this process should or could be accelerated, above all by education.

For Lenin, unlike Plekhanov, religion was less an "intellectual error [than] . . . a social and moral outrage" rooted in rank exploitation. Rather than leave de-faithing and de-churching to gradual self-liquidation aided by small doses of enlightenment, Lenin advocated making the attack on church and religion central to the revolutionary project: one of the main reasons for a Marxist party in Russia was "to carry on the struggle against all religious bamboozling or stultification of the workers."[75]

But notwithstanding this interpretive and tactical discord, Lenin and Plekhanov pulled together in the battle against religion. In 1902, mindful of the struggle over church and religion during the French Revolution, they pressed to make religion a private affair, to separate church and state, and to secularize education. Lenin proposed that all state funds for the Orthodox Church and clerical institutions be ended as an essential precondition for "wiping out the shameful and accursed past, in which the Church was the slave of the State and Russian citizens, in their turn, the slaves of the Church, when medieval inquisitional laws tyrannized over the conscience of men."[76]

But starting with the *fin de siècle*, with the issue of forcing the course of history increasingly agitating and dividing Russian Socialists, other Marxists made a point of insisting that it was neither desirable nor possible to extirpate the religious temper. Often their unorthodox interventions involved rethinking Marxism itself, which they identified as a religious phenomenon in its own right. Anatoli Vasilyevich Lunacharsky's critique of Plekhanov is emblematic of this turn.[77] Of course, he agreed that the old religion served to relieve popular fears of mysterious natural forces and that its doctrine and church were meant to keep in place the underprivileged in favor of the ruling and governing classes. But Lunacharsky challenged the idea that religion had always and everywhere been a repressive force, insisting that in the past it had intermittently inspired or mobilized popular protests against injustice and inequality. Unlike Plekhanov, whom he considered a latter-day *philosophe* trusting in human reason and education, Lunacharsky called attention to the non-reasoning, not to say irrational impulses driving humanity's permanent if unsteady religious quest, culminating in socialism, the "religion of mankind."[78] In his reading, in addition to being a social theorist, Marx was a moral philosopher and prophet in the tradition of Isaiah, Christ, and Spinoza—a combination that was "Judaism's precious gift" to the family of man.[79] Lunacharsky argued that by confining his exegesis to the rational and scientific facets of Marx's theoretics, Plekhanov missed their intense emotional and moral charge. As "the most religious of all religions"[80] socialism was inseparable from a latent collective fervor, peculiar to Russia, waiting to be aroused and harnessed, for "without enthusiasm it is not given to men to create anything great."[81] The assignment, here and now, was to generate myths and rituals, faith and communion, without lapsing into god-worship, mysticism, and otherworldliness. Lunacharsky wanted the Bolsheviks to "propagate Marxism as an anthropocentric religion whose God was Man, raised to the height of his powers, and whose celebration was revolution—the greatest and most decisive act in the process of 'God-building.' "[82] Even if he does not say so explicitly, there is reason to believe that Lunacharsky's thoughts turned to God-building once he discerned the inertia of peasant Russia.

If even hardened Russian Marxists stressed the quasi-religious sides of their project, it is hardly surprising that left-idealists like Berdyaev should have done so as well. Berdyaev considered himself a "radical Christian" or "religious . . . and collectivist revolutionary" distinctly understanding of Marxist socialism, even if "deeply hostile to its authoritarian implications." He and Lunacharsky were aware of each other and basically agreed on the potential of emergent religious-like belief and purpose for the revolutionary movement.[83] A true but disenchanted Christian, Berdyaev blamed the Russian Orthodox Church—as Michelet and Quinet had blamed the Gallican Church—for "failing to carry out its mission," occupying "a conservative position in relation to state and social life," and acting as a "slavish subject to the old regime," thereby preparing the ground for "the false religion of communism which aimed to take the place of Christianity." In addition, conditions and traditions in Russia were not favorable to a "liberal bourgeois revolution," the liberal movement being anchored in the Duma and Cadet party, which lacked popular support and "inspiring ideas." Accordingly, in the Romanov empire the revolution "could only be socialist . . . and totalitarian," leavened by a "spiritual turn of mind" peculiar to Russia. Not surprisingly the country's intelligentsia was tempted by the left in general, which understood revolution as "both a religion and a philosophy," and by Marxism, which was "a faith, a religion, in addition to being a science and a politics."[84]

Whatever their differences, Plekhanov and Lenin were at one in opposing the idealist as well as the Marxist or materialist enchantment with the mystique and spirituality of revolution. Lenin might as well have spoken for both of them in November 1913, when writing to Gorky, who himself was not above hearkening to the religionist Siren: there was no greater difference between "god-seeking, god-building, god-creating and god-making" than between "a yellow and a blue devil, . . . [and] to talk about god-seeking without declaring against *all* devils and gods . . . and to prefer a blue to a yellow devil was a hundred times worse than not saying anything about it at all."[85] Of course, Plekhanov and Lenin were, in the first instance, troubled by discordant voices in their own camps. Plekhanov scorned Lunacharsky, berating him as a "hayseed" and a "God-composer" or "God-spinner."[86] And Lenin criticized him for unwittingly lending support to reaction. Reiterating Marx's condemnation of religion as an "opium," Lenin called it "spiritual booze or schnapps in which the slaves of capital drown their . . . demands for a life in some degree worthy of man."[87] In this way, Plekhanov and Lenin both upheld the orthodox Marxist conception of the nature of religion, as well as the orthodox Marxist interpretation and projection of itself as the most powerful form of secular rationalism. Their views aligned them with many outside the Marxist movement and made them all the more dangerous to the tsarist regime inasmuch as intense criticism of the Orthodox Church, often combined with militant religious disbelief, reached beyond the radical left to the loyal opposition, and it was widespread in the intelligentsia.

Clearly the divisive urgency of the ecclesiastical and religious question during the French Revolution and its immanence in the old Russia combined to precipitate its theoretical discussion by radical members of the latter-day Enlightenment in the late Romanov empire. Not even Lenin could have anticipated that the religious question would soon have to be confronted in a Russian revolution at the same time that this revolution would become the primary host of Marxism, a messianic secular religion whose social catechism would have an even greater echo than the Declaration of the Rights of Man. Indeed, "perhaps not since Christianity was founded" has the world seen "a doctrine combining as much proffered hope with as much militance and zeal . . . as the message offered the downtrodden, the oppressed, and the disinherited by Marx and his followers."[88]

* * *

NOTES

1. Peter L. Berger, *The Sacred Canopy: Elements of a Sociological Theory of Religion* (New York: Doubleday, 1967), pp. 25–27, 35, 39, 80, 100; and Roger Caillois, *L'homme et le sacré* (Paris: Gallimard, 1950), pp. 17–23, 37, 42. Both Berger and Caillois take Emile Durkheim's *Les formes élémentaires de la vie religieuse* (1912) as their starting point.

2. Bruce Lincoln, "Notes Toward a Theory of Religion and Revolution," in Lincoln, ed., *Religion, Rebellion, Revolution: An Interdisciplinary and Cross-cultural Collection of Essays* (New York: St. Martins, 1985), pp. 226–92, esp. p. 282.

3. Crane Brinton, *The Anatomy of Revolution* (New York: Vintage, 1957), p. 194.

4. Machiavelli cited in Roger Boesche, *Theories of Tyranny from Plato to Hannah Arendt* (University Park, Pa.: Pennsylvania State University Press, 1996), p. 136.

5. Edgar Quinet, *Le Christianisme et la Révolution française* (Paris: Fayard, 1984), pp. 229–45. Before Quinet, Hegel had argued along similar lines. See Joachim Ritter, *Hegel and the French Revolution: Essays on the Philosophy of Right* (Cambridge, Mass.: MIT Press, 1982); and Werner Berthold "Weltgeschichtskonzeption und Stellung zur Grossen Französischen Revolution," in Manfred Kossok and Editha Kross, eds., *1789: Weltwirkung einer grossen Revolution*, vol. 2 (Liechtenstein: Topos, 1989), esp. pp. 618–27.

6. Jacob Burckhardt, *Weltgeschichtliche Betrachtungen* (Stuttgart: Kröner, 1978), p. 118.

7. Karl Marx, *Critique of Hegel's 'Philosophy of Right'* (Cambridge: Cambridge University Press, 1970), pp. 129–42.

8. Sigmund Freud, *Civilization and Its Discontents*, in James Strachey, ed., *The Complete Psychological Works of Sigmund Freud*, vol. 21 (London: Hogarth Press, 1961), pp. 57–145, esp. p. 81 and p. 85.

9. Berger, *Sacred Canopy*, p. 107.

10. Brinton, *Anatomy*, p. 194 (italics in text).

11. Carl L. Becker, *The Heavenly City of the Eighteenth-Century Philosophers* (New Haven: Yale University Press, 1932), pp. 8–9, 46, 122–23, 130, 138–39.

12. Nicolas Berdyaev, *The Origin of Russian Communism* (London: Geoffrey Bles, 1937/1948), p. 98, p. 100, and p. 105.

13. Ibid., pp. 106–7.

14. Robert Nisbet, *The Social Philosophers: Community and Conflict in Western Thought* (New York: Thomas Y. Crowell, 1973), p. 265.

15. Eugen Rosenstock, *Die europäischen Revolutionen* (Jena: Eugen Diederichs, 1931), pp. 66–67.

16. Richard Crossman, ed., *The God That Failed* (New York: Harper/Bantam, 1952).

17. Burke, "Thoughts on French Affairs" (1791), in Paul Langford, ed., *The Writings and Speeches of Edmund Burke*, vol. 8 (Oxford: Clarendon Press, 1989), pp. 340–42 (italics in text).

18. Ibid., p. 340.

19. "Remarks on the Policy of the Allies" (1793), in ibid., p. 485.

20. Joesph de Maistre, *Écrits sur la Révolution* (Paris: Presses Universitaires, 1989), esp. pp. 91–217 ("Considérations sur la France"). See also Richard A. Lebrun, "The 'Satanic' Revolution: Joseph de Maistre's 'Religious' Judgment of the French Revolution," in *Proceedings of the Annual Meeting of the Western Society for French History* 16 (1989): pp. 234–40.

21. Alexis de Tocqueville, *L'ancien régime et la Révolution* (Paris: Flammarion, 1988), bk. 1, ch. 3, pp. 105–6. Carl Becker called attention to Tocqueville's religious analogy in *Heavenly City*, pp. 154–55.

22. Tocqueville, *L'ancien régime*, bk. 1, ch. 3, pp. 106–8.

23. Ibid., bk. 1, ch. 2, pp. 102–4.

24. Ibid., bk. 3, ch. 2, p. 245.

25. See François Furet, *La gauche et la Révolution française au milieu de XIXe siècle: Edgar Quinet et la question du jacobinisme, 1865–1870* (Paris: Hachette, 1986), passim.

26. Jules Michelet, *Histoire de la Révolution française*, 2 vols. (Paris: Laffont, 1979), vol. 1, p. 54.

27. Quinet, *Le Christianisme*, pp. 181–82, 231, 233–34.

28. Michelet, *Histoire*, vol. 1, p. 317.

29. Ibid., p. 51, p. 54, and p. 60.

30. Ibid., pp. 61–62.

31. Ibid., p. 62.

32. Ibid., pp. 323–40 and p. 43. See also Michelet, *Cours au Collège de France, 1838–1851*, vol. 1 (Paris: Gallimard, 1995), p. 223.

33. Michelet, *Histoire*, vol. 1, p. 308.

34. Ibid., vol. 2, bk. 14, ch. 1.

35. Ibid., vol. 2, p. 616.

36. Quinet, *Le Christianisme*, esp. chs. (lectures) 6 and 8.

37. Ibid., p. 239.

38. Ibid., p. 242.

39. Ibid., p. 240.

40. Quinet, *La Révolution* (Paris: Belin, 1987), pp. 150–51 and p. 168; and *Christianisme*, p. 234.

41. Quinet, *Le Christianisme*, pp. 240–41.

42. Quinet, *La Révolution*, p. 176.

43. Ibid., pp. 511–17.

44. Ibid., p. 173.

45. Ibid., pp. 471–74, 482–83, 493.

46. Alphonse Aulard, *Le culte de la raison et le culte de l'être suprême, 1793–1794* (Paris: Félix Alcan, 1892), p. 17.

47. Ibid., p. 199.

48. Ibid., p. viii.

49. Ibid., pp. 19–20.

50. Ibid., pp. 34–35.

51. Ibid., p. 200.

52. Ibid., pp. 210–17.

53. Albert Mathiez, *Les origines des cultes révolutionnaires, 1789–1792* (Paris: Société Nouvelle, 1904), p. 9 and pp. 15–16.

54. Mathiez, *Les origines*, pp. 10–12.

55. Barnave cited in ibid., p. 22.

56. Ibid., p. 13.

57. Ibid., p. 62.

58. Ibid., p. 35 and p. 38.

59. Albert Soboul, "Sentiments religieux et cultes populaires pendant la Révolution: Saints, patriotes, et martyrs de la liberté," in *Archives de Sociologie des Religions* 2 (July–December 1956): pp. 75–77.

60. Soboul, "Sentiments," pp. 78–80.

61. Ibid., p. 84.

62. Ibid., p. 80 and p. 87.

63. Reinhard, *Religion, révolution, et contre-révolution* (Paris: Centre de Documentation Universitaire, 1960), fasc. 2, p. 178.

64. Ibid., p. 167 and p. 169.

65. Ibid., p. 164.

66. Ibid., p. 174 and pp. 178–79.

67. Ibid., p. 178.

68. Ibid., pp. 174–75.

69. Ibid., p. 162 and p. 164.

70. Ibid., p. 162.

71. Ibid., p. 182.

72. Berdyaev, *The Russian Idea* (New York: Macmillan, 1948), esp. pp. 156–66; and Christopher Read, *Religion, Revolution, and the Russian Intelligentsia, 1900–1912: The Vekhi Debate and Its Intellectual Background* (London: Macmillan, 1979).

73. Jean Jaurès, *La question religieuse et le socialisme*, ed. Michel Launay (Paris: Editions de Minuit, 1959).

74. All citations in the following three paragraphs are drawn from Karl Marx and Friedrich Engels, *On Religion* (New York: Schocken, 1964), with an introduction by Reinhold Niebuhr; and Nicholas Lobkowicz, "Karl Marx's Attitude toward Religion," *Review of Politics* 26 (1964): pp. 319–52.

75. Cited in George Kline, *Religious and Anti-Religious Thought in Russia* (Chicago: University of Chicago Press, 1968), p. 142. See also Erwin Adler, *Lenins Religionsphilosophie* (Munich: Institut zur Erforschung der UdSSR, 1964), pts. 2 and 3.

76. Cited in René Fulop-Miller, *The Mind and Face of Bolshevism: An Examination of Cultural Life in Soviet Russia* (New York: Putnam, 1927), p. 242. See also Adler, *Religionsphilosophie*, pp. 81–86.

77. Read, *Religion*, pp. 79–85.

78. Cited in Kline, *Thought in Russia*, p. 117.

79. Cited in ibid., p. 118.

80. Cited in ibid., p. 122.

81. Cited in Sheila Fitzpatrick, *The Commissariat of the Enlightenment: Soviet Organization of Education and the Arts under Lunacharsky, October 1917–1921* (Cambridge: Cambridge University Press, 1970), p. 4.

82. Ibid., p. 4.

83. Read, *Religion*, esp. pp. 57–59, 77, 88.

84. Berdyaev, *Russian Idea*, pp. 246–49. See also Marie-Madeleine Davy, *Nicolas Berdiaev ou la révolution de l'esprit* (Paris: Albin Michel, 1999), esp. pp. 25–26, 55.

85. Cited in Read, *Religion*, pp. 91–92.

86. Cited in Kline, *Thought in Russia*, p. 118, n. 5.

87. Cited in ibid., p. 142.

88. Nisbet, *Social Philosophers*, pp. 222–23.

PART TWO

Crescendo of Violence

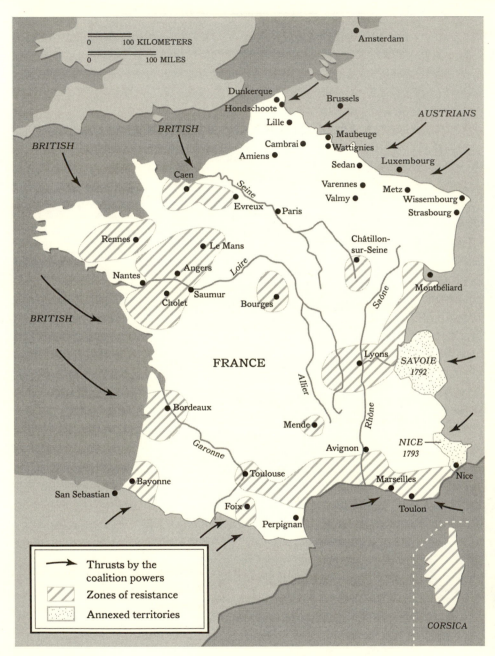

Map labels:

Amsterdam

0 100 KILOMETERS
0 100 MILES

Dunkerque
Hondschoote
BRITISH
Brussels
AUSTRIANS
Lille
Maubeuge
Cambrai
Wattignies
Amiens
Sedan
Luxembourg
BRITISH
Caen
Varennes
Metz
Valmy
Wissembourg
Evreux
Paris
Strasbourg
Rennes
Le Mans
Châtillon-sur-Seine
Angers
Nantes
Saumur
Montbéliard
Cholet
Bourges
BRITISH
FRANCE
Lyons
SAVOIE
1792
Bordeaux
Mende
NICE
1793
Toulouse
Avignon
Nice
Bayonne
Marseilles
San Sebastian
Foix
Toulon
Perpignan

Thrusts by the coalition powers
Zones of resistance
Annexed territories

CORSICA

The Republic Under Siege, 1793

The Return of
Vengeance:
Terror in France,
1789–95

VENGEANCE played a significant role in the unfolding and escalation of the Red and White Terror in the French Revolution. To explore its course is to be attentive to (re)emergences during the radical breakdown of political and legal sovereignty. It is also to avoid exaggerating the role of ideology and of the great leader, or of the two combined. Vengeance has, of course, many faces, above all because it moves and tempts both the classes and masses. It is spontaneous and impulsive, as well as premeditated and theorized.

The *bagarre* or turbulence in Nîmes in June 1790 is emblematic of the vicious circle of vengeance and re-vengeance. In this southern city, premature counterrevolutionaries of ultra-Catholic persuasion denounced Protestants for taking the helm of the revolutionary vanguard with a view to avenging past persecutions. Following several assaults on them, Protestant militants, in their turn, gave two measures for one. They called for revenge despite admonitions from within the Protestant community that only authorized "public vengeance" could break the infernal cycle of reciprocal "hatred, vindictiveness, . . . [and] *ressentiment*" which was being fueled by "private acts of vengeance." Certainly the mutual fear and denunciation driving this violence was well-grounded in local memories, beliefs, and class relations.[1]

Like the contentious Oath of the Clergy of November 27, 1790, the ill-starred flight to Varennes of June 20–22, 1791, was a major defining event. By stoking the fires of mutual suspicion, it undermined the efforts of the moderate triumvirate of Barnave, Lameth, and Duport to save the Revolution from further excesses. On June 26, 1791, General Marquis François-Claude-Amour de Bouillé, supreme commander in the eastern departments and architect of the royal family's escape, proposed to momentarily "suspend" the counterrevolution's imperative vengeance so as to give France's governors a chance to come to their senses. This respite was coupled with the warning that Europe's sovereigns were primed to fight "the monster generated by the National Assembly," which in the capital took the form of a "cannibalistic people drunk with crime, arrogance, resentment, and vice." Bouillé forewarned that should the royal family, following its awkward return to Paris, suffer the slightest harm, "no stone of the city would be left standing" and the National Assembly would have to assume full responsibility for "such an exemplary punishment." In closing, Bouillé noted that his admonition, which was not published at the time, prefigured a forthcoming "manifesto of Europe's sovereigns who will notify [the usurpers in Paris] in even stronger terms what they must either do or fear."[2]

And, indeed, in this dawn of a new and unfamiliar public diplomacy, and judging by the Padua Circular (July 10, 1791), Pillnitz Declaration (August 27, 1791), and Brunswick Manifesto (July 25, 1792), the rhetoric of the king-emperors became increasingly strident and threatening. The cry for vengeance was particularly fierce in court circles and among the émigrés. Count Armand Marc Montmorin, the foreign minister with close ties to Louis XVI, held that "inevitably a terror would be visited upon the population of Paris."[3] Among the émigrés, emotions ran so high that should the French people ever be given over to their vengeance, France "risked being turned into a wretched cemetery."[4] Several émigrés left their imprint on the letter and spirit of the Brunswick Manifesto, which threatened Paris and its citizens with "an exemplary, never to be forgotten vengeance: the city would be subjected to military punishment and total destruction," and the national guardsmen and other *frondeurs* were warned to expect neither mercy nor pardon.[5] The émigrés and their hoped-for foreign supporters saw themselves facing not military enemies but rebels, which meant that the laws of war need not be respected—a view shared, as noted above, by Edmund Burke.[6] But the émigrés and their foreign sympathizers were not the fountainhead of the growing thirst for vengeance, which was located in the Tuileries. In any case, in France the avenging threats from abroad backfired. By arousing "anger" rather than "fear," they gave the Revolution additional ground for deposing Louis XVI, not to say abolishing the monarchy.[7]

In the meantime, the abortive flight to Varennes, in addition to prodding the issue of dethronement at the top, roused the streets and the Commune of Paris from below. The reinstatement of Louis XVI on July 16, 1791, did much to trigger the mass rally of about 50,000 people in support of a petition opposing this move which, on July 17, 1791, culminated in the fusillade of the Champ de Mars. The National Guard units which fired the fatal volleys were under the command of the Marquis de Lafayette, and the two combined embodied the embryonic constitutional monarchy's precarious hold on the legitimate use of violence. In many circles the massacre of some 50 peaceful demonstrators, followed by 200 arrests—without casualties among the men-at-arms—further delegitimated the contested regime; at the same time it sparked the slogan "dethronement or vengeance," which caught fire in December, when Louis XVI vetoed decrees against émigrés and refractory priests.[8]

During the first half of 1792, with the king ever more distrusted for his alleged ties to European courts and the émigrés, the fast-rising military threat from abroad and war fever at home helped channel an increasingly restive popular movement, radicalized by worsening economic conditions, into the drive for dethronement. The declaration of war, the proclamation of the "country in danger," and the Brunswick Manifesto were the backdrop for the investment of the Tuileries in the night of August 9, 1792. Although small by comparison with the mass demonstration on the Champ de Mars the year before, this organized show of popular force turned into by far the bloodiest *journée* of the Revolution to date. Besides, this time the profile of victims was radically different: about 600 of the 1,000 casualties belonged to the Swiss and Royal guards, who killed and wounded the allegedly regicidal protesters by gunshot. Incensed by this fusillade, unarmed members of the crowd and bystanders went on an avenging rampage. Not a few of the Swiss mercenaries and royal servants who were mauled and slain in this access of vindictive rage were mutilated, impaled, and dismembered. Characteristically the

173

arrest and suspension of Louis XVI was tainted by this return of re-pressed personal and collective vengeance, foreshadowed by the lynching of several prominent old-regime officials in July 1789.[9]

Rather than quench the thirst for vengeance, the massacre of Au-gust 10 whetted it even further. Indeed, in the Paris Commune and in the *sections*, it touched off a loud cry for retaliation against the guards who had fired into the crowd, against the king's acolytes who had ordered or countenanced the use of naked force, and against the refractory priests who were suspected of having warranted the repression.[10]

August 10 spelled the fall of the monarchy and heralded the rise of the Commune, whose relations with the Assembly became increas-ingly stormy.[11] Internally divided in what was an extremely fluid and explosive situation, the Commune neither opposed nor incited "the movement for vengeance" which Marat and others made their own. Presently the issue of vengeance became an important touchstone of revolutionary politics: a struggle between, on the one hand, the zeal-ots of wild popular vengeance and, on the other, the advocates of legally grounded retribution, with the latter raising the specter of rampant avenging Furies to advance their position.

As if to calm the streets, on August 11 the Paris Commune called upon "the sovereign people to suspend . . . [their] vengeance" with the assurance that though through the ages justice had been trampled under foot, it was about to carry the day. That same night, in the Legislative Assembly, Danton, the Minister of Justice, backed a pro-posal to bring the captive Swiss Guards to trial before a court-martial or special tribunal. Although he sympathized with the seething popu-lar rage, Danton sought to dampen and canalize it. Stressing that "popular vengeance ends where law begins," he urged that "tribunals should begin to administer justice in order to disburden the people from having to do so." Besides, there were few if any other "antidotes to vengeance."[12] In this same spirit Condorcet, who had justified the massacre of August 10, argued that it behooved the Assembly to pro-tect political prisoners from "illegal vengeance and to have them judged by the law."[13]

Endorsing the Commune's demand that the Assembly set up a spe-cial court, Robespierre proposed that its judges be chosen by popular election. But the Assembly hesitated to set up a tribunal that risked being swayed by avengers at a time that it resisted ceding additional ground to the militants outside its halls and in its corridors. The militants did not, however, relent, judging by a petition presented to the Assembly on August 17 calling for the establishment of a tribunal to judge political criminals, "with one judge from each *section*." Although the *enragés* cried for a court of law, they intended and expected it to be an instrument of vengeance: "Louis XVI and Marie-Antoinette having spilled [the people's] blood, it was now their turn to watch their own followers get their just deserts." Pierre Victorien Vergniaud, one of Danton's associates, instantly retorted that this was a call for something very like "an inquisition, which he would fight to his last breath."[14]

Even so, that very night the Assembly voted to institute an extraordinary tribunal. Elected indirectly, all the judges turned out to be highly professional lawyers and magistrates with Jacobin affinities. The charter set forth legal procedures which were sober by the standards of that time. Entailing traditional elements of sovereignty and spawning new ones, the court was to pioneer new ways of rendering justice as it set about judging and sentencing those accused of having ordered, executed, and brooked the violence of August 10.

Not surprisingly, this emergency tribunal got off to what was perceived to be a slow start: between August 21 and the end of the month it tried only six prominent royalists. All but one were sentenced to death and executed. Louis-David Collenot d'Angremont and Armand Laporte were the first two "political criminals" to be guillotined on the Place du Carrousel. Needless to say, the overheated atmosphere was scarcely conducive to mastering and exercising the due processes of an emergent law. After the Brunswick Manifesto, the Prussians crossed the border to capture Longwy on August 23 and advanced toward Verdun, whose fall seemed imminent. In the capital the air became increasingly thick with fear of foreign military intervention and suspicion of domestic treason.[15]

This tense atmosphere, charged with growing disquiet and unreason, weighed on the national day of lamentation for the victims of August 10, set for Sunday, August 26, and billed as a "day of vengeance."[16] The festivities were centered around "[a] pyramid raised over the ornamental pond of the Tuileries." It was "draped with a black twill," and engraved with the names of places "recalling massacres imputed to the royalists: Nancy, Nîmes, Montauban, Champ de Mars, etc." Unlike the guillotine on the Place du Carrousel, which was designed to put to death in an instant and dispassionately, the pyramid "was virtually an incitement to [wild] slaughter."

The day's three-hour ceremonial cortege was headed by "the widows and orphans of the victims of August 10, dressed in white robes with black waistbands," and carrying a receptacle containing "the petition of July 17, 1791, which had in vain called for a republic." Next came the servants of the law, preceded by a huge male statue holding a symbolic sword, behind which marched the judges of all the emergency courts, including those of the embryonic revolutionary tribunal. The members of the "formidable Commune" fell in behind a statue of Liberty. Bringing up the rear, the deputies of the Assembly wore "civic head wreaths to honor and appease the dead." The air was filled with "the severe chants of Chénier and the austere and fearsome music of Gossec," which aimed to "lift the voice of vengeance to heaven and fill all hearts with deathly tremors and dark forebodings." During the funeral ceremony, Charles-Philippe Ronsin, the main speaker, summoned one and all "to swear on the coffins of the harrowed bodies not to sheathe their swords . . . until France's capital is purged of all the people's oppressors."[17] On Monday a "furious crowd" carried the statue of Liberty to the Assembly "to ask for vengeance" before taking it, along with the Statue of the Law, to the Square of Louis XV for a "frenzied" celebration of both icons.[18]

What little remained of effective state authority had all but melted away. The Legislative Assembly having proclaimed its impending dissolution in favor of a soon to be elected constituent national convention, an interim executive council took the unsteady helm, with Danton at justice, Roland at interior, Clavière at finance, Servan at war, and Lebrun at foreign affairs. This provisional government reigned for forty days, until immediately after the military success at Valmy (September 20, 1792), which was a welcome but fleeting ray of hope in a perilous situation. The Commune of Paris and other municipalities of a radical cast kept pressing for ever greater iron resolve and will. The Assembly grudgingly authorized them to arrest suspects, inviting the establishment of local committees of surveillance.

Especially as seen from the capital, the situation seemed to be going from bad to worse. The Prussians kept advancing, and there were the first signs of peasant resistance in the lands of the future Vendée and Chouannerie. As was to be expected, all levels of political and civil society registered a fast-growing disposition to blame all reverses and perils on a sinister royalist or aristocratic plot. Forthwith several deputies attributed the "infamous capitulation" of Longwy and Verdun to the treacherous influence of local conspirators and threatened severe reprisals following liberation.[19] In the meantime, on August 26, swept by fear and suspicion, the Assembly had issued a decree granting refractory priests two weeks to leave the country or face deportation. By the same token, two days later, at Danton's urging, it ordered private homes to be searched for "suspects" and arms, above all in the capital. The prison population of Paris rose to about 2,800 by early September, of whom about 1,000 were arrested after August 10.

There is no denying the swelling fear behind the first terror, which was largely a panic terror. Brunswick's warning of "an exemplary vengeance" from abroad was as real as the threat of rising resistance at home. Even Roland, less mercurial than Danton, hearkened to the "despair and indignation of a people trembling in the face of imminent peril and [fearing] the cruel vengeance [of] . . . savage counterrevolutionaries."[20] He was joined by Brissot, Condorcet, Gorsas, and Louvet in publicly justifying popular violence against domestic enemies with a view to consolidating the Revolution and bolstering the influence of the Girondins. Their accent was on spontaneous violence, which they expected to be limited and relatively easy to contain.[21]

✳ ✳ ✳

Of course, there were also proponents of preemptive vengeance. Marat repeatedly incited the *petit peuple* to again take matters in their own hands as the focus of the revolutionary animus shifted from the Tuileries to the prisons, which were packed with sworn enemies. He feared that "popular executions" were becoming a "cruel . . . necessity" for a people "reduced to despair" and running out of patience with a "willfully slow-moving justice." As early as August 19, 1792, Marat declared that "the safest and wisest course" was for the people to go "fully armed" to the Abbaye prison to seize the traitors being held there and "put to the sword in particular the Swiss officers and their accomplices," without benefit of a trial.[22] In much the same way,

Louis-Stanislas Fréron decried that even though the prisons were crammed with scoundrels and conspirators, so far the special tribunal, "instead of making a clean sweep," had pronounced only "three death sentences." Even Gorsas, a prominent Girondin zealot, warned that "should the sword of justice fail to strike, the people's sword would have to do so." Whereas heretofore the sacrifice of "a few drops of impure blood would have appeased the cry for a righteous vengeance" by now, with the people "driven to excesses," very likely it would take a "torrent of blood."[23]

This, then, was the context and ambience in which the prison massacres erupted and ran wild during the first week of September 1792. These massacres were the second saturnalia of bloodshed in less than a month and may be considered the culmination of the first, erratic terror of the French Revolution. There is considerable bafflement about their incidental and ultimate causes, the mix of spontaneity and predeliberation being particularly controversial. In terms of the dynamics of their escalation and contagion, the prison massacres might be considered the urban equivalent of the *grande peur* of 1789, which had been largely rural.

It all started early Sunday afternoon, September 2, with the slaying of about twenty refractory priests who, having refused to take the new oath to the republic, were being transferred to the Abbaye prison, pending deportation overseas. During the following five days, patriots driven by "rage and fear" invested nine of the capital's eleven regular jails and improvised detention centers, determined to seize their inmates. About 1,100 of 2,800 prisoners were killed, or over two-fifths of the prison population. Three-quarters of the victims were conventional and nonpolitical inmates, with many thieves and prostitutes among them. The prey comprised about 200 priests, 80 Swiss guards, and 100 nobles. As the killing spread to provincial cities, most of the victims were political prisoners, notably nobles and priests.[24]

If the number of victims did not rise any higher it was, in part, because self-appointed leaders among the vigilantes set up quasi tribunals inside the prisons to interrogate about 2,600 suspects, of whom 1,500 were acquitted. In the words of a member of the Commune, "the people dispensed justice at the same time that they wrought vengeance." Overall, however, there was something distinctly wild and blind about the slaughter of defenseless prisoners who were presumed to embody a ubiquitous domestic enemy with close ties to the *émigrés* and European powers.[25]

Even more terrible than the scale of the killings were the furious and primitive ways in which they were carried out. For the *septembriseurs* the model spectacle of justice was centered around the legendary wheel on the Place de Grève, not around the new-built scaffold on the Place du Carrousel. During four days they "savored" inflicting upon some of their betters torments reminiscent of those suffered by Calas and Damiens.[26] It was not uncommon for prisoners to be cut to pieces "in order to prolong their agonies and amuse the spectators, delighted in the spectacle of the victims' atrocious convulsions and wails of agony."[27]

Although the fate of Marie-Thérèse de Savoie-Carignan, or Princess de Lamballe, was not typical, it was paradigmatic. One of Marie Antoinette's closest confidantes, she emigrated in mid-1791 but soon returned to join the royal family and was confined to the Petite-Force prison after August 10, 1792. On September 3, while being transferred to another jail after having been sentenced to death, a crowd fell upon her. Mme de Lamballe was brutally killed and decapitated: her head fixed on the point of a pike, it was carried, in ominous procession, to the Temple allegedly to force the king and queen to see with their own eyes "how the people wreak vengeance on their tyrants." In the heat of the moment it was widely rumored that the princess had been stripped bare, dismembered, and eviscerated. In actual fact her calvary was comparable to that of de Launay, de Flesselles, and Bertier de Sauvigny in July 1789 which, as we saw, marked a resurgence of ancient rituals of avenging retribution.[28]

Overall the profile of the several hundred deadly assailants was comparable to that of similar partisan, lynch, or pogrom gangs through the ages. Their ranks included "drunks, cowards, and simpletons" alongside respectable artisans, shopkeepers, and (ex-)soldiers. It is uncertain how many of them, if any, acted under the influence of the Jacobin or any other ideological belief system. There were, of course, many times more onlookers than killers. Most likely the former had altogether unexceptional motives for actively inciting or silently condoning the latter. By and large Paris "turned a deaf ear to the war cries of the killers and the wails of the victims," as if "pity had been frozen" and "hearts turned to stone."[29]

Indeed, the absence of any effective restraining force goes far to explain the escalation of the assault on twenty defiant priests into a nearly weeklong and citywide prison massacre. What there was of sovereign power was tenuous and paralyzed. The ministers of the provisional government, most notably Danton and Roland, made little if any effort to intercede. As for the Assembly, it did not "adopt a single [monitory] resolution, directive, or decree"; and its normally "silver-tongued orators," including Rabaut Saint-Etienne, "fell silent."[30] Besides, even if one of the leaders had risen to the occasion, he could not have mustered credible security forces.[31] Although Jérôme Pétion, the mayor of Paris, and Louis Manuel, the *procureur* of the Paris Commune, were as powerless as the Assembly, they kept trying to mediate in the prisons, with modest results. Significantly, on September 7, when informing the Assembly that the situation was not yet entirely back to normal, Pétion noted that "fear . . . [and] terror" were subsiding along with the "return of the rule of law and the reorganization of the *force publique*."[32]

In the meantime, key officials were unnerved and helpless. On September 3 Roland, the interior minister, sent a letter to the Assembly suggesting that "perhaps yesterday's events had best be hushed up." In his judgment "scoundrels and traitors" were taking advantage of a justified popular rage and vengeance, aspiring after a measure of long overdue justice. Roland merely urged the Assembly to calm the waters by openly "conceding that the executive power had failed to foresee and prevent these excesses."[33] Meanwhile the Assembly charged a commission to urge the sections to "stop the effusion of blood and channel the people's fury from domestic vengeance into a more forceful and dignified drive against foreign enemies." This commission promptly reported back that it was powerless "to bring the people to reason" and that the sections were waiting for the National Assembly "to take an energetic stand."[34]

Condorcet also avoided condemning the massacres. On September 4, after the Assembly had received details about the "bloody scenes in the prisons," he wrote in his newspaper that "we are ringing down the curtain on events whose scale and consequences would be difficult to evaluate just now." But in this same article, in which he noted that not a single prison had been spared, Condorcet was perplexed by the "unhappy and awful situation which forces a naturally good and generous people to wreak such vengeance."[35] On September 9, after Pé-tion, confident of the return of normalcy, asked the Assembly to forget all the "bloody scenes," Condorcet insisted that these "dark and random crimes" were perpetrated not by the people but by "brigands."[36] It took another ten days for him to assert that "popular vengeance . . . without legal sanction is murder."[37] In the meantime Roland and Condorcet did nothing to distance themselves from leading Girondins who throughout the bloody week concurred that there was a clear and present danger of a prison conspiracy, with links to local traitors and the émigrés, which the people had done well to thwart in the interest of saving the Revolution.[38]

While the master spirits of the Revolution hedged in public, in private not a few of them must have expressed their consternation about the wildfire of popular vengeance, which they were quick to blame on the dregs of society and the Mountain, or the extreme left. On September 5 Madame Roland, who moved in the inner circles of influence, noted that the Assembly and provisional government were being "cowed by Robespierre and Marat . . . [who] were stirring up the people" with the help of "a small gang cemented by loot stolen from castles and by contributions from Danton, the underhanded chief of this horde." Four days later she told her correspondent, Bancal des Issarts, that in the "ghastly" furor "women were brutally raped before they were torn limb from limb, their insides eviscerated and cut into ribbons and their flesh eaten raw." She closed with a wistful but also half-specious coda: "Now that the Revolution, which I embraced wholeheartedly from the start, has been tainted by these scoundrels and has turned ugly, it mortifies me."[39] Condorcet's wife similarly recorded that the avenging rage "deeply troubled all true patriots."[40]

Even the supporters and sympathizers of direct action were disturbed and mystified by the popular frenzy's raw violence. In the weekly *Les Révolutions de Paris*, under the headline "the people's justice," Louis-Marie Prudhomme advanced an uneasy justification. Giving credence to the widely held conspiratorial view that "aristocrats" were about to break out of prison to join forces with other counterrevolutionaries, he claimed that it was not to whitewash the horrors of "the people's vengeance" to forewarn of even greater horrors should the people "fall back under the aristocratic yoke." But even Prudhomme could not hide his anguish about the mixture of "virtue and vengeance" which had left "a pool of blood and a heap of corpses" in front of the Palace of Justice. In a private letter Babeuf was no less torn. He approved "the people taking the law in their own hands," all the more so since many of the victims were, in fact, guilty. Although he showed concern for the innocents who were murdered, Babeuf asked whether, in this critical pass, justice could have been other than "cruel." Besides, there was the long memory of the old elites having used "the wheel, the stake, and the gibbet" to hold down the people. Indeed, instead of "improving the human condition, they had turned their subjects into barbarians by behaving like barbarians themselves."[41]

* * *

Perhaps most unexpectedly, even Marat was disconcerted by the prison massacres. Ever since 1789 he had, of course, advocated spontaneous popular violence, starting with his justification of the initial assault on the Bastille. Marat saw the direct action of the *petit peuple* serving three purposes: remove the out-of-date rulers and their system of political oppression; secure greater equity for the lower and especially propertyless strata; and promote the *lumières*.[42] In his argument, the common people patiently "endured enormous suffering before, finally, rising and wreaking a vengeance which is just in principle even if not always enlightened in its effects."[43] Troubled by the intemperance of popular insurrection and justice, Marat envisaged the establishment of a community-based committee of "Avengers of the Law" to guide both the restless demos and rudderless justice.[44]

In the fall of 1790, following the massacre of mutinous soldiers at Nancy, Marat denounced the vengeance of the aristocracy for being "barbarian" while hailing that of the people for being "terrifying."[45] A few months later he vowed that he would never soften his "call for the ax of vengeance to be brought down" on counterrevolutionaries.[46] And after the bloodletting of August 10, 1792, he urged the people to visit their vengeance on the suspects in the Abbaye prison.

But then the unenlightened turn of the prison massacres attested to the hazards of rhetorical hyperbole. To be sure, on September 22 Marat played to the crowd when he refuted the charge that it was "a crime to incite the people to take revenge on traitors" and claimed that by listening to him the people had taken steps "to save the nation" and put power beyond the reach of conspirators.[47] But a few weeks later, in October, Marat repeatedly deplored the "disastrous" massacres. He did not, however, disavow them, not least because political "rascals" were seizing upon them "to portray the Paris Commune as a horde of cannibals." It is noteworthy, nonetheless, that at this juncture Marat not only responded "to the instinctive reprobation of compassionate souls" but also became "troubled" to the point of opening himself to the "universal disquiet of a common humanity."[48]

Robespierre's position on violence and terror was not radically different from Marat's, except that at the outset he counseled restraint. In late December 1791 he urged "waiting for the crimes of tyrants to incite an enraged people to wreak their justified vengeance," which, to boot, would be "an expression of enlightenment."[49] Robespierre was confident that eventually an "elemental sentiment . . . would drive the common people to reclaim their dignity by avenging the gross injustices they had suffered in times past."[50]

Robespierre also deplored the excesses of the prison massacres for which the Girondins deftly fixed the full responsibility on him and Marat. Like Marat he did so in heated debate with anyone proposing to exploit them politically. Robespierre conceded that it was natural "to weep for the victims, including those among them who were guilty." But he also wanted France's citizens "to save some tears for [the victims of] other, nay greater calamities," particularly the countless millions who through the ages had suffered the torments of political and social oppression. As for the "pathetic descriptions of the misfortune of Madame de Lamballe and Count Montmorin," they were of one piece with the Brunswick Manifesto. Clearly, with their "avenging" temper, the champions of despotism had appropriated much of the mourning, determined to "defame the infant republic . . . and dishonor the Revolution" which dared to defy Europe.[51]

According to Louis Blanc, looking back, the "contagious frenzy" of the September massacres was reminiscent of the Sicilian Vespers of 1282, which had seen "8,000 Frenchmen strangled within two hours," and of the massacre of the Armagnacs in 1418, which had left the flagstone of Paris prisons "stained with blood." In the past as in the present, there was "an excessive frenzy fueled by an inordinate sense of peril and rage," though in 1792 there were two new elements:

"a fiery patriotic *élan* . . . [and] a philosophy freighted with the fanaticism needed to better counter another fanaticism." The result was that the different "centuries were reduced to wreaking vengeance on each other," a case in point being the hectoring cry, "Remember Saint Bartholomew's Day," which was said to have been hurled at refractory priests as they were being massacred.[52]

＊ ＊ ＊

The September massacres were the apogee of vengeful violence and terror from below. They were more an expression of fear and weakness than of confidence and strength. But then, unexpectedly, in late September 1792 the Revolution's fortunes seemed to take a favorable turn. The victory at Valmy was followed by a successful drive into Savoy and occupation of Nice. These auspicious military developments coincided with the inauguration of the Convention, the abolition of the monarchy, and the proclamation of the Republic. There was nothing to suggest that this upturn would call forth a resumption of terror, or that the chaotic terror from below would be supplemented or replaced by a systematic terror from above.

Of course, to lance the abscess of alleged treason and conspiracy in the prisons without either tightly quarantining the king or somehow removing him from the scene was to leave a potentially dangerous focus and center of resistance. During the first two or three years of revolutionary turmoil the dethronement of Louis XVI, let alone the abolition of kingship, had been all but unthinkable, France having become a constitutional monarchy in practice if not in theory and pretense. It is certainly telling that even after his treacherous flight to Varennes, the king resumed—or was "forced" to resume—his throne, albeit with additional checks on his authority. All along Louis XVI and his camarilla showed an uncanny and cunning staying power. Despite his removal following the massacre of August 10, Louis was not *hors de combat*. Until September 20 he continued to have considerable use and exchange value for politicians at home and diplomats abroad, and he never failed to seize and create promising opportunities for his cause. Besides, his confinement to forced residence in the Temple left his personal future, and that of the monarchy, in abeyance. The discovery in the Tuileries, on November 20, of Louis's strongbox containing incriminating correspondence with foreign courts and chancelleries confirmed the worst suspicions and brought the debate over king and kingship to a head. The call for regicide began to resonate.

Logically there were five options: continuing confinement; deportation and exile; unceremonious execution (in the manner of Tsar Nicholas II in 1918); legal trial; political trial. Realistically the time for unlimited imprisonment was passed, and neither banishment nor precipitate execution was under active consideration. As for a trial by a tribunal founded on law, in the conjuncture of events it was not really a live historical possibility. In effect, any trial was bound to be a political trial. On this score the Jacobins were by far the most open, not to say forthright.

As was to be expected, the "case" was brought before the National Convention, which constituted itself as a special court of justice: its members became at once prosecutors, jurors, and judges. Chrétien Guillaume de Lamoignon de Malesherbes took in hand the defense of Louis XVI. To be sure, few deputies were convinced or plainspoken royalists or constitutional monarchists. Even so, the Convention was not a Star Chamber. Many of its members were moderate republicans and scrupulous lawyers. Though the *Montagne* was not a negligible faction, it was in no position to overwhelm the house, not even by playing to the *enragés* in the galleries, the clubs, and the streets. If the arguments of Saint-Just and Robespierre carried the weight they did, it was largely because in addition to being reasoned and pointed, even if extreme, they struck home in the runaway crisis of confidence in Louis XVI and the monarchy, particularly in the capital.

How to explain, otherwise, the apparent sway or purchase of the political pleadings of the regicides? When Saint-Just intervened in the debate on November 13, he was 25 years old and relatively unknown. With some exaggeration Michelet attributes his instant aura to circumstances having called for "a wholly new man to wield the *glaive de justice*," or sword of justice: Saint-Just "set the tone for the whole trial" because of all the Montagnards, he was best suited to assume "the sinister role of personifying death and speaking on behalf of the people's vengeances."[53] Indeed, Saint-Just argued that a regular trial of Louis XVI was out of the question, since history had already found him guilty for his part in the events of August 10. Louis was neither citizen nor king. Like any ruler he did not rule innocently, and he had on his head the blood spilled at "the Bastille, Nancy, the Champ de

185

Mars, Tournai, and the Tuileries." According to Saint-Just, there being no legal basis for arraigning and sentencing Louis Capet, his trial was bound to be the political act of men taking the responsibility for founding a republic. Since a law court and a political assembly operated on radically different principles, in the event the Convention, in its judicial guise, acquitted him, it would cease to be viable. In sum, Saint-Just "saw no middle ground: this man must either rule or die."[54]

Saint-Just might have spoken to the winds, except that Robespierre, by then a vocal Montagnard tribune, echoed, indeed appropriated his principal arguments. He, too, contended that Louis was not a lawful king but a criminal tyrant who had "long since been judged" and dethroned by events, precluding any presumption of innocence.[55] Besides, the issue was not one of personal liability. Louis embodied the principle of divine right monarchy which, as an institution, had survived the abolition of the monarchy, and it was this principle which at the dawn of this epoch stood before the bar of history. Inevitably the trial would be political, not judicial: just as the king, in his person, was not the "accused," so the members of the Convention were not his "judges."[56]

But Robespierre, even more than Saint-Just, pressed the deputies to consider the political stakes, defiantly asking whether they were prepared to settle for "a revolution without a revolution."[57] It was as risky to allow the "dethroned king to rove around the Republic, or even to keep him in captivity" as it was to "absolve" him, thereby exposing the champions and soldiers of liberty "to the vengeance of despots and aristocrats."[58] Robespierre concluded, "regretfully," that "Louis XVI needed to die so that the *patrie* should be able to live."[59] Although he claimed not to "breathe personal vengeance," Robespierre called for retribution in the form of "the tyrant's death, which would serve to cement both liberty and civil peace." For such a judgment to "benefit the future" it would, however, have to "assume the solemnity of a public vengeance."[60] In this spirit, after urging that Louis be charged with "treason against the French nation and crimes against humanity," Robespierre specified two ways to implement this prescription: "Louis should suffer his punishment on the same square on which the martyrs of liberty had recently met their death [on August 10]; and a monument should be raised on the site of his execution to attest the people's righteous vengeance and admonish future generations to hold tyrants in abomination."[61]

The trial was, of course, a dramatic confrontation among the revolutionaries themselves, many of whom, including (or above all) the Girondins, stressed the drawbacks of pronouncing and executing the death sentence. Some of the moderates advocated continuing the king's confinement until the end of hostilities, at which time he should be exiled. One of them backed this proposal with the argument that the course of man's progress was paved with "moderation, humanity, and prudence" rather than with "grand executions, intense hatreds, and avenging passions," and that a "holocaust of human blood" was an unlikely fount of liberty. Another opposed the "monstrous" suggestion to kill the king for being "informed by vengeance rather than wisdom." Still another cautioned that "such an open act of vengeance would harm rather than help the French nation by giving Europe's despots the perfect pretext to traduce" the Revolution.[62] Ironically the Girondins, initially the foremost warmongers, made a special point of warning that to execute the king would be to inflame the "*ressentiment*, indignation, and horror . . . of all of Europe," thereby feeding the fires of "universal war." Besides, having decapitated "the man rather than the system, the King, dead in France, would be reborn among the émigrés in Koblenz."[63]

Abroad, the reaction was instant. On January 28, 1793, a week after the execution of Louis XVI, the Comte de Provence, speaking as regent, conjured all émigrés and Frenchmen to attest their "attachment to the religion of our fathers and to the sovereign we mourn by redoubling not only their devotion and loyalty to our young and hapless King [Louis XVII] but also their ardor to avenge the blood of his august father." In another proclamation the future Louis XVIII, in his own name and in the name of the Comte d'Artois, his younger brother (the future Charles X), spoke in identically the same key. In a third manifesto, addressed to the French people, the Comte de Provence called for "the reestablishment of the monarchy . . . ; the restoration of religion . . . ; the reinstatement of Frenchmen of all estates in their legitimate rights and possession; and the severe and exemplary punishment of all crimes."[64] Count Antoine François Claude Ferrand, one of his advisors, urged that this retribution run to "44,000 executions, or one in each commune."[65] On June 17,

1793, at the Sacred College, Pius VI had no doubt that the "innocent blood of Louis XVI would rise to heaven . . . and provoke a divine fury," reminding the people of France "that God, the just avenger of crimes, had often inflicted terrifying punishments for altogether lesser transgressions."[66]

Though without a basis in law, the indictment, verdict, and sentence had considerable legitimacy, as did the execution. There was widespread agreement about the king's culpability, even if the bill of indictment remained vague. The Convention was intensely divided; just over half of its members voted for the death penalty, the other half for various lesser punishments. The Girondins' proposal to submit the matter to a popular referendum was defeated by a majority of 137, and so was the call for a stay of execution, by a majority of 70.

The trial, including the execution, was political in every sense of that term.[67] The regicide was intended to bring down a theologically sacralized king and political order. To this end Louis XVI became the sacrificial victim in an improvised rite of passage from the *ancien régime* to a new political and social order. His final stately and public calvary on the Place de la Révolution, witnessed by some 20,000 people, proved to be the founding act for an untried authority system and civil society whose secular liturgy, formulary, and icons were just then being invented and constructed, as well as contested. The solemn killing of the thaumaturgic king, as an act of founding violence, rallied true believers at the same time that it left a legacy of division among the revolutionaries and a reservoir of fear among enemies and neutrals. This irreversible and defining act could only intensify the friend-enemy polarization inherent to the escalating violence and vengeance attending the confrontation of revolution and counterrevolution at home and in Europe.

Although neither Michelet nor Quinet questioned the need to depose and punish Louis XVI and abolish the monarchy, both disapproved of the death sentence and its instant execution. They were above all discomforted by the archaic and magical aspects of the Jacobins' rush to regicide. For them this regicide was a major step toward the Great Terror and provided the counterrevolution with a "royalist myth of the martyred king" who suffered, in Christ-like fashion, for the "redemption" of his nation and people. Curiously, Michelet and Quinet were relatively deaf to the "logic" of the avenging violence inherent to the foundation of a radically new regime whose profane polity and politics turned on the desacralization of king and monarchy.

✳ ✳ ✳

Within weeks after the king's execution on January 21, 1793, the general situation became as tense and perilous as in August–September 1792. The fledgling French Republic declared war on Great Britain and Holland on February 1, and on Spain five weeks later. An emergency levy of 300,000 men for the overstretched French army precipitated antirevolutionary resistance far and wide, but especially in the Vendée, at the same time that the growing war effort intensified social unrest among the hawkish *enragés* in Paris. On March 18 General Dumouriez, the victor of Valmy and Jemappes, was defeated at Neerwinden and evacuated Belgium. Not unlike six months earlier, following the fall of Longwy and Verdun, military confidence was shaken. Once again, the revolutionaries took fright and searched for traitors. In turn, anti- and counterrevolutionaries took heart. As if to head off and defuse an avenging fury reminiscent of the prison massacres, there was renewed pressure for the prompt establishment of a supreme revolutionary tribunal.

This time the initiative came from the Jacobin clubs. By early March 1793 there was a broad consensus among Montagnards and Communards that with the nation strained by war and patriots rushing to the front, the Convention should set up, in the words of Jean Bon Saint-André, "a special tribunal to secure the home front by punishing traitors, conspirators, and agitators."[68] As at the time of the creation of the now dormant tribunal of August 17, Robespierre endorsed this call for emergency justice, and once again, in the Convention, the Girondins opposed instituting what they feared might turn into "an inquisition infinitely worse than that of Venice."[69]

The Convention was still irresolute when in the evening of March 10 Danton stepped forward to openly "assume the historical responsibility for the creation of this terrifying but necessary tribunal." Taking issue with the Girondins' caution, he insisted that Dumouriez's military reverses called for bold steps, to begin with "judicial measures to punish counterrevolutionaries." Danton claimed that it was in the interest of the counterrevolutionaries "that a new-fledged judicial

189

tribunal speaking the law take the place of the ascendant popular tribunal speaking the people's vengeance." Indeed, he told the members of the Convention that "all of humanity was looking to them to save the enemies of liberty from the jaws of popular vengeance."[70]

At the words "popular vengeance," a voice cried out the word "September," a caustic interjection Danton could not ignore. But before joining issue, he conceded "that nothing was more difficult than to define a political crime." In the present crisis, which called for "great efforts and terrible measures," he saw "no middle ground between an ordinary law court and a revolutionary tribunal." Having staked out an extreme and defiant position, and "haunted by the memory of September," Danton addressed his captious critic: "since a member of this chamber dared call back the bloody days which every good citizen deplores," he felt compelled to say that "had a tribunal been in place last fall the people, who are often maliciously blamed for them, certainly would not have stained themselves with blood." Claiming, rather speciously, that in September it had been "humanly impossible to hold back the surge of national vengeance," Danton exhorted "the members of the National Convention to learn from the mistakes of their predecessors . . . in the Legislative Assembly." Specifically, he summoned them "to be terrifying themselves in order to spare the people from having to assume this awesome responsibility." To this end the Convention should "charter a tribunal which, under the circumstances, might not be the best, but neither would it be the worst."[71] Robespierre and Marat were at one with Danton in demanding decisive measures which would at once "put in fear the counterrevolutionaries and save the people from the temptation of joining in wild murder."[72]

On March 10, 1793, the Convention voted to establish the Extraordinary Criminal Tribunal—soon known as the Revolutionary Tribunal.[73] It fixed the methods for the selection of the court's five judges and twelve jurors, and spelled out its operating principles and procedures. Paradoxically, "the momentary triumvirate" of Marat, Robespierre, and Danton played a key role in "formulating the dualistic tenet of enforcement terror and revolutionary legality" as a prophylaxis to blunt and deflect popular vengeance on the order of the September massacres.[74]

190

There was no foreseeing the calamitous course this tribunal would take, along with a panoply of emergency measures and institutions. Certainly the rush of circumstances, intensified by pressure from the streets, thwarted the efforts of the newly appointed judges to fit the tribunal with checks against its circumstantial defects. In particular, the exigencies of war impeded circumspection. Ironically, the war was being urged on by those very political forces which were most apprehensive about the de-democratization of the fledgling regime. Between Dumouriez's first defeat at Neerwinden on March 18 and his defection to the enemy in early April, the Convention instituted a surveillance system, established the Committee of Public Safety, and proscribed the émigrés. Meanwhile the strains of war played havoc with food prices and supplies. To rein in social unrest, the government moved to fix the value of the *assignat* and to enforce the *maximum*. Simultaneously, it was confronted with the federalist rebellion of the major southern cities and the spread of the anti-revolution in the Vendée. This seamless crisis could not help but exacerbate the face-down between the Jacobins, pressed by the sansculottes and *enragés*, and the Girondins, who felt the mailed fist starting with the Parisian *journées* of May 31 to June 2. There seemed no escaping the emergence and hardening of what Lazare Carnot called a "*dictature de détresse*," or emergency dictatorship, driven by the closely entwined failing foreign war and expanding civil conflict.[75]

✳ ✳ ✳

Had it not been for this rising storm, the assassination of Marat, on July 13, 1793, the eve of the fourth anniversary of the fall of the Bastille, most likely would have been an isolated and harmless bolt of political lightning. But with the turbulent weather, Marie-Anne-Charlotte de Corday d'Armont's fatal deed touched off a political firestorm. In death even more than in life, Marat lent himself to being at once apotheosized and demonized—as the incarnation of good or evil, light or darkness, virtue or vice, purity or impurity.

Disenchanted with the Revolution, Charlotte Corday claimed that by killing Marat she meant to "avenge untold innocent victims" as well as "save thousands of lives . . . and prevent many other disasters." When the judges, before sentencing her to death, asked whether she "thought she had slain all the Marats," she replied that with "this one dead, all the others will be put in fear."[76]

Almost instantly Corday was both excoriated and extolled as the arch-avenger. One of the revolutionary papers reported that on hearing of Marat's assassination, several women exclaimed that death by guillotine would be "too mild for such a heinous crime" and vowed to "cut up and devour the scoundrel who had deprived the people of their best friend."[77] After noting in *Père Duchesne* that to curse Corday was to "fire the people's vengeance," Hébert likewise insisted that to "fit the crime" the punishment would have to be "more terrible and degrading than death by guillotine."[78] As for Charlotte Corday, on being turned over to the Abbaye prison, she apparently feared "that the people would tear her limb from limb." She did not breathe easier until she thought she stood fair to be "beheaded by the guillotine, which would be a gentle death."[79]

There was, indeed, considerable apprehension that an overwrought crowd would once again invest the Abbaye prison, this time to touch off an uncontrollable massacre with the vindictive slaying of Marat's assassin. At the Convention several deputies, worried that a popular "clamor for vengeance" would set off "a terrible explosion," urged citizens to remain both calm and vigilant at the same time that they reassured them that they "would be avenged." Likewise François Hanriot, the hard-line commander of the capital's national guard, simultaneously approved the cry for vengeance and stressed that "the best way to keep in check the aristocracy was to trust and support our courts of law." Presently even the firebrand Hébert sought to calm the atmosphere, insisting that "the day of vengeance was not yet at hand" partly because Paris still needed to persuade the provinces that the capital was not "a city of cannibals."[80]

In the meantime, at the main Jacobin club there was a move to enshrine Marat, the martyr of liberty, in the Pantheon. But Robespierre objected, contending that by giving people a false sense of "redress," such a spectacular homage would assuage their "thirst for vengeance." On July 15 a delegation of the Society of the Men of August 10 came to the Convention to "demand that Marat be avenged" rather than given "the honors of the Pantheon," not least because he was, in any case, assured of a "permanent Pantheon in everyone's heart."[81]

By this time several bards of the Revolution were entrusted with planning a solemn funeral rite for Marat. It stands to reason that the iconoclastic intelligentsia, including the unbound artists of the new order, should have turned to celebrating and commemorating the Revolution's major events and heroic leaders or martyrs. In this way they hoped to challenge and replace the resplendent public ceremonials of the *ancien régime*. Jacques-Louis David is emblematic of these self-conscious activist illuminati who came forward to assist in laying the foundations for a future full of promise. An early partisan of reform, he was radicalized by the force of circumstance. With time he became a fervent champion of the nascent republic and Jacobin patriotism. David was elected one of the capital's deputies in the National Convention and eventually served on its Committee of General Security. He had a sympathetic understanding for Robespierre and Marat, with whom he consorted off and on.

David emerged, of course, as not only the peerless painter-artist of the Revolution but also its master *metteur en scène*. Characteristically he idealized and ideologized one of the Revolution's grand founding events in *The Oath of the Tennis Court*, his first and arguably one of his most compelling historical paintings, started in mid-1790. No less exemplary, David was the guiding spirit of the ceremonial transfer of Voltaire's ashes to the Pantheon in June 1791. This sober and grandiose funeral procession, partly mimetic of yesterday's religious prototype and featuring Greco-Roman imagery, was staged to symbolize and herald "the victory of reason over superstition, philosophy over theology, justice over tyranny, tolerance over fanaticism." David was responsible for the overall "organization" and "decoration" of this and several later public rites, while François Gossec and Marie-Joseph Chénier provided, respectively, the music and lyrics.[82]

David does not seem to have had a hand in conceiving and staging the calvary of Louis XVI—procession, execution, burial—on January 21, 1793, which was designed to consummate the king's profanation as a symbol of monarchy while diligently precluding his living on as a martyr. Indeed, David's calling and vision was to construct, represent, and memorialize heroes, not anti-heroes; martyrs, not demons. Nowhere was his revolutionary commitment more intensely tested and expressed than in his orchestration of the funeral of Jean-Paul Marat and his martyr painting of this uncommon revolutionary. A few months earlier David had experimented with new techniques of funeral pageantry and iconography in rendering honor to Michel Lepeletier de Saint-Fargeau. As deputy from Yonne, this aristocrat had voted the death penalty for Louis XVI. In revenge for this apostasy, Lepeletier was mortally stabbed by a former royal bodyguard. David arranged for his semi-nude corpse, with its fatal wound unhidden, to lie in state on the Place Vendôme preceding a memorial service on the floor of the Convention. Shortly thereafter David captured the atmosphere and message of the ceremony in his painted exaltation of Lepeletier. In every respect, Lepeletier's apotheosis prefigured Marat's.[83]

Knowing Marat personally, David was all the more pained by his assassination and disposed to give his all to assure that Marat be given proper homage. Under his direction, by the evening of July 15 Marat's embalmed body lay in state in the erstwhile church of the Cordelier monastery, the meeting place of the Jacobin club bearing that name.[84] The corps rested on a bier "lined with flowers and draped with the tricolor." His head graced with an oak crown, Marat's body was wrapped in a white sheet, giving bold relief to his red chest wound, which was in plain view. Two stones, presumably relics from the Bastille, were set at the base and front of the bier, carved with the rousing epitaph: "Marat, *L'Ami du peuple*, friend of the people, assassinated by the enemies of the people. Enemies of the people, temper your glee, for he will have his avengers."[85] Dignified by the participation of the full body of the Convention, the funeral procession of July 16, likewise designed by David, was of a piece with the mood and purpose of this *mise en scène*. Marat's body, with its prominently displayed stigma "pointing up the wound inflicted on the Republic," focused the outcry against the Revolution's "ubiquitous" domestic and foreign enemies at the same time that it provided an eloquent human relic on which to swear vengeance. Even if unintentionally, to instrumentalize the *corps meurtri* was to "generate emotions, designate enemies, feed vengeance, and exalt the martyr."[86] The rite exorcised uncertainty and fear as much as it fired revolutionary zeal. In this way, the commemoration of the popular idol enabled the revolutionary elites to combine their spoken discourse with a language of images and gestures accessible to the lower orders who were remote from the high culture of oratory and letters.

This was the atmosphere in which David turned to paying pictorial homage to Marat as he had to Lepeletier. Indeed, he invested this second memorial portrait with the same rhetoric as the first. David executed the two paintings while intensely engaged in revolutionary politics on the Jacobin side. In both silent poems or painted sculptures "death and violence are . . . the spiritual center," along with selfless "suffering" and unrequited "pity."[87] David exhibited the two paintings in his atelier until November 1793, when the Convention asked that they be hung on both sides of its presidential chair (which he himself eventually occupied briefly in January 1794): to the left Lepeletier, next to a tablet with the Constitution of 1793; to the right Marat, next to a tablet with the Declaration of the Rights of Man and the Citizen.[88] Two months earlier, when presenting *The Death of Marat*—probably his "masterwork" and possibly the "greatest political painting of all time"[89]—to the Convention, David had told his fellow deputies that he had answered the people's call to once again "take up [his] brush" and "avenge our friend, avenge Marat."[90] He offered this "homage of his brush, . . . Marat's livid and bloody features" serving to recall "his virtues . . . to [p]osterity, which will avenge him."[91]

* * *

The purpose of Marat's instant apotheosis was less "to establish a cult" than to forge a "rallying cry" to divert popular rage into government channels.[92] There is a transparent connection between, on the one hand, the intensification of the push for vengeance by the spontaneous and calculated cathexis on Marat and, on the other, the clamor for an official policy of terror. Of course, the emergency regime kept hardening in the face of intractable domestic and foreign difficulties as well as under the pressure of true believers and militants. In July and August 1793 the antirevolution continued to spread in the Vendée and Lyons was swinging out of control. Although republican forces reclaimed Marseilles on August 25, British and Spanish troops entered Toulon with the help of a local fifth column on August 27–28. In the meantime, on August 1 Valenciennes had fallen to the Austrians. The adoption, on July 26, of capital punishment for hoarding was a sign that the economic and financial situation was still critical.

Although the Jacobins and sansculottes were equally disposed not only to exaggerate the scale and intensity of the emergency but also to blame it on traitors and conspirators, they differed in their prescriptions for dealing with it. The Jacobins, swearing by would-be representative institutions, proposed to give first priority to tightening political controls from above and the center; the sansculottes, standing on direct democracy, advocated pressing ahead with the radicalization of the Revolution from below. But at this crucial juncture both favored an emergency dictatorship, including a war economy. In any case, it is just as important not to overestimate the seriousness of this sectarian in-fighting as it is not to underestimate the gravity and urgency of the situation confronting a precarious and contested provisional government. Notwithstanding the adoption of the Constitution of June 24, 1793, the legitimacy of the infant revolutionary regime remained frail.

These were the defining circumstances for the partisan debates and struggles over tomorrow's terror. Starting in early August, two converts from the priesthood to sansculottism were among the first to urge that terror be forged into an instrument of revolutionary policy. Jacques Roux, a self-appointed spokesman for the *enragés*, proposed to have the terror supported and energized by a *levée en masse*. Jean-Baptiste Royer, from Chalon-sur-Saône, argued along similar lines and in the second half of August became a leading advocate for a terror "in the context of a *levée en masse*."[93] On August 30, at the Jacobin club, Royer invoked Marat's revolutionary precept and fate to legitimate his proposal to "*placer la terreur à l'ordre du jour*," as the "only way to arouse the people and force them to save themselves."[94] In the meantime, on August 23, the Convention had decreed the *levée en masse*.

All this time Robespierre and Danton, along with other leaders of the Mountain, sought to turn the incipient terror inward at the same time that they backed the *levée en masse* in support of the war effort along and beyond France's uncertain frontiers. On August 2 Robespierre, by now a member of the Committee of Public Safety, told the Convention that "the terrifyingly swift sword of the law should hang over the heads of all conspirators, striking terror in the hearts of their accomplices and of all enemies of the *patrie*." Speaking in this same vein, Danton once again commended "the sword of the law" as the best antidote to "popular vengeance," insisting that for want of it the people would "take the law into their own hands." Pierre-Marie-Augustin Guyomar, another Montagnard deputy, urged that timely measures be taken "to prevent the explosion of the sad but necessary vengeance of a people driven to despair."[95] On September 5, following another revolutionary *journée* in Paris, Bertrand Barère, for the Committee of Public Safety, moved a motion in the Convention to "*placer la terreur à l'ordre du jour*," which was passed overwhelmingly. Barère credited the Paris Commune with having coined this "splendid phrase" and promised that the new policy would make it possible to "instantly eliminate all royalists and moderates along with the whole counterrevolutionary pack." He stressed, however, that this repressive violence would be exercised by "special tribunals, not illegal vengeance." Indeed, terror and revolutionary justice increasingly became inseparable. Speaking at the Paris Commune on September 15, Hébert agreed that "the day of vengeance was now at hand," adding that "mercy" was a thing of the past. With the terror high on the agenda, not only "outright aristocrats will be arrested, but so will those failing to actively support liberty."[96] Two days later, on September 17, the Convention adopted the Law of Suspects.

✳ ✳ ✳

Whereas the Jacobins exploited the stirrings for vengeance mainly to serve their struggle against domestic enemies, the Girondins did so primarily with an eye to the conflict with the foreign powers. In October 1791, in one of his first speeches advocating war, Brissot, leader of the Girondins, had warned Europe's crowned heads that although "the vengeance of a free people takes time to build up, once it does explode it will be fierce."[97] He admonished them that their continuing support of the émigrés could not help but provoke "the vengeance of a free people." In turn, Brissot told his countrymen, France "would become fair game for Europe's contemptible tyrants unless it visited its timely vengeance on them."[98] Shortly before the formation of the Girondin ministry on March 15, 1792, he criticized Jean-Marie Antoine Delessard, the foreign minister, for practicing a diplomacy of appeasement which "cooled the ardor of a French nation burning to avenge the insults being hurled from abroad."[99] The Legislative Assembly declared war on Austria on April 20. While the French armies suffered their first reverses in the Low Countries, on April 25, in Strasbourg, Claude Rouget de Lisle wrote the *Chant de Guerre pour l'Armée du Rhin*, soon known as *la Marseillaise;* its final stanza thundered forth "*Amour sacré de la patrie conduis, soutiens nos bras vengeurs.*"[100] Apparently the volunteer corps (*les fédérés*) from Marseilles sang what emerged as the Revolution's emblematic anthem with ever more raging tempos and accents at Valmy and around the Tuileries on August 10.

At the same time, many soldiers of the Republic took to wearing a talisman engraved with the motto "*le patriotisme vengé,*" and in the Convention Pierre Joseph Cambon read out a declaration promising tomorrow's liberated peoples that France would help them "drive out their tyrants and . . . protect them from their vengeance, subversion, and return."[101] But, of course, there were periodic setbacks, as in the summer and fall of 1793. On October 11, during the difficult battle of Flanders, the Committee of Public Safety issued a proclamation—signed by Hérault de Séchelles, Collot d'Herbois, Billaud-Varenne, Barère, Saint-Just, Robespierre—hailing the recapture of Lyons, where "traitors and rebels were being cut to pieces," and exhorting France's soldiers "to exterminate the lackeys of tyrants" who should not be spared "your righteous vengeance." That very day the Imperial forces broke through the French lines at Wissembourg and threatened Alsace-Lorraine. The Committee sent Saint-Just and François-Joseph Lebas to the scene to shore up the morale of the soldiers of the Army of the Rhine. On October 24, from Strasbourg, these proconsuls proclaimed that they had brought them not only "the sword" with which to strike down all "traitors and even trimmers among them" but also the wherewithal to "avenge you and to secure victory."[102]

✹ ✹ ✹

In the spring of 1793, at the same time that the provisional government faced increasing military difficulties along France's borders, it was confronted with the rising defiance of the major cities of the Midi and of the villages and towns of the Vendée in the west. Eventually this challenge to central authority turned into all-out rebellion, giving rise to civil war fraught with the rhetoric and practice of vengeance—on both sides.

The federalist insurgence was essentially urban.[103] Notwithstanding its indigenous reasons, in essence federalism was a struggle for control of local government which mirrored a similar struggle in the capital. In fact, the struggles at the center and in the periphery were symbiotically linked, with the chief actors in all quarters egregiously misperceiving and misrepresenting each other's intentions. On June 2, 1793, with some 80,000 people in the streets, the Paris Commune, in league with the Montagnards, pressured the Convention to take a hard line: twenty-two deputies, including two ministers, were arrested to be tried by the revolutionary tribunal for supporting what was construed and portrayed as a separatist undertaking with links to the émigrés and foreign powers. In the spring of 1793, in Lyons, Marseilles, Bordeaux, and Toulon moderates stood against the emergency measures adopted by the faraway Convention, while their counterparts in Paris remained under fire for continuing to contest the *dictature de détresse*. Presently, whereas the anti-Jacobins got the upper hand in the southern cities, they were decisively defeated in the capital, where they were soon reviled as Girondins.

The southern moderates, or future federalists, seized on the issue of the *maximum* and its latent threat to private property to incite the rising fear of ultra-Jacobinism, which was driven by local sansculottes hearkening to Paris. With time, and in keeping with the polarizing logic of civil war, they were supported by outright reactionaries and counterrevolutionaries. In turn, these collaborations allowed the radicals in Paris to characterize the federalists as sworn to not only the decentralization or breakup of France but also the royalist-directed counterrevolution for a full-blown restoration in league with the European courts.

It is important to note that support for the struggle of the moderates against radicals near and far was quickened by mounting economic stress, disenchantment with the Revolution, and consternation about the excesses of zealous revolutionaries, both indigenous and on mission from Paris. Even so, the restiveness of the southern cities escalated into open revolt mainly because the central government lacked adequate military force and administrative-legal leverage to contain it, leaving the federalists the beneficiaries of the collapse of sovereignty. If the center nevertheless eventually won out, it was largely because the rebel cities, besides going their separate ways, failed to raise credible military forces and rally the surrounding countryside.

Throughout the perilous summer of 1793, with the regime hardening in the face of rising resistances at home and threats from abroad, the Committee of Public Safety fastened on Lyons, France's second city and manufacturing center, as the principal bastion and nerve center of the counterrevolution in the Midi. Not that the leaders in Paris made light of the sedition of Marseilles, Bordeaux, and Toulon, but just then they considered the situation of these port cities to be less threatening and urgent.

Lyons was very much at war with itself before it rose up against Paris.[104] Pressed by their own *enragés*, the local Jacobins called for the city's Girondin governors to establish an emergency regime to deal with, above all, the social question. Joseph Chalier, the most extreme of the radical patriots, came to symbolize and embody this challenge. Like Marat, he inspired either blind devotion or fierce hatred. Both were tribunes of and for the people, with a strong belief in the value of revolutionary violence and vengeance. Of the two, Chalier was less theoretical, coherent, and removed. Whereas Marat was "the last [emblem] of the old Revolution . . . [and] the man of civil war," Chalier was the "first [emblem] of the new Revolution . . . [and], in Lyons, the man of the *guerre sociale*."[105]

In November 1792 the Jacobins managed to take control of the local government, with Chalier figuring as their chief. Modeling their rule after Paris, they tried but failed to arrest the deterioration of economic and social conditions. Partly out of frustration, and incensed by the systematically obstructive behavior of the city's old ruling class, by early 1793 Chalier resorted to increasingly intemperate rhetoric. He vowed that in order to achieve "liberty and equality, as well as security for person and property," he was prepared to "exterminate all that goes by the name of aristocrat, *feuillant*, moderate, egoist, royalist, agitator, hoarder, usurer, and the priestly caste." Though Chalier praised "Jesus Christ for being a good man . . . preaching mercy and moderation," he professed that his own "cry was for vengeance."[106]

On May 29 the anti-Jacobins seized power back again. Within twenty-four hours Chalier was "arrested, vilified, tied up, beaten, and thrown into Lyons' darkest dungeon" pending trial.[107] Before being sentenced to death without appeal, he caustically told the members of the summary court that he expected "justice and leniency," since they were "judges, [not executioners], and as such free of rancor, hatred, and vengeance."[108] While his trial for inflammatory speech was swift, his execution on July 16 was eerie. By reason of the guillotine never having been used in Lyons, the blade fell down three times without fully severing Chalier's head. After finally detaching it with a knife, the executioner reached to hold the head up to the crowd, but "Chalier being bald, he had to grab it by one of his ears." The ascendant moderates were cemented by their expiatory victim, their desire for vengeance momentarily satisfied. In turn, the defeated radicals had their martyr, who cried out to be avenged. In the meantime Lyons had consummated its break with the central dictatorship, a special commission having decided to disregard its decrees henceforth.[109]

It took the Committee of Public Safety three months to dispatch sufficient troops to face down Lyons. After a short siege, the rebel city was brought under control on October 9. There was surprisingly little resistance. General Kellermann having balked at using repressive violence, General Dubois-Crancé was in command. A confirmed Dantonist, he readily collaborated with the representatives on mission whom the central authorities sent forth to direct the city's pacification. The stage was set for a re-revenge. As his troops moved in, Dubois-Crancé issued a fiery proclamation, in a tenor reminiscent of the Brunswick Manifesto, vowing that Lyons was about to be "destroyed" for its transgression. In this same spirit, on October 12 the Convention changed the name of France's second city to *Ville-Affranchie* and ordered that following the city's annihilation a monitory memorial column be erected amid its ruins, with the inscription "Lyons waged war against liberty; Lyons has ceased to exist."[110] Two days later, at the Jacobin club, Robespierre held that Lyons' traitors needed to be mercilessly "unmasked and executed" with an eye to "avenging the memory of their innocent victims."

Paradoxically, Aristide Couthon, member of the Committee of Public Safety and proconsul in charge of political operations, including the *épuration*, was not an all-out avenger.[111] In no time he realized that the local Jacobins who had suffered under the federalist reign were driven by an avenging rage exceeding even that of the government and *enragés* in Paris. Indeed, the soldiers of the liberating army, who were not native to the region, "were less terrifying" than the local leaders of "[punitive] raids, who knew whom to blame and single out for reprisal."[112] To be sure, Couthon set in motion the arrest of thousands of suspects, the establishment of emergency tribunals, and the demolition of the houses of the well-to-do. Even so, Paris recalled him for being too lenient at a time when he himself, for his own reasons, asked to be relieved. On November 4 he was replaced by Collot d'Herbois, another member of the Committee, and Joseph Fouché, a representative on mission in the Nièvre, who arrived a few days later. Both men were breathing vengeance. They urged the tribunals to quicken their pace. When the prisons became overcrowded or the guillotine glutted, they ordered mass executions. In early December, in the plain of Brotteaux, between 350 and 400 "political" prisoners were put to death by grapeshot and musket fire, and then buried in mass graves that had been dug in advance. By the following April "almost two thousand persons had been put to death in Lyons."[113]

To set the atmosphere and signal their ruthlessness, on taking charge Collot d'Herbois and Fouché conspicuously participated in a carefully staged glorification of Chalier.[114] The night following Chalier's execution, several men went to the cemetery to dig up his remains and make a plaster cast of his mangled head to serve as both relic and proof of fealty. Later that same night a woman votary and her son even went one step further: they took the mutilated head home in order to make an exact cast. Replicas of Chalier's head began to figure in public processions and ceremonies beginning with the apotheosis of Chalier on Sunday, November 10. On the eve of this celebration Dorfeuille, the president of the new people's court, pronounced a commemorative oration on the Place des Terreaux: he castigated Lyons as a "latter-day Sodom" and assured the new-born martyr that "we will avenge you . . . and cleanse [your] hallowed soul" with the "blood of the scoundrels."

Starting at daybreak of the day after, the cortège set out from the Place Bellecour and moved along the banks of the Saône in the direction of the Place des Terreaux. A "gigantic statue carrying a large axe of the law on its half-naked shoulders" was in the lead. There followed "a group of *sans-culottes* armed with pikes and wearing Phrygian caps, as well as a bevy of young women dressed in white and crowned with flowers." The focal point of the procession was a shrine supposed to contain Chalier's ashes and topped by his bust, carried by Jacobins from Paris. All this time, "twenty thurifers burning incense" circled around this striking ensemble. Next came a "corps of musicians and singers" just ahead of "an ass wearing a miter, mantled by a bishop's vestment, with a chalice around its neck and a missal attached to its tail." The procession was closed by a mock *muscadin* "dragging a flag of fleur-de-lys through the mud."

Collot d'Herbois and Fouché were the principal speakers at the closing ceremony in front of city hall on the Place des Terreaux, where the funeral urn, very like a relic, was displayed on a new-model, profane altar. In the name of a "prostrate nation" Collot d'Herbois asked God to forgive the slaying of "this most virtuous of men . . . [whose] suffering he swore to avenge." In like manner, Fouché pledged to "avenge Chalier's torment, using the blood of aristocrats as incense." As an iconoclastic finale, the ass drank out of the chalice, the missal was burned, and the urn was taken to the nearby church of Saint-Nizier, to rest on the altar. Meanwhile a popular song, on the air of the *Marseillaise*, vowed to "avenge the honor and virtue" of Chalier, the "greatest of all genuine sans-culottes," by "annihilating infamous Lyons."[115] That same evening Collot d'Herbois and Fouché wrote to the Convention that at Chalier's stately apotheosis the cry for "'vengeance!' repeatedly interrupted the silence of grief," and they assured their colleagues in Paris that they would heed this call.[116]

Though less widely known than Marat's martyrdom, Chalier's did reach beyond the Midi. In December 1793 a self-appointed delegation of incensed citizens of *Ville-Affranchie* traveled to Paris to appeal to the Convention and the Committee of Public Safety to put a stop to the fusillades and rein in the vindictive *épuration*. As soon as he heard about this subterfuge, Collot d'Herbois rushed to the capital to defend his policies and counter his critics. He considered it useful to take with him a cast of Chalier's head as proof of his revolutionary *bona fides*. Shortly after his arrival, on December 21, he took the lead in a cortège of true believers who carried the relic from the Bastille to the Convention in an abortive effort to claim a place for Chalier in the Pantheon. Presently Collot d'Herbois rose to justify his actions for being in line with his original instructions drafted at a time when all deputies "thirsted for vengeance to be visited on Lyons' infamous conspirators."[117]

All told, during the six months following the recapture of the southern capital which, according to Dubois-Crancé, "claimed 1,500 rebel lives," the various nonmilitary emergency tribunals pronounced and enforced about 2,000 death sentences, or more than 10 percent of all official executions during the Great Terror. The repression in Lyons was part of a nationwide system of legal revolutionary terror which, although it superseded yesterday's spontaneous and wild vengefulness, was penetrated by a distinctly punitive and vengeful spirit. Even if, after the fact, the Committee of Public Safety and the Convention sought to distance themselves from the rage of retributive justice, almost from the start they had fired it with their incendiary rhetorical and symbolic ferocity: Lyons to be destroyed, to be re-named, to be mortified. Admittedly, much of this discourse was "full of sound and fury," the bark being louder than the bite: the city "was not laid waste, . . . not all culprits perished or were executed, . . . and relatively few houses were demolished." Still, under the circumstances the official declamations turned out to have been more than empty rhetoric. Besides, along with the vindictive repression, they left a leg-acy of divisive acrimony which seeded the soil for the intensely aveng-ing White Terror after Thermidor.[118]

Quinet emphasized, as mentioned earlier, that since the punishment was inflicted *after* the Republic's soldiers were in full control of Lyons, it was cruelly retributive, and also gratuitous.[119] But mindful of Quin-et's precept to pay close attention to chronology, it is well to recall that so far the Republic had merely won a battle, not the war: the other southern cities and the Vendée remained to be reduced and pacified, and the war with the First Coalition was as yet very much in the balance. As a matter of course the officers and political emissaries of the liberating army were under orders to seize weapons and ammu-nition, raise manpower, and organize war production for the *armée des Alpes*, which promptly moved south.

The *armée d'Italie* reclaimed Marseilles on October 13, its internal war and rebellion having been similar but much less fierce than those of Lyons.[120] In their liberating proclamation Barras and Fréron, the people's representatives, characterized the republican army's "holy mission" to be to "save Marseilles and raze Toulon," as part of a drive to eliminate "moderation and royalism."[121] In their report on the de-liverance of France's first commercial port, they told Paris that 13,000 young men from the Var were on their way to Toulon. Although the proconsuls changed the name of Marseilles to *Ville-Sans-Nom* (City Without Name), the Committee of Public Safety soon nullified this rechristening in a gesture of tactical appeasement. To justify this quick reversal, the Committee claimed that "timeless justice" demanded not only that outrages "against the nation ... and patriotism be avenged," but also that "patriots who had refused to participate in these crimes be spared punishment and infamy."[122]

Bordeaux was retaken on October 21 by about 1,600 men with minimal casualties on either side, thus dramatizing the federalists' military impotence. In the capital of the Gironde, which many Jacobins also perceived as a nerve center of the far-flung urban revolt, the severity of the retribution was somewhere between that of Lyons and Marseilles: of some 900 persons arrested throughout the department, some 300, or one-third, were sentenced to death and executed.[123] But again, the proconsuls assured Paris that they had armed three battalions and were sending "1,500 rifles to Toulouse for the army assigned to march against Toulon."[124]

Since the British had come ashore in late August in support of the rebellion in Toulon, the defection of this strategic port was held up as irrefutable proof of the interpenetration of internal and external counterrevolution. In any case, after a long siege Toulon's recapture on December 19, 1793 was hailed as on a par with the recapture of Lyons two months earlier: Toulon was to be struck off the map and its name changed to *Port-la-Montagne* (Port of the Mountain).[125] About 300 counterrevolutionaries and suspects were executed during the first twenty-four hours and another 800 to 900 thereafter. In Toulon, as in Lyons, a popular song had the "terrifying" refrain: "Vengeance, Citizens, vengeance! Let us take to arms."[126]

※ ※ ※

Along with the federalist defiance and serious military setbacks on the frontiers, the Jacobin authorities also had to confront the revolt of the Vendée, whose military phase—the *Vendée militaire*—ran from March through December 1793. Although the civil war in the Vendée is discussed in detail in a separate chapter,[127] it calls for attention here by virtue of the prominence of the avenging Furies in what was the most taxing domestic challenge to the revolutionary regime in Paris.

Whereas the rebellion of the southern cities, especially Lyons, brought out in bold relief the resistance of urban France, the insurrection in the Vendée dramatized that of rural France. As Quinet saw it, for most of 1793 Paris faced two radically different types of insurgency: "the revolt of Lyons, Marseilles, and Toulon, which was purely political, and that of the Vendée, which was religious." In the west, unlike in the southern cities, the civil war was "a war of religion," with "two fanaticisms set against each other."[128]

Of course, the Vendean imbroglio had no such explosive charge at the outset. It began as a territorial, popular, and spontaneous anti-revolution rooted in latent suspicion of the encroaching distant center, nearby city, and ubiquitous modernity. Between 1789 and 1792 this suspicion was rekindled by a string of intrusive anticlerical, fiscal, and economic measures, and it was brought to a boil in March 1793, by the conscription of local youths for military service far from home, along France's distant frontiers. Presently, around March 20 near Chantonnay, the defeat of General Marcé's regular military corps by a small horde of primitive rebels laid bare the atrophy of the center's sovereign reach. This unexpected military outcome, egregiously misperceived by both sides in line with their respective worldviews, became a powerful catalyst for a friend-enemy dissociation. In sum, the escalation from a bottom-up anti-revolution to an organized counter-revolution battling a determined revolutionary regime with savageries and massacres on both sides was gradual as well as unintended by one and all. The Jacobin authorities in the capital and their proconsuls in the field contributed to the radicalization of the conflict by not only overestimating the ideological and political coherence as well as likely foreign support of the wild-growth soldiery, but also underestimating the military and political capabilities of the rebel peasants, priests, and nobles. This dual misperception had its counterpart in the opposing camp: particularly the White leaders became trapped in their own misconstructions, which were the reverse image of those of their foes.

Needless to say, the avenging Furies of the Whites, on the one side, and the Blues, or Reds, on the other, were radically different. Above all, even at the height of their strength and offensive, once the amorphous peasant bands had been forged into the "Catholic and Royal Army," the Vendean leaders lacked the fixed chain and post of command indispensable for a systematic enforcement terror. Besides, except between March and July 1793, the rebel forces concentrated on outmaneuvering and eluding their superior foes; the cities, which were patriot strongholds, remained beyond their reach; and in the end they were defeated. Indeed, circumstances saved them from being tempted by the demon of collective vengeance. Still, when irregular peasant rebels rushed into the towns of Machecoul and Cholet at the very start of the rebellion, during the second week of March, they carried out large-scale massacres of patriots—public officials, national guardsmen, constitutional priests. Wild and savage, these atrocities of the first hour foreshadowed the naked brutality inherent in any full-fledged civil war. With the institutions and forces of law and order sapped, the furor of the "primitive rebels" was bound to be partly driven by old-fashioned vengeance and, to the extent that they were touched by the Catholic and royalist rhetoric of their leaders, by ideology as well. To repeat, violence and terror were peculiarly pervasive in the Vendée by reason of its civil war being a *Glaubenskrieg* in which both sides feared and fought for their core religious, social, and cultural values.

On the Jacobin side, the clamor for retribution against the Whites stoked the raging Furies of the Terror. On November 7, a month after Lyons was rebaptized *Ville-Affranchie*, the Convention with alacrity accepted the proposal of Merlin de Thionville to change the name of the rebellious province from Vendée to *Département Vengé*. Noirmoutier, the scene of a major massacre, was renamed *Ile de la Montagne*, and the neighboring region of Bouin *Ile Marat*. The site of the mass execution of some 700 rebel prisoners was called the "district of vengeance."[129] These neologisms expressed and sanctioned the ferocious spirit of the fighting and pacification of this fratricide. But above all, just as Collot d'Herbois and Fouché wrought their punitive reprisals *after* the recapture of Lyons, so Jean-Baptiste Carrier and Louis Marie Turreau wrought theirs *after* the defeat of the military Vendée. Precisely because in the Vendée this retribution was charged with the Furies characteristic of religious conflict, the *noyades* of Carrier and especially the twelve "infernal columns" of Turreau, which raged for four months, surpassed even the eruptions of vengeance in Lyons, Bordeaux, and Toulon. The *Vendée-vengée* bore the full brunt of personal revenge, revolutionary justice, and wanton massacre, aggravated by epidemic and famine.

While this repression was under way, leading Jacobins continued to declaim about the logic of vengeance. Evoking the sins of commission of the *ancien régime*, which the defunct power elite had never even bothered to justify, Saint-Just asserted that besides being far less cruel, the new republican regime "perhaps foolishly took pride in making known its principles with metaphysical luxury." The monarchy having "bathed in the blood of thirty generations," it was only fitting that the people should at last "take revenge for twelve hundred years of crimes against their forebears." In Saint-Just's telling phrase, "terror is a double-edged sword: some use it to avenge the people, others to serve tyranny."[130] While Saint-Just spoke of historical vengeance, Robespierre focused on the place of vengeance in the current ideological terror: "as long as the enemies of liberty persecute even a single person of virtue the republican government is duty-bound to rush to his side and avenge him publicly." Robespierre was particularly caustic about moralists who sought to protect internal enemies "from the avenging sword of national justice," insisting that by so doing they blunted "the bayonets of our soldiers" who were risking their lives fighting the armies of foreign tyrants.[131]

Especially in connection with the revolutionary violence and terror in the Vendée, but also with that in the southern cities, it is important—but also difficult—to distinguish the military casualties from the victims of political terror.[132] Whereas in the west the number of military or indirect victims exceeded the number of nonmilitary or direct victims, in the south these proportions were reversed. Taking the terror as a whole, the vast majority of victims were convicted for sedition or treason, or over 90 percent of all indictments. Of course, by itself, and because of its polysemy and inconsistency, the charge of sedition or treason favoring internal or external enemies would not be a good measure of the motive and intention of the Terror. But there was a high correlation between the laying of such charges and the geographic incidence of the Terror: by far the greatest toll of victims was concentrated in the southern and western regions which were the prime theaters of civil war, and also in frontier departments. Furthermore, judging by the chronological chart of the trials and executions, they correspond with the flux and reflux of civil and foreign war, with the peak during the last two months of 1793 and the first two months of 1794. Indeed, terror "was used to crush rebellion and to quell opposition to the Revolution, the Republic, or the Mountain."[133] Of course the line between an internal enemy of, on the one hand, the Revolution and Republic, and the government of the day, on the other, was at once shifting and treacherous. Still, whatever its self-serving and despotic excesses, the Committee of Public Safety, France's provisional government, sought to reestablish an undivided and centralized sovereignty involving a monopoly on the legitimate use of violence both at home and abroad. To the extent socioeconomic factors and conflicts bore upon this struggle, they were more pressing in the provinces, particularly in the southern cities, than in Paris. Among the nonrational reasons and mainsprings of terror, the ardor for vengeance is likely to have been at least as varied and consequential as the fire of utopian ideology and quasi-religious fanaticism, all the more so given, as noted, the high and critical correlation of terror and civil war.

* * *

Thermidor marks less a break than a bridge in the protean unfolding of the French Revolution. Certainly the deficit of political and legal sovereignty was neither eliminated nor reduced, with the result that the climate and terrain remained propitious for the avenging Furies to continue sowing death and chaos. Indeed, the polarizing struggle for power continued in both city and country. Away from Paris this struggle became particularly intense wherever the avenging Jacobin terror had been exceptionally fierce and devastating. The victors of the Year II well-nigh became the losers of the Years III and IV, and vice versa: whereas the Jacobins had eventually taken command of the Red Terror, the anti- and counter-Jacobins in time seized the initiative and secured the upper hand in the Thermidorean reaction and White Terror. Of course, during this great reversal of atmosphere, role, and purpose, the word-concept of terror lost its specificity to become a polemical term which one and all used to excoriate the "other's" intentions and methods.[134] Indeed, there is no appreciating "the true nature of the Terror of 1793–94 without taking into account the Counter-Terror of the year III, . . . which was a sort of collective reprisal for the excesses, threats, brutalities, humiliations, and enthusiasms of the previous year." The two Furies should be placed "back to back in order to bring out" basic similarities and contrasts in government policies and avenging stratagems. Rather than consider the Year III as either "just an epilogue to the year II . . . or simply the year One After Robespierre," the two years ask to be read in terms of each other.[135]

The White Terror lasted over a year, or about as long as the Red Terror. In fact, since it flared up intermittently during the Directory and Consulate, and was not unrelated to the earlier anti- and counter-revolutionary resistances, the life of the White Terror may be said to have been spread over more than a decade.[136] Compared to the Red Terror, it counted fewer victims and was less centrally directed. It also lacked a comprehensive logic such as the need to save the *patrie* and the republic, the more so since by this time the French armies were winning the day abroad. Qualitatively, however, there may be said to have been important family resemblances. In terms of sheer horror and arbitrariness, the two terrors were much the same. Being less top-down than the Great Terror, the White Terror had greater similarities with the bottom-up terror which had culminated in the prison massacres of September 1792, and as such had been disproportionately driven by vengeance, both personal and communal, both utterly wild and at best quasi-legal. For the victims there was little to choose between "the steely bureaucrats of *robespierriste* unanimity . . . [and] the vindictive judges and heartless bourgeois of the Thermidorean regime."[137]

* * *

The new phase in the dialectic of vengeance began immediately following the execution of Robespierre on 10 Thermidor of the Year II, or July 28, 1794. Before long the political world within and beyond the Convention divided along roughly three lines: those fixing the responsibility for the worst excesses on Robespierre and a few of his acolytes; those blaming them on the system of terror of which the Robespierrists were an integral part; and those denouncing Robespierre and the terror as the inevitable outgrowth of the Revolution, whose republican institutions they challenged. The three positions were tied to political agendas that were difficult to reconcile. But in the heat of the moment, with the air heavy with suspicion, hatred, and fear, one and all denounced yesterday's miscreants, each seeking to embody them in a favorite demon.

To be sure, though divided, the Convention presided over the wholesale liberation of political prisoners and recalled not a few representatives on mission, preferring charges of terrorism against several of the hard-liners among them. At the same time, however, cries for reprisals and vengeance intensified not only in the Convention but in the press and the public, especially among those who had suffered personally or through relatives and friends under the Red Terror. Although there were voices calling for clemency and punishment by republican law rather than popular vengeance, they were well-nigh drowned out. The dominant tone was struck by the counterrevolutionary anthem, the *Reveil du Peuple*, composed as an *anti-Marseillaise* in January 1795: now that the "day of vengeance" had arrived, the chief culprits would be plucked from the "savage horde of . . . infamous assassins, . . . brigands . . . and bloodthirsty murderers" to be cast into a "hecatomb of yesterday's executioners . . . and barbarous cannibals."[138]

There was something inexorable about the crescendo of the vengeful White Terror. This was partly because the Convention adopted a set of decrees which half unintentionally fostered it, and also to some degree because it appointed representatives on mission who were as unsteadfast as the central authorities themselves. On January 10, 1795, (20 Nivôse, Year II) the deputies authorized the unconditional return of émigrés who had left France after May 31, 1793, thereby expanding the reservoir of potential avengers. A few weeks later, on February 21 (3 Ventôse), they promulgated the reopening of Catholic churches and the return to France of refractory priests conditional on their taking the loyalty oath of 1792. In nearly the same breath the Convention also passed "a sort of inverted law of suspects" ordering each commune to keep a close eye on all officials dismissed or suspended since 10 Thermidor, exposing to "public contempt and reprisal anyone who had played a role in the revolutionary government."[139]

But the situation was not brought to a head until early spring 1795. On April 1, or 12 Germinal, Paris was shaken by a Jacobin-inspired food riot. Although easily brought under control, it prompted the Convention, obsessed by the specter of the return of Jacobins and sansculottes, to order the disarmament of presumed left-wing terrorists. Loosely applied by hard-line local officials, this law of April 10 (21 Germinal) led to many thousands of suspects being arrested and jailed, so that once again overcrowded prisons became symbolically charged targets for the discharge of seething, politically freighted Furies. To boot, on April 11 the original decree on the qualified return of émigrés was superseded by a law removing all remaining restrictions and restoring all property and political rights. In sum, three major elements favoring collective vengeance came into play: the growth of the reserve army of avengers; the rising ire of the new representatives on mission and their local collaborators; and the convenient cathexis on the prisons.

In the meantime acts of personal retribution multiplied and unsettled the political and social landscape against a darkening economic horizon. The incidence of this private and anarchic vengeance was essentially local. Aggrieved individuals wrought their vengeance on suspects who were personally known to them and about whose wanton misdeeds of the previous year they had, or claimed to have, reliable information. Driven by family- and community-validated values and intentions, the avengers administered the full gamut of psychological, material, and physical punishments, more often than not unmindful of the limiting injunction of "an eye for an eye."[140]

The fact that the local and central authorities lacked the political will and muscle to rein in this rash of personal and irregular violence encouraged wild but partly organized vigilantes and lynch gangs to unleash larger scale avenging Furies. Indeed, the White Terror "was a highly contradictory phenomenon, both anarchical and organized, both deliberate and accidental, both structured and random."[141]

Although protracted, savage, and glaring, the White Terror did not befall the whole of France: the worst of the retributive violence was all but confined to the departments of the southeast. Centered in the lands stretching from the Rhône-et-Loire to the Bouches-du-Rhône, the geography of the fiercest White Terror matched that of the fiercest anti-federalist Red Terror, including its distinctly urban configuration. Of course, there were counter-terrorist outbreaks in the rural west as well. But in Brittany they were part and parcel of the *chouans'* guerrilla warfare against the republican armies, giving this region's White Terror a martial face.[142]

During the first half of 1795 the worst of the anti-Jacobin White Terror, concentrated in the Midi, took the form of gory prison massacres. Counting the storming of the Bastille, this was the third time that evil-starred prisons became focal points of violent confrontation and polarizing consciousness. Due to the rash of post-Thermidorean arrests, the jails of many cities and towns were crammed not only with officials and collaborators of yesterday's short-lived ultra-Jacobin reign but also with their suspected sympathizers and fellow travelers. To would-be avengers, incited by firebrands, these prisons appeared as simmering cauldrons of wild *enragés* on the verge of boiling over. This swelling agitation resembled that on the eve of the September prison massacres in Paris, except that the roles were reversed: in some places inmates were massacred while being transferred from one jail to another, with their escorts unwilling or unable to protect them; in others large crowds surged into the prisons to murder the inmates, here and there mutilating their bodies and throwing them into nearby rivers. As if reenacting its *bagarre* of 1790, Nîmes made a beginning with four victims on February 24. Lyons was next: with a death toll of between 100 and 120 on May 4 its massacre was, as we shall see, emblematic of the White Terror. In Marseilles two prison pogroms on May 11 and June 5 claimed a total of some 110 lives. In late spring prison massacres also caused about 10 deaths in Aix, 50 in Tarascon, and 90 in Toulon.

Easily the best part of the Thermidorean Convention's deputies and representatives on mission either approved or vindicated the White Terror, including its witch-hunt, and some of them did so in the spirit in which Roland and Condorcet had sought to "veil" the prison massacres in September 1792. The bulk of its membership unchanged, the Convention was not a likely beacon of light, moderation, and justice. Its halting efforts at interposition were equivocal, many of its own members having supported the Terror of the Year II in the capital, in the southern cities, and in the Vendée. Besides, half of them had voted the death penalty for Louis XVI, and not a few feared that a runaway de-Jacobinization might provoke a reaction dangerous to themselves and the Republic. In any case, the Thermidoreans proposed to legitimate and focus the avenging Furies without devising political and legal checks and balances. This paradox marked the trial of Carrier, who paid with his life for brashly telling the members of the Convention that they were looking to salve their own consciences by indicting him for a course of action they themselves had charted and ratified.

Apostates from radical Jacobinism helped set the new political tone. Jean Lambert Tallien brazenly called on France's citizens to take "prompt" revenge against all recent "assassins," though he allowed that eventually "terror should give way to justice." In like manner Philippe Auguste Merlin de Douai, one of the prime movers of the post-Thermidorean law of suspects, asserted that the "French people were crying to settle accounts" with the "monsters and assassins" who had "stained the soil of liberty," and claimed that they would continue to do so "until the manes of all the victims were appeased." Ominously, some of the new representatives on mission echoed this vindictive bluster. In Marseilles, Chambon insisted that with all the world "disheartened by the slow pace of the proceedings against [yesterday's] scoundrels," the only way to "head off a terrible reaction was to eliminate them from the territory of the Republic." François Gamon warned that without the swift and drastic punishment "of the assassins of our parents, friends, and citizens no human force could stem the tide of personal reprisals." In Aix-en-Provence, Henri Maximin Isnard incited avengers who lacked weapons to "dig up the bones of their fathers and use them to exterminate" their executioners.[143]

In time the avenging wildfire spread beyond the cities to the countryside. Even if not "every village imitated the city," many of them did so, or else acted on their own initiative, which was more their style. Not propitious to "mass slayings," the countryside witnessed "isolated killings in open fields as well as near and inside homes." Many of these killings were rushed to keep defendants from being tried, even guillotined, since "true vengeance calls for personally killing one's own enemy" and perhaps even mangling his corpse "beyond recognition."[144] Even more than in the cities, in the countryside this popular vengeance was personalized, here and there resembling the blood feud. Often these pains and punishment were inflicted with crowds looking on and bearing witness, their members moved by a broad range of personal motives. The number of victims is impossible to estimate, but it was certainly considerable.[145]

✳ ✳ ✳

Of the "federalist" cities, Lyons bore the deepest wounds and darkest memories of the cruel and humiliating punishment for having rebelled against Paris. For the local anti- and counter-Jacobins, reinforced by returning émigrés, Thermidor provided the enabling conditions for revenge against the Mountain. Admittedly, at first the old moneyed elites and middle classes, having reclaimed their influence and power, advocated republican reconciliation, forbearance, and judicial punishment. Several local songs implored the champions of liberty to forget their "quarrels" and thank the Convention for saving them from the "bloody [Jacobin] hordes" by exorcising the "demon" of vengeance and "forswearing retribution in favor of the rule of law."[146]

But these verses were drowned out by lyrics more in tune with the ascendance of an alliance in which republicans and moderate monarchists made common cause with émigrés, refractory priests, and army deserters eager for reprisals. One poem, claiming that the "blood . . . of Robespierre's victims calls for vengeance," urged that all "traitors . . . and cannibals" be given their deserts. Another thundered that the nation's "*bras vengeurs*" should be armed to "punish the Jacobin Furies," thereby "honoring" Lyons' heroic victims, to be memorialized with a commemorative column to be "erected on the Brotteaux." A local variant of the *Réveil du Peuple* hailed the Convention for "punishing the bloodthirsty villains who had sworn to exterminate us" and vowed "vengeance" for the wives whose "husbands were strangled."[147] The tone was equally incendiary in the *Journal de Lyon*, whose epigraph—taken from Voltaire's *Mahomet*—called for "the extermination . . . of all those who relish spilling human blood."[148]

Lyons' failing economy provided a favorable environment for the agitation of impatient avengers among the classes and masses. One of the first public furors was highly symbolic: a crowd forcibly removed a bust of Chalier from the *mairie* to consign it to a nearby bonfire. The fate of Fernex, member of the revolutionary commission, turned out to be tone-setting: on February 14, after being wrested from fifty guards who were taking him to the Saint-Joseph prison, he was killed and dumped into the Rhône river. Within a month the murder of both prominent and ordinary Jacobin terrorists and their insolent anti-burial in the Rhône or Saône ceased to be out of the ordinary, no doubt because the authorities turned a blind eye.[149] Meanwhile the anti-Jacobin representatives on mission who succeeded Couthon, Collot d'Herbois, and Fouché helped give the Convention's Thermidorean decrees an avenging color. As murderous personal vengeance increased without official reproof, vigilantes and untried constables searched homes and combed streets for proven or suspected Jacobin terrorists to be committed to Lyons' prisons, pending trial by special courts. In an unsettled environment not unlike Paris in August 1792, restive crowds, incensed by the slow pace of legal retribution, surrounded the prisons which they suspected of being redoubts of *enragés* poised to erupt and savage the city. Finally, on May 4, confident of immunity, the counterparts of the *septembriseurs* rushed the Roanne prison and massacred about forty inmates, laying the dismembered corpses before the public. During the next few days roving bands took some sixty additional lives at the Recluses, Saint-Joseph, and Saint-Genis-Laval prisons.[150]

In the midst of this extended prison pogrom, the central government's several local agents at once avowed and lamented their helplessness. On May 5 and 6 Boisset, a profoundly troubled proconsul, rushed alarming reports to the Committee of General Security. Estimating that to date there were sixty to seventy victims, he stressed that nothing short of an official constabulary could bring the excesses under control. Boisset warned that unless Paris promptly enacted "vigorous measures" and provided him with men-at-arms, "blood would continue to tarnish the Republic and his own presence [in Lyons] would be futile." In point of fact, "without army units" there was no keeping apart "the partisans of the Terror and of the Monarchy," since even the local "national guard units were breathing vengeance."[151]

This confidential entreaty to the center was supplemented, on May 7, by a public "Proclamation to the French People and the National Convention" signed by local government delegates, commanders of the national guard, and judges. It claimed that "with human reason and the law helpless in the face of unbound natural convulsions," the people were driven to visit "terrible acts of vengeance" on the "imprisoned monsters."[152]

The central authorities failed to intervene both because they were weak and for fear that by bearing hard on the Jacobins they risked encouraging royalists and counterrevolutionaries, who were not without weight in Lyons, even if the local Thermidoreans overestimated it. Significantly, the population of Lyons seems to have been as reluctant to take a stand as the Parisian and local agencies and agents. Indeed there was little public reprobation. Quinet even held that in Lyons the massacres were widely considered "a pale reprisal for the fusillades on the Brotteaux" and that in local theaters the "killers were showered with flowers and applause."[153]

*　*　*

Not surprisingly, Quinet gives a heuristically powerful comparative reading of the White and Red Terrors. He claimed that at first sight—judging by the indifference of the Convention, the connivance of the proconsuls, the bloodthirsty speeches of right-wing *enragés*, and the inertia of the forces of order—"the system of extermination had changed hands essentially unchanged." But a closer look convinced him that the anti-Montagnards "vastly surpassed" the Robespierrists in "the art of coldheartedly eliminating their adversaries." According to Quinet, although the would-be moderates in Paris received "reports, letters, and official documents" about the ongoing atrocities from their local and regional agents, they kept insisting that they "were not well enough informed to intervene to stop them." In actual fact their denial was a "masterpiece of vengeance" in that they "let others exterminate their enemies" without ever "wielding the ax themselves," all the time affecting "airs of piety . . . and clemency."[154]

Besides, this Thermidorean "reaction was an anonymous enterprise," inasmuch as its "horrors could neither be imputed . . . [nor] traced to particular individuals." With time the counter-terror faded from memory by reason of having "succeeded" and because the *modérés* knew better than to "denounce" either themselves or each other. Furthermore, unlike the *révolutionneurs* of the Year II, who published the names, crimes, and last words of the victims of the guillotine in *Le Glaive Vengeur*, the *réacteurs* of the Years III and IV were not so "foolish as to publish lists of their victims." By dispensing with bold justifications and "sham trials," they covered their tracks and masked the scale of the avenging fury. Partly for that reason, the exact number and identities of the victims of "the Thermidorean reaction" in the southeast may never be known, though sound estimates put them at about 2,000, or roughly the same number "that perished [there] during the Terror of the Year II." In any case, there was no terror-breathing and ideologically emblematic Robespierre for the "White Jacobins" to turn into a sacrificial example, and on whose head and memory to call down the curses. This quick forgetting was also helped by the widespread perception that the moderates were acting in accordance with the *lex talionis*, which tended to "legitimate" the Furies and to facilitate consigning both the victims and their tormentors to a memory gap.[155]

In any case, in spirit the Red Terror and White Terror were quite different. Whereas the "butcheries" committed by the Revolution, including those of September 1792, were "without merriment and song," the ordeal inflicted by the "Reaction", which was in the nature of a "protracted second September," was marked by "levity and mockery." In Quinet's telling, the "respectable people (*honnêtes gens*) enjoyed and savored" the massacres. To further their cause they "killed with the diligence, elegance, or luxury characteristic of hunting parties" at the same time that they gave themselves "the pleasure of vengeance" by "sanctioning" the mistreatment of their victims.[156]

Quinet is at his weakest in his discussion of the rank-and-file vigilantes of the terror of the Year III. Like Louis Blanc, he fails to explore their social profile, *modus operandi*, and leadership. He claims that the "spectacle was more or less the same" in all the cities of the Midi: "gangs of killers, regularly organized by the *Compagnie de Jéhu* [Jesus] and the *Compagnie du Soleil*, putting to death prisoners in plain daylight; populations indifferent to the torment of the victims; cutthroats doing their cruel work unhampered and leisurely, between meals accompanied by song; and officials arriving after everything was over and ordering the killing to stop only once there was no one left to save."[157] Quinet overemphasizes the conterrevolutionary reason and control of the societies of Jesus and of the Sun, centered in and around Lyons and Marseilles, respectively, since their members seem to have been moved as much by personal vengeance as by ideological or political conviction and purpose.[158]

For Quinet, the White Terror resumed the ways of Europe's *anciens régimes*, which by virtue of neither divulging nor justifying their crimes against humanity were not inhibited by memory and moral principles. Unlike autocratic monarchies, however, struggling democracies can neither live with their misdeeds nor forget them. In all conscience they expose and denounce them. They also repent and forgive. But they do so at a heavy price. Quinet holds that while "the Terror seriously damaged the Republic, it was the trials of the Terror that dealt it a fatal blow," the trial of Fouquier-Tinville "marking the Reaction's triumph." Ultimately, however, "not Carrier, Fouquier, and other agents were brought to the bar" but the Convention itself, and with it the Revolution, which was left looking "guilty, hideous, and horrifying." The accused argued, and with reason, that they had merely carried out the policies which the Convention and its executive organs had "adopted, consecrated, and supervised." Rather than assume personal responsibility for any of the excessive excesses, the defendants tried to hide behind the Convention which, in turn, sought to "shift the blame to committees and individuals." This posture was characteristic of "the majority of the Convention which out of weakness first voted to use brute violence and then turned to decry and punish it." Not unlike Robespierre, the members of the Convention "lacked the defiant courage and honor of the leaders of the Ancient World who had answered for the cruelties of their epoch or class." The Convention had none of the Roman senate's patrician resolve and conceit to "uphold" its own image and memory. Besides, it lacked the power to conceal its own transgressions.[159]

Jacob Burckhardt's reading of the White Terror parallels Quinet's, except that he placed greater stress on vengeance. He argued that particularly the Midi, including Lyons, "wanted vengeance, not justice, and knew how to wreak it without fear and trembling." Convinced that the "counter-terror would go unpunished," the south witnessed a wild retribution. Rather than wield the blade of the guillotine, the avengers "shot people whom they encountered, casually, 'between two meals,' " as if driven to "assassinate for amusement." As for the societies of Jesus and of the Sun, Burckhardt traced their origins and members to "relatives of victims and prisoners" of the Red Terror.[160]

As a matter of course, the trope of vengeance gradually all but disappeared from the discourse and rhetoric of the time. It is inapposite and unreasonable in legal briefs and arguments of civil and political trials, be they authentic or spurious. In 1793–94 Danton and other Jacobins had been at once sensible and cunning to maintain that law courts, whether summary boards or formal revolutionary tribunals, were the best, if not the only, antidote to popular vengeance, and variants of this argument resurfaced during Thermidor. Indeed, the language and praxis of vengeance was a language and praxis of political combat under conditions of fractured sovereignty and judicial paralysis. It is, of course, carried by a broad range of impulses and mental predispositions. But it is also instrumentalized: explanation, representation, justification, exorcism, rallying cry, specter. Despite this heavy political charge, the Thermidorean Convention's trials of the terrorists of the Great Terror were a reflection and accessory of the restoration of a single and structured sovereignty and judiciary, or the remarginalization of vengeance.

✳ ✳ ✳

NOTES

1. Jacques-Antoine-Marie de Cazalès, constitutional monarchist speaking on the unrest in Nîmes in the Constituent Assembly on February 26, 1791, and cited in François Furet and Ran Halévi, eds., *Orateurs de la Révolution française*, vol. 1 (Paris: Gallimard, 1989), pp. 216–21 and 248–52. See chapter 13 below, for a detailed analysis of the *bagarre* in Nîmes.

2. Cited in Jean-Eugène Bimbenet, *Fuite de Louis XVI à Varennes*, 2nd ed. (Paris, 1868), pp. 251–55.

3. Cited in Luc Willette, *Le tribunal révolutionnaire: Les erreurs judiciaires de l'histoire* (Paris: Denoël, 1981), p. 16.

4. Jean-Guillaume Lombard, secretary of the King of Prussia, cited in Albert Mathiez, *La Révolution française*, vol. 3: *La terreur* (Paris: Denoël, 1985), p. 104.

5. Cited in John Hall Stewart, ed., *A Documentary Survey of the French Revolution* (New York: Macmillan, 1951), pp. 307–11. See also Albert Sorel, *L'Europe et la Révolution française*, vol. 2: *La chute de la royauté* (Paris, 1885), pp. 503–15; and H. A. Barton, "The Origins of the Brunswick Manifesto," *French Historical Studies* 5:2 (Fall 1967), pp. 146–69; chapter 14 below.

6. Burke, "Letter to a Member of the National Assembly" (1791), in Paul Langford, ed., *The Writings and Speeches of Edmund Burke*, vol. 8 (Oxford: Clarendon, 1989), pp. 294–335, esp. pp. 319–20.

7. Jean Jaurès, *Histoire socialiste de la Révolution française*, vol. 2 (Paris: Editions Sociales, 1970), pp. 606–8.

8. See William Doyle, *The Oxford History of the French Revolution* (Oxford: Oxford University Press, 1990), pp. 152–54; Michel Vovelle, *La chute de la monarchie, 1787–1792* (Paris: Seuil, 1972), pp. 166–67; Donald M. G. Sutherland, *France, 1789–1815: Revolution and Counterrevolution* (Oxford: Oxford University Press, 1986), pp. 126–31.

9. See Doyle, *History*, pp. 189–90; and Sutherland, *France*, pp. 150–55.

10. See Jules Michelet, *Histoire de la Révolution française*, 2 vols. (Paris: Laffont, 1979), vol. 1, p. 793.

11. The discussion of the avenging mood in the Commune in this paragraph and the next follows Michelet, *Histoire*, vol. 1, pp. 784–95, 816–21; and Edgar Quinet, *La Révolution* (Paris: Belin, 1987), pp. 314–15.

12. Cited in Michelet, *Histoire*, vol. 1, p. 795 and p. 801.

13. Cited in Elisabeth and Robert Badinter, *Condorcet, 1743–1794: Un intellectuel en politique* (Paris: Fayard, 1988), p. 473.

14. See Willette, *Le tribunal*, p. 10 ff.; and Pierre Sipriot, *Les cent vingt jours de Louis XVI, dit Louis Capet* (Paris: Plon, 1993), pp. 35–39 and 183–86.

15. Willette, *Le tribunal*, p. 15; and Bernard Lerat, *Le terrorisme révolutionnaire, 1789–1799* (Paris: Editions France-Empire, 1989), ch. 2, esp. pp. 94–95.

16. This paragraph and the next follow Michelet, *Histoire*, vol. 1, pp. 802–3; and Julien Tiersot, *Les fêtes et les chants de la Révolution française* (Paris: Hachette, 1908), pp. 88–89.

17. Ronsin cited in Antoine de Baecque, *Le corps de l'histoire: Métaphores et politique, 1770–1800* (Paris: Calmann-Lévy, 1993), p. 346.

18. Michelet, *Histoire*, vol. 1, p. 803.

19. Sessions of August 31 and September 7, 1792, as reported in *Chronique de Paris*, no. 257 (September 2), p. 982, and n. 264 (September 9), p. 1009.

20. Roland cited in Lerat, *Terrorisme*, p. 97.

21. See Marcel Dorigny, "Violence et révolution: Les girondins et les massacres de septembre," in Albert Soboul, ed., *Girondins et Montagnards* (Paris: Société des Etudes Robespierristes, 1980), pp. 103–20.

22. Marat cited in Frédéric Bluche, *Septembre 1792: Logiques d'un massacre* (Paris: Laffont, 1986), pp. 34–35.

23. See Bluche, *Septembre 1792*, pp. 36 ff. See also Marat, *Ecrits*, ed. by Michel Vovelle (Paris: Messidor/Editions Sociales, 1988), pp. 185–89.

24. Pierre Caron, *Les massacres de septembre* (Paris: Maison du Livre Français, 1935), pp 1–12, 76–102, 469–74; and Bluche, *Septembre 1792*, pp. 95–121.

25. Willette, *Le tribunal*, p. 18.

26. Michelet, *Histoire*, vol. 1, pp. 848–49; and Quinet, *La Révolution*, pp. 318–19.

27. Gustave Le Bon, *The French Revolution and the Psychology of Revolution* (New Brunswick, N.J.: Transaction Books, 1980), p. 72.

28. Sipriot, *Cent vingt jours*, pp. 44–47; and de Baecque, *La gloire et l'effroi: Sept morts sous la terreur* (Paris: Grasset, 1997), pp. 77–106. Cf. Michelet, *Histoire*, vol. 1, pp. 853–56; and Marc Bloch, *Apologie pour l'histoire ou métier d'historien* (Paris: Armand Colin, 1993), p. 69.

29. Michelet, *Histoire*, vol. 1, p. 809 and p. 846; Quinet, *La Révolution*, pp. 319–21; Caron, *Massacres*, pp. 103–20.

30. Quinet, *La Révolution*, p. 319.

31. See Caron, *Massacres*, pp. 472–73.

32. *Chronique de Paris*, no. 263 (September 7, 1792), p. 1002.

33. Roland's letter is cited in *Chronique de Paris*, no. 262 (September 7, 1792), p. 1002.

34. *Chronique de Paris*, no. 261 (September 6, 1792), p. 997.

35. *Chronique de Paris*, no. 259 (September 4, 1792), p. 990.

36. *Chronique de Paris*, no. 262 (September 7, 1792), pp. 1001–2; No. 264 (September 9, 1792), p. 1009.

37. Condorcet cited in Badinter, *Condorcet*, p. 475 and p. 585.

38. Dorigny, "Violence et révolution," pp. 103–7, 110.

39. Madame Roland cited in ibid., pp. 103–4.

40. Cited in Badinter, *Condorcet*, p. 474.

41. Cited in Sipriot, *Cent vingt jours*, p. 48.

42. See Marat, *Ecrits*, passim.

43. Cited in ibid., p. 178.

44. Ibid., pp. 195–97.

45. Cited by Pierre Michel, "Barbarie, civilisation, vandalisme," in Rolf Reichardt and Eberhard Schmitt, eds., *Handbuch politisch-sozialer Grundbegriffe in Frankreich, 1680–1820*, vol. 8 (Munich: Oldenbourg, 1988), pp. 7–40, esp. p. 31.

46. Cited in Helmut Kessler, *Terreur: Ideologie und Nomenklatur der revolutionären Gewaltanwendung in Frankreich von 1770 bis 1794* (Munich: Wilhelm Fink, 1973), pp. 36–39.

47. Cited in Michelet, *Histoire*, vol. 2, p. 48.

48. Jean Jaurès, *Histoire socialiste*, vol. 3 (Paris: Editions Sociales, 1970), p. 107.

49. Cited in Marc Bouloiseau et al., eds., *Oeuvres de Maximilien Robespierre*, vol. 8 (Paris: Presses Universitaires, 1953), p. 69.

50. Gustave Laurent, ed., *Oeuvres de Maximilien Robespierre*, vol. 5 (Paris: n. p., 1951), p. 19.

51. Bouloiseau et al., eds., *Oeuvres de Robespierre*, vol. 8, pp. 93–95.

52. Blanc, *Histoire de la Révolution française*, vol. 7 (Paris: 1864), ch. 2 ("Souviens-toi de la Saint-Barthélemy"), esp. p. 195.

53. Michelet, *Histoire*, vol. 2, pp. 176–78.

54. For Saint-Just's speech of November 13, 1792, on the indictment of Louis XVI, see Michèle Duval, ed., *Saint-Just: Oeuvres complètes* (Paris: Gérard Lebovici, 1984), pp. 376–81.

55. Robespierre, "Lettre à ses commettans," no. 5, in Laurent, ed., *Oeuvres*, vol. 5, pp. 56–74, esp. p. 58, p. 60, and p. 64.

56. For Robespierre's speech of December 3, 1792, on the indictment of Louis XVI, see Bouloiseau et al., eds., *Oeuvres de Robespierre*, vol. 9, pp. 121–34. See this same volume for his subsequent interventions in the king's trial.

57. Ibid., p. 89.

58. Ibid., p. 191.

59. Ibid., p. 130 and p. 133.

60. Ibid., p. 133, p. 184, and p. 120.

61. Ibid., p. 130 and p. 136.

62. Cited in Henri Coston, ed., *Procès de Louis XVI et de Marie-Antoinette* (Paris: Henry Coston, 1981), pp. 443–45, 369, 425.

63. Quinet, *La Révolution*, p. 351 and p.354.

64. Etienne Léon Baron de Lamothe-Langon, ed., *Mémoires de Louis XVIII*, vol. 5 (n. p., 1832), pp. 249–53. See Machiavelli, *Discourses on Livy* (New York: Oxford, 1997), ch. 31 ("How Dangerous It Is To Believe Exiles").

65. Jacques Godechot, *La Contre-Révolution, 1789–1804* (Paris: Presses Universitaires, 1961), p. 183.

66. Cited in Abbé Isidore Bertrand, *Le pontificat de Pie VI et l'athéisme révolutionnaire*, vol. 2 (Paris, 1879), pp. 208–25.

67. For this paragraph and the next, see David P. Jordan, *The King's Trial: The French Revolution vs. Louis XVI* (Berkeley: University of California Press, 1979), pp.

208 ff.; Susan Dunn, *The Deaths of Louis XVI: Regicide and the French Political Imagination* (Princeton: Princeton University Press, 1994); de Baecque, *La gloire et l'effroi*, pp. 107–48.

68. Cited in Jaurès, *Histoire socialiste*, vol. 5, p. 312.

69. Vergniaud cited in Willette, *Le tribunal*, p. 24.

70. Cited in Jaurès, *Histoire socialiste*, vol. 5, pp. 312–13.

71. Cited in ibid., vol. 5, pp. 313–14; and in Gérard Walter, ed., *Actes du Tribunal révolutionnaire* (Paris: Mercure de France, 1986), p. xiv.

72. Jaurès, *Histoire socialiste*, vol. 5, p. 310.

73. For the text of the decree of March 10, 1793, see ibid., vol. 5, pp. 310–12; and Walter, ed., *Actes*, pp. xv–xvi.

74. Jaurès, *Histoire socialiste*, vol. 5, p. 316.

75. Cited in Mathiez, *La Révolution*, vol. 3, p. 22.

76. Corday cited in Henri Wallon, *Histoire du Tribunal révolutionnaire de Paris*, vol. 1 (Paris, 1880), ch. 7.

77. Cited by Jacques Guilhaumou, "La formation d'un mot d'ordre: Plaçons la terreur à l'ordre du jour," in *Bulletin du Centre d'analyse du discours*, no. 5 (Lille: Presses Universitaires de Lille, 1981), p. 153.

78. *Père Duchesne* (15 July 1793) cited in Raymond Postgate, ed., *Revolution from 1789 to 1906* (London: Grant Richards, 1920), p. 50.

79. Guilhaumou, *La mort de Marat* (Paris: Editions Complexe, 1989), p. 31.

80. Cited in Guilhaumou, *La mort*, pp. 33–35, 43–44. See also Ulrich Gumbrecht, *Funktionen parlamentarischer Rhetorik in der französischen Revolution* (Munich: Wilhelm Fink, 1978), pp. 106–8.

81. Cited in Guilhaumou, *La mort*, pp. 38–40. See also Mathiez, *La Révolution*, vol. 3, pp. 23–24.

82. David Lloyd Dowd, *Pageant-Master of the Republic: Jacques-Louis David and the French Revolution* (Lincoln, Neb.: University of Nebraska Press, 1948), pp. 52–54.

83. Dorothy Johnson, *Jacques-Louis David: Art in Metamorphosis* (Princeton: Princeton University Press, 1993), pp. 95–99.

84. This discussion of Marat's lying in state and funeral follows Guilhaumou, *La mort*, esp. pp. 51–60; de Baecque, *Le corps*, pp. 26–27; Mathiez, *La Révolution*, vol. 3, pp. 23–24.

85. Cited in Guilhaumou, *La mort*, p. 51.

86. De Baecque, *Le corps*, esp. p. 21.

87. Warren Roberts, *Jacques-Louis David as Revolutionary Artist: Art, Politics, and the French Revolution* (Chapel Hill, N.C.: University of North Carolina Press, 1989), pp. 81–82, 88. See also Johnson, *Jacques-Louis David*, pp. 106–8.

88. Roberts, *Jacques-Louis David*, pp. 80–81; Peter H. Feist, "Jacques-Louis Davids Gemälde 'Der ermordete Marat': Zum Realismusgehalt des revolutionären Klassizismus," in Kurt Holzapfel and Matthias Middell, eds., *Die Französische Revolution 1789: Geschichte und Wirkung*, vol. 10 (Berlin: Akademie-Verlag, 1989), pp. 197–209; Jörg Traeger, *Der Tod des Marat: Revolution des Menschenbildes* (Munich: Prestel, 1986), passim, esp. p. 415.

89. Kenneth Clark and Antoine Schnapper, respectively, cited in Feist, "Jacques-Louis Davids Gemälde," p. 197.

90. Cited in Dowd, *Pageant-Master*, p. 107.

91. Cited in Roberts, *Jacques-Louis David*, p. 83. Jacob Burckhardt considered that having "saturated the Revolution with his poison . . . the cult of Marat was a grim emetic." Quite the contrary, by virtue of her heroic deed, as measured "by the standards of the Ancient World," Charlotte Corday was "one of the most sublime figures of the revolutionary epoch." Burckhardt, *Vorlesungen über die Geschichte des Revolutionszeitalter* (Basel/Stuttgart: Schwabe, 1974), p. 263.

92. Guilhaumou, *La mort*, p. 91. See also de Baecque, *Le corps*, p. 40.

93. Guilhaumou, "La formation," pp. 171–72, 176.

94. Cited in Guilhaumou, *La mort*, p. 94.

95. Cited in Guilhaumou, "La formation," pp. 172–73, 191.

96. Cited in ibid., pp. 191–92.

97. Cited in Frank Attar, *La Révolution française déclare la guerre à l'Europe: L'embrasement de l'Europe à la fin du XVIII siècle* (Paris: Editions Complexe, 1992), p. 107.

98. Cited in Georges Michon, *Robespierre et la guerre révolutionnaire, 1791–1792* (Paris: Rivière, 1937), p. 22 and p. 37.

99. Cited in Attar, *La Révolution française*, p. 115.

100. Cited in Michel Vovelle, "La Marseillaise: La guerre ou la paix," in Pierre Nora, ed., *Les lieux de mémoire*, vol. 1 (Paris: Gallimard, 1984), pp. 85–136, esp. p. 93.

101. Cited in Geoffrey Best, *Humanity in Warfare* (New York: Columbia University Press, 1980), p. 86. See also Esteban Buch, *La neuvième de Beethoven: Une histoire politique* (Paris: Gallimard, 1999), ch. 2, esp. pp. 40–46.

102. Cited in Duval, ed., *Saint-Just*, p. 543.

103. See René Moulinas, "Le Sud-Est," in Jean Tulard, ed., *La Contre-révolution: Origines, histoire, postérité* (Paris: Perrin, 1990), pp. 234–61; and Alan Forrest, "Regionalism and Counterrevolution in France," in Colin Lucas, ed., *Rewriting the French Revolution* (Oxford: Clarendon, 1991), pp. 151–82.

104. For developments in Lyons, see W. D. Edmonds, *Jacobinism and the Revolt of Lyon, 1789–1793* (Oxford: Clarendon, 1990); and Colin Lucas, *The Structure of the Terror: The Example of Javogues and the Loire* (Oxford: Oxford University Press, 1973), passim.

105. Michelet, *Histoire*, vol. 2, pp. 529–31.

106. Chalier cited in Georges Eynard, *Joseph Chalier: Bourreau ou martyr, 1747–1793* (Lyon: Editions Lyonnaises d'art et d'histoire, 1987), p. 81 and pp. 94–95.

107. Michelet, *Histoire*, vol. 2, p. 535.

108. Cited in Eynard, *Chalier*, p. 163.

109. Michelet, *Histoire*, vol. 2, pp. 537–38; and Eynard, *Chalier*, p. 169.

110. F.-A. (Alphonse) Aulard, ed., *Recueil des actes du Comité de Salut Public avec la correspondence officielle des représentants en mission*, vol. 7 (Paris, 1894), pp. 375–76.

111. For the Red Terror in Lyons, see Edmonds, *Jacobinism*, pp. 282–304.

112. Richard Cobb, *The People's Armies or the armées révolutionnaires: Instrument of the Terror in the Departments, April 1793 to Floréal Year II* (New Haven: Yale University Press, 1987), p. 372.

113. R. R. Palmer, *Twelve Who Ruled: The Year of the Terror in the French Revolution* (Princeton: Princeton University Press, 1941), p. 170. See also Sutherland,

France, pp. 222–23; Doyle, *History,* p. 254; Paul Mansfield, "The Repression of Lyon, 1793–4: Origins, Responsibility, and Significance," in *French History* 2:1 (1988): pp. 74–101.

114. This paragraph and the two following ones draw on Eynard, *Chalier,* pp. 171–72; G. Lenôtre [L. L. T. Gosselin], *La Compagnie de Jéhu: Episodes de la réaction lyonnaise, 1794–1800* (Paris: Perrin, 1931), pp. 545–57; Thomas Carlyle, *The French Revolution: A History* (London: Chapman and Hall, 1903), p. 697. Carlyle gives the *Moniteur* (November 17, 1793) as a source for his reconstruction of the procession of November 10.

115. Cited in Anne-Marie Vurpas, *Les chansons lyonnaises à l'époque révolutionnaire: Collection du bicentenaire de la Révolution française à Lyon* (Lyon: Editions Lyonnaises d'art et d'histoire, 1987), p. 108.

116. Cited in Aulard, ed., *Recueil,* vol. 7, pp. 331–32.

117. Cited in Mathiez, *La Révolution,* vol. 3, p. 144.

118. Dubois-Crancé to the Convention (10 October 1793), in Aulard, ed., *Recueil,* vol. 7, p. 350; Palmer, *Twelve,* pp. 170–76; Sutherland, *France,* pp. 221–23.

119. See chapter 4 above.

120. For the Red Terror in Marseilles, see William Scott, *Terror and Repression in Revolutionary Marseilles* (London: Macmillan, 1973).

121. Barras and Fréron to the Committee of Public Safety (13 October 1793), in Aulard, ed., *Recueil,* vol. 7, pp. 404–5; Godechot, *La Contre-Révolution,* pp. 241–43; Sutherland, *France,* pp. 220–21.

122. Cited in Paul Gaffarel, "Marseilles sans nom (Nivôse–Pluviôse An II)," in *La Révolution française* 60 (1911): pp. 193–215, esp. pp. 211–12.

123. Alan Forrest, *Society and Politics in Revolutionary Bordeaux* (Oxford: Oxford University Press, 1975), ch. 10, esp. pp. 235–38, and *The Revolution in Provincial France: Aquitaine, 1789–1799* (Oxford: Clarendon, 1996), ch. 8, esp. pp. 235 ff.

124. Ysabeau and Tallien to the Committee of Public Safety (November 11, 1793) in Aulard, ed., *Recueil,* vol. 8, p. 345.

125. Malcolm Crook, *Journées révolutionnaires à Toulon* (Nîmes: Jacquelin Chambes, 1989), pp. 83–96; and Crook, *Toulon in War and Revolution: From the Ancien Regime to the Restoration, 1750–1820* (Manchester: Manchester University Press, 1991), ch. 6, esp. pp. 147–52.

126. Cited in Vurpas, *Chansons,* p. 117.

127. See chapter 9 below.

128. Quinet, *La Révolution,* pp. 401–3.

129. Elie Fournier, *Turreau et les colonnes infernales: Ou l'échec de la violence* (Paris: Albin Michel, 1985), pp. 35–36.

130. Duval, ed., *Saint-Just,* pp. 700–1, 706, 714.

131. Robespierre, "Discours sur les principes de morale politique qui doivent guider la Convention nationale dans l'administration intérieure de la République" (17 pluviôse, an II, 4 February 1794), in Bouloiseau et al., eds., *Oeuvres de Robespierre,* vol. 10 (Paris: Presses Universitaires, 1967), pp. 357–58.

132. This paragraph rests heavily on Donald Greer, *The Incidence of the Terror during the French Revolution: A Statistical Interpretation* (Cambridge, Mass.: Harvard University Press, 1935); Richard Louie, "The Incidence of the Terror: A Critique

of a Statistical Interpretation," *French Historical Studies* 3 (1964): pp. 379–89; Gilbert Shapiro and John Markoff, "The Incidence of the Terror: Some Lessons for Quantitative History," *Journal of Social History* 9:2 (Winter 1975): pp. 193–218.

133. Greer, *Incidence*, p. 124.

134. See Gerd van den Heuvel, "Terreur, Terroriste, Terrorisme," in Reichardt and Schmitt, eds., *Handbuch*, vol. 3 (Munich: Oldenbourg, 1985), pp. 89–132, esp. pp. 119–23.

135. Richard Cobb, *The Police and the People: French Popular Protest, 1789–1820* (Oxford: Clarendon, 1970), pp. 196–97.

136. Mathiez, *After Robespierre: The Thermidorean Reaction* (New York: Knopf, 1931), p. 176; and Cobb, *Reactions to the French Revolution* (London: Oxford University Press, 1972), p. 31.

137. Cobb, *Police and the People*, p. 20.

138. Cited in Vurpas, *Chansons*, pp. 167–68.

139. Mathiez, *After Robespierre*, p. 177.

140. Cobb, *Reactions*; Cobb, *Police and the People*; and Colin Lucas, "Themes in Southern Violence After 9 Thermidor," in Gwynne Lewis and Colin Lucas, eds., *Beyond the Terror: Essays in French Regional and Social History, 1794–1815* (Cambridge: Cambridge University Press, 1983), pp. 152–94.

141. Lucas, "Themes," p. 153.

142. See P. M. Jones, *The Peasantry in the French Revolution* (Cambridge: Cambridge University Press, 1988), pp. 240–42.

143. Cited in Willette, *Le tribunal*, p. 44.

144. Quinet, *La Révolution*, p. 624.

145. See Colin Lucas, "The Problem of the Midi in the French Revolution," *Transactions of the Royal Historical Society* 28 (1978): pp. 1-25, esp. p. 24; Lucas, "Themes," p. 182; Cobb, *Reactions*, pp. 24–26.

146. Vurpas, *Chansons*, pp. 124–25, 176–77.

147. Ibid., p. 132, p. 137, and pp. 162–65.

148. Cited in Renée Fuoc, *La réaction thermidorienne à Lyon* (Lyon: Editions de Lyon, 1957), p. 40.

149. Fuoc, *La réaction*, pp. 76–79.

150. Ibid., pp. 130–31.

151. Cited in ibid., p. 136.

152. Cited in ibid., p. 137.

153. Quinet, *La Révolution*, p. 623.

154. Ibid., p. 624.

155. Ibid., p. 625.

156. Ibid., pp. 625–27.

157. Ibid., p. 623.

158. See Lenôtre, *Compagnie de Jéhu*, passim.

159. Quinet, *La Révolution*, pp. 628–31.

160. Burckhardt, *Vorlesungen*, pp. 297–98.

In the Eye of a "Time of Troubles": Terror in Russia, 1917–21

IN 1917 the overexertions of a protracted and failing war gravely unsettled Russia: the imperial army was on the verge of disintegration; famine stalked the major cities; the economy and exchequer were wasted; and industry was paralyzed. Twice before, in the time of the Crimean War and Russo-Japanese War, military defeat had shaken the tsarist regime and called forth prophylactic reforms. But in scale and intensity these earlier upheavals were nothing like the deep crisis brought on and fueled by the inordinate material and human sacrifices of the Very Great War. In February–March 1917, between the fall of the Peter-Paul Fortress and the resignation of Tsar Nicholas II, the forces of law and order crumbled, giving the signal for peasants to seize the land from their overlords and for minority nationalists along the periphery to press for autonomy or independence. This rising peasant and nationality disaffection was both cause and effect of a general dislocation which between 1917 and 1921 spiraled into an altogether peculiar and extreme "time of troubles" fraught with Furies.[1]

The contrast between France in 1789 and Russia in 1917 could not be more striking. When the Bastille fell, the Bourbon monarchy was at peace with Europe. Despite a momentary budgetary squeeze, its public finances and economy were sound, and so was its state apparatus, including the armed forces. Not surprisingly, the French Revolution heated up only gradually: it took between three and four years for France to go to war, for Louis XVI to be tried and executed, for civil war to erupt in the Vendée, and for terror to be put *à l'ordre du jour.*

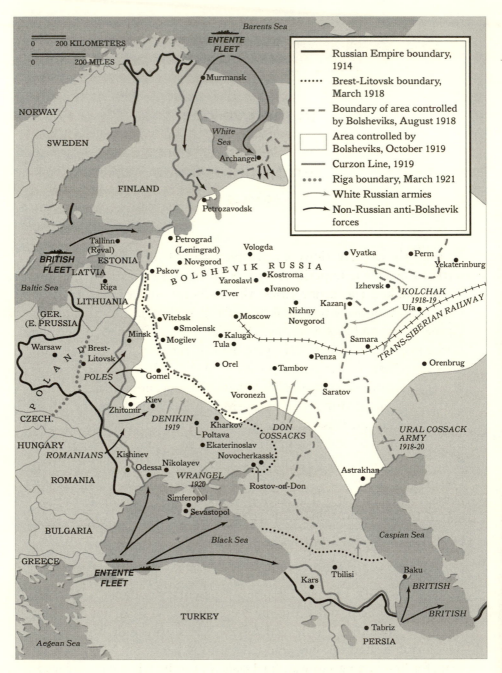

Russia in War and Revolution, 1914 to 1921

In Russia the pace was altogether quicker. The Romanov empire was at war at the time of the uprising in February 1917 in Petrograd, and both civil war and foreign intervention broke forth within less than a year. Nicholas II was executed in mid-July 1918, and mass terror was decreed in early September. In the meantime, earlier that same year, aided and abetted by the Central Powers, Ukraine and several other non-Russian "borderlands" seceded. But above all, the fact of war was omnipresent from the creation, and became an urgent defining issue and force. Whereas the provisional governments of Lvov and Kerensky used the continuation of *war* as a stratagem to tame the revolution, the Bolsheviks envisioned a rush to *peace* to revolutionize it. Especially the moderates, notably the Kadets and Mensheviks, looked to the appeals of nationalism, the flow of Allied financial and military aid, and the discipline of the barracks to help restore a minimum of order and to consolidate a revolution from above, on the model of 1905. The spectacular failure and human cost of Kerensky's military offensive in June 1917 discredited this political strategy. Presently the unreconstructed army was devitalized by the massive desertion of peasant-soldiers bent on joining the fast-spreading *jacquerie* against the nearest squire in the countryside instead of fighting the distant foreign enemy in pursuit of a chimeric "peace without annexations and indemnities."

This irreversible military predicament encouraged Lenin to intensify his drive for immediate "peace, bread, and land." In turn, Kerensky ordered General Kornilov, the new commander-in-chief, to reestablish discipline so that the army would be fit to continue fighting the war abroad and enforce order at home. But convinced that time was running out, and distrustful of non-autocratic government, in late August Kornilov launched an armed insurrection to establish a military dictatorship to be backed by the old ruling and governing classes. With no "national guard" of its own to protect it, the provisional government summoned supporters, including the hated Bolsheviks, to take to the streets so as to parry this diehard defiance. Apart from benefiting the Bolsheviks and their sympathizers, Kornilov's abortive coup further hastened the disintegration of the army, the rebellion of the peasantry, and the restlessness of the industrial proletariat.

Clearly, the inception and early infancy of the Russian Revolution, unlike that of the French Revolution, was marked by the political, economic, and social fallout of an exhausting and unsuccessful war effort. Russia's general crisis in city and country was not the doing of the Bolsheviks and Socialist Revolutionaries, even if their militants exploited it. The ease with which Lenin's inexperienced Red Guards invested the Winter Palace in October–November 1917 was less a measure of the Bolsheviks' strength and perspicacity than of the provisional government's irresolution and impotence in the face of snowballing domestic and foreign problems. To be sure, of all the political parties—which were, in any case, a fragile foreign implant in Russia's autocratic political culture—the Bolshevik party was by far the best organized and disciplined, as well as the most adaptable. Even so, its accession to power was a perverse effect of the rampant destabilization of Europe's largest and most populous, even if least developed, country, compounded by the dislocation of the concert of powers and the hyperbolic war in which it was trapped. While the Bolsheviks, like the Mensheviks and Socialist Revolutionaries, were mentally and theoretically prepared for a conjuncture analogous to 1904–5, they did not anticipate—nor, for that matter, welcome—the colossal implosion which unhinged Russia starting in 1917. Although their decisions and actions were informed by their ideological and programmatic canon, this canon was, in turn, modified in the heat of emergent events which called forth unforeseen intentions, policies, and consequences.

Admittedly, the way the Bolsheviks took power was consistent with their credo of direct and defiant action, and their authoritarian rule following Red October was bound to provoke resistances which they were, of course, determined to counter and repress. But again, just as they were unprepared for the enormity of the crisis, so they were caught unawares by its Furies, which they were not alone to quicken. With the cave-in of sovereignty, it was relatively easy for the Bolsheviks to take the remnant residue of power into their own hands. It was altogether harder, however, to exercise and enforce this vestige of authority; to do so meant fending off a broad range of foes in an incipient civil war that was inseparable from an unbearable foreign war. It may well be that by virtue of its eventual costs and cruelties, this resolve to fight a civil war became the original sin or primal curse of Bolshevik governance during the birth throes of the Russian Revolution. Even in circumstances less wretched than those of 1917 to 1921 in Russia, war and civil war, separately or jointly, are the great scourge of limited or democratic government.

With the overall situation favorable to the intensification of chaos and the attendant friend-enemy dissociation, the Bolsheviks ventured upon a civil war freighted with the founding violence of a new Russia. Eventually this unforeseen internal war, exacerbated by the intervention of hostile foreign powers, became the formative experience of the Bolshevik leaders. This struggle, at once defiant and perilous, fostered their theoretical and mental predisposition, rooted in Russia's authoritarian past, to centralize power, govern by ukase, resort to violence, control the economy, and impose ideological uniformity. At the same time they incited revolutionary zeal and embraced extreme voluntarism. The Bolshevik project was an inconstant amalgam of ideology and circumstance, of intention and improvisation, of necessity and choice, of fate and chance. Perhaps without the guiding historical example of the French Jacobins, which was ubiquitous, the Bolsheviks would have either hesitated to bid for undivided power or flinched once they realized that they faced an even more forbidding situation than their predecessors of the late eighteenth century. But then again, the brazen daring of the Bolsheviks, like that of the Jacobins before them, kept being vindicated by altogether improbable successes which legitimated and strengthened their tenuous and beleaguered regime.

Civil war was of much greater importance in the Russian than the French Revolution. Although the main civil war theaters were in the south and southeast, there was fighting in other regions as well. The Bolsheviks fought, above all, the White generals, who embodied the counterrevolution. Of course, they also did battle with the Kadets, the Mensheviks, and the Socialist Revolutionaries, as well as with several of the minority nationalities. In addition, they fought rebellious peasants in Ukraine, in Tambov province, and in the lands of the Volga. Ultimately, however, the struggle between the Bolsheviks and the White Guards was the crucial one, all the other conflicts being of subordinate importance. Given this primacy of absolute enmity between Reds and Whites, the peremptory dismissal of the Constituent Assembly in January 1918 was of marginal consequence: while it widened the fatal split between the Bolsheviks and the bulk of the Socialist Revolutionaries, it left Kolchak, Denikin, and Iudenich, the White generals, altogether indifferent. Bent on restoring the old regime and empire, even if stripped of the Romanov dynasty, the latter were as hostile to liberal or socialist democracy as they were to proletarian dictatorship.

Actually, Kornilov's stillborn military defiance of Kerensky's government in late August 1917 presaged the counterrevolution in the Russian Revolution. Even though their troops kept deserting them, all ex-tsarist senior officers stayed home to organize resistance rather than go into exile, as so many of their French counterparts had done in 1789. Almost immediately following the Bolshevik takeover in Petrograd, they made their way to the Don territories, with the idea of organizing White Guards of assorted volunteers and seasoned Cossacks to reclaim their world of yesterday. In any case, when, on November 3, 1917, Lenin proclaimed the start of civil war, he and his associates knew that they would have to engage not only the Kadets, but also, and above all, the implacable imperial officers corps.

The French Revolution was constantly present at the creation of the Russian Revolution.[2] Many of the actors in the Russian Revolution modeled themselves after those in the French Revolution: for the Kadets, the Feuillants were the worthy prototype; for the Mensheviks, the Girondins; for the Bolsheviks, the Jacobins. Some "consciously" used the French Revolution "as a pattern or guide for action"; others did so "unconsciously," on the basis of their "implicit or virtual" experience of it. Indeed, the French Revolution served as a road map for some, a model for others, and an incubus for still others. Unlike the Jacobins, who had looked back to ancient Rome for inspiration and guidance, as well as a legitimating pedigree, the Bolsheviks sought their historical referents in a more recent past. Indeed, they became fervent analogists, constantly weighing the resemblances and differences between themselves and the Jacobins. In making these comparisons they drew on the politically informed debates about the French Revolution within the Russian left during the decades before 1917.

The question of violence was central to this critical engagement with the paradigmatic Great Revolution, all the more so because of the repressive violence in its aftershocks in 1848 and 1871. Not only Marx and Engels theorized the role of violence in the unfolding Socialist project, but so did the action intellectuals of the Socialist movements of Central Europe and Russia. Indeed, unlike during the prelude to the French Revolution, violence became an ever more urgent issue during the pre-revolution of the Russian Revolution. In 1905 the tsarist government had not hesitated to crush the rebels and soviets of St. Petersburg and Moscow, and between 1907 and 1917 it had used bold physical and rhetorical violence to curb the reforms introduced with the October Manifesto. Many of the revolutionary leaders of 1917–18 were personally caught up in this repression, so that unlike their Jacobin forerunners, they experienced the state's repressive force at first hand. Indeed, ever so many leading members of the Sixth Congress of the Bolshevik Party, meeting in July 1917, and all fifteen members of the first Council of People's Commissars had spent years in prison, in Siberia, and in exile. Five of the latter had also been jailed by Kerensky's Provisional Government.[3]

The would-be revolutionaries of 1917, compared to those of 1789, were conditioned, not to say hardened, for the exercise of violence. They came upon the political scene steeped in the theory, ideology, and history of its practice. The unprecedented slaughter of the Very Great War merely reinforced them in their conceptual and existential engagement with naked violence, especially since they considered Europe's governors to have unleashed this monstrous conflict as a diversion to unnerve and divide the rising and restive forces of reform and revolution. Besides, of late, throughout Europe, including Russia, the reason of violence had become at least as central to the *idées-forces* of the far right as the far left.

Be that as it may, in the quagmire of 1917–18 there was no governing without recourse to violence. Abroad Russia faced a catastrophic situation, compounded by centrifugal pulls in its non-Russian peripheries, while at home polity, economy, judiciary, police, and army were in headlong decomposition. This external predicament and internal entropy reinforced each other, and the result was an exceptionally grave "time of troubles." These troubles would be all the more furious, and consequently harder to curb, because of the peculiar features of Russia's human geography. Most strikingly, Russia's size was staggering: forty times the land area of France, with eleven time zones. In early 1918, cornered by the Central Powers, at Brest-Litovsk the Bolsheviks were able to cede territories one and a half times the size of Germany without crippling the nascent Socialist Federated Soviet Republic. Even in normal times, let alone in a time of troubles, Russia defied governance as a single unit—a single sovereignty—by virtue not only of its sheer expanse but also its bewildering diversity of cultures, its uneven levels of development, its primitive state of transport, and its encumbrance by a torpid peasant world. This rich but refractory endowment of vastness, diversity, and unsimultaneity was at least as burdensome as the enduring deficit of democratic thought and praxis.

Considering this extreme situation, and especially allowing for Russia's ingrained historical-political traditions, the choice was never really between democracy and despotism, but between different forms of authoritarian rule. Any Russian government was bound to be a severe emergency government prone and indeed obliged to resort to violence as a provisional instrument of rule, and a Bolshevik government would merely be more inclined to do so than a government formed by leaders with a different historical understanding, doctrinal conception, and personal experience of revolution.[4]

This background conditioned the nature and practice of the Bolsheviks' founding violence and enforcement terror of 1917–21, including of its chief executive agency: the Cheka. At the outset, the Cheka was conceived as part of a stopgap for the broken armor—bureaucracy, judiciary, police, army—of the Russian state. Cities and towns experienced the equivalent of the wild land seizures and attacks on notables in the countryside. There was a wildfire of looting of the property of the wealthy classes as well as an explosion of avenging violence against members of the old power elite, especially former government officials and army officers. Further, with prisons and courts crippled, society was overrun by criminals and blackmarketeers who, in turn, provoked wild justice.[5] This rampant lawlessness called for the prompt establishment of a new legal, penal, and police system. In many respects the Cheka was as much an improvisation as War Communism, which was designed less to recast the economy than to reclaim it to provide daily rations and the sinews for political and military survival. Both the Cheka and War Communism were driven by a combination of panic, fear, and pragmatism mixed with hubris, ideology, and iron will.

The development of the Cheka's mission and organization was closely correlated with the spread and aggravation of the civil war, and so was the growth of its ideological furor. With time, and without relenting in its battle against runaway speculation, hoarding, and ordinary crime, the Cheka gave first priority to enforcing security to the rear of the fast changing battle lines of the civil war as well as to deploying special security units among the fighting forces of the Red Army and along vital rail lines and roadways.

Without any deliberate plan but simply in response to all these imperatives, the manpower of the Cheka expanded from some 2,000 men in mid-1918 to over 35,000 six months later and to about 140,000 by the end of the civil war, not counting some 100,000 frontier troops. The central headquarters, first in Petrograd and then in Moscow, eventually established and partially controlled a sprawling network of provincial, district, and local Chekas. As of March 1919 Felix Dzerzhinsky, the Cheka's national chairman, also served as People's Commissar for Internal Affairs, giving him direct and privileged access to Sovnarkom, which presumably defined and oversaw internal security. Gradually, with the civil war raging and calling for instant decisions and resolute actions, at all levels the Cheka tended to stretch and exceed its powers, which were typically ill-defined. Rather than turn criminals and political suspects over to what were intended to be separate revolutionary tribunals for prosecution and sentencing, the Cheka ignored and fended off outside judicial and political controls.

* * *

It is hardly surprising that "the Cheka's original mandate. . . [should have been] modeled on the tsarist security police" whose practices were rooted in Russia's authoritarian past.[6] The Bolsheviks, like the Jacobins, brought back the old methods of criminal and political control, though both foreswore recourse to the old forms of torture. To be sure, there were significant differences between the respective precedents: on the one hand, the religiously fired sack of Béziers and massacre of Saint Bartholomew's Day; on the other, the ungodly exile system in Siberia and the repressive praxis of the Okhranka. These peculiarities in turn made for distinct differences in the configuration of the two terrors, the one having the guillotine as its most distinctive emblem, the other concentration and labor camps. Nonetheless, one might say that in both cases, in Quinet's words, "the weapons of the past . . . were taken out of the old arsenal . . . and used in the defense of the present," with the result that "by way of the terror today's men suddenly and unwittingly reverted to once again become the men of yesterday."[7]

Almost from the beginning, concentration and labor camps were part of the Bolshevik regime's internal security system, and they were grafted onto Russia's age-old internal exile system, a legacy for which there was no equivalent in France. Through the centuries, the experience and memory of religious persecution and prosecution, backed by the Inquisition, left a deep imprint on France's ways and means to "discipline and punish." Russia's methods, for their part, were impregnated with the profane practice of bureaucratic and arbitrary justice, closely overseen by the tsars. The Siberian exile system, dating from the later sixteenth century, was the hub of the Romanov empire's wheel of justice. It was inaugurated by Ivan the Terrible (1533–84), who also initiated Russia's eastward continental expansion.[8] Even if unintentionally, newly opened territories became the entryway to a vast and distant "roofless prison" for "outlaws" sentenced to *ssylka*, or banishment and exile. Ironically, almost from the start exile to Siberia was conceived as a clement alternative to capital punishment.

During the seventeenth century, with the acquisition of huge and sparsely peopled lands in Trans-Uralia, including Siberia, *ssylka* rapidly became "the central and most characteristic feature of the tsarist penal system."[9] The Law Code of 1649 designated several regions in Siberia as places of "external exile" for a sweeping range of lawbreakers, including fugitive serfs and religious dissenters. By now the tsars began to realize the advantage of using *ssylka* along with conscription to populate and develop the empty but economically valuable Siberian spaces, which soon attracted an ever larger flow of more or less voluntary settlers as well. As early as 1662 exiles accounted for 8,000 or over ten percent of Siberia's settler population of 70,000. It was now, too, that torments began to be inflicted on prisoners before they set out on their *via dolorosa*: besides being flogged with the knout, many of them suffered the mutilation of a hand, foot, ear, or nose, as well as the humiliation of being branded. Following this ordeal, many prisoners walked a full year, in leg irons, to reach their destinations, until Tsar Alexander III (1881–94) put an end to these interminable forced marches in favor of transport by ship, and later by train.[10]

Peter the Great updated the Siberian archipelago's "prisons without doors" by supplementing and then surpassing *ssylka* with *katorga*, or forced labor.[11] The moving eastern frontier was to be exploited for the benefit of the imperial regime. More and more convicts were put to work mining silver, gold, and salt as well as, in due course, building roads and railways. *Katorga* became the harshest of tsarist Russia's six categories of penal servitude. Having survived the dual ordeal of the post-conviction torment and the wretched passage eastward, the brutalized prisoners faced a forbidding environment of life and work near the mines of Nerdinsk and Kara, and at many other sites, most of them fairly small: a population of several hundred was the norm, and several thousand the exception. Inadequate housing, clothing, and food made for a high rate of disease and mortality. Weighed down with ten-pound fetters and subject to arbitrary flogging, the convicts worked long hours. They had no time off, until 1885 when they were granted two days of rest per month. Wives were encouraged to accompany or follow their husbands, probably in the interest of colonization, since most convicts settled in the Far East upon completion of their sentences.

The long nineteenth century down through 1917 saw many changes in tsarism's peculiar penal and political security system.[12] Following the Decembrist rising of 1825 Nicholas I established the Third Section, a special political office with a corps of policemen to protect the security of state and regime. In part because of its inadequacy in the face of growing opposition, in 1880 the Third Section was abolished and all security functions were concentrated in a single police department in the Interior Ministry. The next year Alexander III reinvigorated the Okhranka, the tsarist regime's main security organization charged with uncovering, infiltrating, and repressing the political opposition, which was increasingly forced underground and prone to terrorism. Although it was overwhelmed by the great upheaval of 1905, the Okhranka more than recovered between 1906 and 1914, when Nicholas II resumed and intensified the war against the anti-tsarist opposition, which he quickened with his own unbending policies.

The flow of convicts to Asiatic Russia continued all this time, with between 10,000 to 20,000 yearly, unevenly divided between *ssylka* and *katorga*. Although in 1801 Alexander I had abrogated the most extreme forms of cruelty, prisoners continued to be subjected to preliminary branding and knouting for several more decades.[13] There are no reliable figures on the number of political prisoners among them, but according to the best estimates they never made up more than one percent.[14] Indeed, they may be said to have peopled the equivalent of no more than one of the many islands of imperial Russia's penitentiary archipelago. The politicals were neither branded nor whipped. Though they benefited from a privileged status and regimen, they experienced the rigors of the exile system and were in many different ways scarred and marked by it, including by their close if limited contact with lowborn common-law convicts. The political prisoners left a greater mark than their limited numbers warranted by virtue of their notoriety and their role in excoriating the exile system in utterly stark and terrifying terms, which left a dark and haunting imprint on the Russian and European imagination, not unlike the Inquisition.

Dostoevsky was the first of several great Russian writers and political intellectuals to probe tsarism's peculiar prison and exile universe.[15] In his twenties in St. Petersburg Dostoevsky became involved with a half-secret discussion group of young and well-born critics of runaway autocracy. The Third Section being on the watch, Dostoevsky was arrested. He spent eight months in a prison of the Peter and Paul Fortress before, at Christmas 1849, beginning his journey to Omsk, mostly by sledge though weighted down by leg irons. His *Memoirs from the House of the Dead* (1861) is a searing autobiographical but also creatively imaginative telling of his four years of hard labor and military service in this western Siberian city. Dostoevsky's account was followed by those of Chekov, Tolstoy, Bakunin, and Kropotkin.

Solzhenitsyn, too, stands very much in this tradition.[16] In *The Gulag Archipelago* he briefly discusses the history of the exile system, with particular attention to the privileged place of the political prisoners in it. His main concern is to extenuate the evils of the tsarist penal and exile system in comparison with those of the Soviet Gulag. In fact, he means to demonstrate a fundamental discontinuity between the one and the other, making the Gulag exclusively the product of the Communist ideology and the villainy of Lenin and Stalin, without significant roots and parallels in Russia's past. Even so, by describing, however synoptically, the "somber power of exile" and the "miserably clothed, branded, and starving" victims of *ssylka* and *katorga* under the tsars, Solzhenitsyn concedes elements of historical persistence at the same time that he tells the story in the dire and bitter accents of Dostoevsky.

The Bolsheviks themselves were influenced by Russia's prison and exile literature, all the more so because for some of them, as for not a few Mensheviks and Socialist Revolutionaries, it spoke to their own personal experiences. While as of the late nineteenth century the Romanov regime willfully used *ssylka* to deter and intimidate radical critics and revolutionaries, these, for their part, held it up as one of tsarism's basest badges of infamy. Even if Lenin, Trotsky, Stalin, and Bukharin knew the penal and exile system from the inside—albeit under tolerable conditions—they certainly took it for granted that it would be eliminated with the birth of a new Russia. And, in fact, the first Provisional Government abolished it, along with the tsarist police and Okhranka. Eventually the exigencies of the struggle against criminals as well as enemies at home and abroad prompted the Bolsheviks to reach back, selectively, into Russia's storehouse of political strategies and weapons of judicial and political control, and *ssylka* and *katorga* were reshaped to serve the pressing needs of the moment. Presently Paul Miliukov, perhaps the savviest Constitutional Democrat, noted that Bolshevism was a hybrid of "very advanced European theory . . . [and] genuinely as well as deeply rooted Russian" praxis which rather than "break with the 'ancien régime,' reasserts Russia's past in the present." In an evocative simile, Miliukov suggested that just "as geological upheavals bring the lower strata of the earth to the surface as evidence of the early ages of our planet, so Russian Bolshevism, by discarding the thin upper social layer, has laid bare the uncultured and unorganized substratum of Russian historical life."[17]

To come to terms with the Cheka-run concentration and labor camps during the first terror of the Russian Revolution, it is of course important not to go too far in tracing their genealogy and etiology backward into the past. It is equally important, however, not to read their early history in terms of subsequent developments, notably of the Soviet Gulag after 1929 and of the Nazi concentration camps after 1933 and extermination camps after 1941. The term "concentration camp" originated with the colonial wars of the *fin de siècle*: Spain set up concentration camps to hold enemy prisoners and civilians in Cuba, the United States in the Philippines, and England in South

Africa.[18] In all three cases the internment camps were established in wartime, overseas, and as a concomitant of military operations. None of the outside armies faced politically organized ideological enemies to the rear of their lines, which meant that their prisoners, both military and civilian, suffered the miseries of emergency detention rather than institutionalized and willful mistreatment or forced labor. With victory the camps were closed, also because what little there was of insurgent resistance came to an end.

Later on, the concentration camps of post-1929 Soviet Russia and post-1933 Nazi Germany were initially political camps started in peace time and in the absence of active civil war at home. Whereas from the outset the Gulag had the dual mission of enforcing political control and of driving economic growth through the exploitation of the forced labor of its inmates, the concentration camps of the Third Reich did not assume an economic role—nor a genocidal turn—until well after the outbreak of war in 1939.

For their part the camps of the Russian Revolution's first terror were set up in the midst of combined foreign and civil war. Both the external and internal conflicts were highly ideologized, with the result that unlike during the Spanish-American and Boer wars, some of the enemies who were imprisoned in camps were seen as being distinctly political. As for their impressment for forced labor, it was related to the fighting of essentially defensive domestic and foreign struggles rather than to a project of either economic mastery or foreign territorial conquest. But it would seem that the Bolsheviks' readiness to use the labor of camp inmates in the emergency of 1917 to 1921 was conditioned by Russia's past experience with *katorga*, just as the harsh living and working conditions in these camps were due to the extreme rigors of war and civil war rather than to a blueprint for systematic punishment or exploitation, let alone extermination, "there being no Soviet Treblinka."[19]

✳ ✳ ✳

The aristocratic reaction in France, reflected in Louis XVI's repeal of the Maupeau reform in the early 1770s, was mild compared to that in Russia during the decade before 1917. Those were the years in which Nicholas II rescinded many of the liberalizing concessions he had grudgingly made in 1905. By the outbreak of war in 1914 the constitutional experiment had been diluted, the tsar and his acolytes having severely restricted the franchise and civil liberties, as well as broken the Duma. Significantly, this reversal coincided with the growth of a new right sworn to violence, which had the blessing of the Court. As noted, during the Very Great War military misfortune and futility, reckoned in millions of casualties and utter economic exhaustion, once again undermined the old order, and by early 1917 Russia's political and civil society entered a time of unprecedented troubles.

Not surprisingly, the workers of Petrograd, including women textile workers, were in the forefront of the revolt of late February and early March.[20] Clamoring for bread, peace, and the end of autocracy, their swelling strike movement was largely spontaneous. At first, the prospects were dim, as troops loyal to the tsar kept firing upon them, taking numerous lives. But the remonstrants stayed the course, some of them rushing such emblems of repressive state power as police stations, prisons, and court houses. Others wrought their vengeance on public officials, "hunting down, lynching, and brutally killing" policemen.[21] In Petrograd alone there were some 1,400 dead and wounded, about half of them military personnel.[22] It was only with the mutiny of several local army garrisons, urged on by junior officers, that the insurgence stood fair to succeed: the muzhiks in military uniforms who defied the order to open fire on civilians rose against the conceit of their imperial officers, which they considered of a piece with the arrogance of the landed gentry. At any rate, workers and soldiers joined hands to occupy public buildings and seize arms for what quickly turned into a full-scale insurrection. Meanwhile the Octobrists and Kadets, who finally prevailed on Nicholas II to abdicate and Grand Duke Michael to renounce the throne, formed a provisional committee to restore order, composed of thirteen Duma members. Their aim was to fill the emergent political vacuum and prevent a runaway fragmentation of sovereignty. At the same time, the Menshevik Duma deputies, in the spirit of 1905, took the lead in forming a provisional Petrograd Soviet of Workers and Soldiers—in which peasant-soldiers greatly outnumbered proletarian workers—to organize and channel the rebellion. Even if their ultimate political and social objectives as well as their worldviews were very much at variance, Kadets and Mensheviks, one and all fervent westernizers, agreed on the instant establishment of a "bourgeois-liberal" government and the early election of a constituent assembly. Such was the origin and mission of the provisional governments headed first by Prince Lvov and then Kerensky.

But as mentioned before, the Kadets and Mensheviks, now joined by the Socialist Revolutionaries, had one other common, perhaps overriding aim: not unlike the bulk of Russia's traditional power elite, they proposed to see the war through to victory on the side of the Allies. Admittedly, the Mensheviks and Socialist Revolutionaries proceeded to exhort all the world to move toward a peace without annexations and indemnities, to be secured by timely negotiations. But pending this unlikely political and diplomatic reconfiguration, the grueling war continued, with devastating social and political consequences.

Under the circumstances the coalition cabinets headed by Lvov and Kerensky could be little more than emergency governments with a limited and hesitant reformist reach. Still, Russia's new rulers promulgated essential freedoms: association, assembly, speech, press, and religion; as well as disestablishment, amnesty, and the end of capital punishment. But these bold steps, in the spirit of the Declaration of the Rights of Man, touched more sympathetic chords in urban than rural Russia, which had altogether different priorities, notably immediate peace and, above all, land reform. Indeed, especially the Kadets, but also many Mensheviks, dodged the land question, so that at this juncture Russia's embryonic reformist regime produced nothing comparable to France's dramatic night of August 4, 1789, which had brought the abrogation of the "feudal" rights and privileges of the nobility and clergy. Obsessed with the imperatives of war, the Lvov and Kerensky governments sought to restabilize rather than reform Russia's political and civil society, thereby muting their millenarian promise. A certain reading of the dynamics of the French Revolution fortified the members of successive provisional governments in their resolve to prevent any further radicalization favorable to the Bolsheviks and Socialist Revolutionaries, even at the risk of fostering it with their own inordinate caution. Meanwhile the election of the projected Constituent Assembly remained in suspense.

Beginning with the resignation of A. I. Guchkov, leader of the Octobrists, and the removal of Miliukov on May 1, 1917, when Kerensky became war minister, the Kadets kept yielding cabinet positions to the non-Bolshevik left. At the same time that this faction-ridden left gained ground in the straitened state executive, in mid-June it found a home in the First All-Russian Congress of Workers and Soldiers Deputies, a potential rival or alternative to tomorrow's Constituent Assembly. Except for the Bolsheviks, the members of this would-be people's parliament endorsed the policies of the provisional governments. But the country's skyrocketing economic distress and war weariness worked in favor of the dissident and far left, as did the fiasco of Kerensky's politically inspired military offensive on the Galician front in mid-June. Urged upon Petrograd by the Allies, this bold stroke, which cost several hundred thousand lives, was a desperate gamble: an improbable military victory was to be used to consolidate the provisional regime, above all by redeeming the army, without which there was no restoring law and order.[23]

Partly fueled by indignation about the continuing military unreason, the violent anti-government demonstrations of July 3–5, 1917, in Petrograd were primarily carried by the left.[24] The furor was largely spontaneous: considering direct action premature, the leaders of the Bolshevik party and Petrograd Soviet followed rather than led the soldiers, sailors, factory workers, and city poor who took to the streets. Because the riotous crowds lacked discipline and leadership, the provisional government's sparse police and military forces were sufficient to disperse them, with minimal casualties on both sides.

The sequel of these *journées* was mounting discord between the Kadets and the non-Bolshevik left over how to deal with the irrepressible crisis.[25] Lvov and four Kadet ministers resigned as Kerensky assumed the premiership to rule with a coalition in which non-Socialists were now in the minority. He vowed to push for a non-annexationist peace, a constituent assembly, and land reform. At the same time, Kerensky ordered the arrest of leading Bolsheviks, though Lenin and several of his closest associates managed to flee abroad or go underground. He also directed General Kornilov to steel the army. Even so, and as part of a conservative backlash, the Kadets served notice that they were more than ever opposed to a soft peace, social reform, and power-sharing with the Soviets. Indeed, in the wake of the failed June offensive and the portentous July days, the Kadets ceased to support reform as an antidote to further radicalization. Unlike Kerensky, they abandoned the search for a third way or force between the far left and far right.

Not a few prominent Kadets along with liberals and conservatives silently cheered when in late August General Kornilov, with broad backing by senior officers, ordered select regiments to march on Petrograd either to stiffen Kerensky's resolve to stand fast or to establish a government of national salvation controlled by the military.[26] Having tempted the devil, Kerensky dismissed Kornilov and summoned all the forces of movement to rise in defense of the Revolution. These forces rallied under the banner of a Committee for the Struggle Against the Counterrevolution, supported by the Soviet as well as the Bolsheviks, though Lenin stressed that the workers were mounting the barricades to protect the Revolution, not the government. In the meantime the cabinet had invested Kerensky with special, not to say dictatorial, powers to meet the emergency.

Once the challenge from the military was checked, there was yet another cabinet struggle. The third provisional government, headed by Kerensky, was dominated by moderate Mensheviks and right Socialist Revolutionaries. This cabinet was weaker than its predecessors, not least because of the explicit opposition of both the restless forces of order, including the Kadets, and the impatient Bolsheviks.

Unable or unwilling to extricate Russia from the ruinous war and to address the burning land problem, Kerensky simply could not find a social base for his phantasmagoric third way. Conditions were going from bad to worse on the front, in the major cities, and in the countryside, with the result that the disaffection of workers and peasants expanded and quickened. The Bolsheviks were the major beneficiaries of the Kornilov affair. Legitimated as a result of having been asked and armed to help in the defense of the Revolution, they redoubled their agitation and organizing efforts. In turn, the officers corps emerged as the vanguard and nerve center of the inevitable counterrevolution. With little political power, moral authority, and repressive force, the third coalition government was helpless. Here if ever was a situation to which the words of Yeats apply: "Things fall apart; the center cannot hold."[27]

✳ ✳ ✳

In late September and early October, when Lenin, seconded by Trotsky, convinced the inner circle of Bolsheviks to launch an armed uprising, he knew that famine, war weariness, and fear of another right-wing coup would translate into broad popular sympathy or backing for his wager. The Bolsheviks also assumed that few, if any, police and army detachments were likely to stand by Kerensky. Indeed, there were practically no protective forces when on October 25 Bolshevik activists rushed the Winter Palace to arrest the cabinet members, who were briefly held at the Peter and Paul Fortress before being released. While the Red Guards took control of Petrograd, Kerensky hastened off to Pskov, the headquarters of the northern front, expecting to rally loyal troops. But he found none, except for some 1,000 badly armed Cossacks whom General Peter N. Krasnov agreed to rush in the direction of Petrograd. They reached Gatchina, a southern suburb, on October 27. Three days later, "a motley army [of approximately 10,000 men] made up of workers' detachments, soldiers of the Petrograd garrison, and Baltic sailors" defeated Krasnov's forces at Pulkovo Heights, with casualties on both sides.[28] Krasnov was captured, and Kerensky fled to England. It was a measure of the powerlessness of Kerensky's government that during the "Ten Days That Shook the World" there were only several dozen casualties in the capital of the new Great Revolution. In Moscow, however, there was considerable resistance. For an entire week assorted officers, military cadets, and right-wing Socialist Revolutionaries shielded the provisional government, with the result that several hundred people were killed. Still, all things considered, the Bolshevik takeover was relatively bloodless, certainly compared to the February uprising.

It was now the turn of the Bolsheviks to set up yet another—a fourth—provisional government. But theirs was to be a "Workers' and Peasants' Government," to be run by a Council of People's Commissars chaired by Lenin, with Trotsky serving as Commissar for Foreign Affairs. They dropped any pretense of practicing the reason of state and of standing above class or interest. The Bolsheviks had pressed for an early meeting of the Second All-Russian Congress of Soviets, and it opened on October 25–26, in the midst of their bid for power. In addition to looking to avoid the strains of dual power, they sought ratification of their immediate and short-term program: make peace;

distribute land; eliminate food shortages; and elect a constituent assembly. This last point was equivocal in that it implied that ultimately power would be vested in a constituent assembly, which clashed with the Bolsheviks' cry for "all power to the soviets."

In any case, the Congress of Soviets approved Lenin's sweeping Decree On Peace calling for an instant negotiated end of the war "without annexations and indemnities." There followed an equally radical decree expropriating the land of the landlords, imperial family, Orthodox Church, and state. The land was transferred to latter-day *mirs* (village communes) or new-model soviets for distribution, equally, to peasants pledged to work their small plots without hired labor. On January 18 the Decree Socializing the Land confirmed this vast redistribution, without compensation, and reiterated that "the right to use the land belongs to him who cultivates it with his own labor." With these rescripts, which appropriated the platform of the Socialist Revolutionaries, the Bolsheviks meant to broaden their social and political base beyond the urban proletariat. But no less important, they gave evidence of their practical reason: countless peasants having long since seized the land they had now and forever considered their own, the Bolsheviks legitimated the revolution in the countryside which had not been of their doing. Indeed, by recognizing the wild land seizures, the Congress of Soviets and Bolshevik leaders grounded the Russian Revolution much as the National Assembly, moved by the *grande peur*, had grounded the French Revolution in August 1789.[29] Both times the city took the first step, but in countries that were over 85 percent peasant, there was no continuing without the village.

Having spoken on peace and land, the Congress of Soviets elected a Bolshevik-dominated executive committee and approved the new provisional government. In so doing it ratified Lenin's opening programmatic declaration addressed to "All Workers, Soldiers, and Peasants," whose interests now moved to the top of the revolutionary agenda.[30] Except for "ensuring the convocation of the Constituent Assembly on the date set," the new emphasis was—*pace* Hannah Arendt—squarely on the social question, with priority for "the transfer of all land without compensation" to peasants and "the establishment of control over industry by workers." This new course was contingent on securing an immediate and non-annexationist peace, just as the previous course had been tied to staying in the war for war aims fixed before 1917. Indeed, the issue of war and peace remained altogether crucial. The exigencies of war were certain to seriously impede the embryonic Bolshevik regime's efforts to implement its far-reaching program: on the one hand, the Declaration of the Rights of the Toiling and Exploited People of January 16, 1918, signaled a radical break with the past and a headlong rush into a new future, giving Lenin's provisional government the millenarian urge which the preceding provisional governments had lacked or abjured; on the other, in face of an ever more refractory time of troubles there was no dispensing with a *dictature de détresse*. The switches were set for a governance severely torn between contingency and ideology, with the new decision makers mindful of the perils of both pressing emergencies and overweening innovations.

* * *

With the world collapsing about them, none of Russia's provisional governments gave the Constituent Assembly top priority. Both the Kadets and the Mensheviks were wary of elections by universal manhood suffrage, in which they knew they could not fare well.[31] At first set for September 17, 1917, the elections were postponed to November 12. By then, eight months after the fall of the Romanovs, the Bolsheviks were in power. But, as noted, they had pledged to allow the elections to go forward.

About 40 million votes were cast, the rate of participation being between 50 and 60 percent.[32] With about 16 million votes, or 40 percent of the total, the Socialist Revolutionaries secured some 400 seats. The Bolsheviks were second, with about 10 million votes, or 24 percent, which gave them 170 deputies. The outcome confirmed the worst fears of the liberal and social democrats: the Kadets captured only about 2 million votes and 17 seats; the Mensheviks received 1.5 million votes—half of them in Georgia—and 16 seats. The two parties combined accounted for less than 10 percent of the popular vote and 4 percent of the seats.

Perhaps most significantly, the throne and altar, as well as the landlords, were left high and dry, the peasants having voted massively for the Socialist Revolutionaries. While the latter were strongly carried by the countryside, they won only limited support in the cities, taking no more than 8 percent of the vote in Moscow and 16 percent in

Petrograd. The Bolsheviks, for their part, scored well in urban Russia, gaining close to 50 percent of the vote in the "two capitals." Having played on war weariness, they also polled about half the votes in the army garrisons to the rear. As things turned out, the Bolsheviks had a stronger social base than their overall electoral score suggests, especially in 1917–18, when the Revolution's commanding *political* heights were in urban Russia. Even so, although they showed unexpected strength, they would have been in no position to govern democratically, assuming they had wanted to. They did, however, shore up their cramped position by prevailing on the left Socialist Revolutionaries to be their coalition partners, which brought them the support of 40 additional deputies and opened them to the peasantry, in keeping with their land policy.

By the time the Constituent Assembly convened on January 5, 1918, the civil war was getting under way. While the Bolsheviks were not really surprised by the incipient resistance of the White Guards, they were outraged that the Kadets should so fully side with them. Indeed, the Kadets, unlike the Mensheviks, made common cause with the greatest losers of the elections, the Whites, who saw no contradiction between abjuring electoral politics, which put them at a disadvantage, and championing the cause of a free Constituent Assembly. In any case, on December 1, 1917, Lenin called for the outlawing of the Kadets, insisting that they wanted "to simultaneously sit in the Constituent Assembly and organize civil war." His Socialist Revolutionary partners instantly urged the Bolsheviks to "free themselves from their nightmare about the Kadets," particularly since there were no hard and fast criteria for "identifying" them. Instead of hammering away at the Kadets' spurious constitutionalism, the government should challenge the Constituent Assembly to vote "on questions of peace, land, and workers' control," with a view to turning it into a "revolutionary Convention." Blithely ignoring this advice, the all-Russian Central Executive Committee of Soviets adopted a resolution denouncing the Kadets for "heading" the counterrevolution, after Lenin stressed that in "bringing forward a direct political charge against [an entire] political party" the Bolsheviks were merely following in the footsteps of "the French revolutionaries."[33]

The socialists were very much divided on the eve of the opening of the Constituent Assembly in which they would occupy some 85 percent of the seats. The Bolsheviks charged that the slogan "All Power to the Constituent Assembly" embraced by the Mensheviks and moderate Socialist Revolutionaries was really intended to be read as "Down with the Soviets."[34] Clearly, Lenin meant to "counterpose the Congress of Soviets to the Constituent Assembly." Having benefited from their campaign for the soviets, the Bolsheviks valued their symbolic force and expected to have the ascendancy in them. According to Zinoviev, "the duel between the Constituent Assembly and the Congress of Soviets . . . [was] a historical struggle between two revolutions, the one bourgeois and the other socialist, . . . the elections to the Constituent Assembly [being] a reflection of the first [i.e., the] February revolution."[35]

This unseasonable Constituent Assembly convened on January 5, 1918 in Taurida Palace, with Victor Chernov, a leading Socialist Revolutionary, in the chair. In the name of the provisional minority government, Iakov Sverdlov stepped forward to move that the deputies make this government's founding project, as put forward in the Declaration of the Rights of the Toiling and Exploited People, their working agenda. Sverdlov emphasized that just as the French Revolution had "issued the Declaration of the Rights of Man and the Citizen which . . . [sanctioned] the free exploitation of those not possessing the tools and means of production . . . [so] the Russian Revolution had to issue a declaration of rights thundering forth its own project." When his motion was defeated by about 235 over about 145 votes in favor of a proposal to "discuss current questions of policy," the Bolsheviks, as if according to plan, stormed out of the hall, followed by the left Socialist Revolutionaries, signaling the closing and dissolution of the Assembly.[36] Not unlike Stolypin's "coup d'état" of June 3, 1907, which had devitalized the fledgling Imperial Duma, this arrogation aroused little, if any, protest or outrage: once again there was only meager popular support for democratic principles and institutions. In particular the peasants were impervious to democratic chants, all the more so now that they were repossessing "their" land by direct action rather than legislative enactment. As for the industrial workers, who shared the peasants' cruel disappointment with the pre-war Duma, they pinned their faith to the soviets and the factory councils. In effect, the champions of the Constituent Assembly were in no position either to raise volunteers for its defense or to mobilize the streets, the partisans of constitutional democracy being found among the classes, not the masses.[37]

On January 10, 1918 the Third All-Russian Congress of Soviets became the presumptive heir of the Constituent Assembly. The delegates sang the *International* before an orchestra struck up the *Marseillaise*, "to bring to recollection the historical path traversed" since 1789. This Congress promptly adopted a variant of the Declaration of the Rights of the Toiling and Exploited Peoples which the Constituent Assembly had voted down. It proclaimed, *urbi et orbi*, that the Russian Revolution was sworn to "end . . . the exploitation of man by man . . . and the division of society into classes"; to make "all land . . . public property" for transfer "to the working masses without payment . . . and on the basis of equal land tenure"; to establish "workers' control"; and to promote the "right to self-determination." This would-be ecumenical manifesto, which superseded the battle cry "peace, bread, and land," was not without a contingent fighting agenda, in that it vowed to "crush exploiters mercilessly," to raise an "army of working men," and to "put an end to all secret treaties."[38]

* * *

We have seen, then, that civil and political liberties were not high on the reformist agenda in the early dawn of the revolution in Russia. No less striking, the founding violence of the year 1917 was relatively limited, largely because the military was not about to keep repressing it. Indeed, to the extent that the February upheaval culminated in a "revolution from above," the army's senior officers were among its chief sponsors and mainstays. They sacrificed the crown to an accommodation with a legal opposition and Duma which they expected to be moderate and tractable. In any case, if there was no counterrevolutionary resistance and civil war immediately following the February days it was largely because until late August the high command supported the provisional governments, the prosecution of the war being their joint and absolute priority. First Kornilov's defiance and then Krasnov's military drive prefigured the unexceptional counterrevolutionary turn of the ranking generals and their political collaborators. Certainly these hard-liners were not about to rally to a government seeking an early and humiliating exit from the Very Great War as part of a strategy to consolidate and drive on the revolution. In addition to facing the trials and tribulations of Russia's time of troubles, the Bolshevik provisional government had to confront an ominous counterrevolutionary resistance aided from abroad.

Petrograd and Moscow were not promising sites for military resistance. Probably for reasons of logistics as well as because of the prospect of Cossack recruits, the center of opposition moved from the army's general headquarters at Mogilev, east of Minsk, to the Don territories in the south. It was also near Mogilev, in a monastery at Bykhov, that Kornilov was under house arrest along with the other generals who had supported his dare, among them Alexeev, Denikin, Lukomsky, and Romanovsky. Not unlike Kerensky, Lenin treated these star prisoners leniently. Along with the members of Kerensky's cabinet, General Krasnov was released a few days after October 25. In exchange he gave "his 'word of honor' that he would not fight against the Soviet regime," which he instantly broke. In any case, these were the senior officers who formed the original commanding core of the White Guards.[39]

General Mikhail Alexeev, the tsar's chief of staff since 1915, left to go south in early November, and settled at Novocherkassk, northeast of Rostov on the Sea of Azov. By about December 10 he gathered a force of at least 600 men, most of them officers, who were prototypical of the future Volunteer Armies. After escaping from their prison-monastery, the other "Bykhov generals" arrived a few days later, each having made the journey on his own.[40]

The chief of the general staff, General Dukhonin, decided not to take flight. From headquarters at Mogilev he "appealed to the army to remain loyal to the [ousted] Provisional Government and to put an end to Bolshevik violence."[41] He was taken in custody by a local soviet of soldiers before Nikolai Krylenko, with a company of men, came to arrest and take him to Petrograd. Apparently Krylenko failed to restrain an excited crowd, with the result that Dukhonin was shot and his body savagely mutilated. That was December 3, the day cease-fire negotiations with the Central Powers started at Brest-Litovsk. After a skeletal constabulary of Red Guards seized control of Rostov, on December 15 Alexeev's embryonic Volunteer Army dislodged them in a "short but fierce bout of street fighting." With this military action, which gave them their "baptism of fire," the Whites fired the "first shots" in Russia's civil war.[42]

From the outset the generals and the many officers were divided into two factions: one rallied around General Kornilov, who was personally the most ambitious and militarily the most daring; the other around the more sober-minded General Alexeev. In turn, both were at odds with generals A. M. Kaledin and Krasnov, the two main Cossack chiefs. In particular Kaledin, as hetman of the Don Cossacks, was a jealous guardian of his people's autonomy.

In the meantime these White and Cossack generals were joined at Novocherkassk by kindred political leaders, among them Fedorov, Miliukov, Rodzysenko, Struve, and Prince F. N. Trubetskoi. With the Kadets among them setting the tone, they pressed the squabbling officers to settle their differences, insisting that otherwise they could not win support either in Russia or abroad, among the Allies. Persuaded that their enemies' enemies were their friends, on December 18, 1917, one and all agreed on a troika: Kornilov was to be in charge of all White military forces; Alexeev of civil government and relations with the Allies; and Kaledin of the administration of the Don territories as well as of Cossack military forces.[43]

Although there was incidental talk of civil liberties to spare the sensibilities of both liberals and Allies, there was no disguising that the project of this provisional political and military authority was autocratic and ultranationalist, and ultimately counterrevolutionary. Even so, leading Kadets rallied around the generals, who were anything but unpolitical, thereby raising the White Guards' prestige, especially abroad.

Not surprisingly, and with good reason, the untried Bolshevik government forthwith concluded that the Cossack territories of the Don and the adjoining eastern Ukraine were likely to become a major staging ground of resistance. Indeed, within less than two months after the Bolshevik takeover White and Cossack forces were beginning to shoulder arms. Presently Lenin sent Vladimir Antonov-Ovseenko, who had played an important military role in Petrograd during and immediately following Red October, to direct operations on the southern front.[44]

This embryonic counterrevolutionary mobilization coincided with Sovnarkom's initial steps toward the deliberate use of enforcement terror. Sensitized by the Jacobin experience, the Bolshevik leaders were predisposed to such terror, considering it immanent to revolutionary practice. Had there been no "evidence" of implacable resistance immediately following their takeover—which would have been contrary to the "logic" of the situation—the Bolsheviks most likely would have held back on terror. Under the circumstances, however, the issue, for them, was not so much "one of 'principle' " as of "form" and "degree," and hence of "expediency."[45] In any case, on November 28, a decree of the Council of People's Commissars, signed by Lenin, outlawed the Kadet party. Designated "enemies of the people," its members became "liable to arrest and trial by Revolutionary Tribunals." Two days later, on November 30, another decree "declared that civil war had broken out under the direction of the liberal Kadet Party."[46] Trotsky had good reason to charge the "central committee" of the Kadets with being "the political headquarters of the White Guards," although it was gratuitous for him to add that they directed "the recruitment of officers for Kornilov and Kaledin."[47] At any rate, Trotsky announced the arrest of their "chiefs" and the surveillance of "their followers in the provinces." Claiming these steps to be "a modest beginning," he recalled that "at the time of the French Revolution the Jacobins had guillotined more honest men than these for obstructing the people's will." He hastened to add, however, that "we have executed nobody and have no intention of doing so."[48] Although the left Socialist Revolutionaries agreed that the Kadets had joined the enemy camp, they cautioned that "to condemn an entire category comprising countless innocent individuals was to create an all too convenient scapegoat for the sins of the bourgeoisie and a dangerous precedent for other hapless parties."[49]

It is worth stressing that throughout the civil war the bulk of the terror, and the worst of it, was closely correlated with the fighting between the Reds and the Whites. It was much more part of military operations than of political battles against real or perceived enemies and conspiracies. Clearly, the bloodletting of the first terror in the Russian Revolution, like that in the French Revolution, was civil war–related. Although this terror was not preprogrammed by the main contestants, their principal spokesmen proclaimed it nearly from the outset. To be sure, the Bolsheviks' rhetoric of terror was impregnated with the language of class warfare. But their excoriation of the bourgeoisie, landowners, and rural petty bourgeoisie was inseparable from their denunciation of the commanders of the White Armies and their foreign backers. Trotsky called for measures to "wipe off the face of the earth the counterrevolution of the Cossack generals and the Kadet bourgeoisie."[50] But if, as Quinet suggests, the spiral of terror results from the "shock of two irreconcilable elements . . . and of two opposite electric currents,"[51] then the terrorist rhetoric of the anti-Bolshevik camp cannot be ignored or minimized. As Antonov-Ovseenko took charge of the Red Guards in southeastern Russia, and before the Red Army was organized, Kornilov told his associates that "the greater the terror, the greater our victories." Shortly thereafter he vowed that "[w]e must save Russia . . . even if we have to set fire to half the country and shed the blood of three-fourths of all the Russians."[52] In March 1919 Admiral Kolchak ordered one of his generals "to follow the example of the Japanese who, in the Amur region, had exterminated the local population."[53] No doubt a White colonel spoke not only for himself when he held that the biblical injunction "an eye for an eye, a tooth for a tooth" was too mild for the Bolsheviks, who would yield to nothing less than "two eyes for one, and all teeth for one."[54] Eventually even General Wrangel saw the White Guards wielding "the cruel sword of vengeance" rather than bringing "pardon and peace."[55]

As in the early fighting of the Vendée, in the first engagements of the civil war in southern and southeastern Russia both sides committed atrocities which were neither ordered nor reproved by their respective political or military superiors. Around mid-January 1918 in Taganrog, a small port about 45 miles west of Rostov, White forces "blinded and mutilated" a group of allegedly "Bolshevik factory workers . . . before burying them alive."[56] When retaking the town, Antonov-Ovseenko's Red Guards more than matched this ferocity: although they had negotiated a cease-fire "with [the] cadets of the [local] military academy . . . , [they] proceeded to execute them cruelly, . . . [throwing] a batch of fifty . . . , bound hand and foot, into the blast furnaces of a local factory."[57] Denikin later remembered that around this time in this same region he had seen, first hand, "eight tortured bodies of volunteers . . . [who] had been beaten and cut up so badly, and their faces so disfigured, that their grief-stricken relatives could scarcely recognize them."[58]

It would seem that there were few, if any, links between this violence of the first hour, which was wild and inherent to civil war, and the incipient enforcement terror, which was intentional and inherent to revolution. To be sure, unlike Robespierre and Saint-Just before 1789, Lenin and Trotsky had weighed and "experienced" the role of revolutionary violence and terror before 1917, with the result that on this score they did not start their rule with a *tabula rasa*. For them it stood to reason that terror was immanent in the dialectics of revolution and counterrevolution. Haunted, above all, by the specter of a fierce backlash of the sort that had struck Russia after 1905, the Bolsheviks had few qualms about using terror to thwart this historical possibility, nay probability. This fear and resolve became obsessive once the socialist revolution miscarried in central and western Europe, since it foreshadowed greater foreign support for the Whites than the repressive tsarist regime had enjoyed between 1905 and 1917. Indeed, the bitter memory of Sergei Witte and Peter Stolypin explains, in large part, the Bolsheviks' inordinate disquiet about Paul Miliukov and the Kadets.

In the summer of 1917 Lenin overconfidently anticipated a Europe-wide revolution, and hence a favorable international climate for the unfolding revolution in Russia. That was the time he averred that "the 'Jacobins' of the twentieth century would not guillotine the capitalists, because to imitate a worthy model was not to copy it." Lenin seemed confident that in his time it would suffice "to arrest 50 or 100 magnates of banking capital for a few weeks . . . and to place the banks, the syndicate of bankers, and the businessmen 'working' for the state under the control of workers."[59] To be sure, the day following the Bolshevik takeover Lenin wondered how "one can make a revolution without firing squads," since during the civil war, with each side determined to prevail, mere "imprisonment" would be futile.[60] But on November 4 he held, albeit cautiously, that "we have not resorted . . . to the terrorism of the French revolutionaries who guillotined unarmed men," adding that he hoped not to have to "resort to [terror], because we have strength on our side."[61] Even as late as November 1918, when the friend-enemy dissociation was rampant, Lenin claimed, not unreasonably, that "[w]e are arresting but we are not resorting to terror," notably against enemy brothers.[62]

In the meantime, however, the rhetorical terror soared as the opposing sides anathematized and threatened each other, in addition to charging each other with casting the first stone. During the "first weeks of the revolution" it was Trotsky who made the "most militant pronouncements."[63] Immediately following the armed skirmishes attending the takeover in Petrograd, he served notice that for every Bolshevik worker or soldier captured by the enemy the new government would "demand five [of the military] cadets . . . we hold [as] prisoners and hostages." Indeed, Trotsky was of the view that "we shall not enter into the kingdom of socialism in white gloves on a polished floor." When the new regime's harsh security measures were challenged in the Soviet Executive, Trotsky rejoined that "demands to forgo all repression in time of civil war were demands to abandon the civil war." He spoke in this same vein shortly after the proscription of the Kadets, which he characterized as a "mild terror . . . against our class enemies." On this occasion Trotsky warned that this "terror [would] assume very violent forms, after the example of the great French Revolution," within less than a month, when "not merely jail but the guillotine [will be] ready for our enemies."[64] Lenin nodded with approval, charging that the "bourgeoisie, the landowners, and the rich classes, desperate . . . to undermine the Revolution, . . . were preparing to commit the most heinous crimes," including the "sabotage of food distribution" threatening "millions of people with famine."[65]

This was the spirit in which Sovnarkom moved to establish the Cheka, or All-Russian Extraordinary Commission for the Struggle Against Counterrevolution and Sabotage. It is characteristic of the history of the Cheka in the civil war that its creation was not a premeditated step. Rather, it was precipitated by a strike of state and banking employees. On December 19 Lenin asked Felix Dzerzhinsky "to establish a special commission to examine the possibility of combating such a strike by the most energetic revolutionary measures, and to determine methods of suppressing malicious sabotage." Immediately before turning to Dzerzhinsky, Lenin had expressed his confidence that the revolution would find a "Fouquier-Tinville . . . of staunch proletarian Jacobin" temperament qualified "to tame the encroaching counterrevolution."[66] Fouquier-Tinville had been the chief prosecutor of the Revolutionary Tribunal during the French Revolution.

On December 20 the Council of People's Commissars approved Dzerzhinsky's draft proposal for a commission to "suppress and liquidate all attempts and acts of counterrevolution and sabotage; . . . to hand over for trial by revolutionary tribunals all saboteurs and counterrevolutionaries; and to work out means of combating them." The Cheka was "to devote prime attention to the press, to sabotage, to the Kadets, Right SRs [Socialist Revolutionaries], saboteurs, and strikers." As for the "measures" to be used, the text specified "confiscation, expulsion from domicile, deprivation of ration cards, publication of lists of enemies of the people, etc."[67] Dzerzhinsky was appointed chairman of the commission. Local soviets were urged to set up their own branches and to provide the center with information "about organizations and persons whose activities are harmful to the Revolution." Presently Dzerzhinsky ordered that a system of revolutionary tribunals be set up "to investigate and try offenses which bear the character of sabotage and counterrevolution."[68]

It bears repeating that the Cheka was put in place at a time when "the Cossack enemies and other 'White' forces were already mustering in southeastern Russia; Ukraine . . . was in a state of all but open hostilities against the Soviet power; [and] the Germans, in spite of the armistice, were a standing threat in the west."[69] In addition, the army and economy continued to fall to pieces.

Significantly, at the start the Cheka was less a political organ than a makeshift police and judiciary filling the vacuum resulting from the spontaneous decomposition and deliberate dismantlement of the old legal system. The pre-Bolshevik provisional governments, especially the first one, had released thousands of common-law criminals and political prisoners, and where "they acted slowly or released only political prisoners" the streets had forced the opening of jails. This emptying of prisons and break up of the tsarist police went hand in hand with the abolition of the death penalty, the Siberian exile system, and the Okhranka. It was, of course, much easier to liquidate the old legal and police establishment than to put in place a new one, in tune with the new dawn. With authority and law reduced to a skeleton, the successive provisional governments had to proceed on two fronts: to design and establish a new system of *surveiller et punir*; and to set up, overnight, a temporary judicial and police system—martial law writ large—to deal with the spiraling emergency. The paralysis of criminal justice continued even as Kerensky, starting in July, arrested first Bolsheviks and then the generals of the Kornilov affair.[70]

It is not incidental that on the very first day of Bolshevik rule the Military Revolutionary Committee posted and distributed a handbill in Petrograd calling on the people to "detain hooligans and Black Hundred agitators and bring them to commissars of the Soviet in the nearest military unit." This warrant included a warning that "criminals responsible" for causing "confusion, robbery, bloodshed, or shooting . . . would be wiped off the face of the earth." On November 10 this same committee announced that it "would not tolerate any violation of revolutionary law and order," a special military revolutionary court being primed to deal "mercilessly . . . with thievery, robbery, marauding, and attempts at pogroms."[71] The situation continued to go from bad to worse in both town and country. In Moscow in 1918 the rate of robbery and murder rose to between ten and fifteen times the prewar level. Not surprisingly, Lenin "reserved his fiercest anathemas for speculators and wreckers on the economic front."[72] Indeed, they were on a par with those directed against counterrevolutionaries, spies, and pogromists. By mid-April Lenin expressed a view widely shared in the Commissariat of Justice, directed by Socialist Revolutionaries, that to check "increases in crime, hooliganism, bribery, speculation, outrages of all kinds . . . we need time and *we need an iron hand*."[73] In the beginning the Cheka's security operatives and tribunals prosecuted robbers, black marketeers, and thugs, with the result that the "early death sentences of the Cheka were imposed on bandits and criminals."[74] These executions, which apparently became a daily affair, disheartened Gorky, who wondered whether the Revolution, harbinger of a fresh start, would know how to "change the bestial Russian way of life," of which he was a persistent but skeptical censor.[75]

At this critical juncture the Bolsheviks' "almost every step . . . was either a reaction to some pressing emergency or a reprisal for some action or threatened action against them."[76] The incipient terror quickened and broadened its reach in correlation with the exigencies of both civil and foreign war, as well as diplomacy. On February 21, 1918, Sovnarkom issued a declaration warning of German invasion. Subsequently titled "The Socialist Fatherland is in Danger,"[77] this notice recalled the French National Assembly's decree of July 1792 declaring *la patrie en danger*. Within twenty-four hours the Cheka ordered all local soviets "to seek out, arrest, and shoot immediately all members . . . connected in one form or another with counterrevolutionary organizations . . . , enemy agents and spies, counterrevolutionary agitators, speculators, organizers of revolt . . . against the

Soviet government, those going to the Don to join the . . . Kaledin-Kornilov band and the Polish counterrevolutionary bourgeoisie." The injunction was to execute on the spot anyone "caught red-handed, in the act."[78] Significantly, on February 21, the day preceding this sweeping ukase, Sovnarkom had decided to found the Red Army, in face of Germany's renewed military offensive on the eastern front following Trotsky's equivocation in the peace negotiations at Brest-Litovsk.

✳ ✳ ✳

Brest-Litovsk was, without a doubt, a major hinge of the new epoch of world history. It was both cause and effect of the entanglement of revolution and war in 1917–18. In Trotsky's graphic formulation, "the pulse of the internal relations of the revolution was not at all beating in time with the pulse of the development of its external relations."[79] Needless to say, the inescapable choice between continuing the war and terminating it instantly, and cost what it may, was highly divisive among the Bolsheviks themselves as well as between them and the left Socialist Revolutionaries. But more important, whatever the road chosen, it could not help but have momentous and unforeseeable consequences for the course of the Revolution.

The Allied and Associated Powers would not hear of a separate Russian exit from the war, whose military and political outcome remained very much in the balance.[80] As for the Central Powers, notably Germany, they forced the fragile Bolshevik regime to steer between the Scylla of a ruinous dictated settlement and the Charybdis of a fierce terminal onslaught. Either way, the territorial cost to Russia would be enormous: the entire eastern and southern borderlands running from the Baltic to the Black Sea, as well as territories in the Caucasus, coveted by Turkey, were at risk.

Having signed a cease-fire with the Central Powers on December 5, 1917, which was repeatedly renewed, the Bolsheviks kept calling on the Western belligerents to join in a general negotiated peace without victory and annexations for either side. Since this insolent appeal continued to fall on deaf ears, the new rulers of Russia were left to face an impatient and imperious Germany alone, the peace negotiations to start December 22 at Brest-Litovsk.

The debate about war and peace drowned out the polemics about the dispersal of the National Assembly.[81] Starting January 8, Trotsky, back from negotiations at Brest-Litovsk, pressed his "neither war nor peace" stratagem against both Lenin, who advocated an immediate peace on German terms, and Bukharin, *chef-de-file* of the champions of a revolutionary war against the Central Powers.

Past master of the new diplomacy of appealing directly to the peoples over the heads of their governments, Trotsky proposed to gain time for his cunning policy to work. For the long term he looked to revolution in Central Europe. For the short run he overconfidently summoned and expected German workers to pressure their government to agree to a moderate peace, and also nursed the illusion of a general strike in Austria.

Among the Bolsheviks the so-called Left Opposition to a separate peace with Berlin and Vienna very much shared Trotsky's faith in world revolution. In addition to being optimistic about the prospects for revolution in the West, Bukharin, Uritsky, and Dzerzhinsky refused to concede that Russia was militarily spent. Probably swayed by their reading of the *levée en masse* in revolutionary France in 1793, they looked to a popular upsurge not only to resist a German onslaught but to support or carry revolution beyond Russia's European borders. Ultimately Bukharin trusted revolutionary voluntarism to be as decisive in tomorrow's critical junctures as it had been during the October days. Besides, he "regarded 'peaceful coexistence . . . between the Soviet Republic and international capital' as both impossible and inappropriate."[82]

Admittedly, Lenin agreed with Trotsky and Bukharin that without kindred revolutions abroad, the revolution in Russia would be hard-pressed, disfigured, and cramped, also to the detriment of the world at large. But unlike them, he argued against throwing caution to the winds and risking everything on a single throw of the dice. Above all, he took the full measure of Russia's chaos and impotence. Lenin was convinced that the army was *hors de combat* and that Russia's peasants and workers were no longer willing to risk their lives for a nebulous and losing cause. Besides, the economy was wasted. In any event, Lenin was wary of the nostrum of a revolutionary war, not least because of his gnawing skepticism about near-term prospects for revolution in Europe, notably in Germany. He was supported by Sokolnikov, Stalin, and Zinoviev, who also shared his concern that to keep stalling was to risk the enemy setting even stiffer terms.

Respectful of his gainsayers in the Central Committee as well as heedful of the left Socialist Revolutionaries, who reproved any separate peace with the autocratic Central Powers, Lenin agreed that Trotsky be authorized, upon his return to Brest-Litovsk on February 10, to continue to play for time under the pretense of "neither war nor peace." As he feared, the German High Command, eager to free troops for the western front, lost patience and within ten days Berlin ordered its armies to resume hostilities. In no time they advanced to within 100 miles of Petrograd in the north, captured Minsk and Mogilev in Belorussia, moved ever deeper into Ukraine, and occupied Kiev on March 2, the day before the Soviet delegation finally signed an inglorious dictated peace at Brest-Litovsk.

The harshness of the terms imposed on the ex-tsarist empire was unprecedented in the relations between great powers. In European Russia the Bolshevik government was forced to cede control, in the north, of Finland and the Baltic provinces; in the middle, of large parts of Belorussia; and further south, Ukraine and southern Transcaucasia. These territories covered about 800,000 square miles—about four times the area of France—and comprised one-third of imperial Russia's population and agricultural land, over half of its industrial plants, and over three-quarters of its coal mines and oil wells. Between 1789 and 1794 revolutionary France never saw anything like this stinging diplomatic and military reverse. As Lenin told the Seventh Party Congress, the Revolution had been forced to pass "from the continuous triumphal march against . . . [the] counterrevolution . . . of October, November, December . . . on [the] internal front to an encounter with real international imperialism, . . . [making for] an extraordinarily difficult and painful situation."[83]

All the same, the cessions of Brest-Litovsk brought major benefits, even if these were not as evident just then as they became later. Among others, the symbolically important citadel of the Russian Revolution was saved: at the time "the fall of Petrograd would . . . have meant a deathblow to the [revolutionary] proletariat . . . [whose] best forces were concentrated" in and around the capital.[84] Nonetheless, since the city had had a narrow escape and remained strategically vulnerable, on March 10 the Soviet government decided to move its seat to Moscow. The transfer also signaled that the Bolshevik leaders were now more fearful of hostile foreign intervention than they were hopeful of the revolution catching on abroad or the Red Army carrying it there on the point of bayonets. Although Zinoviev stressed the temporary nature of the move, insisting that "Berlin's proletariat will help us move it back to Red Petrograd," he granted that before this would happen the capital might even have to be moved "to the Volga or the Urals," depending on "the course of the world revolution."[85]

Above all, Brest-Litovsk secured Lenin's primary goal which, in fact, one and all embraced: the raw Bolshevik regime won a desperately needed breathing spell to organize Sovdepia, the territories of European Russia that had been salvaged, and to steel itself for a difficult struggle for survival. The life chances of revolution being infinitely better in large than small countries, the Bolsheviks benefited from being left with a territory the size of all the warring countries of Europe combined and a population of 60 million, hence larger than that of any other belligerent, as well as containing most of the ex-empire's war industries and military stores. In addition, most of the non-Russian lands to the west having been lost, Sovdepia was heavily Great Russian, sparing the Bolsheviks certain taxing nationality conflicts in their struggle to reestablish a single sovereignty.[86]

During the time that the Bolshevik leadership was engaged in the political, diplomatic, and military battles of the Brest-Litovsk imbroglio, the civil war was practically in abeyance. At the very time that the Hohenzollern and Habsburg armies resumed their offensive in February 1918, General Kornilov started his so-called Ice March from around Rostov over the frozen steppes southward, toward the Kuban. His host was quite out of the ordinary, in that the best part of his estimated 4,000 men were commissioned and noncommissioned officers, including 36 generals and about 200 colonels.[87] The White officers were still looking for a strategically favorable staging area in which Cossacks would provide the rank and file for an army unlikely to find recruits among the rebellious peasantry.

One of the first engagements of this inchoate army took a dramatic turn. Between April 10 and 13, a chance artillery shell fired by the skeletal Red Guards of Ekaterinodar (Krasnodar), the capital of the Kuban region, struck and killed Kornilov. Eventually, when the revolutionaries found where he had been buried, they disinterred his body and "dragged it to the main square before burning it on a rubbish dump."[88] The succession fell to General Denikin. He abandoned the siege of Ekaterinodar and regrouped his forces in and around Mechetinskaia.

By then the Allied intervention in Russia was underway.[89] Although the British and French made instant contact with the Whites in the south, their feelers were of no great consequence. The main purpose of this intervention of the first hour was to harass the Central Powers on the Eastern Front, where their ascendancy enabled them to free forces for the Western Front and to tighten their control of the vital Ukrainian granary. As in the time of the French Revolution, at the outset the policies of the major powers were guided by interest, not ideology: Berlin bore hard upon Moscow to leave the war and to advance the Central Powers' mastery throughout the eastern European rimland; the Western Allies, having failed to keep Russia fighting on their side, meant to establish a military presence sufficient to create a credible diversion on their enemies' eastern flank. Geopolitically the Allies were at a great disadvantage: with no access by land, they were reduced to using their naval power, which necessarily was stretched to the limit. At any rate, they proceeded to seize some of Russia's major ports: in March the British and the French put ashore small landing parties in Murmansk (on the Arctic Ocean); in April the Japanese and the British established a bridgehead at Vladivostok (on the Sea of Japan); and in early August the United States landed troops in Archangel (on the White Sea). The putative idea was to protect Allied stores and to prevent the transshipment of goods to the Central Powers. After the unhoped-for uprising, in late May, of the 30,000 to 40,000 men of the Czech Legion along the Trans-Siberian railway, there was the additional objective of getting stores to them, possibly to reopen the front against Germany and Austria in the east.

Compared to the intervention of the Central Powers, that of the Allies was negligible. There was no common measure between, on the one hand, the lands ceded under Brest-Litovsk, especially Ukraine, and, on the other, the remote maritime gateways and scant task forces. But the objective reality of the Allied intervention mattered less than the manner in which it was perceived and represented by the Bolsheviks. Besides, even if the intentions of the Allies were essentially "strategic" rather than "political," their rhetoric was as stridently anti-Bolshevik as Lenin's was anti-capitalist. No longer in a position to play the one belligerent coalition off against the other, the Bolsheviks were left without any leverage in an international system which they now considered wholly hostile to them. Lenin viewed and portrayed the intervention as the opening of a counterrevolutionary campaign orchestrated by the great imperialist-capitalist powers, led by Britain and France. By mid-1918 Sovnarkom was at daggers drawn with all the major powers at the same time that it confronted White armies in the south and in Siberia, rebellions by left Socialist Revolutionaries in central Russia, and several defiant political assassinations in the twin capitals. It was this conjuncture that provided the context, precondition, and warrant for the turn toward a more systematic terror of enforcement.

✳ ✳ ✳

The civil war heated up considerably in the summer and fall of 1918, before the guns of the Great War fell silent on November 11. There were two major fronts: in the lands of the middle Volga and western Siberia, under the command of Admiral Kolchak; in the territories between the River Don and the Black Sea, under General Denikin.

In August Kolchak's forces captured Kazan and Samara west of the Urals. Had they succeeded in advancing westward and taking Nizhny Novgorod, "they would have had a clear road to Moscow."[90] They also captured Omsk east of the Urals, a vital rail link to eastern Siberia and the Pacific. Rival counter-governments were set up in Samara and Omsk, further illustrating the runaway fragmentation of Russian sovereignty. Socialist Revolutionaries had considerable sway in Samara, while ultranationalist conservatives, not to say outright counterrevolutionaries, had the ascendancy in Omsk. Partly under Allied pressure, and starting September 8, representatives of the major opposition parties and assorted members of the suspended Constituent Assembly met for a full month in Ufa in an effort to establish a single and effective anti-Bolshevik government for all of Russia.

Kolchak, the most forceful of the White commanders, had originally gathered an army in northern Manchuria and adjoining Siberia, where some of the Socialist Revolutionaries had rallied to him. But just as the White officers' armies in the south looked to the Cossacks to provide the bulk of their soldiers, so those of the center and east looked to the Czech Legion for theirs. Originally the 30,000 to

40,000 Czechs and Slovaks were to be redeployed via Vladivostok to France to resume fighting the Central Powers. But when they balked the Soviets' demand to surrender their weapons in mid-May, Trotsky ordered that they be disarmed by force. By virtue of resisting successfully, the Czechs and Slovaks overnight became the largest as well as the best trained and best equipped military force fighting the revolutionary regime. Within about a month they were the controlling military force in and around Penza, Ufa, Omsk, and Tomsk, and before long they spread along much of the Trans-Siberian railway between Tomsk and Vladivostok, the essential port of entry for Allied aid to Kolchak's forces. Because of their fairly liberal and democratic orientation, the Czechs also formed a praetorian guard for the Samara government.[91]

Indeed, starting in June Samara became the rallying point for the Socialist Revolutionary representatives of the ill-starred Constituent Assembly, who extended their fragile reach northwestward, to Simbirsk and Kazan. They meant to challenge the legitimacy of the Bolshevik regime by setting up a government of democrats and moderate socialists sworn to a progressive political and social program. But the Kadets and Mensheviks begged off: in particular the leaders of the Kadets threw their full weight behind Denikin in Ekaterinodar and Kolchak in Omsk. In addition, the Socialist Revolutionaries lacked significant popular support in the villages and towns of the central Volga. For all these reasons their political drive soon foundered, laying bare the limited historical possibility for a democratic resistance in a political field increasingly polarized between revolution and counterrevolution.

This preclusion of a third way was confirmed by the rising political primacy in the anti-Bolshevik camp of White officers whose illiberal worldviews were a mixture of conservatism, reaction, and counterrevolution, all the more so since the Cossack leaders shared their willful disregard of the land question. In the wake of military successes in western Siberia and southern Russia, the White officers and their political supporters not unreasonably pressed for a strong emergency government along with a moratorium on divisive debates about constitutional, social, and nationality issues until after victory over the Reds. They easily had the upper hand at the Ufa conference which on September 23 proclaimed the creation of a five-man Directory to act as a provisional government for all of Russia until a new Constituent Assembly could be convened.[92]

But the ambience changed radically before the conference closed on October 6. In mid-September the newly formed Red Army, under the command of Trotsky, recaptured Kazan and Simbirsk. Whereas this spectacular first victory fired the confidence of the Bolshevik leaders, it redoubled the resolve of the White generals to exercise power without constitutional restraints and political debate. At the same time, with Red troops closing in on Samara, the Czechs left the local Socialist Revolutionaries to fend for themselves, with the result that this nonauthoritarian outpost in the military resistance collapsed. Even before the end of the Great War Admiral Kolchak had imposed himself as the "Supreme Ruler" of the government at Omsk, and soon he presumed to speak for the resistance of all the Russias. This coup of November 18, 1918, ousting the Socialist Revolutionaries from his government, was merely the *coup de grâce*. Disdainful of limited rule, Kolchak and his ultraconservative supporters kept the backing of the Kadets, whom they humored with shadowy promises of an eventual re-convocation of the Constituent Assembly so as to leave them a semblance of dignity.[93]

Meanwhile in the Don–Black Sea region, within two months of taking command in April 1918, Denikin had raised his army to a strength of about 9,000 men, not counting the cavalry he expected the Cossack hetmans to muster. He resolved to build a solid military base in the Kuban rather than risk his forces in a premature drive to link up with Kolchak and the Czech Legion or in an offensive in the direction of Moscow. In addition to being self-sufficient in grain and oil, the Kuban abutted upon several ports on the Black Sea which Denikin valued for providing access to foreign aid. Moving south he seized Ekaterinodar, the geopolitical hub of the Kuban, on August 16, and Novorossiysk, the Black Sea port, ten days later.[94]

Along the way, in July, there was heavy fighting at Belaya Glina, Tikhoretskaya, and Stavropol which prefigured the peculiarities and Furies of the Russian civil war. Around the first two towns the Whites took large numbers of Red prisoners, who "were either shot or drafted into the ranks of the Volunteers," with the result that Denikin now "had 20,000 under his command." On entering Belaya Glina the

Whites learned that after capture some of their men "had been brutally tortured and then killed," with the result that "for the first time . . . they began to take reprisals." Apparently they, in turn, proceeded to "arbitrarily shoot" their prisoners in small batches, "each batch . . . [being] compelled to first watch the execution of their comrades."[95]

Stavropol experienced the terror of civil war twice. The first time occurred on July 21 when a self-appointed anti-Bolshevik guerrilla leader took the town, using singularly "simple and brutal" methods.[96] Several weeks later the Red Army seized it back, thereby inviting a second White assault in mid-November. This time the charge was led by General Wrangel, perhaps the most notable, even noble, of the ex-tsarist generals. After taking nearly 3,000 Bolshevik prisoners, and determined to make recruits, he had their 370 officers and non-commissioned officers parade under their eyes before having them shot. Immediately thereafter Wrangel gave the terrified rank and file the opportunity to join the Volunteer Army, thereby giving them "a chance to atone for their crime and prove their loyalty to their country."[97]

In the meantime Denikin had set up his military headquarters at Ekaterinodar. Following Alexeev's death he also became the uncontested political master of the counterrevolution's southeastern staging area, though his relations with the Cossack hetmans remained strained. Hereafter at Ekaterinodar the military and their conservative collaborators reigned supreme. Like their comrades at Omsk they invoked the need for absolute military primacy to justify deferring debate on fundamental political and social issues which would at once divide and embarrass them. With both Lenin and Wilson excoriating Europe's old order, they could not publicly avow their unseasonable agenda.

Not that all Whites were counterrevolutionaries.[98] Many of them were instinctive reactionaries or calculating conservatives. Even so, there were few, if any, bona fide constitutional monarchists or liberal democrats among them. To be sure, the generalissimos counted several Kadets among their political advisors. But besides being of little consequence, except to provide a liberal façade for the benefit of the outside world, these ostensible junior partners were either right-wing or renegade members of their parent party. In addition to indiscriminately execrating the three main components of the socialist left—

Bolsheviks, Socialist Revolutionaries, and Mensheviks—the Whites even damned the original Kadets for having been the chief gravediggers of tsarism. All in all the Whites were a microcosm of the ruling and governing classes of the *ancien régime*—military officers, landowners, bureaucrats, churchmen—with minimal popular support. Nor could their Kadet associates have provided them with a social base, since theirs was a party with very few adherents and followers. Indeed, without the engagement of Cossacks and impressment of enemy prisoners the Volunteer Armies would have been all but an officers' army.

To all intents and purposes the main political generals—Kolchak, Denikin, Iudenich, Wrangel—were unreconstructed champions of the Russian empire. To the extent that they had an ideology, it was an all-embracing nationalism or patriotism of uncertain appeal to Great Russia's masses, even if it resonated with its classes. One and all claimed to be fighting for "Russia Great, United, and Indivisible," perhaps even for "Faith, Tsar, and Fatherland." They called for the reestablishment of the borders of 1914 along with a far-reaching restoration. Needless to say, this die-hard posture offended the leaders of the minority nationalities, many of whom put breaking out of imperial Russia's "prison of peoples" ahead of joining the war against the Bolsheviks. Their indignation was all the greater because such talk of empire flew in the face of the promise of national self-determination being held out by Wilson and Lenin. But the Whites could not have renounced their faith in Great Russia without denying themselves. Besides, they had no ideological precept other than one or another variation of muscular nationalism available to press into service. It would have been neither timely nor expedient for them to lay bare their frozen conservatism and reaction, including their fear-inspired condescension toward the lower orders, both peasant and proletarian.

Except for the outright counterrevolutionaries among them—and they were few in number—the Whites were discreet about the negations which animated their worldview and program. They were integral antimodernists as well as fierce adversaries of liberalism, democratic politics, and civil liberties. Their conspiratorial mind-set was of a piece with that of their counterparts in the French Revolution. The Whites of revolutionary France had attributed all the ills of their time to the corrosive force of Enlightenment ideas purveyed by Freemasons, Jansenists, and Protestants, allegedly the principal trailblazers and masterminds of Jacobinism. For their part, the Whites of revolutionary Russia laid the blame for their country's troubles on materialist ideas and on the Jews, who were accused of inventing and manipulating these ideas for their own benefit. Characteristically, the forged *Protocols of the Elders of Zion* imputing a Jewish-Masonic world conspiracy gained a certain credibility among the leaders and backers of the Volunteer Armies.

All in all, the Whites of various persuasions were driven by a common sensibility, temper, and prepossession rather than by a coherent ideology or concrete program. The anti-cum-counterrevolution was less focalized in the Russian than the French Revolution. After 1789 both inside France and outside, in Koblenz, its champions had rallied around the reason and the representative of the Bourbon monarchy as well as the Catholic Church and religion: the "volunteer army" in the Vendée had marched by the name of *armée catholique et royale*, with officers unfurling the *fleur-de-lis* flags and the rank and file flaunting religious amulets. Of course, back then Europe was still intensely monarchist and offered a naturally supportive environment for the exiled successors to Louis XVI. In contrast, after 1917, with the great continental thrones collapsing, expatriate crowns had lost their aura and were out of season.

Although the Russian Whites achieved a certain military consistency, they remained politically inchoate, without coherent civil government and administration. This deficiency was due, in large part, to their reluctance to take a clear stand on the land issue. In a country of peasants in which the peasants had, on their own, revolutionized land ownership, notably in European Russia, the Whites equivocated on the agrarian question and allowed landlords to repossess their estates in areas "liberated" by them. Besides, during military operations the Volunteer Armies lived off the land, pillaged, and requisitioned supplies, so that on this score there was nothing to choose between them and the Red Army.

The problem of the non-Russian minorities was equally vexing to the Whites. Especially in cis-Uralian Russia these minorities were taking advantage of the breakdown of imperial controls to press for autonomy or outright separation. The Revolution and civil war broke into the non-Russian borderlands, intensifying not only national rebellions but above all ethnic, sociocultural, and religious cleavages and conflicts. Not that these peripheries were swept by full-scale national revolts. Indeed, the national awakenings were sparked and carried primarily by small elites of dissident intellectuals, students, and professionals of cities and towns with at best a weak hold on the vast peasantries and countrysides they claimed to represent and mobilize. Certainly they needed the support of outside powers to compensate for their lack of a social base. The appeals of nationalism competed with the trumpets of class warfare as well as with the incitement of age-old and territorially explosive ethnic and religious strife. But all the non-Russian nationalities, both townspeople and peasants, suspected the Whites' great Russian nationalism and dubious land policies. This damaged the military fortunes of the Volunteer Armies at two critical points of the civil war: Ukrainians and Poles would not back Denikin's campaign in the southwest and west; Finns and Estonians would not join Iudenich's drive on Petrograd. Clearly, anti-Bolshevism, by itself, could not carry the day. Nevertheless, the Whites were the single most formidable threat that the Bolsheviks faced—one, moreover, that interacted with and magnified all the other crises to which the Bolsheviks responded with increasingly ruthless terror.

＊ ＊ ＊

On Brest-Litovsk the Bolsheviks stood all but alone. The entire non-Bolshevik left, along with the liberal center and the conservative right, opposed them. Above all, the signing of the dictated peace strained relations with their closest not to say only political allies: the left Socialist Revolutionaries opposed the treaty and bolted the coalition government to step up their campaign against it. Thereafter their good faith became suspect, and their resumption of individual terror from below intensified the regime's enforcement terror from above.

While they functioned as a would-be loyal opposition, the left Socialist Revolutionaries had been forthright in their criticism of the forcible procurement of grain, the reinstatement of the death penalty, and the persecution of political rivals. Brest-Litovsk was merely the last straw. After withdrawing from the Council of People's Commissars on March 19, the left Socialist Revolutionaries went over to active resistance. All the time that they had inveighed against the incipient state terror, they had made a point of not abjuring their party's tradition of political assassination, which some of its disabused adherents now proposed to renew and train upon the Bolsheviks. As if to serve notice of this impending turn, on June 20 a working-class member of a small Socialist Revolutionary direct action group assassinated Moisei Volodarsky, the People's Commissar for the Press, Propaganda, and Agitation in Petrograd. When Lenin learned that the local Bolshevik authorities apparently "held back . . . workers [who] wanted to retaliate with mass terror," he expostulated with Zinoviev, the local party chief, that although "our resolutions threaten mass terror, . . . when it comes to action, *we slow down the entirely justified* revolutionary initiative of the masses." Lenin urged that a "*decisive* example" be set, lest the "terrorists" consider the Bolsheviks "milksops" in what was "an extreme war situation."[99]

The cleavage between the Bolsheviks and the left Socialist Revolutionaries dominated the Fifth All-Russian Congress of Soviets, which met in Moscow from July 4 to 10, 1918. With less than one-third the Bolshevik delegates, who had a clear majority, the left Socialist Revolutionaries were confounded, all the more so since they had hoped against hope that thanks to their sway with the peasants, this revolutionary citadel would be theirs. At any rate, while the congress was in session, a group of left Socialist Revolutionaries, some of whom had stayed on to work for the Cheka after March 19, launched a terrorist campaign to destabilize Sovnarkom. The opening deed was by far the most daring and dramatic. Apparently inspired or encouraged by Marya Spiridonova, a herald of anarcho-terrorism, on July 6 Iakov Blumkin, one of the left SR Chekists, assassinated Count von Mirbach, the new German ambassador in Moscow. The idea was to provoke Berlin to cancel the Treaty of Brest-Litovsk and resume its drive into Russia, thereby triggering a *levée en masse*. This murder was also expected to instantly spark an anti-Bolshevik but revolutionary rising in the capital, followed by insurrections in several provincial cities. Although the streets of Moscow remained calm, the conspirators occupied several public buildings, including the Central Telegraph Office, from which they aimed to rouse the rest of the country.

When Dzerzhinsky, on Lenin's order, went to the German Embassy in an effort to blunt the diplomatic blow, he learned that the assassin had introduced himself with Cheka credentials. To continue his inquiry Dzerzhinsky went to Cheka headquarters, where he himself and Martyn Latsis were arrested by dissident Chekists. Obviously there was need for quick and forceful action to placate the German government and cut short the left Socialist Revolutionary rebellion. Within twenty-four hours, and without bloodshed, Red guards freed Dzerzhinsky, reestablished control over all official buildings, including the Lubianka, and arrested most members of the left Socialist Revolutionary delegation to the All-Russian Soviet meeting in the Bolshoi Theater. Thirteen of the delegates were later executed by the Cheka—all of them Chekists. Strange to say, "the first recorded 'political' victims" of the Red Terror actually had themselves been its agents. All the other prisoners were released and amnestied, including Spiridonova. As for Blumkin, he made good his escape.[100]

As was to be expected, the Cheka was purged of all left Socialist Revolutionaries as Dzerzhinsky reiterated its crucial importance in the civil and foreign war facing the regime. Manifestly "organized terror . . . [was] an absolutely essential element in Revolution." The Cheka was an instrument to defend the Revolution, "just like the Red Army," and in fighting for "victory over the bourgeoisie" neither the one nor the other could afford to stop and ask whether particular individuals were being wronged, even if this meant that "the sword occasionally falls on innocent heads."[101]

No doubt the turbulence in Moscow would have been less disturbing for the Bolshevik leadership had it not coincided, altogether fortuitously, with several uprisings along the upper Volga. Boris Savinkov, the mastermind of this enterprise, was a man of many seasons.[102] As a young terrorist of Socialist Revolutionary temper, in 1904 he had had a hand in the assassination of Vyacheslov Plehve, Nicholas II's ultrareactionary interior minister. In 1917 Savinkov was a deputy minister in Kerensky's government, until he rallied to General Kornilov starting with his August defiance. Expelled from the Socialist Revolutionary party, he became involved with the Union for the Regeneration of Russia, which operated in the twin capitals. Recognizing no enemies to the right, the politicians and military officers of this clandestine organization were resolutely anti-Bolshevik and favored resuming the war against the Central Powers, which commended them to the Allies. In collaboration with members of the Union,

Savinkov planned risings in Rybinsk, Murom, and Yaroslavl. He traveled to the region to complete preparations, arriving there in early July 1918. In the meantime he had made contact with Joseph Noulens and Bruce Lockhart, the French and British agents in Moscow, with a view to coordinating the risings with an Allied landing in Archangel. With this prospect of Allied support, in particular Yaroslavl, with its strategic location 180 miles north of Moscow, assumed critical importance.

Actually the Unionists failed to muster a critical mass of anti-Bolshevik volunteers, with the result that the sparse local Red forces mastered the insurrections in Rybinsk and Murom without difficulty. The showdown in Yaroslavl turned out to be altogether more serious. On July 6 an improvised volunteer militia, led by White officers, seized control of the city, and it took the Bolsheviks two weeks to gather sufficient forces, including Chekists, to retake it. Before starting their assault the Reds summoned "all who valued their lives . . . to evacuate the city within twenty-four hours."[103] The warning was far from empty: the assault was fierce and there were heavy battle casualties on both sides.

But of course the military fighting was accompanied and followed by a deadly terror and counter-terror, with the usual atrocities. During their occupation of Yaroslavl the Unionists summarily executed the three ranking Bolsheviks and "imprisoned as many as two hundred others on a death barge anchored in the Volga."[104] In turn, following the liberation of the city, the new Bolshevik authority issued a fierce victory proclamation which asked, rhetorically, "[h]ow many hundreds of vermin and parasites . . . [local revolutionaries should] exterminate in retribution for the precious lives of our three friends" and gave warning that since "[p]riests, officers, bankers, industrialists, monks, merchants . . . [were] all the same, . . . neither cassock, nor uniform, nor diploma could protect them." Referring to a resolution of the recent All-Russian Congress of Soviets to "reply to all criminal enemies of the people with mass terror against the bourgeoisie," the proclamation vowed that "[n]o mercy [would be shown] to the White Guardists."[105] In the event "fifty-seven of the captured insurgents, mostly officers, were shot on the spot." In addition, a special commission, which included several Chekists, selected another 350 insurgents for execution.[106] Very likely this "was the first mass execution by the Bolsheviks."[107]

The avenging fury following the uprisings in provincial cities during the summer of 1918 marked an intensification of the Red Terror. Since it was widely publicized, this terror was meant to "deter the others," giving it at once a wild and functional cast. This was also the time that the local branches of the Cheka were ordered "to practice the government's [new] policy of unrelenting mass terror," with *Izvestia* carrying "almost daily" reports on their activities.[108] It appears that street crowds and their tribunes did not in any significant way press for this escalation.

* * *

Crowds and the "theater" of revolution were of no moment in another of the Cheka's contingent but ideologically conditioned act of terror: at about the same time that the Cheka played a key role in the repression of the leftist Socialist Revolutionaries in Moscow and the rightist Unionists on the upper Volga, it was the chief agent in the execution of Nicholas II, his family, and his retinue.[109]

Following the tsar's abdication, the imperial family was confined to a wing of Tsarskoe Selo, the former imperial palace near Petrograd. At first the provisional governments were not concerned about the safety and future of Nicholas II, and even gave some thought to allowing if not urging him to seek asylum abroad. But then, with the capital ever more agitated and exile abroad increasingly problematic, in mid-August—between the July days and the Kornilov affair—Kerensky had the imperial family moved to Tobolsk, an out-of-the-way and sleepy Siberian town. They lived there with ease and dignity until the Bolshevik takeover.

For the Bolshevik leaders the question of the Romanovs was of considerable weight, both ideologically and politically. Standing on the shoulders of the revolutionaries of 1789, and bent on transcending them, they, along with many of Russia's socialists, had long since taken the execution of Louis XVI as prefiguring the eventual fate of Nicholas II. The tsar's central role in the subversion of the constitutional settlement of 1905 and in the rise of an anti-Semitically colored ultraconservatism intensified the left's predisposition to regicide. In 1911, at the height of this "aristocratic reaction," Lenin commended it, all the more so since this was merely the Romanovs' latest access of repressive violence: "If in a country as cultured as England, which had known neither a Mongol yoke, nor bureaucratic oppression, nor the tyranny of a military caste, it was necessary to behead one crowned brigand in order to teach [subsequent] kings to be 'constitutional' monarchs, then in Russia it is necessary to behead at least one hundred Romanovs to teach their successors not to organize Black-Hundred murders and Jewish pogroms."[110] Several years later, after his arrival at the Finland Station in April 1917, Lenin drafted a resolution, passed by the party's central committee, declaring that "William II [was] as much of a crowned bandit deserving of the death penalty as Nicholas II."[111]

Soon after taking the reins the Bolshevik leadership hesitated between bringing the ex-tsar to justice in Petrograd or executing him unceremoniously without a trial. While this debate followed its course, in late April 1918 Sovnarkom sent Iakov Yakovlev, along with a detachment of Red Guards, to Tobolsk with instructions to transfer the royal family to Ekaterinburg (Sverdlovsk), capital of the Urals. Southeast of Tobolsk and about 900 miles east of Moscow, Ekaterinburg was a politically safe industrial city under Bolshevik control. The imperial party was assigned to forced residence in a mansion (Ipatev House) confiscated from a wealthy local merchant, in which the ex-tsar's everyday life was shorn of its royal nimbus.

It is unclear whether this mortifying secret internment was a calculated first step toward a trial and execution or a temporary expedient. In the meantime, the tsar's jailers were under strict instructions not to allow any contact with Whites who, inspired by Louis XVI's ill-fated flight to Varennes, might try to organize a rescue or escape with a view to giving the counterrevolution a potent symbolic banner and depriving the Revolution of the benefits of a possible trial. But the fortunes of civil war were about to complicate Yakovlev's mission.

In early July, units of Kolchak's volunteer forces and the Czech Legion were reported to be closing in on Ekaterinburg from the east and southwest. Yakovlev and local Bolshevik officials were disconcerted about what to do with the imperial family, should the enemy invest or capture the city. Presently the members of the Ural Regional Soviet, having voted to execute the tsar and his family, sent Philip Goleshchekin, a reliable Bolshevik, to Moscow to seek approval for their decision. In the capital he conferred with Sverdlov, chairman of the All-Russian Central Committee of the Soviets, and this at a time when the Central Committee opted for the ex-tsar's trial. Apparently Goleshchekin returned to Ekaterinburg with the order to organize a public trial, to be held in Moscow, in which Trotsky would act as chief prosecutor but also with the understanding that should time run out, the local soviet could take whatever steps it considered appropriate. On July 12, after Red officers had notified the regional soviet that the fall of Ekaterinburg was just a matter of days, it voted to put the imperial family to death without a trial. Four days later, during the night of July 16–17, the tsar, the empress, their five children, the family physician, and three servants were summarily shot. The ten executioners acted under orders of Yakovlev and Iakov Yurovsky, the family's chief jailer and a leading member of the regional Cheka. The killing was brutal, without ceremony and without last rites or honors. Unlike the nearly simultaneous repression in Yaroslavl, it was carried out in secret. The remains of the victims were thoroughly disfigured before being disposed of in a grave that was both profane and concealed.

The claim that the Whites were at the gates was neither sham nor pretext. When Ekaterinburg fell on July 25, "a detachment of monarchist officers raced . . . to free their Emperor."[112] Even so, there may have been other historical possibilities. The regional soviet might, in good time, have transferred the imperial family to a zone untouched by civil war, or the opposing sides might have negotiated its safe passage out of Russia. Probably the friend-enemy dissociation had gone too far for half-measures. But since Sverdlov presumably had given large discretion to the Ural Soviet, and in view of the impossibility of a public trial in Ekaterinburg, the local powers could certainly have executed Nicholas II but spared his family and retinue. It is hard to say what combination of impulses accounted for this excessive excess: ideology, fanaticism, vengeance, fear, bewilderment. Admittedly, the Bolshevik leaders may have wanted to consecrate the new order with an act of founding violence doubling as a major milestone of irreversibility. But for such an act to be effective, it would have had to be open, principled, and ritualized, on the order of Louis XVI's calvary. As it was, the Central Soviet Executive Committee in Moscow simply announced that the tsar had been shot because Ekaterinburg was "seriously threatened" by the Czechs and "a new plot of counterrevolutionaries, which had as its objective to take the royal hangman out of the hands of the Soviet Government." It stated, falsely, that "the wife and son of Nicholas Romanov were sent to a safe place,"[113] since all the children were killed and so were prominent members of the extended Romanov family. Incidentally, not unlike the dispersion of the Constituent Assembly, in city and country the killing of the tsar aroused little overt indignation, let alone resistance.

As the civil war intensified and Sovnarkom became increasingly alarmed about the Volga and the Urals, it ordered the terror stepped up in those regions. On August 9 Lenin urged the Bolshevik leaders of Nizhny Novgorod, where "a whiteguardist rising was brewing, . . . instantly to introduce mass terror." Local officials were told "to shoot and transport hundreds of prostitutes who got soldiers drunk, ex-officers," as well as "to make mass searches, . . . to execute for possession of weapons, . . . [and] to massively deport Mensheviks and unreliable elements." That same day, in response to an alarming telegram about rural unrest around Perm, northwest of Ufa, Lenin ordered the organization, locally, of "a strengthened guard of reliable persons to carry out merciless mass terror against kulaks, priests, and White Guards as well as to lock up unreliable elements in a concentration camp outside the town."[114] Presently Latsis, who with Dzerzhinsky had been briefly detained in Moscow on July 6 and now headed the Cheka on the eastern front, expounded on the internal logic of this crescendo of terror. On August 23, in *Izvestia*, he asserted that civil war knows no "established customs . . . and written laws." It calls not only for the "slaughter of those wounded fighting against you . . . [and] the destruction of the active forces of the enemy, but also the demonstration that anyone raising the sword against the existing order will perish by the sword." According to Latsis, civil war knows "no courts of law," since it is "a life and death struggle" in which, "if you do not kill, you will be killed [yourself]."[115]

❋ ❋ ❋

The cumulative radicalization and politicization of the terror were given yet further impetus by the assassination of Moisei Solomonovich Uritsky and the attempt on Lenin's life on August 30, 1918. Like the assassination of Marat in July 1793, these acts of bottom-up insurgent terror brought on a major change in the fragile regime's top-down enforcement terror. Admittedly Marat's murder was intended to undermine the revolution, while the assaults on Uritsky and Lenin were meant to check its betrayal. But notwithstanding their antipodal political purposes, these acts of gestural terror had a similar function in the intensification and institutionalization of both terrors, with vengeance an important ingredient.

Uritsky was chairman of the Petrograd Cheka. He was not a particularly conspicuous, controversial, or hard-line member of the new political class. His killer, Leonid Akimovich Kannegiser, who was close to the moderate Populist Socialist Party, acted alone and without a precise objective other than to lash out at the new regime.

When informed of Uritsky's slaying, and no doubt recalling the recent assassination of Volodnarsky, Lenin instantly sent Dzerzhinsky to Petrograd to conduct an investigation. Upon his arrival there, however, the chief of the Cheka was informed that Lenin himself had just been struck by an assassin's bullet. Dzerzhinsky rushed back to Moscow, no doubt convinced of a link between the two incidents. But they turned out to be as unrelated as July's uprisings in the capital and the upper Volga. Needless to say, such coincidences do not exactly dampen the specious conspiratorial reasoning inherent to politics in revolutionary moments.

Lenin was shot and gravely wounded on leaving an armaments factory in a suburb of Moscow after a speech to workers on the dangers of counterrevolution, which he apparently closed with the coda that "there is only one issue, victory or death!"[116] Fania Kaplan was among several suspects arrested on the spot and taken for interrogation first to the Lubianka and then the Kremlin. Almost immediately she was declared guilty, without a trial. Unlike Charlotte Corday, who hailed from respectable society, Kaplan had an anarchist background. She had met Spiridonova while serving a term of hard labor in Siberia for her subversive activities. Like Blumkin, von Mirbach's assassin, Kaplan was swayed by Spiridonova's anarcho-terrorist gospel. Apparently Kaplan's eyesight was very poor, which suggests that she most likely did not act alone but in concert with a group of Socialist Revolutionaries, even though she seems not to have been a member of their party.

The assassination of Uritsky and the assault on Lenin could not help but fire the Bolsheviks' righteous rage, suspicion, and rancor. The day after Uritsky's murder Petrograd's *Krasnaia Gazeta* thundered that the season of "namby-pambyism" had come to an end: "thousands of our enemies" will have to pay for the death, and the "surviving members of the bourgeoisie will have to be taught a bloody lesson by means of terror." The next day this same paper vowed that "only rivers of blood can atone for the blood of Lenin and Uritsky."[117] In Moscow *Pravda* proclaimed that the time had come "to destroy the bourgeoisie, else it will destroy you," and forewarned that "from now on the hymn of the working class will be a hymn of hatred and vengeance."[118] The daily of Nizhny Novgorod used language found in many provincial papers when it asserted that "the blood of the killed and wounded was crying out for revenge."[119] Although Petrograd's *Krasnaia gazeta* carried a telegram from Bolshevik activists to Zinoviev suggesting that workers be urged to wreak "vengeance on . . . Right-SRs and White Guards,"[120] it remains unclear whether this call for avenging terror in the press was accompanied by a popular clamor for vengeance in the streets, reminiscent of July 1793.

The official reaction was very much in the same key. On September 2 the All-Russian Central Executive Committee adopted a resolution warning that "all counterrevolutionaries and all those inspiring them will be held responsible" for attempts on the life of "Soviet leaders and champions of the ideals of the socialist revolution." Hereafter the "White Terror" of the people's enemies would be countered by "a Red Terror against the bourgeoisie and its agents."[121] The next day *Izvestia* carried a public notice by Iakov Peters, deputy chairman of the Cheka, claiming that "the criminal designs of the White Guards, the Socialist Revolutionaries, and other pseudo socialists" were forcing the working class to use its "avenging hand to break the chains of slavery . . . [and] to reply . . . with mass terror."[122] It served notice that anyone "arrested carrying arms and lacking the necessary identification papers [would] be subject to instant execution," while whoever "agitated against Soviet authority would be seized immediately and confined to a concentration camp." As for "plundering capitalists, marauders, and speculators," they would be set to "forced labor . . . [while] individuals involved in counterrevolutionary plots will be destroyed and crushed by the heavy hammer of the revolutionary proletariat."[123]

On September 4, 1918, *Izvestia* printed one of two official decrees which put the terror of the Russian Revolution *à l'ordre du jour*. In the first decree, addressed to all the soviets, Grigory Petrovsky, the commissar for internal affairs, first justified and then spelled out a new set of repressive measures. He was almost defensive about abandoning Sovnarkom's heretofore lenient treatment of the forces of resistance which, as he told it, were clearly the aggressor. On the enemy side there was "the killing of Volodarsky and Uritsky; the attempted killing and wounding of . . . Lenin; the execution of tens of thousands of our comrades in Finland and Ukraine, as well as in the territories of the Don and those seized by the Czechoslovaks; the endless conspiracies in the rear of our armies; and the open complicity of the Right Socialist Revolutionaries and other counterrevolutionary scoundrels" in these plots. By contrast, there were "markedly few serious repressions and mass shootings of White Guards and bourgeois by the Soviet authorities, [which] shows that notwithstanding the persistent allegations of mass terror against Socialist Revolutionaries, White Guards, and the bourgeoisie this terror does not, in fact, exist." The time had come to "put a decisive end" to this "laxity and weakness." Henceforth "all Right Socialist Revolutionaries known to local soviets must be arrested immediately . . . [and] a considerable number of hostages must be selected from among the bourgeoisie and the ex-officers." Even the smallest attempt or sign of resistance among the White Guards "must instantly be met with mass executions" and, above all, "there must not be the slightest hesitation or indecision in using mass terror to once and for all eliminate them from the rear of our armies."[124]

While Lenin was in his Kremlin apartment recovering, Sovnarkom discussed a special report on internal security by Dzerzhinsky that served as a basis for the formal decree "On the Red Terror," which was issued on September 5 over the signatures of Grigory Petrovsky and Dmitry Kursky, the commissar for justice. Insisting that since it had become "absolutely essential to secure the rear areas by means of terror," this decree declared that the Cheka needed to be reinforced "with as many reliable party comrades as possible." To shield the Soviet Republic, the Cheka would have to "safeguard it from its class enemies by isolating them in concentration camps," and it would have to "shoot all persons involved with White Guard organizations, conspiracies, and uprisings," making sure to publish their names and "the grounds for their execution."[125] Latsis claimed that "the right to execute," heretofore severely criticized by "many party comrades, . . . was now legalized" by virtue of real life having "forced the Red Terror to reply to the White Terror."[126]

Following the rebel terrorist assault on Uritsky and especially on Lenin, "the terror, hitherto sporadic and unorganized, became a deliberate instrument of policy," directed from above.[127] The executions of Kannegiser and Kaplan, which were only to be expected, were overshadowed by a string of wholesale retributive shootings, hostage takings, and arrests, in conformity with the letter and spirit of the new Cheka guidelines. Significantly, the primary victims of this crescendo of violence were members of the old governing and ruling classes who were guilty or suspected of collaboration with the Whites. Although the Socialist Revolutionaries were no less the target of this heightened enforcement terror, relatively few of them were actually killed or taken hostage. Indeed, the hardening terror cannot be said to have given priority to the struggle against ideological and political rivals over the death struggle with the genuine counterrevolution.

The worst reprisals took place in Petrograd. Gleb Boky, the new acting chairman of the local Cheka, published the decree "On the Red Terror" with a covering statement insisting that Uritsky's assassination tragically demonstrated the laxity of past security measures. He announced the execution of "512 counterrevolutionaries and White Guards, including 10 Right-SRs, and the arrest of representatives of the bourgeoisie as hostages."[128] Among the victims and hostages there figured high officials of the *ancien régime* and provisional governments, as well as military officers, bankers, merchants, and factory managers. Moscow counted over 100 victims, and several other cities between 10 and 40.[129]

Judging by the announcements of the local Chekas, there was nothing mysterious or hidden about this repression. In the capital it was declared to be a reply "to the attempted assassination of the leader of the world proletariat," and in Perm "to the assassination of Uritsky and the attempt on Lenin's life."[130] By and large the rhetoric was that of vengeance, intended to both justify and intimidate. In Nizhny Novgorod, where about 40 persons were shot and an additional 700 held hostage, the local paper served notice that for "every real and threatened murder of a Communist," several bourgeois hostages would be shot, because "the blood of our murdered and wounded comrades cries out for revenge."[131] The Cheka of Torzhok vowed that "for every head and life of our leaders, hundreds of heads of the bourgeoisie and their helpers will fall"; the Cheka of Penza announced that "for the murder . . . of one comrade . . . the Whites paid with 152 lives," to be followed by "severer measures against them in the future."[132]

The escalation of indeterminate and erratic terror into specifically and intentionally political terror was closely correlated with the escalation of the civil war, which became an increasingly commanding fact, in the rear as well as on its rapidly shifting battle fronts, all the more so because from the outset it was freighted with colossal international complications, condensed in the treaty of Brest-Litovsk and its aftermath. In the summer of 1918 the Bolsheviks had to contend with the advancing armies of Kolchak and Denikin, at the same time that they had to decide the fate of the imperial family and cut short the resurgent politics of assassination. In addition, following the proclamation of a grain emergency in May 1918 and the introduction of War Communism, the chronic antipathy between city and country began to take a turn for the worse.

Between spring and autumn in 1918, not unlike in 1793, the revolution "became more defiant with every day" by virtue of being "threatened, provoked, and desperate," and the Bolsheviks, much like the Jacobins, began to "turn what burst forth as a fit of anger and an impulse of despair into a principle of government." In fact, "with heartless dispassion the revolutionaries converted . . . [this contingent] fury into a set of rules, thereby not only setting on fire such volatile impulses as indignation and fear, but also transforming rage into a ruthless instrument of governance and salvation."[133] It was also in this mood of systematic ruthlessness, and at the high point of the crisis in the civil war during the summer of 1918, that the Bolsheviks took the first steps toward establishing a system of labor camps.

* * *

The Cheka's camp system grew out of the Bolshevik response to the breakdown of the judicial and penal system which, as previously noted, nearly coincided with the collapse of political sovereignty. Gradually, by the summer of 1918, the regime put in place "three different organs to impose penalties for various kinds of crime." There were, to begin with, "ordinary courts," or people's courts, which dealt with crimes that did not bear upon state security. As for the newly charted "revolutionary tribunals," they were to judge and penalize crimes against the state, in particular counterrevolutionary activities, profiteering, and hoarding. The Cheka was the third branch. Unlike the two others, it was an administrative, not a judicial organ, "whose actions were not subject to any legal rules of procedure or limited in scope by any legal definition or restriction," at least so far as its powers of arrest and incarceration were concerned; its power to carry out executions was, however, limited to cases of armed insurrection, counterrevolutionary activity, and banditry. Needless to say, the revolutionary tribunals and the Cheka were far more ruthless than the people's courts, which "accounted for 97 percent of persons brought to trial" and were sparing of the death sentence and of long imprisonment.[134]

When and why was the idea for concentration camps first raised? Lenin himself had repeatedly invoked the use of forced social labor for penal purposes. As early as December 1917 he had envisaged it as a means of overcoming the resistance of the old elites to economic reforms. In mid-1918 on several occasions he also suggested limited terms of compulsory labor for bribery and black-marketeering.[135] But it was the acute perils of the summer of 1918 that turned general proposals into practice.

On June 4, 1918, faced with the revolt of the Czech Legion, Trotsky threatened internment in a concentration camp for all Czechs and Slovaks refusing to surrender their arms. Three weeks later, on June 26, he urged Sovnarkom "to establish a coercive regime" complete with "concentration camps" to force the "parasitic elements of the bourgeoisie to perform the most disagreeable work" and to pressure tsarist officers "refusing to join the Red Army."[136] On July 23, 1918, the Cheka was in fact authorized to establish and administer "a different and independent penal system . . . for those whose activities or potential activities constituted a threat to security."[137] Presently the Cheka started to run its own prisons as well as concentration and labor camps. But it was not the only agency empowered to do so at this time. On August 8, 1918, in the wake of the fall of Kazan to the Czech Legion and Kolchak, Trotsky announced that with "the Soviet Republic in danger" he had ordered the officer responsible for the security of the 500-mile rail line between Kazan and Moscow "to set up concentration camps near Murom, Arzamas, and Sviyazhsk for the imprisonment of suspicious agitators, counterrevolutionary officers, saboteurs, parasites, and speculators."[138] The next day, August 9, pre-occupied by armed peasant risings near Penza on the vulnerable eastern front, Lenin wired instructions to the local soviet to organize reliable Red Guards to "exercise massive terror against kulaks, priests, and White Guards [and] to lock up suspicious elements in a concentration camp outside the town."[139] In early September, following the attempt on Lenin's life, Cheka headquarters issued the previously mentioned declaration admonishing that "anyone daring to agitate against Soviet authority would be arrested immediately and confined in a concentration camp." Two days later came the "Decree on the Red Terror" which, *inter alia*, declared it "essential to safeguard the Soviet Republic from its class enemies by isolating them in concentration camps" and charged the Cheka with this task.[140]

✳ ✳ ✳

The fall of 1918 saw a major shift in the balance of forces in Russia detrimental to the Bolsheviks, a shift due in large part to a change in the international balance of forces, as crystallized with the end of the Very Great War. As long as the Central Powers had dominated the Eastern Front, the Allies had confined themselves to occupying safe seaports through which to transship military and economic supplies to Kolchak and the Czechs. Immediately after the Armistice and following Germany's withdrawal from Ukraine, the Allies rushed to also seize Russian ports on the Black, Caspian, and Baltic seas, with a view to supplying all three Volunteer Armies. The Allies left no doubt that they meant to transform their intervention from disquieting the Central Powers in the east to helping the Whites overthrow the Bolshevik regime. Compared to Sovdepia, the territories controlled by the Whites were barren of industry and manufacture. This particular handicap accounts for their utter dependence on foreign supplies of weapons, ammunition, and clothing. Although the Allies dispatched ground forces as well, these were of minor significance, except for the regiments securing the strategic ports. The Western powers also provided diplomatic support fashioned to bolster the Whites' legitimacy. In addition they stood behind the governments of Rumania, Poland, and Finland. Among the chief beneficiaries of the decomposition of the tsarist empire, these three countries were primed to participate in the siege of the Bolshevik regime even if they refused military collaboration with the Whites for fear of their persistent Great Russian pretensions.

During the winter of 1918–19 Moscow made several proposals intended to defuse this ominous foreign intervention while at the same time looking for ways to capitalize on the Revolution's appeal abroad, notably in central Europe.[141] The Allies, including the United States, spurned all overtures. They were at once frightened of the specter of Communism hovering over the destabilized Continent and confident that Lenin's weak and amateur regime would come apart in face of insuperable difficulties at home and containment from abroad. Of course, the governments of the major powers were as divided on the Russian as on the German question. As in the time of the French Revolution, each country reacted to the implosion of one of the international system's great powers according to its own reason of state. But following 1917, unlike after 1789, the Allied governments were buffeted by domestic political pressures which, except in the United States and Japan, were fueled by strains of war. By reason of diplomatic rivalry, political prudence, and war weariness, the concert of powers decided for limited and indirect over full-scale and head-on intervention. The Big Four continued to send aid to the White armies, at the same time that they rebuffed Moscow's diplomatic overtures and helped to quell an allegedly Bolshevik takeover in Hungary. When finally, in late May 1919, they conditionally recognized Kolchak as head of all the counterrevolutionary forces in Russia, his "Ufa offensive" was beginning to falter, foreshadowing his fall. Within a few months Denikin and Iudenich were defeated as well, followed by Wrangel.

Admittedly, Allied assistance was not nearly as systematic and extensive as it might have been and as, understandably, the Bolsheviks surmised and charged it to be. It was, in addition, as lacking in coordination as the military campaigns of the three major White armies. Still, without this material, including financial aid, the counterrevolution could not have persevered as long as it did. While Kolchak depended on foreign rifles, guns, and munitions from Vladivostok reaching him in western Siberia, Denikin relied on the ports of the Black and Caspian seas for supplies. The British contribution was considerably greater than the French, while the United States assumed the role of paymaster-in-chief. Apparently "the arms and equipment . . . sent to Kolchak . . . [were] roughly comparable to total Soviet production in 1919."[142] During that same year the British supplied Denikin with "198,000 rifles, 6,200 machine guns, 500,000,000 rounds of small arms ammunition, and 1,121 artillery pieces."[143] To be sure, this material aid could not offset the Whites' manpower deficit: unlike the Bolsheviks, they failed to convince or coerce the peasants to answer their call to arms. But the Allied governments had political and economic reasons for not sending ground forces, notwithstanding the ultra-interventionist arguments of Winston Churchill and Marshal Foch. Portentously, as early as April 1919 even the French, though desperate to maintain an eastern counterweight to Germany, withdrew the combat detachments they had landed in Odessa some six months before.

It would appear that "had Allied aid to the Whites been stopped" after the Armistice "the Russian Civil War would almost certainly have ended much more quickly in a decisive [Soviet] victory."[144] Any substantially shortened civil war most likely would have lessened the military and civilian bloodletting, the militarization of Bolshevik political society, the ravages of famine, and the economic and social woes of major cities. Besides, with a less protracted, ferocious, and taxing civil war, sustained from abroad, the Bolshevik leaders would have contracted neither their phobia about encirclement by a hostile outside world leagued with domestic enemies nor their hubris fed by their unexpected triumph over insuperable odds. But there is, of course, the other side of the picture: in case of a quick victory in the civil war, a "triumphant revolutionary Russia" would have been in a better position to generate sympathy and support in "a Europe fairly quivering with social unrest and upheaval."[145]

In one respect the heightened threat to the Revolution after the Armistice led to an easing of Bolshevik repression of the non-Bolshevik left, which now cautiously sided with the regime. At the outset the Cheka spied out and harassed active oppositionists among the Mensheviks and Socialist Revolutionaries. Throughout most of 1918 the bulk of these enemy brothers, "convinced that the Bolsheviks would be unable to rule for long without their help," adopted a would-be third or independent position expressed in the motto "neither Lenin nor Denikin [or Kolchak]." Of course, the Mensheviks, led by Julius Martov, condemned the Bolshevik seizure of power and establishment of an authoritarian regime, particularly since they persisted in their view that backward Russia was not ready for a socialist transformation. At first the Mensheviks stayed clear of anti-Bolshevik subversion and conceived of themselves as a loyal opposition. The picture was not nearly so clear with the Socialist Revolutionaries. Once their militant left wing had spent itself in the abortive politics of assassination and insurgency in July 1918, for which they paid a considerable price, there remained two factions: one proposed to "follow the Menshevik strategy of dissenting neutrality"; the other "preferred to challenge the regime in the name of the Constituent Assembly" and, as we saw, collaborated with the White Guards in the fall of 1918.[146]

But following the Armistice, both the Mensheviks and the Socialist Revolutionaries denounced the continuing Allied intervention, now that it shifted from countering the Central Powers to supporting the counterrevolution. In particular, with Kolchak's overthrow of the SR-dominated Directory in favor of a military dictatorship at Omsk in November 1918, almost overnight the right Socialist Revolutionaries either began supporting the Bolsheviks, even if reluctantly and fitfully, or else disengaged or emigrated. Indeed nearly all the components of the non-Bolshevik left, both urban and rural, tended to "ignore the Red Terror . . . because, by and large, it did not affect them." To be sure, the Cheka "fulminated against the socialist 'traitors,' " and not always without reason. But the Cheka's "victims were mainly officials of the old regime and well-to-do citizens." At present the anti- and non-Bolshevik lefts therefore had much more reason to fear the White than the Red Terror. In the crunch, they definitely considered the Bolsheviks "the lesser evil," afraid that should the Whites prevail, they "would liquidate [the Revolution] completely." It was "this prospect [that] in late 1918 . . . [prompted] the Mensheviks, followed by the SRs, to move toward reconciliation with Lenin's regime."[147]

This is not to say that mainstream Mensheviks and Socialist Revolutionaries ceased to either criticize the Bolsheviks or press their own agendas. Although indecisive about the Constituent Assembly, they called for free elections, democratic control of the soviets, and respect for civil rights. In exchange for their eventually rallying support for the armed struggle against the Whites, the Bolsheviks decided to leave loyal Mensheviks and Socialist Revolutionaries considerable political leeway: they could publish newspapers, hold public meetings, and speak out in the soviets. To be sure, this semi-legal and semi-loyal opposition, which was intensely disunited, was closely watched. The Cheka blew hot and cold, intermittently censoring or closing newspapers as well as arresting and then releasing known critics. Typically, in June 1919 Martov was placed under house arrest for five days. Even so, it is not to trivialize this repression to note that apparently very few left oppositionists were hounded, brutalized, executed.[148]

Likewise, although left Socialist Revolutionaries repeatedly engaged in active resistance, they were treated with "comparative leniency." Many of them were imprisoned, and often for protracted terms, but "they suffered relatively few casualties": by 1922 "26 LSRs had been executed, 4 had died in prison, and 51 were still in detention."[149]

Oddly enough, compared to the French terror of 1792–94, the Russian terror of 1918–21 permitted voluntary and forced exile for sectaries of the left. In the autumn of 1920 the Politburo allowed Martov, who was seriously ill, to leave Russia for Germany, enabling Lenin to claim that "we willingly let Martov go." It is true that following Kronstadt, the Bolsheviks, who were ever nervous about potential popular resistance, imprisoned leading oppositionists. Eventually some of them were tried on charges of committing "terrorist" acts, receiving long prison terms as well as death sentences. But the death sentences were commuted, and other oppositionists were not tried at all, but released on condition of foreswearing all political activity. Still others were either "permitted to emigrate or sent into internal exile." Characteristically the Soviet authorities granted the request of Fedor Dan, who had been arrested and sentenced to internal exile in connection with the Kronstadt mutiny in February 1921, to go abroad—a request that he had backed with a hunger strike.[150]

* * *

Kolchak opened the second phase of the civil war in the spring of 1919 with a drive toward the central Volga, his ultimate objective being Moscow, 500 miles to the west. His army of some 125,000 men set out from around Perm, Ekaterinburg, and Cheliabinsk in early March and advanced swiftly, to take Ufa in mid-March and close in on Kazan, Simbirsk, and Samara by late April. The forces facing Kolchak were weak. The Red Army was as yet in the early stages of its transformation from a volunteer militia of workers to a conscript army of peasants. Conscious of the shortcomings of their troops, the Soviet field officers opted for a strategic retreat as the Kremlin, desperate to stem Kolchak's advance, rushed tried and true volunteers and political commissars to the endangered front.

In early May the Red forces began to counterattack and within a month, after retaking Ufa, they had gained in self-confidence. By late August Kolchak's armies had been driven back well beyond their starting points. Kolchak had rushed his offensive to take advantage of the rawness of the Red Army and to bid for stepped-up Allied support. But Kolchak also paid a price for his haste: by not working and waiting to coordinate his drive with Denikin's, he drew all the enemy fire onto his own forces, which soon turned out to be overextended.

From the outset Kolchak resorted to terror both because he set much store by it and because he became caught up in the iron logic of civil war. On December 21–22, 1918, local Bolsheviks had seized a prison in Omsk, his capital, and had set free not a few left-wing political prisoners, most of them non-Bolshevik, even anti-Bolshevik. In the ensuing repression some 300 men were killed indiscriminately and about another 150 were executed following summary courts-martial. Ironically, most of the prisoners the Bolshevik rebels had freed voluntarily surrendered to the White authorities, confident of fair and legal treatment. Instead, a White officer arbitrarily selected fifteen to be shot on the banks of the Irtysh river. Spokesmen for the local radical and liberal intelligentsia cried out against the "uninterrupted spilling of human blood" and the extinction of "the feeling and consciousness of humanity, the value of life, and . . . the legal order in the state." They held all the "contending political groups and parties" responsible for throwing Russia back to "prehistoric times," in the process killing its "civilization and culture and . . . destroying the great [and timeless] cause of human progress."[151]

Admittedly, violence was less controlled in Kolchak's indeterminate territories than in the more structured and fixed Sovdepia. Much of it can be traced to the complete breakdown of political and legal sovereignty in large zones of Siberia in which self-appointed Cossack chiefs arrogated unlimited power to themselves, wreaking havoc to the rear of Kolchak's lines. Grigory Semenov and Ivan Kalmykov were representative of these condottiere who during the spring and summer of 1919 plundered, took hostages, tortured, and killed on a large scale, with the Supreme Ruler at once unwilling and unable to restrain them.[152] According to Roland Morris, the American ambassador to Japan, whose government supported several hetmans, "[a]ll over Siberia . . . there [was] an orgy of arrests without charges; of executions without even the pretense of trial; and of confiscations without color of authority." In an atmosphere of "panic fear . . . [m]en suspected each other and lived in constant terror that some spy or enemy would cry 'Bolshevik' and condemn them to instant death." William Graves, the commander of U. S. troops in Siberia, confirmed that in Siberia whoever failed to "support Kolchak and the autocratic class surrounding him" risked being denounced a "Bolshevik."[153]

With Kolchak's failing military fortunes these chaotic conditions went from bad to worse. While anti-Jewish pogroms were one of the mainstays of counterrevolutionary violence and terror in the southwestern theater of the civil war,[154] they were very much the exception in the eastern regions, where Jewish communities were rare and small. It was in July, while Kolchak's armies were in headlong retreat, that some of his "supporters launched a pogrom . . . in Ekaterinburg . . . that claimed some two thousand casualties which, in view of the city's comparatively small Jewish population, counted as an appalling massacre."[155] This pogrom was not, however, an isolated excess late in the second phase of White resistance beyond the Urals. In mid-November 1919, coincident with the Red Army's capture of Omsk, representatives of the remaining Czechoslovak forces in Siberia notified the Allied governments that "under the protection of [their] bayonets the local Russian military authorities permit[ted] themselves activities at which the whole civilized world [was] horrified." There was nothing uncommon, they said, about "the burning of villages, the beating of peaceful Russian citizens by the hundreds, the shooting without trial of representatives of democracy, on the mere suspicion of political unreliability."[156]

Kolchak kept retreating some 1,500 miles eastward along the Trans-Siberian railway from Omsk toward Irkutsk, just west of the southern tip of Lake Baikal. Encouraged by his imminent defeat, on January 5, 1920, Mensheviks and Socialist Revolutionaries backed by Czechoslovak legionnaires seized control of the city. It was a measure of their lack of realism that they represented themselves as a "Political Center" making a renewed bid for a third way. Presently Kolchak and his entourage reached Irkutsk under the patronage of the Allies. Instead of arranging for his flight or exile, General Maurice Janin, the chief Allied representative in Siberia, pressed the newly formed government to imprison and try him. Kolchak's predicament worsened on January 21, when a committee of local Bolsheviks supplanted the "Political Center." He was now in a situation comparable to that of Nicholas II in Ekaterinburg in mid-1918: the plan to put Kolchak on trial, supported by Lenin, was cut short when stray units of his decomposing army closed in on Irkutsk with the declared intention to liberate him. On February 7, 1920 an official of the local Cheka ordered several local Bolsheviks to shoot Kolchak and his chief political counselor. Their corpses were disposed of as unceremoniously as those of the imperial family, in that they were "cast into an icehole in the river Angara."[157]

Whatever the vicissitudes of Kolchak's campaign, it was the first to have held out the promise of successful counterrevolution not only to the resistance within Russia but to the Big Four in Paris as well. In the spring of 1919 this seemed a real historical possibility, in the brief moment when Kolchak's offensive toward the central Volga fortuitously coincided with Denikin's thrust toward the lower Dnieper.

Faced with this peril, Sovnarkom once again stepped up the terror. Starting in the spring and through the fall, hundreds of Mensheviks and Socialist Revolutionaries were arrested on suspicion of disloyalty and complicity with the enemy in cities likely or about to be buffeted by the civil war. This was also the time when in several of these cities the Cheka was charged with reining in labor strikes in industries considered essential to the civil war effort. The workers were driven to remonstrate by sparse rations, runaway prices, and fear of starvation, even though they also clamored for self-rule and political decontrol. Here and there the strikers were joined by soldiers who mutinied when ordered to restrain or fire on them. In March–April 1919 Tula, 120 miles east of Moscow, in Kolchak's reach, and Astrakhan, the Caspian port and mouth of the Volga, in Denikin's, witnessed a terrifying repression. In Tula hundreds of strikers were arrested, and before work resumed 24 alleged "ringleaders" were executed. Infinitely worse, in Astrakhan, under the direction of Sergei Kirov, the political chief of the region, probably over a thousand workers and mutineers were arrested. With the prisons saturated, the local forces of law and order, including Cheka operatives, put the overflow on barges, with the result that scores of them drowned or were thrown into the Volga. All told, between 2,000 and 4,000 strikers and mutineers are estimated to have been killed, followed by the massacre of 600 to 1,000 class enemies, including members of the bourgeoisie.[158]

In mid-winter 1918–19 Denikin had moved south to drive the Soviets out of the northern Caucasus, including Piatigorsk and Grozny. He now prepared to move into the center of Russia. He had even fewer men than Kolchak, but had received timely and ample supplies of British arms and ammunition. In early May the Armed Forces of South Russia launched a three-pronged offensive: northward to take Kharkov and the Donets Basin; eastward to seize Tsaritsyn; and westward to capture Ekaterinoslav (Dnepropetrovsk). By the end of June they had also occupied Odessa, Nikolaev, and Novorossiysk on the Black Sea.

Denikin made these stunning gains at the very time that Kolchak suffered his first reverses, and before long he supplanted the Supreme Ruler as the high hope of the anti-Bolshevik resistance—at home and abroad. Partly because the fledgling Red Army was heavily engaged in fighting Kolchak, it kept falling back on the southern front, and when it finally mounted an attack in August, Denikin managed to hold fast. In the meantime, heartened by his quick success, Denikin redefined his military objective: he would move on Moscow and link up with Kolchak, with a view to shoring up the Supreme Ruler's weakening position. The main axes of his advance would be northward from Kharkov via Kursk and Orel to Tula and from the Don Basin to Voronezh. The drive started in mid-September 1919, and once again Denikin's divisions advanced swiftly. By mid-October, having taken Chernigov and Voronezh on his western and eastern flanks, his main force reached Orel, 250 miles south of Moscow, and within a fortnight it drew near Tula.

But at this point, not unlike Kolchak at his apogee in May, Denikin found his armies to be overstretched, and for many of the same reasons. As a social conservative he, too, had continued to sidestep the land question, which was all the more detrimental in his case, since he had to divert some of his thinly deployed forces to parry an attack from Makhno's peasant bands to his rear. Likewise, Denikin and his supporters were unfeigned champions of a great, indivisible, and centralized Russia, which meant he was not about to receive help from Ukrainians and Poles. To be sure, the White troops were still better trained, officered, and—thanks to the British—better equipped than the Red troops. But by now these advantages could no longer make up for the swelling ranks of the Soviet Army.[159] As for the hope held out by General Iudenich's drive toward Petrograd from the north, it was, as we shall see, short-lived.

＊ ＊ ＊

As we saw, the Cheka stepped up its drive to uncover counterrevolutionary conspiracies and ferret out political enemies during the second half of 1918. The defiance of the left Socialist Revolutionaries, Kolchak's first military moves, and the attempt on Lenin's life were at once the reason and justification for this first escalation of terror, brought out in high relief with the Decree on the Red Terror. Although the Bolshevik leaders, including Dzerzhinsky, exaggerated the scope and conspiratorial nature of the not entirely separable left-populist and counterrevolutionary challenge, it most certainly was no mere phantasm. Just as there is no revolution without counterrevolution, so there is no counterrevolution without conspiracy.

The Cheka broke up a few embryonic cabals of White sympathizers during the fall and winter of 1918–19. But it was only in June 1919, during Denikin's first offensive, that the counterrevolutionary underground again became threatening. In 1918, the Whites had organized the National Center, a clandestine network of members of the conservative elites sworn to help battle the Bolshevik regime behind the lines of the civil war. With branches in both Moscow and Petrograd, it gathered intelligence for the Volunteer forces and sought to stimulate unrest in the Red Army. While ex-tsarist officers ran the military side of this enterprise, the Kadets held the political reins. In 1919, the National Center set about organizing uprisings to coincide with Denikin's advance on Moscow and Iudenich's on Petrograd.[160]

There were attempted risings in Petrograd in mid-June and again in mid-September, and in Moscow on September 18–19, 1919. In all instances the Cheka struck back fiercely. On June 16, following a misfired mutiny by the garrison of one of Kronstadt's forts, the Cheka executed "every fifth man, for a total of 55 . . . in full view of [their] comrades."[161] This cruel and excessive punishment was followed by a massive search for arms and accomplices. In July some of the members of Petrograd's National Center were arrested. Two months thereafter, in September, between 300 and 1,000 alleged conspirators were taken into custody in Moscow, most of them old-regime officers and Kadets, of whom about 65 were shot. In announcing the liquidation of the capital's branch of the National Center, Dzerzhinsky claimed that it had planned to sow confusion, "if only for a few hours," in which to "take over the radio and telegraph . . . and notify front-line troops of the collapse of the Soviet government, thereby provoking a panic and demoralizing the army."[162] In October and November, during Iudenich's advance to the outskirts of Petrograd, what remained of the National Center in that city was reactivated, precipitating the arrest of "a further 300 suspects."[163]

This discovery of a not inconsiderable conspiracy near the center of power, compounded by Denikin's advance toward Moscow, brought about a general broadening of the Cheka's sway. Both the Reds and Whites had already resorted to terrorist violence in the battle zones, as the civil war became increasingly savage and merciless. Certainly on the Bolshevik side there were numerous arrests and executions as well as arbitrary requisitions and confiscations. But in addition to this terror at the front and to the rear, most of it spontaneous and wild, the Cheka now came into action on a larger scale than heretofore, as the embodiment of the regime's institutionalized enforcement terror.

On June 20, Sovnarkom had issued a decree directing the Cheka to go on a full war footing in all "areas under martial law." It was specifically authorized "to impose 'summary justice (up to shooting)' " in dealing with a broad range of political enemies and suspects: individuals "belonging to counterrevolutionary organizations"; committing "treason"; engaging in "espionage"; harboring "traitors and spies"; concealing "weapons . . . , forging documents, . . . touching off explosions or fires for counterrevolutionary purposes"; "destroying or damaging" transportation and communication equipment as well as military and food supplies. Criminals engaging in "banditry, . . . armed robbery, . . . plunder, [and] illegal trade in cocaine" were mentioned last.[164]

Dzerzhinsky instantly distributed this decree to all Cheka sections, insisting that they were now officially responsible for "purging . . . the Soviet Republic of all enemies of worker-peasant Russia." In his covering circular he ordered all branches to turn themselves into "armed camps" primed to "secure the rear of our army, . . . to frustrate the plans of White Guard plotters," and to punish "with a stern hand . . . [even the] slightest attempt to harm the revolution."[165]

In the spirit of this circular, the political prisoners in the jails of some of Ukraine's major cities became hostages to fate. The prisons and the concentration camp of Kharkov held several hundred such captives, many of them former military officers, alongside a cross-section of common-law criminals. As if to warn off the White Guards or exorcize their own fury mixed with fear, in June the local Chekists began to carry out random executions. During the night of June 22— two days before the Whites entered Kharkov—79 of the 350 prisoners of the Tchaikovsky Street jail were summarily sentenced to death and executed.[166] The same scenario unfolded in Kiev: on August 28, on the eve of the fall of Ukraine's capital and largest city, the local terror culminated in several hundred executions.[167]

As might be expected, much of this terror bore the marks of the furious brutality inherent to civil war. In both Kharkov and Kiev the mass killings immediately preceding capture by Denikin's forces were in the nature of massacres, with batches of victims forced to undress and kneel along a ditch before being shot.[168] In Kharkov and other cities, moreover, numerous victims were lacerated and mutilated before being executed, and in Kiev and Ekaterinoslav several of them were "crucified." In Odessa White officers were reported to have been "chain[ed] to planks and push[ed] . . . slowly into furnaces or boiling water."[169]

In addition to the raging civil war intensifying the repression in Moscow and Ukraine, it quickened the establishment of concentration camps. Even though eventually common criminals would be incarcerated in concentration and labor camps, in the beginning the camp population consisted largely of political enemies and suspects, in particular members of the old elite from among whom the Bolsheviks proposed to draw their stock of hostages. Intended as a determent, at this time the camps isolated and punished rather than reeducated or exploited inmates. They also immured members of rival political parties. As the civil war continued, the number of prisoners kept rising. By mid-1919 the Cheka is estimated to have held some 13,000 hostages.[170]

The policy of hostage taking had first been advocated by Lenin and Trotsky the year before, in the wake of the uprising of the left Socialist Revolutionaries, which had inspired the Decree on the Red Terror with its injunction to isolate class enemies in concentration camps. Soon thereafter Dzerzhinsky insisted that hostages would have to be individuals valued by the Whites and their supporters, who would set no store by "just any ordinary schoolteacher, forester, miller, or small shopkeeper, the less so should he be Jewish." They would be more likely to "value high state officials, big landowners, manufacturers, prominent workers, scholars, relatives of persons known to be on their side." But at that time, while local Chekas were urged to identify possible hostages in "these circles," they were still not authorized to seize and put them in prisons or concentration camps "without permission" from headquarters in Moscow.[171] At any rate, the number of hostages kept rising, and a few weeks after his June 1919 circular Dzerzhinsky forewarned that "even the most superficial" contacts with White Guards would bring on "the most severe punishment—execution, confiscation of property, and confinement of all adult members of families in concentration camps."[172]

In the meantime, the Bolsheviks began to envisage a role other than hostage for concentration camp inmates. At the start of 1919, when the situation seemed to take a turn for the better, Dzerzhinsky had proposed cutting back the Cheka's powers of administrative repression in favor of the revolutionary tribunals. But he made a special point of insisting that he did not favor the Cheka surrendering control of the inmates of concentration camps. On February 17, 1919, at a session of the VTsIK (All Russian Central Executive Committee of the All-Russian Congress of Soviets), he urged that henceforth concentration camps should have the additional mission of harnessing the labor of inmates, particularly of "gentlemen without regular occupations and of those unable to work without a certain degree of coercion." Dzerzhinsky suggested that Soviet administrators who were "indolent and negligent" should also be subjected to this labor discipline. All in all, the idea was that concentration camps, besides serving as a place of detention for political enemies and hostages, could serve as a "school of labor."[173] It was an idea that Lenin, too, had occasionally adumbrated, and indeed in May 1919, he "decreed the use of concentration camp inmates for military construction on the southern front."[174]

It was in the spring of 1919 that the Soviet government decided to go beyond mobilizing the labor of concentration camp inmates by setting up separate forced-labor camps. A decree of April 11 charged the provincial Chekas with organizing and running these camps, and a follow-up decree of May 12 called on them to establish a forced-labor camp to hold about 300 inmates in each province. Hereafter, despite considerable jurisdictional confusion, the Commissariat of Justice ran ordinary prisons; the Commissariat for Internal Affairs shared authority with the Cheka over the forced-labor camps; and the Cheka, by itself, controlled the concentration camps. Throughout this improvised and complex universe of preventive and punitive detention conditions of life and work were exceedingly harsh and often cruel. But this state of affairs seems to have been due to the dead hand of Russia's past and the miseries of an unrelenting time of troubles rather than to a Bolshevik warrant for torture or decimation.[175]

Not much is known about the earliest concentration and labor camps. They "were located in the heartland of Russia, not in remote regions of Siberia or the north." Any number of these camps were set up in former monasteries and convents. Apparently their inmates were able to have "contact with the outside world" and were permitted to engage "in political activity," and many of them "survived and regained their freedom."[176] The logic of the situation suggests that many of the camps were set up by new men of power facing local problems and enemies, with little control from the center. Likewise, there is sparse information about the number of prisoners in each of the three types of detention centers, the crimes with which they were charged, and their pains and punishments. According to official accounts in 1919 throughout Russia, but excluding the heavily embattled Ukraine, the Cheka arrested about 80,000 persons—"for such offenses as counterrevolution (21,032), malfeasance (19,673), and speculation (8,367)." While about 3,500 prisoners were executed, some 27,000 were released.[177] In late 1920 the Soviet Union held a total of about 50,000 prisoners, of whom some 24,000 were civil war prisoners and 6,000 inmates in 84 concentration and forced-labor camps spread over 43 provinces. The number of camps rose to 120 in late 1921 and to 132 a year later, and the number of detainees to about 41,000 and 60,000, respectively. Between a fifth and a quarter of the camp population was imprisoned for counterrevolutionary activities, the others were held, in uncertain and changing proportions, for common law crimes, economic crimes, and military desertion. As for the social profile of the camp inmates, between seventy-five and eighty percent were peasants and workers.[178]

* * *

The second phase of the civil war began drawing to a close in the fall of 1919, with the Red Army's counteroffensive against the overextended forces of Denikin.[179] By mid-November the Reds had driven Denikin's northernmost armies back to Kursk, leaving both Orel and Voronezh behind them. They pushed ahead in two directions, southeastward into the Donets Basin and southwestward into Ukraine. In another month they took Kharkov and Kiev, which fell to them on December 16. The fate of Denikin and his original and last bastion on the lower Don and Kuban was sealed, not least because the fighting spirit of the Don and Kuban Cossacks was as broken as that of the southern army. Denikin still tried to make a last stand first at Rostov and then on the Crimea, but to no avail. Overcome by panic and fear—including fear of reprisals—some of his troops visited a fierce avenging fury upon the cities, towns, and villages along their line of retreat.[180] Both the "Volunteers" and the Cossacks finally fell back toward the Black Sea port of Novorossiysk. In mid-March 1920 Denikin was among several thousand soldiers and civilians who were evacuated and exiled through this seaport. Many times their number were taken prisoner.

In the meantime, in late September 1919 General Iudenich stepped up his drive toward Petrograd.[181] While Denikin's forces were reeling near Orel, and partly to relieve them, on October 20 the Northwestern Army of some 20,000 men had unexpectedly penetrated to the outskirts of the capital of the Revolution. Although Iudenich seemed prepared to make concessions to the Finnish government in exchange for military support, he forfeited it by yielding to political pressure to embrace the cause of a "great, united, and undivided" Russia. Since Iudenich, like the other White leaders, also disregarded political and social reform, he deprived himself of support from behind enemy lines, and from within Petrograd as well. In any case, helped by special worker's battalions, Trotsky's troops managed to stem the advance and within three weeks drove Iudenich's host back toward the Estonian border, where they fell to pieces.

Probably the autumn of 1919, specifically mid-October, marked one of the most perilous moments for the embattled Bolshevik regime: Denikin's divisions had drawn close to Tula not far from Moscow and Iudenich's troops stood less than 15 miles outside Petrograd. The fall of Petrograd would have been a severe psychological and symbolic blow for Lenin and his associates, all the more so had it coincided with, or shortly been followed by, the investment and fall of Moscow, which would have been a major, if not necessarily fatal, military setback. As it turned out, the Red Army weathered both storms, largely because by then it had grown to over 2 million men, 80 percent of them peasants, and reaped the benefits of improved organization and battle experience, partly thanks to ex-tsarist cadres. At the start of the new year, shortly after the second anniversary of the October Revolution, the Bolsheviks stood tall, having all but vanquished the White Guards and reclaimed additional territory. In cold realism the great powers discontinued their active if mostly indirect intervention in favor of a policy of containment, focused on eastern and east central Europe.

* * *

Revolutionary Russia's complex relations with Poland laid bare the grave perils and limitations of its peculiarly isolated position in the international system. Any Russian government, let alone Lenin's, would have found it difficult to cushion the shocks of the Romanov empire's decomposition. The Treaty of Brest-Litovsk gave a foretaste of the tangled consequences of this breakup in the western marshes, notably in the territories lying between Germany and Russia and stretching from the Baltic to the Black Sea. When the armies of the fallen Hohenzollern empire evacuated these lands, they became the site for explosive rivalries over intensely contested frontiers among several successor or would-be successor states. These conflicts were magnified by the simultaneous downfall of the Austro-Hungarian and Turkish empires. By virtue of its location, size, and population, renascent Poland was not only the strategically most crucial of the successor states but also the most ambitious and combative. It was, in addition, best prepared to reclaim its independence.

Under the leadership of Roman Dmowski and Jozef Pilsudski, the Poles capitalized on France's desperate search for a replacement for Russia as a counterweight to Germany, as well as on the collapse of Russia, Germany, and Austria-Hungary to recover imagined historic borders. Although the new-born Polish government had no difficulty raising troops, it could not do without the diplomatic and material support of the Allied powers. Warsaw played on the latter's disharmony and irresolution at the same time that it made the most of the unsettled state of European Russia, where Reds and Whites were locked in battle.

Indeed, in the east Pilsudski proposed to restore the borders of 1772 before Russia should recover as a great power and reestablish its hegemony over eastern Galicia, Ukraine, Belorussia, and Lithuania. In the euphoria of an improbable chain of favorable circumstances, Warsaw's new political class even aspired to a Polish-dominated confederation of most of these lands. But should this vaulting ambition be thwarted, a renascent Poland would fight to hold as much of these fiercely disputed borderlands as possible. Indeed, this resolve to recreate a Greater Poland took absolute precedence over helping Denikin's drive to Moscow, the Poles distrusting all Great Russians, be they Red or White.

In April 1919 the Polish forces seized Vilna.[182] There followed the capture of eastern Galicia in June and of Minsk, Kovno, and Lvov in July. By late August Polish troops had penetrated to the Dvina river and past the Pripet Marshes to the Berezina river, just beyond the Curzon Line. Shortly before, on August 12, the Supreme Council of the Allies had proposed this ethnically sensitive boundary line running south from Grodno through Brest-Litovsk to Przemysl as a basis for negotiation between Poland and Lithuania, Belorussia, and Ukraine. Confident of the connivance of the Great Powers, Warsaw ignored their admonitions. Of course, Moscow understood the Polish design but was unable to react, the Red Army being stretched to the limit fighting the White Guards.

In their total isolation, the Bolsheviks could see only two chances for relief: one, a revolt of the Polish working class in the rear of Pilsudski's armies, which never materialized; the other, the long-standing ethnic and cultural antagonisms dividing the peoples of the non-Russian borderlands. These historical enmities were far from negligible, but they were not sufficient to enable the Red Army to win against Poland. Above all, the at best proto-nationalist Ukraine, caught up in civil war and lacking seasoned political and military leaders, was no match for resurgent Poland any more than it was a match for either Denikin's or Trotsky's armies.

Pilsudski resumed his advance in early spring 1920, occupying Zhitomir on April 26 and Kiev on June 7. The fighting became increasingly furious on both sides. On May 10 Trotsky issued an order of the day (No. 217) from Gomel to be read to all fighting units. In it he charged that "unheard of atrocities . . . [were being] committed by Polish White-Guard forces upon captured and wounded Red Army men," who were being "tortured, beaten, shot, and hanged." Although he recognized that such atrocities "arouse justified fury and desire for vengeance," Trotsky expostulated that it would "be wrong and unworthy of revolutionary fighters to take vengeance" on Polish prisoners and wounded, whom he ordered be "spared." In a follow-up order of July 17 (No. 231) from Moscow, Trotsky conceded that "there may have been isolated cases [of misconduct] when more backward Red Army men . . . who were less filled with the liberating idea of communism tore out the hearts of captured Polish soldiers," moved as they were by "thoughtless vengeance" for atrocities perpetrated by Polish White Guards in Kiev, Borisov, and Bobruisk. Referring back to his previous directive, he ordered that the humane treatment of Polish prisoners "be enforced with absolute strictness and without exception," and to that end "the Red forces and, in particular, their new formations" should be given to understand that "Polish soldiers are themselves helpless victims of the Polish and Anglo-French bourgeoisies." Trotsky called for the "thorough investigation of all rumors and reports" of atrocities against Polish soldiers or civilians. In closing, he "firmly reminded all commanders and commissars" that he held them personally responsible "for seeing that this present order is strictly obeyed."[183]

With the Allies looking the other way, Pilsudski, their self-appointed proxy, continued to march east, determined to test the limits of the Bolsheviks' presumably still overstrained military capabilities and political resolve. But having defeated the White armies, except

for Wrangel's as yet unsuspected residual forces, and before confronting Makhno and Antonov, the Red Army, near the top of its numerical
strength, breathed somewhat easier. In mid-1920 several divisions
under the command of generals Semën M. Budennyi and Mikhail
Tukhachevsky struck back. The Polish forces almost immediately
paid the price for being drawn too thin. Zhitomir was recaptured on
June 7, 1920 and Kiev on June 12. In July the Red Army retook
Minsk, Vilna, Grodno, and Bialystok. By August 1 it crossed the Bug
river to seize Brest-Litovsk, thereby overstepping, in its turn, the
Curzon Line.

As one may have expected, the Allies, having shifted to containment
by way of a *cordon sanitaire*, were more alarmed by this transgression
in the direction of Warsaw than they had been by the previous one in
the direction of Moscow. When they hurriedly offered to mediate on
the basis of the Curzon Line, Gregory Chicherin, the commissar of
foreign affairs, curtly demurred. The Soviets were torn between, on
the one hand, the dogged dream of a revolutionary upheaval in Poland
as well as, following the abortive Kapp *Putsch*, in Germany, and, on
the other, the panic fear of a hostile encirclement, of which Greater
and hostile Poland would be the farthest outpost and bridgehead.
Furthermore, by now General Wrangel was threatening to break out
of the Crimea, perhaps with foreign help.

But there was also, of course, the force of ideology and mental disposition. Admittedly the Bolshevik creed did not call for spreading
revolution on the point of bayonets. Although the Bolshevik leaders,
like their enemy brothers, were inspired by the universalism of the
French Revolution, they recognized themselves in neither the Republic's *Grande Nation* nor Napoleon's imperial pretense. Like the Jacobins of before the Year II, they gave a defensive rather than aggressively expansionist reading of the theory and practice of the nation-
in-arms and *levée en masse*.

Whereas three years after 1789 the ultra-Jacobins took over an offensive ideological war from the Girondins, the Bolshevik regime was
from birth enmeshed in defensive conflicts that were turned essentially inward, not outward. Even so, the Bolshevik leadership was forever torn between advocates of the primacy of domestic politics and
champions of the primacy of international politics, with not a few wav-
erers between them. At the time of Brest-Litovsk and until late 1918,

Lenin, Bukharin, and Trotsky were, as we saw, emblematic of these three positions, with Lenin invariably bringing one and all around to his reason. Not unlike Robespierre he gave absolute priority to consolidating the regime and the gains of the Revolution, while Bukharin, like Brissot, espoused the not necessarily peaceful spread of the Revolution to Europe as the key to its future at home and abroad. At critical moments Trotsky reluctantly but decisively and steadfastly sided with Lenin. Meanwhile, no one could be found who did not hope against hope that a workers' revolution further west—in Germany—would help to ease the Russian Revolution's fateful isolation. On two occasions expectations ran high: in November 1918, with the collapse of the Hohenzollern and Habsburg thrones into republics severely pressed by labor risings; and in March–April 1919, with the establishment of rebel republics in Munich and Budapest. But these revolts were contained and reduced with the help of repressive violence.

Although the universalism of the Russian Revolution, including its tenet of national self-determination, made considerable inroads abroad, it did so as something to be invoked or condemned from afar, and not by means of subversion, let alone by force of arms. The Soviets were in no position to foment and help distant revolutions, except by the word, unaided by the sword or rifle. Even the most internationalist-minded Bolsheviks recognized the impossibility of the Red Army rushing to support the uprisings in Central Europe during the winter and early spring of 1918–19. In the meantime, set upon from all sides, and with the proletarian revolution stillborn abroad, Lenin felt more than ever justified in his strategy of momentarily putting revolution "in one country"—in Russia—ahead of world revolution. Ironically the foundation of the Third International, or Comintern, in Moscow in March 1919 coincided with this shift from an international to an internal perspective and strategy.

For well over a year events vindicated this course. But then, in mid-1920, with the Red Army unexpectedly rolling back Pilsudski's legions and making a breach through which to advance to Warsaw, the internationalists reopened the debate they had lost at the time of Brest-Litovsk.[184] Renewing their golden dreams, some Bolshevik leaders advocated seizing this opportunity to move westward to help spread revolution where, in the Marxist vision, it should have started in the first place. Others, moved by a deep-seated fear of counterrevolution, even after the defeat of the Whites, urged marching on Warsaw to abort or roll back the embryonic *cordon sanitaire* rather than to break through to Central Europe. Besides, after three years of total isolation and constant peril, some Bolsheviks were not about to pass up a chance to once again tempt fortune, as they had in October 1917.

In any case, having turned down the offer of Allied mediation, Sovnarkom authorized Tukhachevsky to press his advantage. By early August his troops reached the Vistula and stood a few miles east of the Polish capital. But contrary to the internationalists' prophecy, the approach of the Red Army triggered not a workers' revolt but a nationalist outburst in Warsaw. In mid-August Pilsudski, advised by General Maxime Weygand, Marshal Foch's chief of staff, struck back. Following a chaotic "battle of the Vistula," and with his lines overextended, Tukhachevsky was forced to beat a retreat. Within a matter of weeks, by mid-October, the Polish forces were back to nearly the same positions they had reached in the spring.

Their gamble having failed, the Soviets had to reconcile themselves to Russia's military exhaustion and diplomatic isolation as well as to Poland's emergence as the pivot of the *cordon sanitaire* to the west. Eager to avoid further damage, Moscow sought a negotiated settlement. Although Warsaw played for time to consolidate its position, Pilsudski knew that without substantial Allied help, which was now out of the question, he had gone the limit.

Negotiations started on September 21, 1920, in the Latvian capital, and an armistice coupled with preliminary peace terms was signed and went into effect a month later. The final terms were fixed in the Treaty of Riga signed on March 18, 1921. The Russo-Polish border now ran from Vilna in the north through Grodno and Rovno to Lvov in the south, or some 100 miles east of the original Curzon Line. With its conquest of a large swath of the late tsarist empire's western borderlands, Poland acquired five million Ukrainians and one million Belorussians, making for a considerable irredentist vulnerability.

Although the Poles were the undisputed winners, the Soviets made some gains as well. For one thing, they prevailed on Warsaw to agree to a frontier 50 miles west of their farthest line of advance, thereby snatching Minsk from Poland's jaws. Trotsky was not altogether wrong to proclaim that in March and April "the Polish Government could have had without a war a peace no less favorable than the one which has now been concluded with us."[185] Furthermore, and above all, the cessation of hostilities on the western frontier enabled the Bolsheviks to concentrate on bringing the civil war to a conclusion by facing down General Wrangel, Denikin's successor, in the south.

✳ ✳ ✳

When General Wrangel took over command of Denikin's army on March 22, it counted some 100,000 to 150,000 men, of whom between 30,000 and 35,000 were thoroughly battle-worthy.[186] The army had withdrawn to the Crimean peninsula, which is almost an island unto itself, surrounded by the Black Sea and the Sea of Azov. Not immediately threatened by the Red Army and in control of the remnants of the Black Sea fleet, Wrangel had both the time and space to prepare for battle. The Crimea had, however, one drawback: an insufficient food supply for a population of three million which included more civilian refugees than soldiers.

A hereditary nobleman of monarchist disposition, General Baron Peter Wrangel was a generation younger than the commanding White generals who had gone down to defeat. Probably he was also more open-minded than they, at any rate when it came to learning from their shortcomings, as he understood them. Wrangel took such ex-imperial conservative luminaries as A. V. Krivoshein and Peter Struve to advise him on domestic and foreign policy, respectively. With their counsel he issued a cautious land decree and reached out to Makhno; sought openings to the Poles and Ukrainians; and contemplated the establishment of local government and social services throughout his realm. He also proposed to rein in his soldiers' spoliation of villages and mistreatment of prisoners. Wrangel's policies, which were too little and too late, were designed to rally maximum support on all sides for what he knew would be an uphill struggle, as he said himself, "with anybody at all, but for Russia," if need be "even with the devil."[187] But ultimately he did not shed the friend-enemy rhetoric or perspective of civil war which had left its trace on his operation in Stavropol nearly two years before. When launching his major offensive in the summer of 1920, Wrangel told his associates that his "Russian Army . . . [was] march[ing] to liberate its native land from the Red vermin," and a few months later, when the tide of battle turned against him, he spoke of "our brothers [suffering] in Red butchers' dungeons."[188]

Taking advantage of the Red Army's heavy engagement with Pilsudski, in early June some of Wrangel's troops began to move out of the Crimea: several units established beachheads on the northwestern shores of the Sea of Azov; others moved northward overland in the direction of the Dnieper. Although the season of Allied aid was over, the French recognized and encouraged Wrangel in the hope of his drawing Red troops from the Polish front. While advanced regiments did manage to cross the Dnieper in early October, within a few days they were driven back across the river. Indeed, the beginning of the second withdrawal to the Crimea coincided with the end of the Russo-Polish war. From Kharkov Trotsky served notice that "all our attention is [now] concentrated on the front against Wrangel . . . [and] the whole country has turned its face to the south."[189] On October 20 the Red Army launched a major offensive to the south, forcing a string of engagements, including the decisive battle in the Crimea's far northern isthmus connecting it to the mainland. The fighting took a heavy toll of casualties and prisoners, as well as of victims of atrocities, on both sides. Within three weeks, on November 11, General Michael Vasilev Frunze, the commander-in-chief of the Red Army's southern front, offered Wrangel terms of surrender, including a broad amnesty coupled with the right to emigrate, which astonished Lenin for their "excessive leniency."[190] Spurning the offer, Wrangel and his officers led an orderly fallback of their troops to the major Black Sea ports, for evacuation.

Every aspect of General Wrangel's last stand confirmed, once again, the intrinsic weakness and dependency of the White counterrevolution. Just as his initial success was heavily contingent on the unintended help of the Poles, in the form of Pilsudski pinning down the Red Army, so the safe evacuation of the bulk of his soldiers who escaped capture turned upon the protection and assistance of the Allied powers. As was to be expected, Britain and France provided not a few of the 126 ships which took many thousands of White troops and civilians to safety in Constantinople, though Wrangel himself made a point of leaving Sevastopol for exile on board the Russian cruiser *General Kornilov*. Of course, an even larger number of Whites, both military and civilian, were left behind, along with sympathizers and fellow-travelers, and it was they who were about to suffer the full brunt of the victors' retributive terror. Indeed, "one of the most sweeping outbursts of terrorism occurred in the Crimea after the defeat and evacuation of Wrangel."[191]

The Furies in the Crimea in the aftermath of the civil war took the form of indiscriminate punitive expeditions against Wrangel's collaborators. The number of summary executions in Sevastopol, Simferopol, Kerch, and Yalta ran into the thousands, but it is impossible to advance a close estimate of the total number of victims of this avenging fury which, according to the émigrés, turned the Crimea into an "All-Russian Cemetery."[192] In several towns "[i]mmense numbers of persons suspected of having had any connection with Wrangel's regime were rounded up and shot." Judging by an article in a local newspaper in December 1920, in this terrorist violence there was something of the avenging fury of Turreau's infernal columns in the Vendée. The writer called for a "pitiless, unceasing, . . . [and] death-dealing struggle against the well-hidden snakes," the snakes in question being White Guards, of whom "too many remained at large . . . waiting for the moment to throw themselves on us again." But instead of leaving them "the possibility of attacking us," the workers, wielding the "merciless sword of the Red Terror, . . . shall scour the Crimea and clear it of all the hangmen, enslavers, and tormentors of the working class."[193] Characteristically, in the Crimea, not unlike in the Vendée, execution by shooting was not the only type of punishment. In Sevastopol Chekists "proceeded to hang suspected Whites," while in Kerch they were said to have taken large numbers of victims "out to sea, and drowned them, and their terrorstricken wives and mothers flogged . . . or, in a few cases, shot along with their sons or husbands."[194] The blend between orders from Moscow and local initiatives remains obscure, as does that between official approbation and censure of atrocities.

✱ ✱ ✱

The civil war in the dawn of the Russian Revolution was a mixture of a class war, a war between Great Russians and non-Russians, and a war between city and country. Though these wars overlapped, they did not coincide. Above all, the class war between the Reds and Whites was over before the war between city and country—between Reds and Greens—began to rage full tilt. Even the war with Poland was fought at a time when the class war was over, except for the terminal battle with Wrangel. And both the non-Bolshevik left and the vigilant peasantry, terrified at the prospect of a restoration, gave higher priority to saving the Revolution than to defeating the Bolsheviks.

In most essential respects the Reds had an important advantage. They controlled Russia's densely populated heartland, held together by the centripetal force of the twin capitals. Sovdepia benefited from an effective transportation network; the bulk of the ex-empire's essential industries and military stockpiles; and the symbolic sway of Petrograd and Moscow, including the Kremlin. But above all, its relatively homogeneous population of 60 million provided an ample source of manpower for the old-new Red Army which from a "small volunteer force of proletarians" expanded to some 2 million in mid-1919, 3 million six months later, and 5 million at the end of the civil war. Essentially a peasant army, compared to their enemies the Bolsheviks had a "superior ability" to mobilize the muzhiks, and this despite a high level of resistance to conscription and of desertion.[195] To boot, this mushrooming peasant army was increasingly trained, disciplined, and led by commissioned and noncommissioned officers from the tsarist army,[196] and these were backed by political commissars of non-peasant background. The latter were a link in the chain of command of a centralized government straining to set up and direct a civil administration as part of its overarching goal of reestablishing a single sovereignty. Besides, with their promise of radical social reform, the Bolsheviks touched a sympathetic chord with the younger generation, which disproportionately joined their military and political ranks.

By comparison, the territories controlled by the Whites were widely scattered and had a population of less than 10 million. In addition to being thinly settled, their "peripheral" regions lacked industry, and, in places, were populated by non-Russians. Their evasion, nay refusal of land reform and self-determination stood in the way of their making inroads among the peasants and minorities, all the more so since their call to rally around "Russia, One and Indivisible," their chief ideological plank, had little purchase among ordinary people and non-Russians.

Ultimately the unpolitical pretense and patriotic self-complacency of the White resistance could not dissimulate its narrow restorative intentions. Its ideological poverty may have endured because, unlike its counterpart in the French Revolution, it never systematically turned to account the religious passion. Apparently none of the White generals ever considered calling his armed force an "Orthodox and Tsarist Army." Russia's imperial past was relatively barren of crusades, inquisitions, or religious wars, and, as we shall see, church and clergy were not nearly as ubiquitous as they were in France, the religion of everyday life being more home-centered. Nor was there a Vatican to issue anathemas *urbi et orbi* and to call to order a hierarchical clergy.[197] Without religious agents and agencies, the White generals and politicians must have found it difficult to incite and rally the lower orders of country and town. Besides, they were the rearguard of nineteenth-century conservatism and reaction rather than the vanguard of twentieth-century counterrevolution. Although there were spokesmen for the Black Hundreds and the Union of the Russian People in Omsk and Ekaterinodar, they were neither numerous nor tone-setting. Overall the generals and their political acolytes felt uncomfortable reaching beyond the elites to out-of-doors publics. Apart from being suspicious of mass and populist politics in city and village, they were inept at it, and they never found an intelligentsia to act for them.

Still, even if, except in military affairs, the Whites were out of season, in the context of their time their temperament and worldview partook of the counterrevolutionary persuasion. They were both ultranationalists and intensely hostile to modernity, liberal and democratic politics, and social reform. At the same time they took a conspiratorial view of history and of those who had an agenda different from theirs. At bottom, unrestrained by the Allies, the Whites were driven by the friend-enemy dissociation, and as such in every respect as disinclined to compromise as the Bolsheviks.

✳ ✳ ✳

It is as difficult, if not impossible, to get an accurate measure of the human costs of the first terror of the Russian Revolution as it is to determine those of the terror of the French Revolution. While the scale and incidence of the terror of the guillotine of 1793–94 have been closely reconstructed and admit no serious doubt, the same cannot be said of the bloodletting in the Vendée and its aftermath, which remains in dispute. Indeed, it is not easy to demarcate the casualties of the military battles from the victims of the terror in the main centers of the civil war in France. There is general agreement that the victims of the terror of the guillotine ran to between 35,000 and 40,000, which reckons in the victims of executions, drownings, and deadly conditions in overcrowded prisons. For the Vendée the estimates of battle and civilian casualties, including the victims of the attendant and after-war terror, range between 150,000 and 500,000.[198]

Calculations of the number of people who died at the hands of the Red Terror in Russia differ by similar orders of magnitude. Not surprisingly, in 1921 Soviet authorities published the lowest figure: they claimed that from 1917 through 1920 the Cheka had executed slightly over 12,700 individuals. Fifty years later (1971) it was estimated that 200,000 people had been executed between 1917 and 1923, while an additional 300,000 to 400,000 were said to either have died in prisons and camps or been killed in the suppression of peasant revolts, industrial strikes, and military mutinies. Other rough measures range between these two extremes, one (1935) setting the total for the civil war at 50,000, and another (1981) at 140,000. All these estimates are a mixture of incomplete or flawed data and informed conjectures. Such is likely to continue to be the case even after the surviving Cheka and other archives of the ex-Soviet Union become accessible. For certain, the toll in lives was very heavy, probably corresponding to that in the French Revolution in terms of the proportion of the total population. The contrary would be surprising given the intensity as well as the extent and duration of the Russian civil war.[199]

In pondering the bloodletting in the civil war, which needs to be doubled to take account of the White Terror, it is worth noting that unlike the terror in the French Revolution, it was set in a time when violence was invading every European nation and every other home: in the Very Great War between 10 and 13 million men were killed and close to twice that number wounded. By 1917 Russia had suffered about three million casualties, nearly one-quarter of its fighting forces. There followed the millions of direct and indirect casualties of the civil and foreign war of the Revolution, many of them due to disease furthered by inadequate provisions and medical services.

Indeed, the Red and White leaders fought the civil war to the death, *coûte que coûte*, as Europe seemed once again to be entering a "valley of the shadow of death."

* * *

Evidently "the intensity of the Red Terror varied appreciably with time and circumstance." Its first surge came in the fall of 1918, following the attempt on Lenin's life, the British landings at Archangel and Baku, and the seizure of Kazan by Kolchak and the Czech Legion. It receded in November 1918, with the stabilization of the front on the Volga as well as the upheaval in Central Europe and the German withdrawal from Ukraine.[200] The Red Terror rose to a second peak in 1919, in face of the difficult struggle with the armies of Kolchak, Denikin, and Iudenich. After their defeat there was another reflux, heralded by the decree of mid-January abrogating capital punishment. But in 1920–21, with the Russo-Polish war, the defiance of Wrangel, and various peasant insurgencies, the first Red Terror again worsened until after the end of the civil war.[201]

Not only the menace of the White Armies spurred the Red Terror but so did the White Terror, which was an integral part of the counter-revolution's military operations. It would appear that "by far the largest number of persons who met a violent end under the regime of the Whites seem to have come to their death not as a result of any regular trial, or even of a summary verdict by a drumhead court-martial, but were simply slaughtered by more or less irresponsible bands of soldiers whose leaders certainly kept no records of their actions."[202] Clearly there is even less reliable data for the White than the Red Terror, in part because the Whites had neither fixed ministries nor the equivalent of a separate Cheka, although their armies had special "security units and punitive squads."[203] Apart from not theorizing terror as the Bolsheviks did, they practiced or condoned it without proclaiming or publicizing it. Accordingly the killings and atrocities of the Whites were widely perceived to be altogether more erratic and less organized or premeditated than those of the Reds.

In actual fact, whatever the degree of intention and control, judging simply by the scale and character of the anti-Jewish violence in White-controlled territories, notably Ukraine, it is safe to say that the two terrors, in addition to being interactive, were akin not only in their general order of magnitude but also in their inner nature. Certainly alone the victims of the White Terror ran into not the thousands but the tens of thousands. It goes without saying that when confronting the terror in the Russian civil war, "Red and White authors alike, with few exceptions, display a tendency greatly to exaggerate the numbers of persons killed by their opponents, while minimizing or glossing over the terrorist activities of their own side."[204] Sad to say, even academic historians, let alone *les terribles simplificateurs*, including the apostates among them, are not much more successful at taming their prepossessions.

It does not help the study and understanding of the terror to make the number of victims the ultimate measure of things by either exaggerating or minimizing them. Nor is anything gained by overdetermining the role of dogmatic ideas or demonic key leaders. The terror of 1917 to 1921 was, in the main, a fact of civil war fueled by the dialectic of revolution and counterrevolution. The toll and torment of victims was greatest in areas caught up in the battles of the civil war, with the worst ravages before, during, and following the capture and recapture of cities. Besides, in both town and country it is important to distinguish between wild and intentional savagery. By nature without rules of engagement and retaliation, civil war is a cauldron of wanton and unpremeditated violence with little, if any, ideological leaven. There is, to boot, the calculated and coordinated violence which is ideologically driven and centrally directed.

Needless to say, the opposing sides charged each other with intentional and mandated terror. It is as difficult to estimate the balance between spontaneous and willful Furies as it is to estimate the balance between direct death by execution and drowning and indirect death by undernourishment, cold, and disease. Although the Bolsheviks minimized the ravages of the Red Terror, like the Jacobins they loudly justified them both theoretically and morally. Perhaps less openly, they also valued the terror for having been effective, considering their victory in the civil war. Unlike their enemy brothers, they did not entertain the possibility that the terror may have been, in Quinet's terms, at once politically corrosive and counterproductive. Meanwhile, the Whites proclaimed their innocence. All but silent about their terror, they neither rationalized nor theorized it, except to insist that it was minimal, defensive, and *à contre coeur*. If anything, making a virtue of necessity, the Whites claimed to have lost the civil war because, unlike the Bolsheviks, they did not have the beast in them.

✳ ✳ ✳

NOTES

1. See Moshe Lewin, "The Civil War: Dynamics and Legacy," in Diana P. Koenker et al., eds., *Party, State, and Society in the Russian Civil War* (Bloomington: Indiana University Press, 1989), pp. 399–423, esp. p. 401. Until February 1918, dates are given according to the "Old Style" (Julian) calendar, which was thirteen days behind the Western calendar. Thereafter dates are given according to the "New Style" (Gregorian) calendar in use in the West, and adopted by the new regime.

2. Dmitry Shlapentokh, "The French Revolution in Russian Intellectual Life, 1789–1922," in Joseph Klaits and Michael H. Haltzel, *The Global Ramifications of the French Revolution* (Cambridge: Cambridge University Press, 1994), pp. 72–88; Shlapentokh, "The French Revolution in Russian Political Life: The Case of the Interaction Between History and Politics," in *Revue des Etudes Slaves* 61 (1989): pp. 131–42; Tamara Kondratieva, "Le pouvoir du précédent dans l'histoire: L'impact de la Révolution française en Russie," in ibid., pp. 201–15; Kondratieva, *Bolcheviks et Jacobins: Itinéraire des analogies* (Paris: Payot, 1989); John Keep, "1917: The Tyranny of Paris over Petrograd," in *Soviet Studies* 20:1 (July 1968), pp. 22–35; Shlapentokh, "The Images of the French Revolution in the February and Bolshevik Revolutions," in *Russian History* 16:1 (1989): pp. 31–54.

3. Michael Jakobson, *Origins of the Gulag: The Soviet Prison Camp System, 1917–1934* (Lexington, Ky.: University Press of Kentucky, 1993), p. 18.

4. Martin Malia, *The Soviet Tragedy: A History of Socialism in Russia, 1917–1991* (New York: Free Press, 1994), p. 95 and p. 97.

5. George Leggett, *The Cheka: Lenin's Political Police* (Oxford: Clarendon, 1986), esp. chs. 1–2; and Orlando Figes, *A People's Tragedy: The Russian Revolution, 1891–1924* (London: Cape, 1996), p. 522, p. 525, and p. 533.

6. Richard Pipes, *The Russian Revolution* (New York: Vintage, 1990), p. 801.

7. Edgar Quinet, *La Révolution* (Paris: Belin, 1987), p. 505.

8. Ruslan G. Skryunwikow, *Iwan der Schreckliche und seine Zeit* (Munich: Beck, 1992); and Alan Wood, "Siberian Exile in Siberian Russia," in *History Today* 30 (September 1980): pp. 19–24, esp. p. 20.

9. Wood, "Siberian Exile," pp. 20–21; Wood, "Crime and Punishment in the House of the Dead," in Olga Crisp and Linda Edmondson, eds., *Civil Rights in Imperial Russia* (Oxford: Clarendon, 1989), pp. 215–33, esp. pp. 218–20; Bruce W. Lincoln, *The Conquest of a Continent: Siberia and the Russians* (New York: Random House, 1994), p. 164.

10. Jocelyne Fenner, *Le Goulag des tsars* (Paris: Tallandier, 1986), pp. 145–46, 152–58.

11. Wood, "Siberian Exile," pp. 21–24; and Lincoln, *Conquest*, pp. 163–65.

12. D.C.B. Lieven, "The Security Police, Civil Rights, and the Fate of the Russian Empire, 1855–1917," in Crisp and Edmondson, eds., *Civil Rights*, pp. 235–62, esp. pp. 236–43; Edward Peters, *Torture* (Oxford: Blackwell, 1985), pp. 96–97, 113; Fenner, *Le Goulag*, pp. 144–45, 164–65, 207–14.

13. Wood, "Crime," pp. 221–22; and Abby M. Schrader, "Containing the Spectacle of Punishment: The Russian Autocracy and the Abolition of the Knout, 1817–1845," in *Slavic Review* 56:4 (1997): pp. 613–44.

14. Wood, "Siberian Exile," p. 24; Wood, "Crime," pp. 228–29, 233; Lincoln, *Conquest*, pp. 164–67; Fenner, *Le Goulag*, pp. 159–60, 216–17, 265–77.

15. Feodor Dostoevsky, *Memoirs from the House of the Dead* (Oxford: Oxford University Press, 1983). See the introduction by Ronald Hingley. Also see Wood, "Crime," p. 215.

16. Wood, "Solzhenitsyn on the Tsarist Exile System: A Historical Comment," in *Journal of Russian Studies* 42 (1981): pp. 39–43. See also Tatyana Tolstaya, "In Cannibalistic Times," in *New York Review of Books*, April 11, 1991, pp. 3–5.

17. Cited in Richard Pipes, *Russia under the Bolshevik Regime* (New York: Knopf, 1993), p. 503.

18. Andrzej J. Kaminski, *Konzentrationslager: 1896 bis Heute* (Stuttgart: Kohlhammer, 1982), pp. 34–35.

19. Ibid., pp. 90–92. Apparently, concentration camps were also used by the Turkish government at the time of the Armenian massacre.

20. Tsuyoshi Hasegawa, *The February Revolution: Petrograd, 1917* (Seattle: University of Washington Press, 1981); Alexander Rabinowitch, *Prelude to Revolution: The Petrograd Bolsheviks and the July 1917 Uprising* (Bloomington: Indiana University Press, 1968), ch. 1; Pipes, *Russian Revolution*, ch. 8.

21. Figes, *People's Tragedy*, p. 317 and p. 322.

22. See I. N. Steinberg, *In the Workshop of the Revolution* (New York: Rinehart, 1953), pp. 140–41; Leggett, *Cheka*, p. 53; Figes, *People's Tragedy*, p. 321.

23. See Max Weber, "Russlands Übergang zur Sozialdemokratie" (published April 26, 1917), in Weber, *Gesammelte politische Schriften* (Munich: Drei Masken, 1921), pp. 107–25; and Dmitri Volkogonov, *Lenin: A New Biography* (New York: Free Press, 1994), pp. 137–38.

24. Rabinowitch, *Prelude to Revolution*, chs. 4–6; and Louise Erwin Heenan, *Russian Democracy's Fatal Blunder: The Summer Offensive of 1917* (New York: Praeger, 1987). Cf. Pipes, *Russian Revolution*, pp. 419 ff.

25. William Rosenberg, *Liberals in the Russian Revolution: The Constitutional Democratic Party, 1917–1921* (Princeton: Princeton University Press, 1974), chs. 6–8; and Rabinowitch, *The Bolsheviks Come to Power: The Revolution of 1917 in Petrograd* (New York: Norton, 1976).

26. Geoffrey Swain, *The Origins of the Russian Civil War* (New York: Longman, 1996), ch. 1; Richard Luckett, *The White Generals: An Account of the White Movement and the Russian Civil War* (London: Routledge & Kegan Paul, 1971), pp. 79–86; Rosenberg, *Liberals*, pp. 229–32, 463–68; Volkogonov, *Lenin*, pp. 130–32; Rabinowitch, *Bolsheviks*, pp. 124–33; Richard B. Spence, *Boris Savinkov: Renegade on the Left* (Boulder, Colo.: East European Monographs, 1991), pp. 139–48.

27. William Butler Yeats, "The Second Coming" (January 1919).

28. Rabinowitch, *Bolsheviks*, p. 308.

29. Robert Conquest, *The Harvest of Sorrow: Soviet Collectivization and the Terror-Famine* (New York: Oxford, 1986), p. 43; Malia, *Soviet Tragedy*, p. 94; Sheila Fitzpatrick, *Stalin's Peasants: Resistance and Survival in the Russian Village after Collectivization* (New York: Oxford, 1994), p. 23; Lewis H. Spiegelbaum, *Soviet State and Society: Between Revolutions, 1918–1929* (Cambridge: Cambridge University Press, 1992), pp. 39–40.

30. The text of this manifesto is cited in Rabinowitch, *Bolsheviks*, pp. 303–4.

31. Rosenberg, *Liberals*, pp. 146–48 and 194–95; André Liebich, *From the Other Shore: Russian Social Democracy after 1921* (Cambridge, Mass.: Harvard University Press, 1997), pp. 72–73; Vladimir N. Brovkin, *The Mensheviks after October: Socialist Opposition and the Rise of the Bolshevik Dictatorship* (Ithaca, N.Y.: Cornell University Press, 1987).

32. For the course and outcome of these elections, see Oliver H. Radkey, *Russia Goes to the Polls: The Election to the All-Russian Constituent Assembly, 1917*, updated ed. (Ithaca, N.Y.: Cornell University Press, 1990).

33. John Keep, trans. and ed., *The Debate on Soviet Power: Minutes of the All-Russian Central Committee of Soviets, October 1917–January 1918* (Oxford: Clarendon, 1979), pp. 173 ff.

34. Cited in Pipes, *Russian Revolution*, pp. 546–47.

35. Cited in Keep, trans. and ed., *Debate*, pp. 243–44.

36. Cited in E. H. Carr, *A History of the Bolshevik Revolution: The Bolshevik Revolution, 1917–1923*, vol. 1 (London: Macmillan, 1950), pp. 118–19.

37. Carr, *Bolshevik Revolution*, pp. 120–21. See also Pipes, *Russian Revolution*, p. 553; and Malia, *Soviet Tragedy*, p. 114.

38. Carr, *Bolshevik Revolution*, pp. 126–33.

39. Sergei Starikov and Roy Medvedev, *Philip Mironov and the Russian Civil War* (New York: Knopf, 1978), p. 107; and Carr, *Bolshevik Revolution*, p. 161.

40. Luckett, *White Generals*, pp. 95–96.

41. Volkogonov, *Lenin*, p. 162.

42. Luckett, *White Generals*, pp. 96–98; and Malia, *Tragedy*, p. 113.

43. Bruce W. Lincoln, *Red Victory: A History of the Russian Civil War* (New York: Simon & Schuster, 1989), pp. 80–81; and Luckett, *White Generals*, pp. 99–100.

44. Evan Mawdsley, *The Russian Civil War* (London: Allen & Unwin, 1987), p. 19; and Lincoln, *Red Victory*, pp. 84–85.

45. See Leon Trotsky, *Terrorism and Communism: A Reply to Karl Kautsky* (Summer 1920) (Ann Arbor: University of Michigan Press, 1961), esp. pp. 48–49 and 55–58.

46. Leggett, *Cheka*, p. 13.

47. Isaac Deutscher, *The Prophet Armed: Trotsky, 1879–1921* (New York: Oxford, 1954), p. 338.

48. Cited in Deutscher, *Prophet*, p. 338.

49. Leggett, *Cheka*, p. 13. See also Steinberg, *Workshop*, ch. 4.

50. Cited in Lincoln, *Red Victory*, p. 86.

51. Quinet, *La Révolution*, p. 497.

52. Cited in Lincoln, *Red Victory*, pp. 85–86.

53. Cited in Virginie Coulloudon, *Illusions sibériennes: L'échec du gouvernement Koltchak, novembre 1918–janvier 1920* (Paris: [thèse] EHSS, 1997), pp. 267–68.

54. Cited in Ronald Grigor Suny, *The Soviet Experiment: Russia, the USSR, and the Successor States* (New York: Oxford, 1998), p. 71.

55. Cited in Figes, *People's Tragedy*, p. 564.

56. Lincoln, *Red Victory*, p. 86.

57. Leggett, *Cheka*, pp. 53–54.

58. Cited in Lincoln, *Red Victory*, p. 86.

59. Cited in Kondratieva, *Bolcheviks*, p. 57.

60. Cited in Lennard D. Gerson, *The Secret Police in Lenin's Russia* (Philadelphia: Temple University Press, 1976), p. 133.

61. Cited in Samuel Farber, *Before Stalinism: The Rise and Fall of Soviet Democracy* (London: Verso, 1990), p. 114.

62. Sheila Fitzpatrick, "The Civil War as a Formative Experience," in Abbott Gleason, Peter Kenez, and Richard Stites, eds., *Bolshevik Culture: Experiment and Order in the Russian Revolution* (Bloomington: Indiana University Press, 1985), pp. 57–76, esp. p. 67.

63. Carr, *Bolshevik Revolution*, p. 165.

64. Cited in ibid., pp. 165–66; and in Leggett, *Cheka*, p. 54.

65. Cited in Lincoln, *Red Victory*, p. 134.

66. Cited in Leggett, *Cheka*, p. 16 and p. 22.

67. Cited in ibid., p. 17.

68. Merle Fainsod, *How Russia Is Ruled* (Cambridge, Mass.: Harvard University Press, 1953), p. 358.

69. Carr, *Bolshevik Revolution*, p. 168.

70. Jakobson, *Origins of the Gulag*, p. 3 and p. 16; and Peter H. Juviler, *Revolutionary Law and Order: Politics and Social Change in the USSR* (New York: Free Press, 1976), pp. 18–19 and p. 22.

71. Cited in Juviler, *Law and Order*, p. 15.

72. Carr, *Bolshevik Revolution*, p. 168.

73. Cited in Juviler, *Law and Order*, p. 19.

74. Fainsod, *How Russia Is Ruled*, p. 358.

75. Cited in Lincoln, *Red Victory*, p. 134. Also see Maxim Gorky, *Untimely Thoughts: Essays on Revolution, Culture, and the Bolsheviks, 1917–1918* (New Haven: Yale University Press, 1995).

76. Carr, *Bolshevik Revolution*, p. 161.

77. Leggett, *Cheka*, p. 56.

78. Cited in Fainsod, *How Russia Is Ruled*, p. 358.

79. Trotsky, *Terrorism*, p. 43.

80. Arno J. Mayer, *Political Origins of the New Diplomacy, 1917–1918* (New Haven: Yale University Press, 1959), chs. 5–9.

81. My discussion of this debate draws heavily on Deutscher, *Prophet*, pp. 373–92.

82. Stephen F. Cohen, *Bukharin and the Bolshevik Revolution: A Political Biography, 1888–1938* (New York: Knopf, 1973), p. 43.

83. Cited in Mawdsley, *Civil War*, p. 44.

84. Trotsky, *Terrorism*, p. 43.

85. Cited in Volkogonov, *Lenin*, p. 185.

86. Mawdsley, *Civil War*, p. 70 and p. 76; and Pipes, *Bolshevik Regime*, pp. 10–13.

87. Lincoln, *Red Victory*, pp. 88–89.

88. Mawdsley, *Civil War*, p. 21; and Pipes, *Bolshevik Regime*, p. 21.

89. W. P. Coates and Zelda K. Coates, *Armed Intervention in Russia, 1918–1922* (London: Victor Gollancz, 1935), chs. 7–9; and Richard H. Ullman, *Anglo-Soviet Relations, 1917–1921*, vol. 1: *Intervention and the War* (Princeton: Princeton University Press, 1961), chs. 8–10 and Epilogue.

90. Luckett, *White Generals*, p. 217.

91. Lincoln, *Conquest*, ch. 39; Mawdsley, *Civil War*, pp. 46–49 and passim; Geoffrey Swain, *The Origins of the Russian Civil War* (New York: Longman, 1996).

92. N.G.O. Pereira, *White Siberia: The Politics of Civil War* (Montreal: McGill–Queen's University Press, 1996), ch. 4; and Jonathan D. Smele, *Civil War in Siberia: The Anti-Bolshevik Government of Admiral Kolchak, 1918–1920* (Cambridge: Cambridge University Press, 1996), pp. 79–89.

93. Pereira, *White Siberia*, ch. 5; and Smele, *Civil War*, pp. 104–7 and ch. 2.

94. Luckett, *White Generals*, pp. 177–78 and 182–88.

95. Ibid., pp. 179–80.

96. Ibid., p. 184.

97. Wrangel cited in ibid., p. 192.

98. This discussion of the ideology and program of the Whites relies heavily, above all, on Peter Kenez, "The Ideology of the White Movement," in *Soviet Studies* 32:1 (Jan. 1980): pp. 58–83; Kenez, "Pogroms and White Ideology in the Russian Civil War," in John Klier and Shlomo Lambroza, eds., *Pogroms: Anti-Jewish Violence in Modern Russian History* (Cambridge: Cambridge University Press, 1992), pp. 293–313; Kenez, *Civil War in South Russia, 1919–1920: The Defeat of the Whites* (Berkeley: University of California Press, 1977). See also Moshe Lewin, "The Civil War," in Koenker et al., eds., *Party, State, and Society*, pp. 399–423; William Henry Chamberlin, *The Russian Revolution, 1917–1921*, vol. 2 (New York: Macmillan, 1957), esp. ch. 27 and ch. 32; Mawdsley, *Civil War*, esp. pp. 278–85; Johannes Rogalla von Bieberstein, *Die These von der Verschwörung, 1776–1945: Philosophen, Freimaurer, Juden, Liberale, und Sozialisten als Verschwörer gegen die Sozialordnung* (Frankfurt/Main: Peter Lang, 1976), pp. 199–209.

99. Cited in Volkogonov, *Lenin*, p. 236.

100. Leggett, *Cheka*, ch. 4; and Lincoln, *Red Victory*, pp. 141–43. Eventually Blumkin "repented his deed, joined the Bolshevik party, won distinction in the civil war, and rejoined the Cheka." Later "he was arrested and shot" for his contacts with Trotsky on Prinkipo Island. Deutscher, *Prophet*, p. 403, n. 2.

101. Cited in Boris Levytsky, *The Uses of Terror: The Soviet Secret Police, 1917–1970* (New York: Coward, McCann, and Geoghegan, 1972), p. 28; and Carr, *Bolshevik Revolution*, p. 175.

102. Spence, *Savinkov*, passim; Leggett, *Cheka*, p. 280; Pipes, *Russian Revolution*, pp. 646–56.

103. Cited in Lincoln, *Red Victory*, p. 147.

104. Spence, *Savinkov*, p. 211.

105. Cited in Lincoln, *Red Victory*, p. 146.

106. Leggett, *Cheka*, p. 104.

107. Pipes, *Russian Revolution*, p. 652.

108. Leggett, *Cheka*, pp. 103–4.

109. Edward Radzinsky, *The Last Tsar: The Life and Death of Nicholas II* (New York: Doubleday, 1992), pt. 2; Marc Ferro, *Nicholas II: The Last of the Tsars* (New York: Viking, 1991), chs. 3 and 4; Volkogonov, *Lenin*, pp. 207 ff.; Lincoln, *Red*

Victory, pp. 146–55; Juri Buranow and Wladimir Chrustaljow, *Die Zarenmörder: Vernichtung einer Dynastie* (Berlin and Weimar: Aufbau Taschenbuch, 1994), esp. pp. 286–99.

110. Cited in Leggett, *Cheka*, p. 66.

111. Cited in Volkogonov, *Lenin*, p. 208.

112. Lincoln, *Red Victory*, p. 154.

113. Cited in Chamberlin, *Russian Revolution*, p. 92.

114. Cited in Leggett, *Cheka*, p. 103.

115. Cited in ibid., p. 104.

116. Cited in Semion Lyandres, "The 1918 Attempt on the Life of Lenin: A New Look at the Evidence," in *Slavic Review* 8:3 (Fall 1989): pp. 432–48, esp. p. 432.

117. Cited in Sergey Petrovich Melgounov, *The Red Terror in Russia* (Westport, Conn.: Hyperion Press, 1926/1975 repr.), p. 33.

118. Cited in Steinberg, *Workshop*, p. 147; and Leggett, *Cheka*, pp. 113–14.

119. Cited in Melgounov, *Red Terror*, pp. 9–11 and pp. 33–34.

120. Cited in Mary McAuley, *Bread and Justice: State and Society in Petrograd, 1917–1922* (Oxford: Clarendon, 1991), p. 382.

121. Cited in Carr, *Bolshevik Revolution*, p. 176.

122. Cited in Gerson, *Secret Police*, pp. 131–32.

123. Cited in Leggett, *Cheka*, p. 108.

124. Full text cited in Chamberlin, *Russian Revolution*, pp. 66–67; and Pipes, *Russian Revolution*, pp. 818–19.

125. Full text cited in Leggett, *Cheka*, pp. 109–10.

126. Cited in ibid., p. 110.

127. Carr, *Bolshevik Revolution*, p. 176.

128. McAuley, *Bread and Justice*, p. 382.

129. Ibid., pp. 382–83; Pipes, *Russian Revolution*, pp. 619–20; Steinberg, *Workshop*, p. 233.

130. Cited in Steinberg, *Spiridonava: Revolutionary Terrorist* (London: Methuen, 1935), p. 233; and Lincoln, *Red Victory*, p. 160.

131. Cited in Steinberg, *Workshop*, p. 149.

132. Cited in Lincoln, *Red Victory*, p. 160.

133. Quinet, *La Révolution*, p. 498.

134. Carr, *A History of Soviet Russia: Socialism in One Country, 1924–1926*, vol. 2 (London: Macmillan, 1959), ch. 24, esp. pp. 448–53.

135. Leggett, *Cheka*, p. 176; and Michel Heller, *Le monde concentrationnaire et la littérature soviétique* (Lausanne: L'Age d'Homme, 1974), p. 22.

136. Heller, *Le monde concentrationnaire*, p. 36.

137. Carr, *Socialism in One Country*, p. 449.

138. Cited in Trotsky, *The Military Writings and Speeches*, 3 vols. (London: New Park Publications, 1979–81), vol. 1, pp. 310–11.

139. Cited in Leggett, *Cheka*, p. 179. Cf. Gerson, *Secret Police*, p. 147.

140. Cited in Leggett, *Cheka*, p. 179. See also Aleksandr I. Solzhenitsyn, *The Gulag Archipelago, 1918–1956*, vol. 2 (New York: Harper, 1975), pp. 17–18.

141. See Mayer, *Politics and Diplomacy of Peacemaking: Containment and Counterrevolution at Versailles, 1918–1919* (New York: Knopf, 1967), esp. parts 4 and 5.

142. Mawdsley, *Civil War*, pp. 143–44.

143. Ibid., p. 167.

144. Chamberlin, *Russian Revolution*, p. 171.

145. Ibid., p. 171.

146. Pipes, *Bolshevik Regime*, pp. 42–43.

147. Ibid., p. 43.

148. Ibid., pp. 43–45; Leggett, *Cheka*, pp. 319 ff.; Vladimir N. Brovkin, *Behind the Front Lines of the Civil War: Political Parties and Social Movements in Russia, 1918–1922* (Princeton: Princeton University Press, 1994), pp. 169–73; Israel Getzler, *Martov: A Political Biography of a Russian Social Democrat* (London: Cambridge/ Melbourne University Press, 1967), pp. 182 ff.; Liebich, *Other Shore*, pp. 82–95.

149. Leggett, *Cheka*, p. 114. See also Brovkin, *Front Lines*, pp. 174–84.

150. Volkogonov, *Lenin*, p. 87. See also Liebich, *Other Shore*, pp. 88–95.

151. Cited in Chamberlin, *Russian Revolution*, pp. 187–88. See also Fernand Grenard, *La révolution russe* (Paris: Colin, 1933), p. 328.

152. Lincoln, *Red Victory*, pp. 254–60; and Pipes, *Bolshevik Regime*, p. 116.

153. Morris and Graves cited in Lincoln, *Red Victory*, pp. 258–59.

154. See chapter 13 below.

155. Lincoln, *Red Victory*, p. 263.

156. Cited in Chamberlin, *Russian Revolution*, p. 200.

157. Ibid., pp. 201–4. See also Lincoln, *Red Victory*, pp. 265–89. Cf. Pipes, *Bolshevik Regime*, pp. 116–18.

158. Nicholas Werth, "Un état contre son peuple," in Stéphane Courtois et al., *Le livre noir du communisme: crimes, terreur, répression* (Paris: Laffont, 1997), pt. 1, pp. 97–101.

159. See Orlando Figes, "The Red Army and Mass Mobilization during the Russian Civil War, 1918–1920," in *Past and Present* 129 (November 1990): pp. 168–211.

160. See Leggett, *Cheka*, pp. 283–87; Levytsky, *Uses of Terror*, pp. 31–33; Pipes, *Bolshevik Regime*, pp. 119–21.

161. McAuley, *Bread and Justice*, p. 388; and Farber, *Before Stalinism*, p. 120.

162. Cited in Gerson, *Secret Police*, p. 157.

163. McAuley, *Bread and Justice*, p. 389.

164. Cited in Gerson, *Secret Police*, p. 155.

165. Cited in ibid., p. 155.

166. Ibid., pp. 153–54.

167. Brovkin, *Front Lines*, p. 123.

168. See ibid., p. 124; and Gerson, *Secret Police*, p. 154.

169. Lincoln, *Red Victory*, p. 384.

170. Gerson, *Secret Police*, p. 152.

171. Cited in ibid., p. 152; and Heller, *Le monde concentrationnaire*, p. 41.

172. Cited in Gerson, *Secret Police*, p. 156.

173. Carr, *Socialism in One Country*, p. 451; Gerson, *Secret Police*, pp. 146–47; Heller, *Le monde concentrationnaire*, p. 42; Leggett, *Cheka*, p. 179.

174. Pipes, *Russian Revolution*, p. 836.

175. Cf. ibid., pp. 836–37.

176. Farber, *Before Stalinism*, p. 136.

177. Gerson, *Secret Police*, pp. 158–59.

178. Leggett, *Cheka*, p. 178.

179. Chamberlin, *Russian Revolution*, vol. 2, ch. 33; Mawdsley, *Civil War*, ch. 15; Pipes, *Bolshevik Regime*, pp. 89 ff. and pp. 128 ff.

180. Brovkin, *Front Lines*, pp. 229–30. See chapter 13 below.

181. Chamberlin, *Russian Revolution*, pp. 271 ff.; Mawdsley, *Civil War*, pp. 196 ff.; Pipes, *Bolshevik Regime*, pp. 92–94 and pp. 123–25.

182. Norman Davies, *White Eagle, Red Star: The Polish-Soviet War, 1919–1920* (New York: St. Martin's Press, 1972).

183. Cited in Trotsky, *Military Writings*, vol. 3, pp. 184–85 and pp. 212–13.

184. Thomas C. Fiddick, *Russia's Retreat from Poland, 1920: From Permanent Revolution to Peaceful Coexistence* (London: Macmillan, 1990). See also chapter 15 below.

185. Cited in Trotsky, *Military Writings*, vol. 3, p. 241.

186. See Kenez, *Civil War in South Russia, 1919–1920: The Defeat of the Whites* (Berkeley: University of California Press, 1977), ch. 9.

187. Cited in Mawdsley, *Civil War*, p. 267.

188. Cited in Lincoln, *Red Victory*, p. 434 and p. 441.

189. Cited in Trotsky, *Military Writings*, vol. 3, p. 243.

190. Cited in Brovkin, *Front Lines*, p. 345.

191. Chamberlin, *Russian Revolution*, vol. 2, p. 74.

192. Melgounov, *Red Terror*, pp. 75–81; and Leggett, *Cheka*, p. 465.

193. Cited in Chamberlin, *Revolution*, p. 495.

194. Melgounov, *Red Terror*, pp. 75–83, esp. p. 78.

195. Figes, "The Red Army," esp. pp. 168–69, 183–84, 195, 207.

196. Figes, *People's Tragedy*, p. 591.

197. See chapter 6 above and chapter 12 below.

198. See chapter 9 below.

199. Geoffrey Hosking, *The First Socialist Society: A History of the Soviet Union from Within*, enlarged ed. (Cambridge, Mass.: Harvard University Press, 1990), p. 71; Chamberlin, *Russian Revolution*, pp. 74–75; Mawdsley, *Civil War*, p. 286. Nothing justifies the judgment that "all one can say with any assurance is that if the victims of the Jacobin terror numbered in the thousands, Lenin's terror claimed tens if not hundreds of thousands of lives" (Pipes, *Russian Revolution*, p. 838). This reading does not seem to take account of the victims of the civil war in the Vendée and the repossession of the cities of the Midi whose number greatly exceeded those of the Great Terror of the guillotine. Besides, any such global comparison should perhaps also note that France's population in 1789 was one-sixth of Russia's in 1917, which makes the number of victims of the Jacobin terror proportionately higher than those of the first Red terror under Lenin.

200. Starikov and Medvedev, *Philip Mironov*, p. 109; and Spiegelbaum, *Soviet State and Society*, p. 53.

201. Chamberlin, *Russian Revolution*, p. 73.

202. Ibid., p. 80.

203. Lewin, "Civil War," p. 406.

204. Chamberlin, *Russian Revolution*, p. 75.

PART THREE

Metropolitan Condescension
and Rural Distrust

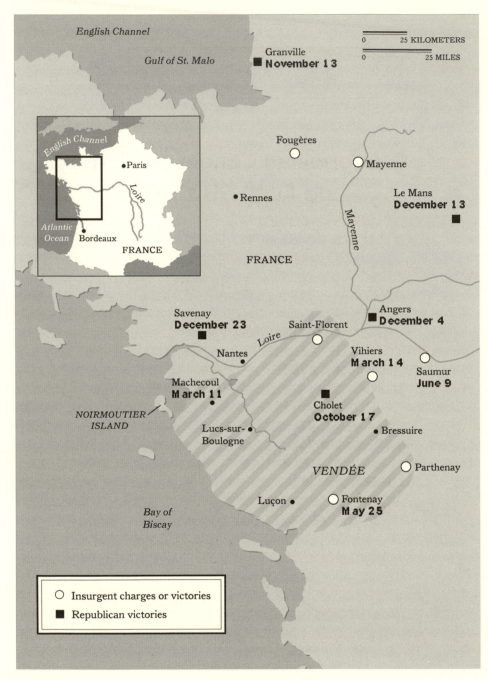

Theater of Military Operations in the Vendée Insurrection, 1793

Peasant War in France:
The Vendée

THE VENDÉE was in essence a civil war, and it is this fact of civil war which accounts for its singular fury. If war is hell, then civil war belongs to hell's deepest and most infernal regions. Except for the two world wars of the twentieth century, which were partly civil wars, Montaigne's lapidary formulation stands: "foreign war is a much milder evil than civil war."[1] Of course, this axiom is counterbalanced by Montesquieu's reflection that "unrest within a country is preferable to the calm of despotism."[2] In any case, in a long-term and universal perspective, civil war is "the oldest and primary form of collective conflict." By comparison, interstate conflict is a "relatively recent development," and notwithstanding appearances, external war has been the exception, internal war the rule. For social man and woman it is more common but also "psychologically more satisfying" to hate and kill a nearby rival or enemy who is personally known than a faraway foe who is a complete stranger. Not surprisingly there is no treatise on civil war on the order of Clausewitz's *On War*, civil war being essentially wild and savage. There are no rules of engagement, and the line between attacker and defender is blurred. With both sides equally driven by "fear and hatred," they increasingly "resemble each other in both their actions and moral attitudes." The fighting zones, beyond control and lawless, become lairs of revenge and re-revenge, as well as of summary justice.[3]

The civil war in the Vendée was, of course, an integral part of the French Revolution which shaped it. Characteristic of the antirevolutionary resistance inherent to revolution, the Vendée's unfolding was typical of the transmutation of anti-revolution into counterrevolution. Probably even more than the federalist rebellion of the cities of the

Midi, with which it coincided, it was the hinge of the civil war within the French Revolution. Without doubt the Vendée marked the culmination of the Revolution's crescendo of violence and terror, as measured by the nature and scale of hate-driven atrocities on both sides. In the western lands not only the revolutionary forces, the Blues, but also their counterrevolutionary opponents, the Whites, freely massacred, raped, and pillaged. Unlike in the Midi, the vicious cycle of retribution and counter-retribution continued well beyond the military defeat of the rebels, in large part because stray bands of insurgents were able to fade into a remote and forbidding countryside to intermittently renew their resistance.

If the Vendée stands out among civil wars for its peculiar but not unique fury, the reason is that the normal social, psychological, and political dynamics of such conflicts were in this case enormously intensified by the religious factor, which Edgar Quinet was among the first to isolate and theorize.[4] He rightly noted that France's urban-based political class and intelligentsia, surprised by the vitality of "an old and supposedly superannuated" faith and cult, only slowly realized "that a religious war was still possible in the eighteenth century." Although he allowed for certain family resemblances between the rural uprising in the west and the urban rebellions in the south, he underscored, as we saw, that "everything was different in the Vendée": while the revolt of Lyons, Marseilles, and Toulon was "purely political . . . , that of the Vendée was religious."

Beyond the clash of two worldviews, the conflict in the Vendée entailed "the collision of two fanaticisms," the one rooted in "a faith of old," the other in "a yearning for liberty turned to the future." But in this aspect of their struggle the "republicans, despite their heroism, were at a disadvantage," in that they were moved by "vague ideas which could not touch people tied to an apodictic faith" like Catholicism. According to Quinet, the Revolution could not hope to "encroach on the old religion" and "exterminate" it without countering it "with an absolute faith of its own." Whereas in the past, when resorting to the sword, "Mohammed had brandished the Koran and . . . the Duke of Alba . . . had been sponsored by the Pope," in the Vendée Carrier and Turreau had no comparable warrant to back their *noyades* and *colonnes infernales*. In this old-new war, in which none of the "rules of the long established art of war" applied, the main weapons were "prayers in churches, public invocations, sacred hearts sewn on outer garments, nocturnal processions, clandestine rallies in woods, tales of miracles, hushed intrigues behind altars, and vows of draft-resistance." Since the religion of the republicans lacked holy places and rituals, they had little beyond the *Marseillaise* to set against the insurgents' prayers, rites, and magic formulas.

Following military victory the pacification was unsuccessful until the Vendeans' principal demand was met, which was "the maintenance of the old regime in the religious sphere." Indeed, they did not spill their blood in vain: they saved "the supremacy of their religion, including their priests and altars" in their own realm and, indirectly and in no small extent, in the rest of France as well.

Michelet was equally insistent on the centrality of church and religion in the beginning of the rebellion, and hence also in the horrors of the ensuing fratricide.[5] In his reading, the region's peasant women and priests, jointly, were the heart of the resistance. Of the two, he considered the women "more sincerely and violently fanatic," determined to "goad their confessors into martyrdom and their husbands into civil war." According to Michelet, the great majority of local women became "champions of counterrevolution," driven by "their love of the past; the force of habit; their natural weakness; and their pity for the victims of the Revolution." They embodied not only the hearth but the church. By virtue of a common "language and mentality" there was an "intimate and deep understanding" between country women and priests, making the former the vital link between peasants and priests who, bolstered by their "esprit de corps" and backed by the "authority of the Pope and the bishops," availed themselves of the pulpit and confessional to promote the antirevolutionary cause. By 1792 an "ecclesiastical terror" pervaded the cult as the parish clergy, assisted by the women, set about summoning "a people inherently opposed to any outside influence . . . for a revolution against the Revolution." With a change in cadence an old hymn was turned into a counter-*Marseillaise* and "the *Dies Irae*, recited with raging passion, became nothing less than a righteous call to murder [the enemy and condemn him to] eternal hellfire."

Both Quinet and Michelet emphasized the autonomous and self-driven nature of the antirevolutionary phase of the Vendée, before it became counterrevolutionary, hence political. Unlike in the revolutionary camp, where "the upper classes spurred on the people," notably in the cities, in the Vendée the peasants "took up arms" before they "called on noblemen to lead them, eventually enlisting Lescure, La Rochejaquelein, Bonchamps, d'Elbée, and Charette." By the way, had the Convention distributed the lands of the Vendean nobility to the peasants, it might well have forestalled this reluctant alliance and cut short the uprising. Ultimately, in Quinet's telling, the Revolution took no "fundamental and irrevocable measures concerning either religion or property," with the result that just as the Catholic church and religion endured despite being severely buffeted and tormented, so did the de-feudalized notables who "saved the bulk of their lands."[6]

＊ ＊ ＊

At the outset the peasant outbreaks in western France were part of the same undercurrent of antirevolutionary agitation which gradually broke to the surface in the southern Massif Central—an undercurrent that sprang from the usual mixture of smoldering discontents and disappointments with the new order. Indeed, the enigma is not the simmering peasant resistance in the west, which was unexceptional, but its escalation, in a confined region south of the Loire, from a desultory jacquerie into a full-scale counterrevolutionary insurgency and the most savage civil war in the French Revolution.

The human geography of the distant region holds the key to this mystery.[7] What came to be known in 1793 as the Vendée was an area of some 830 square miles that was in fact divided among four of the new departments (Vendée, Deux-Sèvres, Loire-Inférieure, Maine-et-Loire) and three old provinces (Anjou, Brittany, and Poitou) of far western France. The area was a homogeneous world unto itself. Communications were primitive, except for two main roads, one running south from Nantes to La Rochelle, and the other running east from Les Sables-d'Olonne to Saumur. Compared to other precincts seething with anti-revolution, the Vendée was nearly entirely rural and agrarian: a land of villages and isolated farms with a dense peasant population. The soil being fertile, the peasants were not only self-sufficient in food but raised a surplus of grain, cattle, and sheep. The urban centers were small market towns with relatively few workshops and government offices, and hence few artisans, clerks, and profession-als. With a population of 8,000, Cholet, the largest town, was nothing like Montauban or Nîmes.[8] It had few social and institutional carriers of modernism and republicanism, so that it was relatively unthreaten-ing to the surrounding countryside. The nearest large city was Nantes, a major merchant and administrative center located outside the Vendée on the north bank of the Loire. Abhorred by the peasants as the local bridgehead of the encroaching central state and modern world, Nantes eventually became the chief republican command and supply hub during the civil war and its appalling aftermath.

Not least significant, unlike the cities of the Midi, the villages and towns of the Vendée were solidly Catholic. Church and religion, satu-rated with superstition, idolatry, and magic, were central to the self-definition and self-affirmation of peasant and village, notably when threatened by natural disasters or outside forces. It is, of course, im-possible to say whether religious faith was any more ardent in the Vendée than in other predominantly rural provinces. But certainly the church was the nerve center of daily life, with religious services, holy days, and processions pacing and structuring every social activity, as well as priest and prayer sacralizing profane popular festivals. Further-more, without a Protestant minority to incite suspicion, hatred, or fear, the region lacked a credible lightning rod for local discontents and frustrations. After 1789 church and religion reinforced the tradi-tional resistance to the state's intrusion, all the more so now that they could direct it against godless republicans and Jacobins, who came to enforce policies and reforms dictated from afar.

The nobility of western France, not unlike its clergy, was opposed to reform, and the two combined were, of course, considerably more influential than the sparse local bourgeoisie, particularly since they reigned over a deferential rural population. In this respect the situa-tion was not unlike in Montauban and Nîmes, except that in the Vendée the nobility and clergy carried greater authority and there were fewer members of the Third Estate to rush forward to organize or join National Guard units and claim elected and administrative positions. To be sure, Maurice Louis Joseph Gigost d'Elbée and François Athanase Charette de la Contrie were among the émigrés of the first hour, but they soon returned and yielded to the insurgent peasants who beseeched them to take command of the emerging Catholic and Royal Army.

As the agents of the revolutionary regime proceeded to enforce political and ecclesiastical reforms in this isolated region of Catholic peasants, priests, and nobles, they aroused growing opposition. The local implementation of the "nationalization" of church property, of the Civil Constitution of the Clergy, and of the clerical oath of allegiance were experienced as offensively profane intrusions into a sacralized universe. Whereas the improbable decrees of the distant National and Constituent assemblies of 1789 and 1790 were suspect, the anathematizing encyclicals of the equally distant Holy See of the spring of 1791 were considered tried and true: the former were mediated, locally, by outside agents or local heretics, the latter by native and trusted priests.

Characteristically, about 90 percent of the priests of the west refused to swear the oath to nation, law, and constitution, compared to the approximately 55 percent nationwide.[9] In the diocese of Nantes, including in its country parishes, only 18 percent of the clerics complied, the vast majority of them ministering to city districts. In Saint Florent 88 percent stood fast, in the district of Cholet 90 percent. Apart from hearkening to superiors and being under the sway of their flock, the refractories were moved to hold out by peer pressure, material interest, and status. The scattering of constitutional priests—of apostates—were captives in their own parishes in which they came to incarnate the ungodly forces falling on the true church and religion from outside. By contrast, the refractory priests blended in with their parishioners, who looked to these, their native sons, to continue administering the sacraments.

Meanwhile, political and military events in Paris further prepared the way for civil war in the Vendée. In January 1793, the execution of Louis XVI dramatized the hardening friend-enemy dissociation. Not long after, despite the overextension of its military forces, the Convention raised the stakes of foreign war by throwing down the gauntlet to England, Holland, and Spain. In March it adopted a harsh anti-émigré law, established the Revolutionary Tribunal, and decreed the deportation of refractory priests. And on February 24, in the midst of this cumulative radicalization, the Convention voted to conscript 300,000 men for military service on the nation's endangered frontiers.

If anything, the struggle against the agents or local collaborationists of the novel and unchristian regime in Paris rallied peasant and noble even more strongly around priest and church as they stood against all encroachments, be they profane or sacred: taxes, conscription, price controls, the sale of ecclesiastical property, the new status of the church, the clerical oath. Just as there was no disjoining the secular and religious aspects of the everyday life of Vendeans, so there was no separating these two facets of their incipient resistance. Even so, as Quinet noted, since with time the main symbols, chants, and incantations of the anti-revolution were taken from the clerical repertoire, it is not unreasonable to assume that the religious element was central to its syncretic driving force. And eventually, as anti-revolution turned into counterrevolution, the rebel fighting forces went by the name of "Catholic and Royal Army," as if to trumpet their religious source and inspiration.

Starting in early March 1793 there were more and more acts of overt symbolic and physical protest, both individual and collective, directed against public officials, constitutional priests, and national guardsmen. It was the implementation of the military draft which unexpectedly triggered the Vendée uprising. Indeed, the Vendée might have remained calm "had the Revolution not come to take the peasant away from his home, field, and cattle in order to . . . send him to . . . fight for what he detested" and run the risk, in the words of Balzac, "of dying without last rites and going to hell for all eternity."[10] Anyhow, the first sustained rioting occurred at Saint-Florent-le-Vieil on March 10–12, touched off by the arrest of several young men who were determined to resist conscription. Apparently the issue was less conscription as such than the method and criteria of selection: public officials, national guardsmen, and constitutional priests were exempt from service, and hence from the draft lottery in which all unmarried men between 18 and 40 years of age were held to participate. Locally those eligible for exemption were reviled as hirelings of the Revolution and its centralizing ambition. Needless to say, there was antidraft agitation in many other rural provinces. But unlike in the west, and more particularly in the lands of the future Vendée, it was choked off in good time. In other words, for the opposition to compulsory military service to snowball into mass resistance it needed to have a comparatively free rein and to fuse with other aggrieved and less contingent interests and passions. In the Vendée, with its sacral universe threatened but as yet relatively untouched by the outside world, that was exactly what happened. News of the arrest of the draft resisters served as a tocsin for thousands of peasants of the surrounding countryside, who exploded with their own grievances. In the eventual facedown on March 12 between several thousand "primitive rebels" armed with pitchforks and some one hundred guardsmen armed with muskets, the former won the upper hand. After killing several soldiers the peasants, who suffered some casualties of their own, plundered the homes of known and suspected patriots and drove them out of town.

During the following days similar but larger and fiercer disturbances or confrontations took place in and around Machecoul (11th), Cholet (14th), and Chantonnay (19th), in which not a few republicans were brutally put to death. The *bagarre* of Machecoul became emblematic of this *fureur paysanne*. Several hundred peasants invaded this town of 5,000 inhabitants and held it for about ten days, during which they not only savagely killed most of the vastly outnumbered local national guardsmen and public officials but also massacred, maimed, and pillaged the households of presumed political enemies. They settled personal scores as well. The number of victims in and around Machecoul ran to several hundred. Presently peasant rebels, instead of returning home after participating in such raids, joined together to form a swelling though still shapeless horde. About 10,000 peasants are estimated to have participated in the attack on Cholet, overpowering some 400 hastily assembled national guardsmen.[11]

Paris and Nantes became seriously disquieted once local riots turned into a regional revolt and volatile rebels into steadfast insurgents. It soon was evident that the rebels' early successes were largely due to the insufficiency of the military and security forces opposing them. This was confirmed on March 18–19 when near Chantonnay a swollen band of peasants routed General Marcé's column of some 1,200 men, half of them regular soldiers, who had been sent from La Rochelle to crush the rebels once for all. Some 500 government troops were killed and nearly that same number were captured. Indeed, there was one striking difference between the western territories north and south of the Loire: to the north republican reinforcements arrived in time to contain and disperse the rebels; to the south there were no military forces to supplement the raw and undermanned militias and their sparse political associates in the small towns.[12]

The bulk of the soldiers of the rebel hordes-turned-army were peasants, and most of them were "day laborers, farm servants, and plot farmers . . . [rather] than peasant proprietors." Of course, the rank and file of combatants also included members of the inchoate lower middle class of town and village: cottage artisans, shopkeepers, innkeepers. As for the leaders, or rather cadres, they were drawn from the local nobility and refractory priesthood. Accordingly, the "Catholic and Royal Army" was a microcosm of the Vendée's rural world, all the more so since the insurgents originating in towns were ex-peasants with strong social and psychological ties to the countryside. To the extent that this irregular army included not only men but eventually also women and adolescents, and in addition, lived and breathed in the countryside like fish in water, it may be said to have activated not individual Vendeans but the entire *Vendée villageoise*.[13]

Most of the instant officers were of the petty nobility and some were commoners, like Jacques Cathelineau and Jean-Nicolas Stofflet, the one a carter, the other a gamekeeper. Whatever the reasons for the initial reticence of members of the secular elite to take command— above all they depreciated and distrusted mass action—they eventually did so, and with considerable effect.[14] Indeed, they forged bands of irregulars into more or less organized battalions, in which refractory priests were not unimportant. Clergymen summoned the faithful to rebel at the same time that they were swept along by them, though perhaps not primarily by the women among them, as suggested by Michelet. There was certainly no conspiracy of martial priests, but neither were the clergymen advocates of moderation or compromise. They sacralized and justified the resort to violence in defense of religion and monarchy, and they became the conscience and chaplains of the "Catholic and Royal Army" which, from its base in the Vendée, was to fight for the restoration of the old political, social, and cultural order, including the full reestablishment of the Catholic Church and religion.

In this way, the antirevolutionary opposition in the Vendée escalated into a counterrevolutionary uprising and consequently into civil war. The ensuing conflict, the *Vendée militaire*, had three fairly distinct phases. During the first, from March through early September 1793, the rebels kept growing in strength and went from victory to victory. While their temporary capture of Saumur and Angers was evidence of their resolve to reach beyond their villages and rural districts, their inability to take Nantes in late June prefigured the limits of their military and political capabilities. The second phase, from autumn through December of that same year, was a season of reflux and disbandment marked by the reversals of the Catholic and Royal forces at Cholet and Granville in mid-October and mid-November, and culminating in defeat at Savenay on December 23. The third or terminal phase overlapped considerably with the preceding one: the late fall through the winter of 1793–94 saw the intersection of the steep fall of rebel military fortunes and the sharp rise of military mastery and ferocious pacification by the revolutionary forces, followed by sporadic irregular warfare until 1796.

This civil war, unlike the one in the Russian Revolution, was a purely internal war without intervention by foreign powers. To be sure, eventually the rebels made a last-minute effort to capture Granville, a Channel port, in a vain bid for English aid. As may be expected, the revolutionaries overestimated the importance of this abortive move, which then served to validate their rhetoric about the international nature of the defiant counterrevolutionary conspiracy. At all events, the civil war in the west remained all but exempt from foreign interference. Besides benefiting the Blues militarily, this insulation meant that there were no external restraints on excessive excesses by either side.

✳ ✳ ✳

It is, of course, difficult if not impossible to say which side in this civil war was the first to commit what in a later age would be called "war crimes" and "crimes against humanity." They were certainly perpetrated by both camps, with their respective actors and zealots believing themselves to be retaliating for the prior misdeeds of their respective "common enemy." Blues and Whites increasingly demonized each other, with the result that they became less fearful of military defeat than of the avenging fury following it. In any case, Michelet's question of yore has lost none of its cogency and actuality: "while there is incessant talk of Carrier's *noyades*, why is there considerably less discussion of Charette's massacres," if not to "stir up some memories . . . while stifling others"?[15] All too often historians and public intellectuals, "unsympathetic to the hapless patriots," make it appear as if "the insurgents were saints who only reluctantly moved to wreak vengeance and perpetrate reprisals for republican cruelties."[16] This one-sided perspective fails to discern that such infamous republican misdeeds as the *noyades* and the "infernal columns" were, in fact, the culmination of a vicious circle of atrocities unanticipated by either side at the outset.

* * *

Dismissive of the far-off peasantry, the revolutionary leaders in Paris at first attached little importance to the unrest in the Vendée. It took some time for them to realize that it had the makings of an antirevolutionary groundswell that could sweep over an entire region. But presently militant Jacobins turned the rising insurgency in the Vendée into a favorite metaphor for the fast-spreading counterrevolutionary perils for which they were sounding the alarm. In addition to the revolt in the west, there was the growing threat of intervention by the émigrés, the Vatican, and the foreign powers. Further, General Dumouriez had just been routed at Neerwinden. Even before news of General Marcé's defeat at Chantonnay reached Paris, on the floor of the Convention several deputies urged severe penalties for participants in civil disorder and draft resistance, which they characterized as "worrisome symptoms of counterrevolution." A more frenzied voice was heard to exclaim that since "the ship of state was foundering and its distress was general, there was need for a solemn debate to forge an overall political strategy to save *la patrie*," to be spelled out along with a "philosophic rationale."[17]

Bertrand Barère de Vieuzac, a prominent montagnard, promptly rose to the occasion. He contended that, emboldened by divisions in the Convention, "the counterrevolution had started and conspiracies were exploding everywhere." Since "exactly the same disorders and plots were erupting in almost all parts of the Republic," it was safe to assume that the émigrés, foreign agents, and priests who were fomenting them "were in league with each other." Barère pointed to "the department of the Vendée" as the most telling example and terrifying portent. It was there that "legions of fanatics were in open counterrevolution . . . while revolt and counterrevolution were brewing throughout Brittany."[18]

The following day, on March 19, 1793, Jean-Jacques Régis de Cambacérès, a newly prominent hard-liner, successfully moved a decree declaring all rebels "outlaws" liable to summary execution by the military. Joseph Cambon applauded, contending that "the time for half measures had long since passed."[19] Presently Barère, in the name of the Committee of General Defense, announced that reinforcements were being sent to the Vendée and that Marcé would be "tried by a court martial sitting in La Rochelle." But Robespierre, considering such a venue too prosaic, urged that Marcé be judged in broad daylight by the Revolutionary Tribunal in Paris: at issue was "not simply a military blunder . . . [but] the conduct of the struggle against tyranny, and hence the very why and wherefore of the Revolution."[20]

Neither the insurgent peasants nor the authorities in Paris set out to fight a protracted civil war: the former were carried away by the momentum of their easy initial victories; the latter were trapped in their extravagant estimate of a very circumstantial uprising. In any case, the continuing upswing of the rebellion in the spring of 1793 was due to concrete military and political developments on the ground and not to any grand ideological design or temptation in Paris. Following the capture of Cholet, Bressuire, Parthenay, Thouars, and Fontenay in late April and May, the rebel offensive reached its highest peak in June. Saumur fell on June 9, Angers on June 18. Cathelineau set out to take Nantes, and hence secure access to the sea, but his forces were repulsed on June 29. Still, notwithstanding this setback, the Republican forces had suffered defeat after defeat, and this at a time when the southern cities were spinning out of control.

Meanwhile the representatives on mission in the west sent alarming reports to Paris about fanatical priests, nobles, and agents of the émigrés taking charge of thousands of equally fanatical "brigands."[21] In no time the rhetoric as well as the operations of the commanders of the "Catholic and Royal Army" took fire. Upon "liberating" Parthenay they proclaimed that they "had taken up arms to uphold the religion of their fathers and to restore the throne and crown to Louis

XVII, their august and legitimate sovereign." As fighters for "the holiest and most righteous cause," they warned that any "clubist" or other miscreant breaking the peace would be punished "without mercy." On May 24, following the capture of Fontenay, the same commanders told all the world "that everywhere and with divine guidance, the holy cross of Jesus Christ and the royal standard of the Bourbons were winning out over the blood-stained flag of anarchism . . . in the struggle for the restoration of altar and throne." The liberators of Angers "strictly enjoined and ordered" the populace "not to recognize any authority other than that of his Most Christian Majesty Louis XVII."[22]

With a touch of hubris, before starting their assault on Nantes the commanders of the White forces, "the sword of vengeance in one hand and an olive branch in the other," called on their enemies "to capitulate, lest they intended to dig their own graves." They were ordered not only to raise the white flag and surrender all weapons but to "hand over, as hostages, the deputies of the National Convention on mission in Nantes, as well as other individuals to be specified." The officers and men of the garrison were warned that unless they "swore loyalty to Religion and King," they would be "put to the edge of the sword and . . . Nantes would be laid in ruin." In early July, in the wake of their victory over General Westermann near Châtillon, the Catholic army celebrated having routed the "horde of [godless] assassins" whose passage had ravaged the countryside with "theft, assassination, arson, pillage, and destruction."[23]

* * *

In actual fact, from the outset the Vendeans took no live prisoners, and when they had time to spare they racked captives before killing them. Their "primitive rebellion" had a distinctly if unexceptionally raw side which was never disowned or curbed. The impulsive torture and massacre of patriots, constitutional priests, and prisoners which exploded in Machecoul on March 11, and continued for several days, was by no means adventitious. During the following week the insurgents' forays into Pontivy, Montaigu, and Cholet were equally brutal. This savagery seems to have been no less in evidence during the high tide of the Vendée during the spring and summer of 1793. No wonder that republicans far and near abandoned their condescending view of what they had taken to be an archaic *fronde* for an attitude of outright enmity for a popular and uncontrolled fury stripped of political innocence.

This new conceit took form in June, around the time of the rebels' threatening (if ultimately miscarried) drive on Nantes. While the atrocities committed by the Vendeans were ferocious and fearsome enough, their enemies, as might be expected, perceived and portrayed them in even darker colors. As the *jacquerie* in the Vendée became increasingly military and political, starting in July Barère repeatedly stepped forward to discuss what he called a "political cancer" harmful to the state. With more indignant perplexity than calculated cunning, he conceded that the "inexplicable [Vendée] continued to smolder . . . [and] threatened to turn into a dangerous volcano." The Blues could not hope to defeat "the brigands unless they mastered their ways of fighting." Measures were being taken "to exterminate this race of rebels by destroying their sanctuaries, burning down their forests, and cutting off their supplies." Barère claimed that the enthusiasm that was now driving the *levée en masse* to crush the Vendeans was reminiscent of "the frenzy of the crusades." For the meantime the Vendée remained the hope of all foreign and domestic enemies. Accordingly the destruction of the Vendée, besides daunting the European powers, would also convince "Lyons to stop resisting, Toulon to rise against the Spanish and the English, and Marseilles to reclaim its republican soul."[24]

Marat's assassination having radicalized Parisian Jacobins of all persuasions, on August 1, 1793, an angry Convention declared war—total civil war—on the Vendée. Impregnated with the friend-enemy spirit, it ordered the war ministry to instruct all local commands to prepare to "burn forests, brushwood, and rebel sanctuaries, as well as to seize cattle and crops." In addition—three weeks before the decree of the general *levée en masse* was voted on August 23—throughout the land "men between the ages of sixteen and sixty were urged to volunteer to fight the rebels."[25]

Until the third phase of the Vendée, however, the decree of August 1 mattered more for what it revealed about the mind-set and rhetoric of the revolutionaries than about their ways of fighting the civil war. The Committee of Public Safety's order implementing the decree included an injunction setting limits to the increasingly merciless warfare: "Women, children, and the aged are to be evacuated to the interior, their subsistence and security to be fully ensured in keeping with humanitarian considerations."[26] This decree was printed, published, and disseminated in Saumur by August 4. Within a couple of weeks there were protests about the excesses of certain military units. After personally confronting General Jean Antoine Rossignol, the ruthless commanding officer of the army of La Rochelle, a patriotic notable from Parthenay wrote to General Westermann to denounce the "unfortunate" measures being taken to "protect [his] city from marauding brigands." He asked, indignantly, whether the soldiers of freedom really planned to "scorch Parthenay . . . and confiscate all livestock and grains," which were the lifeblood of its inhabitants, many of whom had hastened off to fight for the *patrie*.[27] Local authorities arrested Rossignol and his accomplices for their "misconduct and immorality" even before the Committee of Public Safety called him to order, insisting that in applying the decree of August 1 the republican forces should take care to "wreak the nation's vengeance only on supporters and accomplices of the rebellion."[28] On September 8 the civil authorities of Saumur as well as the representatives on mission with the fighting forces stressed the urgent need to protect the property of "refugees and steadfast citizens [and] to evacuate women, children, and the aged." The proconsuls served notice that officers would be held responsible for excesses.[29]

The Convention adopted the Law of Suspects and the Maximum while both the "Vendée of the Midi" and the "Vendée of the West" put Paris in great fear. Between September 18 and 22 the Catholic and Royal Army defeated the republican forces at Torfou and Saint-Fulgent. Incensed, on October 1 Barère asked the Convention to declare that "the nation's safety and salvation demands that the bandits of the execrable war in the Vendée be exterminated by the end of the month."[30] To achieve this goal the Convention, that same day, streamlined the military forces in the west: the garrisons of Brest, La Rochelle, and Mayence were merged into a single Army of the West, under the command of General l'Échelle, "a man of the people and an old soldier."[31] But many of the volunteer recruits, though ideologically motivated, were untried, and so were most of their officers. Of necessity, to turn the tide, the government called in such seasoned commanders as Generals Kléber, Westermann, and Marceau, as well as experienced soldiers who had served under them along the frontiers of the Rhine. At the same time Paris assigned special representatives on mission to the Western Army, to coordinate military and political operations, with special attention to firing the soldiers' patriotic and republican zeal. But initially the mounting ferocity of fighting was due less to ideological fire than to the style of military engagement peculiar to civil war as practiced by both sides.

Before long several republican brigades converged on Cholet and on October 17, under Kléber's command, defeated Charette in what turned out to be the civil war's greatest battle. The political commissioners with the newly formed Western Army informed the Committee of Public Safety that the victory at Cholet in the time fixed by the Convention meant that "the Vendée was done for, even if not all the rebels were exterminated as yet."[32] As it turned out, although Charette had lost the initiative and his army of 30,000 to 40,000 was in disarray, he managed to lead it across the Loire near Saint-Florent. Forthwith the local proconsuls on mission called on the soldiers of liberty to "avenge" the republic by "drowning the tatters of the Catholic and Royal Army in the Loire or exterminate them along its banks," but with "forbearance for comrades and friends."[33]

With the tide of war turning in favor of the patriots, their rhetoric echoed that of the "Catholic and Royal" commanders in their finest hour. From Saint Florent Merlin de Thionville urged the Committee of Public Safety to issue a proclamation announcing that "Lyons was leveled, the Vendée crushed, and the land awash with the blood of traitors."[34] On October 21 the political emissaries extravagantly assured Paris that the triumphant republican forces had "left behind them only heaps of ashes and corpses," and vowed to "pursue the fugitives and frightened horde of rebels throughout the length and breadth of the land."[35] Two days later, and in tune with Merlin's advice, the Committee of Public Safety commended the armed forces for their contribution to the defeat of federalism in Lyons and Bordeaux as well as to the "destruction of the rebels in the Vendée." Over the signatures of Robespierre, Hérault de Séchelles, Carnot, and Billaud-Varenne, and after hailing all fallen heroes and extolling the nation, the committee exhorted republican soldiers "to continue the good fight in order to, within a month, avenge the French people, . . . banish tyranny and slavery, and secure justice, happiness, and virtue."[36]

North of the Loire the increasingly disoriented but still formidable Catholic and Royal Army headed via Mayenne to Granville, on the Gulf of Saint-Mâlo, perhaps in the hope of securing the support of a British fleet, but was repulsed on November 13. In what gradually turned into a rout, the Whites fell back southward by way of Mayenne to Angers. Next they moved northwest to be overpowered at Le Mans on December 13, and then, retreating in a southwestern direction, on December 23 they suffered their final defeat as an organized fighting force, at Savenay. By now some of the rebels' best officers had been either seriously wounded or killed in action.

As the rebels retreated, vast numbers of noncombatants—perhaps as many as 20,000 women, children, seniors, and priests—infiltrated and followed Charette's dispirited host. Some joined out of fear of the enemy, others for reasons of family and community solidarity, and still others as true believers decided to encourage their husbands and priests to stay the course. This influx of noncombatants made the Catholic and Royal Army doubly vulnerable to the inhumanity of civil and religious warfare, which knows no mercy. But as they retreated, the Vendeans themselves became increasingly ferocious in their treatment of republican prisoners. Furthermore, what appears in hindsight as the exhaustion of the insurrection was not instantly perceived as such by either side. Thus the rebels incited, and ultimately justified, the rising punitive fury of their sworn enemies before these realized that victory would soon be in their grasp.

In fact, the ruthless rhetoric of the Committee of Public Safety now began to be reflected in the deeds of its senior field officers. Kléber reported that after the victory at Cholet "the entire land [was] a sea of flames, . . . many of the brigands having refused to surrender," thereby exposing themselves and their sanctuaries "to punishment by hellfire." Two months later, following the victory at Savenay, he notified Paris of his confidence that "the enemy's destruction was now a certainty." But Kléber could not close his dispatch without confiding that his "pen refused to describe the atrocities which we inflicted on these wretches, even if France and Europe know all about them."[37] General Westermann was even more confident than General Kléber that total victory was near, but had none of his scruples. In a letter to the Committee of Public Safety he exulted that "the Vendée [was] no more, . . . our virtuous swords [having] finished it off" at

Savenay. He claimed to have "followed orders" when, in the heat of battle, he "crushed children under the hooves of his horses and slaughtered women," incidentally sparing the world the "progeny of these brigands."[38]

Clearly, with time not only did untried political generals like Rossignol and Henri Ronsin become agents of the brutalization of internal warfare, but so did professional soldiers like Kléber and Westermann. As noted, which of the two sides threw the first stone or bore major responsibility for the upward spiral of atrocities is an all but insoluble problem. Michelet saw the rebel forces as the chief driving force of the vicious circle of revenge and re-revenge. He held that "the fanatic violence of the priests" was of a piece with "the sacred ferocity of the Inquisition which had looked less to kill man than to make him suffer and repent by putting him to torture worthy of avenging God!"[39] The violence of the revolutionaries had a "less exalted" purpose in that it "sought simply and solely to eliminate the enemy, the executions and *noyades* being intended to reduce the pain of death, not to offer a human sacrifice."[40]Quinet held that on both sides of the friend-enemy divide, the ways of killing, no matter how different, were sacralized and driven by an intense millenarianism, the one religious, the other secular. Either way, there can be no doubt that the second phase of the Vendée and its aftermath, or third phase, were by far the bloodiest and most savage. On the republican side, Carrier's "political mission" to Nantes is quintessential of the first phase, and Turreau's "pacification campaign" of the second.

＊ ＊ ＊

Of course, the *noyades* and the "infernal columns" overlapped and had a common matrix. Even so, whereas Carrier's ferocious emergency regime was both consequence and cause of the escalating savagery of the still raging civil war, Turreau's wanton punitive pacification of the rebel territories after victory was an expression of ideologically charged avenging terror. It was correlated with the Great Terror in Paris, whose champions persuaded the Convention to change the name of the department of the Vendée to *Département-Vengé*.

In line with its practice of dispatching representatives on mission to trouble spots or attaching them to field armies, the Committee of Public Safety assigned Carrier to the Army of the West, with his seat in Nantes, where he arrived to assume his duties about October 22, 1793. To be sure, by then the republican forces seemed to be gaining the upper hand. But it would take them another three weeks to prevail at Granville and nearly two months to win the terminal battles of Le Mans and Savenay. As the principal republican strong point near the Vendée, Nantes had long since been staggering under the burdens and perils of civil war. Although its garrisons had warded off a major rebel assault in late June, it still seemed endangered, all the more so because of a widespread if exaggerated fear of a British landing. The port's vital overseas commerce, especially with the Antilles, was at a standstill, which complicated the victualing of a city of 90,000 inhabitants bulging with close to an additional 20,000 refugees and prisoners. Indeed, upon his arrival Carrier "found a virtually desperate situation, the hospitals, prisons, cemeteries, and burial pits of Nantes being filled to overflowing."[41]

The massive inflow of prisoners was the most explosive aspect of the fallout of the civil war in Nantes. Because of severe overcrowding and critical shortages, sanitary and medical conditions went from bad to worse, breeding contagious diseases of epidemic proportions. Many of the republicans and revolutionaries who had fled ahead of rebel forces or had managed to escape them were sick and injured, and so were many of the prisoners.

Even more than the hospitals, the prisons were jam-packed and became precincts of death. At the same time that a growing number of local political suspects and refractory priests were being incarcerated, the city began to be flooded with captive rebels to be held for trial. With these captives running to about 10,000 by the end of 1793, the number of prisons burgeoned from three to twelve. The fear of the spread of communicable diseases from the jails to the city prompted the decision to concentrate some 6,000 prisoners on ships anchored at the main coffee entrepôt at the far end of the port. Many of the rebels were wasted by the time they were thrown into prison, where dysentery and typhus were rampant. Even the guards and doctors of the prisons were not out of harm's reach, nor were the members of the revolutionary tribunals who held court in them. The final victories of December merely aggravated matters: thousands of Vendeans were falling back to Nantes or being herded there. With no ethnic or religious minority to serve as scapegoat for the city's distress, the prisoners became an easy mark, especially since many of them were not entirely blameless or could easily be portrayed as treacherous. The prisoners were blamed for aggravating the food shortage and the related risk of famine and disease; the prisons were rumored to be seething with political mutiny.[42]

Carrier, the emissary responsible for dealing with this hellish situation, was a product of the radicalization of the Revolution in Paris. Close to the Hébertists without being closed to other revolutionary factions, Carrier was the consummate Jacobin, on good terms with the members of the Committee of Public Safety. Shortly after taking charge in the west, he assured his principals that "prejudice and fanaticism were being swept away by the irresistible force of reason and that the flaming torch of the *lumières* was at once irradiating the world and scorching its enemies." Carrier urged the committee to fulfill its popular mandate "by bringing the thunder and lightning of vengeance . . . down upon the heads of all counterrevolutionaries." At the same time he assured Paris that he had ordered the "arrest of all suspects in Nantes" and vowed that "forthwith not a single of the city's countless counterrevolutionaries and food hoarders would remain at large."[43] In turn, Carrier came under pressure from local patriots, who were breathing fear and vengeance. Not unlike their Parisian counterparts in September 1792, they pointed to the prisons, bursting with unrepentant traitors and rebels, as wellheads for counterrevolutionary risings, which would be concerted with Charette and the British. In the name of the Committee of Public Safety, Hérault de Séchelles, vowing that the "proper time for compassion was not now but after victory," pressed Carrier to "purge the city ahead of an English landing."[44]

Responsible not only for Nantes but for the entire region, Carrier acted as the all-out ideological warrior in tune with his superiors in Paris, even if these were not always in concert among themselves. Confident that "he had mastered the art of [civil] war," he promised them that once the insurgents were driven out of the offshore island of Noirmoutier, fifty miles southwest of Nantes, he would instruct General Dutruy and General Haxo to put to death, throughout the liberated territories, "all individuals, regardless of sex, and to apply the torch unsparingly."[45] As if to justify and flaunt his savagery, Carrier told the twelve who ruled that "they should know that women, along with priests, had fomented the war in the Vendée, and that it was the women fighting alongside the brigands who were calling for the execution of our hapless prisoners, strangling many of them themselves." On Noirmoutier, meanwhile, neither side flinched, but once "500 or 600 of our patriots were on shore [they] slaughtered right and left," and of the "900 bodies buried in a salt marsh, the majority were theirs, not ours."[46]

At Barbâtre the republican forces killed everyone in sight, even though the rebels had already fallen back toward the town of Noirmoutier, just to the northwest. Completely cornered, they offered to surrender in exchange for their lives. When the political proconsuls demurred, General Haxo held that being "soldiers, not executioners," he and his men could "not massacre enemy forces once they were disarmed, all the less since most of the islanders were republicans like us." He insistently asked, "in the name of the army, that the lives of civilians be spared, including the lives of monarchists, on condition they lay down their arms."[47] In several instances Haxo prevented the worst, but usually he was overridden by hard-line political delegates. These soon informed the Convention that an intensive *battue* had flushed out numerous civilian rebels who, along with captive combatants, were about to be executed. This ferocity prefigured the vengeful terror of Turreau's twelve "infernal columns," and in fact Turreau took an active part in the "pacification" of Noirmoutier.

All this time Carrier wrestled with the staggering problems of Nantes. As the tide turned decisively in favor of the Blues, he notified the Convention that in addition to many brigands being killed in action, hundreds "were being captured" and channeled to Nantes. Since this influx contributed to a glut of the guillotine, Carrier "decided to resort to the firing squad" and urged Marie-Pierre-Adrien Francastel, his counterpart in Angers, to have recourse to this same "useful and expedient method."[48] Doubtless the triple danger of famine, epidemic, and prison mutiny contributed to the decision to speed the liquidation of the *détenus* by summary executions and *noyades*.

While this triple danger was a grim reality, its specter was also cunningly manipulated as a pretext for staying the repressive course. In Nantes, as in Paris, there were factional rivalries among revolutionaries over the interpretation and application of the decree of total war that had been issued on August 1, 1793. To be sure, no one advocated opting out of the civil war: the debate was over the degree and control, not the principle, of terror. The framework for discussion was one of functional rather than substantive rationality, even if ideological zealots kept exerting a certain influence. In Nantes, in the midst of the local "carnival of death," these zealots protested against "sparing the Vendée" at the expense of their city, insisting that there was no qualitative difference between "killing" in the battle for the city's "public health" and killing in the battle for the Vendée.[49] Under Carrier and until Savenay, local moderates, who were of relatively high social status, came increasingly under suspicion, until in mid-November nearly 140 of them were arrested and sent to Paris for arraignment by the Revolutionary Tribunal.[50]

This, then, was the context in which Carrier presided over emergency trials, summary executions, and mass drownings in Nantes. The local revolutionary tribunal was charged with judging individuals accused "of armed rebellion, of material and moral support of the rebels, of hoarding and speculating in essential foods, and . . . of seditious speech." Apparently both prosecutors and judges were divided between loose and strict constructionists, with Carrier siding with the latter. During its life of fifteen months the tribunal adjudicated some 1,000 cases, handing down 273 death sentences, 168 prison terms, and 42 deportations. Like any emergency court, the tribunal operated in disregard of legal norms, but it also returned about 550 acquittals.[51]

There were, in addition, two military commissions. By the standards of a revolutionary court, the so-called Lenoir commission at least minimally took account of legal procedures and the testimony of the accused. Between November 1793 and May 1794 it rendered about 650 judgments, less than 250 of them death penalties, and 161 of these were pronounced after Carrier's recall to Paris. Dispensing political justice under extreme conditions, the Lenoir commission committed its share of judicial errors and outrages.[52]

The real epitome of the injustice of revolutionary justice in civil war was the Bignon commission, itself evincing the breakdown of political sovereignty and legal authority. It was chartered in mid-December at the initiative of political delegates sent from Paris. Over a period of five months the Bignon tribunal, in its rush to pseudo-justice, passed a total of about 3,000 death sentences, some 660 in three days in

Savenay and some 1,950 during the first three weeks of January in Nantes. At Savenay the defendants were summarily charged and executed for their active participation in the rebellion; at Nantes they were indicted and put to death for a broad range of ostensible misdeeds, the accused being randomly selected primarily from among the thousands of prisoners crammed into the detention center in the port. Using arbitrary procedures, the Bignon court delivered grinding judgments, with little or no regard for the depositions and rights of the accused.[53] Since it was intended to retaliate for past offenses and, above all, to deter future ones, this revolutionary justice was both intemperate and unhidden. Society at large was indifferent. Onlookers at executions were either exultant or solemn, except for twinges of disquiet when children or women were among the victims being carted to judicial slaughter.[54]

Carrier always and everywhere, even if furtively, was a hard-liner. Baffled and troubled by the scope, complexity, and urgency of the problems in his realm, he was inclined to use violence to control events that had spun out of control, thereby exacerbating the crisis. Of course, Carrier's messianic prepossession predisposed him to be implacable. Sworn to the Jacobin vision, he battled the fanaticism of the counterrevolutionaries with a fanaticism of his own. On one occasion, in mid-November 1793, he traced "all the ills of mankind to the throne and the altar," linking "the massacres of Saint Bartholomew's Day, Nîmes, and the Vendée," for which he fixed much of the responsibility on priests.[55] He did so in the city whose name recalled the revocation, in 1685, of Henry IV's edict of religious toleration.

In advocating summary trials and executions, Carrier was at once driven by ideology, pressured by circumstances, and compliant with Paris. The same applies to his recourse to the *noyades*, with the difference that the victims, the bulk of them being refractory priests, were selected by exclusively ideological criteria. It was on November 5, or two weeks after his arrival in Nantes, that Carrier signed an order authorizing the use, if need be, of river barges in the ongoing repression. There is some ambiguity as to whether he meant to sanction their use as floating prisons or as instruments of willful murder. In any case, the men of Lamberty's killing squad thought they had been given a free hand to do their *basse besogne*, and their atrocious drownings were not reproved at the time.

All told there were four mass drownings between November 5 and mid-December, for a total of about 465 victims. It is not to mitigate their absolute horror to note the falsity of later tales of ships being fitted with trap bottoms; of priests and nuns being forced to marry and grovel before being thrown overboard; of hundreds of children being given over to the river of death; and of the number of victims running to at least several thousand. On November 18, when informing the Convention that he had just learned of the drowning of 50 refractory priests who had been "penned up on a boat at anchor in the Loire," Carrier spoke of the *noyade* as "apparently intended to reduce the number of priests."[56]

On December 6 he reported to the Committee of Public Safety that "another 53 priests were about to be laid to rest" in France's longest river.[57] A week later, on December 10, Carrier noted the coincidence of a defeat of rebels west of Machecoul and the transfer of fifty-eight refractory priests from Angers to Nantes "to be held on a ship afloat on the Loire before being swallowed up by . . . the revolutionary torrent."[58] On December 22, in advising Paris that the left bank of the Loire was now in republican hands, he commended "the miraculous Loire for having devoured another 360 [unidentified] counterrevolutionaries of Nantes."[59]

Another point that deserves special emphasis is that the drownings started in early November 1793, after the republican victory at Cholet but well before the defeat of the Vendée in the second half of December. Significantly, there were no *noyades* after Savenay. Manifestly Carrier was the mastermind of a terror which was an integral part of the local civil war. To all intents and purposes Carrier completed his mission with the end of the *Vendée militaire* and before Turreau proceeded to pacify the region during the first four months of 1794. Both quantitatively and qualitatively, the violence of the avenging but also deterrent terror directed by Turreau was of a different order than that directed by Carrier.

❋ ❋ ❋

Before turning to a discussion of Turreau's dark reign of terror in the Vendée, it may be useful to suggest that the savagery in Nantes in 1793 had by far less in common with that in Auschwitz—and other German concentration camps and extermination sites—in 1940 to

1944, than with that in Paris in 1871. Admittedly, the Nazi regime originally intended Auschwitz to be a camp for prisoners.[60] But it was, to begin with, set up beyond Germany's borders—in conquered Poland—for foreign political prisoners, who were earmarked for forced labor. In a second stage it became an industrial center, to serve Berlin's expansionist foreign and military policy. In its final phase Auschwitz also held prisoners captured in the war of aggression against Soviet Russia, and their living conditions were perhaps most analogous to those of the rebel prisoners in Nantes, except that Carrier was not out to systematically decimate his captives. At any rate, in their reason and purpose the deadly prisons of Nantes had nothing in common with Auschwitz. The bulk of Auschwitz's inmates were men and women, regardless of age and state of health, who were foreign, not German nationals, and very few of whom had been combatants. They were willfully worked to the bone, and in the process emotionally and psychologically dehumanized and degraded, before dying an agonizing death or being killed by execution or gassing, which was the fate chiefly of Jews and Gypsies. No tribunal held court within the confines of Auschwitz, and there were no *indulgents* among its masters. Rudolf Höss, the commandant of the camp, was never in danger of being recalled to Berlin to be reprimanded or tried for overstepping (nonexistent) bounds.

Civil war defined the mission and dynamics of Carrier's terror in Nantes, as confirmed by the profile of its victims, which was radically different from that of Höss's terror in Auschwitz. Although there were a few women, children, and aged among the prisoners and the slain, the vast majority of them were adult males. The Vendeans were not victimized because they were captured on a foreign battlefield or belonged to an arbitrarily defined national, ethnic, or religious group marked for enslavement or extermination, but because they had taken up arms in a civil war that turned against them and that caused enormous casualties and miseries on *both* sides. Although not a few of them were wrongfully imprisoned, tried, and executed, the principle of individual responsibility was not entirely set aside. To be sure, the captive rebels and their helpmates belonged to an enemy who was fiercely demonized. Even so, they were not seen and treated as if they were, in their own persons, the embodiment of absolute evil or impurity. The deadly prison conditions, summary executions, and *noyades* in

Nantes grew out of the blind rage of civil war and were meant to generate fear and deter resistance, while the inferno in Auschwitz grew out of the Furies unleashed by a regime battling foreign "enemies" for European domination but free of domestic opposition.

The real homology of the atrocious events in and around Nantes during the Vendée is with the atrocious events in and around Paris during the Commune.[61] In both situations the fact of civil war was crucial: in 1793 the Vendée rebelled against the contested regime, in Paris; in 1871 the capital rebelled against the contested regime, which had moved its seat to Versailles. In March 1793 as in March 1871, a spontaneous and disorderly popular explosion only gradually escalated into an organized uprising. Both times the insecure rulers viewed the insurgents as savage and cruel brigands: in the one case priests and women were excoriated as the chief villains among the Vendeans; in the other the anarchists and *petroleuses* among the communards. General Haxo was no more successful in pressing for forbearance in late 1793 than were the advocates of compromise in April 1871. Mutual distrust and hatred kept spiraling, the rebels of 1793 glorifying priest and church, those of 1871 profaning them in conflicts that were religiously charged on both sides. The Vendée was directed against the perceived threat of the anticlerical and invasive city, and was defeated by Paris; the Commune was directed against the perceived threat of the clerical *hobereaux* and monarchists of Versailles, and was defeated by the countryside. The rebels of the Vendée and the Commune remained all but cut off from the rest of France and Europe, with the result that they had to face, unassisted, the armies of the fragile First Republic and the embryonic Third Republic, respectively.

Both times there was a vast disproportion of power between the rebels and a hard-pressed regime resolved to crush them in a conflict that assumed the logic and violence peculiar to the friend-enemy dissociation. Like the *Vendée militaire*, the battle of Paris culminated in a vindictive fury. During the *semaine sanglante* of May 21–28, 1871, probably over 20,000 Parisian rebels were killed, with fewer than 900 dead on the government side. Relatively few rebels died in battle, the majority of them being shot either as they raised their arms to surrender or simply following capture. In addition, the Versailles forces took about 26,000 prisoners, and arrested about another 10,000 suspects after the end of the fighting. The prisons of Paris and its environs being overcrowded with military and political prisoners, over 20,000 of them were confined to naval pontoons anchored at Brest, Cherbourg, Lorient, Rochefort, and La Rochelle. Although the conditions of confinement were atrocious, there was no disease or famine, and there were no *noyades.*

Even so, Paris was subjected to the terror of retribution. Adolphe Thiers, the chief executive of the Second Empire's equivocal and embattled successor regime, was altogether candid about the need for an updated auto-da-fé. He proclaimed that the punishment to follow upon victory would have to be "at once legal and implacable." Thiers called for a "thoroughgoing expiation, of the sort that honest people must inflict when justice demands it," but vowed that it would be "wrought on the authority and by way of the law."[62] Twenty-eight special tribunals proceeded to dispense an emergency, military-type justice, with limited regard for the rights of the accused. Among the 36,000 prisoners who were charged there were about 1,000 women and 600 children under sixteen years of age. About 10,000 communards were convicted of a wide range of criminal actions and complicities related to the insurrection. The emergency courts pronounced 93 death sentences, of which 23 were executed. They also condemned 251 defendants to forced labor for life or other long terms, 4,586 to deportation overseas, and 4,606 to various prison terms. Fifty children were sent to houses of correction.

Like the rebels of 1793, those of 1871 were not innocent noncombatants. Whatever the circumstances and triggers for their first act of rebellion, they seized and executed hostages, profaned houses of religion and public monuments, set fire to state and municipal buildings, and battled government troops from behind barricades. Still, after using massive military force to crush the uprising, drowning it in blood, Thiers's government of moral order mandated a vast and blatantly pseudo-judicial vengeance intended to terrify and deter the heirs of the Commune. Supported by moderate republicans, it did so despite the fact that the civil war was over and France was at peace with its neighbors, there being no near-term danger of either renewed revolt or foreign invasion.

Any civil war, like any foreign war, must end. But civil wars are more difficult to terminate equitably and without vengeance than international conflicts: compare the peace-making of 1870 and of 1918–19 with the retribution of 1871. Precisely because the *Vendée militaire* was religiously driven, neither side wielded the sword for concrete and limited ends. To the contrary, they both spilled blood for "spiritual" values and ideas, which are by nature non-negotiable. Besides, in the Vendée there was no effective governing authority on the White side with which to treat for a cease-fire, let alone a settlement. In the extreme, in an ideologically freighted international war the opposing sides fight to the death, as they did during the Second World War. In a civil war like the Vendée, the objective was not simply to defeat the enemy in the field of battle but to reduce and convert him.

✻ ✻ ✻

Just as the civil war in the Vendée did not break out overnight, it did not end all at once. Although the republican armies defeated the military rebellion in late 1793, there was no formal end of hostilities. Several units and commanders of the Catholic and Royal forces remained at large and kept eluding capture. Above all, the battles of Le Mans (December 13) and Savenay (December 23), besides not appearing as final at the time as they did weeks later, did not bring about "moral" or "religious" disarmament on either side. Despite being put in fear, the peasants of the Vendée continued to provide cover and support for fugitive rebels, all the more so with the republican military and civil authorities subjecting nearly the entire region to a cruel and indiscriminate punishment.

But above all, the suppression of the insurgent peasants in the northwest and the simultaneous recapture of the defiant cities in the Midi did not mean that the Revolution was triumphant. To be sure, it had won several battles. But the war, including the war with the European powers, remained to be won. Even the most self-assured revolutionaries must have been shaken by the scope and intensity of the rural and urban resistance, which they construed as an integrated counterrevolutionary movement with dangerous conspiratorial and international dimensions. There was a certain logic in this tendentious view, since the decision makers in Paris, torn by partisan and personal discords, had to deal simultaneously with several domestic and foreign trouble spots under extreme and explosive conditions. Perforce they could not change mind-set and policy frame from issue to issue, from crisis to crisis. Their conception of the rebellious Vendée, which was widely shared by their military commanders and political emissaries, was part of their larger understanding of the beleaguerment of the insecure revolutionary regime. This larger understanding, which was ideologically informed, was not about to come apart, particularly since the embers of the Vendée continued to smolder.

The succession of Carrier, the political proconsul, by Turreau, the political general, reflected the overlap between what turned out to be the final battles and the incipient pacification campaign. Carrier was well into his hundred-day reign of terror in Nantes on November 27, the day the Committee of Public Safety appointed Turreau to take command of the Western Army. Promoted out of the National Guard, not the regular army, Turreau had Hébertist affinities and, like Ronsin and Rossignol, distrusted the alleged moderation of attested generals like Kléber, Westermann, and Marceau. In any case, when he replaced General Marceau on December 29, Turreau's assignment was not to pacify the Vendée but to direct the unfinished military operations in that unhappy land.

Though desperate for troops elsewhere, on December 3, 1793, Paris assigned additional detachments to the Western Army and ordered Turreau "to keep the rebels from re-crossing the Loire" and, more generally, to "destroy" them.[63] The next day it was announced that "national agents" would direct the enforcement of the Convention's "revolutionary laws" intended to "avenge the nation but keep in check personal vengeance."[64] Shortly afterward, in the wake of the victory at Le Mans, Carrier, who also cut a military figure, told the Convention that total victory was imminent, the battle having been "so bloody and murderous" for the rebels that their corpses were "scattered along the road all the way to Laval."[65] Other political commissioners added that the "streets, houses, and public squares" of Le Mans were strewn with heaps of corpses, and that this striking success was all the more "satisfying" for having cost the republican forces only "thirty dead and about one hundred wounded."[66]

The good tidings of Kléber's and Westermann's victory at Savenay on December 23 were related to Paris in equally euphoric and callous terms.[67] According to Carrier, in this battle thousands of rebels were killed north of the Loire and "three or four hundred" of Charette's men south of the river, but the general himself, with a band of "about 900 brigands, had managed to flee in disorder" into the forests around Les Herbiers.[68] Simultaneously, from his headquarters in Angers, Francastel advised the Committee of Public Safety of plans to deal severely with thousands of the rebels from north and south of the Loire who were taking flight to avoid punishment for their crimes. He proposed to make sure that innocent and potentially loyal citizens would be spared as part of Angers's garrison moved south "to bolster critical positions inside the Vendée, pending the arrival of reinforcements . . . needed to deliver the final blows."[69]

After Savenay, and without instructions from Paris, local military officers and political representatives set about planning the pacification of the Vendée. Traveling via Alençon, Angers, and Rennes, Turreau finally arrived in Nantes, a month after his appointment. Since he immediately left for Noirmoutier to see to its final "liberation," he did not settle into his headquarters until January 7, 1794. By then General Kléber had framed a plan of pacification. He estimated that between them Charette and Cathelineau still had about 5,000 men whose primary aims were to avoid capture and loot for survival. Rather than pursue these poorly armed irregulars to engage them in battle, Kléber proposed to have generals Haxo and Dutruy "isolate and envelop" them, sending "small, mobile cavalry detachments from fixed strong points . . . to harass them and cut their food supplies." He stressed that the success of this battle plan was contingent on "winning the confidence of the rural population by enforcing strict discipline among the troops," many of whom were raw and reckless.[70]

Turreau, Kléber's superior, turned aside this relatively indirect and restrained strategy in favor of a head-on and indiscriminate flying operation. At the same time that he proposed to rush troops to the western Vendée, the hinterland of the Atlantic coast, to counter a possible British landing, Turreau called for a "prompt . . . [and] frontal assault . . . on all known enemy concentrations."[71] Actually his estimate of the remaining rebel forces was no higher than Kléber's and he quite agreed that the war was no longer "a cause for concern." But Turreau stood apart with his view that the war "would not be over, conclusively, until every last brigand was exterminated."[72] Besides, he was determined to rush ahead both because he wanted to free up troops for service along France's borders and he expected the pacification to be mere child's play.

Turreau informed Paris that he was about to start his "stroll through the Vendée" with a view to "setting on fire everything" except for the sites which would serve as staging areas "for the extermination of the rebels." Of course his superiors would have "to issue the order" for this operation, since he was "merely the Convention's dutiful agent." In particular he asked for a directive on how to deal with "the *women and children* of the rebel territories," since if they were "*to be put to the sword*" he could not do so on his "own responsibility," without a special warrant from higher authority.[73]

Meanwhile starting January 17, and without waiting for instructions, Turreau divided six divisions of some 12,000 men into twelve columns to comb the Vendée for rebels "from east to west," with orders to "search and burn forests, villages, small towns, and farms." The aim was to smoke out and kill "all brigands caught in possession of weapons or likely to use them." No exception would be made for "girls, women, and children" who were implicated, nor should "mere suspects" be spared. But Turreau did order his commanders to see to it that "no harm would come to men, women, and children who were civic-minded and had not participated in the brigands' revolt."[74]

At first, pacification proceeded easily, and Turreau basked in the approval of his superiors. By January 24, in a dispatch from Cholet, he informed Paris that twelve columns were "crisscrossing the Vendée" and that provided he received the necessary support, he expected to have the upper hand "within a fortnight." The province would, of course, be left without "houses, provisions, arms, and inhabitants, except for those slipping away to hide deep inside forests." Bearing in mind the time needed for dispatches to reach the capital, the Committee of Public Safety promptly approved Turreau's mode of operations. On February 6, over Carnot's signature, its members assured him that from their distant vantage point they considered his "measures to be both sound and pure." Indeed, they expected him "to show great results" in a campaign about which "they and the National Convention had so often been misled." They told Turreau that it was his "duty to exterminate all brigands, down to the last" and enjoined him to rid the rebel territories of all firearms lest they be used again in the future.[75] While this letter breathes no word about the treatment of women and children, there is nothing to suggest that this silence was intended to proscribe turning the avenging fury on them.

In the meantime, however, as Turreau received reports from his field commanders about the unexpected difficulties of their mission, he began to shift the blame for all setbacks to others. The gravity of the situation was driven home by news that the brigands "had actually dared . . . to attack . . . and [momentarily] seized" Cholet. On February 10, from Nantes, Turreau reproved the Convention for having included Cholet among cities to be spared, and called on Paris to order that "despite its population's patriotism" it be racked by fire. He reiterated that "the war in the west was not over" and now claimed that "30,000 brigands remained to be destroyed."[76]

Of course, in Paris the Vendée continued to be caught up in the factional and personal rivalries within the revolutionary camp, with no effective sovereign power to discipline them. At any rate, on February 12 Turreau's report on Cholet, which played to the *enragés*, prompted Barère to go before the Convention in an effort to distance himself from the worst brutalities of the *colonnes infernales*: although the Committee of Public Safety stood by "the spirit and terms of the decrees" which ordered the destruction and scorching of rebel strongholds and hideaways, these did not warrant the devastation of "the farms and homes of good citizens." Barère claimed to be particularly "shocked" that the implementation of the Convention's decrees should be so "barbarous and intemperate" as to reinvigorate and swell rebel bands. Instead of giving the green light to make an example of Cholet, Barère announced that Nicolas-Joseph Hentz and Pierre-Anselme Garrau would leave, with "full powers," to join the other representatives on mission with the Western Army, presumably to restrain Turreau.[77]

Meanwhile, with the continuing support of most generals and representatives on mission, Turreau persisted in his course. The pitiless brutality in and around Les Lucs-sur-Boulogne is characteristic of his Carthaginian resolve. Lucs-sur-Boulogne was a small town of about 2,000 inhabitants some twelve miles north of La Roche-sur-Yon. After his defeat at Noirmoutier Charette took his remaining irregulars to this region, where they harassed republican forces at the same time that they were incessantly tracked and intermittently engaged by them. On February 27 General Cordellier's column came upon Charette's cohort and, in an unexpectedly difficult passage of arms, suffered a humiliating, if minor, defeat. Charette's partisans then headed south to La Roche-sur-Yon, where they were forced to scatter into the countryside. Instead of going in pursuit of them, on February 28 Cordellier, ostensibly to avenge his setback, laid waste Lucs-sur-Boulogne, indiscriminately massacring about 500 people, including women and children. What the massacre of Machecoul had been to the incipient antirevolutionary phase of the peasant rebellion, the massacre of Lucs-sur-Boulogne was to its terminal phase of furious revolutionary pacification. Both massacres were inseparable from military engagements, with the result that the lines were blurred between soldiers killed in combat and civilian victims of vindictive terror.[78]

About this same time, and apparently without provocation, General Huché ravaged La Gaubretière and the surrounding countryside, southwest of Cholet, with fire and sword. An extreme hard-liner like Cordellier, he reported to Turreau that, although conditions were not propitious for a "large carnage," his forces nevertheless killed "over five hundred men and women," many of them after being "smoked out of bushes, ditches, hedges, and woods." On his return to Cholet Huché passed through La Verrie, where his men killed the few people they encountered, "except for children," before going on to set fire to Saint-Malo du Bois, where they did not find "a single soul."[79] They were equally destructive when they invested Vezins and Vihiers, northeast of Cholet, in the direction of Saumur.[80]

Eyewitness accounts and secondhand reports dating from the time of the pacification drive testify to a ferocity and barbarity characteristic of former times. Victims are said to have been lacerated, mutilated, and defiled before and after being killed; women raped, disfigured, and burned alive; infants and children impaled on pikes. No doubt many or most of these excessive excesses were less part of the grim and studied reality of pacification than of its inevitable complement of terrifying phantasms, delusions, and rumors. But no matter how uncertain the testimony, there is no denying the merciless and reckless savagery of the infernal columns, with not a few villains and criminals in their ranks. No less certain and fatal, there were few military and political leaders in the field or in Paris to restrain or punish them.

It was not long, however, before in several towns of the Vendée, patriots and men of honor, dismayed and terrified by Turreau's methods, raised their voices in protest. By late January 1794, immediately following the start of Turreau's drive, the municipal leaders of Les

Herbiers petitioned him to "spare" their town, while those of Pou-zauges begged that their "community be exempt from the anathema visited upon the department of the Vendée."[81] On March 1 the popular societies of Fontenay and Les Sables-d'Olonne sent delegates to convince the proconsuls in Nantes that since their communities had been unswervingly loyal to the Republic, had contributed to its victory, and were themselves ferreting out rebels, the "writ to set the entire region on fire" should not apply to them.[82] A few weeks later a local commander asked his superior to help save twelve women, some of them "mothers of infants," who were in jail on suspicion of rebel activities. Yet another officer averred that by burning and killing indiscriminately, without differentiating between "patriots and re-bels," several unsteadfast generals were "alienating instead of winning over the people."[83] On March 28 a delegation from Mortagne told the political emissaries in Nantes that it was "common knowledge" that peasants were again taking to arms "because they were incensed by the killing of men, women, children, and the aged by General Huché's brigade."[84] The military command, municipal administra-tion, and popular society of Luçon protested the failure to "distin-guish between the innocent and the guilty, the patriots and the ene-mies of the state." Likewise, the patriots of Fontenay informed Turreau that the orders he had given to General Huché in Luçon "were in every respect an outrage against the commonweal, . . . in-verting virtue and crime."[85]

Indeed, Luçon and Fontenay, in the southern reaches of the *Dépar-tement-Vengé*, became particularly alarming flashpoints, with suppli-cation and remonstrance growing into outright resistance. In re-sponse to the protests emanating from Luçon, General Huché, ever the sworn intransigent, assured Turreau that the town "was teeming with aristocrats, moderates, and [their] agents" who masterminded the "petitions and remonstrances" as well as the clamor "to identify and spare patriots," which he proposed to ignore.[86] In turn, on April 9 Luçon's "revolutionary control committee" informed Turreau that it had arrested Huché with a view to putting him on trial for what in a later age would be called crimes against humanity.[87]

In the dispatch advising the war minister of this "incredible arrest," Turreau insisted that he had appointed Huché—"a pure republican even if not a great soldier"—to replace General Bard, whose *modéran-*

tisme suited Luçon and the surrounding area, which were infested with the "aristocratic canker."[88] By now, in the absence of Garrau, who was delayed in the Pyrenees, Hentz had taken stock of the local situation and together with Francastel confirmed that "a nefarious temper" reigned throughout much of the Vendée, including in Luçon and Fontenay. From Angers they told the Committee of Public Safety that apparently Charette and Stofflet had combined their forces. However that may be, the "largest horde of brigands no longer exceeds two thousand men, half of them without arms," and wherever the republican forces draw near they vanish into "the countryside they know so well." Meanwhile, even if Charette had faded away, "his name had become a legend that will long outlive him." In any case, Hentz and Francastel hesitated to dismiss or reassign Turreau: while nationally the "cause of liberty" was strengthened by "Delacroix, Danton, and their associates being handed over to justice," the Vendée continued to be "in the hands of men of their ilk," who remained to be brought under control.[89]

Once in Luçon, on April 17 Hentz and Francastel acted on this diagnosis. They declared a state of siege, closed the local popular society, and ordered the transfer of Huché and all the documents concerning his case to Paris. Joined by Garrau, they warned the Committee of Public Safety that the "aristocrats" of cities like Luçon, which were "lairs of counterrevolution," were "deceiving and inciting the people of the countryside." But the three proconsuls also struck a softer note. They urged Paris to distrust generals who gratuitously exaggerate the number of rebels, the pacification having reduced the enemy to a skeletal force: in the Vendée "it was no longer a question of fighting a war but of hunting down [less than 2,000] brigands."[90]

Turreau, it is true, read the military situation differently, still seeing "very dangerous zones of fermentation" on both banks of the Loire. To the north such was the case in the Morbihan, the territories infested by the so-called *chouans*, and the lands along the Mayenne and Vilaine, where "only terror" kept many of the fugitives from the battles of Le Mans and Savenay from "regrouping." There were at least as many brigands on the prowl south of the Loire. Fully aware that troops were needed elsewhere, Turreau claimed that to succeed he needed to double his force of 40,000 men. In early May 1794 he stepped up "the hot pursuit of the brigands; the removal of provisions, fodder, and cattle; and the destruction of ovens and flour mills." Meanwhile Turreau denounced "the moderation of certain generals and the negligence or ignorance" of certain politicians at the same time that he warned that "until all the scoundrels opposing the Republic are purged the Vendée will remain their rallying cry and rallying point."[91]

Despite the difference in their military estimates, the political emissaries endorsed Turreau's political logic. Like him they kept cautioning the Committee of Public Safety not to listen to "the popular societies and established authorities of Sables, Fontenay-le-Peuple, Niort, Luçon, even La Rochelle, etc." so as not to further delay the liquidation of the insurrection. But on April 6, probably before receiving this caveat, the Committee—over the signatures of Barère, Carnot, Billaud-Varenne, and Collot d'Herbois—forwarded the "numerous remonstrances" it had received to the proconsuls with the request that they "consider them seriously without, however, discontinuing the measures necessary to protect the Republic and stamp out the horrible and protracted war of the Vendée." Heeding the criticism that their outlook was distorted by their having remained too close to headquarters in Nantes, the Committee ordered them to go into the field to judge for themselves. In reply, Paris was told that Francastel and Hentz were about to travel "towards Niort, Luçon, etc."; that Garrau would journey "to Machecoul, Challans, les Sables, and La Rochelle"; and that Prieur de la Marne, the visiting member of the Committee, would go to the "Loire-Inférieure and the Morbihan."[92]

Reporting on their foray into the southwest of the Vendée, Hentz and Francastel stressed that much of the region was in the hands of "popular associations which had turned into hotbeds of counterrevolution." They testily noted that those who had falsely charged them with never leaving Nantes meant to discredit anyone determined to prevent the brigands from "renewing their war in the spring."[93] In a report from Niort which reached the Committee of Public Safety on April 22, the two emissaries reiterated that in the southwest "counterrevolution was rife" in several military units as well as in popular associations and in elite circles "tied to the rich." In the city of Niort "brigands were sheltered openly, the maximum was violated, the Lord's day was observed, women did not wear the *cocarde*, and royal symbols were displayed on public buildings." With an eye to the political scene in Paris, Hentz and Francastel concluded that the Vendée was "as far away from republicanism as heaven is from earth."[94]

* * *

Evidently the original estimate that pacification would be mere child's play was mistaken. The end of the *Vendée militaire* did not break the cycle of mutual demonization and hatred, which continued at fever heat. Even if the pacification had been less savage, much of the population of western France would have continued to be hostile to the new regime. The ferocity of the infernal columns merely exacerbated this deep-seated animosity. It helped create a favorable atmosphere for Charette's and Stofflet's elusive armies as well as for stray guerrilla bands to harass, ambush, and raid their enemy. The primitive rebels south of the Loire, not unlike the *chouans* to the north, had the priceless advantage of knowing the terrain and knowing where to hide, with the support of the local population. The unremitting climate of insecurity and fear favored enduring violence by both sides, with the rebels often driven by personal and righteous vengeance, the soldiers of the republic by punitive and retributive venom. There was, in addition, the unabated shock of irreconcilable worldviews. The Blues embraced their secular catechism, and indiscriminately blackened all their enemies as immutable counterrevolutionaries. But the Whites were no less faithful to their credo. On July 1, 1794, five officers of two rebel groups operating around Saint-Philbert, east of Mortagne, addressed a circular to all republicans that laid bare their dogged counterrevolutionary passion. They vowed never to "offer incense to the monstrous Republic" which was devastating and disfiguring Europe's "most brilliant Kingdom." Instead, they swore to keep fighting to reclaim their "King and the Apostolic and Roman Catholic religion by annihilating the so-called Republic." For them and their soldiers there could be no question of "returning to their homes, the [republicans] having burned down their houses and slaughtered their women and children." Pledged to "live and die . . . for King and Religion," they adjured all who had lost their way "to recant and forswear the perverts who were determined to rule France and incite one and all to have their throats cut for a specious and phantasmic liberty and equality." In any case, there could be no question of "either recognizing or negotiating with you as long as you swear by the republican book."[95]

The intensification of the war and pacification in the Vendée was, of course, cause and consequence of the radicalization of the Revolution which was orchestrated in Paris, particularly by the Committee of Public Safety. The twelve who ruled issued all the essential military and political directives and received most major reports from the field. Their council was also the focal point of factional struggles which were replicated on the ground and left their imprint on vital decisions at both ends. Each of the major factions in the epicenter of the Revolution had its local correspondents.

From the outset the politics within the governing circles in the capital bore on the course of the civil war in the Vendée, and it did so ever more intensely once Turreau's forces became mired in the pacification campaign. At the same time politics became increasingly fervent among military and civilian officials in and near the theater of operations, as well as in the towns and cities of the region. Ultimately the political cleavages and dissensions in Paris and in the Vendée were closely entwined, and at both ends they weighed in the balance. But to repeat, at the center as well as in the periphery the infighting was about the ways and means, including the limits, of the local terror, and not about the principle of terror as such. In this respect, the politics of the terror in the repression of the Vendée was the same as in the pacification of the rebellious cities of the Midi.

Needless to say, the political guidelines and general orders sent forth by the executive in Paris left local officials a considerable margin for interpretation and implementation, which included translating habitually swollen revolutionary rhetoric into concrete and precise precepts of political and military strategy and tactics. One and all were unprepared for their unlikely assignment, which brought them face to face with the bane or pathos of novelty. Generals Kléber and Haxo were new to irregular warfare, and General Turreau was a neophyte in the military arts. As Michelet points out, most of the senior emissaries and officers were "lawyers, physicians, and journalists" who overnight became "awkward and inexperienced men of war." They were posted to cities or towns in which "even girondin republicans" were in hiding, leaving them "in terrifying isolation." Fearing for their lives, the "tiny minority" of local Montagnards pressed the proconsuls "to kill all traitors today to avoid being killed by them tomorrow" in circumstances in which "the imminent White Terror invited the Red Terror." Michelet suggests that the men in Paris simply could not fathom "the predicament of those *terribles voyageurs* or fated agents of the Revolution" whom they posted to the great unknown. Facing unsuspected perils, and "far from the center," they wound up "breaking the law in order to uphold it and committing crimes in order to deter them." Tragically, by the time they "returned to the world of the living," or even before, "they sensed . . . that they had become expendable." And, in fact, once back in Paris, rather than hailed as heroes, they were tried by hostile courts and judges.[96]

The reason was that the impasse in the Vendée had become a defining issue in the polarizing struggle between the hard-liners and the moderates for the soul and future of the Revolution. While the *intransigeants* proposed to keep enlisting outside violence to smash and punish the resistance as part of a policy of imposing a radically new society on the Vendée, the *indulgents* urged that the mailed fist be relaxed and combined with clemency in the interest of reconciliation. Roughly speaking, in the battle over policy in the Vendée the affinities of the ultras were with the faction headed by Hébert and those of the moderates with the faction headed by Danton and Desmoulins. Michelet claims that ever since October, when in Lyons one of Robespierre's men had pressed for appeasement, any suggestion to take such a turn was "suspected of being part of a Robespierrist machination."[97]

Certainly the weakening and defeat of the Hébertists in Paris encouraged the opposition first to Carrier and then to Turreau. Both of them shared the precepts of this group. The groundswell of republican remonstrances from the towns and cities of the Vendée, symbolized by General Huché's arrest in Luçon, coincided with the political trial and guillotining of the Hébertists in the second half of March and of the Dantonists in early April. The suspension and reassignment of Turreau followed in mid-May, after the levers of power had come into the hands of Robespierre, whose agents had been instrumental in decrying both Carrier and Turreau for their blunders, not their excesses.

Even Carrier's recall on February 8, 1794, before the climax of the Great Terror in Paris, was linked to the politics of the Revolution. He came under a cloud less for the *noyades* than for his high-handedness with fellow emissaries from the center and fellow revolutionaries in Nantes. In any case, after his return to Paris, Carrier remained an unreconstructed hard-liner, impenitent about his excesses, which were beginning to be denounced as abuses of the Terror detrimental to the Revolution and the Republic. The Convention did not arrest and try Carrier until late November 1794, well after the fall of Robespierre and Thermidor, which he had promoted. By then the vast majority of deputies sought to distance themselves from the worst excesses of the Terror. Especially once Carrier brazenly reminded them that only yesterday they had openly supported or silently condoned drastic measures, he became a convenient expiatory offering for the enormities of a terror they were not prepared to denounce outright, let alone abjure. They were convinced that the Terror had achieved its purpose and might have to be reinstated to root out hidden counterrevolutionaries. Carrier was abandoned and disowned by the surviving members of the Committee of Public Safety and all the other deputies on mission, and his head fell on December 16.[98]

Turreau was at risk first and foremost because his strategy of brutal pacification had failed and was criticized in both Paris and the Vendée for stoking rather than dampening the smoldering peasant insurgency. Besides, the close to 100,000 soldiers still tied up in the Vendée were desperately needed for the taxing war with the European powers. Whereas locally the savagery of the repression stimulated criticism of Turreau, in the capital concern for the regime's international security kept rising. Rather than cashier Turreau, his superiors gave him a minor command in Belle-Île-en-Mer. He was replaced by General Vimeux, who urged his troops "to reach out . . . to those whom perfidious priests and nobles had incited to violence but now were contrite and prepared to obey the laws of the Republic." He further ordered them, publicly, "to respect property, the basis of society, . . . [and] to protect individual life, in keeping with the commandments of humanity." Although they had fought without giving quarter to defeat the enemy, the soldiers of the Republic now needed to be moderate and self-disciplined to "win a second victory over them," which would be "rewarded" by the return of their "misguided brothers" to reason and to *la patrie*.[99]

In late October 1794, when taking command of all forces north of the Loire, General Hoche struck an equally conciliatory note in a proclamation to the population of the Vendée. He assured the rebels that by handing over their arms they would rejoin *la patrie* and recover their French citizenship. Insisting that the Republic was moved by "the magnanimity that the strong owe the weak," Hoche pledged that his soldiers were coming to "free [the Vendeans] from tyranny, not to slaughter or plunder them." They were pledged to "respect . . . [and] protect the vulnerable aged, women, and children . . . who were returning to hearth and home, praying to God, and tilling the soil." In conclusion Hoche called on rebel leaders to turn away from the infamous Charette, all the more so now that the "barbarian émigrés and ferocious English" were powerless to give help.[100]

As for Turreau, he finally faced the revolutionary tribunal in late 1795. Even if less brazenly than Carrier, he, too, argued that his policies and actions had been approved by the entire government as well as by the political emissaries to the Western Army. Besides, since so many respectable officers and men had carried out the protracted pacification by iron and fire, it would have been difficult and unseemly to hold solely Turreau responsible. A full year after Carrier was guillotined, Turreau was exonerated: the president of the military council concluded that "as both soldier and citizen" he had performed the duties of his command in a worthy manner.[101]

Ultimately Carrier achieved a greater notoriety than Turreau, who went on to become an imperial baron and ambassador to the United States under Napoleon. Indeed, Carrier's "sacrificial" execution served the same expiatory and diversionary function for the legion of active and passive supporters of the atrocities of the terror in the Vendée and the cities of the Midi that Robespierre's execution served for those of the Great Terror in Paris. In the fullness of time the two men emerged as the ideal-typical anti-heroes of the French Revolution.

✳ ✳ ✳

What, then, was the place and role of the terror in the Vendée in the overall terror of the French Revolution, and to what extent were these two terrors of the same species? The course of the terror at the center was closely correlated with the civil war in the Vendée and, to a lesser degree, the rebellion of the cities of the Midi. Certainly such was the case until the *grande terreur* of Paris in June–July 1794. Even though highly visible, in terms of numbers this dramatic and terrifying spectacle of the guillotine at the epicenter of the Revolution was outdistanced by the hypertrophied and unrestrained terror associated with the civil war during the preceding fifteen months. To the extent that this link between terror and civil war was important, perhaps even decisive, it reflects the close correlation between, on the one hand, revolution and, on the other, antirevolution and counterrevolution.

Though it is impossible to give an accurate account of the human losses caused by the major components of the terror, there are some sound estimates. The official terror, starting in March 1793 and running through July/August 1794—what Quinet conceived as the "systemic terror"—claimed between 35,000 and 40,000 lives. This total can be broken down into three groups: about 17,000 were condemned to death by special or emergency tribunals and commissions; between 10,000 and 12,000 were summarily executed after capture and without trial; and several thousand died from "natural causes" in overcrowded prisons and detention centers. As we shall see, the bulk of the second and third group of victims were killed or died in and around the Vendée and the cities of the Midi.[102]

Of course, the nonsystemic or bottom-up terror of between July 1789 and March 1793 also took a large toll, in particular the prison massacres of September 1792. In addition, primarily under the official terror, at one time or other between 300,000 and 500,000 "suspects" were thrown into prison: some of them were fined, deported, and sent to the galleys; others died from malnutrition and disease.

The official terror of seventeen months can be divided into three phases: March through September 1793; October through May 1794; and June and July 1794.

The first phase was triggered by the early Vendée uprising and the frontier defeats culminating in the "treason" of Dumouriez. The Convention created the revolutionary tribunal of Paris on March 10. During the following few weeks a succession of measures made "treason, espionage, and correspondence with the enemy" punishable by death, along with "seditious language, seditious cries, and seditious writing." But of all the iron decrees of the spring of 1793, that of

March 19 became the most important, since by itself "it resulted in more executions than all the other legislation of the regime." This decree outlawing rebels was "provoked by the Vendean rising."[103] It specified that rebels captured "bearing arms . . . were to be condemned to death by military commissions and executed within twenty-four hours," the punishment to be only slightly less Draconian for rebels "taken without arms." This summary treatment was to be applied to local "leaders and agitators, [as well as] to priests, former nobles, and their agents and servants, . . . [while] rank and file insurgents were to be detained until the Convention decided their fate."[104]

The spring and summer of 1793 were particularly tense, with the armies of foreign powers advancing deeper into France, the Vendée uprising and the federalist insurrection assuming major proportions, and the streets of the capital exerting mounting pressure for a tight rein. Although the number of executions was not particularly high during these months, in April 175 of 210 executions were carried out in the west.[105]

There was a distinct acceleration of the terror in the fall of 1793, and it reached its peak in the winter, notably in December and January. In the early autumn the Convention put the terror "at the head of the nation's agenda," adopted the Law of Suspects and the Maximum, and declared the government to be "revolutionary" until the end of hostilities with the European powers. The hardening of the regime was prologue not only to the execution of Marie-Antoinette, Mme Rolland, and the Girondins, but also to the first successes over the foreign armies, the recapture of Lyons, and the victory at Cholet. Apparently the advocates of terror considered these victories a "justification" for their strategy, "tacitly recognized in the organic law of December 4." This law spelled out the reorganization of the Revolutionary Government, notably the division of labor between the Committee of Public Safety and the Committee of General Security.[106]

In any case, there were nearly 7,000 executions in December and January, about 6,500 of them concentrated in Lyons, nearby Feurs, and the Vendée. These same regions claimed 83 and 59 percent of all executions in February and March, respectively. In April the west, which was "still turbulent," continued to account for 50 percent of all executions.[107] Mathiez rightly notes that until late 1793 "the bloody [official] terror was all but confined to the regions devastated by civil war and the rear of the front lines of the armies" fighting the European powers. Indeed, the center of France and the great majority of the departments remained relatively untouched.[108] There were no executions in six departments, fewer than 10 in 31 departments, and between 10 and 100 in 32 departments. Of all the executions, 52 percent were in the west and 19 percent in the southeast, or a total of 72 percent in areas racked by insurrection. The toll was heaviest in the lands of the *Vendée militaire*, the Loire-Inférieure accounting for "one-fifth of the total for France." In addition, of the 2,639 executions in Paris during this second phase—16 percent of the total—well over half of the victims came from trouble areas in the provinces.[109]

Of course, the arraignments and verdicts of emergency courts must be weighed with extreme circumspection. But again, "in the regions of revolt and civil war," which suffered the lion's share of "legal" executions, "the proportion of indictments for sedition (93 percent) completely dwarfed all others." All in all, until close to the end of the second phase "there were fewer innocent victims than commonly supposed," the vast majority of those executed for sedition being "guilty" by virtue of actually having been rebels.[110] None of this is to gainsay that there must have been a large number of egregious miscarriages even of emergency justice.

Whatever the taproots of this terror, its objectives were political rather than social and economic.[111] Although during the first two phases the scale and intensity of the terror in the resistant regions and cities largely exceeded that in Paris, the capital was its epicenter. Even if much of this terror eluded central control, Paris provided the impulse and direction for what was a bid to restore a single political and judicial sovereignty by the agency of the Revolutionary Armies and representatives on mission. But the governing authorities in Paris cannot be said to have applied a premeditated plan to fight the civil war they themselves had helped to bring about. Rather, they improvised in the face of runaway chaotic conditions and emergencies. The Jacobins anticipated neither the domestic nor foreign resistances. Certainly the scale, intensity, and tenacity of these resistances were beyond their imagining, as were their cruelties and horrors. One cannot deny or minimize the importance of the Jacobin ideology in the perception and representation of contingencies, as well as in the making and implementation of policy; but just as ideology influenced the responses to unexpected events, it was, in turn, shaped and inflected by them. The exigencies of civil war, like those of foreign war, favored recourse to executive rule and violence as well as to official approval or mobilization of popular *élan* and fanaticism. No less important, in addition to enabling the Jacobins to enlist France's heritage of administrative centralization for their emergency rule, the civil war, particularly in the Vendée, reinforced their predisposition to view and represent themselves as the beleaguered champions of urban-based light, progress, and dynamism in a society of country-based and church-enforced obscurity, backwardness, and stagnation. In any case, there is nothing to suggest that they were driven by an ethnocidal animus. The Jacobin fury was not turned against the Vendeans as a distinct people but against the real and suspected counterrevolutionaries among them at a time when many Vendeans were not "blameless in life and pure of crime."

* * *

NOTES

1. Montaigne, *Essais*, bk. 2, ch. 23.

2. Montesquieu, *Considerations on the Causes of the Greatness of the Romans and Their Decline*, trans. David Lowenthal (Ithaca, N.Y.: Cornell University Press, 1965), p. 93. See also Reinhardt Koselleck, *Critique and Crisis: Enlightenment and the Pathogenesis of Modern Society* (Oxford: Berg, 1988), p. 188.

3. Hans Magnus Enzensberger, *Aussichten auf den Bürgerkrieg* (Frankfurt/Main: Suhrkamp, 1993).

4. All quotations in this and the two following paragraphs are from Edgar Quinet, *La Révolution* (Paris: 1987), pp. 410–12.

5. All quotations in this paragraph are from Jules Michelet, *Histoire de la Révolution française*, vol. 2 (Paris: Laffont, 1979), pp. 15–29.

6. Quinet, *La Révolution*, p. 410.

7. Charles Tilly, *The Vendée* (Cambridge, Mass.: Harvard University Press, 1964); Paul Bois, *Paysans de l'ouest* (Paris: Flammarion, 1971); Jean-Clément Martin, *La Vendée et la France* (Paris: Seuil, 1987); P. M. Jones, *The Peasantry in the French Revolution* (Cambridge: Cambridge University Press, 1988), ch. 7.

8. For the human geography of Montauban and Nîmes, see chapter 13 below.

9. The following paragraph draws on Timothy Tackett, *Religion, Revolution, and Regional Culture in Eighteenth-Century France: The Ecclesiastical Oath of 1791* (Princeton: Princeton University Press, 1986), passim; Jean-Joël Brégeon, "Les guerres de l'ouest," in Jean Tulard, ed., *La contre-révolution* (Paris: Perrin, 1990), pp. 201–33, esp. pp. 206–7; James Roberts, *The Counterrevolution in France, 1787–*

1830 (London: Macmillan, 1990), pp. 34–38; Ralph Gibson, *A Social History of French Catholicism, 1789–1914* (London: Routledge, 1989), p. 51; Jean de Viguerie, *Christianisme et révolution: Cinq leçons de la Révolution française* (Paris: Nouvelles Editions Latine, 1986), pp. 149–51.

10. Michelet, *Histoire*, p. 321; and Honoré de Balzac, *Les Chouans* (Paris: Gallimard, 1972), p. 329.

11. Jean-Julien Savary, *Guerres des vendéens et des chouans contre la république française*, 6 vols. (Paris, 1824–1827), vol. 1, pp. 105–7; and Martin, *La Vendée*, pp. 33–34. See also Michelet, *Histoire*, pp. 325–26; and Alain Gérard, *La Vendée, 1789–1793* (Paris: Champ Vallon, 1992), ch. 8.

12. Martin, *La Vendée*, pp. 36–37; and Michelet, *Histoire*, pp. 332–33.

13. Jones, *Peasantry*, pp. 228–36.

14. Brégeon, "Les guerres de l'ouest," pp. 201–33, esp. pp. 214–15.

15. Michelet, *Histoire*, p. 489.

16. Ibid., pp. 329–30.

17. Martin, *La Vendée*, p. 30.

18. Barère cited in ibid., pp. 30–31.

19. Cambacérès and Cambon cited in ibid., p. 31.

20. Robespierre cited in ibid., p. 39.

21. F.-A. [Alphonse] Aulard, ed., *Recueil des actes du comité de salut public*, vols. 2–12, (Paris, 1889–99), vol. 2, passim.

22. Cited in Savary, *Guerres des vendéens*, vol. 1, pp. 217–18, 233, 305–6.

23. Ibid., vol. 1, pp. 322–24, 358–61.

24. Cited in Reynald Secher, *Le génocide franco-français: La Vendée-vengé* (Paris: Presses Universitaires, 1986), p. 156; and Jean-Pierre Thomas, *Bertrand Barère: La voix de la Révolution* (Paris: Desjonquères, 1989), p. 139.

25. Cited in Martin, *La Vendée*, pp. 195–96.

26. Cited in Savary, *Guerres des vendéens*, vol. 1, pp. 424–30.

27. Cited in ibid., vol. 2, pp. 58–59.

28. Cited in ibid., vol. 2, p. 61 and pp. 100–4.

29. Cited in ibid., vol. 2, pp. 103–7.

30. Cited in Elie Fournier, *Turreau et les colonnes infernales: Ou l'échec de la violence* (Paris: Albin Michel, 1985), p. 27; and Brégeon, "Les guerres de l'ouest," p. 220.

31. See Savary, *Guerres des vendéens*, vol. 2, pp. 204–5, 224–25.

32. Cited in Aulard, ed., *Recueil*, vol. 7, pp. 507–8.

33. Cited in Savary, *Guerres des vendéens*, vol. 2, pp. 288–90.

34. Cited in Aulard, ed., *Recueil*, vol. 7, p. 522.

35. Cited in ibid., vol. 7, pp. 547–50, esp. p. 549.

36. Cited in ibid., vol. 7, pp. 585–86.

37. Cited in Fournier, *Turreau*, p. 20 and p. 23.

38. Cited in Simon Schama, *Citizens: A Chronicle of the French Revolution* (New York: Knopf, 1987), p. 788; and in Jones, *Peasantry*, p. 228, n. 30.

39. Michelet, *Histoire*, p. 329.

40. Ibid., p. 489.

41. Jean-Joël Brégeon, *Carrier et la terreur nantaise* (Paris: Perrin, 1987), p. 127.

42. Brégeon, *Carrier*, pp. 130–37. See also Michelet, *Histoire*, p. 661 and pp. 697–98.

43. Cited in Aulard, ed., *Recueil*, vol. 8, pp. 371–82, esp. pp. 381–82.

44. Cited in Michelet, *Histoire*, p. 687.

45. Cited in Aulard, ed., *Recueil*, vol. 9, p. 332. See also Fournier, *Turreau*, p. 32.

46. "Recollections of a Republican Volunteer," cited in Fournier, *Turreau*, p. 34.

47. Cited in ibid., p. 36.

48. Cited in Aulard, ed., *Recueil*, vol. 9, p. 552, and in Brégeon, *Carrier*, p. 148.

49. Michelet, *Histoire*, p. 698.

50. Brégeon, *Carrier*, pp. 178–79.

51. Ibid., pp. 140–43.

52. Ibid., pp. 146–48.

53. Ibid., pp. 148–51.

54. Ibid., pp. 143–45.

55. Cited in ibid., pp. 180–81.

56. Cited in Aulard, ed., *Recueil*, vol. 8, p. 505.

57. Cited in ibid., vol. 9, p. 222.

58. Cited in ibid., vol. 9, pp. 315–16. See also Brégeon, *Carrier*, pp. 161–64.

59. Cited in Aulard, ed., *Recueil*, vol. 9, pp. 588–89.

60. For this reading of Auschwitz, see Arno J. Mayer, *Why Did the Heavens Not Darken? "The Final Solution" in History* (New York: Pantheon, 1988), esp. ch. 11.

61. For this reading of the Commune, see Jacques Rougerie, *Procès des communards* (Paris: Julliard, 1964). See also Karl Marx, *The Civil War in France* (New York: International Publishers, 1940); Prosper-Olivier Lissagaray, *Histoire de la Commune de 1871* (Paris: Maspero, 1972); Frank Jellinek, *The Paris Commune of 1871* (New York: Grosset and Dunlap, 1965); Georges Bourgin, *La guerre de 1870–1871 et la Commune* (Paris: Flammarion, 1971); Stewart Edwards, *The Paris Commune of 1871* (London: Eyre and Spottiswoode, 1971).

62. Cited in Rougerie, *Procès*, p. 17.

63. Cited in Aulard, ed., *Recueil*, vol. 9, pp. 120–23.

64. Cited in ibid., vol. 9, pp. 177–79.

65. Cited in ibid., vol. 9, pp. 550–52.

66. Cited in Savary, *Guerres des vendéens*, vol. 2, pp. 432–44.

67. See Aulard, ed., *Recueil*, vol. 9, pp. 607–10.

68. Cited in ibid., vol. 9, pp. 645–46.

69. Cited in ibid., vol. 9, pp. 659–60, 729.

70. Cited in Savary, *Guerres des vendéens*, vol. 3, pp. 21 ff.

71. Cited in ibid., vol. 3, pp. 26–27.

72. Cited in ibid., vol. 2, p. 496.

73. Cited in ibid., vol. 3, p. 41. See also Secher, *Le génocide*, p. 158; and Fournier, *Turreau*, p. 43.

74. Cited in Savary, *Guerres des vendéens*, vol. 3, pp. 42–44, 47, 56–57.

75. Cited in ibid., vol. 3, p. 151. See also Fournier, *Turreau*, p. 69; and Secher, *Le génocide*, p. 159.

76. Cited in Savary, *Guerres des vendéens*, vol. 3, pp. 166–72.

77. Cited in ibid., vol. 3, pp. 181–82.

78. For the massacre of Les Lucs-sur-Boulogne see Martin, *La Vendée*, p. 308; Marie-Auguste Huchet, *Le massacre des Lucs-sur-Boulogne* (La Roche-sur-Yon: Delhommeau, 1983); Martin and Xavier Lardière, *Le massacre des Lucs: Vendée 1794* (Vouillé: Geste, 1992); Paul Tellonneau, *Les Lucs et le génocide vendéen: Comment on a manipulé les textes* (Luçon: Hécate, 1993).

79. Cited in Fournier, *Turreau*, pp. 74–76.

80. See Marie Clénet, *Les colonnes infernales* (Paris: Perrin, 1993), esp. ch. 15.

81. Cited in Fournier, *Turreau*, p. 100.

82. Cited in Savary, *Guerres des vendéens*, vol. 3, pp. 257–58.

83. Cited in ibid., vol. 3, pp. 316–17.

84. Cited in ibid., vol. 3, p. 320.

85. Cited in ibid., vol. 3, pp. 326–27.

86. Cited in Fournier, *Turreau*, p. 94.

87. Savary, *Guerres des vendéens*, vol. 3, p. 386.

88. Cited in ibid., vol. 3, pp. 394–400, esp. p. 397.

89. Cited in ibid., vol. 3, pp. 387–88.

90. Cited in ibid., vol. 3, pp. 419–22, 425–26.

91. Cited in ibid., vol. 3, pp. 469–71, 482–83.

92. Cited in Aulard, ed., *Recueil*, vol. 12, p. 389, p. 427, and pp. 469–70.

93. Cited in ibid., vol. 12, pp. 506–7.

94. Cited in ibid., vol. 12, pp. 607–8.

95. Cited in Savary, *Guerres des vendéens*, vol. 4, pp. 6–8.

96. Michelet, *Histoire*, pp. 707–9.

97. Ibid., p. 661.

98. Brégeon, *Carrier*, chs. 15 and 16; and Jacques Dupâquier, ed., *Carrier: Le procès d'un missionnaire de la terreur et du comité révolutionnaire de Nantes, 16 octobre–16 décembre 1794* (n.p.: Éditions des Etannets, 1994). See also Bronislaw Baczko, *Comment sortir de la terreur: Thermidor et la Révolution* (Paris: Gallimard, 1989), esp. pp. 194–207 and pp. 227–54.

99. Cited in Savary, *Guerres des vendéens*, vol. 3, pp. 575–76.

100. Cited in ibid., vol. 6, pp. 27–29.

101. Cited in Gérard, *La Vendée, 1789–1793*, p. 278.

102. Donald Greer, *The Incidence of the Terror during the French Revolution: A Statistical Interpretation* (Cambridge, Mass.: Harvard University Press, 1935).

103. Greer, *Incidence*, p. 14.

104. Ibid., p. 15.

105. Ibid., pp. 112–14.

106. Ibid., p. 115.

107. Ibid., p. 116.

108. Albert Mathiez, *La Révolution française*, vol. 3: *La terreur* (Paris: Denoël, 1985), p. 103.

109. Greer, *Incidence*, esp. pp. 65–70.

110. Ibid., p. 84, and pp. 120–21.

111. Ibid., p. 81, p. 85, and p. 124.

Peasant War in Russia:
Ukraine and Tambov

IN CONSIDERING the eruption of peasant resistance in the Russian Revolution from 1917 to 1921–22, two points need to be stressed at the outset. The first is the bare fact that in 1917 Russia was even more rural and agricultural than France in 1789. Close to 85 percent of the population lived in the countryside and made its living on or from the land. Even large sectors of the urban population were first-generation ex-peasants, with strong attachments to their native villages. Perforce the imperial army was a peasant army. In social, cultural, and religious terms, the world of the peasants was the world of their forefathers. Illiteracy also ran close to 85 percent, and the atmosphere was distinctly obscurantist, especially in the eyes of the urban elites. The magic and ritual of religion, as well as its comfort and terror, pervaded everyday life and bound the cake of custom.

There was nothing exceptional about European Russia, as well as parts of western Siberia, being swept by peasant protests and uprisings. After 1789, France had a single and geographically circumscribed Vendée, although this *jacquerie* had coincided with the federalist defiance of the great southern cities. In contrast, early revolutionary Russia saw four major and geographically dispersed peasant upheavals, in southern Ukraine, Tambov province, the lower Volga basin, and western Siberia, as well as minor uprisings in parts of the Caucasus, Belorussia, and central Asia. Besides, the peasant rebellions in Russia were not accompanied by any urban rebellions comparable to the defiance of Lyons, Marseilles, and Toulon. Many of European Russia's major cities were so intensely trapped in the military flux and reflux of the civil war, notably in the non-Russian peripheries, that they had no chance to affirm themselves. Changing hands a dozen

Area of Makhno Rebellion

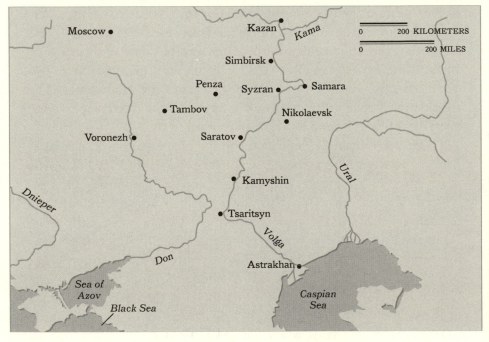

The Volga Region and Surrounding Area

times, Kiev was an object rather than subject of history, claimed as it was by Bolsheviks, Whites, and Poles, as well as by fledgling Ukrainian nationalists.[1] Of course, there was the Kronstadt rebellion in late winter 1921. But even this sizable sailors' mutiny on the small island fortress in the Gulf of Finland some twenty miles west of Petrograd was at least as much influenced by the still raging peasant tempest as by the concurrent workers' unrest in the ex-capital.[2]

Given Russia's larger size and population, it is not surprising that it should have had a larger number of peasant insurrections and rebels than revolutionary France. Overall the peasant bands and armies counted more fighting men than the White Guards. This is not to say, however, that between 1917 and 1922 most or all of peasant Russia was seething with rebellion, let alone up in arms in opposition to the new Bolshevik regime. Although the unrest was widespread, there was little if any military or political coordination even among those rare peasant armies that were somewhat organized. Still, here and there the magnitude and proficiency of these irregulars was such that especially when the Red Army was hard pressed by the White Guards or Polish armies, they momentarily assumed disproportionate importance. At the same time, the peasants had benefited enormously from the October Revolution; they were not about to help defeat the Bolshevik government, for fear of bringing back the old regime, which would be certain to undo the land settlement of 1917–18. Ironically, once the Whites were defeated, it was too late for the Greens to prevail. To be sure, just then the peasant insurgents were at the peak of their strength and primed for battle. But though exhausted from four years of grueling war and civil war, the Bolsheviks managed to muster sufficient forces and resources to defeat them.[3]

The second point that needs to be stated, or rather reiterated, is the conceptual premise that a revolution necessarily calls forth movements of anti- or counterrevolutionary resistance, including revolts by the revolution's disillusioned beneficiaries and fundamentalists. In Russia, even more than in France, at the creation the tillers of the soil were among not only the Revolution's principal beneficiaries but also its chief agents. It is not to minimize the premier role of Petrograd's workers, middle classes, and intelligentsia to insist on the importance of the peasants in the upheaval of 1917. Of course, the ironbound authority system first cracked in the capital. However, the soldiers who fraternized with the riotous crowds and disobeyed the order to shoot strikers in the capital were as much part of village Russia as the soldiers who deserted their regiments at the front and the peasants who seized land from gentry estates and public domains in rear areas. It is a measure of the agony of imperial Russia's *ancien régime* that the normally immutable and meek world of the muzhik, the bedrock of tsarism, should have become unbound. The peasant agitation which fueled the *grande peur* in 1789 was largely an echo of France's urban upheaval, and it was contained and defused by the astonishing abolition of feudal rights and privileges on August 4 and 11, with full respect for private property. In 1917, to the contrary, the peasants instantly emerged as full partners in Russia's great renewal, and their widespread and willful intervention, notably in European Russia, left an indelible mark on the incipient revolution.

Indeed, the spontaneous and formless rebellion of the peasants and peasant-soldiers quickened the dissolution of the ex-empire's essential but brittle centralizing control structures. It also struck both reformists and revolutionaries like a bolt from the blue. Prince Lvov and Alexander Kerensky were perplexed, and for both ideological and political reasons unwilling to face up to the pressing agrarian problem, leaving it to go from bad to worse. Although the Bolsheviks were no less bewildered and caught short by the peasant revolt, they met it by making it their own. Fully conscious of the antirevolutionary role of the peasants in the insurgency of the Vendée as well as in the repression of the European upheavals of 1848 and of the Paris Commune of 1871, Lenin sought to appease the turbulent rural world by satisfying the muzhik's putative land hunger.

The Bolsheviks gave their blessing to a peasant uprising against the landowners that was more far-reaching if less spectacular than the proletarian uprising against the urban notables, including the sparse bourgeoisie. In the year 1917 the petty peasantry seized some 108 million acres from 110,000 large landlords, and 140 million acres from two million smaller landowners. Large landed property was liquidated in favor of small peasant farms, increasing the average peasant holding by about 20 percent and cutting in half—from 16 to 8 percent—the number of landless peasant households by 1920.[4]

Lenin and his associates never really intended their revolution to favor the peasants. Neither Marxist theory nor the Bolshevik program had much to say about the contemporary peasant question. There was, to be sure, a general predisposition to collectivized, large-scale, and streamlined agriculture. But this broad objective, congruent with capitalist modernization and rationalization, was embedded in a worldview that was singularly insensitive to the mentality and condition of the peasant. As men of the city Lenin and the top Bolshevik leaders were steeped in the political and literary culture of Russia's twin capitals. For them, the industrial workers, not the peasants, were the heralds and carriers of the future. Marxists were impatient with the peasantry for being the substructure of the eternal and unyielding past. Following Marx, who, like Voltaire, disdained "the idiocy of rural life," the Bolsheviks considered the peasants half-savage, ignorant, and superstitious. They thought them, in addition, to be the Nemesis of culture and progress, not least because they were open to manipulation by the old ruling and governing classes. In the Marxist vision the peasantry had one major saving grace: the world of petty peasants, like that of petty shopkeepers and artisans, was destined to be reduced by the rush of capitalist and socialist modernization. This warped and condescending vision of the peasantry had prevented the Bolsheviks from striking root in the countryside before 1914, leaving the field to the Socialist Revolutionaries.[5]

In addition, the relationship between Bolsheviks and peasants was troubled by the sheer amplitude of the land seizures, which inordinately complicated Sovnarkom's efforts to consolidate power and restore sovereignty on a revolutionary basis. The vast redistribution and leveling of landholdings entailed a decline in productivity fatal for a broken nation caught up in foreign and civil war. Over and above the paralysis of trade and transport complicating the distribution of food, there was no incentive for peasants to produce a surplus for the market, since with the ruble in free fall, the price of consumer goods had risen beyond their reach. Like the Jacobins at the time of the French Revolution, the Bolsheviks were confronted with the difficult problem of provisioning the cities and armies—but unlike the Jacobins, they had to face it all at once, on a huge scale, and with uncertain access to vital breadbaskets such as Ukraine.

Given the Bolsheviks' resolve to fight *to the death* to hold on to power, they had no other recourse than to stiffen the war economy inherited from the tsarist regime which had aimed to make grain a state monopoly. In May 1918, with the declaration of a food emergency, Sovnarkom turned to rationing, price controls, and requisitioning. These measures became the foundation of War Communism, a scheme to simultaneously manage a political economy of extreme scarcity and take halting steps toward transforming it along socialist lines. But in this makeshift combination of contingent necessity and principled reform, the former was decisive. Precisely because the Bolsheviks were ideologically and politically unprepared to run an overheated war economy at the same time that they were tempted by the pathos of novelty, they plunged headlong into a search for a substitute for Russia's failing market and financial system. As may be expected, in a cumbersome and unhinged agricultural economy the procurement of food, notably grain, became the embattled Bolshevik regime's first politico-economic priority. In a reflex comparable to the one that had prompted the Jacobins to adopt the *maximum* in September 1793, the Bolsheviks arbitrarily fixed prices and delivery targets, which they soon backed by hard-driving requisitioning brigades and harsh penalties for speculators and black marketeers. Marxist scorn for the free market's regulation of supply and demand probably inclined them to resort to administered prices and quotas, enforced by the cudgel. But this does not mean that they sidelined the market as part of a calculated drive to recast Russia's economy in accordance with a nebulous socialist blueprint. Clearly it was less the Bolshevik leaders' preexistent Marxist intentions than their preconceptions about rural and peasant Russia that disposed them to consider the mandatory extraction of grain from the villages the most promising way to relieve the starvation stalking the cities, all the more so since they looked to the beneficiaries of the great agrarian settlement of 1917–18 to be cooperative. Besides, they thought they could use the muzhik's legendary submissiveness to advance his own liberation. And once the Bolsheviks met with peasant resistance, they were confident that the mere threat of force could break it.

✻ ✻ ✻

The principal fuel for all the peasant revolts, without exception, was indignation and protest against the imposition of seemingly unjust prices and exorbitant quotas, compounded by the forced collection of food and impressment for occasional hard labor. This protest turned into active opposition once Red Army units and special requisitioning detachments proceeded to apply increasingly ruthless methods of procurement.[6]

To prevail in their uphill struggle for survival, the Bolsheviks needed to extract from the countryside not only food for the cities and armed forces but also conscripts and horses for the Red Army. As the civil war dragged on, ever more peasants were drafted for military service far from home. As at the time of the French Revolution, the escalating duress and frenzy of war and civil war revolutionized the Revolution. Increasingly coercive food procurement and military conscription triggered and radicalized resistance in village and province, not least because the grain collectors and recruiting agents were distrusted for coming from distant and hostile parts. The fact that these outside officials were Great Russians and urban workers ignorant and contemptuous of local customs and languages merely sharpened the animosity which greeted them.

Yet in spite of all these stresses and strains, the marriage of convenience between Bolsheviks and peasants lasted as long as the counterrevolution threatened and wrought havoc. The White Guards, like the Red Army, lived off the land, pillaged, and requisitioned livestock; and their persistent imperial pretense alienated the nascent political classes of the non-Russian borderlands. Furthermore, the Bolsheviks had a clear policy of granting the land to the peasants; the Whites, for class reasons, sidestepped the land issue, but their actions spoke louder than their equivocations: in territories "liberated" or reconquered by them, the old landed notables readily repossessed their lands. With good reason "the peasants usually regarded the Reds as the lesser of two evils for fear that the Whites, if victorious, would reinstate the landowners."[7] Before long at least 80 percent of the rapidly growing Red Army's recruits were peasants, and despite massive desertions, their willingness to fight and sacrifice their lives was crucial for the Revolution's survival. By and large the showdown between rebel peasants and Bolshevik rulers was suspended or postponed until after the defeat of the Whites. Meanwhile "the system [of War Communism] did work: it got food to the cities and to the armies, saved the Revolution, and prevented famine."[8]

In and of itself the victory over the counterrevolution did not bring the reestablishment of Russia's single and unifying political and legal sovereignty which had cracked in 1917. Rather, the civil war had two phases. The first phase involved, mainly, the struggle between, on the one hand, the Bolsheviks and, on the other, the counterrevolutionary Whites and their foreign backers. This phase came to an end, as we saw, with the defeat of Wrangel, in November 1920, following the war with Poland. The second phase, which overlapped to some extent with the first, consisted essentially of the struggle between the Soviet regime and the antirevolutionary peasant insurgencies. This second phase reached its peak starting in the fall of 1920, hence after the end of the first phase.

Once the first phase of the civil war concluded, Moscow was in a position to reinforce its military and security forces in the regions of major peasant unrest. Indeed, one of the reasons for the initial successes of the peasant *jacqueries* was the sparsity of Bolshevik political cadres as well as military, security, and Cheka forces in much of rural Russia. Overall the administrative and judicial apparatus was even more wasted in 1920 than in 1917. Once the Soviets were free to take on the antirevolution they were bound to get the upper hand, especially since the major peasant rebellions remained isolated from each other and had no links to the world outside Russia.

Meanwhile, however, the peasant resistance capitalized on the infantile disorders of the successor party-state. In critical areas the vacuum of power offered an unexpected opportunity to "reclaim" the personal and communal liberties of an idealized past as a hedge against the reimposition, by Russia's new regime, of central controls complete with levies of imposts and men. In the case of the rebellion headed by Nestor Makhno in southeastern Ukraine, this bid for the recovery of a golden age was leavened by the allure of self-governing and communitarian peasant anarchism concordant with Bakunin's and Kropotkin's vision. In fact, to the extent that the rural rebellions had a social and political agenda it was, paradoxically, to save the essence of the Bolshevik land settlement of 1917–18 favoring small holders and local soviets.

All along and nearly everywhere, military desertion played a considerable role in this antirevolution. Whereas in 1917 peasant soldiers defected from the sclerotic Imperial Army to defy overbearing officers and seize land, starting in 1918 they deserted from the new-model Red Army, some to escape military service, others to join an active resistance. These latest runaways melted into the woodlands of their native up-country, where they joined draft dodgers who formed small bands living off the land and by plunder. These so-called Greens were hidebound and fervent provincials rather than knowing or zealous anti-Bolsheviks.[9] Eventually a great many of them became involved in "spontaneous [and] . . . generally short-lived and easily suppressed . . . village uprisings . . . against local officials, often accompanied by lynch law (*samosud*), pillage, and violent acts of vengeance."[10] Lenin claimed that during the civil war such risings were "a permanent feature of the general Russian scene."[11]

Here and there isolated village uprisings spread to neighboring hamlets and villages, and mushroomed into full-scale *jacqueries*. In the process the leaders of these would-be revolts "developed sophisticated forms of political and military organization, within which local SRs and the odd White Army officer were able to play a subsidiary role." In the rural districts or provinces where these risings originated, the peasants were enraged, as noted, by the exactions of tax and food collectors as well as of army recruiters, backed by the arm of terror. In any case, these revolts were also readily smothered, not least because the rebels had only pitchforks, scythes, and pikes with which to face the firearms of government forces.[12]

Although there were significant differences among the several large-scale peasant insurgencies, they shared important features peculiar to modern guerrilla warfare in terms of deployment, tactics, and weapons, as well as of social matrix and political pretense. Not that any of them, with the partial exception of the Makhno-led uprising, ever was of major consequence. Still, their incipient coherence accounts as much for their relative staying power as their regional expansion and their sizable hosts of peasants and Greens. But then again, for the most part, and characteristically, the field of vision of all the peasant insurgencies, including the most structured ones, was distinctly local, at best regional, and their temper was patently antimodern. This dual myopia showed forth in the rebels' predilection for wrecking railway and telegraph lines, which they considered emblematic of the corrosive intrusion of the outside world driven and accelerated by science and technology.[13]

❋ ❋ ❋

Of all the peasant uprisings in the Russian Revolution, the one led by Makhno was of greatest consequence. Over time his bands and brigades of irregulars ran not into the hundreds or thousands but the tens of thousands. More or less consciously they rallied to the black flag of anarchist self-liberation as well as self-sufficient and cooperative land ownership. Makhno's partisans fought whoever tried to thwart their age-old dream, in broad but disconnected patches of open country in southeastern Ukraine between the Don in the east and the lower Dniester in the west, Ekaterinoslav in the north and the Sea of Azov in the south. This region of Ukraine kept changing hands during the civil war, which meant that the Makhnovites more or less consecutively battled the Austro-German armies; the Ukrainian hetmans Skoropatsky, Petliura, and Grigorev; the White Guards; and the Red Army. With the start of the counterrevolution early in 1918 the Whites, many of whose main bases and lifelines of Allied support were located precisely along the northern coastlines of the Black Sea, became Makhno's sworn enemies, since they meant to restore the reign of both Great Russians and great landowners. This priority was so absolute that Makhno even joined with the Bolsheviks to defeat Denikin's consolidation of White control of the Black Sea coast in 1918 and his northward push against the Red heartland in 1919. The Bolsheviks did not become the categorical enemy until after the defeat of Wrangel in late 1920. This sequence was implicit in the motto "[b]eat the Whites until they're Red, beat the Reds until they're Black."[14]

Born into a poor peasant family in Ekaterinoslav province, just north of the Crimea, in 1889, at the age of twenty-eight Makhno started serving a twenty-year sentence for terrorist activities in a Moscow prison, where he picked up the essentials of peasant anarchism. Set free by the first Provisional Government, he returned to his native land, notably to the Gulai Pole region, southeast of Ekaterinoslav, to organize local artisans and press for the expropriation of big landowners and large peasant proprietors. As noted, he first fought Skoropatsky and his Austro-German patrons. By mid-1918 Makhno began to organize peasant bands, and as of the end of the year these helped the Red Army fight first Petliura and then Denikin. During the spring and early summer of 1919, with an apparent standoff between the Reds and Whites, Makhno, who was allergic to discipline and authority, balked the unified military controls which the Bolsheviks meant to impose on him. He also protested their requisitions and their betrayal of their own principles of peasant economy, local self-government, and national self-determination. To back his remonstrance Makhno ordered some of his 20,000 irregulars to harass the Red Army's military and supply operations.

At this same time, in early May 1919, the chief of the other major peasant insurgency in Ukraine also turned against the Bolsheviks. Nikifor Grigorev was an unprincipled, not to say nihilist guerrilla leader whose host of some 15,000 men was deployed south of the Dnieper in central Ukraine, halfway between Psatikhatki and Uman, north of Makhno's base of operations. He, too, had at first collaborated with the Reds. But now, at the height of the civil war between the Reds and the Whites, he proposed to throw in his lot with the counterrevolution. Grigorev issued a proclamation fiercely assailing both Bolsheviks and Jews, whom he conflated, as his partisans moved out in all directions, with the result that before long they were drawn dangerously thin. Their retaliation for being defeated by the Red Army included avenging pogroms against the Jews, the fiercest of them in Elisavetgrad.

In the meantime, however, Grigorev had approached Makhno to make common cause and join forces. Makhno demurred, since he would neither collaborate with the Whites nor countenance pogroms, even if some of his associated hetmans and cossack bands were prepared to do so. In turn, the Bolsheviks called on Makhno to publicly decry Grigorev as part of their effort to get him to resume collaborating with the Red Army against Denikin. On May 10, 1919, Leo Kamenev, Lenin's representative on mission in the Ukraine, wired Makhno that with Grigorev "refusing to carry out . . . battle orders and . . . turning his coat, the decisive moment has come: either you march with Russia's workers and peasants or you will in effect open the front to the enemy." Insisting that this was no time for hesitation, Kamenev warned that his failure to condemn Grigorev and to answer this summons would "be taken as a declaration of war."[15] In his response, Makhno vowed to continue fighting the Whites, but reiterated that in so doing he would be "fight[ing] for the freedom of the people . . . [and not] for governmental power or for the baseness of political charlatans" responsible for "institutions of violence, such as your

Commissariats and Chekas, which commit arbitrary violence against the working masses."[16]

In mid-1919 central and southeastern Ukraine was in turmoil, and Ukrainian national authority failed to get a solid footing, all the more so with Makhno spurning it. The Reds were forced to fight Grigorev and court Makhno at the same time that they were at grips with the Whites. Denikin benefited from this war behind the Bolshevik lines. During the summer his armies advanced to Kharkov and toward Moscow, with a subsidiary drive in the direction of Rostov, at the same time that Kolchak was sending his forces from western Siberia into the Volga region, which would not be halted and driven back until June.

The Makhnovites spared no effort to hold off the counterrevolutionary forces, which were closing in on them. But the Bolsheviks distrusted Makhno, convinced that whoever was not fully with them was against them. When Makhno summoned a congress of his supporters for June 15 to decide future policy, Moscow banned it. Insisting that there was "no room for 'Greens' in this war," Trotsky preferred "an open White-Guard enemy . . . [to] a low-down 'Green' traitor who crouches . . . in the woods until the Denikins approach, when he sticks his knife in the back of the revolutionary fighters."[17] Presently Trotsky accused Makhno's partisans of having seized critical supplies intended for the Red Army. More peremptory than Kamenev a few weeks before, Trotsky thundered that the time had come to put an end to such "anarchist-kulak abuse" and alleged that to "scratch a Makhno follower . . . [was to] find a Grigorevite."[18] All remaining ties between Makhno and the Red Army were broken.

Caught between the hammer and the anvil of the two archenemies in Russia's civil war, Makhno hung in doubt.[19] Pressed by both sides, he and some of his followers decided to retreat northwestward in the direction of Grigorev's territory, whose partisans were also being forced to give ground. Although Makhno had recently rebuffed Grigorev's overtures, he now proposed a meeting with a view to either come to an agreement or outwit him. Apparently the idea was to join the two partisan movements in a single host, with Grigorev assuming the military command and Makhno the political direction. But the gulf between them would be difficult to bridge. Grigorev refused to recognize any enemies on the right, which meant that he was prepared to collaborate with Denikin to defeat the Bolsheviks. He also persisted in his visceral and militant anti-Judaism. On both points Makhno was intractable. With his call for a plague on both houses falling on deaf ears, Makhno had to recognize that ultimately he conceived of his struggle in social-revolutionary, not counterrevolutionary terms. In addition, he persisted in his repugnance for anti-Semitism. He had several Jews in his military and political directorate and acted together with several Jewish self-defense units. Especially in the wake of Grigorev's monstrous anti-Jewish massacre in Elisavetgrad, Makhno made an explicit disavowal of pogromism a prerequisite for cooperation.

These issues were to be aired on July 26 or 27 at a mass meeting in the village of Sentovo, just north of Elisavetgrad. Coming from the neighboring provinces of central Ukraine, some 20,000 partisans and peasants sworn to agrarian resistance assembled to witness a public debate about which course to follow. Grigorev was the first to speak. He reiterated his position about the absolute priority of defeating the Bolsheviks and driving them out of Ukraine. One of Makhno's lieutenants was the second speaker. He was in the midst of criticizing Grigorev's position when rhetorical jousting gave way to bloody guerrilla theater. Allegedly Grigorev, enraged by the remarks of his respondent, reached for his revolver. But some of Makhno's chief acolytes, presumably forewarned, were quicker to draw. Their shots wounded Grigorev, and Makhno himself is said to have rushed forward to fire the *coup de grâce*.

Without the least delay Makhno's partisans encircled Sentovo and disarmed Grigorev's men. Several Grigorevites were put to death in full view of the assembly, and the rest were urged to join their would-be confederates. For all intents and purposes, hereafter Makhno's movement was the only organized, peasant-based antirevolutionary resistance in Ukraine, now concentrated in Grigorev's erstwhile base of operations. But notwithstanding his political ascendancy, Makhno was unable to consolidate and expand his mastery on the left bank of the Dnieper. In late August 1919, soon after being surrounded by White troops west of Uman, he and some of his men managed to break free and head for his homeland around Gulai Pole.

In the coming months Makhno won support among peasants who had experienced the momentary return, in the train of the Whites, of the old landed and governing elites. At the same time he took advantage of the fact that most of Denikin's forces were engaged in the drive on Moscow, which was about to falter. Meeting with little opposition, in October Makhno briefly managed to occupy several cities near Gulai Pole: Berdiansk and Mariupol to the south and southeast, on the Sea of Azov, and Alexandrovsk and Nikopol to the northwest. Late that month his troops for several weeks also took possession of Ekaterinoslav, the administrative seat of the province of some 110,000 inhabitants which included Gulai Pole. Upon seizing control of this manufacturing and transportation center, Makhno issued a proclamation granting "all political parties and organizations complete freedom to spread their ideas" but also warning that none of these would be permitted "to prepare, organize, or impose political power upon the toiling people." His embryonic government promised to guarantee peasants and workers self-government "from the bottom up," with safeguards against the encroachment of outside powers.[20]

Evidently Makhno was a man of many or no seasons. He was both parochial and tolerant, wild and temperate. In the whirlwind that swept through eastern Europe he spurned becoming either a born-again Great Russian or a new-model Ukrainian nationalist. At the same time he denounced the political instrumentalization of anti-Judaism from within the heartland of pogroms. Shortly before his showdown with Grigorev he had admonished his partisans that among them "there was no place for those who seek, under cover of the revolutionary insurrection, to satisfy their instinct for profit, violence, or looting at the expense of the peaceful Jewish population" which had suffered martyrdom through the ages. On this same occasion he reminded them that their "enemies as well as those of the entire people are [not only] the rich bourgeoisie, be they Russian, Ukrainian, or Jewish, . . . [but also] all those who defend the unjust regime of the bourgeoisie, such as Soviet commissars, members of repressive expeditionary forces, and extraordinary commissions, who go from town to town and village to village, torturing the toiling people who refuse to submit to their arbitrary rule and dictatorship." And just as these usurpers should be "arrested and, . . . in case of resistance, . . . shot on the spot, . . . [so all perpetrators of] violence against the peaceful toilers of any nationality . . . should be punished with death."[21]

Not that in this time of civil war the Makhnovites themselves were altogether harmless. They had briefly, for a week, entered Ekaterinoslav once before, in December 1918. At that time they had burned "archives, records, and libraries," as well as "shops and bazaars . . . in the streets adjacent to the railroad station," with Makhno expressing his "city-hatred" by himself "firing . . . a three-inch cannon . . . point blank into the tallest and most beautiful buildings."[22] Both then and later the partisans made a special point of destroying jails and engaging in widespread looting. The scale and intensity of their retributive violence against political enemies remains undetermined.

Makhno's situation changed radically in the autumn of 1919, when Denikin's batallions retreating before Trotsky's legions, put to flight and broke up Makhno's forces. This military reversal hastened the end of Makhno's incongruous domination of so many hateful and uncongenial cities, which were in any case about to be seized by the advancing Red Army. By this time, having momentarily thwarted the Whites to the east and south, the Bolsheviks were gearing up to repel Pilsudski's forces advancing from the west. Moscow called on Makhno to join the battle on the Polish front. He refused, and in mid-January 1920 he and his movement were outlawed. For much of the remainder of the year the Reds and the Makhnovites were locked in a fierce and violent struggle in which neither side showed mercy.

But once again the Bolsheviks and Makhnovites suspended hostilities in order to stand together against their common enemy: from early October through mid-November 1920 they joined forces to fight General Wrangel, whose offensive was the Whites' desperate last throw of the dice. Wrangel's troops advanced into Makhno's home base, capturing Alexandrovsk and Sinelnikovo, respectively southwest and northwest of Ekaterinoslav, which now was endangered as well. Even so, Makhno rebuffed Wrangel's proposal for "common action against the Soviets by hanging the unfortunate envoy who brought it to him."[23] Instead, true to himself, he offered to temporarily put his warriors under the field command of the Red Army. In exchange, Moscow agreed to respect Makhno's full control of his own troops, to amnesty anarchist prisoners, and to grant a considerable degree of political freedom.[24]

Michael Frunze, the commander of the Red Army's southern front, promptly ordered Makhno to "seize the Gulai Pole area and pursue the retreating enemy," a singularly welcome assignment.[25] All in all, however, Makhno's partisan brigades played a considerably lesser role in Wrangel's than Denikin's defeat. In any case, on all fronts the drive against the counterrevolutionaries moved swiftly, Wrangel having overextended his forces in a sweeping all-or-nothing offensive. By November 15, following the water-borne evacuation of retreating Whites, the Red Army captured Sevastopol and began to invest the Crimea. Not long before, having regained much (though by no means all) of the territory lost in the west, Moscow had also made peace with Warsaw.

The final defeat of the White counterrevolution opened the terminal phase in the struggle between the Bolsheviks and Makhno's anarcho-peasant antirevolutionaries, their mutual suspicion and hostility precluding an accommodation. Makhno was not about to bend the knee to centralized Bolshevik rule any more than Lenin and Trotsky were prepared to bear with the survival and consolidation of an anarchist stronghold around Gulai Pole. Incidentally, at the time no government would "long [have] tolerate[d] an independent or autonomous area within its borders," particularly not Lenin's "authoritarian state," which was determined to assert its all-out sovereignty.[26]

Unburdened of their White and Polish enemies, in late November 1920 the Bolshevik leaders once again outlawed the Makhnovites and ordered the Red Army to bring them to heel at the same time that the Cheka proceeded to arrest and execute several prominent anarchists in Kharkov.[27]

Characteristically the critical military engagements took place in the Gulai Pole region, which was Makhno's principal bastion, and also both defined and circumscribed his narrow political, social, and strategic vision. Indeed, "the village of Gulai Pole, which passed from one side to the other several times, [was] to suffer the most."[28] When the Red Army occupied the village, Makhno managed to escape. Although he reclaimed it for several hours in early December, thereafter an ever smaller number of his men carried out hit-and-run attacks when not scrambling to elude Red forces. With time more and more combatants and supporters became weary of an increasingly futile cause. In late August 1921 Makhno and a band of some 250 mounted partisans finally "gave up the struggle as hopeless" and crossed the Dniester river into Rumania.[29]

Throughout their verbal and military struggle—except during their brief cooperation against Wrangel—both Reds and Greens resorted to terror. Probably the terror was more systematic on the Bolshevik than the rebel side. In their search-and-destroy operations, as well as their punitive expeditions, the Reds arrested and executed proven and suspected peasant insurgents and their fellow travelers, not a few of whom were also taken hostage. Since the partisans usually faded into the countryside as soon as Soviet troops drew near, more often than not the latter "defeated, captured, or shot . . . not insurgents of Makhno's army but local peasants . . . who sympathized with [them]." According to one of Makhno's lieutenants, the Bolshevik retribution "contained all the symptoms of terror inherent in a ruling caste." Whenever the Soviets did "not shoot prisoners on the spot, they imprisoned and subjected [them] to all types of torture so as to force them to repudiate the movement, to denounce their comrades, and to join the police."[30] The Red military and security forces, including the Cheka, proceeded in like manner in the insurgent zones of the Volga and western Siberia. A Soviet newspaper reported that in Saratov "repressive measures were . . . curing the population of its sympathies" for the rebels, with the result that it was "obediently" ferreting out and handing over the "bandits" and their arms caches. According to an eyewitness, beyond the Urals "the Chekists hit the village clergy particularly hard, . . . executing more than a hundred priests . . . in the Diocese of Tobolsk alone."[31]

The Greens, for their part, "replied to the Bolshevik terror with blows no less severe."[32] The objective of many of their raids was to eliminate the entire local leadership of their Red enemies. They "killed all the Communist Party members they could catch, all Cheka and Militia members, and all officials of the Committee of the Poor and of food requisitioning organizations." Although as a rule Makhno's partisans set free captured Red Army soldiers, they shot their officers, "unless the rank and file interceded strongly on their behalf."[33] The degree of needless savagery attending this violence is still uncertain. Apparently excesses were confined to operations in towns and cities—in an overnight raid on Berdiansk the partisans allegedly killed 83 Communists.[34] Presumably, the opposition in the countryside "rarely justified . . . nastier" methods. While some of the Makhnovite killings "were as brutal as those of their enemies, . . . it cannot be said that they . . . [were carried out] with the same methodical cruelty."[35]

The Makhnovite antirevolution in the Russian Revolution invites comparison with the Vendean antirevolution in the French Revolution. One of the more striking differences is the Ukrainian Greens' embrace of anarcho-agrarianism and equalized land ownership; it was this social radicalism which largely accounts for their becoming a beacon of hope for so many peasants and workers who were disenchanted with the Bolsheviks for having betrayed their original promise. But there are some other equally noteworthy dissimilarities: church, religion, and priest seem not to have played a major role among the Greens; there were practically no old-regime military or civilian notables in the leadership; and the rebels neither expected nor solicited help from émigrés or foreign powers. Even so, the family resemblances are no less telling than these dissimilarities. Both the Vendée and Gulai Pole were geographically remote, and the two insurgencies were and remained distinctly regional, exploiting the breakdown of sovereignty, the vacuum of power, and the collapse of the judiciary. The primitive rebels of 1792–94 in France and of 1918–21 in Russia were less newly sworn anti-Jacobins and anti-Bolsheviks than quintessential champions of a perennial provincial world against the forever invasive distant state and nearby city, whose agents became intolerably intrusive once they exceeded the traditional norms governing the levy of taxes, collection of grain, and conscription of peasants. Construing this encroachment as an affront to their time-honored belief system and self-rule, the Vendeans and Makhnovites closed ranks around local customs, institutions, and memories. As for their terror, while it was less systematic than that of their Jacobin and Bolshevik foes, it was no less ferocious. Nor was it less immanent to their cause for being spontaneous and "primitive." Neither side was innocent and, as in all civil wars, terror and counter-terror were, in the main, fatally interactive and avenging. Still, and to repeat, all things considered, the Vendean uprising eventually assumed a distinct counterrevolutionary thrust; the Makhnovite insurgency remained an essentially local if expansive *jacquerie* of olden times.

Compared to Grigorev and to Alexander Antonov, the peasant leader in Tambov, Makhno was tactically much more astute and flexible and hence relatively resilient. He practiced an uneven mixture of regular warfare and wild "banditry," and his versatility gave him a distinct advantage, even if it is not clear whether it was a matter of careful design or hectic improvisation. Though standing against the modern world, Makhno's men fought with not only pitchforks and cudgels but rifles and machine guns. While it had no truck with ex-tsarist officers, the Makhno resistance attracted not a few deserters from the Red Army, even if the hoped-for massive crossover of seasoned soldiers never materialized. Although all calculations of the fluctuating number of partisans are approximate, according to one reasonable estimate, at its "peak in the autumn of 1919" Makhno's host of chiefly poor peasants counted some 40,000 fighters, of whom 15,000 were foot soldiers, 10,000 mounted infantrymen, 5,000 auxiliaries, and 10,000 "on the sick list, mostly with typhus."[36]

But ultimately, precisely because he exulted in the not inconsiderable support of the ambient peasantry, Makhno was blind to his weakness: lacking an overall strategic military and political vision, he remained, above all, fatally isolated. To be sure, he advocated local self-rule and small individual landholding. Makhno never did, however, "clearly say where he stood in relation to Bolshevik land policy as a whole" and how he proposed to fit his anarchist peasant republic of participatory democracy into either a nascent post-tsarist Russia or an at best embryonically independent Ukraine.[37]

✻ ✻ ✻

The second major *jacquerie* was centered in and around Tambov, in the Penza *guberniya*, or province, some 250 miles southeast of Moscow. Eventually Antonov emerged as its most distinctive and effective military leader. Although of petit-bourgeois background, like Makhno he was very much a man of the back country. The villages, small towns, and open fields around the administrative city of Tambov were to him what those around Ekaterinoslav were to Makhno. Compared to the latter's operational lands, Antonov's were more fertile and wooded, as well as much more densely populated, making for an ample supply of labor. While the radical land reform of 1917–18 fired the expectations of the poor peasants at the expense of the very rich, who were driven out, the continuing exactions of war and civil war precluded early economic gains.[38]

Antonov had joined the Socialist Revolutionaries in his youth. A few years after 1905 he was sentenced to twelve years in Siberia, but apparently for robbery, not political opposition. Amnestied in the first dawn of 1917, he returned to his native province, where he drifted into a local militia in the Kirsanov district. The Provisional Government's evasion of agrarian reform prompted Antonov to shift to the Left Socialist Revolutionaries in the manner in which Makhno embraced active peasant anarchism. Following the Left SRs' stillborn risings in the summer of 1918, Antonov fell out with the Bolsheviks. Seeking cover in the forests, he helped form a small peasant band which in the summer of 1919 killed several score Bolshevik activists. By this time the civil war between Reds and Whites had given rise to the forced collection of grain and the military draft, stimulating unrest in the countryside. Antonov proceeded to recruit among draft resisters, army deserters, and irate peasants.[39]

Paradoxically, despite the strength of the Socialist Revolutionaries in the Tambov region, Antonov's insurgency had even less of a clearcut political agenda than Makhno's. Antonov not only had cast in his lot with the Socialist Revolutionaries before 1905 but had switched to their left-wing faction in 1917. One and all were sworn to a peasantism embedded in an "instinctive" distrust, if not hatred, of the city as well as of the city-oriented political class, including the Bolsheviks. Although the Socialist Revolutionaries, not the Bolsheviks, had struck roots in Tambov province, and although the Union of the Working Peasantry, the political agency of the insurrection, issued a program of Socialist Revolutionary coloration, Antonov never really embraced or espoused it. However, even if for prudential reasons—the Bolsheviks had taken several Socialist Revolutionaries hostage—the "national," regional, and local leaders of the party avoided direct involvement with the uprising, they could hardly hide their sympathy for it. Besides, its members, on their own account, were active as advisors, partisans, and covert collaborators. While the Socialist Revolutionaries certainly did not mastermind the Tambov insurgency as the Bolsheviks charged, there is no denying their implication in it. The contrary would have been surprising, for their peasant-focused revolutionary consciousness sensitized them to the rebels' plight and plaint, especially in a time of acute misery.[40]

There were, of course, significant differences between the Makhno and Antonov risings. Unlike Antonov, Makhno forged his movement and its intentions before he broke with the Soviet regime, and thereafter intermittently collaborated with it. In addition, geographically he ranged farther from his original operating base, so that compared to Antonov he was marginally less parochial and inconstant, perhaps because of his immanent social concerns. But at bottom the peasant revolts in southeastern Ukraine and in Tambov province, as well as those in the lower Volga and western Siberia, were cut of the same cloth. Besides practicing identical guerrilla tactics, they all had essentially similar if not identical causes, dynamics, social carriers, sympathizers, and outcomes.

But the Tambov uprising did not really explode until late summer or early fall 1920, well after the defeat of Denikin, in which Antonov had had no part. Because of a poor harvest the peasants were doubly disinclined to part with their grain; at the same time, in face of the shortfall, the Bolsheviks set altogether unrealistic delivery targets. Presently the arrival of the heavily armed and intermittently venal requisitioning detachments triggered spontaneous peasant counteractions which were surprisingly successful on account of the obvious dearth of Bolshevik cadres and security forces in the region. Since the rising coincided with Pilsudski's counterattack against Tukhachevsky, Wrangel's lunge out of the Crimea, and Makhno's intractability, Moscow had few divisions to spare. Antonov crisscrossed the Tambov area to encourage villagers to either resist or attack Bolshevik collection brigades, with the result that before long the peasants looked to him "as the invincible avenger of their violated interests."[41]

At the outset the Bolsheviks were overwhelmed both politically and militarily, making them all the more determined and fierce. Counting the local Cheka units, which were bolstered by December, "the Soviet forces in Tambov province numbered 3500 men."[42] These had to face a fast-spreading wildfire of peasant furies.

Tambov's antirevolutionary rebels never congealed into an organized guerrilla army. Many if not most of their actions were impulsive. Although the city of Tambov, unlike Ekaterinoslav, was never invested or captured, at one point the peasants did advance upon it. Apparently this particular host of *pieds-nus*, armed with farm tools and accompanied by women and children, was in the nature of a "procession both threatening and defenseless, snowballing . . . as more peasants joined upon hearing church bells proclaiming the marchers' approach." Although some Red soldiers, touched by the "ancient and honorable" aspects of this remonstrance, deserted to join the Greens, Bolshevik military and security forces "dispersed . . . the procession ten kilometers from Tambov," killing dozens of marchers "by machine gun fire."[43]

Eventually, starting in late fall and early winter 1920–21, the forces on both sides assumed sizable proportions. At the height of the Tambov uprising the partisan bands of the irregular Green Army consisted of between 20,000 and 40,000 full-time peasant fighters with considerable support at the grass roots.[44] In turn, when Tukhachevsky assumed command of the Tambov region in the spring of 1921—after having directed the rollback of the Poles, the defeat of Wrangel, and the assault on the Kronstadt rebels—he disposed of "more than 50,000 regular troops, three armored trains, three armored units, several mobile machine-gun units, about seventy field guns, hundreds of machine guns, and an aircraft unit."[45]

Even if their numbers were impressive, the partisans were at a distinct disadvantage. Compared to the Red Army, Antonov's brigades, even more than Makhno's, were poorly trained, officered, and armed. To boot, each band mounted its own hit-and-run raids against Bolshevik grain requisitioning squads or punitive detachments. While there was a tactical advantage to such pinprick surprise strikes, the partisans paid a heavy price for the want of military coordination and the absence of a clear political program, a dual deficit rooted in ageless localism. Needless to say, the Greens of Tambov never even thought of linking up with rebels in adjoining provinces, of whom they were totally unaware. This psychologically and culturally conditioned parochialism also explains their having kept away from the alien and threatening cities, which the Bolsheviks managed to keep under their control.[46]

This peasant war was fought with the utmost ruthlessness by Reds and Greens alike. Both gave measure for measure, and were as likely to be avengers as re-avengers. There may have been a qualitative difference in the nonmilitary violence wrought by the opposing camps: "an excess of torture on the side of the Greens, an excess of killing on the side of the Reds." The greater recourse to raw brutality by the rebels may have been due not only to their having been the "weaker party in numbers or in weapons" but also to their having come of age in traditional societies with peculiar cultures and collective memories of "primitive" violence. This is not to suggest that the Reds' violence was altogether "modern," since there were several instances of Bolsheviks savagely flogging, mutilating, and burying peasants.[47]

The Red repression began in December 1920, following Wrangel's collapse. Disquieted by the Tambov uprising, Lenin charged Dzerzhinsky with heading up a special commission to speed and intensify the drive to crush it. Almost simultaneously Bukharin was asked to propose noncoercive measures. On February 2, 1921 he won the support of the Politburo for "a reduction in the confiscation of produce in order to relieve the peasants."[48]

Evidently Moscow resolved to sharpen the use of the mailed fist while exploring ways to appease the restless peasants throughout the realm. Indeed, this was the time that Lenin conceded that with Russia drained and the industrial proletariat a tiny minority, should a teeming and defiant peasantry ever provide the mainstay of a counterrevolutionary front, it would be far more "dangerous than Denikin, Iudenich, and Kolchak put together."[49]

Presently Vladimir Antonov-Ovseenko, who had helped seize the Winter Palace and headed Petrograd's Military Revolutionary Committee, was sent to Tambov to take command of the security and Cheka forces which were being battered by Antonov's partisans. He promptly decided to renew the local political cadres and reinforce the military effectives in preparation for a full-scale and uncompromising pacification campaign.[50] In March and April 1921 his staff drew up lists of rebels, devised a hostage system, and sought to set poor peasants against kulaks.[51] But these steps turned out to be unequal to the task. As early as December 20, 1920, the commander of the Internal Security forces had forewarned Dzerzhinsky that in order to "liquidate Antonov's bands it [would be] necessary to flood the area of rebellion with troops so as to saturate it with a total occupation."[52]

Following the defeat of the Whites, the Bolsheviks diverted additional army and security forces to the Tambov region. By March 1921

Moscow's "military strength . . . stood at 32,500 infantry and 8000 cavalry, besides artillery and machine guns."[53] As a further sign of its concern and resolve, on April 27 the Politburo appointed Tukhachevsky to take command of military operations. On July 16, 1921, after two months on the ground, Tukhachevsky informed Lenin that in Tambov the "causes of the uprising were the same as throughout the entire RSFSR, i.e., dissatisfaction with the clumsy and exceptionally harsh enforcement of the policy of food requisitioning." Besides the danger of the revolt spreading to neighboring provinces, "in five districts of Tambov province the Soviet regime no longer exists." Tukhachevsky wanted his superiors to know that with "a total of up to 21,000 bandits . . . the action to be undertaken had to be considered not as some sort of more or less protracted operation but as an entire campaign, or even a war."[54] In this same dispatch he also insisted, however, that in addition to "extracting bandit elements implanted in revolutionary committees . . . [and] applying terrorist methods against bandit sympathizers," the local Soviet authorities should "split up the peasantry by . . . arming it against the bandits while at the same time providing it with a material interest in the shape of property confiscated from them."[55]

Clearly Tukhachevsky and Antonov-Ovseenko were working hand-in-glove. On June 1, 1921, they issued Order No. 130 directing that in reprisal for "Green holdouts," their families be taken hostage and held "in concentration camps, [soon to be] followed by exile and confiscation of property." This decree also prescribed the death penalty for anyone caught concealing weapons and "for the senior breadwinner of any household in which a weapon is found." While Red military and security forces successfully pacified village after village, they soon realized that more and more rebels managed to vanish into the countryside, thereby raising the specter of their regrouping to resurface before long.[56]

This specter prompted Tukhachevsky and Antonov-Ovseenko, in accord with Moscow, to raise the pressure still further. On June 11 they issued Order No. 171 mandating the establishment of a reign of terror based on collective guilt and punishment. The aim was to deracinate every last rebel. In a preamble, the order praised Soviet troops for having "defeated and dispersed Antonov's bands" and Soviet power for having "reestablished order in the countryside . . .

[and] the peaceful work of the peasants." But the remainder of the text spelled out, in six articles, the measures necessary to "tear out all the roots of SR-permeated banditry." In the spirit of Order No. 130, it established the following schedule of retributions: any citizen refusing to give his name was "to be shot on the spot without trial"; in any village in which weapons were hidden "hostages are to be taken and shot unless such weapons are surrendered"; in any household in which "weapons are found the oldest member of the family present is to be shot on the spot without trial"; any family giving shelter to a bandit was to be "deported from the province, its property confiscated, and its breadwinner shot on the spot without trial"; any family hiding the family members or the property of bandits was subject to having its "oldest breadwinner shot without trial"; and in case a bandit family managed to flee, "its property [was] to be distributed among peasants loyal to Soviet authority and its abandoned house to be burned." To maximize the effectiveness of the proposed reign of fear, this ukase was to "be read out at village assemblies and . . . carried out firmly and mercilessly."[57]

The next day, June 12, Tukhachevsky issued another order, this one confidential, which confirmed that by now the concern was no longer with liberating insurgent villages and punishing proven or suspected Antonovites but with hunting down rebels who had made good their escape. Very much like General Turreau after the defeat of the *Vendée militaire*, Tukhachevsky meant to turn Tambov province into a *département-vengé* with a view to deter the resumption of rebellions near and far. He insisted that since "remnants of defeated bands and individual bandits" were launching attacks on "peaceful inhabitants" from their forest hideouts, these needed to be "cleared with poison gas." As theater commander he ordered the "inspector of artillery . . . [to] immediately release . . . to [designated] localities the required number of poison gas balloons as well as specialists . . . [capable] of making careful calculations . . . to make sure that the cloud of asphyxiating gas spreads throughout the forest and exterminates everything hiding there."[58]

In addition, there were many punitive search-and-destroy expeditions against settled districts and villages. In the small rural district of Estalskai "76 persons [were] executed," among them captured guerrillas and hostages, and 33 houses were razed. Southeast of Tambov, in Kamenka district, "all males were rounded up" with a view to frightening the womenfolk and hostages into "revealing the location of stores and hideouts." In Krivopoliane it took the slaying of 13 hostages for the villagers to "hand over several 'bandits' " and to divulge the hideaway of guerrillas and their caches of arms.[59]

Evidently, probably following orders Nos. 130 and 171, soldiers as well as security and Cheka operatives not only killed captured and presumed rebels and sympathizers but also set fire to houses and villages, and, above all, took hostages among relatives and friends. Many of the hostages were randomly chosen. Relatively few of them were executed or released, most of them being deported. In fact, apparently entire families were forcibly relocated, and so were several villages.[60]

One of the most ferocious punishments—though perhaps exceptionally so—was visited on Belomestnaia Dvoinia, a small town of fewer than 2,000 inhabitants some twenty miles west of the city of Tambov: "154 'bandit hostages'. . . were shot, 227 'bandit families' were seized, 17 dwellings were burned, 24 torn down, and 22 given over to poor peasants." In this same locality a band of guerrillas had previously "burned the quarters of the soviet and killed up to 50 people, including members of the local soviet." Belomestnaia Dvoinia seems to have been caught up in a typical cycle of revenge and re-revenge. But even if such was the case, "the ratio of vengeance was better than three to one and [was] inflicted, vicariously, on the sedentary population instead of the mobile force that had . . . [carried out] the raid."[61]

Belomestnaia Dvoinia was not the only village in which the Green Terror came first, calling forth a Red counter-terror that was much worse than the original rage. In March 1920 in the north and northwest of the Volga region, in addition to cutting communications and terrorizing local Bolshevik authorities, peasant rebels "murdered over 600 party and soviet officials," which led the Bolsheviks to send in "punitive detachments . . . [to] suppress the rebellion mercilessly."[62] Both sides practiced terror and counter-terror. It was this reciprocation that intensified the horrors of the second phase of the civil war in the Russian Revolution. Whereas the terror of the Reds became increasingly methodical and, with victory, ever more gratuitous, the terror of the Greens became increasingly frenzied and bestial, notably once they began to lose heart.[63]

Perhaps by virtue of being "primitive rebels," the Greens practiced a violence and terror that usually if not invariably reproduced those of times of old. To be sure, they perpetrated modern-style mass executions, as in the case of a commune in Tambov province near Rasskazovo, where they allegedly "killed everyone, even the young and the aged." But characteristically such cold violence did not preclude "crude and refined tortures." Gorky claimed that there were instances of Communists being "nailed to trees with railroad spikes" and their "half-crucified" bodies being left to "flop about and dangle in agony." According to a rebel eyewitness, some "captured workers were buried alive up to their necks" after having been charged with both "religious apostasy" and the plunder of peasants. In Tambov there were cases of victims being buried "straight up or in a sitting position with only the head above ground." These torments tended to be publicly staged to enable the in-group to express its utter contempt and loathing for the cursed outsiders. In Siberia captured Red soldiers were buried "head downward," with their legs left "as far as the knees above the ground."[64]

There were other forms of punishment as well. Here and there prisoners and suspects were flogged, maimed, eviscerated, and quartered. When Tishchenko, one of the chiefs of Soviet military operations in Tambov province, was taken prisoner, his captors "carved a red star on [his] back . . . [before] hacking off first his right and then his left arm, and—after further torture—finally beheading him."[65] In the lands of the Volga, it was not altogether uncommon for rebel bands, upon entering a village, "to hunt out and eliminate the Soviet and Bolshevik leaders." Likewise, in the "Nikolaevsk district over 300 party members were killed . . . before October 1921 . . . [and in] the Pokrovsk region more than 100 were killed before April." Judging by the tortures inflicted on some of these officials, this retribution was not without its "archaic" sides: "eyes and tongues were cut out; bodies were dismembered; crosses were branded on foreheads and torsos; heads were cut off; men were burned alive or drowned in ice-packed rivers and ponds." These inflictions, carried out in public, must have been condoned if not acclaimed by villagers whose "hatred and desire for vengeance" were fired by "the terrible conditions at the end of the civil war, when the famine crisis reduced some people to murderous cannibalism."[66] In some places along the Volga "the anger of the

crowd . . . spilled over into personal acts of vengeance and gory murders." In one village "nine members of a food-requisitioning brigade
were drowned under the ice of the Volga River" while in another "the
chairman of the district party was beheaded . . . , his body thrown . . .
into the river and his head put on top of a stake."[67] These saturnalias
of cruelty not infrequently helped set the tone for the destruction of
party offices, railway equipment, and telegraph lines, as well as with
the burning of tax records.[68]

There is no way to make an exact estimate of the human and material cost on both sides of the struggle between revolution and antirevolution in Tambov province. It is equally difficult to get a precise measure of the number of victims and hostages of the "infernal columns"
sent to pacify the province. Apparently, "as at July 20, 1921, 5,000
hostages were held in concentration camps, waiting transportation to
exile."[69] According to the head of Moscow's Committee of the Red
Cross, by September "a large number of peasants, [who were] hostages
from Tambov province," were confined in the capital's "detention
centers." There were "56 people in the Novo-Peskov camp, 13 in
Semonov, and 295 in Kozhukhov, including 29 men over sixty, 158
young people under seventeen, and 42 under ten, and 5 not yet one
year old." All these hostages "arrived in Moscow in pitiful condition,
ragged, half-naked, and so hungry that small children root around
rubbish dumps to find scraps to eat."[70]

❋ ❋ ❋

Before coming to some conclusions about the peasant wars, there is
need for a brief recounting of the rebellion of sailors and soldiers at
Kronstadt in March 1921. This rising took place four months after
the defeat of Wrangel, and hence following the end of the civil war
with the Whites, but before the repression of the Tambov insurgency,
which closed the peasant wars. Especially because the vital naval base
was next door to Petrograd, *prima facie* the resistance in Kronstadt
bade fair to pave the way for an uprising against the Bolshevik regime,
in a city that was both the cradle of the Revolution and the lofty peak
of urban Russia. In actual fact it was closely tied into the agrarian
unrest. Certainly it had little if anything in common with the revolt
of the southern cities during the French Revolution: whereas the
federalist uprisings of 1793 were initiated and led by local elites,

the Kronstadt rebellion swelled up from below and remained self-directed. The bulk of the insurgent sailors and soldiers of the local naval and army garrisons were of peasant origin. They meant to overturn the coercive economic and political practices of the Bolshevik regime, thereby reclaiming the popular and liberating thrust of the October Revolution, including the right to owner-operated landed and artisanal property. They rebelled to regenerate the Soviets of Workers and Peasants, not to revive the Constituent Assembly, as the necessary agency and bulwark for freedom of speech, press, assembly, and association.[71]

Kronstadt utterly confounded the Bolshevik leaders. They faced, to be sure, a disconcerting political and ideological challenge. No less disquieting, although there were fewer rebels on the island fortress than in Tambov, they were trained and well-armed fighting men. In addition, their bastion was in a strategic location open to military intervention by foreign powers rather than in the far interior closed to the outside world.[72] Admittedly, even with the counterrevolution crushed, Lenin and his colleagues loudly decried the Kronstadt revolt as yet another White maneuver, supported from abroad.[73] But among themselves as well as at the Tenth Party Congress, whose meeting in Moscow coincided with the naval rising, they conceded that the reality was considerably more complex. It was a measure of the jolt to the revolutionary sensibility and the "gravity with which Kronstadt was viewed" that on March 10, 1921, a week after the outbreak, over a quarter of this congress, or 300 delegates, "volunteered" for service on the Kronstadt front.[74]

If the Kronstadt revolt became so intensely disquieting it was, in large part, because it coincided with labor disturbances in neighboring Petrograd. In late January the bread ration was temporarily reduced by one-third in a city that for several years had suffered grim shortages and hardships. Presently this cutback triggered demonstrations and strikes among industrial workers, who had expected the end of the civil war to bring relief and usher in the promised future. Partly under the influence of local Mensheviks and Socialist Revolutionaries, these would-be rebels combined their economic demands with calls for free trade and speech, as well as free and secret elections of soviets and the release of political prisoners. Initially perplexed by this defiance, the municipal authorities resorted to both the stick and the carrot. To begin with, they declared martial law, closed select factories, and arrested hundreds of militant workers as well as leading Mensheviks and Socialist Revolutionaries. They also brought in reliable policemen and soldiers, including Chekists, to bolster the local forces of law and order. At the same time, probably after consultation with Moscow, where the Party Congress was about to phase out War Communism, the local Bolshevik leaders made available extra food supplies. The end of forced food requisitions was also adumbrated, promising to pacify the enraged ex-peasants in Petrograd's workforce and their restive cousins in the countryside.[75]

Unexpectedly, the labor unrest in Petrograd was defused by early March. By then, however, it had emboldened the rebels in Kronstadt, who had an inflated view of the neighboring workers' militancy and rage. At any rate, the insurgents were now completely on their own and without the prospect of help from beyond the island. Even so they persisted, in league with the crews of the warships at anchor in the harbor. They demanded essentially the same rights and freedoms as their counterparts in Petrograd, except that they proposed to limit these rights to workers and peasants. They also pressed for self-governing soviets, trade unions, and peasant councils, though they spurned the idea of a constituent assembly. Even if the project of the rebels was vague, their negations were explicit. They cried out that they were rising against the "Communist usurpers" who instead of emancipating workers were putting them in "fear of . . . the torture chambers of the Cheka, whose horrors—including the bayonets, bullets, and gruff commands of the Chekists—far exceed those of the tsarist regime." Indeed, they charged that even the White Guards had not "surpassed the mass executions and bloodletting" wrought by the Communists while quelling "the protests which peasants express in spontaneous uprisings and which workers, driven by [terrible] living conditions, express through strikes."[76]

Arriving in Petrograd on March 5, following the city's appeasement, Trotsky issued a call for the Kronstadt rebels to "surrender unconditionally," which they spurned.[77] That same day Tukhachevsky took command of all forces in the Petrograd military district. He proceeded to reinforce them with politically reliable Red Army units, backed by detachments of Chekists, military cadets, and young Communists. Tukhachevsky launched an abortive attack on March 8, before this buildup was completed. He felt pressed by time: the ice in the Bay of Finland was about to melt, giving the 15,000 rebels, notably their naval units, a major advantage. Having regrouped his effectives and made several dry runs on the ice, and following steady artillery barrages, Tukhachevsky attacked in the early hours of March 17. Some 35,000 men moved on Kronstadt from the southern shore of the Gulf of Finland, 15,000 of them hugging the northern coastline. By then the 300 volunteer party delegates were on the ground urging on the Red forces, their efforts helped by word that on March 15 the Moscow congress had "voted to replace forced requisitions with a tax in kind."[78]

The battle was bound to be unequal. As usual the defense had a significant tactical edge, in this case sharpened by inclement weather. But in every other respect the rebels were at a disadvantage, notwithstanding their high esprit and courage. Since neither the workers of Petrograd nor the foreign powers rushed to their side, they were completely on their own. With the island cut off from the outside world, short of a quick victory, there was no feeding a population of 50,000 and no replenishing military stores.[79]

Their uniforms covered by white cloaks, the Red troops advanced from several directions and in successive waves across the perilously thin ice covering the waters of the easternmost bay of the Gulf of Finland. They suffered very heavy losses. Many drowned as the ice broke either under their weight or from exploding shells, and many more were killed or injured by rebel artillery and machine-gun fire. But eventually and inevitably the key forts of Kronstadt fell in the early afternoon of March 18. Driven by deep but irreconcilable convictions, both sides fought fiercely in what turned into a battle whose cruelty and loss of life were unequalled in Russia's civil war.[80]

A well-informed estimate puts rebel losses at about 600 killed, over 1,000 wounded, and some 2,500 prisoners. These losses would probably have been even heavier if 8,000 rebels, including key members of the provisional revolutionary committee, had not managed to escape to Finland, thereby also reducing the reason for Bolshevik vengeance in the aftermath of a hard-won victory. Indeed, the Red forces paid by far the steeper price: their casualties ran to about 10,000 killed, wounded, and missing. Fifteen of the 300 volunteers from the Tenth Party Congress were among the dead.[81]

It is not clear how many of the rebel casualties can be laid to Bolshevik vengefulness after the revolt was broken. To set a fear-inspiring example, on March 30 thirteen of the prisoners captured during the fighting were summarily tried and executed. In social background, "five [of them] were ex-naval officers of noble birth, one a former priest, and seven of peasant origin." While "several hundred . . . of the remaining prisoners" most likely were shot outright, the Cheka dispatched the others to prisons in Petrograd as well as to concentration and labor camps, their subsequent fate unknown.[82]

The crushing of the Kronstadt revolt and the ensuing punitive pacification sparked another spurt of political repression. In the two capitals as well as in major Ukrainian cities, anarchists who "had been released after their arrest" a few months before "were taken into custody again."[83] As previously noted, the Mensheviks were implicated in Petrograd's industrial unrest, even if they were blameless in the Kronstadt rising. At any rate, and hardly surprisingly, on February 25–26 the Cheka proceeded to detain leading Mensheviks in Moscow, Petrograd, and several provincial cities. There were also "mass arrests . . . in seven Ukrainian provinces." In mid-April, after the Kronstadt revolt, but before Tukhachevsky was sent to put down the Tambov rising, Lenin opposed a recommendation to release certain Mensheviks, Socialist Revolutionaries, and anarchists, insisting that their "place [continues to be] in prison."[84]

The non-Bolshevik left, including the anarchists, heralded the Kronstadt uprising for echoing the insurrection of the Paris Commune. Ironically, Kronstadt fell the very day of the fiftieth anniversary of the start of the mythologized if problematic insurrection of 1871. Whereas in early 1918 Lenin and his associates had rejoiced when their rule had survived the first hundred days, or the life span of the Commune, they now sought to appropriate its commemoration to support their enforcement terror. The Bolsheviks knew their military victory to be morally flawed, and were troubled that enemy brothers would vilify them as the *Versaillais* of their day. The Bolsheviks who fell in the assault, including the fifteen party delegates, "were buried with military honors in a mass funeral" in Petrograd. In Kronstadt, mean-

while, "the battleships Petropavlovsk and Sevastopol were rechris-
tened the *Marat* and the *Paris Commune*, while Anchor Square became the Square of the Revolution."[85]

✻ ✻ ✻

No doubt the terror attending the military operations of the peasant
rebels was more spontaneous and less systematic than that practiced
by their enemies. Even if Makhno and Antonov had left a significant
paper trail, there is little reason to believe that it would have led to a
warrant analogous to Order No. 171. The bulk of rebel terror was
wild, and much of it was raw and cruel. The Greens were, as noted,
primitive rebels whose thoughts and actions were driven by local mentalities and loyalties. They had little if any coherent ideology, political
organization, and military strategy. For all that they did have a set of
goals, even if by and large they aimed to reclaim and regenerate an
idealized pastoral order rather than propose and build a truly new one.
Likewise, the fact that the peasant rebels kept being forced to take
flight and were eventually defeated does not mean that they were
intrinsically defensive and harmless, averse to violence and terror except when driven to retaliate for prior injury.

The rural rebellions faltered and failed despite their solid roots in
the poor and middle peasantry as well as wide backing by the muzhiks
of the surrounding countryside. It is difficult to estimate the level of
support among workers and artisans of nearby towns and cities. In
any case, one of the chief weaknesses of the rural antirevolution was
the inability of its leaders to forge links either between the different
peasant rebellions or with urban revolts. The mentality of Makhno
and Antonov was as insular as that of the rank and file. No doubt the
Socialist Revolutionaries could have done more to de-parochialize and
politicize the *jacqueries* had they not been broken by the failure of
their would-be uprising of July 1918.

Ultimately the course of this mutually brutalizing civil strife was
defined by the intersection of the intrinsic deficits of the peasant
rebellions and the contingent frailties of the Bolsheviks. Despite their
material handicaps, partly compensated by their moral strength and
corporate solidarity, the Greens made good only wherever and as
long as they could benefit from the power vacuum growing out of

the breakdown of political and legal sovereignty. Even assuming more than a modicum of coordination between and among Makhno, Antonov, and other peasant leaders, it is most unlikely that ill-organized, ill-equipped, and ill-articulated guerrilla bands could have defied the Red Army for long, especially with the Bolshevik regime putting in place a new-model centralizing authority in the form of a party-state.

There was, to be sure, another side to the complex relationship of Bolshevik and peasant. At the start of the second phase of the civil war, the Bolsheviks had envisaged combining vigorous repression with economic concessions to the peasants. Even though the moment was inauspicious for this new departure, in the end the Bolsheviks were obliged to blend firmness with appeasement. By and large the height of the peasant wars coincided with the economic collapse and great famine of 1921–22.[86] It is not clear whether, on balance, acute material hardship exacerbated or dampened peasant resistance. It is more than likely that the infernal logic of rebellion and repression aggravated the economic emergency and the risk of starvation. At any rate, whatever the real or perceived causalities, the peasant fury and the portentous famine conspired to precipitate Moscow's relaxation of the iron hand of War Communism for the less visible, not to say invisible hand of the New Economic Policy. In fact, NEP quickly sapped the rural upheaval and bade fair to increase food production. There is reason to believe that the chief legacy of the peasant rebellions was their contribution to speeding up Lenin's shift from War Communism to NEP.

But the leverage of the peasants was short-lived. To be sure, important sectors of the composite peasantry continued to reap the benefits of the land settlement of 1917–18. Overall, however, the sons and daughters of the soil were cheated out of their political and communal rights by the abolition of the system of self-governing soviets. At the same time the barbarous and antimodern side of the rebellion confirmed the Bolshevik leaders in their condescending view, both in doctrine and practice, of peasant, village, and countryside.

It is impossible to estimate, let alone closely calculate, the human costs of the second phase of Russia's civil war. Not only is the death toll on both sides difficult to establish, but so is its breakdown into battle casualties, victims of terror, and deaths due to civil war-related disease and famine. Needless to say, whatever the blood tax, it came on top of millions of battlefield casualties of the Very Great War as well as of military and civilian casualties during the first phase of the civil war. In the aggregate, between 1914 and 1922 Russia's loss of life is likely to have run to well over ten million. This figure includes the millions of victims of disease and of the famine of 1921–22.[87] Alone among the major belligerents of the First World War, Russia counts more civilian than military deaths. The killing of captured enemy combatants and of hostages by the opposing sides in the peasant wars made but a relatively modest contribution to this monstrous pyramid of Russian dead. This judgment is suggested by a considered estimate that in Tambov, in addition to about 5,000 Greens having been killed in action, "not less than 2,000 prisoners and hostages were executed."[88] Needless to say, the horrors of civil war cannot be reckoned exclusively by the number of killed and maimed. Although this quantitative aspect cannot be ignored, it is inseparable from the qualitative damage caused by the terror practiced by both sides.

Of course, the material cost was huge as well, though again it is not easy to evaluate how much of it to attribute to the First World War and the first phase of the civil war, and how much to the peasant wars. By 1922 livestock stood at about two-thirds of the prewar level. There was, likewise, a drastic decrease in the area sown: in Tambov it fell to about 45 percent of the prewar level. As for the grain crop, including potatoes, it went down by nearly 60 percent between 1909–13 and 1921. Nationwide industrial production was reduced to about 30 percent of the prewar figure: in Tambov it was down to about 20 percent in 1921.[89]

One need not pronounce on the ultimate causes of the civil war and the particularities of its attendant terror on the opposing sides in order to reflect on its legacy to the post-civil war political regime and culture.[90] Any such discursive considerations cannot help being colored by the outcome of the civil war, which left the Bolsheviks the undisputed victors and masters. Indeed, the fact of having prevailed against enormous odds fostered a certain hubris among Bolshevik leaders and doubtless legitimated their peculiar pretense and praxis, also in eyes other than their own. Although they had been, to a degree, mentally and theoretically prepared for the eventuality and necessity of civil war, they could hardly have anticipated its scale, duration, and fury.

The civil war furthered and vindicated revolutionary militancy and voluntarism as well as administrative license and centralization. It invited and justified recourse to violence and terror, summary justice, and iron governance. This propensity for rigid, distended, and coercive authoritarian rule was all the stronger by virtue of the new regime's narrow social base and pool of professionals and experts, compounded by the weight of tsarist Russia's autocratic, patrimonial, and Gothic traditions. The militarized Bolshevik party replaced the skeletal and fragmented state, its raw cadres compensating for the deficit of reliable and skilled proletarian and peasant activists and agents.

Actually, the civil war weakened the new social and cultural forces in the symbiosis of Russia's immutable past and late-coming but malleable present, bending the "simultaneity of the unsimultaneous" even more in favor of the gravity of former times. Ever so many members of the modernized and modernizing professional, bureaucratic, and business elites went into foreign exile or to the margin, while the vitality of the industrial labor force of the big cities was undermined above all by the massive reflux of workers to the countryside: the number of workers in large and medium-sized industries was cut by more than half by 1920, and so was the celebrated proletariat of Petrograd. Notwithstanding the removal of the old governing and ruling classes, seared by their defeat in the civil war, Russia was still, or perhaps more than only yesterday, a society of illiterate peasants bolstered by the land redemption and bound by immemorial institutions, values, and traditions from which the Bolsheviks were estranged. This alienation was all the more serious since the "lame and impotent conclusion" of the revolution in central Europe meant that the Bolsheviks were forced to modernize and reform backward Russia with its windows all but closed on the outside world. At the end of the civil war and the beginning of NEP the Bolsheviks were an embattled vanguard with a siege mentality, in both national and international terms. As they turned to building "Socialism in One Country"—by necessity rather than choice—they had to recover and assume a distinctly Russian identity. Not that they abandoned their universal vocation. But hereafter Russia would be as much a model of socialist modernization for the Third World as one of socialist redistribution for the First World.

* * *

NOTES

1. Orlando Figes, *A People's Tragedy: The Russian Revolution, 1891–1924* (London: Jonathan Cape, 1996), p. 698.

2. Robert Conquest, *The Harvest of Sorrow: Soviet Collectivization and the Terror-Famine* (New York: Oxford University Press, 1986), p. 53.

3. Figes, *Peasant Russia, Civil War: The Volga Countryside in Revolution, 1917–1921* (Oxford: Clarendon, 1989), p. 322 and p. 327; Conquest, *Harvest of Sorrow*, p. 56; Vladimir N. Brovkin, *Behind the Front Lines of the Civil War: Political Parties and Social Movements in Russia, 1918–1922* (Princeton: Princeton University Press, 1994), p. 161, p. 322, and p. 390.

4. Conquest, *Harvest of Sorrow*, p. 43. See also Teodor Shanin, *The Awkward Class: Political Sociology of Peasantry in a Developing Society, Russia 1910–1925* (Oxford: Clarendon, 1972), pp. 145–47.

5. See David Mitrany, *Marx against the Peasant: A Study in Social Dogmatism* (New York: Collier, 1961); Moshe Lewin, "Dimensions of Stalinism in Russia: The Social Background of Socialism," in Robert C. Tucker, *Stalinism* (New York: Norton, 1977), pp. 111–36, esp. pp. 120–22; Alvin Gouldner, "Stalinism: A Study of Internal Colonialism," in *Telos* 34 (Winter 1977–78): pp. 5–48. Cf. Brovkin, *Front Lines*, passim.

6. See Peter Holquist, *A Russian Vendée: The Practice of Revolutionary Politics in the Don Countryside, 1917–1921* (unpublished Ph.D. dissertation: Columbia University, 1995), esp. ch. VIII.

7. Sheila Fitzpatrick, *Stalin's Peasants: Resistance and Survival in the Russian Village after Collectivization* (New York: Oxford University Press, 1994), p. 24.

8. Barrington Moore, Jr., *Social Origins of Dictatorship and Democracy: Land and Peasant in the Making of the Modern World* (Boston: Beacon, 1966), p. 87. This is Moore's judgment, based on Mathiez, of the economic policies of the Committee of Public Safety, which can be applied to those of Sovnarkom.

9. Michael Malet, *Nestor Makhno in the Russian Civil War* (London: The London School of Economics and Political Science, 1982), pp. 150–51, 153.

10. Figes, *Peasant Russia*, pp. 323–24.

11. Cited in ibid., p. 324.

12. Ibid., p. 324 and p. 329; and Brovkin, *Front Lines*, pp. 321–22.

13. Figes, *Peasant Russia*, p. 329; and Bruce W. Lincoln, *Red Victory: A History of the Russian Civil War* (New York: Simon & Schuster, 1989), p. 324.

14. Cited in Malet, *Makhno*, p. 83.

15. Cited in ibid., p. 35.

16. Cited in William Henry Chamberlin, *The Russian Revolution, 1917–1921*, vol. 2 (New York: Macmillan, 1957), pp. 233–34.

17. Leon Trotsky, *The Military Writings and Speeches: How the Revolution Armed*, vol. 2 (London: New Park Publications, 1979–81), pp. 326–27.

18. Cited in Chamberlin, *Russian Revolution*, p. 234. See also Malet, *Makhno*, pp. 34–39; and Brovkin, *Front Lines*, pp. 115–16.

19. The following three paragraphs are based on Malet, *Makhno*, pp. 40–45, 84; and Peter Arshinov, *History of the Makhnovist Movement, 1918–1921* (Detroit: Black and Red, 1974), ch. 7.

20. Cited in Chamberlin, *Russian Revolution*, pp. 235–36.

21. Cited in Malet, *Makhno*, p. 171.

22. Richard Stites, *Revolutionary Dreams: Utopian Vision and Experimental Life in the Russian Revolution* (New York: Oxford University Press, 1989), p. 64.

23. Chamberlin, *Russian Revolution*, p. 238.

24. Malet, *Makhno*, pp. 64–66. See also Trotsky, *Military Writings*, p. 285 and p. 291.

25. Malet, *Makhno*, p. 66.

26. Ibid., p. 129.

27. Chamberlin, *Russian Revolution*, p. 239; and George Leggett, *The Cheka: Lenin's Political Police* (Oxford: Clarendon, 1981), p. 335.

28. Arshinov, *Makhnovist Movement*, p. 165.

29. Chamberlin, *Russian Revolution*, p. 39.

30. Arshinov, *Makhnovist Movement*, pp. 166–67.

31. Cited in Brovkin, *Front Lines*, p. 382.

32. Arshinov, *Makhnovist Movement*, p. 166.

33. Leggett, *Cheka*, p. 334. For this violence, also see the excerpts from the diary of Makhno's wife cited by Chamberlin, *Russian Revolution*, pp. 237–38.

34. Malet, *Makhno*, pp. 72–73; and Chamberlin, *Russian Revolution*, p. 239.

35. Malet, *Makhno*, pp. 103–4.

36. Ibid., pp. 85–92, 95.

37. Ibid., p. 118; and Michael Palij, *The Anarchism of Nestor Makhno, 1918–1921: An Aspect of the Ukrainian Revolution* (Seattle: University of Washington Press, 1976), pp. 252–53.

38. See Lincoln, *Red Victory*, pp. 469–70.

39. Leggett, *Cheka*, p. 330.

40. Ibid., p. 332; Lincoln, *Red Victory*, p. 469; Brovkin, *Front Lines*, pp. 363–68; Roger Pethybridge, *One Step Backwards, Two Steps Forward: Soviet Society and Politics in the New Economic Policy* (Oxford: Clarendon, 1990), p. 65.

41. Seth Singleton, "The Tambov Revolt, 1920–1921," in *Slavic Review* 25:3 (September 1966): pp. 497–512, esp. p. 504. See also Brovkin, *Front Lines*, p. 363.

42. Leggett, *Cheka*, p. 331.

43. See Brovkin, *Front Lines*, pp. 362 ff.

44. Figes, *Peasant Russia*, ch. 7; Geoffrey Hosking, *The First Socialist Society: A History of the Soviet Union from Within*, enlarged ed. (Cambridge, Mass.: Harvard University Press, 1990), p. 78; Conquest, *Harvest of Sorrow*, p. 51; Leggett, *Cheka*, p. 330.

45. Dmitri Volkogonov, *Lenin: A New Biography* (New York: Free Press, 1994), p. 344.

46. Pethybridge, *One Step Backwards*, pp. 65–66.

47. Oliver H. Radkey, *The Unknown Civil War in Soviet Russia: A Study of the Green Movement in the Tambov Region, 1920–1921* (Stanford, Calif.: Hoover Institution Press, 1976), pp. 334–36.

48. Volkogonov, *Lenin*, p. 303.

49. "Report on the Political Work of the Central Committee: March 8, 1921," in V. I. Lenin, *Collected Works*, vol. 32 (Moscow: Progress Publishers, 1965), pp. 170–91.

50. Lincoln, *Red Victory*, pp. 471–72.

51. Brovkin, *Front Lines*, pp. 385–86.

52. Cited in ibid., p. 384.

53. Leggett, *Cheka*, p. 332. See also Lincoln, *Red Victory*, p. 472.

54. Cited in Leggett, *Cheka*, p. 330.

55. Cited in Brovkin, *Front Lines*, pp. 384–85.

56. Radkey, *Civil War*, pp. 322–23.

57. The text of Order no. 171 is cited in slightly discordant translations in Radkey, *Civil War*, p. 324; Brovkin, *Front Lines*, pp. 386–87; Volkogonov, *Lenin*, pp. 343–44; Alexandre Soljénitsyne, *Ego* (Paris: Fayard, 1995), pp. 88–89.

58. Cited in Volkogonov, *Lenin*, p. 303; and Soljénitsyne, *Ego*, pp. 89–90.

59. Radkey, *Civil War*, pp. 326–27.

60. Ibid., pp. 328–32, 349–51.

61. Ibid., p. 326.

62. Ibid., p. 320.

63. See ibid., pp. 321–22; and Lincoln, *Red Victory*, p. 473.

64. Radkey, *Civil War*, p. 319.

65. Ibid., p. 320.

66. Figes, *Peasant Russia*, p. 346.

67. Ibid., p. 328.

68. Ibid., p. 347.

69. Leggett, *Cheka*, p. 333.

70. Cited in Volkogonov, *Lenin*, p. 344.

71. Paul Avrich, *Kronstadt 1921* (Princeton: Princeton University Press, 1970), pp. 190–91.

72. Ibid., p. 218.

73. See Richard Pipes, *Russia under the Bolshevik Regime* (New York: Knopf, 1993), p. 382; and Martin Malia, *The Soviet Tragedy: A History of Socialism in Russia, 1917–1991* (New York: Free Press, 1994), p. 143.

74. Avrich, *Kronstadt*, p. 194.

75. Ibid., p. 194; and Brovkin, *Front Lines*, pp. 389–95. Brovkin systematically exaggerates the scale and intensity of the storm and stress of February–March 1921, insisting that the "entire social system" was in crisis, and "the country ungovernable" by virtue of Bolshevik misgovernment. Leggett and Conquest have this same perspective, as does Malia.

76. Manifesto published in the rebels' short-lived newspaper on March 8, 1919, cited in Lennard D. Gerson, *The Secret Police in Lenin's Russia* (Philadelphia: Temple University Press, 1976), p. 189.

77. Isaac Deutscher, *The Prophet Armed: Trotsky: 1879–1921* (New York: Oxford University Press, 1954), p. 312.

78. Avrich, *Kronstadt*, pp. 193–200, 202.

79. Ibid., pp. 200–1. See also Pipes, *Bolshevik Regime*, pp. 382–84.

80. Deutscher, *Prophet Armed*, pp. 513–14; Avrich, *Kronstadt*, p. 205 and p. 210; Pipes, *Bolshevik Regime*, pp. 384–85.

81. Avrich, *Kronstadt*, p. 211.

82. Ibid., pp. 214–15.

83. Ibid., p. 233.

84. Leggett, *Cheka*, pp. 320–22.

85. Avrich, *Kronstadt*, p. 211 and p. 213.

86. See chapter 12 below.

87. Conquest advances the following approximate figures: 2 million killed in the First World War; 1 million in the first phase of the civil war; 2 million in the peasant wars; 3 million by disease; and 5 million by famine. Conquest, *Harvest of Sorrow*, pp. 53–54.

88. Radkey, *Civil War*, pp. 347–48.

89. Conquest, *Harvest of Sorrow*, p. 55; and Radkey, *Civil War*, p. 338 and p. 340.

90. The following reflections draw heavily on the essays by Sheila Fitzpatrick, Leopold Haimson, Reginald Zelnik, and Moshe Lewin in Diane P. Koenker et al., eds., *Party, State, and Society in the Russian Civil War* (Bloomington: Indiana University Press, 1989), pp. 3–23, 24–47, 374–380, 399–423; Fitzpatrick, "Origins of Stalinism: How Important Was the Civil War?" in *Acta Slavica Iaponica* 2 (1984): pp. 105–25; Fitzpatrick, "The Civil War as a Formative Experience," in Abbot Gleason et al., eds., *Bolshevik Culture: Experiment and Order in the Russian Revolution* (Bloomington: Indiana University Press, 1985), pp. 57–76.

PART FOUR

The Sacred Contested

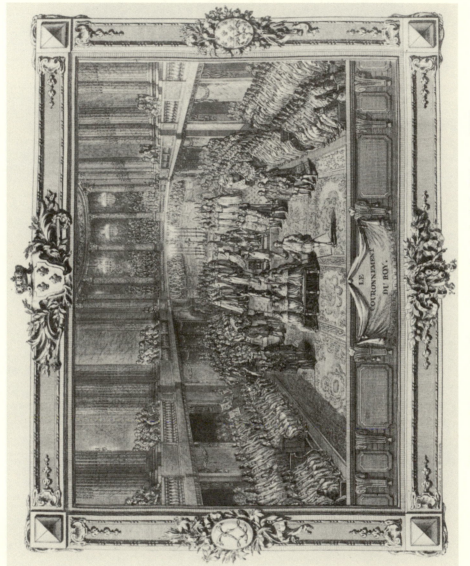

The Coronation (*sacre*) of Louis XVI in the Cathedral of Rheims, 1775

Engaging the
Gallican Church and
the Vatican

IN 1789 FRANCE was 85 percent rural. Twenty-two million out of 28 million French men and women lived in the countryside, the overwhelming majority engaged in agriculture and agriculture-related work. At least one-third of them were poor or destitute. Their households and communities were trapped in inertia and were untouched by the *lumières*. Illiteracy was very much the norm. Peasant traditions and attitudes were inseparable from religious beliefs and practices in which magic at once reinforced and alleviated the fear of famine and plague, as well as of the Last Judgment. The houses and representatives of God were as omnipresent as the landed nobles who were the masters of the seignorial system.[1]

There were, of course, considerable variations in landholding, welfare, literacy, and religiosity. But these do not invalidate this general portrait of a fixed rural society, all the more striking when counterposed to urban France. At the time France counted about sixty towns with over 10,000 inhabitants, Paris towering over all of them with a population of 600,000. Starting in 1789, "the city was opposed to the countryside just as the revolution was opposed to the ancien regime." As we will see, *citadins* and peasants only rarely marched to the same beat. Not infrequently city and revolution made common cause against rural France and the old order.[2]

On the eve of the Revolution, however, both city and country were still spanned by the enormous institutional power of the Church. The Gallican Church was the "eldest daughter of the Catholic Church" by virtue of France being Europe's premier Catholic country in terms of population and religious vocations. France's paramount church probably was also Europe's wealthiest, thanks to its income from tithes and donations and its ownership of 10 to 15 percent of the nation's land. Throughout the length and breadth of the country, cathedrals and churches, monasteries and convents were the commanding focal points of communal life. The clergy occupied a prominent position in the ruling and governing class in both city and country, especially because of the large number of institutions it managed.

The Church establishment counted about 140 dioceses, close to 40,000 parishes, and about 1,000 monasteries and nunneries, as well as hundreds of welfare and educational institutions. In addition to one priest per parish, or a total of 40,000, appointed for life, there were again as many vicars and auxiliaries, plus tens of thousands of monks and nuns. The higher priesthood of 8,000 included some 140 archbishops and bishops, all of them of noble birth. Of course, France's cities had many parishes, both large and small. In addition, they boasted a variety of ecclesiastical institutions along with a wide variety of clerics other than the workaday *curés*. For a population of about 600,000 Paris had fifty parish churches and monasteries, owning a quarter of the capital's land area. Amiens, a city of 35,000 inhabitants, counted 1,200 churchmen and churchwomen for fifteen parish churches, fourteen monasteries, and nine nunneries. And when the Estates-General met in 1789, the First Estate of some 170,000 churchmen sent 296 representatives to Versailles. This delegation included forty-seven bishops, twenty-three abbots, twelve canons, and six vicars, most of them wellborn, along with 208 parish priests, most of them semi-educated and of humble and rural origin.[3]

Rooted in a long-standing alliance with the Roman Catholic Church, the French monarchy itself was in essence Christian and Catholic. His "Most Christian Majesty," the King of France, was king by the Grace of God. He was at once only too human but also sacred and inviolable, with thaumaturgical powers. The millennial ceremony of the *sacre*, or anointment and coronation, of Louis XVI—the fifth Bourbon, the thirty-third Capetian—which renewed the alliance of throne and altar, took place in the cathedral of Rheims on Trinity Sunday, June 11, 1775.[4] Attended by the princes of the blood and preceded by the archbishop of Rheims, Cardinal de La Roche-Aymon, the king entered the cathedral at 7:30 in the morning. He took his seat, his back to the high altar, in the *fauteuil du souverain* standing alone on the dais in the middle of the sanctuary. The assembly in the cathedral was drawn from the apex of the Establishment. Once the archbishop had sung the *Veni Creator* and the holy vessel containing the oil of anointment was brought forward and placed on the altar, he approached Louis XVI to take his promise that he would continue to protect the integrity of the Church and its privileges. As part of this oath Louis XVI pledged to defend the "church against the wickedness of infidels," to "expel heretics from his kingdom," and to live and die in the Catholic faith. Thereupon La Roche-Aymon held high and consecrated first the sword and then the scepter of Charlemagne before handing them to the Bourbon to hold. The twenty-year-old Bourbon and the seventy-three-year-old cardinal then prostrated themselves on a purple velvet carpet while four bishops recited the litany of the saints. Next, Louis XVI rose to kneel on the steps of the altar in front of the archbishop, who was now seated before him. Having anointed his head and body with sanctified oil, the archbishop proclaimed Louis XVI to be consecrated king.

The climax of the ceremony was the moment of coronation: after entrusting Charlemagne's scepter to the king, La Roche-Aymon, assisted by the six great peers of the realm, held Charlemagne's crown over his head. There were several additional prayers and benedictions as the king continued to kneel at the cardinal's feet. Finally, with the scepter and the *main de justice* in his right and left hand, respectively, the king, wearing the "ordinary" crown, ascended the throne. With cannons booming and bells ringing, the general public was admitted through the main portal of the cathedral to join in the acclamation and participate in the closing *Te Deum*. On June 13–14, after resting from the six-hour ceremony, the king touched, one after another, several hundred ragged wretches afflicted with scrofula, thereby reaffirming the miraculous powers proclaimed in the legendary proverb, "the King touches, God heals."

In the normal order of things, and very much in the spirit of the *sacre* in Rheims fourteen years before, a grandiose religious ceremony preceded the opening of the Estates-General on May 5, 1789. Michelet's penetrating eye was drawn to it as glaring evidence that throne and altar remained inextricably linked. Although he did not deem it a premeditated provocation, he did note the "odious detail of this Gothic ceremonial" intended, even if unintentionally, to perpetuate "class distinctions . . . [and] social hatreds" as well as to "humble and humiliate" the common people.[5] The democratic persuasion that inspired Michelet's comment does not invalidate his judgment on the *ancien régime's* last apotheosizing self-celebration, nor his vivid rendering of it.

On April 29 Louis XVI instructed the archbishop of Paris, Leclerc de Joigné, to plan a general procession of the Holy Sacrament for May 4 in Versailles in which "the King, the Queen, the royal family, the princes of the blood, and all court officers would participate." Its purpose would be to ask God's guidance for "the grand and notable assembly of my Kingdom's Estates General."[6] In fixing the order of precedence and dress code for this solemnity, the court's master of ceremonies took the arrangements of the opening of the Estates-General of 1614 as his model.

On the appointed day, following the singing of the *Veni Creator*, 1,200 members of the Estates-General wended their way from Versailles's church of Notre-Dame to the Cathedral of Saint-Louis for the celebration of the Mass of the Holy Spirit. Some forty Franciscan friars and the priests of the local diocese marched at the head of this imposing processional, followed by the 550 deputies of the Third Estate. Representing the least esteemed of the three orders, they were kept at the greatest distance from the king. They wore black woolen costumes with white muslin ties and three-cornered hats without braids or buttons. But despite their "modest dress," the people's delegates, over 300 of them lawyers and magistrates, were "resolute in both step and demeanor." Having been spurned by the nobility, Mirabeau was among them, carrying a sword and "attracting much attention."[7]

There followed the "small but grand body of deputies" of the Second Estate, among whom the ninety leading noblemen stood out for their striking attire.[8] Dressed in black coats with golden facings and wearing white stockings and lace ties, the magnates cut a dash with their swords and plumed white hats in the style of Henry IV.

In the procession the First Estate of churchmen was in third place, but with the privilege of marching immediately ahead of Louis XVI and his notable entourage. The cloth was as if divided into two separate orders. Some 200 priests wearing cassocks and square caps were in the lead. They were separated from the upper clergy by several hundred "vocal and instrumental musicians of the King's royal chapel clad in black, with swords at their sides."[9] Not unlike the preeminent nobles, the nearly fifty cardinals and archbishops of the upper clergy impressed the crowds with their blazing vestments.

The royal party was like a world unto itself. It was headed by the grand officers of the crown and the *gentilhommes d'honneur* of the princes of the blood. Each of these—the Duc d'Orléans, the Duc de Berry, the Duc d'Angoulême, the Comte d'Artois, the Comte de Provence—was surrounded by scores of attendants, some on foot, others in carriages. While each prince had two or three equerries, Louis XVI had fourteen. The king walked immediately behind the Holy Sacrament, carried by the archbishop of Paris, while the chief royal chaplain held His Majesty's candle. He was surrounded by the princes and noblemen of the court. The queen was to the left of the king, her candle carried by her personal chaplain. She was attended by, among others, Madame Elisabeth, the duchess of Orléans, and the Princess de Lamballe.[10]

At the Cathedral of Saint-Louis the Mass of the Holy Spirit was celebrated by the archbishop of Paris, assisted by the archbishops of Toulouse and Bourges, and sung by the royal musicians. The bishop of Nancy, Monseigneur de la Fare, delivered a sermon in keeping with the logic and mystique of the occasion.[11]

The solemn proceedings showed that even now there were no serious fissures in the pretense of sacralized political power. The attending crowds, which included many Parisians, were awed by the grandeur of the spectacle. There were scattered cheers for the representatives of the Third Estate, and for the king. Apparently the nobility, flaunting privilege and vanity, elicited few plaudits, and the queen was viewed with a scornful eye. But overall, reverence for the Establishment seemed intact. Neither the order of precedence nor the *mise en scène* was questioned, and during the early dawn of the revolt the continuing centrality of the Roman Catholic Church and religion was taken for granted by the upper ten thousand as well as society at large. Apparently, few if any delegates of the three estates ever even considered boycotting, let alone publicly opposing, the archaic pageant of sanctified and hegemonic power.

The fact that in June the lower clergy of the First Estate backed the incipient reform movement by voting to join with the Third Estate in no way weakened the union of throne and altar, all the less so since the rebel priests aimed to reform and regenerate the church without undermining its peculiar preeminence. The embryonic National Assembly sought to reshape and loosen rather than sever the bonds between God and Caesar as part of a general renewal of political and civil society. Characteristically, the spectacular abolition of seignorial rights, including those of the Church, during the notable night of August 4–5, 1789, was capped, late that night, with a solemn *Te Deum* in the royal chapel of Versailles, in the presence of the king and the deputies. This unhoped-for reform also called forth many a Thanksgiving mass in different parts of France in which the old clergy and the emergent political class joined together. Thereafter clergymen, considering the Gospel the perfect foundation for the rebirth of France, consecrated the tricolor flags of newly formed National Guard units.[12] They also officiated at ceremonies centered around maypoles and freedom trees, and until 1792 many of the newly invented and staged civic festivals included solemn church services. Not a few clergy and laity seized the hour, in the words of Kierkegaard, "to introduce Christianity into Christendom."

✱ ✱ ✱

Precisely because in France the relationship of state and church was not challenged, let alone recast, before August 4–5, it had to be taken up soon afterward, and this involved "reforming the one and the other" simultaneously. The very strength of the bond meant that it was impossible to reform the government without making major changes in the status of the Gallican Church in both civil and political society; and soon these changes began to be driven also by the contingencies of the Revolution and the Enlightenment views of its leaders. But—again, because of the very ubiquity of church and religion in all spheres of life—there was no way of making or forcing such changes without doing violence to deep-felt interests, sensibilities, and passions. Presently the religious question became a major catalyst of the friend-enemy dissociation, despite the efforts of moderate bishops in 1790 and of Robespierre in 1794 to prevent the rift.[13]

A relatively small number of the Third Estate's *cahiers de doléances* called for reform in the Church, notably for a curtailment of fiscal privileges and a redistribution of the extravagant wealth of religious orders and prelates in favor of the parish priests. Scores of the lower clergy harbored similar reformist notions, and these worldly concerns made for a common ground with the Third Estate in May–June 1789. Of course, while for the former ecclesiastical reform was the key to the regeneration of Church and ministry, for the latter it was an essential precondition for the reform of the commonweal. But even if a vanguard in the Third Estate proposed to press reform within the awe-inspiring Gallican Church as part of a curtailment of the powerful "state within the state," it considered neither questioning its eminent institutional sway nor attacking the Catholic religion per se.[14]

In any case, at the creation of the French Revolution the Third Estate and the reformists within the Church needed each other. Numerically the delegation of the First Estate at Versailles "was dominated by parish priests . . . [and] out of this body came the crucial [if narrow] majority which on June 19 voted to join with the Third Estate." To be sure, nearly 20 percent of the upper clergy finally rallied as well, and so did a liberal fraction of forty-seven members of the nobility. Still, without "the discontent and ideals of the lower clergy," the Revolution "might well have been stillborn."[15]

But politics knows no gratitude. Presently the First Estate found itself confronted with several changes that went alarmingly beyond its ill-defined intentions. In the wake of August 4 and 11, 1789, the priests and, above all, the bishops faced the problems stemming from the renunciation, without compensation, of feudal prerogatives and the tithe. This surrender of economically valuable rights dealt them and the religious orders such a severe material blow that the hierarchy was compelled to rethink and restructure the finances of the Church. Would the men and women of the cloth have to become, as Mirabeau suggested, salaried public functionaries? With the aggravation of the state's budgetary deficit, on November 2, 1789, the National Assembly, by a large majority, voted to have the property of the Church placed at the disposal of the nation, to serve as collateral for the assignat. This measure further increased the Church's dependence on the state—or, rather, on the ill-defined new regime.[16]

Ever more churchmen became alarmed about not only this ominous dependency but also other unforeseen consequences of their alliance with the Third Estate. As early as August 1789 the Declaration of the Rights of Man and the Citizen unequivocally defined civil rights and liberties to include religious freedom for non-Catholics. The following April the Assembly defeated Dom Christophe-Antoine Gerle's motion to proclaim Roman Catholicism France's dominant or state religion. This rebuff was all the more politically divisive because nearly the entire clergy had taken for granted that the Gallican Church would continue to be paramount, with Protestants and Jews held in an inferior status, exposed to discrimination.[17] No less troubling for the hierarchy, about this same time the Assembly decreed the dissolution of all monasteries and convents except those with a charitable and educational mission. The bulk of the clerical deputies in vain protested what they considered the would-be temporal state's unwarranted intrusion into the inviolate ecclesiastical sphere. Although the majority of the Assembly viewed the reformation of the Gallican Church as a normal part and consequence of the reform of France's public institutions, for ideologically charged political reasons, militant reactionaries opposed the decree of dissolution, while reformers pressed it, thereby feeding the incipient polarization of forces opposed to compromise.

The new men of power may be said to have shown greater resolve in dealing with the monarchy and nobility than with the Church. Admittedly, they were critical of the excessive weight of the priesthood and hierarchy in state and society. But they were also daunted by the men of the cloth, not least because they had a sacred aura about them. To challenge the Church head-on was to move into uncharted and treacherous waters. As Quinet suggested, the Enlightenment did not provide legislators and Jacobins with either a canon or guidelines for the separation of church and state, of religion and politics.[18]

Without following a master plan, during the first year the Revolution gradually eroded the autonomy of the Gallican Church: "politically, by associating the *bons curés* with the Third Estate; socially, by abolishing feudal privileges; economically, by nationalizing church property; and [finally] religiously, by enacting the Civil Constitution of the Clergy."[19] This new status for the clergy, voted on July 12, 1790, was inseparable from the intensifying struggles over the future directions of the Revolution in the Constituent Assembly and beyond, and hence stirred the embers of religious strife. From now on, for all sides, but especially for the fundamentalists of the right and left, positions on the church-religion issue became a crucial touchstone of political orientation and engagement: revolutionaries denigrated all critics and opponents of the Civil Constitution for their medieval clericalism and obscurantism; the anti- and counterrevolutionaries at home and abroad traduced their opponents for being enemies of God and the Catholic faith.

Since during the springtime of the Revolution the majority of the National Assembly had "recast vast areas of French secular life unresisted and . . . removed the Church's material foundations without much outcry," it did not expect inordinate opposition as it set about redefining the Church's place in the embryonic new order.[20] To be sure, the majority of bishops in league with die-hard secular notables had seized every opportunity to decry the disestablishment drive for being inherently ungodly. Be that as it may, the immediate purpose of the Civil Constitution of the Clergy was to recast the materially and politically weakened Church in the same spirit and intention as the other institutions of the commonwealth. For reasons of economy and efficiency, the number of dioceses was reduced from 139 to one diocese for each of France's newly drawn eighty-three departments, with one parish for every 6,000 inhabitants. In the future, priests would be popularly elected and adequately paid, with the higher clergy commanding less generous incomes than heretofore.

Clearly, even though the lawgivers professed that with the Civil Constitution they were not exceeding their temporal authority, they certainly did so in the eyes of the clergy. Quite apart from never as much as consulting the hierarchy about the redrawing of France's ecclesiastical map, the brazen secular state presumed to institute an electoral regime for the priesthood and to loosen the Gallican Church's ties to Rome by stripping the Pope of his time-honored prerogative of investiture.[21]

The vast majority of the clerical deputies as well as much of the clergy and laity at large took umbrage and hurled defiance at the Civil Constitution, insisting that such drastic changes in the internal organization of the Church—which they perceived as encroaching on the sacred—called for prior consultation with either a national church council or the Pope in Rome, or with both. Forthwith the decree became a boon for the rearguard of hard-line bishops and noblemen at home and émigrés abroad, and, as we shall see, for the Pope as well. Unintentionally and unexpectedly, anti- and counterrevolutionaries were presented with a salient issue, a fiery battle cry, and a ready-made audience. The sixty bishops and scores of priests who lost their posts and the countless churchgoers who were disconcerted by the diocesan and parochial reorganization were the most natural embodiment of this oppositional potential.[22] With time the countryside in particular was teeming with countless individuals who felt offended, disenchanted, betrayed, or terrified by the Paris-centered Revolution. Among them religious and ecclesiastical concerns ran deep. Although these concerns were on the whole inseparable from political and social discontents, as often as not "unprofane" preoccupations provided the spur to active opposition.

On August 24, 1790, Louis XVI gave the Civil Constitution his royal sanction, albeit reluctantly. He did so as part of the search for a constitutional monarchy, which was still very much a historical possibility, and because he was convinced of broad support for the new arrangements at all levels of the priesthood. But the moderates of both camps, who sought a timely termination of the Revolution, were increasingly hampered by their respective zealots. France's smoldering religious war fostered polarization and, in turn, was fueled by it. When the National Legislative Assembly convened on October 1, 1791, the anticlerical Mountain carried even greater weight than in the Constituent Assembly. In the meantime, a year before, all except two of the thirty-two bishops who had been deputies in the Constituent Assembly had issued an "Exposition of Principles Regarding the Civil Constitution of the Clergy" which was endorsed by all the other bishops, making a total of 120 signatories.[23] Drafted by Jean-de-Dieu Raymond de Boisgelin de Cucé, the archbishop of Aix, it set forth the episcopate's criticisms of what it took to be the new Assembly's intention to make the established church and religion subservient to the state. With an eye to avoiding a schism, this episcopal predication left some room for accommodation. But the patriots read it as a call to disobedience by a Church determined to maintain its privileged status outside and against the regenerate nation. Both sides were preparing for another showdown in an atmosphere of soaring mutual suspicion, with the bishops attentive to Rome and the Mountain to the streets and the Commune of Paris.

On November 27, 1790, with the die-hards boycotting the session, the Constituent Assembly adopted a decree requiring clergymen, like all public functionaries, to take a loyalty oath within two months. They were to swear not only "to be loyal to nation, law, and King," but also "to defend, with all their power, the Constitution decreed by the National Assembly and accepted by the King." Any cleric refusing to take this oath would forfeit his post. He would, in addition, be liable "to prosecution for disturbing the peace" should he persist in exercising his ministry.[24]

The effect of the oath was to widen and intensify the growing schism within Church and clergy, as well as in society at large. The prelates construed and represented the oath as a vote for not only the separation of altar and throne but also the establishment of a church subordinate to the state and on a par with other religious communities, notably Protestant and Jewish. They admonished that to take the oath would be to approve a break with Rome as well as to sanction government interference in matters of doctrine and ritual.

Beyond the highly controversial issue of content, there was that of form. The oath was to be sworn, for all to witness, in the Assembly, in churches, and in broad daylight. Certainly to make the oath-taking public was to give reign to intimidation and rehabilitate an ancient but contested practice. Not unlike the Tennis Court Oath, exalted in David's dramatic painting, the clerical oath epitomizes "the performance of archaic but still meaningful rituals" in support of radical change. At the same time, it "evinces the extent to which the Revolution tried or pretended to be a religion that used collective rites to forge disparate individuals into a communion of the faithful."[25]

While the law-givers fully expected the bishops to be up in arms, they were taken unawares by the scale and intensity of the parish priests' defiance. This resistance was all the more perturbing to them because it took form without clear guidance from either Pope Pius VI or Louis XVI, who had countersigned the decree of the clerical oath on December 26, 1790.

The ecclesiastical deputies were to take the lead in the Assembly, the central theater of power. On December 27 Abbé Grégoire stepped up to the tribune to affirm that the Civil Constitution in no way "violates the holy truths which we must believe in and teach," and solemnly swore the oath. Characteristically, however, in the chamber all but two of the forty-four bishops and nearly two-thirds of the priests were unwilling to follow his example. Outside the Assembly, only an additional two bishops fell in line, so that 156 out of 160 bishops stood their ground.[26]

Nationwide barely one-third of the clergy took the oath, including only slightly over one-half of all parish priests. Obviously, there were enormous regional variations, running from over 90 percent non-jurors in the Vendée to over 90 percent jurors in the Var. In general the zone of widespread defiance comprised the north (including much of Normandy), the west, the mountainous regions of the center, Alsace, and Lorraine. As for the zone of above-average compliance or "constitutionalism," it took in much of the center, including the Ile-de-France, and the southeast, with Lyons, Marseilles, and Nice.[27]

In both zones, and indeed throughout France, a complex mixture of factors bore on the clergy's reasons and motives for taking or refusing the oath: local and regional history and culture; confessional strife; ecclesiastical density; social structure; and political conjuncture. But whatever the interplay of collective and individual considerations, there was a constant "dialectic . . . between the perspectives and attitudes of the clergymen confronting the oath and the opinions of the laity among whom they lived and served."[28] There were strong positive correlations between, on the one hand, refusal of the oath and, on the other, unquestioning loyalty to the bishop, enduring local or regional distrust of the outside world, and deep-running hostility for nearby Protestant communities. There is reason to believe that insofar as the decisions of priests were swayed by parishioners moved by profane considerations, to that extent the oath-taking became in effect a referendum on reform not only in state-church relations and in church organization but in all other spheres as well.[29]

With few of the defiant clergymen reconsidering their position, the rift between the embryonic revolutionary state and the refractory church kept widening. The majority of the Assembly and episcopacy viewed each other in increasingly Manichaean terms: whereas the former could not conceive of placing their trust in a Gallican Church unbound from the state and tied to Rome, the latter, with a majority of bishops now in exile, could not fathom a profane state and a society sworn to religious pluralism and toleration. This hardening of positions coincided with the king's flight to Varennes in June 1791, which exacerbated tensions, all the more with the Jacobins exploiting it to discredit one and all champions of compromise. Had this escape been successful, it might well have brought the "reinstatement of the Church of the Old Regime" as part of a general "restoration." After all, in the public justification for his escape, Louis XVI invoked, above all, religious motives.[30]

On November 29, 1791 the Legislative Assembly proceeded to force the issue. It passed a decree giving clerics one week to swear loyalty to the Constitution. To refuse was to risk not only salary and pension but also two years of prison for standing against the *patrie* and public order. Increasingly hopeful of help from abroad, and tempted by the *politique du pire*, Louis XVI vetoed the measure on December 19, thereby adding fuel to the fire.[31]

During the next six months the church-religion question became ever more entangled with the politics and diplomacy of the foreign war which "revolutionized the revolution." With the first military setbacks, the declaration of *la patrie en danger*, and the Brunswick Manifesto, the patriots intensified their vilification of the refractory priests, who were now charged with the additional and not totally imaginary sin of being subversive agents in the service of foreign powers. On May 27, 1792 the Legislative Assembly passed a decree making refractory priests subject to summary deportation abroad on being denounced for disloyal activities by twenty registered citizens of their canton. Three months later, on August 26, yet another and even harder decree ordered the forcible deportation overseas, within a fortnight, of all refractory priests refusing to leave the country of their own accord.[32] They now had no choice other than to emigrate or go underground. Less than a month later, the escalation of the religious conflict culminated in the killing of about 300 refractory priests in the avenging September prison massacres.[33] Meanwhile the pace of the exodus of clergymen quickened to eventually reach close to 30,000.

This escalation is all but universally deemed to have been the inevitable result of the Civil Constitution of the Clergy and, above all, the mandatory loyalty oath. As Quinet was the first to point out, nearly all commentators and historians took these measures to have been the *grande faute* or supreme and fatal political blunder of the infant French Revolution, and this judgment remains uncontested to this day.[34] Insofar as this position suggests that the church-religion question could and should have been circumvented, downplayed, or ignored, with a view to depriving the upward spiral of polarization and violence of essential fuel, it runs counter to the logic of the struggle over the redefinition of church-state relations in prerevolutionary (and revolutionary) France. As noted above, the age-old interpenetration of the two spheres was so far-reaching that it was impossible to reform the one without the other. This is not to deny the drastic nature of the Legislative Assembly's intervention in the reorganization of the Church, which quite naturally was widely perceived and decried as an attack on both the faith and the faithful. But the escalation of the friend-enemy dissociation was not a one-sided affair: it was spurred on not only by the actions of the revolutionary leadership but also by those of the clerical intransigents and the Holy See.

✳ ✳ ✳

Pope Pius VI could hardly have been expected to welcome the Revolution. Indeed, from the outset he was incensed and alarmed by the course of events in France. He was fundamentally hostile to the ideas of liberty and equality as formulated in the to him presumptuous and perverse Declaration of the Rights of Man, which defied the Catholic creed and worldview as understood and enforced at the time. He also took umbrage at the abolition of annates and tithes, the expropriation of church properties, and, above all, the challenge to his sovereignty in Avignon and the Comtat Venaissin. Like the church leaders in France, the Holy Father had both theological and ideological as well as social and political reasons for dreading the Revolution. But unlike them, his hands were not tied by the perils of having to make hard decisions in the eye of the storm.

In addition, and perhaps not surprisingly, the pontiff's informants and counselors reinforced his animus. In France he listened to Father Jean-Siffrein Maury, an ultrareactionary in both political and ecclesiastical affairs whom he raised to the rank of cardinal after his emigration to Rome in late 1790. His apostolic delegate in Avignon, Siffrein Salamon, was of the same turn of mind. In the Vatican he gave his ear to émigrés, particularly the hard-liners among them; to the French ambassador, Cardinal François-Joachim de Pierre de Bernis, an irreconcilable close to the Comte d'Artois; to the ambassadors of the Great Powers who envisaged the formation of a Holy Alliance against revolutionary France; and to Cardinal Zelada, his secretary of state, who was in accord with Maury and Bernis.

Whereas in public Pius VI moved slowly and with caution, in private he framed his position rather rapidly. Probably he kept his counsel in the belief that the French episcopate would stand fast on its own. Once he did break his silence, the Pope, backed by the Sacred College of Cardinals, breathed fire and fury. His pronouncements were wrathful and uncompromising in both letter and spirit—a *locus classicus* of conspiratorial reasoning, execration, and demonization. The Pope's intemperate intervention was inspired by his apocalyptic view that with Protestantism, Jansenism, and the Enlightenment seeding the ground, the French Revolution was the linear and ultimate descendant of the Reformation, and therefore to be reined in, if not crushed, in good time.

In the wake of his forced move from Versailles to the Tuileries in October 1789, Louis XVI apologized to Pius VI for the Assembly's recent anticlerical measures. Implying that "the new and disquieting order" could not last very long, the king reassured the Pope that as "the eldest son of the Church he would keep watch and ward over the rites of the Holy Church, the union with the Roman Church, and the respect due the ministers of the Gospel."[35]

But with the situation going from bad to worse following the National Assembly's decree against the houses of religion, on March 9, 1790, the Pope addressed the Sacred College of Cardinals, most or all of whose members shared his consternation. To his way of thinking there was "universal" agreement that the "vast and vigorous" French monarchy, Europe's "premier great power, had . . . plunged into an abyss of distress verging on complete ruin." In the beginning "this revolution" may well have been concerned with administrative and political matters. In no time, however, it began to encroach on the realm of religion, foreshadowing its "subjugation and subservience to political interests." Indeed, the situation was growing "more alarming by the day." In the face of heaven, the decrees of the Assembly "attack and subvert the Catholic religion, usurp the rights of the Apostolic See, and violate existing treaties." The pontiff considered these infractions to have their "source in the false doctrines . . . and contagious principles of freely circulating, poisonous, and subversive writings." The Assembly "guarantees every one the freedom not only to think as he pleases, even in religious matters, but to express himself publicly with impunity." Even the primacy of the Catholic religion was being contested and "non-Catholics were declared eligible for municipal, civil, and military posts." Besides, "church property was put at the disposal of the nation and . . . the tithe was abolished." Even now Pius VI held that the Holy See could not continue to be silent in the face of these "sacrilegious decrees." For the moment he was undecided, however, whether to remonstrate with the bishops, the clergy, or the beleaguered king of a nation which was "tempted by the vain phantom of liberty . . . and allowed itself to be subjugated by a council of philosophes." To be sure, there was "a time to keep silent and a time to speak" (Eccles. 3:7). But having been "given the charge to speak," there were limits to his continuing to hold his peace. In conclusion, the Pope wanted his senior advisors to know that his "silence should not be construed as indifference, and even less as approval." Three weeks later, at the consistory of March 29, he specifically denounced the principles of the Declaration of the Rights of Man and the Citizen.[36]

From this time forward the news from France became increasingly alarming: in April, the rejection of Dom Gerle's resolution; in May, the *bagarre* between Catholics and Protestants in Montauban; in June, the *bagarre* in Nîmes and the petition of the Pope's subjects in the territory of Avignon to become part of France; and finally, in July, the Civil Constitution of the Clergy. All the while, Pius VI maintained his public silence, though off the record he intimated that before long he would speak out. On July 10, he wrote to Louis XVI to urge him not to approve the Civil Constitution: the king was admonished that by signing this decree he would not only lead his kingdom "into error . . . and a schism" but might also "ignite the savage fires of a religious war." Pius VI served notice that although until now he had shown restraint, "should religion continue to be imperiled the Head of the Church would [have to] make his voice heard." For special emphasis he added that although the king "had the authority to renounce certain royal prerogatives . . . [he] was not empowered to alienate or abandon those belonging to God and the Church": as a matter of fundamental principle, "no purely civil and political body had the right to change the doctrine and discipline of the Catholic Church," at the risk of endangering its edifice.[37] That same day, July 10, 1790, the Pope sent a letter to Archbishop Jérôme-Marie Champion de Cicé of Bordeaux. He informed this prelate, who had kept an open mind until he finally chose emigration over the oath, that he had just written to Louis XVI to reiterate that "the renovators had no objective

. . . other than to destroy, down to its name, the Catholic cult and confirm the unbelievers in their impious system."[38] Pius VI contacted several other prelates to urge them to prevail on the king not to endorse the unrighteous decrees in order "to save their religion, King, and *patrie*."[39]

The letter to Louis XVI did not reach Paris until July 23, two days after he had announced his approval of the Civil Constitution. For reasons of political expediency, he and his advisors decided to keep the letter secret. On August 28 the king informed the Pope that he had signed in order to avoid a schism in the Church and reassured him that he remained more than ever true to his religion and loyal to the Holy Father. This did not soothe the Pope's indignation, and on August 17 he notified the king that he had set up a special council of 20 cardinals, mostly theologians and canonists, to examine the issues raised by recent developments in France and to advise him on the course to follow.[40] On September 22, as this council was about to start its deliberations, in another letter to Louis XVI he expressed his disappointment about the king's having signed under duress and yielded to "violence." The pontiff repeated that the Civil Constitution was "pointed at the heart of the Catholic religion" and was nothing short of a "criminal outrage." Nonetheless the Holy See did not want to promulgate a "doctrinal judgment" without "thorough consideration" and without the certainty that "the faithful would follow the lead of their pastors."[41]

What finally prompted Pius VI to speak out was not an additional provocation by the revolutionary government but the French episcopate's own "Exposition of Principles" of October 30, 1790. Despite its outright criticism of the Civil Constitution of the Clergy, this text still looked to continue the search for compromise. Above all, it hinted that there might be some way to re-form the relationship of church and state without doing violence to Catholic religious belief. Pius VI considered this stand "weak as water," all the more so since soon thereafter, on November 27, Paris imposed the oath to the Civil Constitution on the clergy. One of the first prelates to take this oath, Cardinal Étienne-Charles de Loménie de Brienne, wrote to the Pope to explain and justify his action. In his reply of February 23, 1791, the pontiff charged Loménie de Brienne with having "greatly dishonored the purple," since in the final analysis the Civil Constitution was "an amalgam drawn from several heresies." The Pope made it clear that the time was past due to show the French bishops "the venom of their errors" and to spell out the "mandatory disciplinary measures." Pius VI put Loménie de Brienne on notice that should he persist in his error he would be "stripped of the dignity of cardinal," a warning carried out on September 26, 1791.[42]

The authoritative pronouncement, in the form of a papal brief, *Quod aliquantum*, was issued on March 10, 1791.[43] It expressed the Pope's unqualified opposition to both the reorganization of the Gallican Church and the founding principles of the Revolution. For doctrinal rationale and precedent, Pius VI reached back to the condemnation of "Luther's heresy" by the Council of Sens in 1527; to the "proscription of a captious, false, impious, and heretic text" by Benedict XIV in 1755; and to the "anathema" issued against a "defiant contravention of the Apostolic See's decrees" by the second Council of Tours in 567. The Pope unequivocally denounced the Declaration of the Rights of Man and the Civil Constitution of the Clergy for seeking "to annihilate the Catholic religion and, along with it, the obedience due to Kings." Regarding the Declaration, the Holy Father stated that it was nothing short of madness to give all men the absolute "freedom to think, speak, write, and print" in matters of religion. As for the Civil Constitution, it was intended to put an end to "the most sacred dogma and discipline of the Church"; to "annihilate" the rights of the Holy See, the clergy, the religious orders, and "the whole Catholic community"; to "abolish" all sacred rites; and to dispossess the Church of "all ecclesiastical properties and revenues."

Pius VI vowed to "protect the sacred rights of the Church and Apostolic See against all attacks" and in so doing meant to "point up what separates such strangers to the Church as infidels and Jews from those whom the regeneration of baptism has submitted to its laws." He enjoined all French prelates to refuse the oath, insisting that it "degrades the primacy of the Holy See" and violates the "Roman Pontiff's prerogative to confirm the election of bishops." It was equally important not to relax the Church's discipline and organization, which was rooted in dogma and could be changed only by ecclesiastical authority.

The Pope claimed that in reading the Civil Constitution, in which "not a single article was free of error," his hands "literally trembled," and he was reminded that one of his predecessors had warned that the innovations proposed at the time of the Reformation were likely to "provoke in France, and against the Apostolic See, the same schism that afflicts Germany." While Pius VI fully recognized man's duty to obey civil laws, he cried out against whoever in France was so "presumptuous and delirious to think that man has the right to take the place of God." He reproved the "new doctrine, . . . hierarchy, and . . . discipline," forged in Paris, holding that they made for a "system that preaches and exalts unrestrained and unlimited freedom at the same time that it denies citizens the freedom of conscience."

In the covering letter for his brief to Louis XVI, the Pope emphasized that the College of Cardinals' examination had fully and unanimously "demonstrated that there was no escaping the charge of heresy for swearing an allegedly civic oath." He also reminded the king of his solemn vow at his *sacre* in 1775 "to defend and maintain, in their full integrity, the rights of the Church and privileges of the episcopate."[44]

Although the French bishops had been apprised of the Pope's fierce objections for well over six months, they decided to keep the brief to themselves, in the hope of finding a way to temper it. But within a month, on April 13, the Holy See issued *Charitas*, an even more stringent brief addressed not just to the French episcopacy but to all the clergy and faithful. With this writing Pius VI took the ultimate step of declaring the Assembly's decrees heretical and schismatic. He unequivocally condemned the "falsehearted bishops" who had taken an oath that was "criminal, illicit, illegitimate, sacrilegious, and in violation of the sacred canon," inasmuch as the Civil Constitution would expose bishops to election by "secularists, heretics, infidels, and Jews." The Holy Father adjured them not to "allow men impressed by the philosophy of their century to lay before the public a monstrous doctrine . . . contrary to the precepts of Jesus Christ . . . ; and not to listen to the beguiling and deathly discourse . . . of the new philosophes who have declared war on the Catholic religion and are leagued against the Church." He admonished the five renegade bishops that unless they retracted their oath within forty days they "would be anathematized and denounced as schismatics." In conclusion, Pius VI exhorted the faithful "to keep away from all usurpers," including "false-hearted bishops, archbishops, and priests," and to maintain "strong ties with the See of St. Peter, for to belong to the Church requires being united with its visible head."[45]

Again, the French bishops held back the papal pronouncement for fear of precipitating an irreparable break, and in a vain effort to keep the Pope's views from becoming public. On April 23, Pius VI issued another predication, this time addressed to the clergy and faithful not only of France, but of all the world. In the encyclical *Adeo nota* he condemned, *urbi et orbi*, the Declaration of the Rights of Man for "denying the rights of God over man," leaving him "amputated" from his Maker and at the mercy of "a febrile liberty and equality which threaten to strangle reason." All in all "freedom of thought and action . . . is a chimerical right contrary to the commands of the Creator." In his righteous wrath Pius VI charged that in addition to "overthrowing the Catholic religion," the National Assembly's "monstrous freedoms" benefited "people who are strangers to the Church, such as infidels [Protestants?] and Jews."[46]

The bishops' efforts to prevent publication of the Pope's pronouncements directed specifically to France were cut short. On May 2, in the wake of rumors in the royalist press, the papal nuncio gave a copy of *Charitas* to Count de Montmorin, the French foreign minister. It was made public on May 4, along with *Quod aliquantum.* By then the war was radicalizing the Revolution: forced-draft military, economic, and ideological mobilization were giving rise to emergency rule as well as resistance to it. Caught up in the logic and dynamics of the political struggle between the forces of revolution and antirevolution which was inseparable from the spiraling war between revolutionary France and the European powers, the Pope and the refractory Gallican Church perforce became essential agents of counterrevolution.

On the very day that he released *Charitas,* the Pope published a brief on the unrest in Avignon and the Comtat Venaissin. From the very beginning he disregarded the demands of the population of these territories, held by the papacy since the fourteenth century, for some of the rights granted to French citizens in 1789. The Pope's rebuff contributed to radicalizing the local disaffection, which gradually swelled into popular demonstrations in favor of accession to France, to be ratified by referendum. Rather than seek an accommodation, Pius VI castigated the remonstrants and summoned the Great Powers to stand with him, warning that France's takeover would wreck the concert of Europe. Now, in this latest pronouncement, after characterizing the insurgence in Avignon and the Comtat Venaissin as an assault on his temporal rights and on the Catholic religion, Pius VI charged the supporters of the new prophecy with following a "small cabal of perverse men" tied to a "nefarious conspiracy" determined to turn the population "against the law of God and country." In conclusion, the Holy Father declared all recently adopted revolutionary measures "void, illegitimate, and sacrilegious" and warned that churchmen who had suffered violence would be avenged.[47]

As was to be expected, the Vatican's intervention instantly became a catalyst of counterrevolution, all the more so because it was not merely a censure and rejection of the Civil Constitution but a wholesale condemnation of the Revolution's philosophical and ideological premises as well. The pronouncements of the Pope sparked popular demonstrations in the streets of Paris: "near the Palais Royal a crowd burned an outsized effigy of Pius VI, with the word 'fanaticism' written in red across his forehead and brandishing a dagger in his right hand, a scroll representing the brief of March 10 in his left."[48] Seizing on the French government's failure to issue an official apology for this affront, the papal nuncio Dugnani left for Rome. A few months before Paris had dismissed Cardinal de Bernis, its ambassador to the Holy See, for refusing to take the oath. In turn, the Holy See now spurned his designated successor, the Comte de Ségur, for having taken it, with the result that "diplomatic relations between Paris and Rome were broken and . . . the schism was consummated."[49]

In Rome as in Paris, the friend-enemy spirit now ruled. Six months after relations were broken, on September 26, 1791, Pius VI presented a report to the College of Cardinals which revealed how extreme his opposition to the Revolution had become. The pontiff began by praising Loménie de Brienne for his past services: in the 1760s he had taken the lead in putting Rousseau's *Social Contract* on the Gallican Church's index of prohibited books and in "warning" the clergy and laity about the "dangers of the freedom of thought . . . [and] the press." But then, after 1787, as one of the king's first ministers, Loménie had balked the Vatican to champion the Act of Tolerance for Protestants, which became "a fatal source of the ills besetting and tearing apart Church and Kingdom." In fact, Loménie was one of the trailblazers of the Revolution launched by the National Assembly: having left state office and taken charge of the diocese of Sens, in March 1790 he publicly "extolled the revolutionary system" and claimed credit for having been one of its "zealous promoters." After all this, and insisting that he had reluctantly yielded to the force of circumstance, Loménie "shamelessly" proceeded to ask the Apostolic See to approve the Civil Constitution, which allowed "Jews, Mohammedans, Calvinists, and sectarians" to participate in the election of priests. Ignoring warnings that he would be severely sanctioned unless he repudiated his errors, Loménie sent a letter to the Pope in which, after spuriously distinguishing between "accepting and approving evil laws," he tendered his resignation as cardinal.[50]

No less revealing of the Holy See's attitude to the events in France, in a brief of March 19, 1792, Pius VI publicly cried out against the "criminal . . . and deplorable" actions of Catholics, especially ecclesiastics, who "foment the disastrous schism, thereby serving the conspiracy which the new philosophes have mounted in the National Assembly, where they have the majority." The Supreme Pontiff conjured "all who were helping to deepen, spread, and prolong the ravages of this schism in France to . . . bear in mind 'the terrifying wait for the Last Judgment and the fury of the jealous fires of divine vengeance which would some day consume' them."[51]

Ten months later, on January 21, 1793, Louis XVI's execution definitely ruptured the alliance of throne and altar, leaving a phantom French monarchy in exile and the universal Roman Church dispossessed of its peerless Gallic branch. To decapitate the king was to desacralize and demystify the immemorial principle of absolute and divinely consecrated monarchy while at the same time sacralizing the untried principle of national or popular sovereignty, the regicide having been voted, even if only with a slim majority, by the Convention.

This spectacular and potentially contagious apostasy could not leave the Pope indifferent, and on June 17, 1793, he delivered a widely disseminated "Allocution on the Death of Louis XVI" to the Sacred College of Cardinals.[52] He imputed the "cruel and barbaric spectacle in Paris . . . to an ungodly conspiracy," and contested the Convention's "legal right or authority" to judge and condemn the king. Having "abrogated the monarchy," it had transferred all power to the people. Ironically, on one score Pius VI had a certain affinity with Voltaire, in that he, too, considered the people, in Shakespeare's words, "a beast with many heads": it listened to "neither reason nor counsel"; it was in no condition to have "sound and virtuous ideas"; and it judged issues not by fact but "opinion." As for this public opinion, it was "always inconstant, easily misled, ungrateful, arrogant, cruel, and open to all excesses as well as disposed to revel in carnage, savor the effusion of human blood, and delight in the last agonies of the dying."

At all events, Louis XVI had done ultimate penance for having "affixed his signature, despite himself, to decrees that were contrary to the discipline and canonical faith of the Church." Indeed, like James I, his sole crime "was that of being King," and the Supreme Pontiff saw an analogy with Benedict XIV's judgment that Mary Stuart's death "was due to hatred of the Catholic religion, which would have prevailed in England had Mary lived to reign." Obviously Louis XVI, like Mary Stuart, was the victim of a furious "hatred" of the true faith. In France Calvinists had long ago started to plot and spread their subversion of Catholicism, and to this end had "leagued themselves with the perverse philosophes." Protestant pamphlets and the writings of Voltaire—this "infamous . . . and irreverent individual"—were "like the natural fruit of a poisonous tree." Pius VI invoked his own encyclical of 1775, at the start of his reign, in which he had urged the priesthood to "forcefully and vigilantly" prevent these pernicious publications from "contaminating your flock." Had his exhortation been heeded, the "vast conspiracy . . . of these depraved minds against kings and empires" might have been choked off long since. By inscribing the false and specious words of liberty and equality on their banners and embracing a freethinking philosophy, the "factionalists" were "corrupting sound minds and customs as well as subverting established laws and institutions."

As Pius VI saw it, the "sacrilegious" Civil Constitution of the Clergy had grown out of this profane counterculture. Both the recasting of the Church and the execution of Louis XVI were fired, above all, by hatred of the Catholic religion, since the king was accused of having refused to sanction the deportation of refractory priests and of having reiterated his resolve to reclaim the lofty place of the Catholic Church as soon as possible. In conclusion, the Holy Father lamented that France, which had been "a mirror of all Christianity and an unbending pillar of the [Catholic] faith," should have unleashed, against the Holy Church, a furor whose "excesses exceed those perpetrated against it by its bitterest enemies" through the ages.

The symbiosis between throne and altar was indeed broken, and the divorce between the old religion and the Revolution was all but complete. The September massacres had already had refractory priests as their principal victims, and there would be much more of the same to come—the drownings of priests in the Loire, the intemperances of the de-Christianization campaigns, the atrocities attending the conflict with the "Catholic and Royal Army" in the Vendée—so much fuel for the doubling of the French Revolution's struggle for political and social reform with a religious civil war. But this radical change may be said to have grown out of not only the National Assembly's vote and enforcement of the Civil Constitution and the clerical oath but also the See of Rome's peremptory and intransigent policies toward the French Church and its fiery execration of the principles of 1789.

* * *

Following the break with the Holy See in the fall of 1791, France had two antagonistic Catholic churches pledged to the same faith and practicing the same liturgy: the fledgling Constitutional Church, reconciled to disestablishment and religious pluralism; and the traditional but now "refractory" Gallican Church, sworn to Rome and the time-honored association with the state. Although the schism was virtually politically driven, in important respects the opposing sides proceeded to reenact the internecine struggles of the past. Whereas the renovators claimed to redeem the Church by recovering its original ethical and moral purity as laid down in the Scriptures, the last-ditchers purported to uphold the True Faith and indivisibility of the universal apostolic Church. The opposing rhetorical pretensions were necessarily accompanied by fierce reciprocal recrimination and damnation: the refractory clergy was charged with being corrupt, obscurantist, and despotic; the constitutional clergy with being schismatic, heretical, and ungodly. A holy war of other times was grafted onto the civil and international wars of the French Revolution in which organized Catholicism played a much greater role on the counterrevolutionary than the revolutionary side. As Burke saw it, "the Catholic religion . . . [being] fundamentally the religion of France, [it] must go with the Monarchy of France." In Burke's view, which on this point was similar to the Pope's, just as "the Monarchy did not survive the Hierarchy, no, not even in appearance, for many months—in substance, not for a single hour," so it could not "exist in the future, if that pillar is taken away, or even shattered and impaired."[53]

In the showdown between the two consanguine churches the traditionalists had a distinct advantage over the constitutionalists. The former had the full weight of ecclesiastical and doctrinal tradition behind them, bolstered by the imprecations of the Apostolic See and the prelacy. Indeed, "between the two essentially similar potencies, power was bound to be with the older, the refractories expelling the constitutionals like shadowy intruders."[54]

No less important, the Constitutional Church received only limited official support. Although it was an ally and instrument of the revolutionary government, it ran into increasing hostility from the radical Mountain, above all because many of the constitutionals "sided with the Girondins and Federalists." As it turned out, the constitutionals failed in their primary political mission, which was to help contain and defeat the non-jurors and their anti- and counterrevolutionary backers, who gathered momentum in the Vendée and at Koblenz. With time, in particular for the sansculottes, there was little to choose between the two clergies, "pro-Girondin constitutionals being as great a danger to the nation as the refractories who were leagued with the kings and émigrés."[55] Ironically, the Constitutional Church fell victim to both traditional Catholicism and the radical Revolution, as the confrontation between these two forces reached its climax with the de-Christianization drive of 1793–94.

De-Christianization was not a *Ding an sich*, but part and parcel of a revolutionary configuration and dynamics. It was far from a systematic campaign: there was no overall project, nor was there a high command. Some actions—notably, the majority of the iconoclastic happenings, including carnivals and autos-da-fé, which at once animated and discredited de-Christianization—were spontaneous and local. Others, such as the taking down of church bells and the collection of valuable sacred objects, were government-mandated. The resignation and marriage of priests fell between these two extremes. The adoption of the Republican calendar, with its non- or anti-Christian overtones, as well as the promulgation of the cult of the Supreme Being, had government authority behind them. And the revolutionary field agents and armies in the provinces played an important and often counterproductive role in forcing de-Christianization, here and there running amok.

Furthermore, de-Christianization was not simply a product of radical revolutionary ideology, but also of the desperate situation of the revolutionary regime. No doubt Alphonse Aulard overloaded the contingency thesis when he argued that de-Christianization was the "necessary and indeed political consequence of the state of war into which the Revolution had been plunged by the *ancien régime*'s resistance to the new spirit."[56] But it is to distort its enabling or defining conditions to minimize the domestic and external dangers facing the infant Republic during the second half of 1793: federalism was spreading like wildfire; the peasant rebellion in the Vendée was at its height; and Marat was assassinated in Paris. Abroad, the First Coalition was draining off scarce military and economic resources needed to deal with this domestic time of troubles, which the counterrevolution, including the Church, exploited for its own benefit. It was in these months that the policies of the regime of public safety were put in place: *levée en masse*, "total" war in the Vendée, the Law of Suspects, the Maximum. On October 10 the government was declared "revolutionary until the conclusion of peace," in keeping with the merciless resolve driving the avenging fury following the "liberation" of the rebel cities and the defeat of the *Vendée militaire*.

It was at almost exactly this moment that de-Christianization got under way, with the adoption on October 5, 1793, of the republican calendar, proposed and fashioned by Philippe Fabre d'Eglantine. Hereafter time was to be counted no longer from the birth of Christ but from the birth of the Republic on September 22, 1792. Just as the rebaptism of cities was intended to refigure space for the new age, so the republican calendar, with its new nomenclature and holidays, was meant to refigure time by extricating it from the grip of revealed religion and by marking the categorical break in historical continuity.

The promulgation of the new-made calendar coincided with the officially encouraged start of the seizure of church bells and church valuables, including sacred objects, for the war effort. Some churches were set on fire or demolished; others were turned into stables and arsenals. Now and again these profanations were accompanied or followed by the ideologically motivated desecration or burning of religious paintings, statues, and crosses, usually on the square in front of the church. Here and there this iconoclasm was part of improvised rituals mocking religious obscurantism. There was also a rush to desacralize everyday life by changing the names of towns and cities and, above all, of streets and squares, the objective being to cleanse the toponyms of "everything which might recall the *ancien régime* (kings, castles, . . .) or previous superstitions (names of saints)."[57]

But the single most salient and far-reaching aspect of de-Christianization may well have been the resignation and marriage of priests. Nothing could match the high drama, on November 7, 1793, in the Convention, of the public renunciation of Jean-Baptiste Gobel, the constitutional deputy-bishop of Paris. Several hundred clerics followed his example, including most of the other constitutional deputy-priests. Ironically, Abbé Grégoire, who the year before had boldly stepped forward to take the clerical oath, now refused to resign, insisting that "I am a bishop and I will remain a bishop."[58] A week later the Convention voted to empower all duly constituted authorities to accept letters of resignation, and held out a financial reward for priests forswearing their sacred calling. But the vast majority of the 17,000 to 20,000 priests who resigned and the 4,000 to 6,000 priests who married were moved to do so by a combination of pressure, intimidation, and duress. Most of them were parish priests, and a clear majority of them had previously sworn the oath. But not a few constitutionals as well as refractories were imprisoned, deported, or executed for refusing to compromise or betray their ministry. In any case, by Thermidor the Gallican Church was seriously weakened. In addition to those who had resigned, 20,000 to 25,000 clerics had emigrated or had been deported—including 118 of 135 bishops and archbishops; some 3,000 to 5,000 had been executed; and many others had gone underground, often to join the counterrevolutionary resistance.[59]

The de-Christianization movement's principal theater of action was in "the departments rather than in Paris, and the *plat pays* was more affected by its brutalities than the towns."[60] It was this that made de-Christianization such an effective stimulus for the friend-enemy dissociation. The ecclesiastical and religious renovationists, both moderate and radical, came face to face with the time-honored religious beliefs, practices, and symbols of an essentially illiterate laity in a predominantly rural and peasant society. Indeed, there was a vast chasm between, on the one hand, the reformist intentions and executives in Paris and major cities, and, on the other, the dead hand of the past in the countryside in which tradition-bound parish priests were the officiants of a popular religion whose liturgies and rites were heavy with mystery, magic, and superstition. A change in any one aspect of the life of church or religion could only be experienced as the derangement of an all-embracing cosmology, all the more so since it tended to be perceived as imposed by agents of an alien and hostile outside world. Accordingly, even if de-Christianization was not entirely dictated and organized from the center and from above, it was bound to run into much more resistance than collaboration or accommodation through most of rural France. The intention was less to de-Christianize a nation that in vital respects had never been Christianized than to break open a "primitive" world which the Catholic Church and religion at once mirrored and sustained.

Even the slightest act of de-Christianization could stimulate resentment and defiance fraught with obstruction, resistance, and even revolt. Opposition was fueled by the violation not only of deep religious sensibilities but of age-old customs and habits in small towns and villages, particularly wherever the representatives on mission and the soldiers of the revolutionary armies were, or were alleged to be, in the vanguard of de-Christianizers. Townsmen and villagers readily conflated their long-standing aversion for the outside world with their current grievances against the revolutionary government, making the agents and carriers of de-Christianization scapegoats for their cumulative discontents. There is no separating or closely weighting the profane and sacred elements in the actions and reactions of the opposing sides. The desecration of churches and resignation of priests, not unlike the conscription of soldiers and requisition of provisions, formed a seamless web of encroachments charged with reciprocal violence. Probably many but not all militant revolutionaries were de-Christianizers, just as many but not all fervent counterrevolutionaries were soldiers of God. That true-believing revolutionaries wound up assailing the Catholic Church and religion in rural France was a measure of the overreach of an essentially urban and urbanizing project. In town and village, to attack church and religion was to lash out at the vitals of traditional society.[61]

Actually, at the revolutionary epicenter in Paris the de-Christianizers were themselves split into two main factions, one of whose chief discussions concerned the wisdom of this frontal assault on traditional belief. On the one hand, there were the zealous antireligionists, not to say atheists, with Hébert as their emblematic spokesman. They championed the instant excision of religious feelings and rites by means of a furious but spontaneous anti-Christian campaign to be carried by the sansculottes of urban France as part of a populist upheaval from the bottom up and designed to radicalize the Revolution socially.

On the other hand, there were those de-Christianizers who simply wanted to consolidate the separation of state and church while at the same time completing the defusion of the Church's anti- or counter-revolutionary sway. Robespierre emerged as the leading voice of this prudent position. He cautioned against any head-on assault on religion, insisting that it was both untimely and impolitic. In addition to considering it unwise to alienate the constitutional clergy, he feared, above all, that "to affront the peasantry's deeply held religious prejudices" was to risk feeding a groundswell of antirevolutionary resistance.[62] He was no less concerned about de-Christianization benefiting the foreign powers, which were poised to seize on it to justify their call to arms.

It would appear, then, that whereas Hébert, with his Paris-centered vision, incited the anti-Christianism of the underclasses and valued its revolutionary potential, Robespierre was skeptical of it and worried that its excesses would trigger a dangerous backlash by the silent majority. Nor was Robespierre prepared to give up on the freedom of religious worship, which the Convention reaffirmed with his strong support on December 5.

❋ ❋ ❋

Meanwhile some of the de-Christianizers coupled their destructive charge against church and religion with the search for a substitute secular religion with its own scripture, symbolism, and liturgy. Although anti-Christian and anti-sectarian, Robespierre was, as we saw, nevertheless drawn to deism, to be practiced and celebrated in the form of a civil religion. But in November 1793, with urban de-Christianization reaching a peak in Paris, where many churches were now closed down, the Hébertists and their sympathizers, including ex-bishop Gobel, stole the march by arranging for the first civic celebration of the Festival of Reason to be moved from the Circus of the Palais Royal to the Cathedral of Notre-Dame. For the occasion the organizers built, within the cathedral, a small mountain topped by a Temple of Philosophy flanked by busts of Voltaire and Rousseau. On November 10 the ceremonial procession which set out for Notre-Dame was headed by the Goddess of Reason. This deity appeared in the form of a living person, the well-known opera star Mlle Maillard, presumably to avoid a statue that would call to mind the Virgin or invite idolatry. Inside the cathedral the participants were witness to a ceremony of rebaptism. Following the emergence from the Temple of Philosophy of a young woman representing the Triumph of Reason over Fanaticism, Notre-Dame was renamed the Temple of Reason to the accompaniment of a hymn of liberty composed by François Joseph Gossec with words by Marie-Joseph Chénier.

The ceremony, like its reenactment in the provinces, was prosaic rather than liturgical: Michelet deemed it "chaste, sad, dry, and boring"; Quinet judged it "distressingly sterile . . . and empty" and a mere "*coup de théatre*." Both historians deplored the absence of novel ideas or sentiments to replace traditional ones, at the same time that they asked for indulgence for the "generous error" of those patriots of 1793 who had rushed to overturn a church and religion that had shackled humanity for centuries. In any case, more than likely, and regardless of intention, the embryonic and stillborn Cult of Reason aroused strong and conflicting passions less through the form, substance, and purport of its ceremony than through the grandeur and fame of its venue.[63]

For all the obvious reasons, Robespierre looked askance at the Cult of Reason. But it took several months for him to begin putting in place the no less hastily improvised Cult of the Supreme Being, which was not intended as yet another articulation or intensification of de-Christianization but as an alternative national religion. The winter and spring of 1793–94 saw, of course, the full horror of the revolutionary paroxysm with the *colonnes infernales* and the liquidation of the Hébertists and Dantonists. But the nascent cult, even if it marked the apogee of Robespierre's reign, was less a part of the climax of this convulsion than of its ebb tide or remission. It was instituted on May 7, 1794, following a speech by Robespierre proclaiming the Supreme Being and the immortality of the soul. The first—and only—grand festival of the Supreme Being was celebrated four weeks later on June 8, or about six weeks before Robespierre's own fall.

Once again Jacques-Louis David, ever understanding of the vagaries of the Revolution, was charged with the *mise en scène*. Attuned to the idea of inventing a vicarious religion and liturgy, and unsympathetic to the spirit and staging of the ceremony of the Cult of Reason, he designed the rites of the nascent religion of nature to be held in the open, on the Champ de Mars. The participants consisted of both citizens and the members of the Convention. As "sad and dry" as yesterday's ceremony in the Temple of Reason, this celebration had, in addition, something official if not forced about it, as was also the case with the satellite ceremonies in the provinces.[64]

But there was also something truly distinctive about this second would-be alternative religious service, in that it was braced by a would-be creed. Jacobins were circulating a "Gospel of Liberty," addressed to the Supreme Being. In these teachings they thanked the "*Père de Lumière* . . . for giving us the courage to break our chains and to punish crime," insisting that they did so not kneeling but "standing up, so as not to debase your work." The Jacobins expressed their gratitude to the new divinity for guiding them to victory and for "visiting vengeance on the heads of the hydra" which was forever seeking to reproduce itself in order to strangle "equality and fraternity." In a "confession of faith" embedded in this gospel, the votaries of this new cult proclaimed their belief "in the new French Republic, one and indivisible, as well as in its laws and the newly received sacred Rights of Man." They also felt sure "that the sans-culottes who had sacrificed their lives for these sacred rights and the *patrie* are seated to the right of the father of us all and bless all their brothers who are wreaking their vengeance on the tyrants." In conclusion, the true believers, certain that the "holy Mountain of the French has purged itself of all traitors," expressed confidence that "the legislators of the French people would continue to hurl thunder and lightning on Europe until all the tyrants who are making war on us are crushed."[65]

Robespierre's reasons for pressing ahead with the Cult of the Supreme Being remain obscure. To some extent he may have done so in the belief that as yet the people could not dispense with God and religion, atheism being a matter for the educated classes. Accepting Voltaire's tenet that "if God did not exist he would have to be invented," notably for the benefit of ordinary people, Robespierre assumed the new society to need a religion and church of its own, all the more so in its founding moment. But there may also have been a political calculus: to counter and marginalize what remained of militant de-Christianizers, so as to appease the mass of traditional believers as well as the European powers, as he envisaged bringing the Revolution to a close. Then again, however, Robespierre, the consummate "*logicien politique,*" may have been looking to put in place a civic religion as a moral foundation for a continuing terror. In any case, it is difficult, if not impossible, to assess his motives and purposes, not least because the Cult of the Supreme Being was every whit as evanescent as the Cult of Reason.[66]

Quinet exaggerated the historical possibility of breaking, overnight, the cake of inherited religious beliefs and practices, notably in rural France. Even so, he shrewdly perceived that in the end Robespierre left France unevenly divided between two cults which were "diametrically opposed and of necessity repelled and spurned each other." One was Catholicism, which was bound up with the counterrevolution. This old belief system and church were an "enormous force" because they were anchored in the "mass of the nation" and in harmony with the "deep-grounded folkways of a countryside intimidated by the Terror." The other was the Cult of the Supreme Being, which rallied at best a "tiny minority," many of them "official votaries." The built-in weakness of this alternative religion was intensified by virtue of its "own founders having condemned the cult based on reason." As if to appropriate a variant of Robespierre's charge that atheism and de-Christianization were for the classes, not the masses, Quinet judged the cult of the Supreme Being to have been "purely rationalist" and addressed to "enlightened minds." In sum, Robespierre had built a "fragile philosophic chapel . . . on enduring Gothic foundations." His "small temple of Greek or Roman inspiration, fated to cave in by reason of its inherent fragility," was overshadowed by the "immensity of the medieval cathedral," custodian of the "soul of the past."[67]

Significantly, when calling attention to the "ideological character of the French Revolution, . . . [which was] its *principal if transitory characteristic,*" Tocqueville stressed that it took the form, in the main, of "antireligious fanaticism." Indeed, the revolutionaries hated the priesthood and religion "with the ardor of proselytes and even of martyrs; a dedication which previously only religion could evoke." In Tocqueville's reading, anti- or ir-religion became "the most vivid and persistent of the revolutionary passions." Characteristically, "the learned," who execrated the terror, continued to be driven by the "irreligious, Voltarian, Encyclopedist impulse" to write and speak in this impious idiom long after "the masses" ceased to hearken to it.[68] The centrality and fanaticism of anti-religion in the revolutionary ideology needs to be considered together with the centrality and fanaticism of the defense of religion in the anti- and counterrevolutionary worldview and ideology. Certainly the attack on and defense of religion, rather than developing separate from each other, were thoroughly interrelated, and their reciprocation contributed not only to their achieving salience and primacy within their respective ideological constructs, but also to the general hardening of the friend-enemy dissociation.

✱ ✱ ✱

NOTES

1. See P. M. Jones, *The Peasantry in the French Revolution* (Cambridge: Cambridge University Press, 1988), ch. 1.

2. Bruno Benoit, ed. *Ville et Révolution française: Actes du colloque international* (Lyon: Presses Universitaires, 1994), p. 7.

3. André Latreille, *L'église catholique et la Révolution française*, vol. 1, *Le pontificat de Pie VI et la crise française, 1775–1799* (Paris: Hachette, 1946), pp. 8–17; Bernard Cousin, Monique Cubells, and René Moulinas, *La pique et la croix: Histoire religieuse de la Révolution française* (Paris: Centurion, 1989), pp. 13–26; Jean de Viguerie, *Christianisme et révolution: Cinq leçons d'histoire de la Révolution française* (Paris: Nouvelles Editions Latines, 1986), pp. 8–54, esp. p. 52; Nigel Aston, *The End of an Elite: The French Bishops and the Coming of the Revolution, 1786–1790* (Oxford: Clarendon, 1992), chs. 7–8.

4. This reconstruction of the *sacre* of June 11, 1775, is based on Duc de Croy, *Journal inédit, 1718–1784* (Paris: Flammarion, 1907), pp. 179–89; Bernard Fay, *Louis XVI ou la fin d'un monde* (Paris: Perrin, 1966), pp. 123–26; Jean-François Chiappe, *Louis XVI*, vol. 1: *Le Prince* (Paris: Perrin, 1987), ch. 1.

5. Jules Michelet, *Histoire de la Révolution française*, 2 vols. (Paris: Laffont, 1979), vol. 1, p. 104.

6. Cited in Georges Lefebvre and Anne Terroine, eds., *Recueil de documents relatifs aux séances des états généraux, mai–juin 1789*, vol. 1 (Paris: Centre National de la Recherche Scientifique, 1953), pp. 117–18.

7. Michelet, *Histoire*, vol. 1, pp. 102–3.

8. Ibid., p. 103.

9. Lefebvre and Terroine, eds., *Recueil*, p. 131.

10. Ibid., pp. 120–22 and p. 133.

11. Ibid., pp. 134 ff.

12. Jean Centini, "Le clergé et la bénédiction des drapeaux de la garde nationale parisienne," in Jean-Clément Martin, ed., *Religion et révolution* (Paris: Anthropos, 1994), pp. 150–57; and Julien Tiersot, *Les fêtes et les chants de la Révolution française* (Paris: Hachette, 1908), p. 15.

13. See Edgar Quinet, *La Révolution* (Paris: Belin, 1987), bk. 5 (*La Religion*), pp. 147–90.

14. See Hans Meier, *Revolution und Kirche: Zur Frühgeschichte der Christlichen Demokratie*, 5th ed. (Freiburg: Herder, 1988), pp. 101–5; and Ralph Gibson, *A Social History of French Catholicism, 1789–1914* (London: Routledge, 1989), p. 31.

15. Gibson, *Social History*, p. 34.

16. Ibid., p. 34; Meier, *Revolution und Kirche*, pp. 106–7; and Timothy Tackett, *Religion, Revolution, and Regional Culture in Eighteenth-Century France: The Ecclesiastical Oath of 1791* (Princeton: Princeton University Press, 1986), pp. 11–12.

17. Quinet, *La Révolution*, p. 87.

18. See ibid., pp. 150–52.

19. Meier, *Revolution und Kirche*, p. 121.

20. William Doyle, *The Oxford History of the French Revolution* (Oxford: Oxford University Press, 1990), p. 140.

21. See Pierre Pierrard, *L'église et la Révolution, 1789–1889* (Paris: Éditions Nouvelle Cité, 1988), p. 54.

22. Ibid., pp. 53–54.

23. See Tackett, *Religion*, ch. 5; and Aston, *End of an Elite*, ch. 12.

24. Latreille, *L'église*, p. 93; and Tackett, *Religion*, pp. 16–33.

25. See Claude Langlois, "Le serment révolutionnaire: Archaïsme et modernité," in Martin, ed., *Religion et révolution*, pp. 25–39, esp. pp. 33–34, 38–39.

26. The four bishops were Loménie de Brienne, Talleyrand, Jarente, and La Font de Savine. See Aston, *End of an Elite*, p. 245.

27. Tackett, *Religion*, esp. pp. 291–98; Cousin et al., *La pique*, pp. 135–40; Michel Vovelle, *Revolution against the Church: From Reason to the Supreme Being* (Oxford: Polity Press, 1991), pp. 171–73.

28. Tackett, *Religion*, p. 287.

29. See François Lebrun, "Religion et révolution dans l'ouest: Publications scientifiques et luttes historiographiques," in Martin, ed., *Religion et révolution*, p. 49.

30. Tackett, *Religion*, p. 6.

31. Latreille, *L'église*, p. 113 ff.; and Doyle, *French Revolution*, p. 177.

32. Latreille, *L'église*, p. 118; and Paul Christophe, *1789: Les prêtres dans la Révolution* (Paris: Editions Ouvrières, 1986), pp. 107–11.

33. See chapter 7 above.

34. Quinet, *La Révolution*, p. 169.

35. Cited in Abbé Jules Gendry, *Pie VI: Sa vie et son pontificat, 1717–1799*, vol. 2 (Paris: Picard, 1906), pp. 111–12.

36. *Recueil des décisions du Saint-Siège Apostolique relatives à la Constitution Civile du Clergé et aux affaires de l'Église de France depuis 1790 jusqu'en 1799*, 2 vols. (Rome, 1900), vol. 1, pp. 5–17.

37. *Recueil du Saint-Siège*, vol. 1, pp. 23–29.

38. Ibid., vol. 1, pp. 39–45, esp. p. 45.

39. Ibid., vol. 1, pp. 31–37, esp. p. 35.

40. Ibid., vol. 1, pp. 53–59, 69.

41. Ibid., vol. 1, pp. 65–79, esp. p. 67 and p. 71.

42. Ibid., vol. 1, pp. 101–19.

43. Ibid., vol. 1, pp. 119–301.

44. Ibid., vol. 1, pp. 301–17, esp. p. 305 and p. 309.

45. Ibid., vol. 1, pp. 333–95.

46. Cited in Pierrard, *L'église*, pp. 83–84.

47. *Recueil du Saint-Siège*, vol. 2, pp. 79–149.

48. Viguerie, *Christianisme*, p. 110.

49. Cousin et al., *La pique*, pp. 142–43.

50. *Recueil du Saint-Siège*, vol. 2, pp. 225–95.

51. Ibid., vol. 2, pp. 295–363.

52. The French translation of "Allocutio Habita in consistorio dei XVII junii MDCCXCIII super obitu regis galliarum" is cited in Abbé Isidore Bertrand, *Le pontificat de Pie VI et l'athéisme révolutionnaire*, 2 vols. (Paris, 1879), vol. 2, pp. 208–26.

53. "Remarks on the Policy of the Allies" (1793), cited in Paul Langford, ed., *The Writings and Speeches of Edmund Burke*, vol. 9 (Oxford: Clarendon, 1991), pp. 452–99, esp. p. 486.

54. Quinet, *La Révolution*, p. 177.

55. Albert Mathiez, *Les origines des cultes révolutionnaires, 1789–1792* (Paris: Bellais, 1904), p. 141.

56. Aulard, *Le culte de la Raison et le culte de l'Être suprême* (Paris, 1892), pp. vii–viii. See chapter 6 above.

57. Vovelle, *Revolution against the Church*, pp. 40–54.

58. Cited by Michelet, *Histoire*, vol. 2, p. 631.

59. See Vovelle, *Revolution against the Church*, p. 64; Christophe, *Les prêtres*, pp. 109–13; Aston, *End of an Elite*, pp. 269–82 (Appendix 5).

60. Richard Cobb, *The People's Armies: Instrument of the Terror in the Departments, April 1793 to Floréal Year II* (New Haven: Yale University Press, 1987), p. 443.

61. See Vovelle, *Revolution against the Church*, chs. 8–10; Vovelle, *Religion et révolution: La déchristianisation de l'an II* (Paris: Hachette, 1976), chs. 4–5 and conclusion; Cobb, *People's Armies*, pp. 442–43.

62. Cited in Mathiez, *Les origines*, p. 109.

63. Michelet, *Histoire*, vol. 2, bk. 14, ch. 3; and Quinet, *La Révolution*, bk. 16, ch. 3. See also Mona Ozouf, "Religion révolutionnaire," in François Furet and Mona Ozouf, eds., *Dictionnaire critique de la Révolution française* (Paris: Flammarion, 1988), pp. 607–8.

64. Michelet, *Histoire*, vol. 2, bk. 19, ch. 4; Quinet, *La Révolution*, p. 473; Ozouf, "Religion révolutionnaire," pp. 608–9.

65. "Evangile de la liberté," cited in Yann Fauchois, *Religion et France révolutionnaire* (Paris: Herscher, 1989), p. 99.

66. Michelet, *Histoire*, vol. 2, p. 615. Cf. Ozouf, "Religion révolutionnaire," pp. 609–10.

67. Quinet, *La Révolution*, pp. 485–86.

68. Alexis de Tocqueville, *"The European Revolution" and Correspondence with Gobineau* (Garden City, N.Y.: Doubleday, 1959), pp. 110–11.

Engaging the
Russian Orthodox
Church

IN 1917 RUSSIA was as much a country of peasants as France had been in 1789, or even more so. However, at the time of its revolution France had been in step with the other major European powers. By contrast, one hundred and thirty years later, Russia stood out for its relative economic and social retardation and torpor.[1] To be sure, Russia was not purely European: its human geography and geopolitics were Eurasian, and its "semi-colonial" level of development was combined with an extraordinary diversity of national, ethnic, and religious minorities. Russia's elite culture could not pretend to a transnational radiance and ascendancy comparable to France's in 1789, all the less so with the limited reach of the Russian language. Still, the intellectual and cultural life of Russia was closely enmeshed with that of central and western Europe. In military and economic terms, the Romanov empire's primary vocation and self-perception was European as well.

The Russian empire was spread over 10 million square miles—five times the expanse of France or three times that of the United States. In 1914 its population was between 140 and 160 million. There were no more than eleven cities with over 100,000 inhabitants, and only Petrograd and Moscow exceeded the million mark, with 2.5 and 2 million, respectively. Broadly speaking, these two cities, along with Russia's other urban enclaves, claimed little more than 15 percent of the population. Russia had at best 4 million industrial workers, including miners and railway workers. The great majority of these workers were concentrated in the twin capitals, and so were the members of the modern middle classes. Since the bulk of Russia's 5 million Jews

The crowning.

The Coronation of Nicholas II in the Assumption Cathedral of Moscow, 1896

were compelled to live in the towns and cities of the Pale of Settlement, they contributed disproportionately to the country's urban population, working class, and pool of potential political rebels.[2]

Russia's cities were rare islands in a sea of peasants, villages, and small rural towns. As in France, there were, of course, enormous variations in the condition of the peasantry. In European Russia the greatest disparity was between the life and work of peasants in the sparsely settled and relatively unfertile regions of the north and the life and work of peasants in the rich but overpopulated black soil country in the southeast, notably Ukraine.[3] But partly because of high rents and taxes combined with age-encrusted farming methods and low crop yields, nearly everywhere the muzhik was under "great economic pressure." Much of his wretchedness was due to the "prescientific and premechanical" level of agriculture: "only half of all peasant holdings had iron ploughs, . . . [the majority] using sickles for reaping [and] flails for threshing." Indeed, ultimately the condition of the Russian peasantry was "more remarkable for the depth of its general poverty than for the extent of its differentiation."[4] And the muzhik's low educational level was an additional handicap.

This peasant society, like that of prerevolutionary France, was braced by a single church: the Christian Orthodox Church, in which well over 100 million of 160 million Russians recognized themselves, many of them without being "members" of it. In 1917 there were over 40,000 parish churches and at least half as many chapels. Moscow alone gloried in over 400 churches. The parish or "white" clergy numbered over 50,000 priests and about 45,000 auxiliaries, among them an episcopacy of 130 bishops. Some 550 monasteries and 475 convents supported 90,000 monks and nuns. The Orthodox Church ran 195 schools, 57 seminaries, and 5 graduate academies staffed by 4,000 teachers and attended by 30,000 students.[5]

The Orthodox Establishment owned about one million acres, which mostly belonged to the village churches. A large proportion of these rented their land to neighboring peasants, some of whom "stood in the same economic relationship to the priest or the neighboring abbot as . . . the tenant to his landlord."[6] In general, however, in material and social terms the village priest was not much better off than the muzhik. Precisely because his income from his parish-church land was minimal and he received at most a pittance from church or state, the priest relied heavily on the meager fees the peasants paid him for officiating at christenings and other religious rites of passage usually carried out in the peasant home, not the house of God. Himself of peasant origin, the *pop* shared the worldview and way of life of the muzhik. His literacy was his only badge of distinction, which fitted him to carry out state functions, notably the registration of births, marriages, and deaths.[7]

In addition to being a powerful and integral element of the social and cultural order, the Russian Orthodox Church was also linked with the state in a tight union that would be difficult to pry apart. While the tsarist regime still recognized itself in the time-worn and contested motto "Orthodoxy, Autocracy, Nationality," in effect the principle of autocracy overshadowed the principles of orthodoxy and nationality. Unlike in France, there was neither a strict hierarchy nor an ecclesiastical council bolstered by the equivalent of an external link to Rome.[8] Very likely the Orthodox Church was "more than any other church . . . the servant of the state, . . . helping it to exploit and repress" with "callous indifference to social and political injustice." Watched over by a chief procurator appointed by the tsar, the Most Holy Synod of the Church was by and large under the tutelage of the state Ministry of Religious Affairs. In exchange the Orthodox Church enjoyed absolute preeminence over all other Christian denominations and religions, along with full control "over the spiritual affairs of Orthodox citizens, a realm of activity that embraced liturgy, missions, education, and religious thought." The net effect was the "systematic and conscious exclusion of the Church from secular matters and confinement to strictly 'spiritual' affairs," except for consecrating and upholding the established civil and political society.[9]

Politically the upper clergy and privileged priesthood were, on the whole, thoroughly conservative and considered their loyalty to the tsarist regime a religious duty.[10] Not that there were no reformist elements in the Orthodox Church. Several leading prelates and religious intellectuals advocated greater independence from the state, less autocratic church government, and greater social engagement.[11] But to the extent that there was a push for reform within the Church it came mainly, as in prerevolutionary France, from village priests, all the more so because of their lowly and precarious status. In turn, with time, and in the face of unremitting liberal-democratic and left-wing calls for religious freedom and for the decoupling of throne and altar, the highest church and state authorities, led by the court, prepared to fight a last-ditch battle for the status quo. With the entire priesthood muting its plaints, the collaboration of state and church was as iron-bound as ever.[12]

As in any peasant nation with a powerful church and polarized class structure in the countryside, there was a wide chasm between the elite and popular spheres of Eastern Orthodox Christianity, in part for want of a strict hierarchy. Whereas at the top, particularly in big cities and large towns, worship was generally centered in and around the church and kept faith with the letter and spirit of the Scriptures and canons, at the grass roots the settings and practices, along with the spiritual climate, were strikingly different. In the countryside the faithful offered their prayers in peasant huts and open fields less to praise God and supplicate saints than to appease evil spirits and demons haunting communities steeped in superstition and magic typical of a timeless agrarian world. For illiterate peasants, as well as for ex-peasants in cities, the link to Christianity was less the Gospel than religious icons and relics of saints. Notwithstanding friction with their flock and resentments of the black and high clergy, local priests were indulgent and essential officiants of a popular religion syncretizing pagan and Christian beliefs at the same time that by virtue of their standing and literacy they were pillars of the existing religious and political order.[13]

To note this subordination of church to state, however, is not to underrate the continuing sway of the reciprocal exchange of "unction and sanction" between the political and religious realms in Russia before 1917 as in France before 1789. The tsar still benefited from a nimbus rooted in the spiritual force of the sacred, while the Orthodox Church relied on the mailed fist of the state to preserve its awesome status as Russia's official religion. Of course, the concern for government support to maintain this monopoly was far less pronounced in ancien-régime Russia than France, the Orthodox Church having been spared a challenge on the scale and force of the Protestant heresy exacerbated by foreign entanglements. But this is not to say that the interpenetration of politics and religion was any less intense.

The coronation of the last tsar of Russia was celebrated on May 14, 1896, in Moscow, the old capital symbolizing Russia's religious and national traditions, not in the younger and more cosmopolitan St. Petersburg. From the outlying Petrovsky Palace, Nicholas and Alexandra drove to the Kremlin. Once inside the walls of the citadel they joined a grand procession to the Assumption Cathedral, the time-honored site for this ever-inspiring ritual. The Protopresbyter Ioann Yanyshev sprinkled the route of procession with holy water, and two metropolitans censed the Imperial Regalia at the entrance to the cathedral. The emperor and empress then ascended the hallowed thrones dating from times of yore. After kissing the cross, which was held by the Metropolitan Pallady of St. Petersburg, Their Majesties were themselves sprinkled with holy water. The tsar then rose to declaim the confession of the Orthodox Faith and make the sign of the cross three times.[14]

In 1896 in Russia, as in 1775 in France, the rites of coronation reconciled essential and closely interlaced religious and political intentions. Both rituals aimed to reassert and focalize not only the monarch's fealty to the official religion and church but also the Church's and ultimately God's consecration of his sovereign power. But there was a difference in emphasis between the two ceremonies, the political aspect being more manifest in the grand cathedral in Moscow than in Rheims. To underscore the throne's ascendancy over the altar, at the climax of the holy rite in the Assumption Cathedral a lay nobleman passed the nine-pound imperial crown to the Metropolitan of St. Petersburg who, in turn, handed it to the Tsar of Russia to crown himself.[15] In his coronation benediction Pallady called for God to favor the emperor as "a truehearted protector of the dogma of the holy Orthodox-Catholic Church" and to guide him as "guardian of his Empire." For his part, in his coronation prayer Nicholas vowed submission to the power of God at the same time that he implored the Almighty to "foster his aptitude to carry out the task for which He had chosen him and to counsel him in the discharge of his great duty."[16]

Characteristically, in Moscow, unlike in Rheims, the general public was not admitted to the grand cathedral for the final act of the coronation. Instead, the tsar's subjects were invited to express their jubilation at popular festivals which were officially orchestrated. The celebration, in February 1913, of the tricentenary of Romanov rule was cast in the same mold. Even at this late date, although throughout Russia the common people were associated with this apotheosis through public celebrations, the heralds of the loyal opposition, including their Duma deputies, were barred from the *Te Deum* and other official functions.

And later still, in August 1915, when several cabinet members pressed I. L. Goremykin, Russia's premier, to adopt a measure which he judged contrary to the tsar's will, he justified his refusal to refer it to Nicholas II with this same concept of God-given monarchy requiring total obedience: after reminding his fellow ministers that in addition to "personifying Russia" the emperor was "the Anointed of God, the Hereditary Bearer of Supreme Power," Goremykin insisted that "when the will of such a man is manifested and the path of action irrevocably taken, loyal subjects must submit, regardless of consequences." Besides, "there was only the Will of God," and the will of the tsar "must be obeyed like the commands of the Gospel."[17] No doubt this same understanding of the essence and scope of the Russian monarch's power predisposed the advisors and ministers of Nicholas II not to challenge his resolve to keep the troops shooting down rebels in Petrograd in February 1917, past the point of no return.

✳ ✳ ✳

The revolt of 1905, precipitated by the tsarist government's sinking military fortunes in the Russo-Japanese War, unsettled state-church relations.[18] Throughout political and civil society, the disunion and weakening of the incumbent ruling and governing classes provided an unhoped for opportunity to press for reforms to revitalize the life of the Church. Partly in response to the lower clergy, by late March the Holy Synod entreated the tsar to convoke a sobor, or council of bishops, lower clergy, and laity to redefine the relation of throne and altar as well as to review internal church governance. But in its bid for a "revolution from above" in favor of a semi-parliamentary system, the tsar's new cabinet proposed to take some additional steps to attenuate the illiberal sway of the Orthodox Church in general. On April 30, 1905, without consulting the Synod, the cabinet issued an Edict of Toleration benefiting, above all, the Old Believers and other Christian denominations. In terms of its impact, this edict can be compared to the decree which granted civil status to French Protestants in November 1787: it at once raised and disappointed the expectations of resolute reformists at the same time that it infuriated political and ecclesiastical last-ditchers.

In the face of mounting political pressure for complete freedom of religion as well as for the separation of church and state, the die-hards, backed by the court, dug in their heels. As part of a concerted drive to emasculate the October settlement and its attendant reforms, and confident of the support of key cabinet ministers and functionaries, the tsar shelved his promise to summon a sobor. Characteristically, the restless priesthood backed down. In concert with the prelacy, the 46 priests in the Fourth Duma of 1912–17 collaborated with the emperor and his even more uncompromising political and military counselors to harden and reinvigorate the ancien regime, including its official church. During these years several prominent churchmen, not unlike Nicholas II, took it upon themselves to lend legitimacy to the Union of the Russian People, or the Black Hundreds.

Perhaps surprisingly, in February–March 1917 the priesthood, high and low, reacted with relative calm to the formation of a provisional government and the abdication of Nicholas II, as well as the desacralization of power.[19] At first the bishops underestimated the crisis partly because they compared it with the upheaval of 1905, which had been mastered successfully. Indeed, in the dawn of the convulsion of 1917 the operative analogy was 1905, not 1789: it was not unreasonable for conservatives to presume that military misfortune was once again momentarily dislocating the tsarist regime. In any case, notwithstanding the quick and all but uncontested removal of the crowned head, which had not been nearly so fast and easy in France, for some of the highest prelates the disestablishment of the Orthodox Church, which they took to be inseparable from the imperial state, was simply unthinkable. Others, however, were ready to capitalize on Russia's renewed turmoil to resume pressing for the church reforms which had foundered between 1906 and 1914. Meanwhile, making the best of a perilous situation, for the time being most of the Church's high priests, not unlike the army's senior officers, were disposed to support the Provisional Government.

Before long, however, there was no denying that the upheaval was deeper and the reformist momentum greater than many of the men and women of God had originally assumed. It did not augur well for Russia's official church that the makeshift cabinets headed by Lvov and Kerensky were altogether more determined to sap, if not snap, the symbiotic relationship of state and church than the cabinet appointed by the tsar and headed by Count Sergei Witte in 1905. As if inspired by Condorcet, almost to a man the liberal democrats and socialists backing the nascent regime advocated the desacralization of political and civil society. In quick succession the provisional governments issued decrees ending both religious and national discrimination; placing primary schools receiving state funds, above all parochial schools, under the Ministry of Education; introducing curricular reform, with a ban on the compulsory study of the catechism. In some places, crowds harassed old-world clergymen; in others, expectant parish priests called for a democratization of the Church as part of the general reform of political and civil society. On July 14, 1917, a decree promulgating religious freedom also prepared the ground for civil marriage.

The status of the Orthodox Church remained to be redefined. On August 5 the Ministry for Religious Affairs was recast to take the place of the Holy Synod. The powers of this ministry were to be fixed following an all-Russian sobor to be convened in mid-August with the Provisional Government's political approval and financial support. In the committee of clerics and laity preparing this conclave, conservatives had the upper hand, with the result that in mid-July it summoned the Church to hold fast not only to *all* its prerogatives, privileges, and functions but also its customary state subsidies.[20]

But there was something reckless about taking such an uncompromising line: the Holy Synod could no more afford to go into opposition than the Provisional Government could afford to fall out with the Church. More and more disquieted by the Bolshevik threat, agrarian unrest, and, above all, military defeat, the Synod urged the priesthood to back the Provisional Government, and this despite the latter's zeal for secularized education and religious toleration. The governors of both state and church now gave first priority to continuing the war, maintaining military discipline, and enforcing law and order. Following the popular uprising in Petrograd in early July 1917, the prelates sought to rein in their wayward reforming priests, determined to close ranks for the battle against the far left.

It is instructive to compare two major funeral rites as a measure of the volatility of the church-religion issue at the creation of the Russian Revolution: on March 23, 1917, for the victims of the February uprising in Petrograd; and on July 15 for the Cossacks who lost their lives repressing the July uprising. The former was the post-tsarist government's first stately act of self-representation. The local soviet and Provisional Government joined hands to stage an imposing funeral for the 184 freedom fighters of the glorious February days. This "Burial of the Martyrs" took the form of about a million people soberly but defiantly "marching in from the working-class districts, through the center of town" to the Field of Mars, for the interment. Mixed honor guards of workers and soldiers carried "the coffins . . . to the strains of the purely revolutionary hymn 'You Fell Victim.' " and "[t]hough traditional forms of religious burial techniques were employed," clergymen were not "permitted to officiate or participate." There was something truly novel about the occasion: "[i]t was the first secular outdoor ceremony in Russian history, the first major non-oppositional and all-class ceremony in the lifetime of the Provisional Government, and the only one also without a central charismatic figure as focus."[21]

By mid-July 1917 the setting, atmosphere, and liturgy were radically different. The "first" Provisional Government had turned March 23 into an inspiring observance for the workers who had made the supreme sacrifice defying the failing monarchy; the "second" Provisional Government designated July 15 a day to exalt the seven Cossacks who had given their lives protecting the fledgling democracy. The mayor of Petrograd summoned "all those loyal to the Revolution and imbued with its spirit" to attend the funeral, and appealed to the workers of each of the capital's large factories to send a thirty-member delegation. Once again there was a huge crowd. It was "packed tightest" in and around the spacious St. Isaac's Cathedral, the focal point of the commemoration. But many people also lined the route of the cortège that accompanied the fallen heroes from the cathedral to the cemetery of the Alexander Nevsky monastery.[22]

Inside St. Isaac's the seven Cossacks lay in state as the capital's notables took their seats in the front rows for the Requiem Mass. The members of the cabinet were joined by representatives of the local soviet, *zemstvo* (county council), and city government, as well as of the "merchant and industrial estates." But in particular the chief diplomats of the Allied and Associated powers, accompanied by their military attachés in dress uniform, caught the eye. With the arrival of

Kerensky, the minister-president, the "archbishop of Petrograd, followed by the exarch of the Georgian Orthodox Church and the members of the Holy Synod," advanced to the altar. As they prepared to start the service, several dignitaries stepped forward to "place wreaths . . . at the foot of the caskets." Most notable among them were "the Kadet leaders Fedor Rodichev, Paul Miliukov, and Vasili Maklakov," whose wreath bore the legend: "To the loyal sons of free Russia who fell in the struggle against traitors to their country."[23]

Following a service lasting three hours the seven coffins were carried to the square in front of the cathedral, the first one being borne by cabinet ministers led by Kerensky. The traditional military honors having been rendered, Kerensky gave the funeral oration. Insisting that the Russian state was "closer to destruction than ever before in its history," he called upon the assembly to swear, "before these fallen bodies," to back his resolve to deal "mercilessly [with] any attempt to foment anarchy and disorder regardless of where it comes from." With bells tolling and military bands playing, the funeral procession set out for the Alexander Nevsky monastery. It was led by "priests in flowing black robes bearing tall crosses, church banners, and incense burners," as well as by church officials, followed by civilian notables and "seemingly endless ranks of military troops."[24] The symbols and speeches at the graveside were entirely in keeping with the day's "spirit of traditional Orthodox patriotic Russia."[25]

The contrast between the two grand observances was really quite spectacular. In Petrograd, four months after the fall of the Romanovs, the incipient temper and language of secularist reformism was eclipsed by a renascent temper and language of Christian Orthodoxy and Russian nationalism, albeit shorn of the carapace of autocracy. Despite official efforts, there were few workers and red banners in the crowd and, according to one reporter, "the military bands did not play the *Marseillaise* even once on the way to the cemetery."[26] The commemoration of July 15 registered and projected the "upsurge of the spirit of order, discipline, stability, state power, and frontline patriotism" under the aegis of the Provisional Government. Indeed, the *mise en scène* and liturgy of this consciously constructed high occasion laid bare the mind-set and orientation of Kerensky's cabinet. Trembling on the verge of collapse and with little symbolic capital of its own, it "drew on symbols and rituals rich in the imagery of patriotism and social order: the Army and the Church."[27]

A month later, on August 15, 1917, the all-Russian Sobor, or Church Council, convened in Moscow—the first in two hundred years. Along with the ministers of the interior and of religious affairs, Kerensky attended the opening session in the Kremlin's Uspensky Cathedral.[28] To mark the occasion, special prayers were also said in 33 other churches in Moscow. Almost evenly divided between clergy and laity, the 564 delegates were "heavily weighted in favor . . . of the upper levels of the church organization . . . and of the upper strata of society." Although convoked to discuss the reform of church governance and the restoration of the patriarchate, the delegates—among them 87 metropolitans and bishops—could not close their eyes to political issues, not least because the opening of the sobor nearly coincided with General Kornilov's defiance of Kerensky. Before this move was foiled with the help of the far left, including the Bolsheviks, the delegates "openly—and largely approvingly—discussed it."[29] Though nothing if not critical of Kerensky, the leaders of the Church perforce continued to back him against Lenin. Having voted to restore the patriarchate, on November 5 the sobor elected Tikhon Belavin, the Metropolitan of Moscow, Patriarch of Moscow and of All Russia, and Supreme Metropolitan of the Orthodox Church. Actually, Antony Khrapovitsky, Bishop of Kharkov and candidate of the far right, had "received the majority of the electoral votes," and only a quirk in the selection procedure gave the office to Tikhon, "the most liberal of the leading churchmen."[30] In the meantime, however, the Bolsheviks had taken the reins of government, bringing with them the ideas of the godless wing of the Russian Marxist movement: religion as a social and moral outrage resulting from an exploitative social order; the symbiosis of throne and altar as one of the worst symptoms of Russia's egregious backwardness; and themselves as the representatives and champions of secular rationalism in the struggle to build a new and just society. Clearly the tempo and scope of change in political and civil society and the tempo and scope of "reformation" in church and religion were closely entwined, with inevitable consequences for state-church relations.

✳ ✳ ✳

In Russia after February–March 1917, not unlike in France after July 1789, the disestablishment and reorganization of the official church and the scrapping of the traditional unction of politics were both consequence and cause of the revolutionizing of the revolution. Of course, the church-religion issue did not really become explosive until after the Bolshevik takeover, when it became a major reason for polarization. Just as Lenin and his associates were determined to continue de-churching without, however, forcing de-faithing, so the leaders of the Orthodox Church made a point of reaffirming their own intractable position, all the more so since they, along with all the world, considered the Bolsheviks' hold on power to be tenuous and momentary.

During their first three months in power the Bolsheviks issued several decrees that could not but inflame the tensions with the Church: the nationalization, without compensation, of all land, including the landed properties of all church institutions; the transfer of all church-run schools not nationalized by the provisional governments, including those not subsidized by the state, to a new Commissariat of Enlightenment; the prescription of civil marriage; the transfer of the registry of births, marriages, and deaths from church to state. In addition, the adoption of the New Style calendar, which "caught Russia up to the West chronologically, . . . was a political act of secularization and de-Christianization" highlighted by the "elimination of a number of traditional religious holidays associated with the Romanov regime."[31]

As was to be expected, the Orthodox Church resolutely resisted this encroachment, not to say assault. Almost instantly, once the confrontation with the new regime took a sharp political turn, this resistance became intensely ideological. Issuing increasingly strident denunciations of the Bolshevik pretense, the episcopate counted on the countryside, confident that local priests would rally the faithful peasantry, the bulk of the population, behind church and religion. Indeed, the Russian Orthodox Church proposed to join battle with a state that was at once secular and un-Christlike.[32]

By November 21, 1917, the sobor exhorted the faithful to "offer penitential prayers for the great sin" of the Church's sons "who through ignorance . . . [and] illusion . . . had fallen into fratricide and the sacrilegious destruction of the nation's sacred patrimony."[33] Latter-day infidels were admonished "to give up the foolish and impious dreams of false teachers who summon you to bring about universal brotherhood by means of universal conflict." On December 2 the sobor adopted a resolution modeled on that of mid-July—and reminiscent of Dom Gerle's motion of April 1790—demanding that the Orthodox Church retain religious primacy and ownership of its lands; keep control of sub-university education, marriage, and divorce; and continue to receive state funding. The council also insisted that "the head of the Russian state, the ministers of religion and of education and their deputies must belong to the Orthodox Church."[34]

Two days afterward, on December 4, with the authorization of Bolshevik officials and in accordance with legendary ritual, Tikhon was formally invested in the Cathedral of the Assumption, inside the ancient and sacred Kremlin citadel. Following a resplendent ceremony the new Patriarch, reviving an age-old custom, "got into a carriage drawn by four white horses which circled the Kremlin's outer walls in order for him to sprinkle them with holy water."[35] Three months later, when the Bolsheviks transferred Russia's capital from Petrograd to Moscow, they fixed the seat of their embattled government in the Kremlin, probably as much with a view to desacralize the citadel as for reasons of convenience and safety.

Meanwhile church leaders readily entered the political fray. Not a few of them campaigned for conservative and reactionary candidates for the Constituent Assembly. At the sobor the archpriest Chotavickij supported the call for the election of religious-minded Russians of Orthodox faith with the exhortation not to vote for candidates with pseudonyms or foreign-sounding names. The men of the cloth also severely condemned Sovnarkom's search for a separate peace with Germany, which would be certain to do grave injury to the Russian people and state, the chief carriers of the Eastern Orthodox Church and faith.

On January 16, 1918, Tikhon engaged his full authority and aura in the battle with the new regime. The German armies were renewing their advance, the country was in an impossible diplomatic predicament, and chaos was spreading like wildfire. This was the grim context in which the Patriarch, backed by the sobor, issued a singularly fierce pastoral letter recalling Pius VI's fervid encyclicals of 1792–93.[36] It was addressed "to all Russia, to the beloved in the Lord, hierarchs, clergy, and all the faithful children of the Russian Orthodox Church."

The text cried out against the "open and hidden enemies" of the Truth of Christ who were sowing "the seeds of malice, hatred, and fratricidal warfare." Branding these "furious enemies . . . outcasts of the human race [and] atheist masters of this century's darkness," Tikhon adjured them to stop their "bloody deeds," which were "not only cruel [but] the work of Satan, and for which [they] shall suffer the fire of hell in the life to come, beyond the grave." Invoking "the authority given us by God," the Patriarch of Moscow and of All Russia barred Bolsheviks and their fellow travelers from "receiving the Sacraments of Christ . . . and placed under anathema whoever bore a Christian name, even if merely on account of [his] baptism." Tikhon adjured the faithful "not to commune" with these monsters and instructed the entire priesthood to summon, "with fiery zeal," their flock to defend the Church and its property and to "convene religious gatherings" in line with Christ's promise: "On this rock I will build My Church and the gates of Hell shall not prevail against it" (Matt. 16:18).[37]

This excoriation and anathema provoked and emboldened rather than intimidated the Bolsheviks. On January 19, 1918, four days after Tikhon's pastoral letter and four days after the dissolution of the Constituent Assembly, in which there were few champions of the Orthodox Church, Sovnarkom issued the Decree on the Separation of Church and State, drafted by Lenin. Besides prohibiting "local laws or decisions obstructing or limiting freedom of conscience," this decree laid down that "every citizen may profess any religion or none"; guaranteed the "free practice of religious rites in so far as this does not violate public order"; and declared "all the possessions of the church and religious societies [to be] the property of the people." To dramatize the break with the stubborn past, the edict proscribed not only "religious oath-taking," but all "religious rites and ceremonies accompanying acts of state and other public official functions." To further the laicization of schooling, the decree prohibited "religious instruction in any state, public, or private institution of learning where general educational subjects are taught," but held that citizens were free to "teach and study religion privately."[38] A ban on state subsidies and church collections left the clergy in revolutionary Russia, unlike in revolutionary France, without living and pension.[39] Later, on July 10, 1918, the new Constitution of the Russian Soviet

Republic confirmed the separation of church and state as well as the freedom of religion, including the freedom of religious and antireligious propaganda.

These and other measures were part of a general if vague project to modernize and secularize society as well as to conquer illiteracy and religious bigotry, including anti-Semitism. Except for the confiscatory and redistributive side of the land settlement, for the time being the Bolsheviks were more legatees of the spirit and logic of the Declaration of the Rights of Man of 1789 than of the *Communist Manifesto* of 1848.

In any case, the Church leaders responded to the decree separating church and state by pronouncing an anathema against anyone collaborating in its enforcement. They called on clergy and laity to organize to protect, in particular, holy objects endangered during the shutdown, takeover, or despoliation of churches, monasteries, and convents.[40]

All this time, and until September 1918, when money ran out, the sobor, approved by Sovnarkom,[41] met irregularly to complete the recasting of the Orthodox Church on the conciliar principle. Building on the restoration of the patriarchate and the election of Tikhon, the delegates vested supreme authority in a sobor of bishops, priests, and laymen to be convened every three years, while a Holy Synod of 13 members, headed by the Supreme Patriarch and the Metropolitan of Kiev, was to keep a watchful eye on dogma, liturgy, and religious education. The country was reorganized into five ecclesiastical provinces whose dioceses and parishes were to be governed by the same rules as the central church council. Before adjourning, the constituent sobor "granted the Patriarch unrestricted administrative powers in case the Soviet government made it impossible for the sobor to meet or the Synod to function." It also instructed Tikhon "to draft a will" designating three persons to act in his place should he "become incapacitated or die or should the Soviets prevent the convocation of a sobor."[42]

By fall 1918 it was clear that clergymen of all ranks, along with nearly everyone else, had underestimated the Bolsheviks' staying power. Tikhon now sought to depoliticize his opposition to the regime, proclaiming that it was not the Church's role to "judge the earthly power." He enjoined both the clergy and the faithful to obey Russia's new rulers on condition they could square their actions with their religious conscience. Although the Patriarch did, of course, favor the defeat of the Bolsheviks, he stopped short of publicly consecrating the cause and sword of the White Guards. This tempered disengagement from the political struggle, which was calculated to see the beleaguered Church through perilous times, added up to a distinction without a difference, not least because Tikhon stopped short of lifting the anathema.[43]

On the occasion of the first anniversary of the October Revolution the Supreme Patriarch addressed an open letter to Sovnarkom bluntly prefaced with the Savior's prophecy that "all who take the sword will perish by the sword" (Matt. 26:52). Speaking "bitter words of truth," he charged its members with giving "the people a stone and, instead of fish, a serpent." Concretely, Tikhon held them responsible for a humiliating peace and for "a fratricide of altogether unprecedented savagery." With the "love of Christ . . . openly replaced by hatred . . . and an artificially stimulated class struggle," everybody was living in "constant terror of search, pillage, expulsion, arrest, execution." Contemptuous of civil liberties, the Bolsheviks proclaimed a man-wrought freedom that consisted of "encouraging the lowest passions of the crowd" and of emboldening the press to publish "the most monstrous slander and heinous blasphemy against the Church and its servants." This verbal assault was part of a campaign to "destroy the traditional framework of the ecclesiastical community," shown forth in the decision to forbid "access to the Moscow Kremlin—that sacred patrimony of all the faithful." After disingenuously insisting, once again, that it was "not for us to judge temporal authority," Tikhon exhorted the Bolsheviks to mark their first anniversary "by giving back their freedom to those who are in prison; by stopping bloodshed, violence, pillage, and the persecution of the faith; by . . . building order and law; and by giving the people a longed-for and deserved rest from fratricidal struggle." Should they, however, fail to see the error of their ways, they "will be asked to account for the blood of all the just men which you have shed" (Luke 11:51).[44]

✳ ✳ ✳

Clearly, during the first year of Bolshevik rule the intensification of the church-state confrontation was correlated with the escalation of the civil war. The two sides were uncompromising in their mutual vilification and malediction, the friend-enemy dissociation being quickened by virtue of the failure of leaders of the Church and the party-state to control their agents on the ground, especially in civil war zones, which were seedbeds for fundamentalism and violence.[45]

Even if in the civil war the Orthodox Church was not the greatest force of resistance to the Bolsheviks, who certainly overestimated and overstated its power, it was not inconsequential. Its strength was, of course, less material than moral, cultural, and psychological. Very likely the bulk of the clergy, high and low, sympathized with the Whites, and not a few of them actively supported them. In particular, self-avowed right-wing clergymen were attached to the military headquarters and political directorates of the White armies, all of which, quite naturally, were attended by Orthodox military chaplains. Some of these men of God consecrated the anti-Soviet struggle as a holy war and appealed to foreign governments and sister churches for support. Several priests are even said to have helped to integrate crusading irregulars into military brigades known as "Jesus Regiments," "Orders of the Holy Cross," and "Brotherhood of the Life-Giving Cross." Throughout the White-controlled territories, priests and monks held divine services and delivered sermons exalting the counterrevolutionary armies. They also thundered against Bolsheviks and Jews. Since in this time of troubles the Church had even less of an effective chain of command than in normal times, in the provinces priests acted without worrying about guidelines from the center or from their superiors.[46]

This clerical activism at once answered and incited the Bolsheviks' strident anticlericalism—some of it premeditated and willful, some of it spontaneous and wild. Besides the Red Antichrist's heretical rhetoric, the religious *enragés* either witnessed anti-Christian outrages or heard about them second hand. Especially in civil-war zones, they knew of unchecked Bolsheviks closing churches and monasteries, confiscating and looting church property, or desecrating icons and relics. During the first half of 1918, here and there churchmen were arrested, mistreated, and taken hostage, and not a few were killed and injured. Most of this local violence of the first hour was frenzied and arbitrary, unrelated to any grand design or campaign. Even the brutal murders of Archbishop Skipetrov in Petrograd on January 19 and of Metropolitan Vladimir of Kiev on February 7 were undirected, although the episcopacy perceived and presented these murders as proof of Bolshevik perfidy.[47] There is reason to believe that the Bolsheviks did not instrumentalize anticlericalism until autumn 1918, after the assassination of Uritsky and the attempt on Lenin's life, as well as the escalation of the civil war.

Up to this point Lenin had either ignored or silently condoned dechurching excesses, but certainly had not encouraged them. Like Robespierre, he was afraid that headlong disestablishment and secularization would unduly offend and enrage the peasantry: both resisted pressures from militant atheists with the argument that the common people could not be expected to abandon or transfigure their religiously freighted beliefs, customs, and rituals overnight. Lenin, following Robespierre, feared that a frontal assault on the deep-rooted faith of villagers and small-town dwellers would stoke their resistance and drive them into the arms of the counterrevolution. Though favoring "scientific education and anti-religious propaganda," even at the height of the civil war Lenin considered it "necessary to take care to avoid hurting the religious sentiments of believers, for this only serves to increase religious fanaticism."[48]

By and large, Sovnarkom followed Lenin's cautious line. Despite the unrestrained hostility of churchmen, and though determined to carry through disestablishment and laicization, to avoid exacerbating tensions relatively few churches, monasteries, or seminaries were closed. In May 1918 P. A. Krasikov was appointed head of a special division in the Commissariat of Justice charged with directing "the ideological struggle against religion," to be promoted by a special periodical, *The Revolution and the Church*. In the first issue, aimed at the countryside, Krasikov recalled that during the French Revolution the closing of churches and coercion of priests had been counterproductive, as measured by the growth of religious "fanaticism." He was confident that "a well-organized Soviet farm is more likely to undermine prejudice than the arrest of a dozen priests."[49]

As noted, spontaneous antireligious outbursts were most common in combat zones. In the villages and towns of regions untouched by civil war, religious life in church, hearth, and field continued as before, with priests attending to christenings, weddings, and burials, as well as to the rites of holy days, as they had done always and everywhere. Had the assault on traditional values and folkways been fiercer and more massive, as was to be the case, as we shall see, during the famine and conflict over church valuables in 1921–22, the faithful would most likely have been more disposed to fight back and hearken to the battle cries of Tikhon and die-hard clergymen and clergywomen, especially in areas in which the hardships and disappointments of the Revolution were sowing the seeds of disaffection.

Just as Lenin at first sought to keep his own zealots at bay, so did Tikhon. But even if Sovnarkom differentiated between its struggle with the Church and its struggle with religion, which remained in a minor key, in the eyes of church leaders this was yet another distinction without a difference: in their perception, disestablishment coupled with the warrant for religious diversity was potentially fatal. The episcopate suspected the separation of church and state to be a thinly disguised prelude to the gradual asphyxiation of the Orthodox Church and clergy in particular, and of religious life generally. In turn, and with equally good reason, the Bolsheviks considered the Church as perhaps the last major all-Russian institutional rampart of nonmilitary resistance, not to say counterrevolution. Hence the friend-enemy dissociation between Bolshevism and Orthodoxy lingered on after the end of the civil war, when the famine of 1921–22 reignited the head-on confrontation between state and church, with each side exploiting the emergency to advance its political agenda.

* * *

Starting in the spring of 1921, a severe famine stalked Russia, particularly in regions of the Volga, Ukraine, and Transcaucasia. As much due to drought, the breakdown of the market, and the wrack and ruin of the civil war as to Bolshevik agrarian policy, this famine—like so many major famines—was both a natural and a man-made calamity. In the spring and summer of 1921 an estimated quarter of Soviet Russia's peasantry was in the grip of starvation and epidemic disease. As part of its effort to meet and master the emergency with excruciatingly lean resources, Sovnarkom called on the Church to collect food and money for famine relief. While the Church, largely moved by its own charitable vocation, answered the call, its drive for voluntary contributions fell short of success, largely because most of the faithful were themselves in narrow circumstances. Presently the government asked the Church to turn over part of its valuable treasures to a special commission which would administer their sale and use the proceeds to purchase essential foods and seeds, particularly on international markets. With hunger and accompanying health hazards going from bad to worse, on February 19, 1922, Tikhon called on the faithful to do their utmost for those in need. He also directed priests to hand over church valuables, but left each priest free to decide which treasures to withhold for being sacred or consecrated for holy rites. Four days later, irked by the excessive voluntarism of Tikhon's rescript, President M. I. Kalinin issued a decree enjoining the Church to sell all valuables—gold, silver, precious stones—not essential for religious services. Presumably because the ukase did not exempt sacred objects, the Supreme Patriarch demurred. On February 29, in a counter-decree, Tikhon protested that the Church could accept neither the voluntary transfer nor forcible removal of consecrated objects. To mark his resolve, he declared their confiscation would be a sacrilege, bringing the excommunication of laymen and the suspension of priests lending a hand to it. This was also the time that Tikhon wrote to his counterpart in Serbia to urge that the leaders of all the great religions join forces to battle "the masters of the darkness of this world," which involved fighting their "poisonous teachings that wreak havoc not only in Russia but the world over."[50]

What made Tikhon's intervention particularly suspect in Bolshevik eyes was that it coincided with a meeting of a synod of influential émigré churchmen and laity meeting in Stansky Karlovci, near Belgrade, which seemed to share his views; and Tikhon did little to distance himself from the synod and its positions.[51]

The conclave was chaired by Metropolitan Antony of Kiev, a hardline supporter of the Whites, backed by fourteen like-minded bishops. The lay delegates were largely drawn from "the Russian nobility, the army, and high official circles, . . . [with] at least nineteen generals and many princes and counts" among them.[52]

Meeting from mid-November through mid-December 1921, this synod-in-exile called for the restoration of an anointed Romanov tsar. It also supported Antony's caustic proclamation in which he blamed the famine and epidemic on the incompetence and brutality of the Bolshevik regime; in it he also urged the great powers not to recognize the Soviet government, and to bar it from the Genoa Conference, which was about to discuss European economic recovery. Antony even advocated that instead of sending famine relief, which would strengthen the regime, the powers should help the émigrés and internal resistance liberate Russia and the world from the scourge of Bolshevism, which was a "cult of murder, pillage, and blasphemy."[53] This brazen defiance could only feed Lenin's worst fears and suspicions and spur his resolve to bring the Church to heel.

In Russia, as in France, the threat to church property triggered resistance, though perhaps on a smaller scale. Particularly in the countryside, the forcible removal of church valuables precipitated disturbances, priest and peasant viewing it as a frontal assault on the sacred core of their steady-state universe. While some of these disturbances were spontaneous, others were led by refractory priests who presumably answered Tikhon's call to protect Orthodoxy's sacred objects. Not a few such resisters—bishops, priests, monks, nuns, laymen— were arrested and tried.

One such showdown and its consequences are rather well documented. Between March 12 and 15, 1922, in Shuia, a small textile town near Ivanovo some 200 miles northeast of Moscow, the confrontation over the sacred articles of the local church took several lives on both sides. On March 16 a troubled Politburo, "in Lenin's and Trotsky's absence, voted to delay further confiscations and . . . sent instructions to all provincial party organizations to suspend such actions until further notice."[54]

While this restraining order was in line with Lenin's circumspection in this domain, he now proposed to harden official policy. He held that the government had to persist in removing church valuables, whose proceeds were essential to "carry out economic construction, and especially to uphold our position at Genoa." Lenin deemed the moment "uniquely favorable" to join battle with those determined "to test the policy of militant resistance to a Soviet decree," particularly in famine-stricken areas in which "there is cannibalism and the roads are littered with hundreds if not thousands of corpses." He assumed that with hunger threatening "the broad peasant masses," the regime would have to settle for "their sympathy, or, at least, their neutrality." In sum, there were contingent economic and political reasons for "decisively and mercilessly joining battle with the Black Hundred clergy and subduing their resistance with such brutality that they will remember it for decades to come." At Lenin's urging, the Politburo sent a representative to Shuia with verbal instructions to "arrest no fewer than a few dozen representatives of the local clergy, local burghers, and local bourgeois on suspicion of direct or indirect involvement in violent resistance to the decree . . . concerning the removal of church valuables." Guided by the report of this "representative on mission," the Politburo should instruct "the judicial authorities . . . to conduct the trial of the Shuia rebels . . . as quickly as possible" so as to secure "the execution of a very large number of the most influential and dangerous Black Hundreds of Shuia, and, insofar as possible, . . . also of Moscow and several other church centers."[55] Incidentally, on this occasion Lenin apparently once again made a point of suggesting that Trotsky, probably because of his Jewish ancestry, should not be publicly involved in this matter.

On March 20 a skeletal Politburo, "made up of Trotsky, Lenin, and Kamenev," with Molotov acting as secretary, ordered that "secret supervisory committees" be established throughout the land to "seize valuables" and "split" the clergy, "extending protection to those clergymen openly speaking in favor of seizure." While refractory priests who were "well known" were not to be "penalized till the campaign's termination . . . they should be officially warned that in case of excesses, they would be the first to have to answer for them."[56]

The resistance to the confiscation drive gave rise to many political trials. In Shuia three defendants were sentenced to death. But the spotlight was, above all, on the trials in Moscow and Petrograd, which were intended to foster compliance by fear far and wide. At the Moscow trial held in the Polytechnic Museum in Moscow from April 26 to May 6, 1922, fifty-four defendants, both priests and laymen, were charged with counterrevolutionary activity in the form of obstructing the removal of church treasures. Of the eleven defendants who were condemned to death, five were executed and six had their sentences commuted to prison terms, presumably at Trotsky's urging.[57]

In Petrograd the tribunal sat in "what was once the club of the nobility."[58] The Metropolitan Benjamin of the ex-capital was the most prominent of eighty-six accused. Although he had actually taken a relatively moderate position on church valuables, Benjamin was charged with preaching resistance and having contact with the émigré synod.

But the unwritten text of his indictment may well have been his refusal to recognize the Living Church and his excommunication of Alexander Vedensky, a zealous reformist priest of his diocese. In any case, Vedensky and Vladimir Krasnitsky were hostile witnesses, and their presence and testimony proved singularly damaging.[59] Benjamin and "many of his codefendants were defrocked," and along with a former Duma member and two professors, during the night of August 12 he was "secretly executed" so as to avoid a backlash among his broad popular following.[60] Eventually, "ten of the principal accused were sentenced to death and the sentences of six of them were commuted to ten-year imprisonment."[61]

As of now there are no detailed and reliable estimates of the number of victims of the ecclesiastical and religious terror in the time of the civil war and the conflict over church valuables. According to one estimate, "in the course of 1918–1920 at least twenty-eight bishops were murdered, thousands of clerics were imprisoned or killed, and twelve thousand laymen were reported to have been killed for religious activities alone."[62] Regarding the church valuables conflict, there is, in addition, recent evidence that "over 8,000 persons were executed or killed in the course of 1922," including "2,691 secular priests, 1,962 monks, and 3,447 nuns."[63] In a third estimate, the trials of 1922 "seemed to have eliminated, either permanently or temporarily, many of the hierarchs most hostile to the Soviet regime," and to achieve this outcome "only a small proportion of those found guilty in court were executed, the remainder [being] given various terms of prison or exile."[64] In late 1923 "sixty-six bishops were in prison or exiled, . . . among them Mgr. Alexis, the future Patriarch."[65] Quite apart from the imprecision of the overall figures, there is no breakdown of the number of victims killed by free-acting revolutionary zealots, by organized special forces, and by reason of direct or indirect involvement in civil war engagements.

Nor have the qualitative aspects of this violence, on both sides, been closely reconstructed. According to one account, Archbishop Andronik of Perm "had his cheeks lacerated, his ears and nose cut off, and his eyes gouged" before being "driven through the city and then thrown into the river to drown." In like manner, "Bishop Hermogen of Tobolsk [was] reported to have been drowned with a rock tied to his neck."[66] It remains unclear whether this type of brutality was a hallmark of this violence and whether it was perpetrated spontaneously or on higher orders. In one reading, a government of "atheists and anti-clericals" ordered ordinary Orthodox Russians to "shoot down fellow Christians for attempting to defend their churches . . . [and] executed ordained priests of God" without the country expressing "its displeasure by the general insurrection that one would have expected."[67] Indeed, the frontal attacks on the refractory church and clergy generated less popular resistance in Russia than in France, perhaps because they were less systematic, were geographically more widely dispersed, and came to a head after the end of the civil war rather than at its peak.

* * *

At the same time that the Bolsheviks intensified the use of force against the Church, they benefited from a split in the Orthodox ranks which they, of course, did their best to aggravate.[68] Especially in famine-stricken areas, not a few bishops and priests stood against Tikhon's policy on church valuables, notably his refusal to surrender articles consecrated but not essential for liturgical use. The Patriarch's vocal critics mostly belonged to a minority of progressive clerics and laymen who were moved in particular by the Revolution's social gospel and took strong exception to the prelacy's blanket and inflexible opposition. Their aim was to revive the spirit and mission of early Christianity, insisting that "Christ himself had been a Socialist."[69] With an eye on the Reformation in the time of Luther and Calvin, these self-styled "renovationists" accepted the need for restructuring state-church relations, perhaps along lines of some of Europe's Protestant countries. They considered a radical political reorientation an essential corollary of ecclesiastical and cultic renewal. Specifically, they advocated the democratization of church governance at all levels, from parish and diocese to synod. In the realm of worship, the renovationists called for the simplification of holy rites, making them more accessible by having them performed in vernacular Russian instead of Old Church Slavonic. Ultimately one of their chief aims was to throw critical light on popular religion, especially on such deep-rooted but pagan practices as the veneration of relics.

In March 1922 this movement for an Orthodox reformation gave birth to the Living Church. The chief bearers of this secession, fraught with heresy and schism, were married "white" lower clergy who reproved the celibate "black" priesthood of the monasteries for being of another time, obscurantist, and over-privileged. These rebels with a cause were joined by clerics advocating marriage and remarriage for all ranks of the priesthood, as well as by the usual opportunists, once the Bolsheviks seemed to be winning the day. Bishops Antonin and Leonid probably were the most prominent dissenters. But it was three priests—Kalinovsky, Vedensky, and Krasnitsky—who provided the energizing leadership. In particular, Father Krasnitsky seems to have brought a Luther-like fervor to the task of reforming, purifying, and revitalizing the Orthodox Church.

These three priests headed a delegation of renovationists which in May 1922 called on Tikhon to ask him to relinquish his primateship pending the convocation of a new sobor. This démarche was fired by their indignation about the Patriarch's unbending and ultra-sectarian public policy and church governance. Moreover, they held Tikhon responsible for the plight of many of the churchmen whose lives were at risk in the ongoing political trials. For the dissenters, Tikhon's failure to unequivocally disavow the Stanski Karlovci synod was not the least of his missteps.

Under house arrest and facing trial, Tikhon yielded to the entreaties of the self-appointed spokesmen for the reformists. He handed his reins to Metropolitan Agafangel Preozhajensky of Yaroslavl, pending the election of a new patriarch. When Agafangel proposed to hold to Tikhon's course and shun the Living Church he, too, was arrested.[70]

Meanwhile the Living Church held its constituent congress in Moscow and in July 1922 established a provisional all-Russian Higher Church Administration presided over by Metropolitan Antonin, with offices in "the Patriarch's residence and chancery."[71] This alternative sobor proceeded to discuss such questions as "the recognition of the social revolution, the purification of the Church from reactionary elements, the dissolution of the monasteries, the abolition of celibacy, the reformation of Church services, the examination of all Church doctrine, and the marriage laws."[72] Within less than a year these deliberations resulted in the adoption of a series of significant reforms: "the translation of the liturgy into the vernacular; the acceptance of the new (Gregorian) style calendar [as] the Church calendar; and the stipulation that married clergy [might] be elevated to the episcopate and that widowed priests may remarry."[73] Parish autonomy and lay control gained at the expense of higher church authorities. Reform priests abandoned their flowing cassocks for plain clothes. They also began to wear their hair short and cut their beards.

In December 1922 Tikhon "anathematized the Higher Church Administration and everyone connected with it for doing the 'work of Antichrist' and exhorted Christians to brave death in defense of the True Church." Of course the Bolshevik leadership aided and abetted the breakaway sobor, which in April 1923 lent its backing to the Soviet government, acclaimed Lenin as "a fighter 'for the great social truth,' " commended the new socialist system, condemned and deposed Tikhon for his "reactionary" policies, lifted the anathema, and "abolished the Patriarchate." The schism was consummated.[74]

The reformation of church and religion made greater headway among the priesthood than the faithful. According to one estimate, "by August 1922, . . . of the 143 bishops, 37 supported the Living Church, 36 opposed it, and the remaining 70 sat on the fence."[75] At the end of the year "the majority of the bishops still at large" are reckoned to have "been induced into formally accepting the Renovationist administration." Obviously the Bolshevik authorities encouraged and helped the insurgents, using both carrot and stick. Presently they entrusted the renovators with "nearly two-thirds of all churches in the RSFSR and central Asia, or close to 20,000," including all but four of the several hundred Orthodox churches which continued to function in Moscow.[76] In addition to benefiting from this official warrant and support, which could take the form of the forced removal of refractory priests, the Living Church made inroads among the white clergy.

But even the renovationist clergy had trouble rallying their flock. There was a large gap between the cadres of the Living Church and the rank-and-file parishioners, whom the reformists failed to persuade and hold, even in urban centers. In Moscow the churches "held by the 'Tikhonites' . . . were packed while those held by the Renovationists were empty."[77] This unresponsiveness may have been stimulated by "mock religious celebrations . . . in major cities" during the Orthodox Christmas in early January 1923. According to one less than sympathetic eyewitness of the iconoclastic and "hideously carnivalesque" Christmas procession in Moscow, the "population, and not only the faithful, looked upon . . . [it] with dumb horror," though there "were no protests from the silent . . . [and] empty streets, the years of terror having done their work." For fear that such "ridicule only intensified 'religious fanaticism,' " and eager to abjure it, in March the Twelfth Party Congress called on "atheists to refrain from offending the sensitivities of believers."[78]

Predictably, the resistance was widespread and intense in the countryside.[79] The faithful were less incensed by the renovators' political stands and their proposals for ecclesiastical reorganization than by their projected reforms of everyday religious life. Indeed, they actively opposed and circumvented all efforts to forcefully challenge, change, or prohibit their age-old religious practices and folkways, which they took for sacred. They would brook no offense to their saints, feast days, and rituals. The men and women of rural Russia stood against abandoning Old Church Slavonic for modern Russian in the liturgy, against eliminating monasteries and monks, against tampering with holy relics, and above all, against replacing the Julian with the Gregorian calendar.

To be sure, by virtue of its radical novelty the Living Church lacked the nimbus and authority to sway local parishioners and parish councils. But this deficit was compounded by the renovationists' "insensitivity to the power and vitality of popular religion" and the hazards of breaking in upon it. Even Vedensky eventually "conceded 'that nothing good will come of abolishing the liturgy in Church Slavonic' " and that there was need for "great caution" in introducing such changes if the faithful were not to be scared away. But in any case, the Living Church's days were numbered, as the first era of open and violent conflict between the Bolshevik regime and the Church neared its end.

✳ ✳ ✳

Paradoxically, the famine of 1921–22 had precipitated the move toward both an easing of the emergency economy and a hardening of the showdown with the Church. But once they had won the civil war and survived the famine, the Bolshevik leaders felt increasingly secure and self-confident, as well as less truculent. In turn, confounded by the conflict over its treasures and alarmed by the inroads of the Living Church, the Old Church needed to reconsider its general policy. At any rate, still under house arrest and scheduled for trial, in June 1923 Tikhon was set free in a mutual search for accommodation. His hand partially forced, in exchange for his release on June 16 the confounded Patriarch, concerned about the disarray in the Orthodox camp in face of the consolidating party-state, issued a quasi-penitent declaration of loyalty to the new order. He conceded that heretofore he had been "hostile to the present regime" by reason of his upbringing "under a monarchist regime . . . [and] the influence of people opposed to the Soviet." What was more, his hostility had not been "merely passive." He had issued a statement opposing the peace of Brest-Litovsk; an "anathema against the regime"; and a protest against the seizure of church treasures. Tikhon recognized that the indictment of the "Supreme Tribunal" charging him with these "anti-Soviet actions . . . was well founded" at the same time that he "deplored" them in broad daylight. In asking for the commutation of his punishment, Tikhon declared that he was no longer "an enemy of the Soviet regime," now that he had separated himself "from both the foreign . . . and internal counterrevolution."[80]

Tikhon's address to the bishops, clergy, and faithful, published in *Izvestia* on June 28, 1923, had exactly the same tenor. In this second profession he went out of his way to stress his ongoing efforts to depoliticize the policy of the Church and dissociate it from the Whites. Indeed, at this point he claimed never to have been "as much an enemy of the Soviet authorities, nor as counterrevolutionary, as I have been represented by the Council of the Living Church." Tikhon vouched that henceforth he would "resolutely condemn" any "falsehood and calumny" leveled against the Soviet authorities by monarchists and Whites at home and abroad.[81]

Tikhon's change of course and his political rehabilitation broke the momentum of the renovationist Church movement.[82] Many of the parishes which had defected returned to the old fold. At this juncture the Soviets had less reason to back the Living Church in its struggle with the Old Church; indeed, of the two the latter seemed a more effective partner for tomorrow's *modus vivendi*, or cold accommodation. To be sure, the Bolsheviks had won the battle of the church valuables. In the process, however, they had learned to appreciate the strength and resilience of the Orthodox Church and religion which, as Lenin knew full well, could not simply be wished away. At the same time, experience had taught them the difficulties and costs of rural de-churching and de-faithing in which they had looked to the Living Church as a handmaiden. The patriarchate having renounced its systematic hostility to the regime, the two branches of the Orthodox Church were left to compete for the future. In this competition the Living Church received only limited support from the party-state, which, controlling the purse strings, became less concerned with the reorganization and control of church institutions than with the development of strategies of education and propaganda to contain and erode deep-set religious beliefs and practices in the spirit of Voltaire's injunction: *écrasez l'infâme*. All sides realized that the struggle over church valuables had been a short-term battle in a very long-term struggle.

In particular, not unlike the Bolshevik *énragés*, though for different reasons, the diehards of the Church, including their associates among the émigrés, opposed the move toward mutual appeasement and compromise for most likely reducing the potential for popular outrage. Indeed, analogous to the White generals, the last-ditchers among the princes of the Church found it difficult to rally the men and women of the fields and streets. Admittedly, in 1921–22 there had been widespread spontaneous resistance to de-churching and de-faithing. But there had been no rush to either join the refractories or protest the summary trials of bishops. Most likely the rank and file distrusted the high clergy of the Church, as they had distrusted the generals of the White Armies, for being too closely tied to the old ruling and governing classes sworn to a restoration of the *ancien régime*.

✻ ✻ ✻

NOTES

1. Teodor Shanin, *The Awkward Class: Political Sociology of Peasantry in a Developing Society, Russia 1910–1925* (Oxford: Clarendon Press, 1972), p. 9.

2. See chapter 13 below.

3. Robert Conquest, *The Harvest of Sorrow: Soviet Collectivization and the Terror-Famine* (New York: Oxford University Press, 1986), pp. 14–16; and Sheila Fitzpatrick, *Stalin's Peasants: Resistance and Survival in the Russian Village after Collectivization* (New York: Oxford University Press, 1994), p. 20.

4. Conquest, *Sorrow*, p. 17; and Shanin, *Awkward Class*, pp. 21–22.

5. Igor Smolitsch, *Geschichte der Russischen Kirche, 1700–1917*, vol. 1 (Leyden: Brill, 1964), pp. 709–13.

6. Geroid T. Robinson, *Rural Russia under the Old Regime: A History of the Landlord-Peasant World and a Prologue to the Peasant Revolution of 1917* (Berkeley: University of California Press, 1967), pp. 135–36.

7. Pierre Pascal, *The Religion of the Russian People* (Crestwood, N.Y.: St. Vladimir's Seminary Press, 1976), pp. 20–21; and Geoffrey Hosking, *Russia: People and Empire, 1552–1917* (New York: HarperCollins, 1997), pp. 212–23.

8. Dimitry Pospielovsky, *The Russian Church under the Soviet Regime, 1917–1982*, vol. 1 (Crestwood, N.Y.: St. Vladimir's Seminary Press, 1984), pp. 19–20; and William C. Fletcher, *The Russian Orthodox Church Underground, 1917–1970* (Oxford: Oxford University Press, 1971), p. 16.

9. Gregory Freeze, "Handmaiden of the State? The Church in Imperial Russia Reconsidered," in *Journal of Ecclesiastical History* 36:1 (January 1985): pp. 82–102, esp. p. 83 and pp. 89–90. See also Nicolas Berdayev, *The Origin of Russian Communism* (London: Geoffrey Bles, 1937), pp. 14–15.

10. Hosking, *Russia*, pp. 227–28.

11. Catherine Evtuhov, *The Cross and the Sickle: Sergei Bulgakov and the Fate of Russian Religious Philosophy* (Ithaca, N.Y.: Cornell University Press, 1997), passim, esp. pp. 90–91.

12. Freeze, *The Parish Clergy in Nineteenth Century Russia: Crisis, Reform, Counter-Reform* (Princeton: Princeton University Press, 1983), esp. pp. 466 ff.

13. Felix A. J. Haase, *Die religiöse Psyche des russischen Volkes* (Leipzig/Berlin: Teubner, 1921), ch. 5; Berdayev, *Origin*, passim; Pascal, *Religion*, pp. 10 ff.; Moshe Lewin, *The Making of the Soviet System: Essays in the Social History of Interwar Russia* (New York: Pantheon, 1985), ch. 2; Hosking, *Russia*, pp. 211–14, 245.

14. Arno J. Mayer, *The Persistence of the Old Regime: Europe to the Great War* (New York: Pantheon, 1981), pp. 143–44.

15. Ibid., p. 144.

16. Smolitsch, *Geschichte*, pp. 151–52. See Richard S. Wortman, *Scenarios of Power: Myth and Ceremony in Russian Monarchy*, vol. 2 (Princeton: Princeton University Press, 2000). The page proofs of this magnificently researched and subtly argued study of imperial ceremonial, including the coronation of Nicholas II (ch. 10) and the tercentenary of Romanov rule in 1913 (ch. 13), reached me after my book went to press.

17. Minutes of the August 21, 1915, meeting of the Russian Council of Ministers, cited in Michael Cherniavsky, ed., *Prologue to Revolution* (New York: Prentice-Hall, 1967), pp. 150–67, esp. p. 158 and p. 163.

18. For the issue of church and religion in Russia from 1905 to 1917, see Mayer, *Persistence*, pp. 252–53; Pospielovsky, *Russian Church*, pp. 21–24; Smolitsch, *Geschichte*, pp. 315–30; James W. Cunningham, *A Vanquished Hope: The Movement of Church Renewal in Russia, 1905–1906* (Crestwood, N.Y.: St. Vladimir's Seminary Press, 1981); Freeze, "Handmaiden," pp. 101–2; Hosking, *Russia*, pp. 243–44.

19. For "state-church" relations from the February uprising through the Bolshevik takeover, see Efraim Briem, *Kommunismus und Religion in der Sowjetunion: Ein Ideenkampf* (Basel: Friedrich Reinhardt, n.d. [1948?]), pp. 163–74; John Shelton Curtiss, *The Russian Church and the Soviet State, 1917–1950* (Boston: Little, Brown, 1953), ch. l; Smolitsch, "Die Russische Kirche in der Revolutionszeit von März bis

Oktober 1917 und das Landeskonzil 1917 bis 1918," in *Ostkirchliche Studien*, 14 (1965): pp. 3–34; Roman Rössler, *Kirche und Revolution: Patriarch Tichon und der Sowjetstaat* (Vienna: Böhlau, 1969), chs. 1–2.

20. Pospielovsky, *Russian Church*, pp. 26–27; Fletcher, *Orthodox Church*, pp. 17–18; Briem, *Kommunismus*, pp. 167–70.

21. Richard Stites, *Revolutionary Dreams: Utopian Vision and Experimental Life in the Russian Revolution* (New York: Oxford, 1989), pp. 81–82.

22. Alexander Rabinowitch, *The Bolsheviks Come to Power: The Revolution of 1917 in Petrograd* (New York: Norton, 1976), p. 39.

23. Rabinowitch, *Bolsheviks*, p. 40.

24. Ibid., pp. 40–42.

25. Stites, *Dreams*, p. 83.

26. Rabinowitch, *Bolsheviks*, p. 42.

27. Stites, *Dreams*, p. 83.

28. See Smolitsch, "Russische Kirche," pp. 18–30; Pospielovsky, *Russian Church*, pp. 27–31; Evtuhov, *The Cross*, pp. 191–92.

29. Fletcher, *Orthodox Church*, p. 18.

30. Pospielovsky, *Russian Church*, pp. 30–31; and Briem, *Kommunismus*, p. 171.

31. Robert C. Williams, "The Russian Revolution and the End of Time, 1900–1940," in *Jahrbuch für Geschichte Osteuropas*, 43: 3 (1995): pp. 364–401, esp. pp. 365–66 and 368–69.

32. Evtuhov, *The Cross*, pp. 219–24.

33. Cited in Nikita Struve, *Christians in Contemporary Russia* (London: Harvill, 1967), p. 27.

34. Cited in Pospielovsky, *Russian Church*, p. 37.

35. Briem, *Kommunismus*, pp. 172–73.

36. See chapter 11 above.

37. The text of Tikhon's brief is cited in William Henry Chamberlin, *The Russian Revolution, 1917–1921*, vol. 1 (New York: Macmillan, 1957), pp. 495–97. See also Briem, *Kommunismus*, pp. 201 ff.; Rössler, *Kirche*, pp. 51 ff.; Evtuhov, *The Cross*, pp. 224–27.

38. The text of the decree separating church from state and school from church is cited in Chamberlin, *Revolution*, vol. 1, pp. 497–98.

39. Richard Pipes, *Russia under the Bolshevik Regime* (New York: Knopf, 1993), pp. 343–44.

40. See Fletcher, *Orthodox Church*, pp. 24–25.

41. Briem, *Kommunismus*, pp. 180 ff.; and Evtuhov, *The Cross*, p. 228.

42. Struve, *Christians*, pp. 30–31; and Pospielovsky, *Russian Church*, pp. 33–34, 36.

43. Rössler, *Kirche*, ch. 5; and Pospielovsky, *Russian Church*, p. 39.

44. Cited in Struve, *Christians*, pp. 345–49.

45. See Curtiss, *Russian Church*, ch. 3 ("Decrees and Anathemas").

46. Rössler, *Kirche*, pp. 113–19; and Peter Kenez, *The Birth of the Propaganda State: Soviet Methods of Mass Mobilization, 1917–1929* (Cambridge: Cambridge University Press, 1985), pp. 66–69.

47. Curtiss, *Russian Church*, pp. 47–48; Struve, *Christians*, p. 27 and p. 29; Pipes, *Bolshevik Regime*, p. 343.

48. Reference unfortunately mislaid. But see Robert Service, *Lenin: A Political Life*, vol. 3 (Bloomington, Ind.: Indiana University Press, 1995), p. 109. At the Eighth Party Congress, March 18–23, 1919, Lenin repeatedly warned against affronting and coercing the middle and poor peasants whose economic and cultural uplift would take "many, many years." See V. I. Lenin, *Collected Works*, vol. 29 (Moscow: Progress Publishers, 1977), pp. 139–225.

49. Cited in Kenez, *Propaganda State*, p. 69.

50. Briem, *Kommunismus*, pp. 212–20; Curtiss, *Russian Church*, ch. 6; Charles M. Edmondson, "The Politics of Hunger: The Soviet Response to Famine, 1921," in *Soviet Studies*, 29:4 (October 1977): pp. 506–18, esp. pp. 506–10.

51. Pospielovsky, *Russian Church*, pp. 113–18; Rössler, *Kirche*, pp. 135–37; Pipes, *Russia*, pp. 348–49.

52. Curtiss, *Russian Church*, p. 108.

53. Cited in Rössler, *Kirche*, p. 136.

54. Pipes, *Bolshevik Regime*, p. 349.

55. Cited in ibid., pp. 350–52. In Pipes's reading, the "rambling, hysterical manner" in which Lenin expressed these "apparently sincerely held beliefs . . . suggests that by this time, [two months before his stroke], his mind was no longer balanced" (pp. 352–53). See also Pospielovsky, *Russian Church*, pp. 94–96.

56. Cited in Pipes, *Bolshevik Regime*, p. 353.

57. Ibid., pp. 353–54.

58. Ibid., p. 355.

59. Struve, *Christians*, pp. 36–37. Pipes speaks of the "spurious evidence produced by renegade priests from the so-called 'Living Church' " at this Moscow trial, and by "two turncoat priests, Krasnitski and Vedenski . . . with close links to the security police" at the Petrograd trial. Pipes, *Bolshevik Regime*, pp. 354–55.

60. Ibid., p. 355.

61. Struve, *Christians*, p. 37.

62. Pospielovsky, *Russian Church*, p. 38.

63. Pipes, *Bolshevik Regime*, p. 356; Struve, *Christians*, pp. 37–38; Nicolas Werth, in Stéphane Courtois et al., *Le livre noir du communisme: Crimes, terreur, répression* (Paris: Laffont, 1997), p. 142; Orlando Figes, *A People's Tragedy: The Russian Revolution, 1891–1924* (London: Cape, 1996), pp. 748–49. See also Briem, *Kommunismus*, p. 200.

64. Fletcher, *Orthodox Church*, p. 28.

65. Struve, *Christians*, pp. 37–38.

66. Briem, *Kommunismus*, pp. 198–99; and Pipes, *Bolshevik Regime*, p. 355.

67. Francis McCullagh, *The Bolshevik Persecution of Christianity* (London: John Murray, 1924), p. 27, cited by Pipes, *Bolshevik Regime*, p. 356.

68. For this and the next two paragraphs, see René Fülöp-Miller, *The Mind and Face of Bolshevism: An Examination of Cultural Life in Soviet Russia* (New York: Putnam, 1927), pp. 249–51; Briem, *Kommunismus*, ch. 11; Rössler, *Kirche*, pp. 139–53; Fletcher, *Christianity*, pp. 31 ff.; Pipes, *Bolshevik Regime*, pp. 359–60.

69. Vedensky cited in Briem, *Kommunismus*, p. 229.

70. Fletcher, *Orthodox Church*, pp. 27–28, 31.

71. Pipes, *Bolshevik Regime*, p. 361.

72. Fülöp-Miller, *Mind and Face*, p. 251.

73. Fletcher, *Orthodox Church*, p. 32.

74. Pospielovski, *The Russian Church*, p. 56; and Pipes, *Bolshevik Regime*, p. 361.

75. Pipes, *Bolshevik Regime*, p. 361.

76. Pospielovsky, *Russian Church*, pp. 55–56 and pp. 61–62.

77. Ibid., p. 55, n. 32.

78. Pipes, *Bolshevik Regime*, pp. 357–58.

79. This paragraph and the next follow and draw on Gregory Freeze, "Counterreformation in Russian Orthodoxy: Popular Response to Religious Innovation, 1922–1925," in *Slavic Review* 54:2 (1995): pp. 305–39; Glennys Young, *Power and the Sacred in Revolutionary Russia: Religious Activists in the Village* (University Park, Pa.: Pennsylvania State University Press, 1997), chs. 1–3; William B. Husband, "Soviet Atheism and Russian Orthodox Strategies of Resistance, 1917–1932," in *Journal of Modern History* 70:1 (1998): pp. 74–107.

80. Cited in Struve, *Christians*, p. 39.

81. For excerpts from Tikhon's message as published in *Izvestia* see Struve, *Christians*, pp. 350–55.

82. Briem, *Kommunismus*, pp. 243–47; Curtiss, *Russian Church*, pp. 160 ff.; Rössler, *Kirche*, ch. 7; Pospielovsky, *Russian Church*, passim.

Perils of Emancipation:
Protestants and Jews in the
Revolutionary Whirlwind

ALTHOUGH in the long run revolutionary situations benefit oppressed and persecuted religious minorities, in the short run they put them in peril. In 1789 the Protestants and in 1791 the Jews of France gained full emancipation; in 1917 the Jews of Russia. Each time, however, there was a price to be paid. In terms of lives, the cost of religious liberation was, of course, infinitely greater during the Russian than the French Revolution. But while adverse reactions against emancipation were very different in scale, their causes and dynamics were uncommonly alike. During both revolutions, antirevolutionaries and counterrevolutionaries were the chief instigators and carriers of religious intolerance. Following the emancipation of 1789, anti-Protestantism played a considerable role in the resistance to the nascent *nouveau régime* in southeastern France, particularly in the lower Languedoc. Following the emancipation of 1917, anti-Semitism played a similar role in southwestern Russia, mainly in Ukraine.

The theorists and public intellectuals of the Enlightenment of the eighteenth and nineteenth century were sensitive to the disabilities affecting, respectively, French Protestants and Russian Jews. For many of them, prejudice and religious discrimination against minorities were emblematic of the old order's iniquity, and Protestants and Jews its preeminent victims. The battle against religious intolerance was a vital part of the battle against autocracy and obscurantism. In the same manner that the Calas affair of 1762–65 enraged French Voltaireans, the Beilis affair of 1911–13 incensed their Russian descendants: in the one trial a Protestant was condemned for allegedly murdering his son to prevent his conversion to the Catholic faith; in the other a Jew was

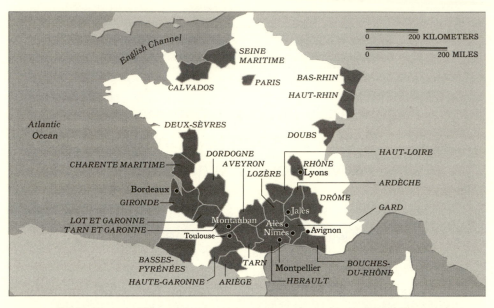

Departments of Strongest Protestant Concentration, End of 18th Century

The Pale of Settlement, End of 19th Century

charged with the ritual killing of a Christian child. Both before and after the fall of the Bastille, French Voltaireans pointed to the Wars of Religion and the Saint Bartholomew's Massacre as characteristic of the immutable villainy of the *ancien régime*. By the same token, before as well as following the fall of the Peter and Paul Fortress, Russian reformers and revolutionaries, in addition to recalling the persecutions of the Jews in the seventeenth and eighteenth centuries, stressed that the anti-Jewish pogroms of 1881–82 and 1903–6 as well as the anti-Semitic agitation of the Black Hundreds revealed the intrinsic infamy of tsarism. Needless to say, in the one case the responsibility of the Catholic Church was underscored, in the other that of the Orthodox Church, the throne and altar being inseparable in both instances. But to *écraser l'infâme* was to denounce less church and religion than intolerance, superstition, and fanaticism.

Protestants and Jews were the perfect scapegoats on whom to discharge a broad range of anxieties and resentments activated or intensified by the revolutionary turbulence. In particular, the last-ditchers of the old order portrayed these most prominent and vulnerable outgroups as incarnating a treacherous plot to desacralize, modernize, and level civil and political society. Of course, in absolute numbers, Protestants and Jews were small minorities. But their heavy geographic concentration in southeastern France and southwestern Russia made them prominent in these regions and led to their being turned into victims through whom to strike at much larger targets. Especially once they aligned themselves with the architects of a new undivided sovereignty, the dominant classes and masses of the Languedoc and Ukraine combined their age-old anti-Protestantism and anti-Judaism with their deep-rooted hostility to invasive tax collectors and magistrates, which they now directed at the agents of the centralizing revolutionary state. As may be expected, conditions of decomposing sovereignty simultaneously favored the freeing of religious or ethnic minorities from bondage and the reawakening and incitement of chronic inter-religious or inter-ethnic animosities.

The conspiratorial logic was central to this dialectic, but of particular import to the anti- or counterrevolutionary side. There are several prerequisites for a stereotypical fantasy or myth about the boundless and wily power of a designated enemy to take hold. Not the least of these is a thoroughly ingrained belief in the importance of conspiracy as a decisive agency of history. In this mind-set a select but half-hidden and alien few can manipulate the many who are presumed supremely ignorant and gullible. For the conspirators of evil to be credible, they must lend themselves to being portrayed as constituting a distant and sinister cabal bent on seeking control of both civil and political society. If this anti-minority strategy is to be effective, the "object" that is to serve as the focus of hostility or enmity cannot be inconsequential or trivial. Indeed, to serve as designated scapegoat, the targeted minority must be endowed with a historically well-established mythos and persona suitable for rigid stereotypical representation and projection. It must be "tangible, yet not *too* tangible, [and] it must have a sufficient historical backing and appear as an indisputable element of tradition," susceptible to a "minimum of reality testing."[1]

In France in 1789 and Russia in 1917, conditions ripened for the insidious myth to take hold that, respectively, Protestants and Jews were at the core of the diabolic conspiracy responsible for the overthrow of the time-honored monarchy and church. This mutation of the traditional conspiratorial demonology was under way during the prerevolutions, which were fraught with aristocratic reaction, well before the fall of the Bastille and the Peter and Paul Fortress. In France, anti-Enlightenment Catholic clerics and public intellectuals had started to assign the Protestants a growing if not decisive place in a deep-laid conspiracy sworn to undermine the established moral, cultural, religious, and intellectual order.[2] In this plot they were said to be leagued with sects of Jansenists, *philosophes*, and Freemasons. Similarly, in Russia, Jews were increasingly vilified and denounced for their allegedly pivotal role in a plot to corrupt and sap the foundations of the tsarist regime, as string-pullers of the liberal-democratic and Socialist movements.[3] In both cases, the scapegoated minority was charged with having a religiously informed basis for its rebellion against the existing authority principle and social system.

Both anti-Protestantism and anti-Judaism were fueled by the religiously sanctified nativism and hostility to modernity rampant in predominantly traditional and peasant societies. The religious dimension was, in fact, all-important, since the reactivation of the conspiratorial predisposition in all strata of society was contingent on a reinflammation of latent popular anti-Protestantism and anti-Judaism. It stands to reason that the conservative and reactionary action-intellectuals, politicians, and priests who proposed to instrumentalize distrust and fear of Protestants and Jews knew that in France and Russia particular audiences were prepared to respond to their demonizing and paranoid predications. With societal values and political institutions breaking down, the encounter of upper-tier orchestrators of collective fears of outsiders and their lower-tier and anxiety-driven followers was bound to be explosive. In such moments panic-stricken local and national notables keyed their cries in defense of the established order so as to engage or reinforce the pressing concerns and forebodings of political and civil society's subalterns. This Faustian convergence placed Protestants and Jews at the center of conspiratorial anxieties and hatreds in 1789 and 1917, respectively.[4]

* * *

In 1789 Protestants counted between 600,000 and 700,000 souls, or less than 3 percent of the French population.[5] About one-third of them were Lutherans settled in Alsace, but the rest were Calvinists anchored in the Huguenot tradition, and almost half of these were concentrated in the Languedoc, the cultural center of French Protestantism. This was a region saturated with collective memories of fiery revolts and bloody repressions. Protestants occupied a disproportionately large place in the economic elite of the cities, where they all but controlled commerce and manufacture. But the overwhelming majority of them were, like the French working population as a whole, peasants and artisans, albeit with a distinctly higher literacy rate than among their Catholic neighbors.

During the 1770s and 1780s the leaders of French Protestantism were negotiating with the royal authorities to lift disabilities deriving from Louis XIV's Revocation of the Edict of Nantes in 1685. These efforts culminated in the Edict of Toleration of November 1787, drafted by Lamoignon de Malesherbes with the advice of Marquis de Lafayette, Baron Breteuil, and Jean Paul Rabaut Saint-Etienne, a politically engaged pastor from Nîmes. Although the edict reaffirmed the state's unalterable tie to the Catholic Church and its continuing support for the promulgation of the Catholic faith "by instruction and persuasion," it granted Protestants certain civil rights, including the right to record births, marriages, and deaths in special civic registers, as well as to bequeath and inherit property.

Despite these gains, the Protestants remained second-class citizens. They were still enjoined from worshipping in public, and continued to be barred from positions in the state bureaucracy, judiciary, and university, as well as in municipal government.[6] While many Protestants were disappointed that the Edict of 1787 fell short of granting them full religious freedom and citizenship, they were not about to press for additional concessions, all the less so because they realized that they faced dogged opposition. Few of the *cahiers* (grievance lists) of the Third Estate took heed of the "Protestant question," and almost none called for further liberalization: those that did call for comprehensive religious liberty originated in districts with large Protestant populations. But the Third Estate's disinterest in the venom of intolerance was made up for by the First Estate's counteractive sectarian zeal. Nearly "three-fifths of the clerical *cahiers* of 1789 . . . specifically request[ed] that the Edict of 1787 be revoked or, at least, that Catholicism be the sole religion practiced in public."[7] The Second Estate, though less strident, was equally hostile to full religious emancipation. Immediately in the wake of the first tremors of 1789, several members of the first two estates and of the ultra-conservative press began to denounce Protestants for conspiring with Jansenists, *philosophes*, and Freemasons to subvert, nay overthrow Catholicism, the Church, and the monarchy. In fact, they anticipated Pope Pius VI's pronouncements of 1790 which excoriated the Reformation for being the Revolution's fountainhead and Calvinism its evil genius.[8]

Whatever their ideological differences, Protestants and *philosophes* were agreed on the importance of religious toleration as a test and warrant of progressive reform. There is good reason to believe that "the ideologies of 1789 were a perfect expression of Protestant aspirations . . . : free inquiry, freedom of conscience, political liberty, civil liberty, respect for the individual and of his rights."[9] Not surprisingly, therefore, from the very outset most Protestants enthusiastically supported the assault on royal absolutism, all the more so since the Edict of 1787 had at once raised and disappointed their expectations. Characteristically, Rabaut Saint-Etienne proclaimed that religious dissidents demanded "not tolerance but liberty."[10] And by December 24, 1789, as if to fulfill and seal a tacit covenant, the National Assembly adopted a decree granting Protestants full freedom of worship and admitting them to all elective and appointive public offices as well as to all professions.

In the meantime, throughout southeastern France, progressive politicians of Protestant faith or origin began to cut a figure in local electoral meetings, notably in Montauban, Montpellier, Nîmes, and Uzès. Some of them were among those chosen to represent this region in the Estates-General, about to become the Constituent Assembly. Fifteen Protestants sat in that body and the ensuing Legislative Assembly, and double that number were elected to the National Convention. Of course, they were a mere handful in assemblies of over six hundred members; few of them were stellar figures; and on critical issues they fell out among themselves. Still, Rabaut Saint-Etienne was elected to preside over the Constituent Assembly; Antoine Pierre Barnave (Grenoble) of the feuillant triumvirate was a Protestant; and so was Pierre Joseph Cambon (Hérault). All three "had what Sainte-Beuve called the Girondin temperament" by virtue of "their optimism and enthusiasm for liberty,"[11] for which Rabaut Saint-Etienne and Barnave paid with their heads during the Great Terror.

But not all politicians of Protestant origin were moderates. Although Marat was not Protestant, his most intemperate detractors seized upon his father's allegedly furtive conversion from Protestantism to Catholicism to blacken him as such. But there certainly were some genuine Protestants who were hard-liners: Thomas-Augustin de Gasparin (Bouches-du-Rhône) and (Pastor) Jean Bon Saint-André (Montauban) served on the Committee of Public Safety; (Pastor) Jean Julien de Toulouse (Haute Garonne), Jean-Henri Voulland (Gard), and Moïse Bayle (Bouches-du-Rhône) on the Committee of General Security.[12] Clearly, Protestant politicians were as divided as their non-Protestant peers in the fluid revolutionary camp. Characteristically, at the king's trial, even though nearly all the Protestant members of the Convention found Louis XVI guilty and approved the death penalty, nine voted for a stay of execution, and twelve against. Nevertheless, there is no denying the political minimum on which all Protestants were agreed: to prevent the return of the *ancien régime*, which they feared would spell the revocation, once more, of their emancipation. Indeed, while the Protestants bade fair to be among the great beneficiaries of the Revolution, they were also in danger of becoming preeminent victims of its miscarriage or deformation.

In the southeast, events since 1787 had quickened the political activism not only of Protestant supporters of the Revolution, but also of its Catholic foes. From the onset in 1789 the two sides were "prepared for either course": while leading Protestant activists seized the hour to turn it to their advantage, their Catholic counterparts were ready not just to contain them but, if possible, to press for the clock to be turned back.[13]

Locally, Protestants were in the vanguard of the challenge to the old regime.[14] In several cities, including Montauban and Nîmes, their daring activism was reflected in their rush to join, not to say control, local National Guard units and municipal councils with a view to at once redress and avenge the great wrongs of the past. This new-found self-assurance and presumption could not help but lash die-hard Catholic royalists into fury. The region's ancient and pervasive, even if abeyant, Protestant-Catholic hostility was about to resurge to become the essential catalyst for the eruption of communal violence and terror.

The sources of this eruption were complex. There were, to begin with, underlying social discontents. These were fed by built-in and contingent strains and stresses in the regional silk industry which increased the dependence of small operatives, artisans, and peasants on merchants and tradesmen, many or most of them Protestant. In turn, since large sectors of the majority Catholic population resented the perceived wealth and weight of Protestants in general and of the middlemen (including the moneylenders) among them in particular, their conspicuous bid for political power was all the more grating.

Militant counterrevolutionaries of the first hour did not hesitate to play on anti-Protestant biases and fears as they linked local with national developments. Within a few months after July 14, members of the landed and clerical orders of the lower Languedoc looked for ways to rally popular support in town and country for the *ancien régime*, including their extensive rights and privileges within it. They represented themselves as guardians, in particular, of the innocence and purity of the rural world against the baneful and cunning encroachment of the forces of modernity. To achieve their purpose, they did not shy away from "fomenting jealousies and . . . rivalries."[15] They fired deep-seated resentments, intensified by the fallout of economic recession, against moneyed wealth, the corrupting city, and the intruding state. In their portrayal, Protestants embodied all three of these evils, especially now that they took the lead in the upheaval which redounded, above all, to their own advantage. In the Languedoc zealots of Catholic royalism instinctively affirmed "that to grant the Protestants freedom of religion and admission to civil and military offices and honors was tantamount to committing an evil act," with dire consequences for individual Catholics, the Church, and the State. Insisting that in earlier times "the Calvinist heresy had only ceased to be contagious once its public cult had been put under the ban and abolished," they called for the revocation of the measures of both 1787 and 1789: to "reestablish the Edict of Nantes" was to court disaster, since the Protestants were still what "they have always been." Should the doors be fully thrown open to them, "they will only think of despoiling" their hosts. Whereas Catholics "suffer" Protestants to be Protestants, the latter "will never pardon" Catholics for being Catholics. Indeed, the Protestants, who visited "horrible excesses upon your forefathers," were "loathsome vipers" certain to "put you to death."[16] Revived and updated, the Protestant stereotype was given pride of place in the anti-revolution's conspiratorial imagination.

For their part, the Protestants rushed forward to exploit the highly unstable conditions in the cities of the lower Languedoc to break into political society, from which they had been excluded through the ages and which was the key to their emancipation. They eagerly joined the forces of change which, should they prevail, would ensure the consolidation of the liberties proclaimed in the Declaration of the Rights of Man and the Edict of Protestant Emancipation. Whereas militant Catholic royalists battled to maintain or restore the old political order as the essential bulwark of religion and church, militant Protestants fought to transform this order with a view to securing basic secular rights, including the unqualified freedom to worship.

Meanwhile, the growth of the religious friend-enemy dissociation in the capital left its mark on the Languedoc. By the end of 1789 the National Assembly had all but eliminated feudal privileges, adopted the Declaration of the Rights of Man and the Citizen, curtailed the authority of the king, placed ecclesiastical property "at the disposal of the nation," and extended full religious and civil liberties to Protestants. Then, in the first half of 1790, came the proscription of monastic vows; Pius VI's condemnation of the Declaration of the Rights of Man; the investiture of Rabaut Saint-Etienne as president of the National Assembly; and the defeat of Dom Gerle's motion to make Catholicism the established state religion. All of this lashed the diehards into an aggressive furor trained upon the Protestants, charged with masterminding the Revolution for their sectarian cause. Nothing was easier than to project both the insurgence against king, church, and nobility in Paris and the "patriotic" breakthrough in the Languedoc as part of a vast conspiracy by Protestants to seize the political, social, and cultural reins, by means fair and foul. Local counterrevolutionaries stirred up long-standing distrust and loathing of the ever-intrusive central state by warning that its encroachments were all the more baneful now that they were being effected by Protestants.

The Protestants, for their part, became more and more convinced that their own fate hinged on the survival of the embryonic *nouveau régime*. Increasingly, they saw themselves as a "small herd trapped among Catholics, and marked for slaughter."[17] Unlike their enemy brothers, who sought to stir the embers of Catholic fanaticism with a view to reviving the internal crusades of old, Protestants rallied to a temporal cause which for them only gradually, in the face of intense and all too familiar hostility, assumed a quasi-religious character. But either way, both communities were being swept up in an atmosphere reminiscent of the wars of religion.[18]

Indeed, "the past survived in the memories which transmitted it, and the two groups came face to face: Protestants and Catholics were equally defiant, hostile, and prompt to claim to be on the defensive while perceiving the deterrent moves of their adversary as a plan of attack, making a clash inevitable."[19] As they confronted each other, ready to strike, "the two sides in Nîmes, Toulouse, and Montauban looked to Paris," with each side putting its own construction on the radicalization in the capital.[20] The zealots of the one side pressed for smiting the Protestant Hydra before it would be too late; those of the other favored seizing the opportunity "to wreak the vengeance they had been waiting for since days of yore."[21]

This, then, was the general context in which the first popularly based and religiously impregnated resistance to the Revolution exploded in the early summer of 1790. Unlike the antirevolutionary revolt in the Vendée three years later, this resistance broke forth in a region with a long history of conflict between Protestants and Catholics; it started from the top down, not from the bottom up; and it was centered in and around dynamic cities.

* * *

The spiraling imbroglio came to a head first in Montauban and then in Nîmes.[22] Montauban was a city with a population of about 25,000, approximately 6,000 of them Protestants, who formed a separate but vibrant community. Protestant business- and moneymen well-nigh dominated the all-important manufacture and commerce of cloth of the city and its environs. Although economically powerful and relatively wealthy, they were shut out of the local political and cultural life, which was the preserve of the Catholic elite of land, church, and public office. Montauban's workforce, which included the artisans and laborers of the textile sector and the clerks in numerous religious and government establishments, was of course heavily Catholic.

Nîmes had a similar profile, except that it had a proportionately larger and economically more powerful Protestant population. France's tenth largest city, Nîmes counted between 40,000 and 50,000 inhabitants and was second only to Lyons in the production and distribution of silk textiles, which also bore upon the economic life of the surrounding countryside. Between one-quarter and one-third of the population was Protestant. As in Montauban, the Protestant community comprised an important group of relatively wealthy manufacturers and moneylenders in the textile sector who were ascendant in the region's economy; the nonagricultural workforce of the region was mostly Catholic.

From the start, the Protestants of Montauban and Nîmes were in the forefront of the forces seeking to have their cities join in with the dramatic changes taking place in Paris. With the old elite firmly entrenched in the municipal councils and churches, the challengers rushed to join the hastily improvised and new-model popular assemblies, action committees, and, above all, national guards, with an eye to outflanking rather than storming the old power centers. Needless to say, the incumbent governors viewed this drive with a mixture of suspicion, fear, and hostility.

By the end of 1789 the Protestants of Montauban were vastly over-represented in the militia and patriotic committees, in which they also all but held the reins. The National Assembly having decreed new municipal elections throughout France, the Protestants proposed to contest them locally, in league with the forces of change. Ironically, the enlarged franchise worked against the challengers. Montauban's traditional notables were able to not only benefit from the customary deference of the Catholic lower orders but play on their anti-Protestantism, all the more so in these increasingly hard economic times. In addition, the clergy provided the old guard with an as yet unequalled agency for mobilizing voters. In any case, on February 1, 1790, the traditional notables of blood, land, and church easily and decisively won the elections: the municipal government remained a bastion of uncompromising Catholic conservatives, if not reactionaries, standing over against the Protestant controlled national guard of middle-class patriotic reformists, not to say revolutionaries. Hereafter, in Montauban, the former hastened to organize national guard units of their own while the latter, in addition to jealously guarding their military advantage, intensified their bid for a commensurate political say.

Here things stayed until, in the face of the National Assembly's increasingly radical anti-ecclesiastical policies, which were imputed to Protestant cunning, the clergy of Montauban convoked a special meeting in the Church of the Cordeliers on April 23. This assembly exhorted the king and the National Assembly to recognize the Catholic religion on the lines of Dom Gerle's resolution, to maintain the local religious orders and foundations, and to exempt Montauban from the mandatory inventory of church property. Similar meetings were held in other houses of worship, all of them with sharp anti-Protestant overtones. In fact, the vicars "fomented a crusading spirit in the churches" at the same time that they "galvanized their flock by urging them to make the forty-hour devotion for their imperiled religion."[23] While there is no denying that "the clergy displayed remarkable organizational skills," it is perhaps going too far to claim, as Michelet does, that they also "excelled at inciting a civil war that by and large the population did not want."[24]

The *bagarre* of Montauban erupted on May 10, 1790, triggered by the start of the Paris-mandated inventory of the local religious establishments to be put "at the disposal of the nation." Whether intentionally or not, the day which municipal officials chose to implement the National Assembly's decree was the first of the three Rogation Days before Ascension, complete with processions intoning chants of solemn supplication. In any case, the official inventory takers had their access to convents blocked by women whose fury was primed by the ideological intoxication of the moment. Encouraged by this success, in the afternoon some of these same women, joined and encouraged by other popular Catholic elements, marched to the city hall, where Protestant national guardsmen were rumored to have assembled. Having surrounded the building and the eighty militiamen guarding it, the demonstrators called on the latter to disperse. When they stood their ground, the crowd, abetted by like-minded municipal officials, surged past them and stormed the building. Several Protestant guardsmen were killed or gravely wounded.

The timely arrival of patriotic military units prevented the situation going from bad to worse, but the incident was far from over. Although the Protestant guards were successfully evacuated, on their way to Montauban's prison they were reviled and manhandled by the still-seething crowd. Apparently, none of the city fathers made any effort to interpose themselves. According to Michelet, the throng "ripped apart the national uniforms of the poor unfortunates, tore off their cockades, and trampled them under foot." Still in physical danger, the guards were "stripped of all but their shirts and made to hold candles . . . as they advanced through bloodstained streets to the cathedral where they were forced to kneel, plead guilty, and make honorable amends."[25] Incidentally, Taine, sympathetic to the Catholic cause, also pictured the Protestant guardsmen as having been "forced to advance, two at a time, covered by a shirt, to the cathedral, to make honorable amends on their knees."[26] In the words of Jean Bon Saint-André, "we apprehended this day of vengeance for over a hundred years."[27]

In the wake of this *journée* there was a massive exodus of frightened Protestants from Montauban. The discomfiture of the patriots, despite their hold on the local national guard and their tie to Paris, emboldened the *enragés* among the old elite. These turned against their own moderates who sought to pour oil on the troubled waters and protect the imprisoned guardsmen, who for all intents and purposes were being held hostage. At the same time, the diehards resolved to strengthen the military forces loyal to the municipal council.

It took external intervention to make the patriots feel secure and to align Montauban with Paris. The reformist municipal authorities of Bordeaux and Toulouse sent detachments of their national guards to the outskirts of Montauban with orders to press for the release and safety of all Protestant prisoners. At the same time, alarmed by the challenge to government authority and eager to discourage the elites of other cities, the National Assembly publicly guaranteed the safety of all non-Catholics in Montauban. To prove its resolve, it sent a special commissioner to the scene to act on its behalf as well as in the name of the king. Mathieu Dumas arrived at the end of the month. Lacking both military force and outside help, the defiant local authorities set free the prisoners and momentarily abandoned their revolt. In contrast to similar showdowns in other cities at a later stage of the Revolution, Montauban was extricated from the defiant grip of would-be counterrevolutionaries without avenging reprisals.

Compared to the *bagarre* of Montauban, the *bagarre* of Nîmes was much larger and more savage, but its underlying causes, driving forces, and stakes were essentially the same. Since it began a month later—on June 13, 1790—the conduct of politicized Catholics and Protestants in Nîmes most likely was influenced by their respective readings of the course of events in Montauban. Also specific to Nîmes was that well before 1789 ultraconservative Catholics and radical Protestants had clashed over the major issues of their day, including, of course, Protestant emancipation. As previously noted, local Protestants had ventured out of their "desert" under the leadership of their pastor Rabaut Saint-Etienne to press for the Edict of 1787. They had also considerably influenced the drafting of the *cahiers* and the elections to the Estates-General. Not too surprisingly, all six of Nîmes's deputies to the National Assembly were Protestants. In reaction, a faction of Catholic intransigents began to pressure the established elite of land, office, and church to mount a vigorous defense of "the ancient and the honorable." In sum, the vanguards of both camps were poised to press for a showdown.

In Nîmes, as in Montauban, within days of the fall of the Bastille Protestants rushed to form a national guard and join it. They provided the bulk of the rank and file of the *légion nîmoise* of over 1,300 men, and nearly all of its commissioned and noncommissioned officers. In the fall of 1789 the old elite reacted by raising several Catholic companies of its own. While the Calvinist "patriots" flaunted new national emblems, the Catholic royalists took pride in the white cockade. The former were heavily middle and lower middle class, the latter from distinctly more modest social and economic strata. To the extent that there was cooperation between the two forces, it was minimal and strained.

The decomposition of sovereignty took the form of confrontation between military force and political power, for over against the reformist Protestants national guard, there stood the old municipal authorities controlled by hard-line Catholics. Starting in January 1790 in Nîmes, as in Montauban, the polarizing friend-enemy struggle focalized on the municipal elections decreed by Paris. Needless to say, the old guard was desperate to maintain or even bolster its traditional political and social ascendancy, which bade fair to stand or fall with that of King and Church. One of their most visible and effective organizers was François Marie de Froment. A former treasurer of the diocese, he was a fervent Catholic royalist who had already gone to Turin to do homage to the Comte d'Artois. He worked closely with local churchmen, high and low, to weight the new electoral lists heavily against the Protestants. The Establishment scored a sweeping triumph, capturing thirteen of the seventeen seats on the town council. The new mayor, Jean-Antoine Teissier, baron de Marguerittes, was of the Catholic party as well, even if he was not one of its firebrands.

The Protestants were less outraged and frightened by their defeat than its unseemly proportions. Aware of the risk of not having sufficient political influence and power to legitimate the force of their militia, they created the *Société des amis de la Constitution* to face the new city administration. Presently well over 80 percent of the over 400 relatively well-to-do members of this purposely nonsectarian club were Protestants. More than ever insecure and in quest of a political base, especially in the wake of developments in Montauban, in early June the Protestants set their sights on winning the impending departmental elections. Control of the local national guard became the focal point of the showdown between the opposing sides. Encouraged by their victory at the polls, Froment and his associates portrayed the conflict as the local equivalent of their Parisian confederates' losing battle against the Protestant-conspired anticlerical campaign, which they excoriated for being the motor of the Revolution. In preparation for a meeting called for April 20, 1790 in one of Nîmes's major churches, they circulated a tract giving the supporting arguments for Dom Gerle's motion, which had just been defeated. The rally in the church, after calling for the closing of the fledgling constitutional club, approved a petition asking the National Assembly to restore the king to his full powers, to declare Catholicism the state religion, and to halt the scheduled inventory of church properties. The themes of this petition were, in turn, integrated into a pamphlet distributed throughout regions with large Protestant minorities. In addition, this broadside proclaimed that the public "welfare" and personal "happiness" depended upon "the preservation of the monarchy and the religion of the Catholic, Apostolic, and Roman Church," and this in turn required "that no other cult be granted the right of public ceremony."[28]

At the beginning of May some of Froment's partisans took to the streets of Nîmes shouting "*vive le roi*! *vive la croix*!" and in one of their many clashes with the forces of order a patriotic soldier was killed. Even after martial law was declared on May 4 the situation remained tense, in part because Mayor de Marguerittes, even if reluctantly, winked at the zealots of Catholic royalism.

Finally, on June 13 several Catholic militiamen went to the bishop's palace to protest its transformation into an encampment of Protestant national guardsmen, some of whom proceeded to seize one of the protesters. One of the firebrands was seized by the guards. When word spread that the Protestants were holding a Catholic militiaman inside the palace, a crowd of true-believers gathered to press for his release. At this point the Protestant guards, taking fright, fired into the throng. There were several casualties, including one killed. The crowd broke up, only to regroup and rally additional militants, inviting further scuffles and casualties. Hereafter "each side saw the other as bent on extermination: the Protestants were certain that they faced another Saint Bartholomew's Day Massacre, the Catholics that they were confronted with another '*Michelade*.'"[29] But in fact there was a crucial difference: in 1790 in Nîmes, unlike in 1572 in Paris, the Protestants had forged a military shield, which they wielded quite effectively.

While dancing the war dance inside the city, the two sides summoned or anticipated help from their respective coreligionists of neighboring towns and villages, near and far. Given the customary solidarity of oppressed minorities, the circuits of mutual aid functioned rather better among Protestants than Catholics. In any event, starting June 14 Calvinist artisans and peasants from the region around Alès, including the Cévennes mountains—"the *rudes cévennois*"[30]—arrived in not inconsiderable numbers, presumably imbued with the collective memory of the revolt and persecution of the *camisards* of 1702–10. That very day, in confused circumstances, a shot was fired allegedly from the Convent of the Capuchins, killing a Protestant national guardsman. This fatal bullet triggered a two-day pogrom in which Protestants massacred and pillaged Catholics. The Protestants vented their rage and perhaps also wrought their historical vengeance on religious houses, beginning with the devastation of the Capuchin Convent, slaughtering several monks in cold blood. Outnumbering and outgunning Froment's militiamen, Protestant guardsmen and irregulars from within and outside Nîmes mercilessly hunted down and killed Catholic royalists and their sympathizers. When the national guard of Montpellier finally succeeded in restoring order, the Catholic side counted about 300 dead, the Protestant side about twenty.

The breakdown of sovereignty had created the possibility for the Protestants of Nîmes to affirm themselves, successfully, in the face of tried and true Catholic political, social, and cultural power. The cost of defeat was high for yesterday's overlords. Had the outcome been the reverse, however, most likely the Protestants would have paid at least as heavy a price. Neither side was in a position to prevail without outside help. The zealots of Catholic royalism were completely isolated, and short of a successful counterrevolution they and their patrons perforce reconciled themselves to losing their timeless ascendancy. In turn, the Protestants were able to capitalize on the fragility of the holdout *ancien régime*, at both the local and regional level, to secure the rights and liberties which had been denied them for too long. Ironically, they resorted to violence and terror to force compliance with the emancipatory and promissory decrees of the National Assembly before vacillating revolutionary governments in Paris condoned their use at the center and nationwide. In the meantime, the Protestants of Nîmes knew only too well that their own new-found and contested freedom was contingent on the survival of the nascent new regime in the capital and nationally, lest there be a virulent backlash.

Having gained a hold upon the streets of Nîmes the Protestants proceeded to consolidate their political position. The Protestant elite, heretofore only a ruling class, now also became a governing class. Protestants were prominent among the political leaders who took over the municipal council and occupied major administrative positions. This meant that they were also centrally involved in the disarmament of the Catholic militias, and the imprisonment and eventual trial of those Catholic militants who had failed to escape. Before long they were disproportionately powerful in the government and administration of the department of the Gard as well. Of course, the Parisian authorities sanctioned and encouraged this radical shift. This made it all the easier for the counterrevolutionaries of the Languedoc to portray their battle against Protestants as a local variant of the battle against the Protestant-engineered Revolution which threatened to overwhelm and rack the whole country, with nefarious consequences for the rest of Europe.

Forced to yield the southern Languedoc's urban bastions to the enemy—not only Montauban and Nîmes but also Toulouse and Montpellier—the adepts of Catholic royalism turned to organizing resistance in the countryside. Fearful of Protestant vengeance, not a few members of the old elite fled the cities, and so did militant zealots like Froment. They rightly assumed that the calamitous *bagarres* of Montauban and Nîmes would send shockwaves through the departments of the Ardèche, Lozère, Aveyron, and Tarn, whose population was partly Protestant as well.

The upshot was the so-called Jalès movement, named after the town in or near which the counterrevolutionaries held three huge open-air meetings in order to rally resistance to the Protestants and the Revolution.[31] From the beginning this movement was at once fostered and cemented by fear and hatred of Protestants. Its initial camp meeting of August 18, 1790, which apparently assembled some 20,000 Catholic peasants along with Catholic-royalist national guardsmen, demanded the release of all Catholics imprisoned in Nîmes and the removal of Protestants from power in all the municipalities that had fallen to them. The conveners also set up a committee to prepare a regional uprising; this effort was stillborn, as were similar schemes at the meetings of February 1791 and of July 1792, both of which were swiftly dispersed by patriotic military units, the last with a considerable loss of life. But to the bitter end the Comte de Saillans, one of the leaders of the counterrevolutionary resistance in the southeast, urged one and all to hold in mind the "diabolical and tyrannical cunning . . . [with which] the Protestant sect was ruling throughout the Midi, usurping vested authorities and controlling the armed forces," their objective being "the destruction of both the Catholic religion and the Monarchy."[32] By then, of course, the pace of the Revolution was quickening and the challenge of the clerical oath had further strengthened the religious and anti-Protestant element in the mixture of impulses driving the resistance in the Languedoc.

None of this is to suggest that Protestantism and Catholicism were the essential and prime movers, respectively, of revolution and counterrevolution. To be sure, in the Languedoc the counterrevolution followed in the "indelible footsteps of the old religious wars, with millions of Catholics lording it over a few hundred thousand Protestants who risked being strangled as surrogates for the Revolution, should Protestantism and the Revolution be construed as being one and the same." But this "ingenious formula" did not succeed with "the Catholics of the Rhône, specifically of Avignon, who proved to be as revolutionary as the Protestants of the Languedoc." Even if the conflict in Avignon became "violent and bloody . . . it did not become a religious war" by virtue of not being "grafted onto the old, hateful, and many-layered undergrowth running from the Albigensians to Saint Bartholomew's Day and the massacres of the Cévennes." In sum, while in the Languedoc the issue "became entangled with a dark and infinitely dangerous element, the day which broke over the Rhône was terrible without, however, being quite so explosive." Even so, there were family resemblances between the one and the other "epileptic fanaticism, that uniquely contagious disease."[33]

In any case, on October 16, 1791, in an atmosphere of simmering civil strife, Lescuyer, the secretary of Avignon's patriotic municipal administration which favored annexation to France, was fatally mutilated in the Church of the Cordeliers.[34] In retaliation, a throng of patriots, who exaggerated the antirevolutionary hostility of the opposition to the newly established government, brutally killed and mangled some sixty inmates, including several women, whom they seized in the prisons of the Papal Palace. To a certain extent this "massacre of la Glacière" was influenced by the "example of Nîmes," where "the massacre of 1790 was presumed to have contributed to the foundation of the Revolution." The trail of "horrid crimes ran from the Albigensians to the Saint Bartholomew's Day Massacre, and from there to the dragonnades and the carnage of the Cévennes." There was, indeed, a fateful concatenation of memory and mimesis: "Nîmes remembered the dragonnades; Avignon imitated Nîmes; Paris followed the example of Avignon."[35] Since the deed was done by patriots who did not bear the stigma of Protestantism, and also because of the raw savagery of the avenging violence, "the sixty victims of Avignon troubled not a few of the minds unaffected by the 300 dead of Nîmes." To the extent that the victims included both "moderate revolutionaries and enemies of the Revolution," the Avignon prison massacre of October 1791 was the "hideous prototype" for the Paris prison massacres the following September. Both contributed to staining the Revolution and lessening its attraction for the outside world.[36]

✳ ✳ ✳

In the Russian Revolution, the liberation of religious minorities exacted an immeasurably steeper price than in the French Revolution. There were, as noted, striking similarities in the size, geographic concentration, and economic profile of the respective minorities, as well as in their segregation, stereotyping, and demonization. There were, in addition, remarkable homologies in the circumstances conducive to their becoming imperiled in their moments of liberation: the breakdown of political and judicial sovereignty; the intensification of centrifugal forces; and the reawakening of dormant prejudices and collective memories of past paroxysms of blind ethnic violence. These conditioning and radicalizing circumstances were, however, significantly more intense in 1917 than in 1789. To begin with, even if during the prerevolution a few enlightened officials urged a relaxation of Jewish disabilities, Russia's old order never promulgated a liberalizing edict comparable to that of 1787. In fact, notwithstanding a minimal opening in 1905, the tsarist regime's policies went from bad to worse during the prewar years, when sectors of the state bureaucracy and imperial court integrated anti-Semitism into their strategy of aggressive social and political defense. Whereas anti-Judaism and Judeophobia became a living part of the conservative and reactionary political formula as well as of popular culture, left-wing radicalism made considerable inroads among Jews, who with time ceased to look to government for protection and emancipation. But above all, almost from the very outset in 1917, and without cease until 1921, attacks on Jews were closely correlated with the fortunes of civil and foreign war. This correlation was all the more intense because this twinned struggle was entangled with nationalist and anarchist risings in the would-be secessionist peripheries where Jewish communities were heavily concentrated. Russia perhaps best illustrates that in modern times Jewish emancipation has not progressed along a straight path.

The *philosophes* of the eighteenth century had stressed that both the torments and vices of Jews were a function of Christian persecution and societal iniquities. In September 1791 the Jews of France, following the Protestants, became full-fledged citizens and, like their Protestant counterparts, kept vigil to prevent the return of the old regime. Thereafter French Jewry, bent on assimilation, trusted the march of progress to erode the need for Jewish separateness and singularity, except in denominational terms. Outside France, in central Europe, the political reaction to the revolutionary aftershocks of 1812 and 1848–49 entailed reversals in emancipation, foreshadowing the eruptions of discriminatory violence in Russia between 1880 and 1917, and again in 1918–21. During these forty years Russian Jewry increasingly sought relief first by way of emigration and then, through its new-fashioned secular leaders—who, incidentally, also spearheaded the unbinding from orthodoxy within their own community—by joining the tsarist empire's embattled political opposition.

In this era, and notwithstanding the Dreyfus affair, republican France represented the positive pole of Jewish emancipation, while autocratic Russia stood for its notorious antithesis. As Lenin wrote in 1913, "of the ten and a half million Jews in the world," almost half live "in the civilized world" where there was no caste-like segregation, no Pale of Settlement, and no *numerus clausus*, and conditions were favorable to assimilation. As for the other half, "they live in Galicia and Russia, backward and semi-barbarian countries, where the Jews are *forcibly* kept in the status of a caste."[37] Of the approximately six million Jews within Russia's 1914 borders, the vast majority was forced to live in the Pale of Settlement, consisting of the provinces of the Kingdom of Poland and of fifteen of the empire's western and southwestern guberniyas. While they made up about 5 percent of Ukraine's population of some twenty-eight million, owing to their being barred from acquiring and farming land, they claimed a much larger share of the population of many cities and small towns or shtetlach, not only of Ukraine but of Belorussia as well, in which they were petty traders, middlemen, shopkeepers, and artisans. Although many of them were mired in relative poverty, by virtue of their peculiar occupational and social cast, Jews tended to be mistrusted as strangers in their own land and reviled as parasites and usurers.

With at best only limited possibilities for geographic and social mobility, this disproportionately literate, skilled, and adaptable non-peasant population looked to emigration as a way out of the Pale and the ghetto: hundreds of thousands of Jews migrated abroad, notably to the United States. At the same time, among those who continued to suffer their condition, and despaired of emancipation, an ever larger number began to sympathize with the far left. As of the late nineteenth century, apart from beginning to organize self-defense units, more and more Jews banded together in the culturally and nationally sectarian Bund, which soon became Russia's largest Marxist party. But after the pogroms of 1903–6, which in every respect vastly surpassed those of 1881–82, Jews also joined the Socialist Revolutionaries and Social Democrats, determined to make common cause with non-Jews in the battle for political, civil, and social rights.

At most 5 percent of Russia's Jews resided outside the Pale, by special permission, subject to revocation. Most of these privileged Jews and their families lived in the two "capitals," where they were active in banking; railway development; the processing and export of sugar, oil, timber, and grain; the professions; and the arts. Except for being smaller, this socioeconomic layer was the equivalent of central and western Europe's stratum of secularizing, assimilating, and acculturating Jews. At all levels of imperial Russia's civil and political society, know-nothings and nativists hawked stereotyped fantasies about the corrosive and immoral influences of this nontraditional element of the Jewish out-group. Indeed, in Russia, unlike farther west, the bulk of the ruling and governing classes, including most of their progressive and reformist elements, took it for granted that tsarist society faced a serious "Jewish question" which called for urgent attention. After 1881, and until 1917, in addition to extenuating the segregationist Pale, the imperial elite supported or condoned quotas for physicians and lawyers as well as quotas for higher education. It also accepted that Jews be barred from the state bureaucracy, judiciary, and officer corps.

Just like the anti-Protestant violence in the French Revolution, the anti-Jewish violence in the Russian prerevolution and Revolution was marked by the logic and memory of past torments. In urban as well as rural Russia the pogroms against Jews were embedded in a long and deep tradition of popular violence sporadically fomented and sanctioned by respectable leaders of society, government, and church—local, regional, national.

Historically the southwest of the tsarist empire, notably Ukraine, was Russia's primary zone of anti-Jewish outbursts, just as the southeast, specifically the Languedoc, had been the heartland of France's anti-Protestant eruptions. When rebelling against Polish rule in the mid-seventeenth century, the freebooters, or Cossacks, led by Bogdan Khmelnitzky, had massacred several thousand Jews, laying waste many of their settlements. There was a second wave of these prototypical pogroms in southwestern and western Russia in the middle third of the eighteenth century, with by far the worst massacre in Uman, halfway between Kiev and Odessa. Both times Jews were the victims of violence aimed at other and larger social and political targets.

Starting in the spring of 1881, for the first time in post-1789 Europe, the Jews of the Pale of Settlement once again "had to face anti-Semitism not simply as a permanent inconvenience but as an immediate threat to their established way of life, as an explosive force, as a dynamic rather than static phenomenon." In the wake of Alexander II's assassination, a wave of pogroms swept over 200 Ukrainian and Bessarabian cities, towns, and villages with large Jewish populations. Kiev and Kishinev were struck, and so was Odessa, with the result that overall "some forty Jews were killed, many times that number wounded, and hundreds of women raped." Although there was no killing in Belorussia, the Jewish quarters of several of its cities suffered arson and looting, leaving "tens of thousands of Jews . . . homeless and penniless."[38]

This anti-Jewish violence of 1881–82 marked more a fresh start than a last gasp of official and populist anti-Semitism in imperial Russia. In many important respects the Jews became the most severely harassed and vulnerable of the Romanov empire's several major religious, ethnic, and national minorities, or, in Lenin's words, "no nationality [was] as oppressed and persecuted as the Jewish."[39] Shortly after the turn of the century, Jews were cruelly reminded of their vulnerable pariah status among the host people of southwest Russia. This time the Jews of Kishinev, the capital of Bessarabia, were the prime victims: on April 6, 1903, Easter Sunday, street gangs fell upon them with the silent complicity of local authorities, in the wake of rumors that local Jews had murdered a Christian boy with a view to mixing his blood in their Passover matzoth. Close to fifty Jews were murdered, several hundred were injured, and quite a few girls and women were raped. In addition, over a thousand homes, workshops, and stores were looted or destroyed.[40]

By now Jews were being anathematized not only for causing the latest ills of Russia's civil and political society but also for being the kingpin of the irrepressible revolutionary movement. When economic strikes misfired, even semi-skilled and unskilled workers turned on Jews for allegedly having recklessly urged them on.[41] Then, as defeat in the Russo-Japanese War triggered the uprisings of 1905, the tsar and the court camarilla, as well as the diehards in and out of government, embraced the conspiratorial creed. Indeed, they denounced the Jews, along with the faithless intelligentsia, for masterminding the would-be revolution from above which forced Nicholas II to issue, *à contre-coeur*, the October Manifesto promulgating limited representative government and civil rights.

Characteristically, the momentary destabilization and dislocation of sovereignty in 1905–6 was accompanied by a new brushfire of about 700 anti-Jewish disturbances, the bulk of them in southwestern Russia, including in Ekaterinoslav, Kiev, and Bialystok. Odessa was the scene of the single most deadly and vicious of these pogroms: during four days in October 1905 some 300 Jews were killed in cold blood, several thousand were wounded, and over 10,000 were left homeless.[42] This was a new-model pogrom not only on account of its scope but also by virtue of its inner springs, in that the police of Odessa, instead of merely turning a blind eye, had a hand in organizing and arming the frenzied and savage crowds. Compared to those of a quarter of a century earlier, the anti-Jewish attacks were blatantly political: the agitators and thugs brandished "the national flag and the tsar's portrait." Whereas "before government had been inactive" and had let pogroms run a limited course, now "it cooperated . . . in organizing [what had become] murder and massacre."[43] The tsar became the self-proclaimed patron of a counterrevolution intended to save but also subvert the old world. Sharing the conspiratorial vision, he let it be known that he considered the Jews the chief instigators and carriers of Russia's revolutionary unrest and violence. In a letter to his mother, he himself claimed that "the people were enraged by the audacity of the socialists and revolutionaries, and since nine-tenths of them were Jewish, they directed their full fury against them, which accounts for the anti-Jewish pogroms."[44]

In fact, Jews were overrepresented not only among the rebels but also among those arrested for revolutionary activity in 1905. In his analysis of the events of 1905–6, Lenin noted that "the Jews furnished a particularly high percentage (compared to the total Jewish population) of leaders of the revolutionary movement" and that "tsarism adroitly exploited the basest anti-Jewish prejudices of the most ignorant strata of the population in order to organize, if not to lead directly, pogroms—over 4,000 were killed and more than 10,000 injured in 100 towns."[45]

After 1906 anti-Semitism became an integral part of the political reason of the hard-liners who recaptured the initiative from liberals and other moderates in order to scuttle the October settlement. This became transparent during the Beilis affair of 1911–13, which, following a Jew's involvement in the assassination of Stolypin, became something in the nature of a "judicial pogrom."[46] Even though the courts eventually found Mendel Beilis, a prototypical scapegoat Jew, innocent of the spurious charge of ritual murder, for two years the champions of the *ancien régime* kept pressing for his conviction, as if to appropriate traditional anti-Judaism and Judeophobia for their new-wrought political anti-Semitism. For Lenin the Beilis case meant that there was nothing "resembling legality in Russia" and that the police and administration were free to engage in the "unbridled and shameless persecution of Jews—everything was allowed, including the cover-up of a crime." No less appalled, leading public intellectuals raised "their voice against the new surge of fanaticism and superstition of the unenlightened masses," and against their governors who were fomenting "religious enmity and ethnic hatred . . . [and] inciting national prejudices, increasing superstition, and stubbornly calling for violence against compatriots of non-Russian origin."[47] They knew that this aggressive know-nothingism permeated the Romanov court, the interior ministry, and the secret police, the triangle of power in which the counterfeit *Protocols of the Elders of Zion* were given their imprimatur and instrumentalized.[48]

Indeed, reputable members of the old ruling and governing elites now embraced a Manichean worldview, and foisted the responsibility for the crisis of Russian civil and political society, and their own endangered standing in it, upon the Jews, who best lent themselves to being portrayed as the incarnation of the principle of evil. Jews became the subversive and conspiring Protestants and Freemasons of their day, all the more so now that the opposition increasingly denounced the persecution of Jews as symptomatic of the *ancien régime*'s depravity. Every accusation, traditional and new-fashioned, was fastened upon them: they were charged with being not only modernizers, strangers, and infidels, but also Christ-killers and westernizers, as well as master revolutionaries.

✳ ✳ ✳

The Great War was ominous for the Jews, whatever its outcome: victory would regenerate the tsarist regime and reinforce its illiberalism; defeat would be blamed on the Jews, to be saddled with the additional stigma of treason. To be sure, the Jews, like all Russians, fought and died for the Romanov empire and regime. But by reason of the Pale of Settlement being the principal theater of war, it was there that they became hostage to military misfortune. With the advance of the armies of the Central Powers in 1915, the Russian command, suspecting the loyalty of Jews, ordered the relocation of many thousands to the interior, while still others hastened off on their own. At the same time that in some battle zones the military tried and executed several Jews for treason, it disseminated the charge that the Jews were spying for the enemy. It was but a short step to fasten the reverses of the imperial armies on the Jews.[49]

Once again, as in 1904–5, military defeat unhinged the tsarist regime. The Jews were not in the vanguard of the February revolution, having well-nigh given up on reformist constitutionalism following its betrayal after 1905–6. Rather, they were conspicuous by their absence from the liberal and democratic parties which once again took the reins in a moment of disarray at the top and rebellion from below. This time, however, conditions seemed more favorable: the Romanovs had abdicated, Russia was allied with the democratic powers, and the insurgents were more numerous and better organized than in 1905. Above all, on March 22, 1917, within weeks of the fall of the Romanovs, the Provisional Government issued a decree guaranteeing the same rights to all citizens and abrogating all disabilities, including those bearing on the Pale of Settlement. This instant and sweeping edict of emancipation could not but fire the enthusiasm of Jews, without exception. Even so, haunted by the memory of the avenging pogroms of 1905–6, many of them were at best guardedly optimistic as they rushed to support and broaden the emergent revolution in the hope of making the crisis of the hateful *ancien régime* irreversible. In sum, the Jews were exhilarated by "the dawn of freedom" at the same time that they apprehended a new "Bartholomew's Night of pogroms."[50]

Some Jews openly and significantly contributed to intensifying the rolling thunder of revolution as members of the Menshevik, Socialist Revolutionary, and Bolshevik parties. All of these had long before condemned the *ancien régime*'s unbending anti-Semitism, above all its growing political exploitation by conservatives and reactionaries, the forerunners of counterrevolution. But in the parties of the socialist left the Jews were noticed less for their numbers than the prominence of their positions.

In February 1917, when the Bund counted about 33,000 adherents, fewer than 1,000 of the approximately 23,000 members of the Bolshevik party were of Jewish descent, or under 5 percent. Close to 3,000 Jews joined the party in 1918, and nearly four times that number in 1919 and 1920, the high tide of the pogroms. But bearing in mind the enormous growth in party membership as a whole, the proportion of Jews remained relatively small. In the leadership, however, they figured rather more conspicuously. From 1911 to 1914, the troika which ran the Bolshevik party, with Lenin as first among equals, included two Jews, Lev Kamenev and Grigorii Zinoviev; and Zinoviev remained through much of the war. At the next level, in 1907 three of the fifteen members of the Central Committee were of Jewish descent, and in 1917 three out of nine: Kamenev, Zinoviev, and Iakov Sverdlov. Four months later, in August, when the committee counted twenty-one members, the former three were joined by Grigorii Sokolnikov, Trotsky, and Moisei Uritsky. Thereafter, throughout 1918–20, the proportion of Jews on the Central Committee remained steady at about 20 percent.[51]

After the Bolsheviks took the reins, several militants of Jewish ancestry assumed important positions in the central executive of the Soviet as well as the Council of People's Commissars. Following Sverdlov's appointment to chairman of the All-Russian Central Executive Committee of the Congress of Soviets, Lenin proposed that Trotsky head up Sovnarkom. Trotsky declined, insisting that Lenin needed to take the helm himself. Lenin yielded, but then asked Trotsky to become Commissar for Home Affairs. Again Trotsky begged off. Apparently he was concerned that since "the counterrevolution would whip up anti-Semitic feeling and turn it against the Bolsheviks . . . [especially in this position] his Jewish origin might be a liability," a concern shared by Sverdlov.[52] At all events, presently Trotsky agreed to serve first as Commissar for Foreign Affairs and then as Commissar for War. Particularly as chief of the Red Army, he became as much a focus for the Whites' anti-Semitic wrath as he would have been as interior minister, charged with enforcing revolutionary law and order. Along with members of other heretofore subject nationalities, Jews also began to take up posts in the Cheka: during 1918–20 they eventually filled many of the highest positions in the Cheka, and ever so many of them served as Cheka agents in Ukraine, including Kiev.

Probably to a man, these Bolsheviks of Jewish background had long since turned their backs on Judaism. They were thoroughly assimilated, acculturated, and secularized Jews, who considered themselves fully Russian. To mark their turn away from their native roots and communities many of them, their "souls seared by tsarist persecutions," had adopted Russian surnames.[53] In doing so they converted not to Russian Orthodoxy but to a secular religion and creed promising a world not only without class inequalities but also free of religious and national oppression. Even though they forswore their respective Jewish communities, they remained "non-Jewish Jews" in what they retained of prophetic Judaism's social precepts.[54]

For many reasons Jews were now able to enter worlds that heretofore had been hermetically closed to them. After the Bolshevik takeover, the incipient new regime needed new cadres, the old ones being discredited, in hiding, or in exile. All things considered, the Jews were at once qualified, impatient, and vigilant. With illiteracy running to over 80 percent nationwide, including in Ukraine, the Jewish population stood out for its literacy.[55] In addition, by virtue of their experience in left-wing organizations, including the Bund, not a few Jews had acquired basic political skills. From the Jewish perspective, the new order provided unimagined channels of mobility: the previously forbidden and forbidding civil service opened up, as did the army and new institutions like the Bolshevik party. As if to make up for centuries of humiliating exclusion, young men of Jewish origin lost no time filling posts in particular in political society, which had been completely out of bounds for them. This opening of party and state, as well as of higher professional schools and cultural institutions, coincided with the abolition of the Pale, clearing the way for taking residence in major cities, which many Jews perceived as nerve centers of opportunity, assimilation, acculturation, and modernization.

The ascent of Jews in the nascent strategic elites of the fledgling Bolshevik regime was remarkable: almost overnight they became unexceptional members of the commonweal's ruling and governing class. For Maxim Gorky, in the early afterglow of 1917, the emancipation of the Jews was "one of the finest achievements of our Revolution." By liberating the Jews, who contributed more than their share to the fight "for political freedom . . . , we have erased from our conscience a shameful and bloody stain." At the same time, to release "the Jews of the Pale of Settlement from their . . . slavery" was to enable this country "to make use of the energies of people who know how to work better than we ourselves."[56]

Of course, the old elites took a radically different view of the penetration of Jews into Russia's sanctum sanctorum of power and influence. They fixed on this aspect of the Revolution to validate their conspiratorial and Manichean view of it. Their own political anti-Semitism was deeply anchored in the age-old anti-Judaism and Judeophobia which possessed the mind of large sectors of Russia's masses and classes and which they proposed to mobilize quite ingenuously. Indeed, many counterrevolutionaries of the White Armies and antirevolutionaries of the Ukrainian Greens made the Jew their surrogate archenemy: the former excoriated the Bolshevik regime and party in general for being a Jewish usurpation; the latter held local Jews responsible for all the intrusions, exactions, atrocities, and blighted hopes of the Revolution. And just as after 1789 the Whites had defamed Marat for his alleged Protestant origins, so after 1917 their Russian counterparts stigmatized first Kerensky and then Lenin for their supposed Jewish ancestry.

In turn, Lenin and his associates inveighed against anti-Semitism as a dangerous political weapon in their enemies' arsenal. As early as July 27, 1918, in reaction to "sporadic outrages against the toiling Jewish population [incited by] agitation for pogroms in many cities, especially in the frontier zone," the Council of People's Commissars issued a resolution declaring "the anti-Semitic movement and pogroms against the Jews . . . [to be] fatal to the interests of the workers' and peasants' revolution and [calling] upon the toiling people of Socialist Russia to fight this evil with all possible means." After warning that "the counterrevolutionaries" were exploiting the "hunger and exhaustion" as well as the "remnants of Jew hatred . . . among the most retarded masses," this resolution directed "all Soviet deputies to take uncompromising measures to deracinate the anti-Semitic movement" and see to "the proscription of pogrom-agitators."[57] Not surprisingly, it was Lenin, rather than his colleagues of Jewish descent, who spoke out against anti-Semitism. In any case, the salience of the issue of anti-Semitism in the passage of ideological arms prompted even hitherto skeptical and nonpolitical Jews to rally around the hardpressed Bolshevik regime: as party activists, sympathizers, or supporters, they feared the worst should the Whites carry the day in the civil war. If the resolve to fight and win the civil war, at great cost, was the original sin or curse of the Bolshevik leaders and the infant Russian Revolution, then probably most Jews of Russia—and many abroad—shared in it. Obviously the field of forces, ideas, and actors, as well as of perceptions and representations, was far from being that simple or binary. Still, the Jewish issue simultaneously fostered and illustrated the bent to polarization characteristic of revolutionary situations.

* * *

From 1918 to 1921, Ukraine was the site of the most decisive and fiercest fighting of the civil war as well as of by far the highest waves of murderous pogroms. Ukraine was home to about 1.5 million of pre-1917 Russia's six million Jews, or nearly a quarter of the entire Jewish population. The population of Kiev and Odessa, its two largest cities, was somewhere between 400,000 and 500,000 each, with Jews accounting for about 10 percent in Kiev and over 30 percent in Odessa. Ukraine had a long history of pogroms, from the seventeenth century to the renewed anti-Jewish outbreaks during the decades before 1914. All along the fury of pogroms was correlated with the intensity of ethnic, social, or political struggles, periods of general tranquility going hand in hand with "mere" apartheid, which was in the nature of a chronic "cold" pogrom. If the "hot" pogroms of 1918–21 were so uniquely extensive and savage, it was because they were linked to the rising and falling tides of civil and foreign war. In Ukraine the civil war between Reds and Whites was complicated by intermittent war with foreign powers and, in particular, resurgent national and ethnic conflicts as well as old-fashioned peasant rebellions. Indeed, of all the regions of the imploded Russian empire, Ukraine was the most severely struck by the fallout of the breakdown of sovereignty, all the more so because of its critical geopolitical location and economic importance. Depending on rapidly shifting contingencies, the Jews were execrated and victimized for being pro-Russians, Bolsheviks, Socialists, or Shylocks. By virtue of their polymorphous quality, they became the chosen surrogate victims of many adversaries and enemies of the Russian Revolution in the protracted struggle in Ukraine.

The pogroms unfolded in four distinct but overlapping periods, each corresponding to a different "regime": the Central Rada from January through April 1918; the German-sponsored rule of Hetman Skoropadski from late April through November 11, 1918; the (socialist) Directory led by Simon Petliura, alongside countless minor hetmans, past mid-1919; and the White Volunteer Army from June 1919 through the fall of 1920. As noted, of all the peripheries of the multiethnic ex-Romanov empire, Ukraine was the most completely consumed by the creeping anomie accompanying the wreck of political and legal sovereignty. Of course, there was a resurgent and insurgent nationalism which aspired to autonomy or secession. Although this nationalism had its political pacemakers and ideological drummers, it was above all driven by a burgeoning *jacquerie* of peasants whose latent animus against Russians, Poles, Jews, and cities was easily inflamed and manipulated, just as the Vendean hatred for the cities and agents of the French state had been turned against the Jacobins in 1793.

Not that in its political disposition the Ukrainian disaffection was Vendeé-like from the outset. The Central Ukrainian Rada, which was set up in Kiev in July 1917, shared the liberal democratic orientation of the Provisional Government in Petrograd. On January 9, 1918, it issued a decree guaranteeing equal cultural rights to all minorities. Several Jews served in the government and sat in the Rada. At the same time, local Great Russians lost no time blaming Jews for the disastrous dislocation of the old empire and old regime.

But above all, unlike not only the *bagarres* of Montauban and Nîmes but also the Vendée, all of which remained isolated and remote, the turmoil in Ukraine was carried by the tidal currents of the Great War and the foreign intervention in Russia's civil war. In March 1918, with the Treaty of Brest-Litovsk, the embryonic Bolshevik regime ceded Ukraine to Germany, making Germany the midwife and temporary protector of its independence: the semi-autocratic Kaiserreich sponsored a short-lived republic before backing a congress of conservative parties which on April 28 made Skoropadski chief of a Ukrainian state more in tune with the old order of the Central Powers. This satellite regime promptly cancelled the liberalizing minorities decree. Presently Jews began to be held hostage for all opposition, both real and imagined, to the making of Ukrainia by indigenous Russians, socialists, liberals, and Bolsheviks. Under conditions of rising lawlessness and economic hardship, in the provinces of Kiev and Poltava Jews were subjected to looting and extortion, often combined with physical violence.

While the Treaty of Brest-Litovsk had made the Germans master of a secessionist conservative Ukraine, the Armistice of November 11, 1918, enjoined the Central Powers to evacuate it. Their departure, along with that of the Skoropadski collaborators, cleared the way for a Directory run partly by outright separatists, and partly by nationalists with Socialist convictions or affinities. Once again the Jews cheered, but soon again met their nemesis. Just as Skoropadski had almost immediately put an end to the Ukrainian Rada and republic, so Petliura used his military strength to cut short the Directory. With the overall situation going from bad to worse, Petliura tapped into peasant unrest to raise partisan bands, and so did a score of other hetmans. Meanwhile, in the far south several Cossack units were moving into action as well.

Like any newly emerging and orderless secessionist state, Ukraine needed a measured external cementing force in order to congeal. The Red Army might have provided it, except that even in its embryonic and overstretched condition it was too powerful to simply serve as a force of negative integration. For a host of reasons, the Bolshevik regime never even considered keeping hands off Ukraine: it was of vital importance by virtue of its strategic location and its granary, all the more since it was fast becoming the chief redoubt of the foreign-backed White Guards.

In any case, within a few weeks, by February 6, 1919, Kiev fell to Bolshevik forces, which had started their advance in December.[58] In the meantime a clear pattern emerged: wherever Ukrainian military forces, of whatever sort, were overrun or routed, they tended to vent their avenging rage on the Jews. As of late December, and beginning with the pogrom in Sarny, south of the Pripet Marshes and half way between Lublin and Kiev, Jews were in acute danger of being made to pay, first, for the reverses of the hetmans' militias and second, as of July 1919, for those of the fighting forces of the White generals and their confederates.

The Jews of the ex-Pale were trapped in what became the main combat theater of the Russian civil war, in which were opposed Reds and Whites, Russians and Ukrainians, centripetal and centrifugal forces. Although Red Army units also committed excesses against Jews, such incidents were relatively infrequent, and the Bolshevik authorities publicly reproved and denounced them. In any case, the field of action came to be so structured that for the captive and defenseless Jews, control or liberation by the Red Army was, if not the star of hope, nevertheless by far the lesser evil. Accordingly, especially with this realization prompting Jews to cheer or help their circumstantial saviors, they could not help giving credibility to the allegation—feeding the self-fulfilling prophecy—that all Jews were pro-Bolshevik and anti-Ukrainian.

The scourge of pogroms erupted in January 1919 in the northwest, in Volhynia province. During February and March it spread to the cities, towns, and villages of many other regions of Ukraine. After Sarny it was the turn of Ovruc, northwest of Kiev. Hetman Kozyr-Zyrka, who was aligned with Petliura, ravaged the Jewish community of this small town in mid-January—robbing, killing, and terrorizing. But perhaps the most deadly pogrom erupted a month later, on February 15, in Proskurov, between Ternopol and Vinnitsa, in the west-central province of Podolia, controlled by Petliura. The population of this medium-sized city of 50,000 was about 10 percent Jewish. In this instance, exceptionally, the pogromists struck not to avenge military defeat at the hands of the Red Army but in retaliation for an attempted Bolshevik takeover within Proskurov, in which Jews had participated. Hetman Semossenko ordered his troops to massacre the Jews but forgo plunder and arson. Within a matter of hours well over a thousand Jews were slaughtered.

In districts where the Reds prevailed, liberation—or, as many local people considered it, subjugation—by the Red Army was followed by the establishment of Bolshevik, and hence centralizing control. Most of the new-wrought officials and administrators, including their local helpers, spoke Russian, thereby flaunting their status as outsiders and offending the indigenous population. Not surprisingly, the latter were suspicious of alien food and tax collectors as well as Cheka operatives: they perceived them as agents of the new governors in Moscow bent on not only winning the civil war and consolidating their regime but reimposing Great Russia's ascendancy over Ukraine.

Forthwith, in addition to individual acts of violent resistance, there were organized counteractive campaigns under the leadership of the various hetmans. These traditionally self-appointed chiefs rallied their partisans, most of them peasants, with slogans focusing hatred upon encroaching and extortionate outsiders, notably Great Russians, Bolsheviks, and Jews. Although they called for Ukrainian independence from Russia, sometimes with distinctly populist-egalitarian inflections, their strident war cry was, above all, a categorical imperative to fight Bolshevism and its proxies, principally the Jews. The hetmans had an essentially localist or at best regional vision and definition of their respectively invented homelands as well as of their "primitive rebellions." They were not fighting to transform the myth of a nation into the reality of a nation-state. Even though some of them, to a degree, had ties to Petliura, they all proceeded, characteristically, in utter isolation. Their main zones of action—which for the Jews became zones of blood—were contained in a rectangle bounded on the north by a line running eastward from Sarny to Chernobyl; on the west by a line running down to Kamenets-Podolsk; on the south by a line running eastward to Uman; and on the east by a line running up from Uman and passing through Kiev. This area included the core of the ex-Pale east and south of its Polish and Belorussian regions.

Hetmans Zelenyi and Struk rallied their peasant partisans, who operated west and north of Kiev, with the incendiary slogan "Death to the Jews and down with the Communists!" Around Tarasca, south of Kiev, Hetman Yatsenko proclaimed that "all Jews [were] Communists" and were "defiling our churches and changing them into stables." On April 10, 1919, Hetman Klimenko, who had a considerable following in the district between Uman and Kiev, led an attack on the Ukrainian capital in which local citizens joined his partisans in thundering "Death to the Jews! For the Orthodox Faith!" And Hetman Tiutiunuk cried out against "our age-long enemies, and their agents, the Jews."[59]

Above all, the bandit-Hetman Nikifor Grigorev was emblematic of the leaders and presumptions of the "primitive rebellions" within the Russian Revolution, though his exceptionally frequent and unscrupulous changes of course made him an extreme case.[60] Adept at partisan warfare, Grigorev had a considerable following east of Uman. His worldview was chameleonic, without either core or contour. Grigorev was a weathercock in the turbulence which defined his fortunes. After following in the trail of Petliura, he had his partisans fight alongside units of the Red Army. But no sooner had he rallied to Bolshevism than he pulled back and prepared to join Denikin. In early May 1919

Grigorev vowed to fight and defeat Bolshevism at all costs. Convinced that Bolshevism was dominated by Jews, he became fiercely anti-Semitic, apparently to the point of personally participating in pogroms.

Grigorev perpetrated his worst pogrom in mid-May in Elisavetgrad, a medium-sized town east of Uman, whose Jewish community had been struck in April 1881. In preparation he leveled a broadside against Bolshevik commissars for being agents of "ever-greedy Moscow and from the country where they crucified Christ"[61] and summoning the "tormented people of Ukraine" to rise up in arms against "Jew-Communists . . . [who were] converting our holy houses of God into stables."[62] The proclamation was not without success: in the three-day pogrom that followed, Grigorev's gunmen and torturers had the collaboration of townspeople and peasants from surrounding villages. Some 400 Jews were murdered, and hundreds were injured. Many of the dying victims were abused, defiled, and mutilated. Hereafter, and through July, there were scores of minor pogroms not only in nearby provinces where Grigorev had considerable sway, but beyond as well. It was at this point that Grigorev had his fatal encounter with Nestor Makhno. To be sure, at the time the former was by far the weaker party, the Red Army having dispersed and broken his irregular and uncohesive bands. Still, Makhno publicly upbraided his would-be ally for his pro-landlordism and anti-Semitism before Grigorev met his end in a shoot-out.[63]

It bears repeating that all this time Ukraine was in totally "unharmonious harmony." To speak of its political order during the first half of 1919 as the "Petliura regime" is to overstate the degree of structured authority and leadership. Petliura had, it is true, played a considerable role in the opposition to Skoropadski, all along advocating a democratic and socializing peasant state. Following the withdrawal of the Germans and their myrmidons, he had become a member of the Directory as well as commander-in-chief of the military forces of the fledgling Ukrainian republic, originally spawned by the Rada. In February 1919, with the support of the intervening Allied and Associated Powers, he also assumed the presidency of the Directory. But Petliura's regime was no less a phantom than Skoropadski's, except that as backers the Allies were a mere shadow of what the Germans had been. In fact, for all intents and purposes Petliura was left on his own to face not only the Red Army and the Whites but also a country in headlong decomposition. Petliura was unable either to discipline his own would-be army or to coordinate the operations of Ukraine's uncounted partisan bands, each under its own more or less independent hetman. Lacking a firm and stable center, Petliura's government was in no position to bring order to a chaotic realm. One of the consequences of this disjointed sovereignty was that the hetmans were free, and indeed obliged, to act on their own, which meant that they were also free to strike at the Jews.

Not that Petliura himself or his government was conspicuously anti-Semitic, at any rate not at the outset. In fact, officially Jews were emancipated. But during the first half of 1919, in his uphill fight against the Red Army, Petliura blinked at the pogroms carried out or sanctioned by his own troops or by the hetmans who were beyond his control. In his eyes the Jews were at once anti-Ukrainian and pro-Bolshevik, and given the logic of the situation, the incitement and explosion of deep-seated popular anti-Judaism served his purposes. He did eventually issue a manifesto denouncing pogroms and forbidding anti-Jewish agitation. But that was in July–August 1919, and by then the war against the Jews within the war against the Bolsheviks had taken its hideous toll.

✳ ✳ ✳

The White Armies in general, and the Volunteer forces in Ukraine in particular, were, of course, more disciplined, efficient, and coordinated than the hetmans' bands of irregulars. Accordingly the Whites had it in their power not only to feed the anti-Jewish Furies but also to curb them.[64] Whereas the pogroms of the hetmans were fueled by the blind and age-old Judeophobia and anti-Judaism of volatile peasants and Cossacks, those of the White generals and officers were, in addition, informed by ideologized political anti-Semitism. Given the largely similar social composition of the rank and file of the partisan bands and Volunteer armies, the ways of their pogroms nevertheless had strong family resemblances. Both killed thousands of Jews in cold blood, and many of their victims were beaten, mutilated, raped, hanged, burned, dumped into wells or thrown from rooftops, and buried alive. This physical cruelty was accompanied by verbal abuse, pillage, and extortion on an ever larger scale.

Although there was a chronological overlap between the pogroms of the hetmans and the generals, those of the latter only really began with the start of operations against the Red Army in mid-1919. To be sure, the White troops fell upon Jews in western Ukraine during their successful advance in the course of the summer. But again, the worst of their anti-Jewish excesses coincided with military setbacks, most notably the decisive defeats later that year. These pogroms were less acts of measured and ritualized revenge than of unbound vengeance. In addition to being fueled by military reverses, they were fired by mounting economic hardships.

The driving forces behind the White pogroms, however, were not only circumstantial but also ideological. Indeed, these two sets of factors were closely entwined and mutually reinforcing. Naturally, Denikin and most of the officers of his "officers' army" blamed the Jews for the Revolution, all the more so once in their vision it became incarnated in Trotsky, the commander-in-chief of the unseemly but increasingly formidable Red Army. With the unexpected defeats of the civil war intensifying their humiliation, they increasingly imputed all their trials and tribulations to the Jews. Lacking a comprehensive ideology and program capable of mobilizing popular support, the Whites assigned anti-Semitism an ever more central and conspicuous place in their essentially arrogant and bitter, as well as uncompromising, creed. While Denikin, unlike Kolchak, was neither a declared nor a furtive political anti-Semite, he was consumed by traditional anti-Judaism, which partly accounts for his not disavowing those who were. Even if he himself never said so publicly, Denikin considered the Jews to be the original architects and past masters of the Bolshevik Revolution. Osvag, his government's propaganda agency, disseminated strident versions of this conspiratorial cunning, and so did some of his senior associates. A prototypical proclamation issued by one of his generals incited the people to "arm themselves and rise against the Jewish Bolshevik communists, the common enemy of our Russian land," with a view to extirpate "[t]he evil [diabolical] force which lives in the hearts of Jew-communists."[65] In this way, the Revolution radicalized the prescriptive anti-Judaism of the conservative field officers.

It should be emphasized that in the highest political and military echelons of the counterrevolution in Ukraine, few voices protested this rampant anti-Semitism. Denikin, like Petliura before him, did issue a declaration disavowing anti-Semitism. But this was essentially tactical, to court the favor of the Allies, since Western champions of the anti-Bolshevik forces in Russia kept cautioning that anti-Semitic excesses were alienating public opinion and complicating continued aid to the Whites. Incidentally, the White generals counted on kindred spirits among the Allies. In August 1919 Sir Eyre Crowe, a high functionary at the British Foreign Office, urged Chaim Weizmann, who called on him to protest the pogroms, to consider that what for Weizmann were "outrages against the Jews, may in the eyes of Ukrainians be retaliation for the horrors committed by the Bolsheviks who are all organized and directed by the Jews."[66] And at Denikin's headquarters, even the Kadets did not take a stand against the pogroms. Indeed, their parent party eventually went to the execrable extreme of "calling on the Jews to repudiate Bolshevism in order to save themselves."[67]

The Orthodox Church spoke in a similar key, thereby providing a powerful religious sanction for pogromism. Practiced in the art of playing on anti-Judaism and Judeophobia, the clergy charged that having subverted the God-given *ancien régime*, the Jews were now using Bolshevism to subject Russia to anti-Christian rule. While there were hawks among the priests, high and low, who stirred up support for attacks on Jews, there were few if any active doves among them. Remarkably, Patriarch Tikhon, the head of the Orthodox Church, issued a remonstrance on July 21, 1919, declaring that anti-Jewish violence brought "dishonor for the perpetrators, dishonor for the Holy Church."[68] But except for this statement, which apparently fell on deaf ears, in the provinces the churchmen condoned even the worst excesses by their silence.[69] When a delegation of Russian Jews asked the Metropolitan of Kiev to raise his voice against pogroms, he, like the Kadets, responded by urging them to "first turn to their coreligionists and ask them to leave the Bolshevik establishment forthwith."[70] In sum, there were no dams to obstruct the wave of pogroms which swept over Ukraine as part of the flux and reflux of the fight to the death in the civil war.

From incidental and relatively mild actions against Jews in June and July, when the White forces seized control of much of Ukraine and made it the chief bastion of counterrevolution, the anti-Jewish assaults spiraled to reach their peak in November–December 1919, which saw the final disarray and fall of Denikin's host. As the pogroms rose in number they also became more ferocious, with pillage and extortion declining in favor of wholesale murder and savagery.[71]

In late summer and early fall the Red Army began to face down the Volunteer forces around Kiev in western Ukraine, from where Denikin had meant to march upon Moscow. The stepped-up fighting, involving the usual cruelties of civil war, boded ill for the Jews. This became clear in late September, when a savage pogrom racked the Jewish community of Fastov, a small town immediately southwest of the Ukrainian capital. In the course of several days, and without hindrance from higher military or civil authority, a brigade of Cossacks slaughtered over 1,000 Jews, most of them "older people, women, and children," many of the younger men having fled in time.[72] This wildfire of death was coupled with an orgy of massive rape, profanation, and plunder. With the Jewish quarter ravaged, "the flourishing town of Fastov [was] transformed into a graveyard."[73]

Before long, in early October, the Jewish community of Kiev was once again set upon. Red forces unexpectedly made a brief incursion into the city, only to be driven out by Volunteer troops a few days later. Once they returned, the Whites intensified their castigation of Jewish Bolshevism and denounced local Jews for having collaborated with the enemy. Like the Jews of Fastov, the Jews of Kiev suffered a tempest of death, plunder, and destruction which took over 250 lives. In the wake of this deadly onslaught V. V. Shulgin, a conservative politician close to Denikin and editorialist of the local *Kievlianin*, claimed that "at night . . . a dreadful medieval spirit stalked the streets of Kiev," with the "heartrending wails" of Jews breaking the city's "general stillness and emptiness." How would the Jews respond to this "torture by fear"? In effect they had only one of two choices: either "confess and repent . . . before the whole world . . . [for their] active part in the Bolshevik madness," or else, and despite "these dreadful nights, full of anguish," organize "a league to combat anti-Semitism, thereby denying well-known facts and inflaming anti-Jewish feelings still more." Insisting that the " fate" of the Jews was in their own hands, Shulgin was confident that this "torture by fear would . . . show them the right way."[74]

With local variations, the crescendo of anti-Jewish violence, as practiced in Fastov and Kiev, was closely correlated with the climacteric of the civil war in Ukraine, notably with the losing battles which the Whites fought to defend, capture, or recapture small towns and villages with sizable Jewish communities. Unlike the Protestants in the Languedoc in 1790, the Jews in Ukraine were in no position to form or join "national guard" units. Completely defenseless, they were reduced to hoping and praying for the timely arrival of government forces.

The record of the Red Army was not spotless either. Soviet forces are estimated to have committed slightly over 8 percent of all anti-Jewish pogroms in Ukraine. Usually the troops that turned on the Jews had fought with either a hetman, or Denikin, or both, before going over to the Red Army. It does seem, however, that higher echelons sought to identify and punish the soldiers of the Boguny and Tarashchany regiments who committed most of these outrages. Indeed, the military command of the Red Army, like the political command of the Bolshevik regime, repeatedly declaimed against anti-Semites, and several pogromists were brought to account. And in June 1919 the Soviet government assigned funds to help "certain victims of pogroms."[75]

To be sure, the Jews of Ukraine were disproportionately favorable to Bolshevism and welcoming of the Red Army, and undoubtedly in some towns there were Jewish elements that were something in the nature of a Trojan horse. This preference and conduct were not, however, a function of predetermined and conspiratorial pro-Bolshevism. Rather, the Jews acted as they did because they were terror-struck by their helplessness in the face of certain peril in a situation in which the hetmans and Whites left them no other choice.

It is striking that the non-Jewish Jews in the Bolshevik leadership as well as among the Mensheviks and Socialist Revolutionaries remained curiously silent. Although Trotsky received many reports about the pogroms of the summer of 1919, apparently he did not cry out against them either in public or behind the scenes. Ironically, Red and White leaders were equally reluctant to confront the issue head on: the former were concerned about "playing into the hands of those who accused them of serving 'Jewish' interests . . . [and about] encouraging pro-White sentiments among its population"; the latter were afraid of alienating the anti-Semites among their officers.[76]

Perhaps there was a tacit understanding that the non-Jewish colleagues of the Bolsheviks of Jewish background would speak up. Certainly, throughout the areas they controlled, by and large "the Bolsheviks did not tolerate overt manifestations of anti-Semitism, least of all of pogroms, for they realized that anti-Semitism had become a cover for anti-Communism."[77] On July 27, 1918, over Lenin's signature, Sovnarkom "issued an appeal against anti-Semitism, threatening penalties for pogroms."[78] In March of 1919, when asked to "make sixteen three-minute records for propaganda purposes, Lenin chose as one of his themes 'On Pogroms and the Persecution of Jews.' "[79] Insisting that with an eye to "divert the hatred . . . [and] attention" of workers and peasants "from their real enemy," the late tsarist monarchy had "incited" them against the Jews. Lenin emphasized that "hatred of the Jews persisted only in countries in which slavery to landowners and capitalists had created abysmal ignorance among workers and peasants, that only the most ignorant and downtrodden people can believe the lies and slander that are spread about the Jews," and that such practices and beliefs were "a survival of ancient feudal times, when priests burned heretics at the stake." Clearly, among the Jews, as "among us," the working people "form the majority" and "are oppressed by capital." Accordingly, Jews were not "enemies of the working people . . . [but] our brothers . . . [and] comrades in the struggle for socialism." To be sure, there were "kulaks, exploiters, and capitalists" among the Jews, just as "among the Russians, . . . [and] rich Jews, like rich Russians, and the rich in all countries, are in alliance to oppress, crush, rob, and disunite workers," sowing and fomenting hatred "between workers of different faiths, nations, and races." Lenin concluded with a denunciation of both "the accursed tsarism" which in the past had "tortured and persecuted the Jews . . . and of those who nowadays are fomenting hatred toward the Jews as well as other nations."[80] Whatever the shortcomings of Lenin's highly ideological but ingenuous pronouncement, it was in stark contrast to the all but total absence of plain-spoken public censure of pogromism by the Whites—not to mention the contrast with the declamations of those who gloried in the idea of weaning the Jews from Bolshevism by subjecting them to "torture by fear." This discrepancy in rhetoric matches the discrepancy in deeds, between the relatively small number of pogroms perpetrated by Red Army units and those committed by the partisan bands and regular divisions of the various resistances, for which the Whites must take most if not all of the responsibility.

✱ ✱ ✱

It is difficult to get a precise measure of the extent and intensity of the Jewish suffering.[81] Indeed, there will never be an exact reckoning of the number of Jews killed in pogroms during the civil war. In Ukraine alone more than 1,000 pogroms struck over 500 Jewish communities, most of them in the Kiev, Volhynia, and Podolia provinces, which had been the center of anti-Jewish Furies in the seventeenth and eighteenth centuries as well. Estimates of the number of Jews who were killed or died in pogroms in all of Russia during the civil war range between 60,000 and 150,000. At all events, the death toll ran into the tens of thousands. In addition, countless Jews were maimed, wounded, orphaned, traumatized, and despoiled; and the rape of women and girls knew no bounds.

It is, of course, equally difficult, not to say impossible, to separate the pogroms perpetrated, respectively, by Whites, Ukrainian nationalists, Greens, and Reds. Certainly the Whites, including the Cossacks who provided the main body of their troops, bear a heavy burden, perhaps even the palm. Neither their senior officers nor their political leaders made any concerted effort to restrain the indiscriminate massacre of Jews. To the contrary, since they conflated Bolshevik and Jew in their perception of the enemy, they considered the drive against the Jews inherent to their counterrevolutionary precept and practice. The Jews were as much the target as the victims of their rage: they were trapped in the vicious circle of vengeance and re-vengeance peculiar to "religiously" fired civil war. Probably Shulgin, the aforementioned conservative politician-journalist, came close to capturing the White outlook and temper: "We reacted to the 'Yids' just as the Bolsheviks reacted to the *burzhoois*. They shouted 'Death to the *Burzhoois*!' and we replied 'Death to the Yids!' "[82] By contrast, among the Greens—and Ukrainian nationalists—Makhno stands out for having stood against the torment and victimization of Jews. Likewise, although several Red Army units carried out pogroms, the Bolsheviks opposed anti-Semitism and sought to discipline those who practiced it. All in all, the wages of Jewish emancipation were exorbitant, and the ways and means of achieving and securing it left a perplexing and perilous legacy for the future within Soviet Russia, and beyond.

* * *

NOTES

1. J. M. Roberts, *The Mythology of the Secret Societies* (London: Secker & Warburg, 1972), passim; T. W. Adorno, Else Frenkel-Brunswick, et al., *The Authoritarian Personality* (New York: Harper, 1950), pp. 607–8; Bruno Bettelheim and Morris Janowitz, *Dynamics of Prejudice* (New York: Harper, 1950), pp. 32–33; Franz Neumann, "Anxiety and Politics," in Herbert Marcuse, ed., *The Democratic and the Authoritarian State* (Glencoe, Ill.: Free Press, 1957), ch. 11.

2. Roberts, "The Origins of a Mythology: Freemasons, Protestants, and the French Revolution," in *Bulletin of the Institute of Historical Research* XLIV (1971): pp. 78–97.

3. Hans Rogger, *Russia in the Age of Modernization and Revolution, 1881–1917* (New York: Longman, 1983), esp. pp. 199–206.

4. Richard Hofstadter and Michael Wallace, eds., *American Violence: A Documentary History* (New York: Knopf, 1970), pp. 11–13, 22, 30–31, 39; and Johannes Rogalla von Bieberstein, *Die These von der Verschwörung, 1776–1945: Philosophen, Freimaurer, Juden, Liberale und Sozialisten als Verschwörer gegen die Sozialordnung* (Bern: Herbert Lang, 1976), passim.

5. The following profile of French Protestantism is based on R. R. Palmer, *Catholics and Unbelievers in Eighteenth-Century France* (Princeton: Princeton University Press, 1939); Burdette C. Poland, *French Protestantism and the French Revolution* (Princeton: Princeton University Press, 1957); Timothy Tackett, *Religion, Revolution, and Regional Culture in Eighteenth-Century France: The Ecclesiastical Oath of 1791* (Princeton: Princeton University Press, 1986), esp. ch. 9.

6. Barbara de Negroni, *Intolérances: Catholiques et protestants en France, 1560–1787* (Paris: Hachette, 1996), pp. 212–13; and André Dupont, *Rabaut Saint-Etienne, 1743–1793: Un protestant défenseur de la liberté religieuse* (Geneva: Labor et Fides, 1989), pp. iii–xi.

7. Tackett, *Religion*, p. 209.

8. See Augustin Theiner, ed., *Documents inédits relatifs aux affaires religieuses de la France, 1790–1800*, 2 vols. (Paris, 1857–58); Abbé Isidore Bertrand, *Le pontificat de Pie VI et l'athéisme révolutionnaire*, 2 vols. (Paris, 1879); Joseph de Maistre, "Réflexions sur le Protestantisme dans ses rapports avec la souveraineté (1798)," in Maistre, *Écrits sur la Révolution* (Paris: Presses Universitaires, 1989), pp. 219–39, esp. p. 227 and pp. 231–32. Also see chapter 11 above.

9. André Siegfried cited in Poland, *French Protestantism*, p. 141.

10. Cited in Negroni, *Intolérances*, p. 214.

11. Pierre Chazel cited in Poland, *French Protestantism*, pp. 189–90.

12. J. F. Robinet et al., eds., *Dictionnaire historique et biographique de la Révolution et de l'Empire, 1789–1815*, 2 vols. (Kraus Reprint, 1975).

13. Colin Lucas, "The Problem of the Midi in the French Revolution," in *Royal Historical Society: Transactions*, Fifth Series, 28 (1978): p. 5 and p. 15.

14. See Poland, *French Protestantism*; Hubert C. Johnson, *The Midi in Revolution: A Study in Regional Political Diversity, 1789–1793* (Princeton: Princeton University Press, 1986); Gwynn Lewis, *The Second Vendée: The Continuity of Counterrevolution in the Department of the Gard, 1789–1815* (Oxford: Clarendon, 1978); James N. Hood, "Protestant-Catholic Relations and the Roots of the First Popular Counterrevolutionary Movement in France," in *Journal of Modern History* 43 (1971): pp. 245–75; Lucas, "The Problem of the Midi," pp. 1–25.

15. Jules Michelet, *Histoire de la Révolution française*, vol. 1(Paris: Laffont, 1979), p. 303.

16. A diehard pamphlet cited in Poland, *French Protestantism*, p. 119.

17. Michelet, *Histoire*, p. 304.

18. Cf. Poland, *French Protestantism*, p. 135

19. Hippolyte Taine, *Les origines de la France contemporaine*, vol. 1 (Paris: Laffont, 1986), p. 488. Taine stretches a point when insisting that with the Edict of 1787 the Protestants had "all their civil rights restituted to them, but in vain."

20. Michelet, *Histoire*, pp. 304–5.

21. Jean Bon Saint-André cited in Taine, *Les origines*, p. 488, n. 1.

22. For the *bagarres* of spring 1790, see Lucas, "The Problem of the Midi," pp. 1–25. See also James H. Hood, "The Riots in Nîmes and the Origins of the Counterrevolutionary Movement," Ph.D. diss., Princeton University, 1968.

23. Michelet, *Histoire*, p. 305.

24. Ibid., p. 302.

25. Ibid., p. 306.

26. Taine, *Les origines*, p. 489.

27. Cited in Roberts, "Origins of a Mythology," p. 88.

28. Cited in Lewis, *Second Vendée*, p. 21.

29. Taine, *Les origines*, p. 490.

30. Ibid., p. 490.

31. Johnson, *Midi*, pp. 130–32; and P. M. Jones, *The Peasantry in the French Revolution* (Cambridge: Cambridge University Press, 1988), pp. 220–21.

32. Cited in Lewis, *Second Vendée*, p. 36.

33. Michelet, *Histoire*, pp. 622–23.

34. René Moulinas, "Violences à Avignon: Les massacres de la Glacière, Octobre 1791," in Bruno Benoît, ed., *Ville et Révolution française* (Lyon: Presses Universitaires de Lyon, 1994), pp. 93–104.

35. Michelet, *Histoire*, p. 639.

36. Ibid., pp. 646–47.

37. Lenin cited in Robert C. Tucker, ed., *The Lenin Anthology* (New York: Norton, 1975), pp. 655–56.

38. Jonathan Frankel, *Prophecy and Politics: Socialism, Nationalism, and the Russian Jews, 1862–1917* (Cambridge: Cambridge University Press, 1989), pp. 51–52. See also John D. Klier and Shlomo Lambroza, eds., *Pogroms: Anti-Jewish Violence in Modern Russian History* (Cambridge: Cambridge University Press, 1992), pts. 1–3.

39. Lenin writing on February 5, 1914, cited in Hyman Lumer, ed., *Lenin on the Jewish Question* (New York: International Publishers, 1974), p. 126.

40. See Lambroza, "The Pogroms of 1903–1906," in Klier and Lambroza, eds., *Pogroms*, ch. 8; and *Die Judenpogrome in Russland*, 2 vols. (Koblenz/Leipzig: Jüdischer Verlag, 1910), vol. 2, pp. 5–79, esp. pp. 5–37.

41. See Charters Wynn, *Workers, Strikes, and Pogroms: The Donbass-Dniepr Bend in Late Imperial Russia, 1870–1905* (Princeton: Princeton University Press, 1992).

42. See Robert Weinberg, "The Pogrom of 1905 in Odessa," in Klier and Lambroza, eds., *Pogroms*, ch. 9; *Judenpogrome*, vol. 1, esp. pp. 109–32; Walter Laqueur, *Black Hundred: The Rise of the Extreme Right in Russia* (New York: Harper Collins, 1993), ch. 2.

43. Simon Dubnow [Doubnov] cited in Frankel, *Prophecy*, p. 136.

44. Cited in Simon Doubnov, *Histoire moderne du peuple juif, 1789–1938* (Paris: Cerf, 1944), p. 1485, n. 1.

45. Lenin cited in Tucker, ed., *Lenin Anthology*, pp. 289–90.

46. Doubnov, *Histoire*, p. 1526. For the Beilis affair, see Rogger, "The Beilis Case: Anti-Semitism in the Reign of Nicholas II," in *American Slavic and East European Review*, 25:4 (December 1966): pp. 615–29.

47. Cited in Arkady Vaksberg, *Stalin against the Jews* (New York: Vintage, 1995), pp. 9–10.

48. Laqueur, *Black Hundred*, ch. 3.

49. Richard Pipes, *Russia under the Bolshevik Regime* (New York: Knopf, 1993), p. 100; and Sonja Margolina, *Das Ende der Lügen: Russland und die Juden im 20. Jahrhundert* (Berlin: Siedler Verlag, 1992), p. 37.

50. Dubnow's memoirs cited in Margolina, *Ende der Lügen*, p. 39.

51. Benjamin Pinkus, *The Jews of the Soviet Union: The History of a National Minority* (Cambridge: Cambridge University Press, 1988), pp. 77–82.

52. Isaac Deutscher, *The Prophet Armed: Trotsky, 1879–1921* (New York: Oxford, 1954), pp. 325–26.

53. Doubnov, *Histoire*, p. 1526.

54. See Deutscher, *The Non-Jewish Jew and Other Essays* (London: Oxford University Press, 1968).

55. See Joel Perlmann, "Russian-Jewish Literacy in 1897: A Reanalysis of Census Data," in *Proceedings of the Eleventh World Congress of Jewish Studies*, 3 (Jerusalem, 1994): pp. 23–30.

56. Maxim Gorky cited in Salo W. Baron, *The Russian Jew under Tsars and Soviets* (New York: Macmillan, 1964), p. 216.

57. This resolution is cited in Lumer, ed., *Jewish Question*, pp. 141–42.

58. The following discussion of anti-Jewish pogroms through July 1919 is based on William Henry Chamberlin, *The Russian Revolution, 1917–1921*, vol. 2 (New York: Macmillan, 1957); Arthur E. Adams, *Bolsheviks in the Ukraine: The Second Campaign, 1918–1919* (New Haven: Yale University Press, 1963); Ilya Trotsky, "Jewish Pogroms in the Ukraine and in Byelorussia, 1918–1920," in Gregor Aronson, Jacob Frumkin, et al., eds., *Russian Jewry, 1917–1967* (New York: Thomas Yoseloff, 1969); Peter Kenez, *Civil War in South Russia, 1919–1920* (Berkeley: University of California Press, 1977); W. Bruce Lincoln, *Red Victory: A History of the Russian Civil War* (New York: Simon & Schuster, 1989); Pipes, *Bolshevik Regime*; Isaac Babel, *1920 Diary* (New Haven: Yale University Press, 1995).

59. For all quotations in this paragraph, including their contextualization, see Adams, *Bolsheviks*, pp. 232–36; and Chamberlin, *Russian Revolution*, pp. 224–25.

60. This discussion of Grigorev is based on Chamberlin, *Russian Revolution*, p. 230; Adams, *Bolsheviks*, pp. 326–27, 402; Adams, "The Great Ukrainian Jacquerie," in Taras Hunczac, ed., *The Ukraine, 1917–1921: A Study in Revolution* (Cambridge, Mass.: Harvard University Press, 1977), pp. 247–70; Peter Arshinov, *History of the Makhnovist Movement, 1918–1921* (Detroit: Black & Red, 1974), pp. 136–37; Lincoln, *Red Victory*, pp. 320–21.

61. Cited in Chamberlin, *Russian Revolution*, p. 225.

62. Cited in Lincoln, *Red Victory*, p. 320.

63. See chapter 10 above.

64. The following discussion of the anti-Semitic predisposition and discourse in the counterrevolutionary camp in Ukraine relies heavily on Peter Kenez, "Pogroms and White Ideology in the Russian Civil War," in Klier and Lambroza eds., *Pogroms*, pp. 291–313; and Lincoln, *Red Victory*, pp. 321–23.

65. Cited in Kenez, *Civil War*, p. 175.

66. Cited in Richard H. Ullman, *Britain and the Russian Civil War: November 1918–February 1920* (Princeton: Princeton University Press, 1968), pp. 218–19, n. 40. See also Pipes, *Bolshevik Regime*, p. 112.

67. Kenez, *Civil War*, pp. 173–74.

68. Cited in Pipes, *Bolshevik Regime*, p. 111.

69. See William C. Fletscher, *The Russian Orthodox Church Underground, 1917–1970* (London: Oxford University Press, 1971), p. 25.

70. Cited in Kenez, "Pogroms," p. 306.

71. Kenez, "Pogroms," p. 298, adapts this periodization and taxonomy of the pogroms of the second half of 1919 from N. I. Shtif.

72. Pipes, *Bolshevik Regime*, p. 109.

73. Report in the *Kievan Echo* cited in Lincoln, *Red Victory*, p. 323.

74. Cited in Chamberlain, *Russian Revolution*, pp. 230–31.

75. Pipes, *Bolshevik Regime*, p. 111.

76. Ibid., pp. 101–4.

77. Ibid., pp. 101–2, 111.

78. Ibid., p. 111.

79. Dmitri Volkogonov, *Lenin: A New Biography* (New York: Free Press, 1994), p. 204.

80. V. I. Lenin, *Selected Works*, vol. 29 (Moscow: Progress Publishers, 1965), pp. 252–53.

81. This summary estimate of casualties, etc., is based on Chamberlin, *Russian Revolution*, p. 240, n. 8; Baron, *Russian Jew*, pp. 220–21; Trotsky, "Jewish Pogroms," pp. 79–81, 87; Kenez, *Civil War*, p. 170; Kenez, "Pogroms," p. 302; Doubnov, *Histoire*, p. 1633; Orlando Figes, *A People's Tragedy: the Russian Revolution, 1891–1924* (London: Cape, 1996), p. 679.

82. Cited in Figes, *A People's Tragedy*, p. 677.

PART FIVE

A World Unhinged

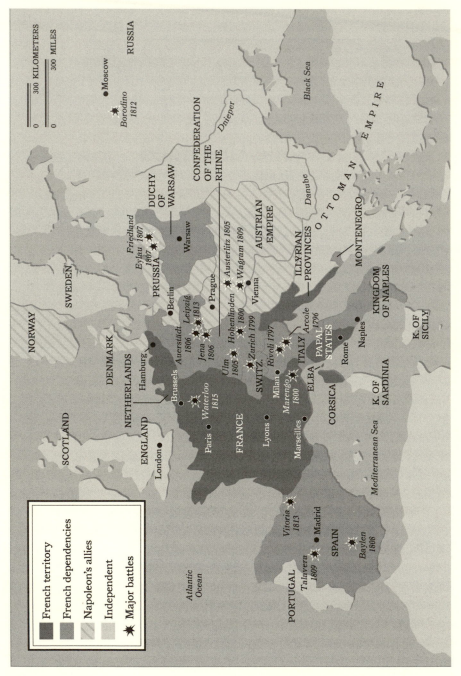

Napoleonic Empire in 1812 (Battle Sites to 1815)

Legend:
- French territory
- French dependencies
- Napoleon's allies
- Independent
- ✶ Major battles

300 KILOMETERS
300 MILES

RUSSIA

Moscow

Borodino 1812

Black Sea

CONFEDERATION OF THE RHINE

Dnieper

DUCHY OF WARSAW

Danube

OTTOMAN EMPIRE

AUSTRIAN EMPIRE

MONTENEGRO

ILLYRIAN PROVINCES

Friedland 1807
Eylau 1807

PRUSSIA

Warsaw

Austerlitz 1805
Wagram 1809

Vienna

Berlin

Leipzig 1813

Prague

SWEDEN

NORWAY

Hohenlinden 1800

Zurich 1799

KINGDOM OF NAPLES

K. OF SICILY

DENMARK

Hamburg

NETHERLANDS

Brussels

Auerstädt 1806

Jena 1806

Ulm 1805

SWITZ.

Rivoli 1797

Milan

Marengo 1800

Arcole 1796

ITALY

PAPAL STATES

Rome

Naples

ELBA

K. OF SARDINIA

CORSICA

Waterloo 1815

Paris

FRANCE

Lyons

Marseilles

ENGLAND

London

SCOTLAND

Atlantic Ocean

Mediterranean Sea

PORTUGAL

Talavera 1809

Vitoria 1813

Madrid

SPAIN

Baylen 1808

Externalization of the French Revolution: The Napoleonic Wars

SINCE 1945, with few exceptions,[1] historians of the French Revolution have tended to minimize if not ignore the fact of war with foreign powers for being extraneous or unessential to the revolutionary phenomenon. With their French-centered, not to say Paris-angled perspective, they have all but shut out foreign policy, the international system, and war in order to closely focus, first on the economic and social causes and dynamics of the French Revolution, and then on the sway of mentality, discourse, ideology, culture, and everyday life.[2]

In fact, revolution and foreign war are inseparably linked. Although there can, of course, be war without revolution, there can be no revolution without war. The fate of revolutions in small or medium-sized powers perhaps best dramatizes the centrality of interstate relations and war: they are either crushed by military intervention from abroad or, alternatively, shielded or imposed by foreign bayonets. But the fact of war is equally essential to the life of revolutions which have their epicenter in a great power. Defeat in war was the incubator of the Russian Revolution, and the flux and reflux of foreign policy, diplomacy, and war significantly shaped and radicalized the French and Russian revolutions. Both revolutions survived infancy less by virtue of the inherent military strength of their fledgling regimes than because of the divisions between and among the powers seeking to strangulate them by military force and quarantine. In turn, the termination of the French and Russian revolutions, including the configuration of their respective after-revolutions, significantly hinged on the policies of the outside world.

Not only at the beginning and end, but at every point in between, international politics impinges on the course of a revolution. Precisely because France and Russia were great powers, their internal upheavals severely unsettled the world system, to the advantage of other states, large and small; the collapse of both countries into dual or multiple sovereignty greatly weakened their diplomatic and military muscle. Besides losing their ascendancy in the concert of nations, France and Russia became vulnerable to secession, intervention, and amputation. In turn, the context and play of international relations, or of power politics, affected the internal life of their revolutions: they bore, above all, upon the struggles over the construction of a new civil and political society. In addition to disturbing the international system of their time, the French and Russian revolutions troubled the internal political, social, and cultural life of the other states by threatening them with epidemic contagion.

There simply is no denying "the reciprocation and mutual dependence of war and revolution," nor are they "ever conceivable outside the domain of violence," since violence is "a kind of common denominator for both."[3] Jacobins and Bolsheviks treated this interconnection of revolution and war as a fact of life, and so did their enemies. Jacques Mallet du Pan claimed that "revolution and war were inseparable because they had a common root."[4] As for Maistre, he went so far as to insist that once the "revolutionary movement" had won the upper hand, alone Jacobinism, favored by "Robespierre's infernal genius, could accomplish the prodigious feat of saving France from a coalition bent upon destroying its integrity."[5] Of course in this vital sphere, Lenin was guided by his own critical reading not only of the Jacobin moment but also of *On War* by Carl von Clausewitz. Specifically, Lenin, following Engels, emphasized that steeped in the warfare of the French Revolution, Clausewitz considered war less a mere extension of foreign policy and diplomacy than an agency of political reason. Lenin even went so far as to argue that because war is grounded "in a set of political circumstances, it is not only a political act, but truly a political instrument, a continuation of political relations, an implementation of these [relations] by other means, . . . [or] rather by the admixture of other means."[6]

Clearly, in this conceptual construction, in revolutionary moments the purposes and methods of war are singularly varied and changeable.

In 1791–94 and 1917–21, when debating questions of war and peace the stakes were, above all, political: the logic and reason of politics prompted Brissot to press for war; Robespierre to oppose going to war; Kerensky to persevere in war; and Lenin to disengage from war. This is not to say that the protagonists dismissed the reason of state and were blind to the diplomatic and military realities of their time. But it is to insist that their perceptions and evaluations of these realities were significantly skewed by their political and ideological prepossessions. Needless to say, such prejudgments also colored the views of foreign leaders who had to assess, from afar, developments in the homeland of the revolution and their impact on the international system. In the course of time, in the epicenter of revolution as well as in the surrounding world, ideology assumed increasing importance as both a distorting mirror and an instrument of international politics.

The aphorism that "war revolutionizes revolution" is as applicable to the French as the Russian Revolution.[7] Of course, revolution-related foreign war is particularly perverse by virtue of being not only intrinsically ideological and absolute but also entwined with civil war, which is likewise inseparable from international relations. Such being the case, foreign war is not merely a "locomotive of history" or a "midwife of revolution." It is also a hothouse for terror.

The causal relationship of war and terror in revolution is of course highly complex. Prima facie it would seem, however, that in 1789 as in 1917, entanglement in war preceded the crescendo of terror. Even in ordinary times, warfare entails hardening the state and curtailing liberties, both individual and collective. This is all the more the case when vulnerable and untried revolutionary regimes are embattled at home and abroad: they find it particularly difficult to mobilize and discipline a country for war. Reflecting on developments in France, Mathiez considered it unexceptional that "the governors of a country fighting a foreign war complicated by civil war should have resorted to summary and emergency justice to repress treason, conspiracies, and revolts."[8]

Although terror was present from the outset in 1789 and 1917, it only became systemic with mounting complications in civil and foreign war. Of necessity there is a strong but not perfect or automatic correlation between escalating strains of war and spiraling pressures for terror. Indeed, when considering the linkage of war and terror, it is well to remember Quinet's dictum that to study them in isolation from each other and without close attention to the diachrony of their interaction is like "telling the story of a military battle without taking account of the enemy army."[9]

Just as the fortunes of foreign war act upon revolution, so the internal dynamics of the revolution act on foreign policy and war. Revolution is a peerless forcing house for the primacy of domestic politics, with *all* sides exploiting foreign policy, diplomacy, and war for partisan purposes. Louis XVI did so up to his trial, and so did the Brissotins and Robespierrists, judging by their war of words over war and peace in 1791–92. In the dawn of the Russian Revolution issues of international politics forced apart first Mensheviks and Bolsheviks and then Bolsheviks and Socialist Revolutionaries, at the same time that they tested the coherence of the Bolshevik leadership. Similarly, after 1789 and 1917, on the counterrevolutionary side, the reason of diplomacy and war soon became essentially political for much of the internal resistance as well as for the émigrés and their foreign sponsors.

✳ ✳ ✳

In France revolution and war were closely linked for nearly a quarter of a century. Between 1792 and 1815, war first revolutionized the revolution before saving and sustaining it. As suggested before, had France been a small power the revolution of 1789, not unlike the Dutch revolt of 1787, would most likely have been aborted by external intervention. But France was Europe's most powerful state in demographic, military, and economic terms; besides, for twenty years the other great powers of the European system were too much at cross-purposes to be able to mount a winning challenge.

In any case, the fact of war was as central to the fall of the monarchy and establishment of the Jacobin reign as it was, after Thermidor, to the rise and fall of the Directory, Consulate, and Empire, as well as to the Bourbon restoration in 1814–15. The rulers of all these would-be regimes considered successful war necessary to save the Revolution, or, in the case of the Bourbons, to strangle it. Not that one and all envisaged war in the same spirit and for the same purpose. Initially it took foreign invasion to convert the Jacobins to the war whose reverses became their great reason to intensify the terror. The Girondins, for their part, looked to war to unite France and consolidate the fragile revolutionary regime, thereby obviating terror at home. A similar way of thinking came to the fore after the fall of Robespierre: from Thermidor until 1814, war served at once to *consolidate* the political, social, and cultural gains of 1789 to 1792 inside France and to *impose* them, along with Napoleon's pioneering measures, beyond France's expanding borders. Paradoxically, the wars of the *Grande Nation* and *Grande Empire* were in the nature of a diversion of pent-up and unresolved internal conflicts into the international environment. The Thermidoreans, including the Bonapartists, meant to contain both revolutionary Jacobins and counterrevolutionary royalists. Forever fearful of their respective conspiracies, they presumed that successful war, which few wanted or dared to end without an extravagant victory, was indispensable for the survival of a middle course at home: military setbacks invited a hardening of government designed to defuse a Jacobin resurgence in the face of the triumph of royalism and the return of the Bourbons in the train of enemy armies; military successes favored measures of political relaxation calculated to win the support of moderate elements which might be tempted to join the monarchist opposition.

Obviously, the war continued because Thermidor marked the ascendance of members of the Convention, most of whom shared a proud if burdensome past as well as a minimum but firm consensus as to where and how to steer the ship of state. They had stood together not only to liquidate the seignorial system, overthrow the monarchy, and behead the king, but to save the republic by tempting war and establishing a *dictature de détresse*. Here and now they were agreed not to tolerate or risk a return of the old regime, also because not a few Thermidoreans had enriched themselves by way of bargain-basement purchases of *biens nationaux* or nationalized property, most of it former church lands. But above all, they embraced the Girondin view of the interrelation of domestic and foreign policy, which had framed the thrust into war in 1792: to have the glories and benefits of a crusading war against monarchic Europe reduce domestic strife in favor of a moderate or anti-Jacobin (if not anti-sansculotte) settlement of the Revolution. The Thermidoreans purged Robespierre without heeding his warning about the two-fold peril of a war of liberation: caesarism at home and resistance to freedom-bringing armies abroad. Ironically, they brought down Robespierre largely because the Jacobins had put the revolutionary armies on the road to victory beyond the northeastern borders, thereby legitimating the Girondin stratagem of exchanging the use of the guillotine within France for the arbitrament of the sword on the far side of France's frontiers. On this score of beating guillotines into swords, the Directory, Consulate, and Empire were essentially seamless, with Napoleon the master blacksmith.

❋ ❋ ❋

The balance between the grim realities and constructive engagements of Napoleon Bonaparte has been controversial ever since his extravagant reign. Pieter Geyl, who lived in the time of Hitler, recalled the difficulty of coming to an equitable reading: "The difference is that under Napoleon French civilization, albeit stifled and narrowed by him, still accompanied his conquest, while the character of the conquest that it has been the lot of our generation to endure is incompatible with any civilization at all." Evidently he agreed with Tocqueville that as "propagandist as well as conqueror" Napoleon at least partially continued the "ideological character of the wars of the Republic, mixing violence with philosophy and enlightenment."[10] Although he stressed the "constraints and atrocities" of the Jacobins and of Napoleon, Geyl wondered whether these had any common measure with the Third Reich's "annihilation of all opposition parties in jails or concentration camps . . . [and its] persecution of the Jews." Geyl wanted to make sure that this comparison should not unduly benefit the "reputation" of Napoleon. Having experienced, firsthand, Hitler's subjugation of his native Holland, which had also come under Napoleon's heel, Geyl emphasized that except for the persecution of the Jews, which "remained singular," there was a "difference in degree, not in principle" between the French and German drive for the mastery of Europe.[11]

This caveat against reading the past through the warped lenses of the present also applies to the comparison of the military furors of the epochs of the French and Russian revolutions. Admittedly, the ravages and miseries of the revolutionary and Napoleonic wars pale next to those of the Thirty Years Wars of the seventeenth and twentieth centuries. On the whole, except in Spain, where they met with popular resistance, the French armies spared civilians and there was little scorching of the earth. Also, military casualties were short of catastrophic by the standards of religious wars. Still, even if the wars of 1792 to 1815 did not escalate into total warfare, they were, as Clausewitz made clear, thick with novelty and unprecedented in scale: the Jacobin revolutionary regime pioneered in forging, even if imperfectly, the nation-in-arms and the conscript peasant army; and taking account of these innovations under the Directory, Consulate, and Empire, Napoleon developed new strategies of warfare, notably the speed of movement and concentration of superior force. One result was a quantum jump in human sacrifice in international conflict. Especially starting in 1812, when his military fortunes along with his reformist intentions began to falter, the imitation emperor held cheap the lives even of his own soldiers.

None of this is to minimize Napoleon's social and administrative reforms not only in many of the distant provinces of the makeshift and refractory empire but also at home, where his violence was less deadly, precisely because so much of it was channeled abroad. For Napoleon Bonaparte was the heir and executor of the French Revolution, not its gravedigger or liquidator. His stewardship of the revolutionary legacy was so effective that when the Bourbons were restored in 1814–15 some of its principal elements were preserved, even if reluctantly and at the insistence of their foreign sponsors. To be sure, France was forced to settle for the borders of 1789, which meant renouncing all recent territorial conquests and spheres of influence. Still, notwithstanding their ultimate cost as well as their "lame and impotent conclusion," the revolutionary and Napoleonic wars contributed significantly to the survival and consolidation of the Revolution. To the extent that Napoleon had a clear aim, it was not to "rationalize" the old regime in the interest of "the society of orders . . . based on inequality and privilege." Rather, he emerged, in the first instance, as the executive agent of an untried political class which had swept away France's "traditional social structure, along with noble privilege, the guilds, the *parlements*, and provincial autonomies."[12]

Above all, Napoleon never even considered undoing the sweeping political and social changes of 1789 which cost the nobles their tax exemptions and fiscal privileges, their time-honored deference and preference, and their right to separate political representation and corporate powers. For them, this headlong degradation was at once massive and traumatic: well over 15,000 nobles emigrated, some 1,200 were executed, and many more were imprisoned. Admittedly, after Thermidor not a few of the émigré nobles returned and bought back some of their lands or purchased other landed properties, not unlike the members of the bourgeoisie and liberal professions who braced their class and status position by acquiring more than their share of the *biens nationaux*.[13] But rather than recover their hegemony, the prescriptive nobles of before 1789 folded into an imperial nobility of old and new men—a "mass of granite"—which Napoleon turned into one of the main pillars of the post-Thermidorean state. Although they were the core of the power elite under Bonaparte and the prime beneficiaries of his rule, the members of this new nobility were more in the nature of a ruling than governing class, a social amalgam in which the inveterate nobles weighed disproportionately in both city and country, both before and after 1815.[14]

As heir of the secular state, Napoleon charged a professional bureaucracy and magistracy, heavily drawn from the incipient imperial nobility, with "substituting interest for privilege and contract for hereditary dependence and protection."[15] The *Code Napoléon* became symbolic of the spirit and intention of the rationalization of public administration and the rule of law. The regime brought to an end the fragmentation of political and judicial sovereignty: western France was pacified, and factional conflict in the central executive and legislature died down.

Napoleon certainly betrayed the Revolution by violating the political and civil liberties of 1789. Encouraged by his sponsors in the Directory and driven by his own despotic temperament, Napoleon throttled parliamentary institutions as well as political and intellectual freedoms. His reach for authoritarian rule was marked by successive coups which were ratified by specious plebiscites and which intermittently entailed the execution, deportation, and imprisonment of ever-suspect Jacobins and even more suspect royalists.[16] But overall, Bonapartism took infinitely fewer lives at home than abroad. Whereas the victims of the coup d'état of the 18 Fructidor of the Year V (September 4, 1797) and of the 22 Floréal of the Year VI (May 11, 1798) ran into the hundreds, the casualties of the wars of the Directory, Consulate, and Empire ran into the millions. As previously noted, the human costs of internal and foreign war are forever judged differently: the killings and horrors of external conflict are considered more natural, justifiable, and intelligible than those of civil strife. But this double standard becomes all the more problematic when applied to the dyadic violence between 1792 and 1815, when internal and external war were intensely intertwined, with the discords of domestic politics conditioning and causing foreign war as much as the vicissitudes of foreign war bore upon the heartbeat of violence back home.

In any case, as Engels and Marx made a point of stressing, there was a strong correlation between, on the one hand, the small toll of Napoleon's internal repression, and, on the other, the heavy casualties of his foreign wars. Friedrich Engels posited that in Germany Napoleon had been "the representative of the Revolution, the propagator of its principles, and the destroyer of the old feudal society." Although Bonaparte had proceeded "despotically, . . . he had been only half as despotic" as the deputies of the Convention and the "princes and nobles" he brought to heel. In fact, Napoleon's stratagem was to "apply *the reign of terror*, which had done its work in France, to *other countries in the shape of war*." As Engels saw it, the Revolution having been "stifled" in Paris, his armies carried it across France's borders. In the Germanies, in addition to "dissolving the Holy Roman Empire and reducing the number of little states," Napoleon spread around "a code of laws which was vastly superior to all existing ones and which recognized the principle of [legal] equality." Ultimately, however, rather than "destroy every vestige of Old Europe . . . he sought to compromise with it . . . by assimilating his own court as much as possible" to those of the other ruling monarchs.[17]

Jointly Marx and Engels carried this analysis one step further. They suggested that precisely because he had understood that the essential basis of the modern state was "the unhampered development of bourgeois society . . . [and] the free movement of private interest, etc. . . . Napoleon decided to recognize and protect [them]." While considering the "state as *an end in itself*," which Bonaparte had meant to keep "*subordinate*" to himself, he had "*perfected* the *Terror* by *substituting permanent war* for *permanent revolution*." In so doing he had "fed the egoism of the French nation" at the same time that he demanded the "sacrifice of bourgeois [interests]" whenever necessary "to advance the political aim of conquest."[18] Presumably the consolidation of the Revolution at home and its export by means of endless foreign war were closely connected.

Because of his deficit of legitimacy, Napoleon was acutely aware of his dependence on the inexorable logic and hazard of war. As he noted himself, whereas a "sovereign born on the throne can be [militarily] defeated twenty times and still return to his capital," as "an upstart soldier" he could not do so, his "domination" being based on "fear" of his arms.[19] Bonaparte knew that his regime hinged on "continual warfare and repeated victories" which helped him maintain his political position in Paris.[20]

Meanwhile, beyond France's old borders, wherever Napoleon took his armies his reception was mixed. He was at once feared and hailed: general on horseback and Jacobin missionary of Girondin inflection. Ironically, when transplanting French reforms abroad, Bonaparte tended to find more collaborators among the classes of the cities than the masses of the countryside. In fact, most of the Continent being even more in the grip of rural obscurantism, illiteracy, and insularity than France, to press parts of the agenda of 1789 to 1791 and of 1800 to 1804 was to call forth resistance driven by a Vendée-like logic.

* * *

Almost from the outset of the Revolution the partisans of the old order, notably the crown and court, expected the European powers to come to their rescue by threatening or using armed intervention. While the king eventually looked for what he was confident would be a short and easy war to reclaim the old order, Lafayette envisaged it to further the establishment of a constitutional monarchy. Brissotins, for their part, proposed to induce a "splendid little war" for the purpose of strengthening and consolidating their political power, discharging unmanageable internal problems into the international environment, and terminating the Revolution on their terms. In turn, Robespierre, Marat, and (until December 17, 1791) Danton advocated avoiding war in the interest of giving first, if not absolute, priority to anchoring and radicalizing the Revolution at home. To the extent that both Brissotins and Robespierrists meant to master the common enemy, they advocated opposite strategies to that end: the former looked to make war on the Revolution's external enemies, including the émigrés, and to spread its physical reach as the best way to defeat domestic enemies and win support abroad; the latter insisted that the war against domestic enemies and the construction of a new order at home were the key to success. Michelet saw a stark contrast between the Gironde, which called for "a crusading war abroad, [complete with] propaganda," and the Mountain, which wanted a "war against traitors and enemies at home" in the form of "domestic purification, the punishment of bad citizens, and the crushing of resistances by way of terror and inquisition."[21]

The Girondins were plainspoken about being partisans of foreign war. Starting in the early fall of 1791 and until France declared war on Austria in April 1792, they raised and orchestrated a strident appeal to arms. Their chief drumbeaters—Brissot, Roederer, Vergniaud, Hérault de Séchelles—charged that the foreign courts, incited by the émigrés, were encircling revolutionary France and conspiring with internal enemies sworn to foment political strife, economic chaos, and social unrest. They created a sense of hostile beleaguerment and fear in the face of what they portrayed to be a virtual state of war or murderous peace. According to Roederer, this confrontation was as much a "foreign war . . . as a civil war between Frenchmen," since the émigrés, who had their collaborators inside France, were being welcomed by Europe's kings and princes. The time had come to convert this "ruinous and debasing" hidden conflict into an "overt" war, for, given the circumstances, "to attack is to defend ourselves." Roederer thundered that to launch out against "Koblenz" was to strike at the "most dangerous enemies . . . among us." In addition to "disguising" themselves, these internal enemies were using the constitution, which they "hated," to further their counterrevolutionary ends. Roederer claimed that "a state of open war" would have the great merit of unmasking these traitors and of enabling all "real friends of the constitution" to declare themselves.[22]

Brissot, the war party's most prominent spokesman, was quite direct about the reasons for France to go to war: "to bolster its honor, external security, and internal tranquillity; to restore its public finances and prosperity; and to put an end to terror, treason, and anarchy." Besides, in a war that would be unlike any other in history, French soldiers would go forth not as conquerors but as liberators of oppressed peoples yearning for help to throw off their chains. Brissot feared, above all, that unless France went to war, society would continue to be "consumed by the poison of subversion." As for a diplomatic solution, it could neither root out this poison nor "overthrow the aristocracy, consummate the Revolution, cement independence, and stimulate prosperity." But there was also a tactical reason for launching a preemptive war: time was on the side not of revolutionary France but of the concert of powers.[23]

Although virtually drowned out, the antiwar party kept raising its voice. Robespierre countered Roederer's and Brissot's summons to march upon "Koblenz" by asserting that the counterrevolution's main headquarters and recruits were inside France, not outside. Following Marat, who stressed that to "crush the enemies within" was an essential precondition for proceeding "against those abroad," Robespierre maintained that the consolidation of the Revolution's gains at home was essential for its éclat in foreign parts. He warned, in particular, that most likely war would strengthen the executive—king, ministers, generals—at the expense of the fledgling republic, perhaps even in favor of a military despotism. Robespierre disputed the "airy hope of rapidly spreading the Revolution abroad" by means of bayonets: the military campaign would be risky and costly, not least because "nobody likes armed missionaries." He advocated furthering the Revolution by defeating the men of Koblenz within France and their outside supporters rather than aborting it "by taking the scourge of war to [foreign] peoples, who, not having attacked us, should be seen and treated as friends."[24]

Of course, cross-border war results not from the actions of a single state but from the interaction of two or more states. The mounting war fever in France was the product of an intensifying friend-enemy dissociation, which had two poles: the unfixed new regime in Paris and the inveterate old regimes of the European concert. From its creation, the French Revolution was at minimum a trans-European event, as measured by its reverberations abroad. Far and wide it stimulated both avowed and latent critical spirits to challenge the accepted, if not God-given, conventions and institutions of established civil and political society. At first, following the storming of the Bastille, the abolition of seignorialism, and the adoption of the Declaration of the Rights of Man, these free thinkers rejoiced and were heartened by what they perceived to be a promising new dawn breaking over France. The response was particularly enthusiastic and vocal in intellectual, artistic, and scholarly circles, which were moved to imagine and debate the recasting of the unbending world of the established order. Indeed, the roll call of idealistic and supportive voices reads like the *Gotha* of the European intelligentsia. Not surprisingly, "the most radical of the 'foreign' revolutionaries or sympathizers, whether . . . those who congregated in Paris or those who in greater numbers remained in their own countries, were seldom more than advanced political democrats."[25]

Early on, even the chancelleries of the great powers were well disposed toward the Revolution, not least because they expected the turmoil in France, which they viewed as mere chaos, to weaken Paris in Europe and overseas to their benefit. But before long the rush of political, social, and cultural changes began to trouble them for being dangerously liberal-minded and progressive. At this point, it was the outward projection of exemplary principle and reform, not of power, that bewildered the European governments and establishments. Even at that, the fear of the new reason bursting forth in Paris did not immediately become an important factor in the diplomacy of the great powers, nor did it prompt them to prepare for war.

Especially with foreign and military affairs reserved to the executive, Europe's staid political class did not debate questions of war and peace with the same abandon as the new men of power in Paris. Even in England, with its parliamentary institutions, the discussion was muted, certainly until Burke set it on fire. Not that the royal courts and chancelleries were unaccustomed to political in-fighting. But since all factions belonged to a relatively narrow ruling and governing class, their discords were intramural, undisturbed by the clamor of counter-elites and popular crowds.

This internal calm conditioned the continuity of traditional statecraft. While the mental sets and diplomatic precepts of old-regime statesmen and generals were adequate to exploit France's foreign-policy paralysis between 1789 and late 1791, they were ill-suited to assess the domestic developments which hereafter contributed to its uncommon foreign-policy bellicosity and novel ways of generating military energy. The chancelleries eventually understood and certainly welcomed the massive defection and emigration of French army officers. At the same time, they were disconcerted by the weakness of counter-revolutionary resistance, the upward spiral of radicalization, the groundswell for war, and the conscription of a vast army. Imprisoned in their traditional worldview and mentality, ultimately Europe's political class continued to "believe that the end of monarchy could only lead to anarchy and powerlessness."[26] Indeed, the emergence of the nation-in-arms and citizen army staggered their belief of the old elites even more than it staggered the belief of the new men of power who invented and organized them. The external world's civil and military leaders needed time and the march of events to shed their incredulity and to take a more realistic measure of things. But this reorientation was complicated by the unforeseen intrusion of ideological predilections which soon fed a chronic fear of revolutionary contagion and subversion. Since a similar mixture of realism and intoxication crystallized in the minds of the revolutionary leaders, the stage was set for mutual misperception, miscalculation, and miscommunication.[27]

✳ ✳ ✳

From 1789 until mid-1791 the major capitals welcomed France's impaired position in the international arena.[28] Actually this unsteadiness was prefigured in 1787, when Paris had failed to deter Frederick William II from sending Prussian troops, commanded by the Duke of Brunswick, to the United Provinces to restore Prince William V, his brother-in-law, to his throne. But the Tennis Court Oath and the fall of the Bastille foreshadowed even greater diplomatic and military irresolution, which the great powers hastened to feed on: Russia and Prussia maneuvered to promote their interests in Eastern Europe and the Balkans; Austria in the Low Countries, Central Europe, and Italy; and England overseas. Characteristically, with France preoccupied with domestic affairs, Russia and Prussia felt free to thrust and parry over Poland, in preparation for a second partition. Of course, developments in France touched the Habsburgs much more directly: Marie-Antoinette was the sister of Leopold II, and the émigrés played on this dynastic link; further, Austria's Belgian provinces were particularly endangered by France. Even so, the Emperor and Prince von Kaunitz, his chancellor, followed a cautious and moderate course as long as it looked as if France would continue to be disabled. To the extent that they expected the dislocation to last and disquiet the surrounding world, they proposed to "encircle France with a solid *cordon sanitaire* which gradually turned into a thick wall of bayonets or, in their own words, *un cercle de fer.*"[29]

London was even less eager to intervene than Vienna, though for strategic reasons England also closely watched developments in the Low Countries. By contrast, Russia was the most aggressively hostile of the great powers. But the bellicosity of Catherine II took the form of urging Austria and Prussia to intervene in France with a view to keeping them from interfering with Russia's designs in eastern Europe, notably in Poland.

The first concrete diplomatic engagement between France and the European powers was a by-product of an essentially domestic measure adopted by the National Assembly. The "abolition" of feudal rights and privileges during the night of August 4–5, 1789, bore upon several German princes of Alsace, which in 1648 had been ceded to Louis XIV. Having previously contested French violations of their rights, these princes now loudly protested the application of this radical enactment to their domains. Rather than court a confrontation, the diplomatic committee of the Assembly encouraged Count de Montmorin, the foreign minister, who was close to the Court, to seek a negotiated settlement. In May 1790 he offered the princes an indemnity in exchange for their recognition of France's full sovereignty over Alsace. Rather than treat with Paris, however, the princes called on the Imperial Diet to back their demand, if need be with the sword, for the unconditional restoration and guarantee of their prescriptive rights. Although Leopold II issued an official protest, he would go no further. He refused to turn the clash over the feudal rights of several princes in Alsace into a conflict of values, all the more so because as yet he did not consider the upheaval in France a threat to the European order.

It took the royal family's abortive flight to Varennes in June 1791 to galvanize the existential fears of the great powers and embroil them in the rising friend-enemy dissociation of the French Revolution. It deserves special emphasis that when Louis XVI decided to make his escape, the Revolution was nowhere near its fever stage. To be sure, on October 5–6, 1789, popular pressure had prompted him as well as his court and the Assembly to move from Versailles to Paris. Moreover, a year and a half later, on April 18, 1791, a crowd had prevented Louis XVI from leaving the Tuileries for Saint-Cloud. Quite understandably his supporters, and particularly the ultras among them, considered the king to be a prisoner in his own realm. Even so, the historical possibility of a constitutional monarchy was by no means foreclosed, its champions being neither inconsequential nor dispirited, even if divided. Admittedly, the price for such a settlement would be severe restrictions on the prerogatives of crown and church. Still, when Louis XVI opted to take flight, the fusillade of the Champ de Mars, the decrees against émigrés and refractory priests, the declaration of war, the storming of the Tuileries, and the prison massacres all lay in the future.

Within France Varennes strengthened the suspicions of radicals and their sympathizers concerning the intentions and capabilities of the old guard. Naturally they dismissed out of hand any suggestion that the king had either been trapped into fleeing or had escaped *à contre-coeur*, for the good of his subjects. Indeed, Varennes gave the idea of an "aristocratic plot" added credibility.

It was reinforced by the vengeful rhetoric of the letter of General Marquis de Bouillé, commander of the armies on the northeastern border, to the National Assembly on June 26, 1791.[30] Bouillé had played a key role in organizing the escape: since his theater of command was not too far from Paris and faced the Austrian Netherlands, it was a natural destination for the royal family. But there was another reason why Bouillé was suited for his assignment: when repressing a military mutiny at Nancy on August 31, 1791, he had not hesitated to have "one soldier . . . broken on the wheel, twenty . . . hanged, and forty-one sentenced to galleys for life."[31] His was an authentic and representative counterrevolutionary voice when he denounced the members of the National Assembly for having spent two years "giving birth to a monster," by making the common people "ferocious, bloodthirsty, . . . delirious, . . . [and] cannibalistic." In addition to the royal family being at the mercy of "bloody savages," France's polity and society were rife with "injustice, extortion, and crime." In Bouillé's telling, the king had fled to Varennes with the intention to forestall a dangerous if understandable attack from abroad by acting as a "mediator between the foreign powers and his people."

Now that the escape had failed and Louis XVI and his family were again in the hands of the Assembly, its members would have to answer to all the kings of Europe for their safety. Bouillé served notice that should any member of the royal family "be harmed ever so slightly, before long not a single stone would remain standing in Paris" and the members of the Assembly "would be made to pay with their heads." Insisting that "the King had not issued a single order," Bouillé assumed full responsibility for the Varennes strategem and adjured the deputies "not to charge anyone with any so-called plot or conspiracy against what you call *la nation* and against your infernal Constitution." In accordance with the heightened friend-enemy dissociation, Bouillé concluded his letter "without sending my compliments, my true sentiments being all too well known to you."

Meanwhile, the fiasco of Varennes reinforced the European courts' apprehension about the apostasy in Paris. Heretofore hesitant, Leopold II now edged toward military intervention. On July 6, 1791, he issued the Padua Circular, summoning Europe's crowned heads to confer about concerted actions to "secure the liberty and honor of the Most Christian King and his family and to set bounds to the dangerous extremism of the French Revolution." Soon thereafter, on July 17, Kaunitz called on the great powers to break all commercial and diplomatic relations with France. A week later, on July 25, Austria and Prussia signed a convention in Vienna laying the groundwork for the meeting of Emperor Leopold II and King Frederick William II at Pillnitz, near Dresden in Saxony, in August 1791, after the two had settled their disputed Ottoman affairs.

By this time the situation in France was becoming increasingly explosive: the furious and divisive debate about the so-called abduction of the king (who was suspended by the Constituent Assembly); the massacre of the Champ de Mars; the summons by the National Assembly to the émigrés to return within two months; and the secession of the Feuillants from the Jacobin club to found their own group. Although the death of Mirabeau unsteadied the "vital center" caught between militant Jacobins and hard-line royalists, it was by no means exhausted. While Europe's statesmen became increasingly skeptical about a quick and auspicious denouement of the crisis in France, whose military disablement they had overestimated, the émigrés and moral-ideological censors—Burke, Mallet du Pan, Pius VI—won an ever wider hearing among the classes, not the masses.

Significantly, though self-invited, the Comte d'Artois was at Pillnitz when the Emperor of the Habsburgs and the King of the Hohenzollerns framed a policy of active support for the Bourbon King of France but short of systematic containment or direct military intervention.[32] Declaring the situation of Louis XVI "a matter of common concern to all European sovereigns," they proposed to explore with them ways of "employing, in proportion to their forces, the most effective means to enable the King of France to consolidate with complete freedom the foundations of monarchical government." Admittedly, Leopold and Frederick William were "resolved to act promptly, in mutual accord, with the forces necessary to secure the proposed common objective [only] if and when (*alors, et dans ce cas*)" the other monarchs answered their call. But not too much should be made of this proviso. In keeping with the normal diplomatic practice of raising pressure by degrees, the two sovereigns announced that in the meantime they would "give their troops such orders as are necessary to have them ready for active service." That they did not just say one thing and mean another became clear on February 7, 1792, when they met again to sign an alliance under which each partner committed 40,000 troops for joint "defense."[33]

But of equal importance, the Pillnitz Declaration of August 27, 1791, was less a conventional and confidential diplomatic dispatch addressed to the French foreign office and other chancelleries than a radically new departure in European statecraft. Indeed, this declaration—nay, proclamation—was intended to intervene, indirectly, in the internal affairs of France by going over the head of its established government, much as the revolutionaries in Paris, both French and foreign, were issuing appeals to incite popular rebellion against the old regimes. Pillnitz inaugurated the politicization of foreign policy and diplomacy, changing international relations for all time, most intensely during revolutionary epochs.[34]

Besides signaling a mounting vigilance and potentially coordinated action by the concert of European powers, the Pillnitz rescript was meant to frighten the moderates in Paris—constitutional *monarchiens* and *feuillants*—into abandoning their search for a vital center. In other words, external pressure was brought to bear to further the termination of the Revolution along essentially restorative lines. The *démarche* of Pillnitz was based on a misreading of political conditions in France by old-regime statesmen influenced by the tendentious advocacy of the émigrés, which any reader of Machiavelli would have taken with grains of salt. It backfired in large part because in the wake of Varennes it was all too easy for reformists and revolutionaries to perceive and portray this latest foreign intervention as confirming, once again, their worst suspicion: the convergence of a major threat from abroad with a refractory resistance at home to make for a seamless counterrevolutionary defiance.

Whereas the outside world could still get an open hearing in the Constituent Assembly, which was anything but a hotbed of extremism, the other spheres of France's fragmented polity were beyond its reach, except the high cadres of the army, state administration, and church, as well as nascent centers of royalist resistance. In mid-September Louis XVI accepted the Constitution, and his suspension was lifted. The new Legislative Assembly, which convened on October 1, was more volatile and impatient than its predecessor. Within three weeks, on October 20, Brissot and his colleagues began their parliamentary campaign for war, and in November the Assembly voted hardened decrees against émigrés and refractory priests, which Louis XVI vetoed, ever hopeful of support from abroad and the provinces.

And yet the sovereignty of Europe's strongest state continued to crack. During the winter of 1791–92, aggravated social, economic, and fiscal problems fueled political unrest in Paris and many parts of the country. Some of the plebs who were being radicalized expressed their protest by joining the cry for war, and certain economic interests had equally contingent reasons for supporting a forward course in foreign affairs. The Girondins did not hesitate to use this popular agitation and special-interest pleading to bolster their own bid for power in which the clamor for war played an increasingly central role. As noted, they propounded war as a cure-all at a time when they—and scores of other politicians and public intellectuals—were ever more baffled by the complexity of France's protean crisis. The problem was less that they and the better part of the deputies were political novices—large numbers of them had considerable experience in public affairs on the provincial and local level[35]—than that they came face to face with the "pathos of novelty." As if calling for a *fuite en avant*, the Girondins commended preventive war as a panacea: to forestall a military attack; to choke off resistance by striking at "Koblenz" abroad; to create an *union sacrée* around the Host of the *patrie*; and to channel mounting domestic difficulties into the world at large. Ultimately they propounded foreign war as the master key to the consolidation—the termination—of the Revolution on terms they never really spelled out.

When Robespierre proceeded, unsuccessfully, to oppose war, he was no less bewildered than Brissot and no less vague about his end purposes. He gave first priority to securing and enlarging the gains of the Revolution at home, not least because war risked strengthening the king and the generals. Besides, Robespierre was less confident than the warmongers of a swift and easy victory.

In this rampant time of troubles, the issue was less the "real" circumstances than the perception and construction of them by the chief actors. By a feedback process, mutual distrust and hostility kept escalating and, short of one or the other side backing down, only a miracle could have checked this polarization. The flight to Varennes, the Pillnitz Declaration, and the Austro-Prussian alliance merely confirmed the revolutionaries' self-fulfilling prophecy regarding their enemies' intentions. Inside France, issues of principle were crowded out by questions of political strategy, to be resolved in an atmosphere of utmost urgency.

The crowns and statesmen of the concert of Europe certainly were less pressured and more poised, all the more so since they continued to consider time and the military advantage to be on their side. Their traditional notions of society and statecraft made it difficult for them to discern that the political transformation in Paris was making France into a radically novel state in the world system. Nor could they imagine that the upstart foreign-policy actors of this so-called government, paralyzed by chaos, would ever dare or manage to measure themselves with Europe's experienced diplomats and generals, especially since the cream of the French officer corps had gone into emigration. Leopold II died on March 1, 1792. Even if Francis II, his son and successor, had been less hawkish than his father, Vienna would disdainfully have rejected Paris's ultimatum of April 5, following the formation of the Girondin ministry, demanding the instant removal of émigré military formations from along the Rhine. Clearly, here was the reverse side of the "pathos of novelty": unshaken in their worldview and their scorn for the revolutionary pretense, the officials of the European chancelleries kept taking diplomatic steps which could not help but play into the hands of the war party in Paris. Whereas at the outset the hawks had been able to count on at most one-third of the deputies of the

Legislative Assembly, on April 20, 1792, the vote for war with Austria and Prussia was nearly unanimous. No doubt, though perhaps innocently, the Brissotins had rallied this overwhelming support by forcing the friend-enemy dissociation and interweaving its foreign and domestic aspects: in this "war assembly" and beyond, they exalted the thaumaturgic powers of war as part of their effort to fuel a "national élan against the enemy at home and abroad."[36]

It would seem, then, that the war of 1792 originated in the political struggles attending the crisis of instability inside France, intensified by the purblind policies of the European courts. Although the ideological factor contributed to both, it cannot be said to have been the final or prime mover. It did not really burst forth until hostilities were under way: hereafter the war revolutionized the Revolution as much as the Revolution revolutionized the war.

* * *

Within ten days following the declaration of war the French armies suffered their first setbacks along the northeastern border, casting doubt on the optimistic assumptions and expectations of the Brissotins. These reverses were bound to complicate the search for a third way. Defying Louis XVI, on May 27 the Assembly adopted a decree intensifying the drive against refractory priests. The king vetoed it on June 11 and two days later dismissed the Girondin ministry in favor of an essentially *feuillant* cabinet. A week thereafter, on June 20, a throng of sansculottes invaded the Tuileries to protest the monarch's renewed self-assertion which on July 8 marked the royalist mass rally at Jalès, in the southeast. But above all, pressed by the embattled Girondins, on July 11 the Legislative Assembly declared *la patrie en danger*. Almost overnight the street construed this credo as a call for the defense of both Nation and Revolution, which hereafter were extolled for being indivisible. Here, then, were the twin pillars of the forcing house of emergency rule in which the symbiosis of war and terror would be nurtured.

The Padua Circular and Pillnitz Declaration paved the way for the Brunswick Manifesto of July 25, 1792, in which the European sovereigns specified their bill of indictment, attainder, and retribution against the Revolution. Whereas the Comte d'Artois had been in the wings at Pillnitz, the émigrés wielded considerable influence in the precincts in which this latest diplomatic document was formulated. That it was drafted by the Marquis de Limon, an inconsequential financier moving in émigré circles, was less significant than that it was endorsed by Count de Fersen and Charles Alexander de Calonne, who hailed it for speaking in an idiom at once European and French. After approving the draft submitted to them, Francis II and Frederick William II had it published, in their names, over the signature of the Duke of Brunswick, the commanding general of the combined Austro-Prussian armies. By late July his troops, after taking Valenciennes and Cambrai, were closing in on Saint-Quentin and Péronne. Although subsequently Brunswick allegedly claimed that, skeptical of the émigrés, he had signed the manifesto with great reluctance, his name and position gave it enormous weight.[37]

Three months after France had declared war, the leaders of the Austro-Prussian coalition, with their troops on French soil, laid out the full range of their intentions in a conflict that they claimed, one-sidedly, had been forced upon them.[38] They wanted the people of the French kingdom to know that they had no purpose other than to stand up to their illegitimate governors who had taken a long series of illegal and provocative actions: "the arbitrary suppression of the rights and possessions of the German princes in Alsace and Lorraine; the disturbance and overthrow of public order and legitimate government in France; the perpetration of daily outrages and violence against the sacred person of the King and his august family; and finally, the last straw, the declaration of an unjust war against His Majesty the Emperor and the attack on his provinces situated in the Low Countries." But the two sovereigns had one additional "and equally important" concern: "to put an end to anarchy in the interior of France, to check the attacks on Throne and Church, to reestablish the legal order, and to restore the King's security and liberty . . . so as to enable him to exercise the legitimate authority which is his due." They felt sure that abhorring the "excesses of a small faction which subjugates them, . . . the sane and . . . great majority of the French nation . . . and people were impatiently waiting [for external help] to declare openly against the odious actions of their oppressors . . . and return to the ways of reason, justice, order, and peace."

Spuriously, but also brazenly, the Continent's two peerless sovereigns declared that "they had no intention of interfering in the internal affairs of France," their sole objective being "to deliver the . . . [entire] Royal Family from captivity." The manifesto promised that the liberating armies "would protect the cities, towns, and villages, as well as the persons and properties of all who submit to the King and support the immediate re-establishment of order and security throughout France." To the contrary, resistance would be dealt with severely: not only national guardsmen "captured bearing arms would be treated as enemies and punished as rebels," but public officials would have to "pay with their lives and property . . . for not exerting themselves to prevent [abuses and acts of violence] in their territories." As for those individuals "daring to defend themselves by firing on the advancing armies either in open country or from . . . their homes, they would be punished instantly according to the rigor of the laws of war, and their houses would be demolished."

But, of course, the city of Paris was the nerve center of the revolutionary dragon to be slain. The capital's inhabitants were admonished to instantly submit to the king and "place him fully at liberty." Their "Imperial and Royal majesties" gave warning that "all the members of the National Assembly, [officials] of the municipality, and [members of the] National Guard of Paris" would be held strictly accountable for the king's welfare. If need be, they would have to "answer with their lives," after being tried by military courts, "without hope of pardon." But above all else, "should the Palace of the Tuileries be entered by force or attacked," or should the king and the royal family "suffer even the slightest violence or outrage," the Habsburg and Hohenzollern Majesties vowed to wreak "an exemplary and ever-memorable vengeance": Paris would be subjected "to military punishment and total destruction, and any rebel guilty of an outrage would be given his just deserts."

To the extent that it was issued in a time of resurgent "religious" strife transcending national borders, the Brunswick Manifesto recalled the ways of medieval crusades and modern wars of religion, not unlike the crusading rhetoric of the banners and marching songs of the French armies. But it was also characteristic of the "first epoch of the counterrevolution," which was singularly artless. Quite unwittingly the Duke of Brunswick and his principals had "revealed the essence of [their] designs, thereby ruining them in advance." To have a chance at success, "instead of threatening the Revolution Brunswick

. . . should have caressed it . . . by loudly proclaiming that his peaceable troops were charged with strengthening the liberty of the noble French nation." At the time, however, the counterrevolution had not yet learned to "cover its hatreds and projects . . . [or] to lie with serenity."[39]

The Brunswick Manifesto, like the Pillnitz Declaration, was meant to bear upon the political situation inside France, particularly in Paris, which was once again misread. Since Pillnitz the caucus of the center had contracted, and so had that of the king. Even though he and his champions more than ever looked to the outside world for salvation, Louis XVI continued to protest his innocence. The royalist press, which published the Brunswick Manifesto, was not nearly so discreet. It conjured the specter of an imminent and devastating military onslaught, unless "the sane part of the Nation" preempted it by itself putting an end to the madness.[40]

This ultimatum by old-regime Europe—"a milestone in diplomatic impertinence"[41]—enraged and provoked more than it unnerved or terrified the temperate revolutionists who, though fearful of true believers, were not prepared to knuckle under and risk a return to the status quo ante. Besides, the thunder of the Brunswick Manifesto was so undiscriminating that throughout the land even the champions and architects of radical reform—of revolution without revolution— feared that the impending lightning might strike them as well.

Above all, however, the manifesto radicalized the radicals and their sympathizers when the news of it fell upon an increasingly restive Paris on July 28–29, 1792. The clubs and sections of militants were lashed into fury by this conspicuous confirmation of the complicity between the king and Europe's crowned heads, or the collusion between the internal and external "Koblenz." They now became the principal centers of agitation for the dethronement of Louis XVI. At the Cordeliers, Danton, who had vacillated all along, now sounded the trumpet for both war and deposal.[42] Within less than a week the Assembly was flooded with petitions calling for the king's removal and the Bourbons' dispersion.[43]

It is not too much to say that the Brunswick Manifesto triggered and focalized the popular demonstration and rush of the Tuileries on August 10 which culminated in the overthrow of the throne and the convocation of a National Convention. This extraordinary *journée* produced a watershed in the French Revolution: "the first period was dominated by the Revolution's struggle against the Monarchy; the second by its struggle against Europe as well as against itself."[44]

Following the Brunswick Manifesto the revolutionaries, with notable exceptions like Robespierre, forgot about their own contribution to the coming of the war. They not only put the entire blame on the foreign powers but portrayed these as being diplomatically united and primed for an all-out military assault. In actual fact, although the powers were determined to curb, if not crush, the new regime in France, they were not about to sacrifice their conflicting interests to this common cause, which also meant that they committed only limited military forces to it. Although they kept their eye on, for example, the Polish imbroglio, in the Brunswick Manifesto they spoke as if they were sworn to restore the old order in France and tranquillity in Europe. This ideological hyperbole played into the hands of the war party in Paris, which used the threat of the oncoming counterrevolutionary armies to justify and energize their own drive to transform a conventional war into a revolutionary crusade.

Soon after the overthrow of the monarchy, the fall of Longwy on August 23, 1792, and Verdun on September 2 dampened the crusading impulse and fed the fear and fury that found expression in the September prison massacres.[45] Indeed, for the crusading spirit to be fired, it had to wait for the unexpected military successes of the French armies during the fall of 1792: in September Valmy, Chambéry, Nice; in October Speier, Worms, Mainz, Frankfurt; in November Jemappes and the conquest of Belgium.

On November 19 the legislature of the fledgling Republic, proclaimed on September 22, issued a decree vowing fraternity and promising help for the would-be rebel peoples of Europe.[46] Four weeks later, on December 15, it declared that far and wide the armies of the Republic would, "in the name of the French nation, proclaim the sovereignty of the people and the suppression of all existing imposts . . . and privileges." In occupied territories the military command would see to the convocation of "primary or communal assemblies in order to create and organize a provisional administration and judiciary." The new civil authorities would "be in charge of regulating and paying local expenses and those necessary for the common defense," with tax levies sparing "the indigent and hard-working portion of the population" but also with "security for person and property."[47] According to Michelet, with the decree of December 15 the Convention gave its war "of conquest, nay, liberation . . . a social character." Raising "the true flag of France . . . above all parties," it proclaimed a "crusade" to set the world free of all tyrants. Although Michelet applauds this project, he anxiously asks "when and how such a war could ever be brought to a close."[48]

✳ ✳ ✳

Overall the same calculations and purposes which had informed the declaration of war on April 20 informed the decrees of November 19 and December 15. The Brissotins, though out of government, continued to lead the charge. But now Joseph Cambon and Danton, as well as their followers, did not merely intone the call to arms but beat the war drums, even if for a different agenda. An all but unanimous Convention, not the street, put the revolutionizing of Europe *à l'ordre du jour*.[49]

Although Robespierre did not organize opposition to this externalization of the Revolution, he did, once again, criticize it, marshaling most of the same arguments he had adduced before. He not only stressed that each of Europe's many peoples had its own individuality, but also wondered how many of them had "the degree of enlightenment and predisposition to adopt the constitution which the French people favored." To simultaneously warrant and violate a people's "sovereign right to freely give themselves a constitution . . . was to run the risk of alienating them": it was unreasonable to expect to "found liberty with the help of outside violence . . . [since] those issuing laws by force of arms would be considered foreigners and conquerors." Rather than make a stand against the universalizing war as such, Robespierre urged that France's "generals and armies be enjoined not to interfere in the political affairs" of foreign peoples.[50]

The radicalization of foreign and military policy of late 1792 was not an alternative to a general radicalization of the Revolution, as envisaged by the Brissotins, but an integral part of it: the thrust into absolute war and the rush to regicide were linked and coincided to make for one of the crucial defining and irreversible moments of the epoch.

Hitherto terror had been largely spontaneous and random in the provinces and in Paris: the violence of the Bastille, the *grande peur*, the successive *journées*, Nîmes, Avignon. This terror was, in the first instance, a terror from below. It took place in the absence of war, without imminent and credible threats from across the borders, except for the agitation of the émigrés of the first hours.

Even if war was not the incidental, sufficient, or final cause for the Great Terror, it was certainly a necessary cause. Just as war became an instrument of policy—both foreign and domestic— starting in mid-1792, so did terror. It ceased to be a string of irregular outbursts of popular violence to become, in Quinet's words, "a cold instrument of government and salvation" wielded from the top and directed from the center. The switches were set for an accelerated and intensified reciprocation of war and revolution and of foreign force and internal violence. The correlation was uneven and erratic, as well as opaque, particularly because of the undisciplined mix of "reality" and "perception" in the ways of the principal actors. Still, it defies common, conceptual, and temporal sense to deny a strong if indeterminate correlation between the facts and atmospherics of war and the revolutionizing of the Revolution: the proclamation of *la patrie en danger*; the September massacres; the trial and execution of the king; the establishment of the Revolutionary Tribunal and the Committee of Public Safety; the call for the *levée en masse*; the placing of terror *à l'ordre du jour*; the adoption of the Law of Suspects; the edict of the general *maximum*; the trial and execution of thirty-one Girondins; the avenging reprisals in the cities of the Midi; the infernal columns in the Vendée.

At the very least, in the same way as the Pillnitz Declaration contributed to the ascendancy of the Girondins, the defeat at Neerwinden and the defection of General Dumouriez furthered the ascendancy of the Mountain. Likewise, the "close interrelatedness of war and revolution," which was "bound to counterrevolution as reaction is bound to reaction,"[51] both at home and abroad, in some significant measure conditioned the interactive resistance and counterresistance in Lyons, Marseilles, Bordeaux, and Toulon. While this interrelatedness is least transparent in the singularly tangled dynamics of the origin and course of the Vendée, given "the logic of the situation," it certainly played a role there as well.

The Girondins had politicized and ideologized the war, and in the process accentuated the externalization of the Revolution. Savoy, Nice, Brussels, and Mainz were the first way stations of the incipient crusade for the liberation of Europe from tyrannical rule. But then the untoward military reverses of early spring 1793 put Robespierre in the saddle, all the more so since they coincided with the eruption of the Vendée and Federalist defiance. More than ever anxious about the fragility of the revolutionary regime, and obsessed with the perils of conspiracy, both domestic and international, Robespierre tried to reverse priorities. In the winter of 1791–92 he had warned of the risks of using external war as a prophylaxis for the growing pains of revolution. By now, however, the Mountain needed to address France's urgent domestic problems and stresses at the same time that they needed to master the headlong war which was aggravating them.

Accordingly, Robespierre and the Jacobins steered a course halfway between the primacy of domestic politics and foreign policy.[52] They revolutionized the ways and means of fighting an essentially defensive war. Instead of billing the war as a messianic crusade, the Jacobins increasingly defined the war in super-patriotic terms, firmly yoking the nation and the Revolution to each other. In fact, the Jacobins sacrificed the radical political, economic, and social revolution within the Revolution on the altar of the nation's war effort. By freezing the Revolution in the interest of military necessity and efficiency, they also consolidated and exploited their hold on power in a still-festering predicament of multiple sovereignty.

The Girondins were, then, the chief architects of a crusading foreign policy and war as an expression of the Revolution's inborn universalism. Apart from the intrinsic enormity, if not impossibility, of their project of "regenerating the world," they were rather ingenuous about it. Brissot and his confederates assumed or pretended that this task would be child's play. Theirs was the temperament of prophets trusting in "the word" as well as in popular "enthusiasm" and *élan vital*. They were all the more "confounded when they ran into the first obstacles." Since the Girondins expected an "effortless triumph," they envisaged using "ordinary means" to achieve their "extraordinary" ends. For them, the benefits of foreign success could be applied to solve the internal problems which they had, to begin with, channeled abroad.[53]

By contrast, the Jacobins had "a clearer feel for reality." They saw themselves "confronted with a superhuman task which they pledged to accomplish with honor and barbarism." Theirs was an "*ancien-régime* temperament" in that they proposed to use "despotic" means to establish a new order. Robespierre and his ilk realized that "liberty could be founded neither without mastering the nature of things" nor without "forcing a people to be free."[54] They were "neither the apostles nor prophets" of the Revolution but its "rabid advocates and prosecutors." Not surprisingly, therefore, they were not among its prime founders and movers. They had not been in the vanguard either of the Bastille or the federalist movement; had opposed the war; and had "played only an indirect role on August 10 . . . [and in] the foundation of the republic." Not that they lacked "faith." But their faith was "neither caring nor inspired." In sum, whereas the Brissotins were prophets, the Robespierrists were zealots.[55]

The crusading war soon assumed a life of its own. Between February 1 and March 7, 1793 war was declared on England, Holland, and Spain. With the French armies on the march, there was need to raise, equip, and deploy additional men. In early spring there were growing signs of hypertrophy: the defeat of Neerwinden; the conscription of 300,000 men which intensified the insurgency in the Vendée; and the overheating war economy and finances, which gave rise to shortages, inflation, and social unrest. The prophets having overreached themselves and being bewildered as well as discredited, the zealots took over, perhaps because there was no one else to assume the Brissotins' poisoned legacy.

The situation they faced was grim. Summoned to both save the Revolution and win the war, the Jacobins saw themselves "forced to organize, in the midst of anarchy, a violent minority government," to be driven by "an explosive combination of interest and fanaticism."[56]

✳ ✳ ✳

The Thermidorean Convention and the Directory were the incubators of Bonapartism. After toppling and executing Robespierre in the name of reclaiming the republic, the Convention proceeded to put an end to the terror, the *maximum*, and the *levée en masse*. But although there was broad agreement on the dismantlement of the Jacobin emergency dictatorship, whose purport remained controversial, there was little concord on the direction in which to take the ever-unsteady republican commonweal. The core of the ruling political class, centered in successive legislatures, consisted of new men of new landed wealth bent on conserving the essential social, economic, and political gains of 1789. Lacking broad popular support, this political class felt threatened by unreconstructed ultra-Jacobins, lying in wait on the left, particularly in Paris and a few other cities, and by resurgent monarchists, on the right, principally in the provinces, heartened by the rifts in the revolutionary camp. Although the Thermidoreans overestimated both perils, they were particularly nervous about the royalist danger. Its multiple and potent components at home and abroad seemed all the more awesome since the moving spirits of both the Convention and Directory disregarded the deep divisions between moderate and intransigent royalists. Because of the weakness of political society's executive authority, there was constant concern that the center, which itself was faction-ridden, might not be able to hold fast long enough for a sober republic to at last consolidate a full and effective political and legal sovereignty.

It is of capital importance that Thermidor's dismantlement of the *dictature de détresse* did not include the termination of the war which had been one of its chief reasons and radicalizers. Presently the issue of war and peace became the touchstone of political debate, with each faction using it and structuring it to advance its own goals. In fact, this issue lost its autonomy, to become a pawn on a political chessboard that was increasingly polarized between royalists and Jacobins. The former were the doves of their time, advocating a negotiated settlement with few if any territorial annexations, in the conviction that an early peace without victory would be most likely to further some form of monarchist restoration. By contrast, the Jacobins stood forth as hawks: the more moderate elements among them pressed for "natural borders," while the war aims of the ultras were without precise limits, except that for them the Rhine became something of a polestar. But by and large the Mountain, torn between minimalists and maximalists, looked to successful war and expansion to rally popular support and to cement the inchoate political class around the Directory and its executive committee. Whereas the doves, counting on the great powers and the Bourbon pretender, considered an early and self-renouncing peace the key to the overturn of the Revolution, the hawks, confident in the nation-in-arms and the revolt of the liberated peoples, considered limitless warfare and enlargement of the *Grande Nation* necessary to preserve its essential gains. On the whole both doves and hawks treated foreign and military policy in purely instrumental terms, their eyes firmly fixed on its domestic political dynamics and consequences.

Actually, the fall of Robespierre was in keeping with this logic. The war with the First Coalition of enemy powers (Austria, Prussia, England, Holland, Spain) began to take a favorable turn with General Jean-Baptiste Jourdan's victory at Fleurus in southern Belgium on June 26, 1794, followed by the capture of Brussels on July 10, some two weeks before 9–10 Thermidor. This was the first of many dramatic interplays between the erratic course of external war and the vicissitudes of the political struggle in Paris. In this instance, military victory prepared the ground for the relaxation of the revolutionary regime.

Although this correlation between the twists of domestic politics and the turns of foreign war was rarely perfect, there is no denying its dynamic. The capture of Koblenz in October 1794, Russia's recognition of the French republic in April 1795, and the defeat of the émigré landing at Quiberon in July encouraged the Thermidoreans to forge ahead with the normalization of the regime, culminating in the adoption of the directorial Constitution on August 22. But then, following the annexation of Belgium, during the autumn and winter of 1795–96 the campaign against the First Coalition ran aground in both southern Germany and northern Italy. It was in this period, on October 5, 1795, that Napoleon, seasoned by his participation in the recapture of Toulon in December 1793, directed the repression of a would-be royalist rising in Paris. Almost simultaneously the Convention reactivated the curb on refractory priests.

The French armies resumed their offensive in the spring of 1796, and Bonaparte was given the command of the Italian army. He won a succession of victories over the Austrians in the Piedmont, and on May 15 seized Milan, forcing the payment of a heavy indemnity. The French forces then moved east to take Verona and Venice before closing in on the northern Papal States, which brought financial dividends as well. In the meantime they also resumed their offensive on the German front, with Jourdan capturing Frankfurt in mid-July. But then, during the autumn and winter of 1796–97, although Napoleon continued to prevail over the Austrians in Italy, on the other fronts the French armies once again failed of success. On August 24 Jourdan was beaten at Amberg, east of Nuremberg, his troops being forced to fall back south of the Rhine. In December Hoche's amphibious expedition to Ireland, aimed at England, suffered shipwreck. Clearly, Bonaparte was the rising star among the generals, with the Austrians signing a preliminary peace with him at Leoben, southwest of Vienna, on April 18. By now he was taking considerable diplomatic and political liberties in what had become his military realm, with the Directory disinclined, if not powerless, to restrain him.

In May 1797 Bonaparte resumed his attack, which culminated in Austria finally signing the Treaty of Campo Formio on October 17. In this treaty, which marked the end of the First Coalition, Vienna not only ceded Belgium, the Ionian islands, and the Austrian part of the Rhine's left bank, but recognized France's hegemony over Italy. With Prussia neutral and Russia watching from the sidelines, England was the only great power to remain an active enemy. But without a major continental ally London was relatively unthreatening, its capacity for a cross-Channel strike being nil. Everything now depended on whether the Directory could muster the cohesion and resolve to press a foreign and military policy designed to keep England isolated while proffering reasonable peace terms. Such a course would require reining in the generals, in particular Bonaparte, whose standing was boosted by the stunning victory over the First Coalition.

Predictably the triumph of French arms appeased or disarmed neither doves nor hawks. The doves, troubled that military and diplomatic accomplishments were bolstering the legitimacy and viability of the Republic, spared no efforts to destabilize it. At home the royalists took advantage of the relaxation of the regime to activate the ex-émigrés, the *chouans*, the refractory clergy, and the *déçus* of the Revolution, while abroad the Bourbons and émigrés urged England to stand firm and the other powers to resume the struggle. As for the hawks, they were dissatisfied with the terms of Campo Formio, particularly because it did not secure, outright, the whole left bank of the Rhine.

But above all, they feared that a peace without victory, or the absence of war, would pave the way for an all-out de-Jacobinization, perhaps even counterrevolution.

At this juncture, however, the inchoate executive of the weak Directory considered the royalist *fronde* to be a greater danger than the Jacobin defiance. Accordingly the coup d'état of 18 Fructidor of the Year V, or September 4, 1797, was intended to put the royalists and their sympathizers *hors de combat*. In the partial elections of April 1797 royalists of all stripes had won 180 out of 260 contested seats, giving them considerable leverage in both chambers. Not willing to take a chance on an anti-republican challenge, and confident of legislative support, three of the directors resolved to strike preemptively. They called in the capital's army garrison, under the command of a Bonapartist general, to arrest some fifty royalist representatives with a view to their deportation to Cayenne in French Guiana. There followed the annulment of elections in forty-nine departments, the arrest of thirty-two journalists, and the proscription of forty-two Parisian and provincial newspapers.[57] But perhaps most telling, the two most prominent members of the Directory's five-man executive, Lazare Carnot and François de Barthélemy, were targeted for arrest for favoring an early termination of both the war and the Revolution along moderate lines. Whereas Carnot managed to flee abroad in the nick of time, Barthélemy wound up being deported. The months following 18 Fructidor saw a renewal of the persecution of émigrés and refractory priests, with over 150 put to death and between 1,400 and 1,800 sent to the islands of Ré and Oléron off France's western coast, the British fleet blocking their joining the vanguard of prisoners in the embryonic penal archipelago overseas.[58]

Of course, the left benefited from this repression of the right, which was coupled with a resumption of official "anti-clerical and anti-Christian persecution and propaganda, the worst since 1794."[59] In this climate of resurgent Jacobinism, and mindful of the difficulty of bridling the military to which it was increasingly beholden, the Directory stayed on a forward foreign-policy course. Determined to emend Campo Formio, from late November 1797 it pressured the Diet of the Holy Roman Empire to recognize France's sovereignty over the entire left bank of the Rhine. In early 1798 French troops intervened in Switzerland to help found a kindred regime and occupied Rome, exiling Pope Pius VI to Tuscany. In other words, the *Grande Nation* continued its policy of expansion, not to say conquest, fully aware that it risked driving two or more of the major continental states to again stand together, providing England with the land forces without which its leverage for intervention was slight. To boot, on May 19 Bonaparte and his expeditionary force of 30,000 men set sail for Egypt. The objective was to strike at British world power. On August 1, 1798, in the battle of the Nile, Nelson destroyed the French fleet off Aboukir, ending all hope of seizing colonial holdings from Britain or seriously damaging its economic lifeline. But the harm was done, in that the antirevolutionary government in London was confirmed in its estimate of France's resolve to challenge England's position as *primus inter pares* in the concert of great powers. By late December 1798 Russia and England signed a treaty of alliance prompted by expediency.

In the meantime the Second Directory, having seen the infant republic safely past the Scylla of the right, became alarmed about the ship of state veering toward the Charybdis of the left. Indeed, the outcome of the partial elections of May 1798, which renewed about sixty percent of the membership of the assemblies, was the obverse of those of the preceding year: they brought forth a sizable if loose group of democratic and Jacobin representatives. This time the directors raised the specter of a revival of the Terror to justify the coup of 22 Floréal of the Year VII, or May 11, 1798. Confident of the army, they "purged 127 deputies from the legislature even before they took their seats."[60]

Whereas "at the time of Fructidor [the Directory] had accused the assemblies of being excessively royalist, at Floréal they were charged with being excessively republican."[61] Even if for a noble cause, these two coups subverted the Constitution, cheapened elections, and heartened the army. To be sure, "France was still a republic, with the widest franchise in Europe."[62] Although "the sword replaced the law," the Directory did not reinstate "the scaffold." Instead, it chose to deport political prisoners to an overseas island, albeit with a "homicidal" climate. Clearly, it continued to oscillate between two extreme parties "without ever considering annihilating either one at a time or both simultaneously."[63] Still, "having antagonized the Right in 1797 and the Left in 1798," the Directory, the unsteady bulwark of the republic, "stood alone," except for the army, whose achievements braced the government at the same time that they paved the road to Brumaire, or the overthrow of the Directory.[64] In hindsight, Tocqueville judged the Directory's repressive measures very severely, insisting that they were more "barbarous . . . than the cruelest laws of 1793": whereas the latter were "heatedly debated" and widely opposed, "the laws of the Directory were silently accepted." All in all the scaffold was replaced by deportation, "a penalty often more severe than death," which satisfied "popular vengeance" but spared it "the unpleasant sight of suffering."[65]

✳ ✳ ✳

Although the war was not without reverses, these were never serious enough for the second or third Directory to earnestly consider ending it short of an outright victor's peace. Still, between 22 Floréal and 19 Brumaire France suffered the most serious setbacks since the summer of 1792, reaching a climax in the spring and summer of 1799. In early March Paris resumed its offensive on the German front and again declared war on Austria, confident that the Second Coalition (England, Russia, Austria, Turkey, Portugal, Naples) would be as divided and ineffective as the first. But within a matter of weeks Jourdan was once more forced to retreat to the Rhine. At about the same time French forces had to yield ground in Italy and evacuate Milan. Although General André Masséna managed to foil an Austrian offensive in Switzerland in early June, his situation remained precarious. Meanwhile the occupation of Naples had precipitated a Vendée-like rebellion in Calabria, and Bonaparte continued to flounder in the Near East.

This adverse military situation "revived memories of the imperiled *patrie*" and fostered a "Jacobin atmosphere." By this time patriots experienced the real and potential losses of recently conquered lands as wounds inflicted to the very heart of the French nation. In any case, the government adopted the elements of a *"levée en masse, . . . an emergency loan, . . . a law of hostages, . . . a rhetoric of apprehension and passion."* Presently, in August, "there were [also] scattered royalist disturbances in the Midi."[66]

In late September Masséna defeated Austrian and Russian forces near Zurich, the Egyptian foray having prompted Russia to join the war to contain France. Not that this military success, though important and welcome, completely redeemed the situation. Meanwhile, having left Egypt a month before Masséna's victory, Bonaparte arrived in France on October 9, and a few days later in Paris. Despite the glaring failure of his grand expedition, whose troops he abandoned to their fate, his reputation was essentially untarnished in Paris, as well as among the bevy of obsequious intellectuals, scientists, and artists who had followed in his train. France was about to live through her third coup d'état since 9 Thermidor, and once again there would be little if any popular or organized opposition.

Bonaparte did not seize the government by force of arms or by raising the masses against the Directory. To the contrary, leading members of the political class maneuvered to have him enter the inner sanctum of power. The Abbé Sieyès, by now the most influential member of the Directory's five-man executive cabinet, articulated their view that the regime needed a stronger executive if it was to uphold the political center, protect the social compact, and confront the enemy powers in pursuit of a strong—a victor's—peace. Needless to say, Sieyès and his associates were confident that they would keep the upper hand over their chosen military coadjutor.

In the coup of 19 Brumaire (November 9–10, 1799), much as in the preceding coups, the army played a certain but not leading role. It provided the show of force attending the violation of the assemblies, with only a platoon of soldiers needed to remove a few defiant deputies who, unwilling to say amen to the liquidation of the severely battered Republic, including representative government, refused to comply with the order to disperse. Once again the imminent danger of a renascent Jacobin terror served as justification. The engineers of the coup, with Sieyès in the lead, were "like men who, having seen a specter . . . in the form of all the ghosts of 1793, threw themselves, with their heads bowed, at the feet of the general designated to protect them." Countless champions of freedom shared Sieyès' obsessive and exaggerated fear, among them "Daunou, Cabanis, Grégoire, Carnot, and even Lafayette," thereby signing their political death warrant.[67] The Brumaireans, many of them "new men who had made it rich thanks to the Revolution," were prepared to sacrifice all moral advances "to material gains."[68] To the extent that the essence of the project was "conservative" it seduced moderate royalists, including the peasantry determined to safeguard the land settlement.

Immediately before the forced dissolution, the deputies of the Directory dutifully designated Napoleon, Sieyès, and Pierre Roger Ducos consuls of a provisional executive charged with drafting a new constitution. Not surprisingly, the Constitution of the Year VIII, proclaimed on December 15, 1799, turned out to have a distinctly authoritarian bent. Of the three consuls of the executive, only one exercised real power, and by August 2, 1802, Napoleon was the sole and lifetime First Consul. As for the three chambers of a putative legislative branch, they were designed to offset each other. In addition, the Consulate's electoral system was far and away more restrictive than that of the defunct Directorate. France now had a nondemocratic government with a strong executive which stood fair to overcome the breakdown of political and judicial sovereignty dating from 1789. To this end, and building on a strong legacy of centralized government, it streamlined the administration, established a police force, and restructured and unified the judicial system. Eventually, in March 1804 this new judiciary was capped with a civil code, or the *Code Napoléon*, which became a model for much of Europe. As we will see, the Concordat of July 15, 1801, with Pope Pius VII was in keeping with this nondemocratic and unifying design. Somewhat outrageously, Quinet considered this bid for a revived if rationalized sovereignty a throwback to the *ancien régime*. In his reading, "the thunderstorm having passed, with the beginning of the century three weighty elements glaringly resurfaced: absolute power with the First Consul; Roman Catholicism with the Concordat; and centralization for the new administration."[69]

In fact, the reality of Napoleon's position and task was far more complex. In the words of François Guizot, it is "no small matter to be, as one man, the incarnation of the nation's glory, a guarantor of revolution, and a principle of authority."[70] As warrant of the populist, democratic, and secularizing sides of the Revolution, Napoleon appealed to the left. In his authoritarian guise he rallied those "terrified by a second terror" and those looking for a resolute defense of the new social order. Last, but certainly not least, with his representation of the super-patriotic conceit, Napoleon "rose above all parties and used the blinding light of national grandeur to eclipse their petty partisan quarrels."[71]

❋ ❋ ❋

But while the 19 Brumaire ushered in the calm after a furious storm at home, the atmosphere remained charged with thunder and lightning abroad. Indeed, the domestic appeasement and realignment along centrist lines, which consolidated some of the basic political and social gains of the Revolution, was contingent on the future course of diplomacy and war. There is no separating the constructive side of Napoleon's internal reign, especially between 1799 and 1804, from his external design and strategy. Napoleon was, above all, a soldier, and he was appointed consul above all for his military genius of proven anti-Bourbon and anti-aristocratic persuasion. At the outset Sieyès is likely to have envisaged keeping political affairs mainly in his own hands while leaving war and diplomacy to his martial confederate. This division of labor was premised on their agreement that a peace without victory, or without at a very minimum natural borders, was precluded, not least for domestic reasons. In any event, there was no question of renouncing the annexations and forward spheres of the revolutionary decade.

When Napoleon became consul, France had annexed Belgium, the left bank of the Rhine, Savoy, and Nice. Furthermore, with its unmatched army, France exercised considerable influence beyond these expanded borders, in Switzerland, Holland, and parts of Italy. After the great powers of the Second Coalition spurned an unrealistic peace proposal from Paris, Napoleon resumed personal command of the Italian campaign, which on June 2, 1800, culminated in victory over the Austrians at the Piedmontese village of Marengo. His aura reinvigorated, he consolidated his hold on power in Paris and summarily spurned Louis XVIII's feelers about a restoration while waiting for Vienna to back down. On February 8, 1801 Austria made a separate peace, in the Treaty of Lunéville, which recognized not only France's annexation of Belgium and the left bank of the Rhine but the independence of several satellite states along with French hegemony over most of northern Italy. A year later, on March 25, 1802, with the Treaty of Amiens, even Britain, now completely isolated, agreed to swear off all further seizures of overseas colonies, except Dutch Ceylon and Spanish Trinidad, in exchange for France yielding Egypt.

If the Second Coalition went the way of the First, it was primarily because the great powers were chronically weakened by conflicting interests and war aims, mutual distrust, and lack of military coordination. Should they ever pull together, even the excellence of the French armies and Napoleon's mastery would be insufficient to stay France's extravagant course. Meanwhile, the treaties of Lunéville and Amiens must be reckoned a cessation of hostilities rather than a genuine peace: the ex-belligerents and old-regime Europe in general considered them excessively unequal, France having given up very little. Here was a clear sign that the ever-suspect government in Paris had no intention of abandoning France's bid for European hegemony. Besides, the French violated both the letter and spirit of the treaties. They fed the chancelleries' worst suspicions by repeatedly intervening in Switzerland, refusing to evacuate Holland, proceeding to several annexations in Italy, and remaining intrusive in the eastern Mediterranean. In addition to their ideological disquiet, the great powers were centrally concerned for their own interests and security. England was, of course, the most disposed to look for ways to mount another anti-French coalition, its own hegemonic pretensions clashing with those of its chief rival.[72]

Ultimately, Paris was the chief hector of the European system. There was, to be sure, Napoleon's insatiable quest for glory, peculiar to the warlord whose legitimacy is contingent on his continuing to "perform heroic deeds."[73] In this instance this personal dynamic was all the stronger by virtue of its being grafted onto the persistent interdependence between the internal life of successive revolutionary regimes, since 1792, and their aggressive strategy abroad. More than ever there was the fear that a no-win peace, let alone a defeat, would result in a restoration or counterrevolution at home. Whatever the strains of perpetual war, there was no danger of an "internal" revolution as long as the armies were successful. Indeed, "Napoleon was never imperiled from within, and . . . his empire would never have collapsed from domestic difficulties."[74]

Under the Consulate, not unlike under the Directory, military success underwrote the ongoing consolidation of regime and state.[75] In the wake of his victory at Marengo, Napoleon pressed ahead with his search for a reconciliation with Pope and Church. Not unlike Voltaire, Napoleon believed in the ultimate rationality of man and society at the same time that he disdained and feared the masses, which for their own good and for the good of society needed to be kept in check by religion and church. Short of a perpetual use of force, not to say violence, Napoleon saw no way of consolidating the new order without defusing the religious schism precipitated by the clerical oath; but he felt no less sure that the state should have control of the church. At this time, standing strong, he could afford to ignore the left and proceed to heal France's religious rift with a view to depriving the advocates of "a return to the *ancien régime*" of "millions of potential recruits," the Roman Church remaining "one of the main pillars of counterrevolution." Meanwhile, with the French in control of Italy, Pope Pius VII, who was less intransigent than his predecessor, was likely to be open to an accommodation. In any case, following arduous negotiations, Napoleon and Pius VII reached a settlement which, unlike Lunéville and Amiens, was equitable save in the eyes of the ultraroyalists and ultra-Jacobins. Under the Concordat of 1801, concluded and ratified in the exultation of Amiens, the Vatican accepted that in France the episcopate and clergy be appointed and paid by the state, and swear loyalty to it. The Holy See also agreed that confiscated church properties not be returned. Although, in exchange, Napoleon recognized Roman Catholicism to be the "religion of the greater majority of French citizens," he insisted upon its being only one of several religions.

Catholic true-believers and Louis XVIII opposed the Concordat because besides treating with an ungodly and regicide government, the Vatican sapped support for an all-out restoration by depriving the refractory church and clergy of the aura of martyrdom. As for the fundamentalist liberals and Jacobins, they decried the attenuation of the separation of church and state as well as of state-supported anticlericalism. In their eyes Napoleon had put the secularization of civil and political society in jeopardy, along with religious toleration. Meanwhile, with the "triumphant re-establishment of Catholicism" Napoleon braced his authority with what he considered an "essential foundation, consecrated by the Concordat."[76]

All things considered, the Concordat was the domestic expression of the centrist alliance and dynamic driving the external war. In this logic, having dealt a blow to the far right, there was need for a corresponding strike against the far left. Dead against the politics of the streets, Bonaparte seized upon the unsuccessful attempt on his own life on December 24, 1800, to proceed against the presumably ever-lurking *enragés*. He backed his charge that the Jacobins and Babou-vists, or proto-Communists, were responsible for this would-be assassination with the claim that he had "a dictionary of the September murderers, conspirators, Babeuf and others who had figured at the worst moments of the Revolution."[77] Napoleon hastened to tell the Council of State that the procedures of "a special tribunal would be too slow and limited . . . [to punish] this atrocious crime, [which called for] a vengeance as swift as lightning." The time had come "to purge [these wretches] from the republic," all the more so since "to make 'a great example' of their chiefs would help dissolve the party, persuade 'workers' to return to work, and 'attach the intermediate class to the republic.' " The Council decided to summarily deport 129 presumed Jacobins to the Seychelles and to Cayenne at the same time that former terrorists or revolutionaries were arrested in several cities. Within two weeks Joseph Fouché provided Napoleon with conclusive evidence that ultraroyalists, not neo-Jacobins, were responsible for the outrage, as part of an effort to destabilize the moderate regime that seemed to take hold with Marengo and the Concordat. But the First Consul stood fast, and so did the Council and the Senate. Napoleon was quoted as saying that "we deport them for their share in the September Massacres, the crime of 31 May, the Babeuf Conspiracy, and all that has happened since."[78]

✹ ✹ ✹

With renewed confidence in the strategy of harnessing the prestige of successful warfare, sanctified by blood, to consolidate and energize the regime, Napoleon resumed the war that had started in 1792 and was to last another decade. He made the most of the rivalries among the great powers, engaging and defeating them almost one by one.

Napoleon continued to reap the political benefits of successive victories, all the more since he fought all his battles on foreign soil and financed them by imposts on conquered lands, so that "the French population was spared the heaviest burdens of warfare."[79]

As we saw, with the balance of power impaired, each of the great powers had good reason to distrust Paris: England feared for its primacy; Austria was "deeply concerned about the growth of French preponderance in Germany and Italy; Prussia found itself with a French army in the midst of its dominion and cheated of a prize which had always been one of its major foreign-policy goals; and Russia objected to any move that presaged renewed French interest in the Levant as well as a destabilization of the German settlement."[80] On top of engaging in this unexceptional calculus of realpolitik and geopolitics, the governments of the great powers took exception to the insolent pretense of France's upstart ruler: on May 18, 1804, Napoleon declared himself hereditary Emperor of the French, with Pius VII celebrating the Mass at which Napoleon crowned himself in Notre Dame on December 2. The political and ruling class acquiesced as meekly as during the recent coups d'état.

Provoked by several additional annexations on the Italian peninsula which violated the Treaty of Lunéville, England and Russia issued a joint warning to Paris while Austria, falling in with this nascent Third Coalition, invaded Bavaria in September 1805. By October 20 Napoleon defeated the Austrians at Ulm. Three weeks later he solemnly led his troops into Vienna, his greatest prize to date. Heartened by this triumph, he went on to defeat, on December 5, the Russian and Austrian forces in the Battle of the Three Emperors, at Austerlitz, halfway between Vienna and Prague. Characteristically, the Allies had nearly three times the number of killed, wounded, and prisoners as the French, or a total loss of between 25,000 and 30,000 men. Two weeks thereafter Austria signed another humiliating peace agreement: by the Treaty of Pressburg (Bratislava), in addition to paying an indemnity, the Habsburgs ceded considerable lands to the Kingdom of Italy, now ruled by Napoleon, and to Baden, Bavaria, and Wurtemberg, which became independent kingdoms. For all intents and purposes France supplanted Austria in both Italy and southern Germany. All in all, the second half of the year 1805 was one of Napoleon's most brilliant seasons, except that on October 21 Nelson's defeat of the French and Spanish fleets at Trafalgar, near the northwestern shore off the Strait of Gibraltar, confirmed Britain's naval supremacy.

Prussia had stayed out of the conflict, and Frederick William III's indecision had facilitated Napoleon's defeat of the Third Coalition. But following Pressburg the Prussian king could no longer temporize without risking either gradual subdual or outright defeat, should his armies have to fight Napoleon by themselves. In any case, in mid-July, as Napoleon went about creating the Rhenish Confederation and unhinging the Holy Roman Empire, Frederick William united with Russia and Saxony in a Fourth Coalition. As was his wont, Napoleon promptly attacked the Prussian-Saxon forces, decisively defeating them in the twin battle of Jena and Auerstadt in mid-October 1806 before triumphantly riding into Berlin on October 27. Especially when outnumbered and without the support of its main ally, even Europe's strongest and most sophisticated old-style army was no match for France's new-model legions. Napoleon pursued the retreating Prussians to the northeast. In early February he fought a bloody but inconclusive battle against a combined Prussian and Russian force at Eylau, near Königsberg. This time the French counted some 25,000 to the Allies' 15,000 casualties, with the inclement weather intensifying the fatal but normal agony of the wounded. Still, not long thereafter, in mid-June, he managed to crush a Russian army further east, near Friedland.

The time had come for both Russia and Prussia to bend the knee in a landmark treaty signed in July 1807 at Tilsit, a port on the Niemen. Napoleon extended France's hegemony to central and eastern Europe, in the process sponsoring the establishment of the Duchy of Warsaw. Whereas he imposed harsh territorial, financial, and military terms on Prussia, Napoleon was rather lenient with Russia. At present his primary concern was to win over Alexander I for his compulsive but uphill struggle with England. Russia was given a free hand in Turkey and the Baltic in exchange for joining the Continental System. Except for a shared hostility to England, this tacit alliance between the two emperors and polities was *contre-nature*. But be that as it may, Tilsit marked Napoleon's apogee, with a multinational army of nearly one million men mounting guard over a French empire extending from the Pyrenees to the Pripet Marshes. No one inside France even dreamt of challenging him, particularly since except for the limited conscription and casualties of native Frenchmen, the domestic costs of perpetual war were as yet minimal.

✳ ✳ ✳

With nearly the entire Continent under French military sway, England was the last holdout. Basking in the hubris of his recent triumphs, Napoleon was not about to be daunted by the difficulty of bending or breaking London's will. Emboldened by his diplomatic marriage of convenience with Alexander I and by England's utter isolation, Bonaparte proposed to high-pressure Britain with a blockade and boycott of its exports, the lifeblood of its domestic and imperial economy. Napoleon issued the Berlin decrees proclaiming his strategic economic policy on November 21, 1806, during the months separating Jena and Tilsit. To implement this policy Napoleon needed to convince and, if necessary, coerce all European coastal states to help enforce the Continental Blockade or System, the objective being French control over every state fronting the seas between the Baltic and the Mediterranean.

After Tilsit Napoleon's unflagging bid for European hegemony was heavily driven by this strategic plan, which England was determined to thwart with a counter-blockade, neither of the two great powers being fitted for autarky. It took French pressure to see to the closing of Hamburg, Lübeck, Bremen, and Rotterdam on the North Sea; and Genoa and Livorno on the Mediterranean. In late 1807 the French began their intervention in Spain and Portugal, the objective being to close in particular the Portuguese coast which remained open for trade with Britain. Even if costly in lives, the march to Lisbon was easy enough. In Spain, to the contrary, the French intervention from the outset intensified a severe rift in the Bourbon ruling house which destabilized its *ancien régime*. By May Napoleon had removed both the ruling king, Charles IV, and his son, Ferdinand VII, in favor of his own brother Joseph Bonaparte, who entered Madrid as King of Spain on July 20.

Meanwhile the French became caught up in Spain's internecine struggle between the immovable governing and ruling classes and the high-spirited champions of enlightened but moderate reform.[81]

Whereas the former resisted the invaders for being armed crusaders for the ideas of 1789, the latter proceeded to collaborate with them to further their liberal(izing) cause. At the same time, there were popular uprisings in Asturias and Andalusia analogous to yesterday's rebellion in the Vendée. Localist and variably spontaneous, some of these risings were incited; others were led by traditional clerics, notables, and officers who cursed the French and their collaborators as unbelievers, Freemasons, and demons, and Napoleon as Antichrist. In every respect the forces of the old order, both well-born and popular, were vastly stronger than the forces for change: journalists, lawyers, and intellectuals without much of a social base, their fortunes rising and falling with those of the enemy armies. Indeed, the strife surrounding the French presence was entangled in an incipient civil war with vast regional and local variations. But by and large the struggles in Spain, even more than those in France from 1789 to 1795, were fueled by unexceptional strains between city and country, cosmopolitanism and provincialism, enlightenment and obscurantism, tolerance and zealotry.

From mid-1808 through early 1814 the French forces were bogged down on the Iberian peninsula, fighting both regular armies and partisan bands.[82] On July 20, 1808, at Bailen, in northeastern Andalusia, General Dupont's army of fewer than 10,000 men was overpowered by General Castanos, whose force of fewer than 20,000 men was a loose mixture of trained soldiers and raw peasant recruits, many of them wielding not rifles but pitchforks. Not unlike the rout of General Marcé at the start of the internal war in the Vendée, this defeat was fortuitous, and for similar reasons.[83] Both times distant citified leaders disdained and underestimated the back-country enemy, with the result that they committed insufficient and ill-trained troops. The situation worsened in August when Wellington landed north of Lisbon and drove French troops out of Portugal as he advanced into Spain. Hereafter Napoleon had to battle the divisions of Spain's regular army, Wellington's expeditionary force of some 40,000 men, and countless bands of primitive rebels. Although totally uncoordinated, these three arrays of armed resistance pinned down large French forces—some 300,000—beyond the time they would be urgently needed elsewhere, particularly in the Russian campaign. This, then, was the bleeding "ulcer" which kept draining Napoleon's strength: in excess of 200,000 casualties over seven years.

Napoleon's style of warfare was not suited to battling irregulars, with the result that when engaging them in battle the French forces came to grief. Indeed, the guerrilla side of the war in Spain became characteristically brutal and savage. The line between soldier and civilian was blurred, and it was open season for terror and counter-terror, vengeance and re-vengeance, by both sides. The brutalization of war carried over to the sieges of Gerona, Saragossa, and Tarragona: especially after the French finally stormed them, these cities suffered cruel punishment. This intermittent conjunction of regular and irregular warfare is reflected in Goya's *Disasters of War*. Goya was emblematic of the dilemma in the several Spains. He was neither a supporter of Ferdinand VII nor a partisan of Napoleon and the *afrancesados*. Goya was at once a critically minded patriot for Aragon, his regional homeland, and an enemy of obscurantism, if not a champion of enlightenment. Not unlike Jacques Callot in his *Miseries and Calamities of War* during the Thirty Years War of the seventeenth century, Goya came face to face with the sheer horror of crusading warfare, both international and civil, which his mind's eye viewed as eclipsing the political reason of the opposing sides. In the terrifying etchings of the *Disasters of War* he transcends and universalizes the Peninsular War by showing that it brought out the beast in both man and soldier.[84] In any case, this conflict wrought enormous physical and mental suffering on both sides, and casualties ran into the hundreds of thousands.

Ultimately the fate of constitutional monarchy and liberalism in Spain was tied to the fate of Napoleon, which the multiple Spanish resistances and Wellington helped to seal only to a small extent. Keeping in mind the different starting points, it is hardly surprising that following Bonaparte's defeat and the withdrawal of the French armies the restoration in Spain should have become considerably more far-reaching than in France. Unmindful of his own collaborationist past, Ferdinand VII imperiously abrogated the Cortes of Cadiz and its constitution. Indeed, he all but reinstated absolutism. With the support of most of Spain's power elite, Ferdinand not only ordered the purge of liberals and *afrancesados* and the abrogation of all freedoms but reestablished the full rights of the landed oligarchy and the Church, including some of the latter's most benighted features.[85]

* * *

Napoleonic France was Europe's *Land der Mitte* of its time. In pursuit of its hegemonic designs on the Continent, Paris had to keep at bay both London and St. Petersburg or gain ascendancy over either the one or the other. By late December 1810 not only was England holding out and pressing its intervention in Spain, but Russia was becoming restless. Alexander I was chafing at the humiliation of the Treaty of Tilsit and at Napoleon's continuing meddling in Poland, now compounded by the latter's marriage to the Austrian emperor's daughter. But above all, increasingly concerned by the economic fallout of his unholy alliance with Bonaparte, the tsar bolted from the Continental System. Not about to tolerate this defiance of his strategic design, Napoleon set out to close the breach. Still in a position to divide and conquer, he prevailed on Frederick William III and Francis II not to unsheathe their swords as he moved to bully Alexander back into line. In case of war he was, as always, confident of a quick victory, which would also redound to his benefit at home, where the impasse in Spain was beginning to dampen some spirits.

At any rate, Napoleon readied the greatest military force ever assembled to face down Moscow. The French army had first expanded, by conscription, to 750,000 in 1794. Though falling short of the vaunted nation-in-arms, this army was unprecedented in both scale and social makeup. Napoleon was the heir of this army, whose organization, personnel, and strategy he recast to fit his intentions. After shrinking in size following the Year II, it rose from 400,000 under the Consulate to 500,000 in 1808, to reach to over one million in 1812. Satellites and conquered lands were forced not only to provide their share of this cannon fodder but also to bear a large part of the expense, since the Napoleonic armies, apart from living off the land, also levied war indemnities, maintenance costs, and taxes.[86]

Napoleon deployed 700,000 men for the assault on Russia, 350,000 of them in the front lines. There were soldiers of at least ten "nationalities" among the troops primed for battle. Opposite them was a Russian army of 175,000 men which Bonaparte disdained; he also made light of road, logistical, and weather conditions. The campaign was expected to take no more than a month when on June 22, 1812, the *Grande Armée*, without declaration of war, crashed into Russia. Its main force crossed the Niemen between Vilna and Minsk in the direction of Moscow. Smolensk was captured on August 18, several weeks later than anticipated. Casualties were heavy on both sides, with Napoleon losing 100,000 men to combat, disease, and desertion. He lost another 60,000 men before the battle of Borodino on September 7, in which each side sacrificed some 40,000 killed and wounded. A week after this bloodbath, the vanguard of the French army entered Moscow, parts of it, including the Kremlin, in flames. His overextended army facing decimation by starvation and exposure to freezing weather, on October 19, in the eleventh hour, Napoleon ordered a total withdrawal. During this inglorious retreat countless thousands of soldiers—fewer officers—were killed by enemy soldiers and Cossacks, and many more died from disease and exposure. The *Grande Armée* was reduced to 60,000 men by the time it retreated across the Berezina river in late November, and to 30,000, in late December, as it fell back over the Niemen, or a mere fraction of the legions which had crossed this river in June. Overall the Russian campaign cost the French side about 400,000 casualties and prisoners, the vast majority of whom must be counted as dead.

Not surprisingly, first Prussia and then Austria joined Russia in the pursuit of Napoleon. In May 1813 at Lützen, southeast of Leipzig, and Bautzen, on the Spree river, Bonaparte still managed to hold off the Prussian and Russian forces with heavy losses on all sides. Even so, the renascent coalition held. Napoleon sought to gain time for reinforcements to reach him, but in vain. The three-day battle of Leipzig, the most awesome and costly of the Napoleonic wars, was fought in mid-October. A combined force of 300,000 Russians, Prussians, and Austrians came together for this supreme clash of arms. By now Napoleon was reduced to fewer than 200,000 men, among whom in particular the foreign conscripts and volunteers began to hang back. For the first time he failed to hold the line, and his troops were torn to pieces and routed: barely a quarter of them managed to retreat west of the Elster river. Although the Allies had suffered about 50,000 casualties, they stayed on the heels of Napoleon, whose remnant of 60,000 men fell back across the Rhine. By early January the 250,000 troops of Field Marshal von Schwarzenberg and General von Blücher had crossed into France and forged ahead practically unopposed. On March 31, 1814, they entered Paris. In the meantime, Wellington had occupied Narbonne and Toulouse in southwestern France. With the "liberation" of Germany, Holland, and northern Italy, the grand empire and nation came to an inglorious end, along with the Continental System.

This vast revolutionary and Napoleonic reflux did not set off popular uprisings anywhere in Europe to either stem or quicken the tide. Except in Spain, the fighting was not attended by significant partisan warfare. The formidable and new-model French armies were defeated by the at best partially remodeled armies of the unchanged old regimes. Terrified by the plebeian irruptions during the high tide of the revolution in France, Alexander I, Frederick William III, and Francis II had no taste for a *levée en masse*. Nor had conditions ever been propitious for popular risings in support of the French armies, even in the event Napoleon had proclaimed the end of seignorialism. It is equally striking, however, that faced with the invading royal armies and the return of the Bourbons, there was no patriotic or neo-Jacobin irruption in support of the French armies during the terminal battle of France from early January through late March 1814.

* * *

Predictably, starting with the rout at Leipzig, the rising prospects of defeat fed pressures in France, particularly from within the new political class, for a timely negotiated peace and political re-formation. Besides, fiscal problems were breaking forth, civilian morale was flagging, and military desertions and draft evasions were on the increase. Indeed, there was no avoiding the political consequences of military defeat: Napoleon's glaring defeat was bound to spell his downfall along with that of the imperial regime. What was undetermined was the form of the successor regime, the course of the transition, and the role of the victorious Allies.

During the week following the fall of Paris, the Senate dethroned Napoleon before he abdicated on April 6. As part of their effort to facilitate or smooth the transition, the Allies granted him full sovereignty over the Island of Elba, to which he repaired with some one thousand soldiers sworn to him. Meanwhile, in Paris, under the watchful eye of enemy troops, an improvised provisional government assumed power, presided over by the protean yet steady Talleyrand. This government proposed to facilitate a "soft" Bourbon restoration acceptable to both the Allies and the composite elite of notables which had crystallized inside France since Thermidor. Clearly, the Bourbons were brought back not by reason of a royalist groundswell but because Viscount Robert Castlereagh, the British foreign secretary, and Talleyrand, the self-appointed chief mediator, considered them indispensable for a compromise settlement, in France and in the concert of Europe.

Louis XVIII may be said to have countenanced rather than espoused a measured restoration.[87] After nearly a quarter century of exile and surrounded by ultraroyalist émigrés, headed by the Comte d'Artois, this position was neither natural nor easy. In any case, touched by the constitutional monarchy he had observed firsthand in England since 1807, Louis XVIII was open to a "compromise between, on the one hand, the new society forged by the Revolution and the Empire and, on the other, the old society grounded in a feudal, monarchist, aristocratic, and religious past."[88]

Ten days after landing in Calais, on April 24 Louis XVIII stopped in Saint-Ouen to meet with emissaries from the Senate and *Corps Législatif*, the chief pillars of the provisional government. But rather than accept their constitutional proposal, which would have made him king by their leave, he insisted on defining his legitimacy and authority himself. In a solemn proclamation he claimed not only to be "King of France and Navarre by the Grace of God," but to have been "recalled by the love of our people for the throne of our fathers." Having called to mind his divine right and lineage, he promised to adopt a "liberal constitution." Meanwhile, "representative government" would be maintained in its present form, along with an "independent judiciary" to guarantee the full range of civil liberties and rights, including access to the civil and military service for all Frenchmen. Louis XVIII declared property to be "inviolable and sacred," and the sale of *biens nationaux* "irrevocable."[89] Judging by his words, and on the face of it, Louis XVIII, like Napoleon, proposed to preserve and enlarge vital elements of the revolutionary heritage.

Ironically, although this declaration of distinctly liberal-minded intentions stood in contrast to the illiberal rule in three of the four great powers, the Allies continued in their support for an orderly transition in Paris. They did so by framing a peace settlement that was neither vindictive nor punitive.[90] The Treaty of Paris, signed on May 30, 1814 well-nigh recognized France's borders of 1792, which included some of the territorial accessions and conquests of the Revolution's first hours, and most of overseas France was left intact as well. Besides, the victors spared the embryonic successor regime the shame of foreign occupation and financial reparation. Presently the Congress of Vienna began to act in this same conciliatory spirit, and France's readmission to the Concert of Europe happened almost overnight when Austria and England signed a treaty with post-Napoleonic France against Prussia and Russia. Evidently France's soft restoration at home and pragmatic reintegration abroad were closely linked.

On June 4 Louis XVIII made good on his Saint-Ouen declaration by presenting the holdover "legislative" chambers with a Charter which became France's fifth constitution since 1789.[91] In addition to embodying the promised rights and freedoms, with an eye to the new political and ruling class this Charter safeguarded all imperial ranks, honors, and pensions. But it also laid down two major, if partially incompatible, defining precepts. Although Article 5 of the Charter assured religious toleration, Article 6 defiantly restored Catholicism as France's state religion. Probably with the best of intentions, but also unrealistically, Article 11 prohibited "all investigations of opinions and votes expressed before the Restoration" and asked "both the courts and the citizenry" to heed this injunction.

As to the system of government, it was less liberal than its professed spirit. Though constitutional, the old-new monarchy of the Charter was not really parliamentary. His person sacred and inviolate, Louis XVIII repeated and refined his claim that the people had freely called him, "the brother of the last King," to assume the throne of France. The king had the power to sanction, promulgate, and emend the laws. As regards the bicameral assembly, he and he alone appointed the members of the upper house of peers, whose tenure was hereditary and whose membership had no upper limit. The members of the chamber of deputies were to be elected by a narrow property-based franchise entitling fewer than 100,000 Frenchmen to vote; the property qualification for candidates for the lower house was three times higher than for the voters, restricting the pool to about 15,000. Further, the king's ministers were responsible to him, not to the house, which he could dissolve. Ultimately Louis XVIII, not unlike Napoleon, embraced the principle or pretense of parliamentary government, *not* its essence.

Even so, from the very outset the ultraroyalists, the only effective opposition of the time, fiercely criticized him for steering a treacherous middle course. Determined to excise the revolutionary legacy and purge the state bureaucracy, and with hardened and avenging émigrés setting the tone, they were supported by large sectors of the nobility and church. These diehards were not about to be appeased by symbolic gestures attuned to their sensibility, such as the solemn commemoration, on January 21, 1815, of the death of Louis XVI in the form of a stately reburial of his and Marie-Antoinette's remains in the royal sepulcher at Saint-Denis, "with the bells of all the churches throughout the land ringing the hour of national expiation and repentance."[92] Slighting the spirit of Article 11 of the Charter, this high celebration was to expunge the memory of the dramatic reburial of Voltaire's remains in the Pantheon in 1791.

✳ ✳ ✳

Within less than a year of the Bourbons' return, during his renewed rule of the Hundred Days, Napoleon wrecked what was a temperate if contested restoration. The ex-emperor and his armed retinue sailed from Elba on seven ships, to land near Cannes on March 1, 1815. Rather than meeting with resistance, in not a few places Napoleon actually was cheered on his march to Paris, where he arrived on March 20. In addition to the popular enthusiasm, especially among the lower classes of certain cities, there was the acclaim of part of the military, including twelve of France's twenty imperial marshals.

While Napoleon was again lionized, Louis XVIII was virtually abandoned. During the night of March 19–20 he stole away from Paris, and eventually, at the end of the month, settled in Ghent for his second exile. By then he had delegated the Comte d'Artois and his two sons—the Duc de Berry and the Duc d'Angoulême—to go to the Midi where, as in the west, King and Church were in disproportionately high favor. Although Angoulême managed to raise several regiments to fight local Bonapartist forces, the entire enterprise instantly misfired. In his predicament, with the moderate restoration shattered, Louis XVIII viewed his ultras with indulgence mixed with trepidation.

As was to be expected, the Allied statesmen gathered at the Congress of Vienna were dumbfounded, by the apparent recrudescence of pro-Bonapartism in France as much as by Napoleon's actions.[93] They momentarily suspended their rivalries to declare Napoleon a European outlaw and order their generals to prepare to reduce him once and for all. Each of the great continental powers pledged 150,000 men, and England agreed to finance much of the combined operations.

On his arrival in the capital to reclaim power, Bonaparte faced a problem similar to Louis XVIII's in 1814. He had to decide upon his political allies and compromises. Taking up where he had left off, Napoleon sought to chart a middle course between two extremes: the royalists whom he loathed and feared; and the neo-Jacobins whom he scorned and distrusted. Actually, he lacked a commanding public reason for this, his ultimate wager, also because the imperial notables of office and wealth were loath to tempt Providence. Still, and as usual, Napoleon had no difficulty finding respectable and obeisant paladins to provide him with an uplifting purpose. Lazare Carnot accepted to serve as interior minister and Benjamin Constant as member of the Conseil d'Etat. The mere presence of Carnot, the "architect of the victory" of 1793–94, in Napoleon's inner council spoke volumes. Driven by a febrile Sieyès-like ambition, Constant supervised the drafting of a constitutional warrant to justify defying not just France but Europe. In any case, by this time Carnot and Constant were advocates of a moderate constitutional settlement. They gave their tacit blessing even though they and their soul mates understood that Napoleon redivivus was a most unlikely agent to this end. In particular, they must have realized that in his logic, the drive for the preservation of the core ideas and interests of 1789 at home was contingent on the resumption of deadly and endless war abroad.

Benjamin Constant and other "liberals" were prepared to blink at Napoleon's quest for European hegemony and military glory, the source of his erstwhile legitimacy, in exchange for his dubious promise to uphold the founding principles of 1789 and the essentials of parliamentary government. In effect the "Additional Act to the Constitutions of the Empire" amounted to little more than a somewhat liberalized version of the Bourbon Charter: the Emperor replaced the King as the principal fount of power, leaving little scope for legislative control and initiative. The act was approved by a spurious plebescite, followed by the hurried election of a new lower chamber with a large majority of *soi-disant* liberals and nonroyalists.

Napoleon was not uninterested in this political remodeling. But he was first and foremost concerned with the ominous military situation. With a negotiated peace on Napoleon's hazy but ambitious terms precluded, a military showdown was inevitable. Whereas the Allies could, in fairly short order, put one million men in the field, Napoleon could muster at best 200,000, of whom some 30,000 would have to fend off royalists in the west and the south. Under the circumstances he needed to strike preemptively: he proposed to defeat the British and the Prussians, preferably one at a time, before taking on the Austrians and Russians. Napoleon hurriedly moved his core army, with seasoned veterans, into southern Belgium, to prevent Wellington and Blücher from joining their forces, for a total of nearly a quarter million men. Although he worsted Blücher at Ligny in central Belgium, the latter pulled around and managed the decisive juncture. On June 18 the combined English and Prussian armies defeated Napoleon at Waterloo, south of Brussels. The casualties ran to some 60,000 out of a total of 350,000 combatants, with 25,000 for the two Allies and 35,000 for the French.

Four days later, on June 22, Napoleon abdicated a second time. This time, to make doubly sure, the Allies banished him to Saint Helena, a British island in the south Atlantic, remote from Europe. Once more the form of the regime was at issue in a situation in which a provisional government, with difficult relations with the Allies as well as with the chambers, was called upon to rule in a vacuum of power. Having crossed into France on June 21, Wellington followed on the heels of the retreating French armies at the same time that Louis XVIII prepared to return to Paris. Again the Allies saw no alternative to Louis XVIII. Presently Wellington urged the French king to follow close upon his forces. Just as in late May 1814 Louis XVIII had stopped at Saint-Ouen to negotiate and proclaim the conditions of his return, so in late June 1815 he stopped at Cambrai to issue a policy declaration, countersigned by Talleyrand, who was about to head the king's new ministry and renew negotiations with the Allies. In fact, this declaration was grafted on to the Charter. But whereas the original Charter, in a spirit of unreal appeasement, had prescribed a massive amnesia and remission of past sins, the revised version vowed that the Chambers would subject all those responsible for the return of Napoleon "to the vengeance of the law."[94]

In any case, the Allied armies continued their advance into France. By July 3 Paris capitulated, and in no time over one million foreign soldiers occupied large parts of the country: the Russians the Île-de-France, including Paris, and Lorraine; the Prussians Normandy and Brittany; the Austrians Burgundy and the Languedoc; the English the Aisne and French Flanders. Meanwhile, on July 8, Louis XVIII returned to Paris "in the baggage of the Allies."[95] Talleyrand's provisional government was equally beholden to the victors.

✳ ✳ ✳

The diplomatic consequences of Waterloo were, of course, considerable. The second treaty of Paris, signed on November 20, was distinctly harsher than the first. France was now forced back from her borders of 1792 to those of 1789, the loss of the Saar to Prussia ending the dream of a Rhine frontier. This territorial cutback was compounded by a war indemnity of 700 million francs and a yearly payment of 150 million francs to cover the cost of 150,000 Allied soldiers occupying strategic zones of the northern and eastern departments for five years. In addition, France was to return some of the art treasures the *Grande Armée* had looted throughout Europe.

Though punitive, this peace was not Carthaginian. The four victors were still and always eager to reintegrate a chastened and normalized France into the concert of powers at the same time that, appalled by the widespread support for Napoleon during the Hundred Days, they signed the Quadruple Alliance committing themselves to military collaboration in the event Paris violated the terms of the peace treaty.

It was not, however, the Treaty of Paris and the Quadruple Alliance but the Holy Alliance of the Throne and the Altar which signaled the twilight of the revolutionary epoch. The former two were consistent with the diplomatic practices and rules dating from the Treaty of Westphalia which had ended the Thirty Years' War in 1648. The Holy Alliance, for its part, enlarged the mission of foreign policy and diplomacy, investing the reason of state with a religious or moral imperative prefigured in the Brunswick Manifesto. Proposed by Alexander I, and inwardly approved by all the crowned heads and the Pope, it caught and propagated the spirit of Europe's *retour à l'ordre*. It marked the spillover into the international system of the triumphant restoration and regeneration of domestic institutions and values throughout Europe and prefigured by the reinstatement of Ferdinand VII rather than Louis XVIII. Having thwarted and defeated the foreign and domestic challenge of the new order, the old regimes stood tall and strong, probably taller and stronger than before 1789. All of them experienced some degree of rebirth of monarchy, nobility, and church, with religion serving as the principal cement of civil and political society. This revival inspired their majesties to declare, "in the face of the whole world, their fixed resolution," in both domestic administration and relations among states, "to take for their sole guide the precepts of [their] Holy Religion; namely the precepts of justice, Christian charity, and peace, which . . . must guide all their steps, as being the only means of consolidating human institutions, and remedying their imperfections."[96] Although at first Metternich sympathized with Castlereagh's caustic quip that the Holy Alliance was a "piece of sublime mysticism and nonsense," with time he valued it as a useful premise for antiliberal or antirevolutionary intervention in the internal affairs of destabilized states.[97]

The political costs of the fatal Hundred Days were much greater than the diplomatic ones. Whereas the first restoration had been essentially conservative and nonconfrontational, the second was reactionary and fiercely contentious. It even precipitated a renewal of civil strife. Particularly the ultraroyalists benefited from Napoleon's brazen return. They underscored his support among senior state servants, military officers, ex-Jacobins like Carnot, and shameless political trimmers like Constant to vindicate their alarm about the perils of moderation and their call for a radical purge of the bureaucracy, army, and chamber. The legislative elections of August 14–22, 1815, at once reflected and encouraged this ultraroyalist resurgence. Of the 380 deputies in the new chamber, close to 90 percent were royalists, nearly 50 percent nobles, and 20 percent ex-émigrés. The mood of the vast majority of this house, swamped with political neophytes, was uncompromising and avenging. In the fall and early winter of 1815–16 the deputies voted four emergency laws to facilitate the implementation of their purifying and retributive agenda. They thereby legalized and encouraged the "second White Terror" which had broken out in the summer of 1815, immediately following Napoleon's second abdication, and which lasted through much of 1816.[98]

This nonofficial terror was centered in the Midi, where the Napoleonic relapse not only was quite marked but was also countered by the Duc d'Angoulême's regiments and the Chevaliers de la Foi, a secret royalist society. Especially in the power vacuum following the Hundred Days, royalist militias, bolstered by volunteers from the surrounding countryside, easily overwhelmed the National Guard constabularies in several cities, including Marseilles. These militias, in turn, connived at attacks against Bonapartists and their fellow travelers. They took a considerable human toll, with Marshal Brune and General Ramel among the most notorious victims, in Avignon and Toulouse, respectively. This was the context and atmosphere in which Nîmes once again suffered the agony of religiously charged civil conflict.

We had occasion to examine the conflict between revolutionaries and counterrevolutionaries in Nîmes in the summer of 1790, its Furies fired by the deeply rooted enmity and distrust between Catholics and Protestants.[99] Back in the dawn of the Revolution, not unlike in its twilight, the *enragés* among the majority Catholics would not tolerate the emancipation of the local religious minority. From 1789 through the empire the Protestants of Nîmes seized the hour to put their segregation and persecution behind them. In short order, besides enjoying full religious freedom, they secured more than their share of influence and power, judging by their weight in the municipal council and National Guard, as well as in the state administration and judiciary.

This integration continued during the first restoration, which accepted the local Protestant leaders' professions of loyalty. But in Nîmes, as in so many places in the south, the return of Napoleon from Elba proved profoundly divisive. Alarmed by the rise of ultraroyalism, which was confirmed by the Duc d'Angoulême's regional inroads, Protestants struck in with the Hundred Days. Inevitably they became prime victims of the anti-Bonapartist and counterrevolutionary backlash during the second restoration. Unlike in 1790, the Protestants of Nîmes were without defense, having been expelled from the local regiment of the National Guard, with the result that royalist bands had the run of the city as they did of the entire department. In July and August 1815, some 100 civilians were killed in the department of the Gard, "most of them Protestants from Nîmes." In addition, these bands backed the vigilantes who "carried out citizen's justice" and participated in the plunder and destruction of Protestant homes, helped by the absence of a protective police force and the paralysis of the law courts. In the face of this violence, which was half spontaneous and half organized, and which was "abetted by the royalist authorities," an estimated 2,500 Protestants fled the city between July and October 1815.[100]

Clearly, in this White Terror, as in the original *bagarre de Nîmes*, zealous anti- and counterrevolutionaries instrumentalized anti-Protestantism for political ends. Both times local notables of the old order enlisted popular anti-Protestantism, leavened by the thirst for vengeance, in a drive to reclaim lost political, social, and cultural ground, including above all the undiminished hegemony of the Catholic Church and religion.

During the second restoration the unofficial White Terror from below coincided with an official White Terror from above. In line with the promise of the Cambrai declaration, and with an eye to the Allies, the chambers prepared to try and punish the Bonapartists of the last hour. As a first step they accepted a government proposal to court-martial some twenty promoters of Napoleon's return and to place nearly twice that number under police surveillance pending agreement on an appropriate venue. Meanwhile, what Marshal Brune was to the unofficial terror, Marshal Michel Ney was to the official terror: for having thrown his weight to Napoleon during the Hundred Days, the house of peers found Ney guilty of treason, for which he was shot on December 7, 1815.

Ney's execution was merely the most dramatic retributive punishment. Between mid-1815 and mid-1816, nationwide, ordinary courts condemned 5,000 to 6,000 persons for political offenses. In addition, under the chamber's emergency laws over 3,000 individuals were arrested and kept under surveillance, and special courts tried about 240 political cases, though the sentences were light. Over and above this legal repression, between 50,000 and 80,000 public servants were dismissed. This purge, which affected "a quarter to a third of those on the government payroll," struck nearly every branch and level of the state apparatus, "civil or military, local or national."[101] Unless added up with the first White Terror, the second White Terror, including the *épuration* of the civil service, cannot be compared with the great Red Terror, even if it was far from inconsequential.

＊ ＊ ＊

Louis XVIII was no more popular and respected after the Hundred Days than before. If he resumed his reign after the interregnum of his second exile it was because neither the Allies nor the political class could think of a credible alternative. Once again, Talleyrand was the chief intermediary in triangular negotiations between the Bourbons and the Allies, only this time the victors weighed even more heavily than the year before. Indeed, the king had to rule in the face of two impediments: the heavy and embarrassing intervention of the foreign powers, evinced by the military occupation and war indemnity; and the relentless censure by integral royalists who questioned his *bona fides*. Certainly, with the army and police still in disarray, he was at once hesitant and helpless to join issue with the ultras. It was not until September 1816, after their rage had crested, that, nervous about the Allies, Louis XVIII affirmed his ascendancy by dissolving the *chambre introuvable*. The removal of an intractable "parliamentary" majority was in the nature of a coup d'état, all the more so with the king's ministers brazenly manipulating the elections, as was becoming common practice.

In any event, in the new lower chamber the ultras were reduced to ninety out of 238 members. This did not mean that they were fatally weakened. A like-minded and coherent political family, also in the house of peers, they were tied to the Comte d'Artois, who was the lodestar for all hardened royalists nationwide.[102] By comparison, the new majority of moderate royalists, sworn to the Charter, lacked cohesion: half of them accepted the existing constitutional balance, with the king, backed by the clergy, firmly in charge; the other half looked to protect and expand the scope of individual freedoms. François Guizot and Pierre Paul Royer-Collart, respectively of Protestant and Jansenite background, were emblematic of this variety of moderate royalism. On the far left of the lower house there was a handful of liberals who were wary of the embers of the *ancien régime* and championed the principles of 1789. After another change of mind, Benjamin Constant, also of Protestant background, stood out among them.

The king had "found" a relatively moderate chamber with which his first ministers, the Duc de Richelieu and the Duc Decazes, were expected to consolidate a sober restoration. Between 1816 and 1820 the chamber voted to slightly liberalize the electoral and press laws. It also adopted a law establishing a new system of recruitment and promotion for France's army, in which the soldiers of yesterday's grand campaigns would have pride of place. Guizot drafted the speech in which Marshal Laurent Gouvion-Saint-Cyr, the minister of war, justified this law, which was fiercely contested. With this speech the restoration government made its own the glories of the soldiers and officers of the revolutionary and imperial armies. Their "ardor, courage, and heroism" were woven into a seamless national destiny by virtue of their never having "doubted that they were sacrificing their lives for the honor of France," and for which "all of Europe admired them."[103]

Louis XVIII and his ministers also sought to reconcile the nation by reclaiming its untrammeled sovereignty, thereby bolstering the regime's legitimacy. Especially Richelieu labored to remove the stigma of the continuing Allied intervention. By contracting loans with private foreign banks, he managed to pay off the war indemnity well in advance, with the result that the military occupation ended in 1818, two years ahead of schedule. Simultaneously, at the Congress of Aachen, France was readmitted to the concert of great powers.

There was, however, no appeasing the ultras. Smarting from their defeat at the polls, they spurned anything less than a wholesale excoriation of the Revolution and a pervasive restoration of the *ancien régime*. Their fortunes were at a standstill but far from hopeless when, on February 13, 1820, Louis Pierre Louvel, a lone Bonapartist faithful, assassinated the Comte d'Artois's younger son, the Duc de Berry, who was third in the line of succession. The ultraroyalists seized on this assassination, much as they had seized on the Hundred Days, to denounce the king's ministers for being soft on political enemies. In their telling, Louvel was part of a vast liberal conspiracy against the monarchy whose ideas and intentions were being freely diffused by the lower chamber and the press. Intimidated by this rising furor, which brought down Decazes, the chamber voted to reinforce the executive, tighten censorship, and revise the electoral laws to favor true royalists over constitutional monarchists and liberals. Thanks to a radically narrowed franchise and the usual government manipulation, the elections of November 1820 spelled the rebirth of the *chambre introuvable*. Starting in December 1821, when Joseph de Villèle, a confirmed but astute ultraroyalist, replaced Richelieu as the king's first minister, the second restoration kept moving to the right, as if to anticipate and prepare the accession of the Comte d'Artois to the throne.

✳ ✳ ✳

The European context was not without influence on the strife between moderate monarchists and ultraroyalists inside France. All things considered, Castlereagh and Wellington were distinctly more supportive of the former than Francis II, Frederick William III, and Alexander I. Indeed, as intimated before, despite their conflicting national interests, after 1815 the three emperors gradually warmed to the idea of forging the Holy Alliance of Throne and Altar into an instrument of statecraft. During the postrevolutionary years they took the slightest liberalizing flicker at home and abroad as evidence of continuing life in the embers of the Great Revolution. Presently they construed any pressure or revolt for a quasi-parliamentary monarchy as a harbinger of more radical things to come. Nervous about the dangerous example France continued to set with Louis XVIII's measured restoration—especially between 1816 and 1820—the crowned heads of the Continent's three major unreconstructed *anciens régimes* warmed to the critique of his ultraroyalist adversaries.

In any case, in the fall of 1819, in Carlsbad, under Metternich's guidance, the delegates of several of "Germany's" princely states decided to curb anti-absolutist agitation with censorship of the press as well as with police surveillance of student fraternities, university curricula, and political dissidents. The following spring, at Laibach, with Britain hanging back, the powers of the Holy Alliance authorized Austria to send military forces to bring under control political unrest in Naples and Turin. By 1822, at the Congress of Verona, France was asked to prepare to intervene in Spain, where following Napoleon's ouster the integralist restoration of Ferdinand VII, noted above, called forth a political backlash. When an unholy alliance of disgruntled generals and constitutionalists forced him to restore the Cortes, encouraged by the nobility and clergy Ferdinand looked to the Holy Alliance for help to stem the tide.

Meanwhile the issue of French intervention became caught up in the struggle over the future orientation of the restoration regime in Paris. At this juncture the ultras were the hawks: they advocated a timely military operation to save Ferdinand VII as Louis XVI could and should have been saved in 1792. Such a move would, in addition, rally the army behind the fleur-de-lis, give the government an explicitly counterrevolutionary coloration, and commit France to the precepts of the Holy Alliance. Presently Villèle, pressed by Chateaubriand, the unabashedly combative and ambitious foreign minister, hearkened to the ultras. In April 1823, under the command of the Duc d'Angoulême, an army of over 100,000 men marched into Spain. Unlike in the days of Napoleon, this intervention encountered little popular resistance and, with the Spanish forces no match for the French, it was terminated, successfully, within six months. In Madrid Ferdinand resumed his absolutist and clerical reign, distinguished by purges and reprisals. In Paris the military success and political outcome in Spain benefited and heartened the ultras in their drive against the moderates. Villèle seized the moment to further increase the ultras' hold on the upper house and to call elections for early 1824. Probably even without the government's brazen perversion of the election, the "left," which had fiercely opposed the intervention in Spain, would have been routed. A few months before his death Louis XVIII, whose health was failing, faced a chamber that was at least as *introuvable* as the one of August 1815, and his ministers were relying increasingly on the Comte d'Artois, who, like Ferdinand VII, had "learned nothing and forgotten nothing." Both embodied the spirit of the Holy Alliance, which was permeated with religion even if Metternich swore more by the axioms of Machiavelli than the teachings of the Gospel.

* * *

There is no explaining the tenacity and irresistible rise of ultraroyalism, focused by the Comte d'Artois, without close attention to the life and role of church and religion.[104] Between 1789 and 1815 the Catholic Church had suffered more than any other institution. Even

Napoleon's concordat with Pius VII had at best closed minor wounds. To be sure, during this quarter century the Church had lost more power than influence, since mentalities and creeds weather even the worst of times. In fact, the losing battle against the Civil Constitution of the Clergy and the clerical oath had fired the faith of not a few believers, many of whom went underground, encouraged by their priests. Pius VI's anathema of the Revolution had a lasting impact and most certainly carried over to the Empire.

After 1814 Church and Vatican quite naturally portrayed the defeat of the Jacobins and Napoleon as a divine punishment and a triumph for the Scriptures over the Enlightenment. The clergy, high and low, were not about to be either charitable or forgiving. Rather, they were self-righteous, irate, and vengeful, and they were determined to resume and intensify the battle against the philosophical, political, and cultural ideas of 1789. Upon his return to Rome in 1814, true to form and swept along by ultramontanism, Pius VII reestablished the Jesuit Order and reinstated the Index. In the ecclesiastical realm, unlike in the political, there was no struggle between advocates of a moderate and integral restoration. The twilight of the revolutionary epoch faded into the dawn of a religious reaction seeking a stark return to the status quo ante. Neither pope nor cardinal could be expected to do battle for religious equality and toleration.

Needless to say, the French clergy could not hope to reclaim their privileges, positions, and properties by themselves. As a matter of course they enlisted the help of the king and the clerical nobility in their effort to recover church lands as well as to regain control of education and the parish register. In turn, king and noble eagerly "used the influence of the Church [and of religion] to impose their political regime," convinced that these were an essential bulwark of the state.[105] The common fortunes and interests of altar and throne made them natural partners, as they had been in good times past.

Although Louis XVIII and the moderates prized this mutuality, at first they drew, above all, on the Church's symbolic capital to further the restoration. By contrast, the ultras were altogether more far-ranging in their instrumentalization of the symbiosis of throne and altar. Partly under their pressure, primary education was placed under clerical control in early 1821. The pace of clericalization quickened with Villèle's premiership. On August 24, 1824, immediately before the death of Louis XVIII, he set up a Ministry of Public Instruction and Religious Worship (*Cultes*), headed by Monseigneur Comte de Denis Frayssinous, with close ties to the Comte d'Artois. During the two years preceding this appointment, as *grand maître* of the university system, Frayssinous had pursued a clerical policy involving a selective purge of the faculty, the suspension of courses, and the closing of certain schools. In his new office he had the power and funds to press the clerical cause at all levels of education as well as in the revival of the Church.

When Louis XVIII died on September 16, 1824, the Comte d'Artois succeeded to the throne as Charles X. During his long exile he had made no secret of his religious-mindedness, which bolstered his predisposition to put church and religion at the center of his counterrevolutionary vision and formula. After their return he and the exiles who had rallied around him had severe reservations about the Charter for being both too "liberal" and, above all, too secular and profane. As leader of the ultraroyalist opposition he had pressured the king and his ministers not only to reinforce the royal prerogative over the legislature but to expand the political and social role of the Church.

Once at the helm of the state, Charles X hastened to implement his agenda. Besides seeing through to final passage a law contrary to the Charter, to indemnify especially ex-émigrés for confiscated properties, he introduced a highly controversial bill to punish sacrilegious acts committed willfully and in public. The bill, which was slightly softened before adoption, prescribed forced labor for the theft of sacred objects, the death sentence for the theft of receptacles containing hosts, and the amputation of a hand followed by public execution for profanatory actions. This law, making the state the guardian of the official religion, was of course more symbolic than practical in its effect. As such, it paralleled another act with which the counterrevolutionary king opened his reign: his *sacre*, performed on May 29, 1825, at Rheims.

Earlier we discussed the *sacre* of Louis XVI, exactly fifty years before, which the Comte d'Artois had, of course, witnessed.[106] The youngest brother of the martyr king proposed to reenact exactly the same ceremony except for three changes, each of them reflecting the impossibility, even for him, of blotting out the last quarter century.[107] First, for fear of gratuitously provoking his irreconcilable foes, Charles X dropped a clause of the royal oath which even in 1775 had been super-annuated: "to extirpate heresy and combat infidels." Second, although he had never relented in his criticism of the Charter, Charles X decided to swear to uphold it. Third, four marshals of the army only too eagerly took the place of the grand peers near the climax of the ceremony: Moncey, Soult, Mortier, and Jourdan carried the crown, the sword of Charlemagne, the scepter, and the *main de justice*. All four had served Napoleon—with time in Spain—and some of them had been at his coronation in 1804. Save for these modulations, the time-honored crowning ritual was unchanged, complete with prostration and unction, followed the next day by Charles X going to Saint-Marcoul to attest to God's healing powers by ministering to the swellings of wretches suffering from scrofula. Over and above the generally affirmative intent of past coronations, this one had a polemical purpose as well. The dramatization of the reforging of the bond between throne and altar was intended to further the exorcism of the demons and the reparation of the injuries of the Revolution, including the Empire. Inevitably the opposition of moderate constitutionalists and liberals saw the coronation for what it was: metaphor and way station for the forced march back to the *ancien régime*. The hereditary and divine monarchy bolstered by the political Catholicism of the Church was stealing a march upon what there was of semi-parliamentary government.

✳ ✳ ✳

It is, of course, easier to fix a clear-cut and meaningful beginning than a pregnant end of a revolutionary epoch. The French Revolution began sometime between the fall of the Bastille on July 14, 1789, and April 20, 1792, the critical turning point when it "sallied forth beyond Paris and France into the Continent which opposed it and to which it needed to impart itself if it was not to be destroyed inside France as well." As "decisive historical hinges 1792 and 1917 were of a kind, except with signs pointing in opposite directions": whereas "three years of European war preceded the revolution within Russia," with the French Revolution "three years of revolution at home preceded the quarter-century war with Europe." Accordingly, as of 1792 "the French Revolution became more and more a European event," whereas after 1917 the Russian Revolution became increasingly "a

Russian affair," especially judging by developments from 1918 through the early 1930s.[108]

The French Revolution roamed all over Europe, "planting the nation-state, establishing the supremacy of the city over the country, and liberating the bourgeoisie from the nobility and clergy." It proceeded both peacefully and by war, with Napoleon "the military pioneer." Bonaparte pulled back from Russia in 1812 less because he was militarily defeated than because "the actions and ideas of 1789" could not penetrate and take root there as they had in "Westphalia, Venice, or Poland." Subjugated by "neither Church nor nobility," the ruling and governing classes of this Russia had "altogether different worries" than their counterparts in France. By virtue of this unreceptive "vacuum," the Russian campaign was without reason, and there is nothing more "unsettling than the discovery that a heroic action is politically senseless."[109]

From the turn of the century through 1812 Napoleon had ascendancy over most of western and central Europe, making his strongest mark on the lands of western "Germany," northern "Italy," and the Low Countries. As noted, the Treaty of Tilsit confirmed that imperial France remained the *Land der Mitte*, without the capability to gain a hold upon either Russia or England, let alone upon both. Accordingly, when Napoleon "consummated the Terror by substituting permanent war for permanent revolution," depending on the location and time of the French occupation the impact of his rule varied enormously, with some places not touched at all. He saw to the consolidation of the Revolution in France at the same time that he exported it to the heartland of his empire. The two processes were closely linked, though with time perpetual and successful war abroad became the lifeblood of the imperial regime. Whereas the revolutionary wars revolutionized the Revolution, the Napoleonic Wars—the externalized terror—provided the *union sacrée*, strong government, and necessary time for the consolidation of some of the Revolution's principal reforms, and perhaps ideas as well. In turn, Napoleon's defeat and the attendant territorial retrocessions had the opposite effect, culminating in the third restoration, or the ascendance of the ultraroyalists, confirmed with the *sacre* of Charles X.

Strangely enough, the crowned sovereigns and elites of the *anciens régimes* perceived Napoleon in much the same terms in his time as

Marx and Engels did in the 1840s. Blind to his antiparliamentarism and his constant repugnance for not only kings—notably Bourbons—and aristocrats but also Jacobins, like Germaine de Staël they saw Bonaparte as "Robespierre on horseback," riding full tilt against monarchy, feudalism, and religion. This viewpoint informed the debates and decisions of the Vienna Peace Congress, which aimed to guard Europe against a renewal of a military and revolutionary threat from Paris until Metternich considered France sufficiently conservative and reliable to help carry out the emergent policing mission of the Holy Alliance.

If in crucial respects Europe's old regime persisted until 1914—in some countries until 1945—it did so in large part because of its remarkable recovery from the stormy epoch of the French Revolution. Overall the time-honored ruling and governing classes, including the dynasts and prelates, effectuated a restoration in which the balance between continuity and reversion, on the one hand, and discontinuity and reform, on the other, decisively favored the former. Certainly until 1830, with the lower orders of city and country quiescent, the restoration era was one of political reaction, with the principle and practice of hereditary and sacred kingship rehabilitated. This revival was not incompatible with the rationalization—modernization—of the state apparatus, including the armed forces, and the administration of justice, Napoleon's principal legacy. Political reaction, which had its social side in the reinforcement of the old elites, went hand in hand with a religious revival and the restrengthening of the official churches, which worked against toleration and emancipation. Culturally and intellectually, the backlash against the Enlightenment was in full force. Burke triumphed over Voltaire.

✳ ✳ ✳

If the French Revolution, including the Napoleonic wars, was a tragedy, so was the Restoration. It spoke volumes about the resistances to revolution, including their counterrevolutionary variety, all too often estimated and represented as inconsequential, impolitic, and innocent. In assessing the costs of revolution, there is no ignoring or minimizing these resistances abroad and at home, for without them there would have been neither foreign nor civil war, neither red nor white terror. Needless to say, in 1789–90 the governing and ruling classes of the *anciens régimes* could not be expected to be indifferent to either the humbling of king and monarchy or the proclamation of the Rights of Man and the Civil Constitution of the Clergy. Considering the enormous power of the elites—in France and outside—it is nothing short of astonishing that the challenge of the revolutionaries was not snuffed out straightway. With time both sides gathered strength and resolve, escalating and hardening the showdown between them.

The nature and scale of the casualties and horrors of the Great Terror and the Vendée, entwined with the war with the European powers, are essentially indisputable, even if their mainsprings and reasons remain highly controversial.[110] As for the casualties and miseries of the revolutionary and Napoleonic wars, they elicit little interest and even less debate. While the intelligentsia, including historians, are horrified and perplexed that death and destruction should be the wages of civil conflict, they consider these altogether normal as the wages of foreign war. The murderous dragonnades of the Vendée are a black page in the history of France, but not the deadly battles of the *Grande Armée*, which are grandiosely, not to say shamelessly, exalted, mythologized, and memorialized. And yet both were an integral part of the struggle for the survival of the Revolution. To repeat, the Napoleonic rule, including its wars, provided extra time as well as the political, administrative, and legal climate and conditions for the crystallization of several revolutionary measures that even Charles X could not deracinate, most notably the radical land settlement inaugurated in August 1789. But the blood-tax of the wars of the *Grand Empire* was many times that of the Great Terror and the Vendée. Indeed, "the bloody scenes of the Terror were episodes of relatively small import compared to the enormous hecatombs of the wars." To boot, "the resounding triumphs of the revolutionary imperial armies precluded all adverse criticisms."[111]

Indeed, the revolutionary and Napoleonic wars took several million French and other European lives. Even if the nation-in-arms was largely a myth, these wars saw the dawn of the mass army, engaging more men in set battles than ever before. Probably as many soldiers died from hunger, disease, and medical neglect as from outright battle injuries, making the warfare of the time doubly cruel, also for the prisoners of war. It is gratuitous to suggest that compared to the warfare of the twentieth century it was child's play because weapons were less lethal, battles were shorter, civilians were rarely directly targeted, and wrack and ruin were the exception.

Certainly measured against the armed conflicts of the eighteenth century the toll was very high.[112] French losses ran to about one million from 1792 to 1802, with perhaps another million by 1814, or a total of some two million out of a population of less than thirty million. To be sure, these casualties were spread over nearly a quarter of a century. Still, the bloodletting was considerable, especially in certain age groups. Besides, many of the battles were singularly deadly. In June 1800, at Marengo, the French and Austrians lost about 20 percent of their respective effectives. Of course, the slaughter rose dramatically during and following the Russian campaign. In September 1812, at Borodino, outside Moscow, the French suffered between 30,000 and 50,000 casualties, and so did the Russians. Napoleon sacrificed at least another 100,000 men during his impossible retreat. Altogether the Russian campaign cost the French armies between 400,000 and 500,000. A year following Bonaparte's defeat on the Moskva, some 300,000 Allied troops defeated about 170,000 French troops in the greatest and goriest battle of the epoch, near Leipzig, at the cost of over 100,000 casualties, nearly evenly divided between the belligerents. Estimating the "dead amongst the military alone . . . [on all sides at] nearly 3,000,000," and adding nearly "another 1,000,000 for civilian losses," the wars between 1792 and 1814 are likely to have claimed "little short of 4,000,000 dead."[113] This total does not include the relatively large number of non-combatants who were killed and died in the peninsular war in Spain which may be said to have been less of its own time than of the future.

Except for the cost in lives, the wars were relatively inexpensive for France, at any rate until far down the line, when the British counter-blockade began to tell. In the liberated, conquered, or occupied territories the French lived off the land, collected war indemnities, levied special taxes, and conscripted manpower. Most certainly this displacement of the economic and fiscal burdens of the bid for European hegemony combined with the psychic dividends of military glory facilitated the "consummation of the Terror by the substitution of permanent war for permanent revolution."

✻ ✻ ✻

NOTES

1. Jacques Godechot, *La grande nation*, 2 vols. (Paris: Aubier, 1956); and R. R. Palmer, *The Age of Democratic Revolution*, 2 vols. (Princeton: Princeton University Press, 1959/1964).

2. It is not to depreciate the recent and current historiography to point out the confining limits of its major paradigms. See Michael Wagner, *England und die französische Gegenrevolution, 1789–1802* (Munich: Oldenburg, 1994), pp. 2–4.

3. Hannah Arendt, *On Revolution* (New York: Viking, 1968), p. 7 and p. 9.

4. Mallet du Pan, *Considérations sur la nature de la révolution en France, et sur les causes qui en prolongent la durée* (London, 1793), ch. 4.

5. Joseph de Maistre, *Écrits sur la Révolution* (Paris: Presses Universitaires, 1989), p. 106.

6. See Werner Hahlweg, "Lenin und Clausewitz," in *Archiv für Kulturgeschichte* 36:1 (1954): pp. 30–59; and 36:3, pp. 357–89.

7. This is Marcel Reinhard's formulation, which informs both Godechot, *La grande nation*, and Palmer, *Democratic Revolution*. See Elisabeth Fehrenbach, "Die Ideologisierung des Krieges und die Radikalisierung der französischen Revolution," in Dieter Langewiesche, ed., *Revolution und Krieg: Zur Dynamik des historischen Wandels seit dem 18. Jahrhundert* (Paderborn: Ferdinand Schöningh, 1989), pp. 57–66.

8. Albert Mathiez, *La Révolution française*, 3 vols. (Paris: Denoël, 1985), vol. 3, p. 90.

9. Edgar Quinet, *La Révolution* (Paris: Belin, 1987), p. 71.

10. Alexis de Tocqueville, *"The European Revolution" and Correspondence with Gobineau* (Garden City, N.Y.: Doubleday, 1959), p. 146.

11. Pieter Geyl, *Napoleon: For and Against* (New Haven: Yale University Press, 1967), pp. 8–10.

12. Martyn Lyons, *Napoleon Bonaparte and the Legacy of the French Revolution* (New York: St. Martin's, 1994), pp. 296–97.

13. William Doyle, *The Oxford History of the French Revolution* (Oxford: Oxford University Press, 1989), pp. 395–96.

14. See Arno J. Mayer, *The Persistence of the Old Regime: Europe to the Great War* (New York: Pantheon, 1981), passim.

15. Norman Hampson, *The First European Revolution, 1776–1815* (London: Thames and Hudson, 1970), p. 136.

16. Maurice Agulhon, *Coup d'état et république* (Paris: Presses de Sciences Po, 1997), pp. 23–35.

17. Engels, "The State of Germany," in Karl Marx and Friedrich Engels, *Collected Works*, vol. 6 (London: Lawrence and Wishart, 1976), pp. 19–21 (italics in text).

18. Marx and Engels, "The Holy Family," in *Collected Works*, vol. 4 (London: Lawrence and Wishart, 1975), p. 123 (italics in text). By "ending the permanent revolution" at the price of "transforming it into permanent war," Napoleon substituted "conquest . . . and the cult of the state for virtue." François Furet, *Marx et la Révolution française* (Paris: Flammarion, 1986), p. 35.

19. Cited by Charles J. Esdaile, *The Wars of Napoleon* (London: Longman, 1995), p. 10.

20. Lyons, *Napoleon Bonaparte*, p. 299.

21. Jules Michelet, *Histoire de la Révolution française*, 2 vols. (Paris: Laffont, 1979), vol. 1, p. 660.

22. Roederer's speech of December 18, 1791, is cited by Anne Sa'adah, *The Shaping of Liberal Politics in Revolutionary France: A Comparative Perspective* (Princeton: Princeton University Press, 1990), pp. 139–40.

23. Brissot's speeches of December 20 and 30, 1791 and January 17, 1792, cited by Georges Michon, *Robespierre et la guerre révolutionnaire, 1791–1792* (Paris: Marcel Rivière, 1937), pp. 46–48, 65.

24. For Robespierre's speeches on the issue of war and peace of December 9, 11, 12, and 18, 1791 and January 2 and 11, as well as February 10, 1792, see *Oeuvres de Maximilien Robespierre*, vol. 8 (Paris: Presses Universitaires, 1953), pp. 35–116 and 157–92.

25. Palmer, *Democratic Revolution*, vol. 2, p. 35.

26. Mathiez, *Révolution*, vol. 2, pp. 80–81.

27. T. C. W. Blanning, *The Origins of the French Revolutionary Wars* (London: Longman, 1986), esp. pp. 208–9.

28. For the coming of war between revolutionary France and the European powers, see Albert Sorel, *L'Europe et la Révolution française*, vol. 2 (Paris, 1885); Kyung-Won Kim, *Revolution and International System* (New York: New York University Press, 1970); T. C. W. Blanning, *The French Revolutionary Wars, 1787–1802* (London: Arnold, 1996); Frank Attar, *La Révolution française déclare la guerre à l'Europe: L'embrasement de l'Europe à la fin du XVIII siècle* (Paris: Editions Complexe, 1992). See also Stephen Walt, *Revolution and War* (Ithaca: Cornell University Press, 1996), pp. 46–89; and David Armstrong, *Revolution and World Order: The Revolutionary State in International Society* (Oxford: Clarendon, 1993), esp. pp. 79–84.

29. Michelet, *Histoire*, vol. 1, p. 607.

30. For the full text of this letter, written in Luxembourg, and discussed in this paragraph and the next, see Eugène Bimbenet, *Fuite de Louis XVI à Varennes*, vol. 1 (Paris, 1868), pp. 251–55.

31. Simon Schama, *Citizens: A Chronicle of the French Revolution* (New York: Knopf, 1989), p. 551.

32. The text of the Pillnitz Declaration is cited in John Hall Stewart, ed., *A Documentary Survey of the French Revolution* (New York: Macmillan, 1951), pp. 223–24.

33. See Sorel, *L'Europe*, pp. 369–71; and H. A. Barton, "The Origins of the Brunswick Manifesto," in *French Historical Studies* 5:2 (Fall 1967): pp. 146–69.

34. See Mayer, *Political Origins of the New Diplomacy, 1917–1918* (New Haven: Yale University Press, 1959), passim.

35. See Timothy Tackett, *Becoming a Revolutionary: The Deputies of the French National Assembly and the Emergence of a Revolutionary Culture, 1789–1790* (Princeton: Princeton University Press, 1996), esp. ch. 3.

36. Michelet, *Histoire*, vol. 1, p. 598.

37. Sorel, *L'Europe*, pp. 509–10.

38. The full text of the Brunswick Manifesto is cited in Stewart, ed., *Survey*, pp. 307–11; and in Jean-Paul Bertaud, *Les amis du roi: Journeaux et journalistes royalistes en France de 1789 à 1792* (Paris: Perrin, 1984), pp. 240–43.

39. Quinet, *La Révolution*, p. 329.

40. See Bertaud, *Les amis*, pp. 244–47.

41. Sorel, *L'Europe*, p. 510.

42. Ibid., pp. 512–13.

43. Bertaud, *Les amis*, p. 245.

44. Sorel, *L'Europe*, p. 515.

45. See chapter 7 above.

46. The text of the decree of November 19, 1792, is cited in Stewart, ed., *Survey*, p. 381.

47. The text of the decree of December 15, 1792, is cited in ibid., pp. 381–84.

48. Michelet, *Histoire*, vol. 2, p. 188 and p. 190.

49. Ibid., vol. 2, p. 191; and Michon, *Robespierre*, pp. 128–30.

50. Cited in Michon, *Robespierre*, pp. 130–32.

51. Concern with the nexus of war, revolution, and counterrevolution is central to the introductory chapter, titled "War and Revolution," of Arendt, *On Revolution*, esp. pp. 8–9.

52. See Kim, *Revolution*, pp. 88–89.

53. Quinet, *La Révolution*, pp. 348–49.

54. Ibid., p. 349.

55. Michelet, *Histoire*, vol. 2, pp. 150–51.

56. Ibid., pp. 378–79.

57. D.M.G. Sutherland, *France, 1789–1815: Revolution and Counterrevolution* (Oxford: Oxford University Press, 1986), p. 302 and p. 305.

58. Ibid., p. 306; and Doyle, *Oxford History*, pp. 334–35.

59. Palmer, *Democratic Revolution*, vol. 2, p. 257.

60. Doyle, *Oxford History*, p. 336.

61. Quinet, *La Révolution*, p. 689.

62. Hampson, *European Revolution*, p. 119.

63. Quinet, *La Révolution*, pp. 688–89.

64. Palmer, *Democratic Revolution*, vol. 2, pp. 259–60.

65. Tocqueville, *"The European Revolution,"* pp. 119–20.

66. François Furet, *La Révolution française: De Turgot à Napoléon* (Paris: Hachette, 1988), p. 207.

67. Quinet, *La Révolution*, p. 700 and pp. 715–17.

68. Ibid., p. 674.

69. Ibid., pp. 729–30.

70. Cited by René Rémond, *Les droites en France*, 4th ed. (Paris: Aubier, 1982), p. 107.

71. Ibid., pp. 106–8.

72. Esdaile, *Wars*, pp. 12–14.

73. See Max Weber, "The Sociology of Charismatic Authority," in H. H. Gerth and C. Wright Mills, eds., *From Max Weber: Essays in Sociology* (New York: Oxford University Press, 1946), pp. 245–52, esp. p. 249.

74. Quinet, *La Révolution*, p. 734.

75. This paragraph and the next follow Lyons, *Napoleon Bonaparte*, pp. 78–92.

76. Quinet, *La Révolution*, pp. 722–26.

77. Cited in Louis Bergeron, *France under Napoleon* (Princeton: Princeton University Press, 1981), p. 21.

78. Cited by Sutherland, *France*, pp. 352–53.

79. Lyons, *Napoleon Bonaparte*, p. 196.

80. Esdaile, *Wars*, p. 22.

81. For developments in Spain, or rather in "the Spains," see Raymond Carr, *Spain, 1808–1939* (Oxford: Clarendon, 1966), chs. 2 and 3; Gabriel H. Lovett, *Napoleon and the Birth of Modern Spain*, 2 vols. (New York: New York University Press, 1965), esp. vol. 2; Jan Read, *War in the Peninsula* (London: Faber and Faber, 1977); David Gates, *The Spanish Ulcer: A History of the Peninsular War* (New York: Norton, 1986); Lyons, *Napoleon Bonaparte*, pp. 220–25; Esdaile, *Wars*, pp. 218–31.

82. John Lawrence Tone, *The Fatal Knot: The Guerrilla War in Navarre and the Defeat of Napoleon in Spain* (Chapel Hill: University of North Carolina Press, 1994); and Claude Morange et al., *La Révolution française: Les conséquences et les réactions du "public" en Espagne entre 1808 et 1814* (Annales Littéraires de l'Université de Besançon [no. 388], 1989).

83. See chapter 9 above.

84. Jean-François Chabrun, *Goya* (London: Thames and Hudson, 1965); Gwynn A. Williams, *Goya and the Impossible Revolution* (London: Penguin, 1976); James A. Tomlinson, *Goya in the Twilight of Enlightenment* (New Haven: Yale University Press, 1992); Hilliard T. Goldfarb and Rava Wolf, *Fatal Consequences: Callot, Goya, and the Horrors of War* (Hanover, N.H.: Hand Museum, Dartmouth, 1990).

85. Carr, *Spain*, pp. 115–29.

86. See Esdaile, *Wars*, passim; and Stuart Woolf, *Napoleon's Integration of Europe* (London: Routledge, 1991), pp. 156–71.

87. For the politics and diplomacy of the restoration(s), see G. de Bertier de Sauvigny, *La Restauration*, rev. ed. (Paris: Flammarion, 1955); and Emmanuel de Waresquiel and Benoît Yvert, *Histoire de la Restauration, 1814–1830: Naissance de la France moderne* (Paris: Perrin, 1996).

88. Bertier de Sauvigny, *Restauration*, p. 457.

89. Cited by ibid., pp. 56–57.

90. Paul W. Schroeder, *The Transformation of European Politics, 1763–1848* (Oxford: Clarendon, 1994), pp. 495–509.

91. For an analysis of the Charter, see Bertier de Sauvigny, *Restauration*, pp. 68–74; and de Waresquiel and Yvert, *Restauration*, pp. 56–63.

92. Furet, *La Révolution*, p. 278.

93. See Schroeder, *Transformation*, pp. 548–57.

94. Bertier de Sauvigny, *Restauration*, p. 117.

95. Ibid., p. 126.

96. The text of the Holy Alliance is cited in G. A. Kertesz, ed., *Documents in the Political History of the European Continent, 1815–1939* (Oxford: Clarendon, 1968), pp. 8–9.

97. See Henry A. Kissinger, *A World Restored: Metternich, Castlereagh, and the Problems of Peace, 1812–22* (Boston: Houghton Mifflin, 1957), pp. 175–90, esp. 189–90.

98. Bertier de Sauvigny, *Restauration*, pp. 129–31.

99. See chapter 13 above.

100. Daniel P. Resnick, *The White Terror and the Political Reaction after Waterloo* (Cambridge, Mass.: Harvard University Press, 1966), pp. 50–54.

101. Ibid., p. 118.

102. André Castelot, *Charles X: La fin d'un monde* (Paris: Perrin, 1988), ch. 16; and J.-J. Oechslin, *Le mouvement ultra-royaliste sous la restauration: Son idéologie et son action politique, 1814–1830* (Paris: Pichon and Durand-Auzias, 1960).

103. Cited in Charles H. Pouthas, *Guizot pendant la restauration: Préparation de l'homme d'état, 1814–1830* (Paris: Plon, 1923), pp. 184–85; and de Waresquiel and Yvert, *Restauration*, pp. 216–19.

104. Oechslin, *Mouvement ultra-royaliste*, ch. 4.

105. Bertier de Sauvigny, *Restauration*, p. 321.

106. See chapter 11 above.

107. For the *sacre* of Charles X, see Bertier de Sauvigny, *Restauration*, pp. 377–79; Castelot, *Charles X*, pp. 394–409; Landric Raillat, "Les manifestations publiques à l'occasion du sacre de Charles X ou les ambiguités de la fête politique," in Alain Corbin, Noëlle Gérôme, et al., *Les usages politiques des fêtes aux XIX–XX siècles* (Paris: Publication de la Sorbonne, 1994), pp. 53–61.

108. Eugen Rosenstock, *Die europäischen Revolutionen* (Jena: Eugen Diederichs, 1931), p. 22.

109. Ibid., pp. 436–37.

110. See chapter 7 and chapter 9 above.

111. Georges Sorel, *Réflexions sur la violence* (Paris: Seuil, 1990), p. 90.

112. This discussion of the human cost of the revolutionary and Napoleonic wars follows, in particular, David G. Chandler, *The Campaigns of Napoleon* (New York: Macmillan, 1966); and J. Houdaille, "Le problème des pertes de guerre," in *Revue d'histoire moderne et contemporaine* 17 (1970): pp. 411–23.

113. Esdaile, *Wars*, p. 300.

Internalization of the Russian Revolution: Terror in One Country

STALIN, LIKE NAPOLEON, should not benefit from comparison with Hitler. The rule of Stalin was an uneven and unstable amalgam of monumental achievements and monstrous crimes. There is, of course, an angle of vision which completely shuts out the former for fear that to take note of anything positive about Stalin is to extenuate his unpardonable sins and mistakes. But for a historian of my background and generation it is difficult, if not impossible, to take such a narrow field of view and equate Stalin with Hitler, to see them as identical twins. Historians are themselves "products of their society and their period," very much like historical actors.[1] Soviet Russia's unequaled and uncontested contribution to the defeat of Nazi Germany was closely bound up with Stalin's willful Second Revolution, starting with the Great Turn of the late 1920s. This judgment is all the more compelling inasmuch as in the 1930s the diplomacy of Moscow toward the Third Reich was neither more cynical nor more shortsighted than that of London, Paris, and Warsaw. Besides, in the 1930s, and again after 1945, the policies of the great powers furthered the consolidation and hardening of Stalin's power.

The moral deadness of Stalin is self-evident, and so is his psychological iciness, even if it remains unfathomable. Nevertheless, by now the ritualized demonization of Stalin—unscrupulous, deceitful, secretive, cruel, paranoid, tyrannical—hinders rather than advances the critical study and understanding of the Soviet regime during his close to thirty-year rule. Evidently Stalin—not unlike Napoleon and Hitler—simultaneously shaped and exploited the forces which carried him to power: he was "at once a product and an agent of the historical pro-

Eastern Europe, 1939 to 1948

cess, at once the representative and the creator of social forces which change the shape of the world and the thoughts of men."[2]

Stalin was the heir and executor of the Russian Revolution. Although in this regard he was very like Napoleon, in another he was radically dissimilar: whereas Napoleon turned the French Revolution outward to spread it far and wide by force of arms, Stalin virtually turned the Russian Revolution inward, to build Socialism in One Country. Both rulers suffered from an acute deficit of legitimacy: Napoleon bolstered his authority by fighting triumphant military campaigns abroad; Stalin sustained his by winning the battle to self-strengthen Russia through willful industrialization and collectivization. This internalization of the Revolution was dictated by the utter backwardness of the Soviet Union relative to the other great powers, which were hostile. Ironically, although Stalin's project was not Bonapartist, he eventually secured his and his regime's legitimacy by reason of the Red Army's spectacular victory over the German Wehrmacht.

Stalin is inseparable from the dual context which conditioned his rise and ascendancy: Russia's protracted time of troubles following seven years of grueling foreign and civil war; and the peril of renewed general war growing out of the spiraling instability in the surrounding world. During the epoch of the French Revolution the post-Thermidorean governments faced nothing remotely approaching this dual imperilment. To be sure, judging by its frequent and unpeaceful "regime changes," France's constitutional system was unsteady. But after mid-1791 France was not a polity, society, and culture in random and consuming chaos, nor was its great-power status ever seriously endangered.

By contrast, during the interwar years the leaders of the Soviet party-state understood that they were condemned to solidify Russia's new foundation in an unfavorable international environment, especially once they realized that in central and east-central Europe the end-of-war crisis of 1918–19 would not turn to revolution. At the start of the New Economic Policy internal conditions were catastrophic. Since 1914 the country is estimated, as noted, to have suffered well over 10 million military and civilian deaths. This demographic and psychological hemorrhage was compounded by the rush to emigration of a substantial part of Russia's educated elite and by the collapse of the state apparatus. In addition, both the economy and exchequer were wasted. The railway system was run down, the production of vital raw materials, especially of coal, was at an all-time low, and industrial production was a mere 20 percent of its prewar level. With hunger and unemployment stalking many cities and towns, the anomalous flight of workers back to the countryside continued.

This return of factory hands to their villages and hamlets, along with millions of demobilized soldiers, furthered the reagrarianization of Russia, set in motion by the land settlement of 1917–18. Although this reform had appeased and neutralized the peasantry, it had done so at the price of falling agricultural output. Overwhelmed by home-coming soldiers and homebound workers, and incensed by forced requisitions of grain and food, peasants tended to withdraw into subsistence farming, turning their back on domestic and international markets.

In essential respects Russia's civil society was even more "pre-capitalist" and less ripe for socialism at the start of NEP than in 1914 or 1917. The Bolsheviks were weighed down by this massive burden of backwardness when they turned to restoring the economy to its prewar level, a precondition for building a new order. To the extent that the new men of power shared a consensus, it was the conviction that there was no alternative to a fast-paced economic modernization entailing a rapid and massive rollback of the refractory countryside.

The Bolsheviks were in a weak position to take on this Herculean task. Theirs was a minority party without a substantial popular mandate or solid social base. Although the Communist Party built up a basic institutional network across the land, it was not up to filling the vacuum left by the extinction of state and local government. Admittedly, the Soviet authorities could rely on the Red Army and the Cheka, though both were radically curtailed after the civil war. Still, with at best limited support or sympathetic understanding among the peasantry, the Bolsheviks continued to be strangers in their own land. They had difficulties inventing a substitute for the Orthodox Church and religion which had cemented the hegemony of yesterday's tsars and governing class. Nor could the Bolsheviks unfurl the national flag: besides running counter to their worldview and precepts, such a stratagem would have been out of season in a country that was in neither mood nor condition to hearken to a *levée en masse* for diversionary war. This assessment was validated by the war with Poland in 1920, which confirmed that in the short run the Revolution could not reach beyond Russia's truncated western borders, especially with the great powers on the watch.

✱ ✱ ✱

Lenin intended NEP to repair the damage of foreign and civil war as well as to reduce Russia's crying backwardness. Not that he and his supporters, including Stalin, framed and followed a grand design. Like War Communism, NEP was an improvisation, though much less focused: it lacked not only the equivalent of the military imperative, which had driven the war economy, but also the basic elements of planning. Just as in early 1918, to secure their survival, the Bolsheviks had beaten a strategic diplomatic retreat at Brest-Litovsk, so now, with the shattered economy taking another turn for the worse in the fall and winter of 1920–21, they opted for a strategic economic retreat, or a "peasant Brest."[3] Indeed, Lenin concluded that there was no saving the revolution of the workers without, once again, placating the peasants. He and his associates appreciated that even with the streamlining of agriculture it would take several generations to transform rural Russia's fixed mentalities and customs. In the meanwhile, however, the emergency dictated trying to win over the indomitable community-rooted smallholders by relaxing state controls and offering material incentives. Above all, the free market now replaced mandatory quotas, levies, and prices. NEP was premised on the idea that the steady procurement of food for the cities and grain for export was the master key to economic reconstruction and modernization. To make small-scale farming the locomotive of economic recovery meant encouraging petty retailing and light manufacture, largely to meet the widespread hunger for consumer goods, also among the urban lower middle class and the professional and technical cadres, who were in short supply. All in all, NEP marked a turn toward a mixed economy in which the state retained ownership and centralized control of large-scale industry, mining, and banking. But by virtue of the continuing predominance of agriculture, this modern sector was not the "commanding" but the "beleaguered" heights of the Russian economy.

By 1926 leading sectors of the economy were approaching their prewar levels. Although impressive in its own right, this recovery was

611

contested and frail: in the countryside nepmen, or hard-driving businessmen, became a focus of jealous suspicion; in the industrial and mining centers workers chafed at their declining living standard. But above all, the economic backwardness of before 1914 persisted. Be that as it may, in a transnational perspective NEP was Soviet Russia's counterpart of the capitalist world's fragile Indian summer of peace, prosperity, and political tranquillity. Whereas before long in Russia a severe contraction of grain production and supplies, complicated by a war scare, would precipitate the termination of the improvised NEP, abroad an unprecedented stock market crash would undermine the makeshift edifice of the Dawes Plan, Locarno Pact, and Weimar Republic. At first essentially unrelated, these two breakdowns were destined to fatally bear on each other.

* * *

From the outset Stalin belonged to the innermost circle of revolutionary Russia's governors. He alone was a member of each of the "small overlapping groups of high officials [of party and state who] made the most important and wide-reaching decisions."[4] In the time that Lenin was *primus inter pares*, Stalin headed three People's Commissariats, belonged to the Politburo and Orgburo, served as political commissar with the Red Army during the civil war, and sat on several major task forces. In 1922, when the Eleventh Party Congress elected him member of the party secretariat with the prosaic title "general secretary," his appointment was widely considered "trivial," most likely by Stalin as well.[5]

With Lenin's health failing as of mid-1922, as may be expected, the struggle for succession started behind the scenes, before his death on January 21, 1924. At first Kamenev, Zinoviev, and Stalin pulled together to block Trotsky, perhaps Lenin's most ambitious would-be heir. While his three rivals suspected him of Bonapartist pretensions, Trotsky, in turn, distrusted them for their uncritical support of NEP, which he considered excessively Thermidorean or unrevolutionary. This unexceptional political in-fighting had a potentially explosive subtext: dissonant appreciations of the correlation of agrarian and industrial policy. Although both Stalin and Trotsky were "industrializers without any special tenderness for the peasantry, in the mid-1920s Stalin's public stance v. as more moderate than Trotsky's."[6] Eventually

Trotsky lost this first round, with the other three members of the Politburo—Bukharin, Rykov, and Tomsky—siding with Stalin. Before long the latter turned against Kamenev and Zinoviev, who now joined Trotsky in a short-lived "United Opposition." Having tightened his hold on the party, by 1926 Stalin felt strong enough to force the removal of Zinoviev, Kamenev, and Trotsky from the Politburo in favor of his own associates, among them Molotov, Voroshilov, and Kalinin.

By this time there was a growing internal debate about the prospects of NEP achieving not merely economic recovery but comprehensive industrialization. This debate was nourished by the emergence of the idea of planning in several government bureaus, particularly in Gosplan. Strange to say, this idea, including the guidelines for translating it into action, owed more to advances in macroeconomics and to recent wartime planning in Germany than to the theoretical and ideological writings of Marx and his epigones. In any case, the concept of economic planning clashed with that of a market-driven mixed economy. So did the concurrent appointment of Dzerzhinsky to also be chairman of the Supreme Economic Council: he was charged with "molding it into a powerful ministry of industry which, like its tsarist predecessors, would focus largely on the development of the metallurgical, metalworking, and machine-building industries"[7]—only now this agency would operate within the parameters of Socialism in One Country.

As previously noted, the miscarriage of revolution in Central Europe and Russia's ensuing isolation left a deep scar on the Bolshevik psyche. In the mid-1920s, when adumbrating the notion of building Socialism in One Country, Stalin merely articulated an idea that had for some time been circulating in inner party circles. Besides, beginning with War Communism the Bolshevik leaders practiced national self-reliance less by choice than necessity, owing to the well-nigh quarantine by the outside world. Of course, the end-purpose of the incipient *idée-force* of Socialism in One Country was at once intelligible and indeterminate. But at the time the only rival *idée-force* was equally general: the precept of "Permanent Revolution," espoused by Trotsky and his associates, which postulated that socialism could not triumph in a single country, particularly not in one as backward as Russia, without a simultaneous breakthrough to socialism in other countries, or without an all-European revolution. Of the two formulas, which unwittingly emerged in radical antithesis, Stalin's appeared more down-to-earth and practicable as the discussion of planning reached its season. During the time that they debated the link or passage between a revised NEP and embryonic Five-Year Plan, the Bolshevik leaders faced a pressing situation calling for policy choices fraught with "the enormous evils . . . of dreadful innovation" or the "strange pathos of novelty": the willful and rapid industrialization of a whole country, according to a would-be plan, substituting administrative for market controls, in peacetime, but in a volatile international environment.

Of course, like any great turn in history, the turn from NEP to the First Five-Year Plan will forever remain open to debate.[8] The outrageous costs of forced collectivization, which were neither anticipated nor intended, raise the question whether the overexploitation of the peasants was an essential precondition for purposeful and high-speed industrialization. In addressing this issue it is important to distinguish between, on the one hand, how this linkage of industry and agriculture was perceived, theorized, and portrayed by the actors of the time and, on the other, how it is seen, calculated, and constructed by historians and economists who dispose of empirical data and analytic tools—as well as retrovisions—which were not available in the late 1920s and early 1930s. It may well be that, in hindsight, in strictly economic terms the collectivization of agriculture "did not, in fact, contribute resources to the industrial sector," and that rapid industrialization under the first two Five-Year Plans took place "without any net accumulation from agriculture."[9] This thesis begs the question, however, of where and how the surplus product for industrial growth was generated in a predominantly agrarian economy without access to large-scale foreign loans or investments. At any rate, such retrovisionary estimates and judgments tend to presume that, except for Stalin's wiles, NEP could and would have been continued with revisions to allow for industrial growth at the same rate as that achieved by a command-and-control economy, without betraying the promise of the October Revolution.

The deliberations about industrialization and collectivization were at once complex and heated, and this despite an underlying consensus that the growth of industry and construction of socialism could not be left to the play of supply and demand alone. The in-party disputes and cleavages were less about objectives than means: the mix of market and state command, of capital and consumer industry, of persuasion and coercion of the peasantry. There was, in addition, not to say above all and increasingly—as we shall see—the critical issue of pace. Without theory or practice to guide them in the face of this *terra incognita*, none of the principals were consistent or self-confident, and not a few advanced unsound and rash arguments. By and large the "left" advocated maximum investment in heavy industry as the locomotive for comprehensive modernization, to be fueled by a combination of iron will, raw enthusiasm, and fierce coercion reminiscent of the difficult if heroic days of the civil war. This faction did not conceive planning, which was as yet opaque, in primarily or purely economic terms. The "right," for its part, called for economic development mindful of the merits of a dynamic equilibrium between heavy and consumer industry, as well as industry and agriculture. Its protagonists trusted the scientific calculation of "objective" economic forces and tendencies to fix the limiting conditions for intervention in support of balanced economic but chiefly industrial growth.

Above all, however, neither side—nor anyone in between—looked through rose-colored glasses or fitted them with restrictive blinkers. Stalin and Bukharin were equally aware of the peculiar Russian obstacles to rapid modernization aggravated by Moscow's virtual banishment from the international economy. Presently it was clear that the new course would work toward several objectives at once: to catch up to the West; to lay the foundations for the socialist transformation of society; to improve living standards; to consolidate the party-state; to inspire foreign Communists and sympathizers; and to develop a modern arms industry.

Before 1934 there was nothing to suggest that by opting for the pursuit of the breakneck noncapitalist modernization of Russia, Stalin was more intensely bent on reaching for personal power than his chief rivals. Like everyone, he was "neither a consistent moderate, nor radical": he "shifted from center-right (during his alliance with Bukharin in the mid-1920s) to left (during the period of so-called cultural revolution at the end of the 1920s and the early 1930s), and then back to a more moderate position in 1931–32."[10] Of course, beginning in 1929 the forced collectivization of agriculture left no doubt about his readiness to use extreme violence to bring to heel the recalcitrant world of the peasants. By then the reason for the maximalist position began to be reinforced by the end of the Indian summer in the capitalist world, which seemed likely to foreclose foreign loans and bring war closer.

* * *

Although Stalin was one of the least cosmopolitan of the veteran Bolsheviks, he very much shared the ambient scorn for and impatience with the muzhik. At the same time, he all but discounted the prospects for foreign aid. As a "conservative revolutionary" Stalin proposed to combine the furious modernization of Russia with the "reestablishment of hierarchies, the affirmation of certain traditional values like patriotism and patriarchy, and the creation of political legitimacy based on more than victorious revolution." While the Revolution was "powerfully present in the First Five-Year Plan period" the revival of things past "dominated in the middle thirties," with all the tensions inherent to this strange symbiosis.[11]

Even if he had not fixed his defiance on Trotsky, whose internationalism informed the rival precept of Permanent Revolution, Stalin was as unlikely to look for help from foreign revolutionaries as he was to order the Red Army to march to their support. The forced and linked industrialization and collectivization unfolded as something in the nature of an internal military campaign. At the time "war metaphors were even more common than revolutionary ones: Communists were 'fighters'; Soviet forces had to be 'mobilized' to the 'fronts' of industrialization and collectivization; 'counter-attacks' and 'ambushes' were to be expected from the bourgeois and kulak class enemy." This imagery was intended to at once evoke the "spirit of the Civil War and War Communism" while simultaneously discrediting the "unheroic compromises of NEP." It was consonant with a Soviet Union which "during the First Five-Year Plan, in fact, resembled a country at war." There were constant calls for unity and self-sacrifice, as well as for "vigilance against spies and saboteurs." With Stalin at the helm and setting the tone, "political opposition and resistance to the regime's policies were denounced as treachery" and imaginary internal enemies were charged with doing the bidding of hostile foreign powers.[12]

Under Stalin the terror, both functional and—as we shall see—political, was directed against domestic enemies behind the front of an internal war to catch Russia up to the other great powers.

This predisposition to fuse despotic rule and catch-up modernization had deep roots in Russia's past.[13] Peter the Great (1682–1725) stood out as at once a pacesetter and emblem of Russia's ingrained autocratic tradition. He had strengthened the central state at the expense of the council of the hereditary boyar nobility at the same time that he had forced the buildup of the army and navy, with help from the West. As part of his effort to reduce Russia's military backwardness, Peter the Great also had seen to the state-directed development of war-related manufacture. He had furthermore impressed convict and serf labor to advance his grand design. This urge and necessity to measure up to the West continued through the reign of Nicholas II, with military imperatives driving the government-supported development of railways, heavy industry, and arms production.

In the time of the late empire, Peter the Great was a notorious foil for discordant criticisms by Slavophiles, reformists, and socialists. But as early as 1928, shortly after propounding the precept of Socialism in One Country, Stalin began to advance a more positive reading: "When Peter the Great, having to deal with more developed countries in the West, feverishly constructed factories and mills to supply the army and strengthen the defense of the country, this was a unique attempt to break the constraints of backwardness."[14] At the same time, Stalin remained critical of the old elites who for reasons of class had turned to modernization to strengthen the *ancien régime* without conquering underdevelopment and furthering social reform. It was not until the mid-1930s that Peter the Great, along with Ivan the Terrible, began to be officially praised, as if to satisfy the Russian people's alleged predisposition to see even their most autocratic rulers as good tsars and to prepare the ground for Stalin's emergence as *vozhd*, the supreme leader or "tsar with a populist aura."[15]

All things considered, Stalin had the advantage over his rivals, which is not to say that his rise was foreordained. There certainly were other alternatives of both person and program. But there were confining conditions as well: the logic of the situation precluded a liberal political and economic course free of violence. One possibility was to rethink rather than discard NEP, with an eye to foster a measured economic development with industrialization as focal point. But then again, much of the sworn political class of the roughhewn party-state suspected "a long-term basic incompatibility between Bolshevism and NEP" and became increasingly reluctant "to tolerate the logic and consequences of a market economy [at the mercy of recurrent] stresses and strains," perceptible starting in 1925–26. Even then, the Five-Year Plan with the moderate targets of the first hour emerged as a credible option. But the unexpected domestic reverses and international perils of the late 1920s narrowed the corridor of time and room for maneuver. Much argues for the view that Socialism in One Country increasingly became "a slogan of survival, of national defense." Even allowing for a certain conscious exaggeration of the impending dangers to country and regime, the situation was urgent.[16]

Besides calling for a vigorous forward policy, the critical convergence of events called for a strong leader. On essential questions—priorities, pace, coercion of kulak and peasant, and foreign aid—the disagreements between and among the major contestants and factions were too ambiguous and inconstant to clearly set them apart. A Machiavelli might well have found it more difficult to consider Trotsky or Bukharin a credible alternative to Stalin than to "imagine Stalin himself acting differently . . . [or] adopting different policies."[17] At the time, none of the leading Bolsheviks either conceived of relaxing the grip of regime and party dating from the civil war or foresaw "the possible consequences of the total power [accruing to] the party apparatus, a total power which they all sought."[18] Certainly Lenin's parting warning about Stalin's "rudeness" was too circumspect to help focalize the personality factor.[19] Apart from Trotsky and Bukharin not making a stand against violence and terror, and notwithstanding Stalin's decisive use of his powers of general secretary, there were as yet few portents of his blunted sense of limits. With a different psychology or mentality, or both, Stalin "could have sent Bukharin off to teach marxism-leninism in the provinces, and left Kamenev to work in the 'Academia' publishing house, and not issued instructions about harsher conditions in labour-camps, or to kill the bulk of senior army officers."[20]

✻ ✻ ✻

Although Russian industry recovered its prewar level in 1926–27, in both industrial production and technology the gap between Russia and "the advanced capitalist nations [remained at least] as wide as in 1913."[21] There was, in addition, the hopelessly low productivity of the bulk of peasants and artisans. By the mid-1920s, hence "two or three years before the grain crisis," leading "Soviet politicians and economists, whatever their school of thought," were debating not the need for radical modernization but the speed at which it should and could proceed.[22] At first Evgenii Preobrazhensky and Trotsky urged a faster tempo than Bukharin. For one and all the comparison of Russia's industrial development with that of the advanced capitalist countries was second nature, and in November 1926 the Fifteenth Party Congress resolved to overtake the First World "in a relatively minimal historical period."[23] The grain crisis of 1927–28 merely intensified the industrialization debate. By 1928–29 not only Bukharin but Trotsky urged momentarily slowing the pace of development for fear of perturbing the economy, particularly the market relationship between city and country, worker and peasant.

By contrast Stalin, standing on his new-wrought but inchoate platform of Socialism in One Country, "increasingly insisted that the pace of industrialization must be accelerated even if this caused difficulties on the market." He and his supporters in the Supreme Economic Council and Gosplan stressed not only the danger of Russia falling further behind in technology and productivity but also the urgent need to provide an industrial base for both the mechanization of large-scale agriculture and the modernization of weapons production. The war scare of 1927 renewed the concern about military vulnerability, to become nearly an obsession following the Great Crash.

Indeed, diplomatic and military considerations were crucial in the constellation of preconditions and causes for the Great Turn of the late 1920s. Of course, as we saw, from the very start world politics bore significantly, if not decisively, on the Revolution and the new regime. At the outset the Bolshevik leaders assumed that they could simultaneously spread the contagion of the Revolution they had raised, and protect the national interest of the Russian state they had inherited. By early 1918, however, they began to subordinate the ideological and crusading temptation to the reason of power politics, with an eye to saving and consolidating their rule.

The war with Poland did not mark a change in course. Without provocation Pilsudski invaded Ukraine in late April 1920. The Red Army counterattacked by midyear, driving enemy troops out of Ukraine and Belorussia and pursuing them to the outskirts of Warsaw. Having winked at Pilsudski's attack, the Allied powers were confounded by the efficacy of Moscow's counterattack. Although at the Paris Peace Conference Woodrow Wilson and Lloyd George had resisted pressures for large-scale military intervention in support of the Whites, they had agreed to the continuation of indirect aid and to the establishment of a *cordon sanitaire* in Eastern Europe, with Poland as its center of gravity. The direct interventionists considered the lands making up this buffer zone equally suited to shut in or invade the Soviet Union. In any case, Marshal Ferdinand Foch, advocate of a greater Poland pointed against the new Russia, approved Pilsudski's eastward reach beyond Kiev and Minsk. Winston Churchill, like Foch, considered Poland "the linch-pin of the Treaty of Versailles." Ever since 1918, in terms reminiscent of Burke and the Duke of Brunswick, Churchill flayed revolutionary Russia for being "a poisoned Russia, an infected Russia of armed hordes not only smiting with bayonet and cannon, but accompanied and preceded by swarms of typhus-bearing vermin" and insidious proselytizers.[24]

In the summer of 1920 Lenin and nearly all his top associates were not about to risk the life of the Soviet regime on a battle for Warsaw in which, should the Red Army prevail, the Allies would be likely to rush to Pilsudski's side. Indeed, very few of them looked to using bayonets to establish a sister republic in Poland as a point of departure for conquests further west, where the prospects for revolutionary risings were negligible. Besides, and above all, conscious of the regime's extreme weakness, Lenin gave full priority to fighting General Wrangel and repressing the indomitable Greens.[25]

Only two major figures stand out for having peered to the far side of the Vistula, and they were linked: Trotsky and Tukhachevsky. Certainly Trotsky was more favorable to a "tough, risky, and adventurous" course than Lenin. But apparently his stance was less a function of his own "personal preference than . . . of pressure exerted by Tukhachevsky's independent initiative."[26]

It is noteworthy that unlike France's revolutionary government, which following the fall of Longwy and Verdun in 1792 had hurled defiance at Europe's old regimes, Sovnarkom exercised self-restraint when Pilsudski pushed back Tukhachevsky in 1920. Compared to the Girondins and Jacobins, the Bolsheviks, ruling over a wasted country, lacked the muscle and self-confidence to simultaneously end the civil war, fortify their regime, and engage the great powers. By signing the Treaty of Riga ending the war with Poland on reasonable terms, the Kremlin also meant to reassure Allied Wilsonians who advocated lifting the quarantine. Indeed, with the outside world much less monolithic than in 1792, Lenin sought to encourage the forces favoring peaceful coexistence.

Of course, had Tukhachevsky managed to take Warsaw, and this without Lenin's approval, he "might very well have become the Bonaparte of the Bolshevik Revolution," backed by impatient internationalists. It would have been difficult for Soviet leaders to "retain civilian control over the Red Army," since Tukhachevsky had defied and "dangerously weakened" the commissar system. Forever on the lookout for analogies with the French Revolution, the Bolsheviks were "aware that a Napoleonic figure might arise in the Army to challenge their rule," and their system of dual command "was designed, in part, to prevent [this]."[27] One time, when Lenin discussed such a possibility with Trotsky, who himself was later taxed with Bonapartist ambitions, Lenin said to him, "very seriously, almost threateningly, 'Well, I think we'll manage the Bonapartes, don't you?' "[28]

The resolution of the Russo-Polish war marked an important milestone in the internalization of the Russian Revolution. Extricated from foreign war, the Bolsheviks proceeded to complete the defeat of the Whites, to repress the peasant rebellions in Ukraine and Tambov, and to crush the sailors' rebellion on Kronstadt. This reestablishment, after four years, of a single and unifying sovereignty coincided with the conclusion of the Treaty of Riga and the Anglo-Russian Trade Treaty in March 1921. In turn, the signature of these two treaties concurred with the adoption of NEP by the Tenth Party Congress that same month. It was as if an unspoken introversive Socialism in One Country had stolen the march on the extroversive Permanent Revolution, with its millenarian acclaim.

✳ ✳ ✳

NEP was premised on "peaceful coexistence" between a shallow-rooted socialist regime and a speciously stabilized capitalist world. Although the First Cold War between the opposing camps momentarily gave way to peaceful coexistence, neither side disarmed ideologically. The Soviets were caught in a contradiction: through the Comintern they encouraged revolution in Europe and Asia, at the same time that they looked abroad for loans, for markets for grain and timber, and for technology transfers. In turn, in reality, the great powers refused to recognize the revolutionary regime. For the Kremlin, the search for foreign loans and imports for economic reconstruction and development was a matter of foreign policy and diplomacy. Lenin and Chicherin appreciated the importance of moderating the Comintern's foreign agitation in order to better exploit the divisions in the concert of nations. For a couple of years Moscow turned to good account Berlin's resolve to circumvent and obstruct the Versailles Treaty, starting with the Treaty of Rapallo of 1922. But by 1925 the Locarno Treaties and the Dawes Plan radically narrowed this avenue: Germany ceased to be the great diplomatic spoiler to become the pivot of the American-brokered restabilization of the capitalist world. Indeed, the danger of "capitalist encirclement" resurfaced at the same time that economic prosperity sapped the European forces pressing for a new deal and for understanding with Russia.

In any case, during this period of peaceful coexistence, with the Red Army's command held to a defensive strategy, NEP made no special provision for arms production, which was to grow along with the economy, with emphasis on improving old weapons systems rather than forging new ones. Evidently NEP's design to expand heavy industry, the key to military production, with foreign capital and technology, was contingent on an extended period of relative normalcy at home *and* abroad. Should peaceful coexistence break down suddenly, ahead of major industrial advances, the old-new Russia would be reduced to mobilizing a peasant army and backward economy to face one or more of the world's most modern military powers. Political and military leaders took stock of this security predicament at the very time that discussions of planned industrialization and Socialism in One Country came to a head.

✳ ✳ ✳

Even at the peak of NEP, there were latent fears of renewed economic and diplomatic isolation accompanied by rising international tensions. As of mid-1926 the first clouds appeared on the horizon: in England the General Strike, which the Comintern had cheered on, triggered fierce anti-Sovietism in the Conservative party and press; and Pilsudski's coup d'état in Poland could not help but cause concern. This renewed anxiety may well have born upon the previously mentioned party resolution of November 1926 stressing the urgency of closing the industrial gap with the capitalist powers "in a relatively minimal historical period."

But it was in the year 1927 that a series of foreign events put political and military leaders on edge: in April Soviet advisors were attacked in Peking, and in Shanghai Chiang Kai-shek arrested and persecuted thousands of Communists and trade unionists; in May the Baldwin government raided the Soviet trade mission in London; in June a Soviet diplomat was assassinated in Warsaw.[29] Most seriously, there was a break in Anglo-Soviet relations, and the Poincaré government lashed out at the Comintern and set upon the French Communists. On the instant Moscow feared an untimely end of makeshift coexistence, which would complicate the industrialization that was about to be given first priority.

Europe's conservative chancelleries and parties overestimated and overstated Moscow's anti-capitalist plot as much as the leaders in the Kremlin and Comintern overestimated and overstated the capitalist world's anti-Soviet counterplot. Presently the latter publicly claimed that the latest anti-Soviet and anti-Communist thrusts were part of a concerted campaign, directed by London, to tighten the quarantine. On June 7 the explosion of a bomb in Leningrad believed to have been masterminded by Russian émigrés further heated the atmosphere of fear and suspicion, with the press conjuring up the twin specter of foreign war and domestic subversion.

Although leading Bolsheviks at once exaggerated and exploited the foreign danger, it was not entirely spurious. Profoundly marked by the Allied intervention in the civil war, they were acutely aware of the uncertainty of external relations; of the anti-Communist *consensus omnium* spanning the outside world; and of Russia's military weakness. Needless to say, Moscow was anything but innocent, even if it was David facing Goliath. Chicherin kept cautioning that the Comintern's strident encouragement of rebellious Chinese peasants and striking British coal miners, coupled with groundless repression inside Russia, was feeding the fires of hostility in the outside world.

Naturally the renewed urgency of international politics precipitated a major debate within the party, with the result that foreign policy once and again became intensely politicized. With broadened support among impatient gadflies, the United (Left) Opposition, led by Trotsky and Zinoviev, renewed the attack on Stalin and Bukharin. Trotsky's denunciation of the failure of Moscow's China policy served as cutting edge for a critique of the bid for peaceful coexistence, which he cast as bound up with Socialism in One Country. The United Opposition's arraignment of Stalin and Bukharin was rather incongruous: on the one hand, it charged them with being unduly sanguine about the stabilization of capitalism and failing to adopt measures to attract foreign loans and investments to speed up industrialization; on the other, it criticized them for not doing enough to incite the workers of the world to rise up against their governments. Ultimately, even with war presumably around the corner, Trotsky held fast to his precept of Permanent Revolution. He looked to rouse particularly the European working class to liberate itself while at the same time saving the Revolution in Russia from itself.

The debate between the Trotskyites and Stalinites had some of the elements of the debate over war and peace between Girondins and Jacobins in 1791–92: Girondins and Trotskyites tended to argue the primacy of foreign policy, which presumed to raise the European revolution in support of the "national" revolution; Jacobins and Stalinites stressed the primacy of domestic policy, and on this score Stalin bore resemblance to Robespierre before the Convention's peremptory rush into general war. In 1927 Trotsky unintentionally facilitated Stalin's task by fostering the polarization of the political and rhetorical field. To be sure, Stalin stepped forth as a sober patriot and instrumentalized the war danger. But for him, as for Trotsky, the external menace served to frame and set forth a clear-cut policy choice. Rather than feed an anxiety hysteria, Stalin, along with Bukharin, argued that although not imminent, war was inevitable by virtue of the intrinsic incompatibility between capitalism and socialism. Under the circumstances Moscow needed to play for time to develop Russia's industrial and military muscle.

This foreign-policy debate, triggered and focused—as well as dramatized—by the war scare, predated the decision for forced-draft industrialization and collectivization. The expulsion of Trotsky from the Communist Party in November 1927 coincided with an access of doubt about the continuance of peaceful coexistence; of skepticism about the staying power of capitalist prosperity; of awareness of military inadequacy; and of fear of diplomatic isolation. Not that on the eve of the Great Turn there was no revolutionary excitement and impatience, especially among true-believers who considered NEP a betrayal of the millenial promise of 1917–18. But to neglect or minimize the swelling disquiet about the international situation is to make light of a key argument in the urgent resolution of the Fifteenth Party Congress in December 1927, following the Politburo's decision to embark on systematic industrialization: "Bearing in mind the possibility of a military attack . . . it is essential in elaborating the Five-Year Plan to devote maximum attention to a most rapid development of those branches of the economy in general and industry in particular on which the main role will fall in securing the defense and economic stability of the country in war-time."[30] As of this moment, military considerations weighed heavily on the political debates and economic decisions bearing on the pattern, method, tempo, and financing of deliberate industrialization.

✳ ✳ ✳

NEP's premise of trusting the future of military preparedness to gradual industrialization was abandoned in favor of the party-state's intervention to promote both in proportions which aroused heated controversy. Encouraged by the heightened sensitivity to the war problem, senior generals asked to be heard. In early 1928 Tukhachevsky, the chief of staff, submitted a report urging rearmament, with emphasis on a rapid buildup of armored and air power. True to his position during the Russo-Polish war, he combined this recommendation with a summons to "use the Red Army as a spearhead of world revolution."[31] When Voroshilov and Stalin demurred, Tukhachevsky resigned to assume a lesser command, but not without continuing to press his views. Under his influence Soviet strategic doctrine shifted from preparing to fight "a protracted defensive war with full-scale mobilization" to acquiring a defensive-offensive capability turning on the combined use of armored and air power. This strategy was, of course, contingent on an industrial sector capable of sustaining the production of modern armaments in peacetime, to be deployed before the start of hostilities.[32] Obviously, these military requirements would compete for scarce resources with urgent civilian needs.

In July 1929 the Politburo resolved that under the Five-Year Plan "a modern military-technical basis for defense must be established." The Sixteenth Party Congress endorsed this injunction in mid-1930. On this occasion Voroshilov exhorted planning officials to stress military factors, since in every major respect "our war industry, and industry as a whole . . . is still hobbling quite badly."[33]

By the end of 1930, although the growth of war industries had quickened, "they were . . . still of lower priority in practice than the tractor or iron and steel industries."[34] Stalin and the Bolshevik leadership continued "to tilt the delicate balance between long-term and immediate military strength toward construction of a powerful heavy industry as a basis for future defense."[35]

Meanwhile, Tukhachevsky kept arguing for a comprehensive military overhaul: "the successes of our socialist construction . . . pose the urgent task of reconstructing the armed forces, taking into account all the latest technical factors, the possibilities of military-technical production and developments in the countryside."[36] Not unlike Heinz Guderian and Charles de Gaulle, his contemporaries, Tukhachevsky swore by mobile warfare and cried for the coordinated use of airplanes, tanks, and artillery. Rejecting "the strategy of defense in depth" on the model of 1812, he disputed two tenets: "that it was 'better to give up Minsk and Kiev than take Bialystok and Brest' . . . ; [and] that the proletarian state had no right to overthrow the bourgeoisie of another country by [armed] force." Once again Stalin and Voroshilov demurred, with Stalin insisting that to follow Tukhachevsky's recommendations would be to open the door "to 'Red militarism' " and to the militarization of society at the expense of the construction of socialism.[37]

Despite this rebuff, for which Stalin apologized after eventually embracing parts of Tukhachevsky's ground plan, the imperatives of the new warfare began to leave their imprint on the discussion of economic policy and allocation of resources for the production of modern armaments. Hereafter the emphasis was increasingly on creating a separate modern arms industry to equip the armed forces and build up strategic stores *before* the start of hostilities. Under the First Five-Year Plan, defense considerations unexpectedly at once drove and warped industrialization.

Stalin emerged as Russia's absolute despot by virtue neither of the egregious miscalculations of his sponsors or rivals, nor the irresistible force of his calculating and ruthless will to power, but by reason of the cunning of history. Circumstances were particularly propitious to his becoming the embodiment of the shift to accelerated industrialization and rearmament, a shift that was necessary but not inevitable in an increasingly uncertain and hostile international environment. But by itself the war scare of 1927, including its political exploitation by Stalin, might not have provided a sufficient rationale for an irreversible switch, from peaceful coexistence and NEP to galloping industrial development and military modernization predicated on the compulsory collectivization of agriculture. The Great Crash of the American Stock Market in October 1929, which mushroomed into the Great Depression of the 1930s, was a godsend for Stalin, consolidating his political hold by vindicating his general stance.

At the Sixteenth Party Congress, which met seven months after Black Friday, Stalin artlessly counterposed the failing capitalist system to the promise of the Five-Year Plan. In his rendering, the world was at a crossroad: "for the USSR . . . a turn in the direction of a new and bigger economic *upswing*; for the capitalist countries . . . a turn towards economic *decline*." Stalin noted that until yesterday "a halo formed around the United States as the land of full-blooded capitalism," and the world over "groveling to the dollar" was accompanied by "panegyrics in honor of the new technology . . . [and] of capitalist rationalization." He mockingly recalled that yesterday's celebration of capitalism's roaring prosperity was punctuated by a "universal noise and clamor about the 'inevitable doom . . . and collapse' of the USSR." The reverse was now happening, exactly as the Bolsheviks had predicted "two or three years ago."[38]

Indeed, the perils of contingent novelty were about to be compounded by a flush of hubris fueled by the conceit of "correct" prediction. Building on Eugen Varga's forewarnings about the impermanence of the capitalist revival and the likelihood of a major downward cycle, many Bolshevik leaders, including Stalin, now prophesied that world capitalism was fated to enter a terminal crisis.[39] Compared to past crises, this one was expected to be universal, deep-seated, and chronic. To boot, with Keynesian economics still unsuspected, the Marxist diagnosis presumed that the panic-stricken governments had no remedial therapies: they were obliged to fall back on protective tariffs and autarky, thereby aggravating the situation, but also vindicating the precept of Socialism in One Country.

But perhaps most important, in Marxist readings there was no confining the runaway depression to the economic and financial realm. At the Sixteenth Party Congress Stalin forewarned that "in a number of countries the world economic crisis will grow into a political crisis," with the "bourgeoisie seeking a way out . . . through further fascistization in the sphere of domestic policy" and "utilizing all the reactionary forces, including Social Democracy, for this purpose." At the same time, "in the sphere of foreign policy the bourgeoisie will seek a way out through a new imperialist war."[40] For a little while the buffeted capitalist governments would again play at cross-purposes, providing Moscow some room for diplomatic maneuver. But this favorable prospect was offset by heightened fear of isolation as war clouds threatened to thicken and burst over Eastern Europe. Stalin was more than ever convinced of the necessity to buy sufficient time to further industrialization and military preparedness before the inevitable clash of arms. By early February 1931 Stalin averred that if the "socialist fatherland" was not "to be beaten and lose its independence," it would have to "end its backwardness in the shortest possible time and develop a genuine Bolshevik tempo in building up its socialist economy." He cautioned that to proceed at anything less than full speed would be to perpetuate the protean backwardness responsible for Russia's string of military defeats in modern times. Stalin concluded on an ominous but rousing note: being "fifty or a hundred years behind the advanced countries," Soviet Russia had to "make good this distance in ten years, and either we do it, or we shall go under."[41]

* * *

The idea for a major backward power to gain upon, nay overtake, the most advanced industrialized nations, overnight, was as novel as it was brazen and contested. It was not adumbrated in either the *Communist Manifesto* or any of the other socialist scriptures. Presently the unknown notion of planned and telescoped economic development, incorporated and expressed in the Five-Year Plan, eclipsed the venerable Communist idea in the prophecy and eschatology of the Russian Revolution. The fact that the crystallization of the untried precept of Soviet planning fortuitously coincided with the dramatic breakdown of free-market capitalism made it all the more compelling, as well as threatening.

There was something preposterous about the Soviet leaders' presumption to radically transform a vast agrarian society of endemic scarcity and poverty in less than a third of a generation. Ironically and fatally, agricultural production came to hold the key to this mad rush to industrialization: surplus grain would be essential to provision the cities and armed forces as well as to sell abroad for advanced capital goods and technologies. Even in the mid-1920s, under NEP, poor harvests and grain exports had forced a rift in the party on this critical nexus: one faction advocated a momentary deceleration of industrialization compatible with the preservation of NEP; the other favored staying the course, even at the risk of dangerously straining it.

The die was by no means cast when untoward international developments broke in upon the situation and debate in Russia. It became increasingly difficult for Bukharin to keep arguing for a slowdown, possibly a pause in industrialization, especially since his sober estimate of the stabilization of world capitalism was being refuted by the course of events. All things considered, the new disquiet about defense, foreign loans, and falling grain prices on world markets played in favor of the maximalists. Though not discounting foreign trade and loans, Stalin was not prepared to allow them to dictate the pace of industrialization, *a fortiori* since he was prepared to resort to a "military-feudal exploitation" of the peasantry, which Bukharin reproved.[42]

At the direction of the Politburo and in cooperation with concerned government departments, Gosplan worked out general guidelines for a Five-Year Plan for submission to the party congress. Against the background of the intensifying industrialization debate of the mid-1920s, the yearly growth rates of Gosplan's first draft of March 1926 kept being revised upward. The version of the plan accepted in April 1929 projected a 230 percent increase of industrial production over the level of 1927–28 within five years, with the growth rate of heavy industry two and a half times that of consumer manufacture.

The bulk of capital investment was earmarked for plants to produce iron and steel, machine tools, and tractors—plants of potential military value. Overriding cautionary voices within Gosplan, the plan of 1929 was premised on five years of good harvests and exports as well as commensurate foreign loans. Furthermore, in 1930 it was decided to meet the projected production targets in four years, instead of five.

Without the benefit of a precedent in the planning of a national economy to guide them, both experts and politicians were at once unsure and reckless. Not cast in stone, the First Five-Year Plan kept being revised to take account of rampant imponderables and bottlenecks. There were inadequate provisions for the development of transport, hydroelectric power, and coal production, as well as for the training and deployment of engineers and skilled workers. But above all, the first plan did not reckon with the headlong collectivization of agriculture, which, as we shall see, was not adopted and forced until 1929–30, and which in the short term proved disastrous. Even so, the Five-Year Plan became myth overnight.

Leaving aside the human costs, the economic achievements of the First Five-Year Plan were astonishing. By increasing industrial production by 250 percent, Soviet Russia took giant steps toward becoming a major industrial power. The average annual rate of industrial growth was close to 20 percent. Some of the old economic centers grew by leaps and bounds, and so did new ones, like the steel center at Magnitogorsk in the southern Urals and the hydroelectric complex on the Dnieper.[43] Factories were being built to produce agricultural machines, tractors, and machine tools. Characteristically, by "the early 1930s the cult of steel and pig-iron production exceeded even the emerging cult of Stalin," with everything being "sacrificed to metal in the First Five-Year Plan."[44] The Second Five-Year Plan (1933–37), with an annual industrial growth rate of 17 percent, consolidated and built upon the achievements of the first, which involved raising living standards and real wages, which had fallen by 50 percent during the previous plan. Because of ominous international developments, particularly the belligerence of Japan and Germany, the second plan kept being revised to increase the scale and pace of arms production. Indeed, during the 1930s military expenditures and investments weighed "ever more heavily upon the Soviet economy." Between

1934 and 1936 the armed forces more than doubled in size to 1,300,000 effectives, and they continued to grow at the same rate for the rest of the decade, along with their equipment with tanks, trucks, and aircraft. Whereas at the end of the First Five-Year Plan only "3.4 percent of the [total] Soviet state budget went [directly] to the military," the proportion rose to 16.1 percent in 1936 and to 32.5 percent in 1940.[45] Obviously, the "great leap forward" in Soviet Russia's industrial economy entailed a "great leap forward" in its military sector, armaments expenditures rising fivefold between 1929 and 1940. No doubt this enormous military effort and burden added significantly to the exorbitant costs and monstrous sacrifices of the domestic side of the battle to protect the regime and nation, which, of course, involved maintaining the power of the ruling elite. There is nothing to suggest that Stalin pushed the military build-up in preparation for either the export of the Revolution by force of arms or the discharge of Soviet Russia's—the Communist regime's—staggering domestic problems into the international environment. Meanwhile, the steep growth of the military, including its industry, increased the political weight of the army.

✳ ✳ ✳

While city and industry were the womb of socialist construction, village and agriculture were at once its lifeblood and nemesis. Russia was nearly as much a country of peasants, wooden ploughs, and sickles at the creation of the First Five-Year Plan as at the time of the October Revolution. The cultural and social abyss separating city and country remained forbidding, and in vital respects the latter held the former hostage. With the Socialist Revolutionaries cast out, Russia's new political class was at one in considering the peasants unwieldy and troublesome at the same time that it realized, increasingly, that without their grain surpluses, taxes, and labor power the party-state would flounder. Ultimately the idea of modernizing and shrinking the agrarian sector through instant and wholesale collectivization with a view to harnessing it for forced-draft industrial development was no less audacious than the idea of planned industrialization. Besides destroying the fabric of private, small-scale, and communally interwoven landholding and farming, collectivization entailed the massive and convulsive transformation of an age-old peasant culture and society. Stalin's impatience with the unbending peasant was peculiar neither to him nor to most Marxists far and near. As we have seen, it was rooted in the Enlightenment.

Following the land decrees of 1917–18, which sanctioned the peasants' spontaneous land seizures, only about one percent of Russia's cultivated surface survived as large estates. This remnant was confiscated to be exploited by peasant communes, collectives, or cooperatives. Under NEP this embryo of "collectivized" agriculture was all but ignored. Like the military sector, it was expected to develop along with the growth of a mixed economy. By 1928 "the socialized sector of Soviet agriculture . . . was responsible for only 2.2 percent of gross farm production, the rest being produced by some 25 million individual peasant households."[46]

All this time Bolsheviks of all schools continued to reject small- and middle-sized family farming, emboldened by the belief that eventually, with greater efficiency and reduced human toil, large-scale collectivized agriculture would and should become the norm. Stalin's project of Socialism in One Country could not avoid confronting the peasant conundrum. By contrast, Trotsky's precept of Permanent Revolution may be said to have sought to sidestep it by holding fast to a concept, rooted in Western Europe's experience, of industrial workers and large cities becoming ascendant in the time that an "enclosure movement" or its equivalent reduces the weight and resistance of the awkward peasantry. To be sure, Lenin had all along insisted on the exigencies of the peasant-worker alliance. But neither he nor any of the other Bolshevik leaders had ever put forth a credible analysis of the simultaneity of Russia's two radically unsimultaneous cultures and societies which was to vastly complicate the furious breakthrough into noncapitalist modernization, and drench it with blood.

Agricultural production, like industrial production, recovered its prewar levels around 1926–27, with a strong performance in grains, livestock, and industrial crops. But productivity was as low as ever when the issue of rapid industrialization came to a head. Indeed, the incipient Five-Year Plan would be heavily dependent on a sluggish and inconstant agrarian economy dominated by unchanging peasants. The harvest of 1927 was average. But deliveries of grain and industrial crops fell off sharply during the winter, and so did grain exports. Although these complications were not out of the ordinary, they were difficult to reconcile with the logic of economic planning, and called in question the optimistic assumptions about the contribution of the undisciplined agrarian sector to forced-march industrialization.

In early 1928 the Politburo decided to spur collectivization and rationalize grain collection by means of inducement and exhortation rather than coercion. By this time, however, the party leadership was becoming torn, not to say polarized, over the peasant question, specifically about how to extract rising and reliable deliveries of grain for both the short and long term. Presently Stalin insisted that, especially with foreign loans highly problematic, the pace of industrialization should not continue to hinge on the vagaries of peasant agriculture which the NEP's market mechanisms could not keep in bounds. He began to argue for forced collectivization and forced procurement at the same time that he charged the kulaks, or prosperous peasants, with playing the market for reasons of personal, class, and political advantage.

Stalin and his closest associates did not stand alone. Their "new approach . . . was welcomed enthusiastically by an influential group of party intellectuals, by some of the party rank and file, by many young communists and students, and by an unknown number of industrial workers." But above all, "support from most members of the party central committee, and from many local party officials, provided the basis for Stalin and his group to prevail over the Right in the course of a protracted struggle between July 1928 and April 1929."[47]

Less alarmed than Stalin about the worsening domestic and international situation of the late 1920s, the Right Oppositionists favored adjusting rather than discarding NEP, as well as revitalizing rather than abandoning the worker-peasant alliance. Overall, however, their affirmations were less forceful than their negations: rejection of coercion and class war in the countryside; opposition to quickening the tempo of industrialization; and disapproval of the absolute priority for heavy industry.

The Right Opposition had three emblematic leaders: Rykov, Lenin's successor as chairman of the Council of People's Commissars; Tomsky, head of the Central Council of Trade Unions; and, above all,

Bukharin, now editor of *Pravda* and head of the Comintern. Only yesterday all three had sided with Stalin against Trotsky and the Left Opposition. Bukharin sought backing in the upper echelons of the party, but without diffusing the Right's arguments or reaching out for broader support. His forte was the arbitrament of the *word*, not political infighting and leadership. Still, Bukharin's position was backed "by a substantial group of senior party officials and by virtually all the leading non-party experts in the major government departments; and it found ready sympathy among one section of the party rank and file, and among most peasants and many workers—when they had the opportunity to hear about it."[48]

In the heated debate of the main issues, control of the party and fixity of purpose gave Stalin the edge over his rivals. But he did not prevail by strong-arm tactics and craft alone. This inner-party struggle, unlike previous ones, bore upon "clear-cut issues of principle and policy." The Right, compared to the Left, projected a certain complacency. Its "platform involved less danger of social and political upheaval, and did not require party cadres to change the habits and orientation of NEP." But this also meant that it promised "much less in the way of achievement" at a time when the party "was hungry for achievement," as well as unsuspecting of its costs. Indeed, the Right proposed "a moderate, small-gains, low-conflict program to a party that was belligerently revolutionary, felt itself threatened by an array of foreign and domestic enemies, and continued to believe that society could and should be transformed."[49]

Stalin did not have a clear blueprint and timetable for mandatory agricultural and industrial development in defiance of the laws of the market. The original plan of December 1927, before its successive radicalizations, projected the collectivization of about 20 percent of the land over five years, without specifying either the form collectivization would take—state or cooperative farms—or the level of financing for the projected mechanization of agriculture at a time when Russia counted only about 25,000 tractors. The plan's intentions and instructions being overly general, at the start its implementation in the countryside here and there reflected "historical class hatreds, Civil War legacies, zealotry, personal rivalry, and the needs of official 'family circle' cliques."[50] Although the critical decisions were made at the center, there was no power structure fitted to direct and control their implementation in distant towns and villages. Besides, when Stalin first resorted to force to meet the stubborn difficulties of grain procurement, he "did not know where the process set in motion by his 'emergency measures' would ultimately lead him."[51]

* * *

Industrialization set the pace, not collectivization: in 1928–29 the intensification and speed-up of the former spurred the latter. Party leaders, and not only Stalin's votaries, more and more doubted that the peasants, for want of material incentives, would be able and willing to step up production. Faced with growing resistance in the village, by the summer of 1929 the Politburo fixed mandatory quotas for grain procurement. Instead of blaming the continuing shortfalls on the breakdown of the market and the defects of official price policy, Stalin denounced the hoarding and stockjobbing of the kulaks. In December the Politburo braced itself to forge ahead with collectivization: it established a special commission headed by Molotov; and Stalin announced a "*turn* toward the policy of eliminating the kulaks as a class."[52] On January 5, 1930, the Central Committee, in a decree "On the Tempo of Collectivization," vowed to all but complete the collectivization of agriculture in 1931–32. The authorities claimed that over 60 percent of peasant households were collectivized within about two months. Even though vastly overstated, this figure suggests the fury of the operation, including the attendant chaos, resistance, and violence. To be sure, there were no peasant risings on the order of those of the Greens in 1919–20. There was, however, formidable passive resistance: peasants slaughtered and sold their animals rather than hand them over to their village kolkhoz, with the result that between 1928 and 1934 Russia's stock of cattle, horses, and sheep was halved.

But it was primarily the kulaks who were subjected to brute force and violence. Unlike the poor and middle peasants, they had prospered by using hired labor, renting out agricultural machines and draught animals, or engaging in commerce. In the late 1920s the kulaks probably constituted slightly less than 4 percent of all peasant production units. But in association with nepmen, they provided a disproportionate share of the marketable surplus of food for the cities, raw materials for industry, and commodities for export. Although there undoubtedly were "genuine exploiters" among the kulaks, more than likely most of them were "simply successful and hard-working peasants."[53] In any case, by proclaiming that they were to be eliminated as a class and kept out of the village kolkhozy, Stalin set the stage for their forced expropriation, deportation, and relocation.

In no time the campaign, which was unprepared and unmindful of village solidarity, gave rise to a surfeit of disorder, unrest, and resistance which alarmed the center. On March 2, 1930, *Pravda* carried Stalin's article "Dizzy with Success": blaming all excesses on overzealous local officials, he countermanded the collectivization of livestock and suggested a moratorium. Presently commissions were charted to examine the grievances of dekulakized peasants, and not a few dispossessed families recovered their property. In addition, 25,000 true-spirited industrial workers were mobilized to go to the countryside to enlighten the peasantry about the merits of collective farming. They were, however, unable to penetrate the "all-pervasive backwardness" of the world of their fathers, which turned a deaf ear to the Siren of progress.[54] Meanwhile many peasants took advantage of the pause to back out of "their" kolkhozy. But even after this withdrawal, in March and April 1930 "6 million peasant households, 24.6 percent of the total number, belonged to 86,000 kolkhozy, compared to less than 4 percent in June 1929, . . . the size of the average kolkhoz [having] increased from 18 to 70 households."[55]

A month after he had issued his stay, Stalin declared it to have been "not a retreat but a temporary consolidation," and in mid-1930 the Sixteenth Party Congress reaffirmed the principle of collectivization.[56] This was the same conclave which approved completing the First Five-Year Plan in four years and accelerating the production of tractors. Full-scale collectivization resumed in early 1931, with the result that 62 percent of peasant households were collectivized by 1932, and 93 percent by 1937.

The socialization of agriculture was well-nigh completed in less than ten years. In the major agricultural regions the "traditional pattern of peasant agriculture . . . was in large part destroyed," the machine tractor station, symbol of the modernizing impulse, playing a major role.[57] Still, the break was not nearly as radical as appears at first sight: by and large "the typical kolkhoz was the old village, with the peasants . . . living in the same wooden huts and tilling the same fields as they had done before."[58] Even so, the cake of custom was being cracked. In many villages "the *mir* ceased to exist . . . and the church was closed," the local priest having "fled or been arrested."[59] The enormous and unforeseen out-migration was no less disruptive: during the 1930s, with the number of cities of over 100,000 inhabitants rising from thirty-one to eighty-nine, between 16 million and 19 million peasants left their villages to enter the urban and industrial workforce. This vast migration "was part of the dynamics of Russia's industrialization . . . [and was] as much a part of Stalin's revolution in the countryside as collectivization itself."[60] But what was good for the city and industry was not necessarily good for the village and agriculture. The out-migrants were mostly "the young, the skilled and educated, the more enterprising peasants fearful of dekulakization, and, in general, a greater percentage of males than females," bleeding the provinces of vital forces.[61]

Such a sweeping and feverish transformation, dictated from above and afar, could not be carried through peacefully. With the Bolshevik leaders resolved, as during the civil war, to persevere at any cost, the human cost was horrendous. In their quasi-military campaign they fixed and revised objectives—targets—as well as strategies and tactics with little regard for casualties—peasant victims—and material losses—declining production and wasted livestock. Victories, such as the bumper harvest of 1930, bred overconfidence; defeats, such as the famine of 1932–33, further hardened the mailed fist. Winning through on the agrarian front was considered crucial for winning through on the industrial front.

This campaign, especially its battle against the kulaks, raged with particular ferocity in 1930–32. The number of kulak family households to be dekulakized was arbitrarily set at about one million out of a total of about 25 million households, or between 5 million and 6 million individuals. In 1930–31, of this total some 63,000 heads of household were arrested, expropriated, and deported to remote regions for being "counterrevolutionary activists." About another 150,000, after being dispossessed of their land, but not of all their non-landed property, were forcibly relocated, along with their families. The remaining 400,000 to 700,000 families were turned out of house and home and forced to settle on less fertile land in or near their village. Naturally dekulakization took the greatest toll of life among the heads of households and families deported for either confinement to camps or resettlement in distant climes. In early 1932 Stalin was informed that "since 1929 . . . 540,000 kulaks were deported to the Urals, 375,000 to Siberia, more than 190,000 to Kazakhstan, and over 130,000 to the far northern region." In all, it is estimated that between 10 and 20 percent of them, or between 315,000 and 420,000, lost their lives, mostly from disease, hunger, exhaustion, and exposure. Many of the deported kulaks were put to work in industry and public works.[62]

In part the ranks of victimized kulaks were so large because, the category of kulak being vague, they were "joined by other intended and unintended victims of repression, most notably *byvshie liudi*, outsiders, and marginal people within the villages," including real and suspected counterrevolutionaries of the civil war as well as members of outlawed leftist parties. In any case, in villages and country towns "the campaign against *byvshie liudi* often merged with and became indistinguishable from dekulakization." This conflation fed upon the collectivization-induced chaos, poverty, and starvation, with party and state officials looking for scapegoats. The spiraling repression, cause and consequence of the trumped-up denunciations of kulaks and outsiders, "seems also to have been shaped by the dynamics of a traditional rural political culture and to have resulted in a kind of traditional victimization."[63]

In the short run and not surprisingly, collectivization failed to remedy the chronic ills and fitful shortfalls of agricultural production. In fact, it aggravated them. To be sure, in 1930 there was a "record [cereal] harvest . . . followed by record grain collection" and exports. But this "spectacular victory, . . . [which] encouraged great complacency," was largely due to good weather. *A fortiori* the disastrous harvests of the three following years confounded the Bolshevik leaders. But rather than reconsider or retreat, they opted for yet another *fuite en avant*. The massive slaughter of livestock is perhaps the best measure of the peasant's recalcitrance. In 1930 alone, the destruction of "animal power" was greater than the "tractor power made available to the kolkhozy . . . and the losses of cows, pigs, and sheep were so great that . . . [the output of] meat and dairy products could not recover to its 1929 level for at least two years."[64] Thereafter, disillusioned by the shortage of tractors to lighten their toil, the collectivized peasants, rather than sweat and slave for their kolkhoz, attended to their household plots and animals. The authorities' reaction was to step up the pressure by raising and fiercely enforcing delivery quotas. In addition, not unlike blue-collar workers, peasants were restricted to their workplace.

These strong-arm measures could not prevent serious food shortages from escalating into the great famine of 1932–33 which, like the famine of the early 1920s, was caused by both man and nature in proportions that remain in dispute. It took 4 million to 6 million lives and inflicted widespread suffering. Some regions were racked more severely than others, and among the worst hit, Ukraine stood out. Collectivization had proceeded perhaps most rapidly and violently in Ukraine, still one of Russia's chief breadbaskets, producing between a quarter and one-third of the country's grain harvest. By mid-1932 about 70 percent of Ukraine's peasants were in kolkhozy and the government claimed about 40 percent of its grain production. In Ukraine the famine was at its worst during the early winter of 1932–33, but subsided starting in early spring, when grain requisitions were relaxed and then ended.

No doubt in Ukraine, as well as in other regions struck by famine, benighted and overzealous local officials of the party-state aggravated the Furies. Ultimately, however, Stalin and his partisans bear full responsibility by virtue of their resolve to forge ahead in the face of forbidding obstacles, regardless of cost, blinded by their commitment to force-paced industrialization and military preparedness as well as by their impatience with the muzhik. To the extent that their violence was in the nature of an enforcement terror, and notwithstanding their recourse to scapegoating and conspiracy mongering, it was essentially instrumental. It seems most doubtful that Stalin willfully mounted a genocidal war against, in particular, the peasantry of Ukraine with a view to abort the embryo of Ukrainian nationalism. Indeed, the Irish famine of the second half of the 1840s, in which over a million out of 8 million people perished, is a much closer parallel than the Judeocide of the 1940s.

* * *

The establishment and extension of the Gulag was closely correlated with the drive for industrialization and collectivization. It became at once an important instrument of political control and a vital agency for the furtherance of planned industrial growth. Indeed, the Gulag had a dual function: to serve as an instrument of enforcement terror; and to serve as an economic resource, notably as a source of unfree labor. These two roles were "inseparable and interdependent, with each role more important at different times."[65]

As we noted above, almost from the outset of the Bolshevik regime, proven, suspected, and imagined enemies from among the old ruling and governing classes were either executed or confined to "concentration camps."[66] In addition, black marketeers and common law criminals were sent to work camps for rehabilitation by forced labor. In the time of Lenin and until the late 1920s the concentration camps for political prisoners were administered by the OGPU, the Cheka's successor, while the work camps, along with regular prisons, were under the NKVD, or People's Commissariat of Internal Affairs. Whereas during this decade the economic role of the double-track penal system was at best marginal, it became increasingly important during the following decade, under Stalin. In other words, even though "the camp system of the Gulag had firm roots in the years *preceding* Stalin's assumption of power, [starting with the Second Revolution] it assumed its defining characteristics in the time of the centrally planned economy."[67]

The Gulag had two tasks. The one was "to imprison criminals, to isolate presumed and proven political enemies or rivals, and to put in fear the population." In this capacity the Gulag was "not only a penal system but also an instrument of terror and sovietization." The other function was "to methodically supply the planned state economy with the labor force of its convicts, thereby contributing to economic development and the settlement of virgin lands." Whatever the relative importance of the penal, political, and economic reasons for the new departure, beginning in the late 1920s "the new economic demands contributed decisively to the expansion of the Gulag."[68] The reserve army of forced labor was used in logging, in the construction of strategic roads, canals, and railways, as well as in the building of industrial plants and the operation of mines in remote regions. This compulsory labor contributed to lowering labor costs and saving foreign exchange. As we shall see, millions suffered and died in the wanton Gulag, which was half-hidden and half-public.

Forced labor played a role in the treatment of all categories of prisoners. Most likely the presumption in favor of this penal measure was rooted in the previously discussed *katorga* for criminals deported to far-off regions under the tsars.[69] The Bolsheviks, for their part, distinguished between the "reform-intended labor of convicts of working-class origin and the forced labor for 'counterrevolutionaries, socially dangerous elements,' and class enemies."[70] In economic terms, this incidental unfree labor was at best expected to cover the costs of the prison and camp systems of the NKVD and OGPU. In other words, the economic utility of forced labor was inconsequential until the decision of the late 1920s to exploit the "potential" of the growing prison and camp population for the advancement of the Five-Year Plan.[71]

This decision emerged, of course, from the same debate which starting in the mid-1920s looked to frame the general parameters for planned economic growth at the expense of NEP. From early on the interpenetration of the regime's policies of internal security, economic development, and labor mobilization were embodied in Dzerzhinsky: besides being master of first the Cheka and then the OGPU, he headed a bureau of labor recruitment for economic reconstruction and the Commissariat for Transportation which directed the construction of new rail lines. Not least important, from early 1924 until his death in mid-1926 Dzerzhinsky was chairman of the Supreme Economic Council. All along, as a "resolute champion of rapid industrialization he concentrated on the transport system and on industry, especially heavy industry." He took an early interest in plans for what became large-scale public works, such as the Stalingrad tractor plant and the Dnieper hydroelectric power complex, in whose construction forced labor eventually played a considerable role. Indeed, in Dzerzhinsky's judgment, "an intimate collaboration between the economic apparatus and the security forces was indispensable" for the success of industrialization.[72]

The Great Turn of 1928–30 was driven by four convergent impulses: the impetus of the First Five-Year Plan; the drive for the forced collectivization of agriculture; the conversion and activation of the OGPU for economic functions; and the centrifugal force of Stalin's rising ascendancy. There is no question but that the momentum of this second foundation of the Bolshevik regime carried over to the expansion of the Gulag. On March 3, 1928, the Council of People's Commissars urged that the penal regimen be hardened to inflict longer sentences and reduce early releases. It did so largely to facilitate the organization and allocation of prison labor. Three weeks later, on March 26, an official decree "ordered the 'greater use of inmates' in the fulfillment of economic projects." Following the Communist Party's adoption of Stalin's conception of forced industrialization in April 1929, the swelling prison population was increasingly considered a "work force" and the OGPU "began to develop an extensive and economically grounded system of forced-labor camps."[73] Within a year the authorities introduced a clear distinction between, on the one hand, prisoners sentenced to terms of less than three years, who were to serve their time in the work colonies of the NKVD, and, on the other, prisoners sentenced to longer terms, to be served in the camps of the OGPU. Hereafter the OGPU's camps mushroomed into the sprawling Gulag holding millions of inmates, hundreds of thousands of them deployed as forced laborers, typically in the construction of the infrastructures essential for the fulfillment of the Five-Year Plans—railway lines, canals, dams, and roads. With the stress on the economic utility of prisoners—also in mining and logging—the camps of the OGPU easily stole the march upon those of the Commissariat of Justice, which kept faith with the precepts of rehabilitation and reeducation. In any case, in great measure for reasons of functional rationality, both political and economic, the prisons and camps of both the OGPU and the Commissariat of Justice were placed under the All-Union Commissariat of Internal Affairs. As a subdivision of this restructured NKVD, the Gulag—the Main Administration of Corrective Labor Camps and Labor Settlements—assumed control of all places of confinement, including their labor reservoirs.

The flux and reflux of the prison population was closely related with coercive and terror-freighted political moves whose reasons and consequences were never purely or primarily economic. Between the Great Turn and the outbreak of the Second World War there were two major waves of mass arrests which swelled the number of prisoners in the Gulag: the first, between 1929 and 1933, consisted of "the opponents and victims of 'dekulakization' and forced collectivization, almost exclusively peasants, disproportionately many from Ukraine;" the second, from 1936 through mid-1938, consisted of the victims of the *Ezhovshchina*, including the "great purge," who came from "all walks of life."[74] In the camps of the Gulag the authorities distinguished between nonpolitical and political inmates. The latter "were used unproductively and allowed to die at the height of the Terror with little or no thought for economic purposes."[75] While under the *ancien régime* and NEP political prisoners had enjoyed a special status, they now tended to be relegated to the depths of the Gulag's hell on earth, along with great criminals. Except for the politicals, one and all were impressed for forced labor "in the service of the second and third Five-Year Plan."[76]

There was, then, a vast increase in the camp population starting in the late 1920s, when it stood at about 30,000. It is estimated to have reached over 500,000 in the mid-1930s, and between 1.5 and 3.5 million by 1939.[77] The overall number of individuals who died is reckoned at between 1.5 and 3 million, unevenly divided between those executed in the camps and those who died there of "natural causes," such as hunger, disease, and exhaustion. Conditions were particularly harsh in "the camps of Kolyma, the camps serving the construction of the Kotlas-Vorkuta railway, the logging camps, and the camps in the far north" of European Russia.[78] There is nothing to suggest that the Gulag was conceived and operated with an autogenocidal or ethnocidal intention, or unwittingly turned into a autogenocidal or ethnocidal fury.[79] The vast majority of inmates—probably over 90 percent—were adult males between the ages of twenty and sixty. There were relatively few children, women, and aged in the camps. Reflecting Russia's social profile, peasants constituted the greatest number of inmates and victims, vastly overshadowing industrial workers and miners. As for the element of ethnocide, even if Ukrainians intermittently were victimized disproportionately, non-Russians were not preyed upon more than Russians.

Of course, all figures bearing on the Gulag are controversial, there being few reliable and exact statistics. Historians know all too well that it is impossible to be accurate and precise about the intemperance of man's inhumanity to man. They can advance more or less well-grounded orders of magnitude, and even these can be treacherous. It is equally misleading to systematically inflate or deflate, usually for polemical reasons, the numbers pertaining to the pyramids of victims and their sufferings. Eventually, as the empirical data is sifted, passions cool, and contexts are framed, plausible figures carry the day, but not without remaining subject to debate and correction.

Meanwhile, the Gulag did not stand by itself: it was part of a large configuration of violence and terror. Whatever the total number of "excess" deaths from 1917 through 1939—between 10 million and 20 million—they cry out for chronologically informed disaggregation, key to critical analysis: the civil war and famine of 1921–22; dekulakization and the famine of 1932–33; the show trials and the *Ezhovshchina*, 1936–38. In the grand total of ravaged lives, the two famines account for by far the greatest number, and they were nearly all peasants, and "unknown." By contrast, the victims of the show trials and *Ezhovshchina* accounted for a much smaller, if disproportionately large, share of the victims. Predominantly urban and educated, they were, above all, high and mid-level officials and functionaries of the party-state, including the military. By virtue of ever so many of their recorded life histories, their identity and fate are easier to reconstruct than those of the wretches of starvation. As we shall see, not everyone who was purged in 1937–38 was arrested, and not everyone who was arrested was executed.

* * *

The violence and terror of Stalin's regime became uniquely fierce and extensive between 1934–35 and 1937–38, the years of the "great purge." Both at the time and since, the word "purge" has assumed a variety of meanings. In the narrow sense, it denotes the periodic, albeit irregular, cleansing of the Communist Party; in a wider sense, the big show trials of 1936–39; and in the broadest sense, all the internal violence and terror that started with the civil war and culminated in the great trials and the *Ezhovshchina* of 1936–38.

Under the *ancien régime* the Bolshevik party had been a clandestine party with a small and select membership, the very opposite of a mass movement. For obvious reasons its membership increased from about 20,000 in 1917 to about 570,000 in 1921. The purges of the 1920s were designed to preserve the party's "original revolutionary fervor" by screening and weeding out, above all, "careerists and flatterers," the chief agents of bureaucratization and corruption.[80] The largest purge of the decade was in 1921, in the wake of the civil war, when roughly one-fourth of the party members were excluded. Although "ideological 'enemies' or 'aliens' " were also targeted, in the purges of the 1920s "*political* crimes or deviations pertained to a *minority* of those expelled."[81] With time, not a few ordinary citizens shared "a grim feeling of satisfaction at the sight of the downfall of frequently oppressive bureaucrats and party officials."[82]

Not unlike the large purge of 1921, that of 1933 followed a huge and rapid growth of party ranks. Starting in 1929, this influx answered the party's need to meet the challenge of industrialization and collectivization. With membership rising by 1.4 million within a few years, there was growing concern about the party being flooded with time-servers and mediocrities. Some "18 percent of the party was expelled," about 23 percent of them peasants, 14 percent of them employees, and 60 percent workers. Although the criteria for expulsion were "slightly more ideological" in 1933 than in the 1920s, the principal objective was, as before, to limit the perverse effects of wild party growth, not to persecute "members of the [political] opposition."[83] There was, however, a noticeable change starting in 1935. In the purge of that year the proportion of "politicals" expelled from the party rose to about 25 percent, reflecting a growing disposition and resolve to "hunt for enemies" within the party, although not as yet in its higher circles.[84]

The political trials of the late 1920s and early 1930s were in the same key as the party purge of 1933. They, too, unfolded in the heat and turbulence of the Great Turn. The Shakhty trial, in the spring of 1928, and the trial of the so-called "Industrial Party," in the winter of 1930, were meant to cow non-party specialists and experts, many of them from the old technical intelligentsia, which was of growing importance to Russia's industrialization. In the first trial fifty-three engineers, including three German nationals, were charged with sabotage and treason for allegedly engaging in deliberate "wrecking," corruption, and mismanagement. Eleven of the defendants were sentenced to be shot, of whom five were executed. The others were judged less severely: four were acquitted, while four received suspended sentences and ten prison terms ranging from one to three years. In the second trial the court pronounced life sentences for most of the accused who confessed their guilt, but political authorities commuted them to prison terms. At a third trial, in March 1931, fourteen ex-Mensheviks working as experts in several economic and planning bureaus were accused of subversive "wrecking" for having pressed for a slow-paced tempo of industrial growth. After making confession they were given prison terms of between five and ten years.

Even if "not all the repression of those years was unjustified," many of the arrests, indictments, and sentences were "completely unwarranted."[85] The charges were shadowy, not to say groundless, the imputation of willful sabotage linked to foreign powers or émigrés being particularly insidious. Clearly, the trials were exercises in political justice in which "legal forms [were] coopted for extra-legal purposes," making for a "fusion of law and terror."[86] This is not to say, however, that the trials of 1928 to 1931, any more than the purges of those same years, were a necessary and logical link or way station between Lenin's reign of dictatorial violence and terror from 1917 to 1924 and Stalin's reign of unbounded and unpredictable terror starting in the late 1920s. Such a linear vision blinks at the perplexities and resistances attending the Great Turn into the second foundation of the Revolution. Presumable Stalin, compared to Hitler, was neither hesitant nor remote, and he played an active and "personal role" in the terror.[87] There is, however, no need to portray him as "an omniscient and omnipotent demon" or as a "master planner" and consummate schemer in order to show his terrifying sides, including his iron will, arrant suspicion, and moral indigence. Indeed, he was "a cruel but ordinary mortal unable to see the future and with a limited ability to create and control it."[88]

Judging by Mikhail Riutin's remonstrance and Sergei Kirov's assassination, political dissension and opposition were very much astir during the first half of the 1930s.[89] A deposed high official of the Moscow party, Riutin was one of the moving spirits of a faction critical of furious collectivization and industrialization. In August 1932, two years after his expulsion from the party for spreading rightist propaganda, he circulated a lengthy memorandum advocating slowing the pace of collectivization and capital investment in order to give relief to peasants and workers. His urgent plea might have gone unnoticed for being on many tongues, except that it was combined with a plain-spoken denunciation of Stalin's rule as "the most naked, deceitful, [and perfectly] realized . . . personal dictatorship" which was "killing Leninism [and] the proletarian revolution." Riutin looked to the "struggle for the destruction" of this dictatorship to "give birth to new leaders and heroes." Following Riutin's arrest in September 1932, at Stalin's urging twenty of his associates were expelled from the party for "counterrevolutionary" activities, among them Zinoviev and Kamenev, who were suspected of sympathizing with them.[90] Stalin having failed to convince the Politburo to prosecute Riutin, he was committed to forced residence until 1937, when he was swallowed up in the fires of the Great Terror.

Kirov was even closer to the center of power than Riutin. Member of the Politburo and chief of the Communist Party in Leningrad, he was assassinated on December 1, 1934. Until recently Stalin was widely presumed to have abetted, if not masterminded, this murder with an eye to remove a dangerous rival who, to boot, was said to have been of democratic disposition. It now appears that through the years Kirov "supported Stalin on every major policy issue," which did not, however, preclude his having a considerable personal following in the party.[91] Be that as it may, Stalin exploited the assassination, putting all the blame on the opposition. In January 1935 nineteen adherents of a so-called "Moscow Center" were arrested for complicity in the murder, including Zinoviev and Kamenev, who were sentenced, respectively, to ten and five years of close arrest. Still, as with Riutin, the fate of Zinoviev and Kamenev was not sealed until two years later, when both succumbed in the first of the big show trials in August 1936. Meanwhile Kirov's assassination, which was to figure prominently in the Moscow trials, carried enormous weight for allegedly providing concrete proof of the ominous conspiracy subverting Soviet society.

The initially relatively mild treatment of Riutin and the alleged accomplices of Kirov's assassin was consonant with a certain political thaw following the worst ravages of the dekulakization and famine.

On May 8, 1933, Stalin and Molotov "ordered the release of half of all labor-camp inmates whose sentences were connected with collectivization." The following year the regime began "to rein in the police and courts and to institute substantial reforms within them." Paradoxically, Andrei Vyshinsky, the ferocious Inquisition-like prosecutor in the coming show trials, pressed for the establishment and observance of legal norms and procedures. This modulation of the terror continued after Kirov's assassination, perhaps in part because the economy was doing well in the mid-1930s, early in the Second Five-Year Plan. In August 1935 "the government declared an amnesty for all collective farmers sentenced to less than five years if they worked 'honorably and with good conscience' on the kolkhozy." Between 1934 and 1936 "arrests in general declined rapidly and steadily," and so did prosecutions, convictions, and imprisonments for "counterrevolutionary activity." These years also saw the debates surrounding the preparation of the new constitution of 1936, which was to reflect a certain normalization. None of this means that Stalin's regime was emptying the Gulag and clearing the way for a transition to democracy in the party or political society at large. But it is to suggest that there was "no pattern . . . of increasing terror," which makes its subsequent escalation that much more past comprehension.[92]

✻ ✻ ✻

It is difficult to grasp, let alone rank the preconditions, causes, and precipitants for this escalation. What were Stalin's reasons for the skyrocketing violence and terror in the late 1930s: to secure his and his associates' rule by eliminating personal or factional rivals; to hold down a restless population by fear; to combat real and perceived enemies at home and abroad; to regain mastery of a political and civil society that was spinning out of control? In addition there is the greatest enigma of all: the regime's insistence on public confession, and the compliance of so many of the victims with this dictate.

Amid the ambiguities and riddles, one certainly stands out. By the mid-1930s, the general situation of state and society became as complex and imperiled as it had been at the time of the Great Turn—except that international tensions were much greater than at the time of the war scare of 1927, and weighed much more heavily in the balance.

In domestic affairs the good years of 1934–36 gave way to a decided economic slowdown aggravated by the world depression and the bad harvest of 1936. The worst since the famine of 1932–33, this crop failure served as a stark reminder that the agrarian sector remained the regime's Achilles' heel. With time the purges exacerbated the situation by fostering considerable economic disorganization. As of September 1936, when Stalin appointed Nikolai Ezhov head of the NKVD, "the focus of the terror expanded to include growing numbers of industrial managers, administrators, and engineers, and the main accusations leveled against purge victims also changed from conspiracy to assassinate Soviet leaders to economic sabotage and 'wrecking'," first leveled in the political trials of 1928 and 1930. The many failings and blockages of the awkward and untried planned and command economy were "attributed to deliberate economic sabotage . . . and espionage."[93]

By themselves "the economic problems . . . of the second half of the 1930s would not have . . . resulted in political terror." They were politicized by "a suspicious and voluntarist leadership that expected 'miracles' and refused to accept economic constraints." Soviet leaders acted in a "political culture and [faced] a populace accustomed to blame hardships on demonic forces and conspiracies." But above all, ominous international developments, with foreign enemies at the gates, bolstered the credibility of wild conspiracy mongering at the same time that they dictated an ever faster military buildup which further strained and deformed the economy.[94]

In the east Japan's conquest of Manchuria in 1931 was a harbinger of worse things to come. Hitler's assumption of power in Germany was particularly worrisome, both politically and militarily. Fascism, or what Moscow perceived as such, spread like wildfire, judging by the ascendance of new-model conservative and reactionary forces in Austria, Hungary, Bulgaria, Rumania, Greece, and Portugal, as well as the Baltic countries, including Poland. Mussolini invaded Ethiopia in October 1935, a move which was condoned by London and Paris and diverted attention from Hitler's unilateral reoccupation of the Rhineland in March 1936. In November Berlin and Tokyo signed the Anti-Comintern and Anti-Soviet Pact, to which Rome adhered the following year, in keeping with Mussolini's tried and true anti-Communism. In the meantime, in July 1936 General Franco's uprising against Spain's republican government rallied not only the political support of all Spanish right-wing parties and the Catholic Church but also the military cooperation of Germany, Italy, and Portugal. The Pope's encyclical *Mit brennender Sorge*, which criticized the Third Reich's treatment of the Church without condemning National Socialism, was nothing as virulent as his *Divini redemptoris*, condemning atheist Communism.

The Soviet Union was not totally blameless for this raging destabilization of the world system. Apart from having unintentionally helped Hitler's rise to power with the Comintern's campaign against German Social Democracy prior to 1933, with their terrorist repression at home the Soviets vindicated the anti-Communism of Fascists as well as conservatives and moderate democrats. Overall, however, Moscow was on the defensive and terrified by the prospect of being left to stand alone against, above all, Germany and Japan. Pushed by foreign Communists, notably French and Italian, Stalin and his associates in 1934 changed Comintern policy from fighting "social fascists" to pressing for hybrid popular and united fronts in the outside world, but with Soviet Russia's security needs taking precedence over class warfare.

Stalin must have realized that it was not Comintern stratagems but Soviet diplomacy that would be decisive. Eager to break out of Russia's isolation, he looked for a rapprochement with the Western democracies. France promised to be most receptive.[95] As much as Moscow, Paris was looking for a continental counterweight to the bellicose Third Reich. In addition, the fascist danger had precipitated Europe's pioneering Popular Front in France, first in the streets of the French capital in 1934–35 and then with the formation of the government of Léon Blum in 1936. To be sure, the Franco-Russian mutual security pact of 1935 was stillborn. Still, Stalin and Maxim Litvinov, his commissar of foreign affairs, were agreed that in the short run Paris, not London, was critical for putting Berlin under restraint. Although it backfired, the Soviet intervention in Spain was intended primarily to improve relations with France. Admittedly, London deterred Paris from intervening in support of the Loyalists. But Blum was no less held back by the moderate reformists in his own coalition as well as France's traditional conservatives, the same forces which had scuttled the Franco-Soviet pact in 1935. In any case, Stalin's intervention in the distant Iberian peninsula was not a self-confident and sly move to expand Soviet power and spread the Communist ideology. Rather, it was a frantic but risky bid for allies by the worried governors of a militarily endangered great power. Not unlike Napoleon, Stalin contracted a bleeding and debilitating "ulcer" in Spain, except that his ulcer gangrened to become fiercely ideological and moral, not military: the cold-blooded torment of Trotskyites, syndicalists, and anarchists on the ground as well as of blameless Soviet officers, advisors, and agents after their return home.

Domestic and foreign affairs were interlocked, and there was no debating them separately. In the mid-1930s the far "left" at home and abroad became fiercely critical of Stalin's new international course. The Comintern's call for a popular front recognizing no enemies on the left and Litvinov's pursuit of collective security through the League of Nations were denounced for undermining revolutionary internationalism. The charge was that instead of adding fuel to the general crisis in the capitalist world and exploiting it for the proletarian cause, Moscow was helping to dampen it as part of the strategy to reassure the Western powers. For the "left" critics Stalin's diplomacy, soon including his military intervention in Spain, was of a piece with his domestic policy, which they scorned for being ever more Thermidorean "in spirit if not in practice."[96] It is difficult to say whether considerations of world or domestic politics weighed heavier in Stalin's decision to step up the terror as he perceived himself to be under growing partisan fire for both. His failure to prevail on the Western democracies to reverse their appeasement of Hitler at Russia's expense is bound to have deepened his predicament, if not bewilderment.

* * *

The first of the great show trials, in August 1936, opens the most horrifying and inscrutable chapter in the life of the Bolshevik regime and Stalin's reign. In comparing the "mutual slaughter" of the French revolutionaries and those of Russia, one difference stands out above all others.[97] In the time of the Great Revolution the terror of the guillotine started some few years after 1789; it was over within fourteen months; and the "centrist" rule of Robespierre, following the elimination of first the "left" and then the "right" Mountain, lasted less than four months. By contrast, "the Bolshevik regime was nearing the close of its second decade without showing signs of Jacobin-like insanity." Of course "there was no lack of terror in the years of the [Russian] civil war," as there had been during the French civil war. But the Bolsheviks, unlike the Jacobins, "did not execute their Girondins." They either "allowed . . . the most eminent spokesmen of Menshevism . . . to leave or . . . exiled [them] from Russia after their party had been banned." Although "a handful" of the Mensheviks who stayed behind were imprisoned, most of them, "reconciling themselves to defeat, loyally served in the Soviet administration and even on the staff of leading Bolsheviks." The pattern of repression was essentially the same with the Socialist Revolutionaries.

Apparently the "Russian Mountain, having spared the lives of its Girondins," was not about to "wallow in the blood of its own leaders." Indeed, even in the early 1930s "the story was still current among Bolsheviks that at the outset . . . their leaders had . . . [sworn] never to set the guillotine into motion against one another." It seems that having "pondered" the French example, Stalin repeatedly said that it "deterred him from resorting to the most drastic means of repression." In the mid-1920s, when Zinoviev and Kamenev "demanded blood" against Trotsky, Stalin objected that "chopping off [heads] and blood-letting . . . were dangerous and infectious: you chop off one head today, another one tomorrow, still another on the day after—in the end what will be left of the party?"[98] In 1929, when Trotsky was exiled from Russia, "it was still inconceivable that Trotsky should be imprisoned, let alone put before the firing squad."

When the French Revolution devoured its own children it did so with an unremittingly "blind but still fresh passion." The Russian Revolution, for its part, took this turn only after "its lava . . . seems to have cooled down." Unlike the Jacobins, the Bolsheviks had elements of a pre-established program and organization, which meant that rather than "being part of the revolutionary flux" they were able to control it and resist "the irrational urges inherent in a despotism . . . issued from revolution." When they finally "succumbed to . . . the gods that were athirst [after having withstood] them for nearly two decades, [the] prostration of the Bolsheviks was even more frightful than that of the Jacobins." Ultimately, this controlled premeditation, "no less than the confessions . . . which contrasted so sharply with the proud and defiant behavior of most of the Jacobin leaders in the dock, made Stalin's purge trials appear even more mystifying than Robespierre's 'amalgams.' "

Certainly Stalin must have approved the first great show trial, that of sixteen eminent Bolsheviks, including Kamenev and Zinoviev, in August 1936. Patently political, this trial resorted to "legal forms for extra-legal purposes" and fused "law and terror."[99] Although it was public and publicized, it crudely transgressed judicial rules and practices. There was no presumption of innocence and no hard evidence to support the indictment; the accused were denied legal counsel. They were arraigned for belonging to a Trotsky-Zinoviev United Center that ostensibly was planning to assassinate Soviet leaders. Kirov's murder was said to have been their dress rehearsal. Straining for a semblance of plausibility, the prosecutor made Trotsky's subversive intrigues the gravamen of his charge. Primarily through Lev Sedov, his son, Trotsky was alleged to have carried on a correspondence with oppositionists inside the Soviet Union as well as maintained personal contacts with them abroad.[100] Although Trotsky was not "blameless in life and pure of crime," and doubtless looked to unseat Stalin, the polemical pamphlet, not the Trojan horse, was his preferred weapon. Still, though Vyshinsky's charge was trumped up, it impressed those credulous souls who presume that there is no smoke without fire. In any case, Zinoviev, Kamenev, and most of the other defendants, the majority of whom were one-time followers of Trotsky, in open court confessed their complicity in Kirov's assassination and their ties to a so-called "Terrorist Center." For all one knows, at the outset the defendants could not imagine that they might, in fact, be put to the sword. Zinoviev and Kamenev had been tried once before, and until 1936 oppositionists of most persuasions and factions had been spared though marginalized. But this time Stalin crossed the Rubicon. All sixteen were executed on August 24, 1936, followed by the arrest and execution of two score suspected sympathizers.

The transition from the relative political moderation of the three good years to the unbounded repression of the infamous years was completed when Ezhov became chief of the NKVD. Since the late 1920s he had occupied several high posts in party and government. In 1935, in a position paper submitted to Stalin, Ezhov had argued that the Trotskyites at home and abroad were aware that Zinoviev's "counterrevolutionary band" had chosen "terror as the weapon in

[its] battle against the party and working class." A member of the Central Committee, he followed up this text with a circular to local party organs asserting that the collaboration of Trotskyites and Zinovievites was premised on their agreement that "terror directed at party and state leaders [was] the only and decisive means to gain power."[101] In any event, Stalin acted with his eyes wide open when, on September 25, 1936, he notified the Politburo of the "absolute necessity and urgency to appoint Comrade Ezhov to the post of People's Commissar of Internal Affairs," to replace Genrykh Iagoda, whom he held responsible for "the OGPU being four years behind . . . in bringing to light the Trotskyist-Zinovievist bloc."[102]

In their forced confessions Zinoviev and Kamenev had intimated that they had sympathizers among former right-oppositionists, thereby unintentionally contributing to spreading the net of suspicion. In September Karl Radek was arrested and Tomsky committed suicide. Three months later Ezhov told the Central Committee that leading rightists, including Bukharin and Rykov, "completely shared [the] aims" of the Trotskyite-Zinovievite center. Presently Bukharin was summoned to explain himself to the Central Committee. He firmly denied any wrongdoing or any familiarity, let alone complicity, with either Riutin or the subversive terrorist center at the same time that he commended the party for its vigilance. Bukharin expressed relief that these nefarious activities were being uncovered before the inevitable and approaching war, adding that "now we can win." Even if unwittingly, and with the execution of the sixteen weighing on him, Bukharin vindicated the reasons and charges of the persecuting prosecution, only to become its star victim a year later, in March 1938.[103]

The second major political trial was held during the last week of January 1937. Piatakov, Radek, Sokolnikov, and fourteen other high party officials were in the dock. In the late 1920s nearly all of them had been expelled from the party for supporting Trotsky, only to be readmitted in the early 1930s and appointed to important positions. Procedurally this trial was no different from the first, except that the authorities now resorted to physical and psychological torture to break the defendants, and have them confess publicly. The indictment, however, had a new tonality. In addition to being accused of conspiring to assassinate party leaders as part of an "Anti-Soviet Trotskyite Center," the seventeen were charged not only with the sabotage and "wrecking" of planned industrialization and collectivization but also, or above all, with espionage in the service of Germany and Japan. The burden of the presentment was that the accused were sapping the Soviet Union's economic and military strength in a time of intense foreign dangers. All seventeen were found guilty, and thirteen were executed.

This obsession with foreign dangers also weighed on the next plenum of the Central Committee in late February and early March 1937, to which Bukharin had been summoned. Its backdrop was Moscow's lone intervention in Spain, the Anti-Comintern Pact, and the Western democracies' continuing appeasement of Hitler, Mussolini, and Franco. Molotov took the floor first, with a report entitled "The Lessons of Wrecking, Diversion, and Espionage of the Japanese-German-Trotskyite Agents."[104] When grilling Bukharin before his peers, Molotov interjected that "if you don't confess, that will prove you're a fascist hireling."[105] Ezhov struck the same note in his "Lessons Flowing from the Harmful Activity, Diversion, and Espionage of the Japanese-German-Trotskyite Agents." He accused Bukharin of knowing of the treasonous Trotskyite conspiracy, whose "threads . . . extended farther than originally thought."[106] Stressing the importance of taking account of the links between foreign treason and domestic subversion, Stalin criticized party leaders for not "paying attention to such things as the international position of the Soviet Union, capitalist encirclement, strengthening political work, struggle against wrecking, etc., supposing all these questions to be second-rate, and even third-rate matters."[107]

No matter how crude and contrived the charges, the perceived logic of the world situation gave them a ring of plausibility, all the more so since a time of troubles was inherently conducive to conspiratorial thinking among masses and classes alike. Indeed, when espousing the paralogism of the plot, Stalin and his votaries may have been as artless and unstudied as they were cunning and calculating.

* * *

If anything, the Tukhachevsky affair at once attested and reinforced the conspiratorial ambience and pretense. Hero of the civil war and Russo-Polish war, as well as modernizer of the Red Army, Tukhachevsky was probably the best known and most popular military leader in the armed forces and the party. He was chief of staff and deputy commissar of war when he was promoted to candidate member of the Central Committee in 1934 and Marshal of the Soviet Union in 1935. On May 1, 1937, he "stood by Stalin's side at the Lenin Mausoleum reviewing the May Day parade."[108] In the heavy atmosphere of the time it must have been shocking and disquieting to learn from the press, on May 11, that Tukhachevsky had been removed from office and, a month later, that he and seven high-ranking generals had been arrested, judged, and executed for treason and espionage for Germany. Tried by a summary court-martial, behind closed doors, Tukhachevsky was severely tortured before he confessed.

Since Tukhachevsky and other officers were mentioned during the proceedings of the recent show trials, it is tempting to argue that Stalin meant to eliminate them for the same ostensible crimes as the members of so-called Trotskyite centers. But the alleged conspiracy of the military leaders seems altogether more complex, and it is also more difficult to dismiss out of hand.

Four theses can be distinguished. The first holds that Tukhachevsky headed a generals' plot, without foreign connections, to remove Stalin and substitute military for civilian rule. According to a second thesis, Nazi Germany's secret services planted forged evidence of a Tukhachevsky-led generals' conspiracy with a view to panic Stalin into eliminating the Red Army's chief officers, including its most talented and daunting general. In a third construction, an émigré White general hatched the idea of a Tukhachevsky plot with links to the Wehrmacht, and inveigled German intelligence services into feeding it to Moscow, his objective being to avenge Tukhachevsky's apostasy to the Red Army after 1917. The fourth suggests that once rumors of disloyalty in the military reached Stalin, he seized on them to spread his terror to the army and to prepare the ground for a rapprochement with Berlin by "placating the Germans . . . by destroying his best military officers."[109]

In any event, Stalin could not completely rule out a generals' plot, all the more worrisome in light of yesteryear's covert collaboration between senior Soviet and German officers. There is also the likelihood that by unduly crediting and stretching the evidence, Ezhov reinforced Stalin's foreboding of "a vast [military] conspiracy against him" and bolstered his resolve "to root it out."[110] Even a less hardened tyrant than Stalin, harried by insuperable problems at home and abroad, would have been shaken by flying rumors of a possible *fronde* in the supreme command of his armed forces, which is not to say that he would have reacted as ferociously as he did. To make matters worse, the conspiracy was presumed to be headed by the premier general of the army, who alone among "all the military leaders of that time . . . showed a resemblance to the original Bonaparte and could have played the Russian First Consul."[111] Even though Soviet advisors, pilots, and arms were engaged in Spain at the time of the Tukhachevsky affair and the ensuing military purge, nothing suggests that Stalin wanted to be his own Napoleon. Incidentally, little is known about Tukhachevsky's position on the intervention in support of the Spanish Republic.

Among the officers who perished in the furiously unfolding military purge, not a few, after fighting in the Russo-Polish war, had risen to top commands. All the marshals of the Red Army, except Budenny and Voroshilov, were executed. An estimated 20,000 to 35,000 army officers and 5,000 to 6,000 air force officers, or one-fourth to over half of the officers of these two branches, were expelled from the party and cashiered. In 1937–39 8,785 army officers and 892 air force officers who were "discharged for political reasons or arrested were returned to their posts, . . . leaving a total of 24,624 in both branches, whose fate is unknown."[112] It is still unclear how many of the officers "whose fate is unknown . . . remained in the Gulag; how many were [acquitted and] freed but not reinstated in the army"; or how many were executed. Although not all were shot or imprisoned, the purge was at once massive and bloody.[113] Officers in politically sensitive field commands or administrative posts were disproportionately at risk. As a matter of course, in May 1937 the civil war practice of assigning political commissars to military commands was reinstated.[114]

The radical purge in the military was part of the *Ezhovshchina*—in reality the *Stalinshchina*[115]—in polity and society at large. Indeed, "to the extent that the terror expanded to become 'great,' it did so now," following Tukhachevsky's execution, and not before. This was the time that, instructed by Stalin and the Politburo, Ezhov fixed on wholly arbitrary categories of perpetrators of past and present transgressions, to be subjected to arbitrary punishment. The NKVD had nearly complete license for the selection of victims. As for the objectives of this excessively excessive terror that was utterly disproportion-

ate to any imaginable purpose, they remain mysterious: the completion of a system of "totalitarian" terror giving rise to a reign of fear
pointed against largely imaginary enemies; or the intensification of a
functional terror against largely real enemies at the expense of innocents. But then again, perhaps there was no fixed purpose, and the
Ezhovshchina, including the open political trials and the closed military trial of Tukhachevsky, was in the nature of an "explosion of madness or [panic] fear" in the highest reaches of an unhinged and intractable party and state, embodied in Stalin.[116]

Ezhov's instructions divided suspects "into two categories, the one
marked for execution and the other for [internal] exile," a quota being
set for each. He stipulated that in 1937 in the two largest oblasts of
Moscow and Leningrad, respectively, 5,000 and 4,000 "were to be
shot," and 30,000 and 10,000 "exiled." Ezhov also fixed at 10,000
the number of inmates to "be executed in the labor camps." The
NKVD set a total of "72,950 executions and 177,500 exiles" for the
country as a whole. In January 1938 Stalin personally "approved an
additional 48,000 executions and 9,200 exiles in 22 jurisdictions."
With local NKVD branches free "to raise or lower the numbers," arrests ran considerably higher than originally fixed by the center. It
appears that in 1937–38 all told the maximum number of people "arrested on all charges" was 2.5 million, while "[t]he number shot 'was
more likely a question of hundreds of thousands rather than of millions.' "[117] The ravages were most devastating in the higher and highest reaches of the political class. Seventy percent of the members of
the Central Committee elected in 1934 were sent to the Gulag or
executed, and so were 50 percent of the delegates of the 1934 Party
Congress, as well as 80 percent of the sitting Central Committee and
30 percent of People's Commissars. Between 1934 and 1939 party
membership was reduced by 36 percent. In the government, the purge
struck savagely at the upper echelons of Gosplan and the Commissariat of Foreign Affairs, in which "a minimum of 62 percent . . . of the
top officials . . . who served in the 1920s . . . fell in the Terror." To
the extent that the Great Terror's primary aim was to put in fear the
inner circles of power rather than the population at large, it is emblematic that "except for Stalin, every member of the Politburo who had
served under Lenin was destroyed, including Trotsky, who was murdered by an NKVD agent in Mexico in 1940."[118]

The third and last great political trial marked at once the crest and reflux of the *Ezhovshchina*. From March 2 to 13, 1938, Bukharin, Rykov, Iagoda, and eighteen others were tried as affiliates of a "Right-Trotskyite Bloc." They stood accused of a composite of the charges preferred at the 1936 and 1937 trials, except that those relating to the economic, military, and diplomatic subversion and weakening of the Soviet Union in favor of foreign powers weighed even more heavily than heretofore. All of the defendants had occupied leading positions in party and state, and most of them had been actively involved in the internecine political struggles of the past decade.

Probably this third trial had greater resonance than the first two because Bukharin was among the accused. Of all the old Bolsheviks his standing was the most irreproachable. Intermittently member of the Central Committee of the Politburo and of the executive committee of the Comintern, as well as editor of *Pravda* and *Izvestia*, Bukharin was also, in Lenin's judgment, the party's "most brilliant and valuable theoretician."[119] As noted, Bukharin fully sided with Stalin against the Left opposition and Trotsky before opposing him during the Great Turn to planned industrialization and collectivization, which led to his being attacked as the leader of a Right Opposition. At the same time the Great Depression, by invalidating his analysis of the staying power of capitalist stabilization, somewhat attenuated his theoretical renown. Although excluded from the Politburo and the executive of the Comintern, from 1929 to 1932 he still occupied important if not commanding positions in two economic commissariats and continued to edit *Pravda* until he was forced to leave it for *Izvestia* in 1934. However, following his implication in the alleged crimes before the first two show trials, Bukharin was completely frozen out of politics. Also, under pressure and disoriented, he gave contradictory testimony. It took another year for him to be brought to trial. In the meantime, on December 10, 1937, he wrote to Stalin, his nemesis, from prison to ask that he be allowed "either to work at some cultural task in Siberia or to emigrate to America, where he would be a faithful Soviet citizen and would 'beat Trotsky and company in the snout.' " But should he have to die, he pleaded that "it be from an overdose of morphine, not by shooting."[120]

At the trial Bukharin and Nikolai Krestinsky sparred with the prosecution, but to no avail. Under relentless compulsion, including threats to their loved ones, they and their codefendants confessed, and most of them, including Bukharin, were executed instantly, while those sentenced to prison terms paid with their lives at a later date.

The three pseudo-trials and Tukhachevsky's court-martial were the controlled part of the Great Terror, which had otherwise veered out of control and developed "a momentum of its own," perhaps to the point of "endanger[ing] the system itself."[121] By the time of the third trial there were rising criticisms within the party of the excesses and mistakes of the *Ezhovshchina*. These were first formally voiced at the plenum of the purged Central Committee in January 1938. They also made their way into the press, and there were individual remonstrances. In the course of the year the generalized and arbitrary Great Purge was curbed in favor of a return to the limited and essentially nonviolent intra-party purges of the 1920s and early 1930s. Arrests, tortures, and executions decreased radically: conditions improved in the prisons and camps; the NKVD's security police was put under restraint; and the autonomy of the judiciary began to make its mark. In November 1938 the Central Committee cashiered Ezhov, as both a gesture of appeasement and an act of self-exoneration; and before long he was arrested and executed.

At the Eighteenth Party Congress, meeting in Moscow from March 10 to 21, 1939, Stalin declared that the fight against internal enemies had run its course and that the "edge" of the security services was "no longer turned to the inside of the country, but to the outside, against external enemies."[122] It may well be that he and his closest associates concluded that the disruptions and rancors stemming from the *Ezhovshchina* needed to be reduced if they were not to impede the call to arms against the foreign enemy. The castigation and proscription of internal enemies was about to be replaced by the exaltation of army and fatherland as Russia was forced to prepare to fight a defensive war, the polar opposite of a military crusade to spread Communism abroad. Hereafter the difficult refoundation of Russia would be fraught primarily with the Furies of foreign war rather than domestic terror.

* * *

The Great Terror of the 1930s defies explanation, let alone comprehension, and divergent interpretations, old and new, will generate critical debate till the end of time. In one reading, Stalin knowingly "sent thousands to their death and tens and hundreds of thousands into prisons and concentration camps," determined to "destroy the men capable of forming an alternative government." No matter how exaggerated his estimate and fear of political rivals and their potential support, Stalin struck all precincts of the party-state to prevent any opposition from coalescing, in the process building a new political class loyal to him.[123] Another thesis, which also slights foreign dangers, denies the existence of any "active organized opposition." Insisting that the collapse of significant resistance is the essential precondition for total(itarian) terror, it holds that in resorting to it Stalin was at best marginally "concerned with known or suspected opponents." Ultimately the Great Terror " 'punished' [for] 'objective' reasons . . . , independently of any subjective guilt," with both the accuser and victim knowing not only "that the victim was innocent" but that he could never have committed any of the "crimes" imputed to him.[124]

In reality, starting with the Great Turn, and judging by the Riutin affair, Stalin and his inner circle considered the internal opposition to be both "real and dangerous," in part because they presumed it to be bound up with escalating international perils. No doubt Stalin conflated the threat to his personal leadership with the threat to the Soviet regime and Russian state. But no matter how intense his disquiet and smoldering his mistrust, in the second half of the 1930s Stalin acted "with great self-control" and was guided by "clear-cut political . . . considerations and calculations."[125]

In another construction, the Furies of 1936–38 were neither an expression of "the uncontested power of an omnipotent dictatorship" nor the "triumphant and carefully planned extermination campaign of a master strategist thirsting for vengeance and absolute power and executed by monolithic and obedient [security] operatives."[126] Indeed, it can be argued that the Great Terror was at once cause and effect of a polity and society with multiple and severe strains between rival governing factions, between Thermidoreans and true believers, and between an overstrained center and refractory periphery. The resulting distempers were magnified by the deficiencies of the party-state's administrative structures and cadres: far and wide the ouster or withdrawal of the old elites had left a vacuum inviting bureaucratic conceit and arbitrariness by unfitted officials of untried local security agencies and judicial organs. To the extent that the Great Terror was the *ultima ratio* of an unbending but insecure regime, its "implementation was chaotic, uncontrolled, and manipulated by nearly all the [party-state's] dignitaries." In sum, the *Stalinshchina* was anything but a logical system with a coherent purpose: it unfolded and raged in an "atmosphere of panic . . . reminiscent of the European witch hunts, lynchings in the American South, or McCarthyism."[127]

It is, of course, difficult to gauge the extent and intensity of the fear generated by the Great Terror. It is not unreasonable to suggest, however, that "to say that all, or probably even the majority, were terrorized is as incorrect for the USSR [even] in the second half of the 1930s as it is for Germany at the same time." Just as in the Third Reich "voluntary support was considerably more important . . . than coercion," in Soviet Russia factors other than fear "were more important in securing popular compliance."[128]

At the height of the Great Terror Stalin was, in the first place, concerned with maintaining and reinforcing the regime's whip hand over the elite.[129] As noted, the great trials struck at the top, not the bottom, of the pyramid. Besides, the unmasking of the misdeeds and deceits of public officials, near and far, corresponded with the ordinary people's predisposition "to lend credence to the regime's propaganda about the subversive activities of [domestic] plotters and foreign agents." In an as yet heavily traditional society buffeted by a whirlwind of change it was not uncommon for people to "attribute [their] everyday misfortunes to the activities of evil spirits" and to "suspect office holders of plotting against them."[130]

Incongruously, Stalin was neither a Thermidorean nor a Man on Horseback. He was, if not a revolutionary, a radical modernizer, as much by necessity as by choice. Russia's "revolution from above" was unlike Germany's in 1918–19, when Social Democrats and left liberals had effectuated a radical reform of political institutions, leaving economy, society, and judiciary essentially unaltered. Stalin, to the contrary, steeled the new political regime for a central role in an all-out economic, social, and military transformation. During the 1930s Russia became a major industrial power, with gigantic metallurgical complexes, hydroelectric power stations, and tractor plants. In sheer volume, but not quality, heavy-industry production caught up with Germany, Great Britain, and France. The number of industrial workers jumped from less than 3 million to over 8 million, and the urban population rose by almost 30 million. At the same time, in economic weight the industrial sector outstripped the agricultural sector, in which Russia's 25 million individual production units were regrouped in 240,000 collective farms.

The social costs of this hurried modernization were, of course, egregious: housing was woefully insufficient and unsanitary; workers, including the women who rushed into the labor force, labored long hours; wages and living standards were all but stagnant; and consumer goods remained scarce. Clearly, the party-state's socialization of property and throttling of the free market did not short-circuit the "primitive capital accumulation" on the back of the working class at a time that the peasantry was also being squeezed to help finance industrialization. Indeed, with collectivization having met with less economic success—and more resistance—than industrialization, peasants would have been as indigent as workers, had it not been for the food they wrested from their family plots.

But there was the other side. In the city and, to a lesser extent, in the countryside, the educational system developed rapidly at all levels, fostering upward social mobility alongside advancement by geographic relocation and on-the-job training. As a matter of course, the hothouse growth of industry and city, of party and state bureaucracy, demanded and furthered the expansion of technical and professional cadres drawn from more modest social origins than under the old regime. It is an index of this trend that between 1934 and 1939 the party admitted or recruited at least as many members as it purged.

Clearly the situation was simultaneously closed and open, terrifying and full of promise. At the same time that "party and state leaders were being arrested as 'enemies of the people' new schools, factories, and palaces of culture were rising everywhere; while military leaders were being arrested as spies . . . the Party was building a strong modern army; while scientists were being arrested as wreckers . . . Soviet science . . . developed rapidly with the Party's support; while writers were being arrested as Trotskyites and counterrevolutionaries . . . some literary works appeared that were real masterpieces; and while leaders in the minor republics were being arrested as nationalists . . . the formerly oppressed nationalities were improving their lot." This "obvious progress" could not help but "engender confidence in the Party that was organizing it and the man who stood at its head."[131]

Besides, if the inevitable social, political, and cultural discontents did not explode, it was on account not only of fear of the NKVD but of the continuing hold of the Communist promise, the absence of a credible programmatic alternative, and the cementing force of foreign dangers.

* * *

The heightened danger of war, shamelessly used to fuel the campaign against domestic enemies, was only too real. Especially as of 1936, the Allied appeasement of the Axis powers, without the least regard for Soviet Russia, quickened Stalin's sense of diplomatic and military encirclement. For all one knows, in his predicament he recalled the foreboding, in 1907, of Alexander Bogdanov, then still a Bolshevik, that by reason of the hostility of the outside world the first socialist state "would be profoundly and lastingly distorted by the many years of its besieged condition, of unavoidable terror, and of a military regime."[132]

Almost from the outset the Bolsheviks could do no more than play on the conflicts of interest among the great powers, beginning with the treaties of Brest-Litovsk (1918) and Rapallo (1922), followed by the Franco-Soviet Pact (1935). Moscow's intervention in Spain was yet another futile and self-defeating attempt to make a breach in the *cordon sanitaire*. The Kremlin seemed helpless in the face of an international situation that went from bad to worse. In March 1938 Nazi Germany "annexed" Austria. On Russia's European doorsteps, the governments of Poland and Rumania, not unlike those of the Baltic republics, turned further to the right and reinforced their pro-Western, or anti-Soviet, orientation. Along its "far eastern" borders, Japan continued its rampage in Manchuria with complete impunity. The appeasement of Nazi Germany, Fascist Italy, and militarist Japan reached its climax with the Munich conference of September 29, 1938, at which Britain and France agreed to the dismemberment of Czechoslovakia, Prague being forced to cede the Sudetenland to Berlin. Six months later, in March 1939, the Third Reich liquidated the rest of Czechoslovakia: Bohemia-Moravia became a German protectorate; Slovakia a sham independent state. Overnight, England and France pledged military support for Poland, Rumania, and Greece in case of attack.

All this time the Allies disdainfully ignored Moscow, and there was no denying that Stalin had suffered a stinging and humiliating diplomatic defeat: neither the policy of collective security nor the intervention in Spain had brought about an opening to the Western powers.

Seven weeks after the Wehrmacht marched into Prague, Molotov replaced Litvinov, the agent and symbol of Moscow's spurned courtship of Paris and London.[133] The appointment of Stalin's closest associate as foreign commissar was a signal that Soviet foreign policy was being reappraised. Not that the Kremlin, embarrassed and indecisive, considered the appeasement of Britain and France beyond recall. But the mutual distrust between Soviets and Allies, dating from 1918–20, was undiminished, with each side suspecting the other of seeking to provoke or incite Hitler to turn, first, against the other. Besides, whereas the Allies had little confidence in the Red Army, especially after its purge, Moscow doubted the political will and military capability of London and Paris to make good their eleventh-hour pledge to stand by Poland, the gateway to Russia. At any rate, Molotov now pressed the Allies to change their unilateral guarantee to Warsaw and Bucharest into a multilateral military alliance. London in particular hesitated to brace a new-model Triple Entente with a binding military commitment. The governors of Poland and Rumania would not agree to Russian troops crossing their borders to engage the Wehrmacht further west, and the Allies were loath to high-pressure them as they had high-pressured Czechoslovakia, albeit in a different logic.

It was while these cross-grained and erratic negotiations were deadlocked between July 24 and August 12, 1939, that the Kremlin made its first overtures to Berlin, which all this time continued its contacts with London and Paris. Disquieted by the prevarication of the Allies, the Soviets became increasingly anxious about the security of their western frontier. Poland was of infinitely greater strategic importance than Czechoslovakia: bordering on Russia, it was the hinge of the buffer zone running from the Baltic to the Black Sea. In the international arena Stalin and Molotov were dealing from weakness and fear, not strength and self-assurance. If they found a receptive ear in the German capital, it was largely because, not entirely unbeknown to them, Hitler was determined to break Poland before the onset of winter. Not about to risk another Munich-like debacle, the Kremlin meant to keep the Axis and the Allies from coming to an agreement much as the Allies were looking to block a rapprochement between Moscow and Berlin. Stalin and Molotov were still creatures and masters of the unfinished refoundation of Russia. But at this perilous juncture they were, above all, practitioners of real- and machtpolitik.

There is, of course, a radically different interpretation of Moscow's diplomacy, which gives absolute primacy to Stalin's ideological intention and thirst for personal power. In this alternate reading, framed with the concept of totalitarianism, the Soviet and Nazi regimes are cut of the same cloth: with Stalin and Hitler as all-powerful leaders, the political, social, and cultural structures and dynamics of both systems are all but identical. Both are considered as inherently bent on unlimited expansion, essential to bolster and maintain total domination.[134] The *Vozhd* and the *Führer* are seen as enemy brothers, the one determined on a *Drang nach Westen*, the other on a *Drang nach Osten*, seeking the military subjection of neighboring states as stepping stones to the mastery first of Europe, then the world. Moscow and Berlin are presumed alike in their resolve to tear apart bourgeois democracy and western civilization, each with the intent of establishing, by force of arms, a new transnational order based on the guiding principle, respectively, of class and race.

In this interpretation, from before the Great Turn, Stalin was sworn to execute Lenin's warrant to revolutionize the Continent, as prefigured by the military offensive toward Warsaw in 1920. Admittedly, the road to the Soviet-Nazi Pact was twisted. But it kept moving forward, with Stalin relentlessly seeking to embroil the capitalist nations in a mutually devastating war certain to seed the ground for the spread of Communist regimes across Europe and overseas. Supposedly the Kremlin worked within this logic when blinking at Hitler's rise to power and, thereafter, when cynically contriving and exploiting the appeals of antifascism to serve the interests of the Soviet state and elite by infiltrating and subverting nations far and wide. In keeping with this reason, Stalin is said to have rushed arms production not to bolster Russia's security but to strengthen his expansionist hand. At last, in August 1939, he took advantage of the looked-for, if unexpected, opportunity to divide and conquer the crisis-torn capitalist world. In sum, Molotov's last-minute negotiations with the Western powers were a calculated deception, all the more so since allegedly not Berlin but Moscow pressed for a deal which entailed Stalin's premeditated seizure of Eastern Europe, way station to the rest of the Continent.[135]

The unreality of this retrovision from a frozen and narrowly western cold-war perspective shuts out the grim reality of the Phony Peace of 1938–39: the Axis powers were the aggressors, and Hitler had a relatively rigid timetable for spreading Berlin's dominion over Europe. Presently Stalin, like Chamberlain and Daladier before him, sought to avoid or postpone war with Germany, eager for a breathing spell to further military preparedness.

In any case, the Third Reich was primed to liquidate Poland in the manner of Czechoslovakia, only more nakedly so. Even in the unlikely event the French army launched an attack on Germany's fortified western frontier, it would lack the striking power and the time to keep the Wehrmacht from overrunning Poland up to Russia's border. Deeply apprehensive about continuing isolation in the face of Germany's impending move to the east, Stalin and Molotov decided to entertain Joachim von Ribbentrop's insistent offer to pay for the Kremlin's momentary neutrality with strategically valuable territories.

With the Soviet-German Non-Aggression Pact of August 23 Moscow and Berlin agreed not to attack each other for ten years, nor to aid a third party that might attack either of them. This unexceptional if startling compact was coupled with an unseasonable secret protocol dividing the ill-starred eastern European rimland—prized by all geopoliticians of pre-atomic times—into two spheres of influence: Soviet Russia secured hegemony over eastern Poland, Bessarabia, Finland, Estonia, and Latvia; Nazi Germany over western Poland and Lithuania. With a stroke of the pen, Stalin and Hitler nullified the treaties of Brest-Litovsk and Riga, as well as Versailles. Above all, the imprudently overexpanded Third Poland was about to pay the price of a fourth partition for having willingly, nay zealously, served as the linchpin of both the Paris Peace Settlement and the *cordon sanitaire*.

Unlike the Allies, Hitler was in a position to offer both time and space: he yielded lands which he himself coveted for the Thousand-Year Reich, confident that he could reclaim them, at will, from a militarily weak, politically unsteady, and racially blighted Soviet regime. Having robbed the Allies of the strategic advantage which had emboldened them in 1914, Hitler expected them to back down and leave Poland at his mercy. When they stood firm, he invaded Poland on

September 1, confident that, in the short run, he need not worry about an Allied attack in the west.

As for Stalin, by averting and deflecting war, even if only for a short while, he got a reprieve to improve Moscow's military preparedness in anticipation of a later reckoning. By virtue of the secret protocol, he held the "deployment positions of the German armies as far to the west as possible,"[136] as several of his senior generals demanded. Predictably, although they declared war on Germany and stepped up rearmament, the Allies took no military action. Bound by a dated defensive mentality and war plan, the French high command marshaled its forces behind the Maginot Line, while across the Channel conscription was barely getting under way. By September 17, 1939, with German troops racing eastward, but ten days before Warsaw's surrender, Stalin sent the Red Army into eastern Poland to at once test and turn to use the letter and spirit of the Russo-German compact. He made a point of occupying "only areas taken from Russia by the Poles in the Treaty of Riga and largely inhabited by Ukrainians and Belorussians."[137] Before long the Kremlin also forced the three Baltic republics—Berlin having ceded Lithuania to Moscow in exchange for Polish lands between the Vistula and Bug rivers—to agree to Russian bases and garrisons on their soil. The Soviets made the same demand on Finland, looking to facilitate the defense of Leningrad and the northeastern salient. When Helsinki balked, on November 30 at least twenty-five divisions moved into Finland to become mired in an embarrassing and costly three-month winter war, sustaining the outside world's understandable doubts about the soundness of the Red Army. The Finnish government eventually ceded the Karelian Isthmus and the shores of Lake Ladoga, but remained master in the rest of the country.

Meanwhile the pact between the two sworn ideological enemies struck Europe's chancelleries and political precincts like a bombshell. It confounded, in particular, millions of Communists as well as millions of sympathizers of Communism and the Soviet Union. In Europe's united-front left, Stalin's cold-blooded sectarian policy in Spain had precipitated a certain disquiet and some prominent defections. No doubt this incipient schism would have snowballed had the secret protocol—reminiscent of the cursed secret treaties of before 1917—been known at the time, along with the ravages of Stalin's terror. But ultimately the disastrous consequences of the democracies' appeasement of the fascist regimes understandably became the grand justification for turning half a blind eye and embracing the lesser of two evils. This was all the more the case since this Allied diplomacy was widely perceived to be deeply marked by the right-wing politics underlying not only most of the outside world's unrelenting animosity to the Russian Revolution, but also its heartless management of the Great Depression.

At home Stalin benefited from seemingly having correctly anticipated the international crisis and the urgency to prepare for it by means of an all-out drive to overcome Russia's dangerous backwardness. Indeed, the cunning of history continued to help Stalin invest the warrant for Socialism in One Country with the fervor of traditional nationalism: by reason of an improbable turn of events, he reestablished Russian control over nearly all the lands ceded after 1917, thereby recovering the strategically critical glacis from Estonia to Bessarabia, along with some 22 million souls, most of them non-Russian. To be sure, his Faustian bargain with Hitler was totally unprincipled. But bearing in mind that Stalin faced a virtual Hobson's choice in a time of extreme peril, perhaps the Nazi-Soviet Pact "should not be added to [the long] list of [his] errors and crimes."[138] Indeed, though "cold-blooded, it was also . . . realistic in a high degree, . . . and it marked the culminating failure of British and French foreign policy and diplomacy over several years."[139]

Between the outbreak of war in September 1939 and Nazi Germany's invasion of the Soviet Union in June 1941, the Kremlin strained every nerve to put off a German attack as long as possible in order to push the training of troops, the production of weapons, and the fortification of frontier zones. A few weeks after the lightning fall of France in June 1940, Hitler ordered his commanders-in-chief to redeploy the bulk of Germany's armed forces from west to east, for an all-out assault on Russia in the fall. When his senior generals insisted that there was not enough time to make preparations and defeat the Red Army before the onset of winter, Hitler reluctantly postponed the assault for one season. Eventually the invasion was set for June 22, 1941. Hitler repeatedly boasted that the scale, speed, and ferocity of the onslaught would be such that the world would "hold its breath." The objective of Operation Barbarossa would be to smash the Red Army, conquer eastern *Lebensraum*, and extirpate "Judeobolshevism."[140]

While Hitler underestimated the Soviet regime and army, as well as the difficulty of the terrain, Stalin kept misjudging Hitler and the dynamics of the Nazi system. In particular, in the spring of 1941 he refused to believe that, notwithstanding the risk of a two-front war, Hitler would strike in June 1941, convinced that the Wehrmacht would not have sufficient time to complete its campaign ahead of Russia's forbidding weather. Overall, however, his incredulity, in the face of credible and convergent indisputable warnings of an imminent invasion, was of the same order as that of France's political and military leaders during the Phony War of the year before. By late spring Stalin was "in a state of confusion, anxiety, demoralization, even paralysis."[141] Only at the eleventh hour did he agree to position additional forces further west.

Lately this frontward deployment has been taken as evidence that in reality Stalin, rather than act indecisively and defensively, was preparing to attack Germany some time in 1941–42, upon completion of his military buildup. Accordingly, mid-1941 "was just about the last possible moment for [the Third Reich] to launch and fight a 'preventive' war" and it is "left to the imagination to contemplate what would have been the fate of Germany and other European countries if instead of giving the order to attack on June 22 Hitler had waited for Stalin to wage the war of extermination he had planned."[142] Actually, in the spring of 1941 Stalin probably was at least as bewildered as on the eve of the Nazi-Soviet Pact; and there is nothing to suggest that he and his generals ever envisaged, let alone planned, either to carry Communism to the heart of Europe or to conduct a Barbarossa-like campaign of premeditated conquest, enslavement, and ethnic cleansing.

Meanwhile, between September 1939 and June 1941 the Soviets tightened their grip on their newly annexed territories, particularly on Poland.[143] Ethnically the Third Poland was severely burdened by the Treaty of Riga: the eastern half had a population of 13 million, of whom over 7 million were Ukrainians, over 3 million Belorussians, and over 1 million Jews. Not surprisingly, unlike the Wehrmacht in German-occupied western Poland, the Red Army was, to a degree, welcomed by these three minorities which, historically, had suffered at the hands of the ruling Polish minority. With some success the Soviets claimed to come as liberators, not conquerors, and here and there they even were met by peasants and workers—led by local Communists and their sympathizers—calling for social and economic reform. But the Kremlin's primary objective was to establish an efficient civil and military administration, which typically involved repressing resistances and enlisting local "collaborators."

Military considerations were paramount. The Red Army created fortified positions inland as well as along the new western border, along the Bug river, and it did so with little regard for local norms, interests, and mores. It also looked to foster security behind military lines.

The drive for political control and security was, of course, by far more systematic and violent. The governments of all the Soviet-annexed countries and territories had been at once politically right-wing and diplomatically anti-Soviet, in several instances overtly pro-German. Immediately following the occupation, the Soviet authorities arrested, above all, high and middle-level government officials as well as army and police officers, and many of them, along with landed magnates, were deported to Russia. Apparently on Stalin's direct order, between 5,000 and 6,000 captured Polish officers were executed, no doubt to cut the ground from under future resistance.

While, for obvious reasons, there were few Jews among these political and military hostages to Fortune, they were disproportionately pounded by the unfolding social-economic sovietization, notably in commerce, banking, and industry. On the other hand, Jews were overrepresented among the collaborators, in that Jews accepted party and government positions, many of them embracing the new regime as the lesser of two evils, all the more so with deadly anti-Semitism ravaging the German half of Poland as part of the Third Reich's conquering racist fury. Incidentally, with the annexed territories, the Jewish population of the Soviet Union rose from 3 million to over 5 million, or fully one-third of all Jews worldwide. Although popular anti-Judaism persisted, probably exacerbated by Jewish collaboration with the Soviets, there seems not to have been any willful or official anti-Semitic discrimination. Indeed, Stalin's agents, unlike Hitler's, were not driven by a cosmic sense of racial and cultural superiority. In the Soviet-occupied territories there was no equivalent of either Reinhard Heydrich or Heinrich Himmler. At the time "the Soviets were . . . somewhat awed, insecure, and intimidated . . . [and] their intentions were [neither] vicious [nor] evil." They applied policies that "were no different from those of the administration at home," which means that they shared and imposed the everyday "hardships . . . [and] arbitrariness of power" that were the earmark of their world.[144] But above all, Hitler considered his part of Poland a corridor for the conquest of *Lebensraum* in the east; Stalin considered his part a defensive bulwark.

There was a second and greater wave of arrests and deportations in 1941, not long before the German invasion. With inordinate concern for military security, many thousands of suspects were exiled to the remote Russian interior. All told, during the twenty-two months of the Phony Peace in the east probably close to one million civilians were deported from the Soviet-annexed lands, some to be confined to work camps, others to be resettled. There were nearly 100,000 Jews among them, mostly refugees from western Poland. Because of the terrible conditions of transport and climatic rigors, the suffering and loss of life is bound to have been considerable. Ironically, in the topsy-turvy world of Europe's most hapless borderland, many of the Jews who were forcibly deported were spared the fires of the Judeocide.

By this time the German half of Poland had become the essential staging ground and logistical base for the ultramodern and superbly equipped army of 3.2 million men which burst into Russia on June 22, 1941. Holding its breath, the world was divided between those who were heartened and those who were terrified by Hitler's prediction that the Wehrmacht needed do no more than "kick in the door" of Soviet Russia for "the entire rotten structure to come crashing down." By all odds the old-new Russia should have crumbled, and it nearly did. Stalin had not made optimal use of his play for time to make the armed forces battle-ready, and he had ignored all storm signals. Clearly, he was momentarily unnerved, not to say panic-struck, by the sheer might of the onslaught which tested the logic of his policy and governance since the Great Turn. Compared to the German assault in the west, which had brought down France in less than six weeks, the blitzkrieg in the east, though infinitely more power-packed and furious, soon began to lose momentum and falter, largely because of the handicap of space. In any case, in terms of space-time the Red Army was able to keep falling back to regroup for defense, compelling the Wehrmacht to keep overextending its supply lines as it raced against the meteorological clock. This forced and improvised defense in depth succeeded despite the loss, during the first six months, of half of Russia's military aircraft, one-third of its capital stock, and one-third of its resource base for grain. Casualties were equally enormous, and the Wehrmacht captured over 2.5 million prisoners. Because of its large demographic reservoir, especially of peasants, the Red Army eventually was able to sacrifice three Russian soldiers for every German soldier.

Of course, there were also less "natural" forces than vast space, ample cannon fodder, and inclement weather to account for the Soviet Union's staying power in the fall of 1941, and its eventual, if difficult and ruinous, victory. Above all, the defense-oriented forced industrialization of the 1930s provided the sinews of modern warfare, and the technique and experience of planning was invaluable. In addition, Russia's immemorial culture of discipline and deprivation turned into an inexhaustible fount of civil and moral energy. On July 3, after recovering his iron will, Stalin proclaimed a *levée en masse* and *dictature de détresse*—in the spirit of the declaration of total war of August 23, 1793[145]—in defense of the Fatherland of Socialism: he called for a Great Patriotic War against Fascism, not a revolutionary war or crusade for Communism. In this "war of the entire Soviet people against the German-fascist armies" there could be "no mercy for the enemy," the rear of the lines would have to be strengthened, "panic-mongers and deserters" would be ruthlessly dealt with, and in case of "forced retreat" the earth would have to be "scorched."[146] From the start the preplanned and wanton savagery of the Wehrmacht and Einsatzgruppen incited and justified Stalin's martial terror in what became a quasi-religious life-or-death struggle between the two largest land armies in recorded history.

In bloodletting, brutality, and destruction there was no common measure between the war in the west and that in the east. The latter felt the full brunt of Nazi Germany's military and genocidal rage: for three years "Barbarossa" was fought on Soviet soil, and it was on the eastern front that the German armies counted four-fifths of their dead, wounded, missing, and prisoners. The USSR suffered between 26 million and 30 million casualties out of a population of 200 million (including the inhabitants of the annexed territories of 1939): over 6 million were killed; some 15 million became invalids or were wounded; and over 4 million were captured or missing, of whom over one-half were slaughtered or died. The 900-day siege of Leningrad, which was wrenched by cannibalism, cost about one million civilian dead and half of Russia's total war dead were civilians. These miseries and disasters of war were compounded by colossal material damage. In this unthinkable total war Ukraine, Belorussia, and the Black Sea region were all but laid waste. With both sides scorching the earth, 1,700 towns and 70,000 villages were leveled, and so were close to 32,000 industrial enterprises. Countless bridges, roads, and railway tracks were destroyed, and the loss of livestock and draft animals was no less massive.

Evidently the Soviet Union paid a monstrous and crippling price for its narrow brush with catastrophe but eventual triumph. Even so, not altogether unexceptionally, the uphill war rallied the people around Stalin and the Soviet leaders, who unfurled the flag of time-honored patriotism and Orthodoxy. It also fostered the legitimacy of the regime, the latest blood sacrifice vindicating the foundation of 1917. The awesome victory seemed to validate the reason of Stalin's Great Turn and the preeminence of the party. Paradoxically, the war which brought wrack and ruin functioned as a forcing house for continuing modernization: it reinforced the system and culture of the command economy along with the party-state, including its radically renovated political, technical, and professional cadres. On the brink of the precipice in late 1941, four years later, in 1944–45, Soviet Russia stood out as the Continent's strongest military power, the Red Army having advanced to the Oder-Neisse line. At first sight Stalin had every reason to gloat or, at any rate, be self-confident. This reading prompted Solzhenitsyn's penetrating but chilling syllogism that in war "governments need victories and the people need defeats": whereas defeat in the Crimean War, the Russo-Japanese War, and the First World War brought Russia "freedom and revolution, . . . the victory over Napoleon [and Hitler]" hardened the existent regimes, "with victory [giving] rise to the desire for more victories."[147]

In reality Stalin was apprehensive and wary. With much of Russia reduced to rubble, Stalin worried that the Allies, in particular the United States, would soon realize that the awe-inspiring Red Army was a Potemkin village dissembling the country's general prostration.

Indeed, not unlike after the civil war and through the 1930s, the Kremlin faced, once again, the impossible problem of integrating Soviet Russia into the world system, including its economy, necessary for reconstruction. The Soviet leaders feared that the Allies would exploit the weakness of the USSR now that its military utility was at an end.

Of course, Allied aid, particularly American Lend-Lease, had been of considerable military importance, notably in 1941–42. But, clearly, the wartime alliance, forged in a time of common peril, was *contre-nature*. On June 22, 1941, when extending unconditional assistance to the Soviet Union, Churchill had been disarmingly plainspoken: conceding that since 1918 he had been the most "consistent opponent of Communism" and insisting that he would "unsay no word [he had] spoken," the British prime minister swore that "all this fades away" now that "the Russian danger is . . . our danger and the danger of the United States."[148] This opposition, which was mutual, was bound to resurface with the turn of the military tide. As the war moved to a close, and the Red Army got the advantage, Stalin and Churchill looked for ways to extend their false-hearted alliance into the immediate afterwar. In October 1944, at Churchill's initiative, they seemed to find common ground in a secret (percentage) agreement defining their respective spheres of influence in eastern and southeastern Europe: Rumania, Bulgaria, and Hungary largely in the Soviet orbit; Greece in the British or Western orbit; Yugoslavia under fifty-fifty tutelage of the two camps. This diplomatic barter was implicitly ratified and broadened at Yalta and Potsdam, where the United Kingdom and the United States assigned to the Soviet Union eastern Poland up to the heretofore contested Curzon Line, compensating Poland with German lands in the west. In any case, this diplomatic logrolling was contingent on the continuing reign of realpolitik, with the reason of state prevailing over ideology.

✳ ✳ ✳

Just as the First World War left a deep imprint on the politics and diplomacy of the period leading into the Second World War, so the First Cold War weighed on the start and development of the Second Cold War. Both cold wars were driven by unstable mixtures of power politics and ideological pretense. At the inception of both, military and diplomatic factors were out front before ideology pulled even or ahead. Whereas ideology was relatively muted during the quarantine years of the 1920s, it again became manifest and strident during the diplomatic death dance of the 1930s.

In 1941, while in the Axis camp the Cold War exploded into hot war, in the Allied camp it went into remission. Since misbegotten wartime alliances are destined to come apart, it is not surprising that the Cold War resurfaced in 1944–45 when Russia and the Western powers recalled their mutual suspicions and conflicts of interest. The Soviets revived bitter memories of the Allied intervention in the civil war, the establishment of hostile regimes along Russia's western borders, the ostracism of Russia from the concert of powers, and the Allied appeasement of Fascism. In turn, the Western powers recalled the cunning of the Comintern and the treachery of the Nazi-Soviet Pact. On both sides, after three years of "normal" relations, there was a surfeit of negative and raw remembrances to feed mistrust and antagonism. In the meantime, incompatible with the spirit of both the Nazi-Soviet Pact and the Grand Alliance, the contrapuntal terms of revolution and counterrevolution vanished from all the belligerents' propaganda, which is not to say that the reality attached to these terms vanished as well. Stalin and Churchill embodied the close kinship between the First and Second Cold War: they were "present at the creation" of both, and they were critical agents of major twists and turns during the transition from the one to the other.

There were, of course, major discontinuities as well. Though bled white, in 1945 the Soviet Union stood forth as the Continent's only militarily credible great power. Simultaneously Berlin, Paris, and London handed over the baton of anti-Communism and anti-Sovietism to Washington, whose instruments of containment would be not only military but also, or markedly, financial, economic, and cultural. Marshal Foch and General Weygand were emblematic of the daybreak of the First Cold War; General George C. Marshall, as secretary of state, was symbolic of the dawn of the Second Cold War.

Neither Soviet Russia nor the United States was practiced and world-wise in international politics. Both were unprepared to assume the responsibilities of their unexpected and unexampled great-power status and to become each other's sworn adversary, not to say enemy.

Indeed, they would have to learn how to engage: the Soviet Union was a Eurasian land power with concrete but vulnerable territorial frontiers to be protected primarily by conventional armed forces; the United States a continental island without exposed strategic borders but with vital if contested spheres of influence to be shielded chiefly by naval, air, and economic power. In terms of security, there was no American equivalent for Soviet Russia's cathectic focus on Eastern Europe. Neither power had a blueprint for ideological or military expansion. Even when making what appeared to be offensive moves, Moscow and Washington believed and claimed to be acting defensively, putatively to preempt an imminent threat from the other. The objective was to improve security or attenuate insecurity, in keeping with the legendary wisdom that in a time of troubles the security of one power or alliance is perceived to be the insecurity of another power or alliance.

In 1944–45, as victorious great powers, the Soviet Union and the United States had radically different profiles. The USSR was, above all, utterly drained and exhausted. The civilian economy was wrecked. Probably Stalin was desperate to conceal the desolation of the Russian economy, especially since it stood in such stark contrast to the American economy, which came out of the war immensely enriched and strengthened. By early 1946, however, military security analysts in Washington concluded that in the short term economic weakness would force Soviet Russia to limit itself to "consolidating its power in Eastern Europe primarily to strengthen its own security" rather than take actions "which might develop into hostilities with the Anglo-Americans."[149] At this same time George F. Kennan, the astute American chargé d'affaires in Moscow, advised the State Department that "gauged against the Western world as a whole the Soviets were still by far the weaker force," which meant that the United States and its Allies could "enter with reasonable confidence" upon a firm course.[150] Frank K. Roberts, Kennan's British counterpart, informed London that partly because of the atom bomb, Russia's rulers realized the "inadequacy" of their navy and air force and that, although confident of the Soviet Union's "ultimate strength," they knew that it was "nothing like so strong at present as the Western democratic world."[151] A year later John Foster Dulles, a hard-line Republican counselor to the

State Department, insisted that with Russia still "weak in consequence of war devastation," its leaders were not about to "consciously risk war," also because its "military establishment is completely outmatched by the mechanized weapons—particularly the atomic weapons—available to the United States."[152]After 1945, with the country bled white, the Kremlin radically reduced the manpower of the Red Army. It did so although worried about sedition in the western periphery, scores of Ukrainians, Belorussians, and Balts having collaborated with the German Wehrmacht and security forces during the war. In any case, preoccupied with security in Eastern Europe and economic reconstruction, and more than ever obsessed with catching up with the West, Stalin was not about to launch his armies on a march to the Atlantic. Like Lenin in the dawn of the First Cold War, he gave absolute priority to making safe the Soviet state and regime.

Meanwhile Stalin and his associates were at once awed and disconcerted by America's daunting capability to project its power to the four corners of the world, partly by claiming the legacy of Europe's overseas empires for itself. By force of habit, and bearing in mind the Great Depression, the Soviet leaders were still convinced that ultimately capitalism carried the seeds of its own destruction. At this juncture, however, they had to come to terms with the unexpected renaissance of capitalism, especially now that America occupied its commanding heights, accounting for a major part of the world's finance capital and industry. In the immediate after-war the Kremlin was less concerned with capitalism's economic inconstancy than its political force: unlike the Soviet economy, the American economy was a formidable source and instrument of instant international power and influence. By 1946, especially in the wake of diplomatic skirmishes between the Soviets and Anglo-Americans along the southern Eurasian rim, Nikolai Novikov, the Russian ambassador in the United States, advised Moscow that "expenditures on the army and navy [were] rising colossally": driven by an "unofficial bloc of reactionary southern Democrats and the old guard of the Republicans," Washington was "establishing a very extensive system of naval and air bases in the Atlantic and Pacific Oceans . . . with many points of support located outside the boundaries of the United States." In Europe and Japan "American occupation authorities . . . were [supporting] reactionary classes and groups" with an eye to "the struggle against the Soviet Union." To this same end, American policy was "directed at limiting or dislodging the influence of the Soviet Union from neighboring countries."[153]

* * *

The first engagements of the Second Cold War came not, as one might have expected, in Eastern Europe, but in Iran, Turkey, and Greece. Britain's imperial decomposition, not to say collapse, left a power vacuum along Eurasia's southern salient, which Moscow could not ignore. Testing wartime agreements with the Allies, the Kremlin looked to refuse the removal of troops from northern Iran with a view to negotiate keeping a foothold there; it also concentrated troops along the Turkish border in an effort to negotiate a revision of the Montreux Convention to give Russia a substantial voice in the control of the Dardanelles. In one reading, in this area, as in Eastern Europe, the Kremlin was moved by a "traditional and instinctive [not to say] neurotic . . . sense of insecurity . . . [and] fear of the outside world."[154] In another, fashioned in London and gradually embraced by Washington, the USSR was heir to tsarist Russia's endemic propensity to expand into a region historically on Britain's imperial watch. As yet no one seriously suggested that this was an early expression of Soviet Communism's inherent expansionism. In any case, once the United States dispatched several warships into the Indian Ocean and eastern Mediterranean to shore up England's failing strength, the Kremlin drew back, partly to husband its limited energy and diplomatic capital for more essential and less risky confrontations, notably in Eastern Europe.

Increasingly with one voice, the United Kingdom and United States considered Soviet Russia's interest in Greece part of the same geostrategic design as its probe in Iran and Turkey. In 1944–45, in line with his agreement with Churchill, Stalin countenanced Britain quelling the resistance-rooted and Communist-led rebellion in Greece and installing a would-be parliamentary monarchy. But starting in mid-1946, during the discord over the Dardanelles, the left-wing partisans rose up again in northern Greece, with help from the Communist regimes of neighboring Yugoslavia, Albania, and Bulgaria. In keeping with the logic of the division of spheres, Stalin reined in the Communists of these embryonic People's Democracies, leaving the rebels at the mercy of the rightist Greek government, backed by British troops and warships. His active non-interference in Greece was intended as a signal to the Allies that he expected them to continue to condone his muscled intervention in Poland, where the Red Army gave Russia the sway that British and American naval and air power exercised in the Arabian and Aegean seas.

Indeed, his eyes fixed on Eastern Europe, Stalin had jumped at Churchill's proposal for mutual accommodation. Bearing in mind the Nazi-Soviet Pact—as well as the treaties of Brest-Litovsk, Versailles, and Riga—Stalin was at once sober and cynical about yet another division of spheres in Eastern and Balkan Europe. To be sure, at Yalta the Big Three had issued the American-made Declaration on Liberated Europe calling for Eastern Europe's provisional governments to be "broadly representative of all democratic elements," to be established "through free elections."[155] But Stalin and Churchill attached little if any importance to this Wilsonian will-o'-the-wisp. Stalin meant to keep control of the western borderlands which in less than thirty years had twice been the staging area and invasion route for enemy armies. In military terms, he considered the rimland running from the eastern shore of the Baltic Sea to the western shore of the Black Sea, particularly its Polish hinge, a question of "life and death." At the time the future status of Germany was altogether uncertain, and Stalin, who "hated" the Germans, expected them to be back on their feet in "twelve to fifteen years."[156] No less important, since he and his inner circle basically thought in conventional military terms, unmindful of long-range aircraft, let alone guided missiles, strategically the forward western space seemed all the more crucial.

This was the mind-set which Stalin brought to the recasting of the polities and societies of the countries liberated by the Red Army. It is important to remember that only yesterday Eastern and Balkan Europe had been a bastion of unmitigated conservatism and reaction. Of course, the countries of this region differed greatly from each other. Even so, by and large, with the partial exception of Czechoslovakia, in major respects they were old regimes.[157] They had been, in addition, the warp and woof of the *cordon sanitaire*. In different degrees their governors had yielded to the Fascist temptation, some to the point of having their countries participate in Operation Barbarossa and the Judeocide. As one might expect, the Kremlin was intent upon aborting the rebirth of governments disposed to resume an anti-Soviet foreign policy and to restore regimes likely to favor such a course.

Meanwhile, throughout Russia's close vicinity as everywhere in Europe, the miseries and disasters of war had considerably strengthened the not inconsiderable opposition to the old ruling and governing classes. To be sure, the presence of the Red Army would weigh very heavily in the transformation of the borderlands. But there was also a powerful indigenous groundswell for a sweeping renewal. A broadly based popular and united front, inclusive of agrarians, pressed for radical de-fascistization as well as drastic land and social reform, along with an entente cordiale with Soviet Russia. The provisional governments which were put in place under Moscow's control were left-leaning but not Communist-dominated coalitions. Depending on the country, they were validated by more or less free elections, and they allowed for considerable civil and cultural freedom. The fledgling regimes—People's Democracies—faced an enormously difficult task. Until the second half of 1947 Stalin had no set mold for the new regimes, nor a blueprint for their satellization.

And yet, almost overnight, in the Western world critics cried out against Moscow's allegedly wily and concerted drive to turn Eastern Europe into a captive and closed sphere of influence impermeable to outside democratic and liberal influences. In turn, this vociferous censure prompted the Kremlin to be on its guard and fight shy of risking continuing openness. Presently not a few sober Allied voices cautioned against prejudging and denouncing the Soviets instead of trying to understand and reassure them. In the United States, where there was a feverish resurgence of anti-Communism and anti-Sovietism fomented by right-wing Republicans and newspapers, Henry L. Stimson, the secretary of war, was troubled that some Americans had "exaggerated views of the Monroe Doctrine" at the same time that they "butt[ed] into every question that comes up in Central Europe . . . and the Balkans."[158] Sharing this concern, Henry A. Wallace, the secretary of commerce, thought it important to "recognize that we have no more business . . . [interfering] in the *political* affairs of Eastern Europe . . . than Russia has interfering in the *political* affairs of Latin America, Western Europe, and the United States, . . . [and] in stirring up . . . native Communists." Wallace considered unexceptional "that the Russians will try to socialize their sphere of influence just as we will try to democratize our sphere of influence" in Japan and Germany. Insisting that Russia would have to meet the Western powers "halfway," he nevertheless cautioned that "the tougher we get the tougher the Russians will get."[159] Subscribing to Stimson's scruples about unilateral nuclear diplomacy, Wallace asked how it would "look to us if Russia had the atomic bomb and we did not, if Russia had 10,000-mile bombers and air bases within a thousand miles of our coastlines and we did not."[160]

✳ ✳ ✳

In 1939, when he repossessed the Eastern European security zone in his Faustian pact with Hitler, Stalin had negotiated from a position of extreme weakness and vulnerability. Eventually the Wehrmacht swept through this zone with lightning speed and ease, and the Red Army did not recapture it until three years later. Henceforth Stalin faced the Western Allies from a position of strength by virtue of Soviet troops occupying the buffer zone and having fought their way to Central Europe.

In any case, Stalin did not flinch when Harry Truman began to harden America's Russian policy and to step up support for Britain: the American president abruptly ended Lend-Lease aid and refused reconstruction loans for Moscow at the same time that he extended financial assistance to London, soon followed by efforts to simultaneously prolong and usurp Britain's role of keeping Russia landlocked. Characteristically, it was Churchill, driven from power by Labour in 1945, who begged off the letter and spirit of his agreement with Stalin to become the first prominent herald of the reversion from realpolitik to ideologically saturated foreign policy and diplomacy. Churchill had declared his impassioned anti-Communism in 1918–19, and between the wars it had informed his sympathy for Mussolini and Franco. But finally the bankruptcy of the tendentious diplomacy of appeasement jolted him into recognizing the sharp pinch of power politics and the reason of state: in 1939 he expressed his understanding for Stalin's pact with Hitler;[161] in 1941 he extended unconditional aid to Moscow; in 1944 he rushed to Moscow to win Stalin for a division of spheres.

On March 6, 1946, speaking in Fulton, Missouri, Churchill, introduced by Truman, predicated that the ancient states and people of Central and Eastern Europe "lie in the Soviet sphere, . . . behind an iron curtain, . . . subject in one form or another, not only to Soviet influence but to a very high and increasing measure of control from Moscow." Although he conceded that the Soviets did not want war, he asserted that they wanted "the fruits of war and the indefinite expansion of their power and doctrine." Especially since there were no limits to the Kremlin's "expansive and proselytizing tendencies," the Western powers, in particular their English-speaking peoples, needed to stand fast and strong so as to give all other peoples a chance at freedom.[162]

Truman applauded Churchill when he sounded the alarm about the Soviets lowering an Iron Curtain from Stettin on the Baltic to Trieste on the Adriatic—a *cordon sanitaire* in reverse—and about their ideologically fired intention to spread "police government" near and far beyond it. Within a year, on March 12, 1947, before a special joint session of Congress, Truman took an additional step from *realpolitik* to *ideopolitik*. To be sure, the Kremlin recently had backed down in Iran, the Straits between European and Asian Turkey, and Greece. But at this juncture, in February 1947, London advised Washington that for budgetary reasons Britain needed to reduce its military and foreign-aid expenditures, necessitating the recall of 40,000 troops from Greece and the termination of financial assistance to Athens and Ankara. This notice was the trigger for Truman and his foreign-policy team to dramatize and justify the need and urgency for a *Pax Americana* to replace the *Pax Britannica*, whose collapse had left a vacuum of international power dangerous for military and economic security across the oceans and continents.

Of course, in keeping with the ongoing projection of U. S. power into the eastern Mediterranean, in his congressional address Truman announced that Washington would guarantee not only the military security of Greece and Turkey but also their economic and political stability, to the amount of 250 and 150 million dollars, respectively. But this conspicuous intervention, which was consistent with wartime agreements, was supported by a sweeping ideological warrant. Truman attributed the crisis in Greece to the "terrorist activities of several thousand armed men, led by Communists," who were "exploiting human want and misery . . . to create political chaos" subversive of economic recovery and government stability. He vowed that henceforth the United States would "support free peoples [everywhere?] who are resisting attempted subjugation by armed minorities or by outside pressures" seeking to impose "totalitarian regimes" on the model of those in Eastern Europe, which violate the Yalta agreement. Indeed, the world had to choose between two "alternative ways of life": that in the Communist orbit feeding on the "evil soil of poverty and strife . . . and based upon the will of a minority forcibly imposed . . . [by] terror and oppression" and the suppression of all civil and political rights; or that in the democratic orbit, based upon the Four Freedoms.[163]

Clearly Truman turned the renewed discord in the eastern Mediterranean into a great virtue and cause, as well as a welcome occasion to put the full weight of the nascent imperial presidency behind the Churchillian vision and tocsin. He raised the ideological wager less to win over a reluctant Congress to vote the credits to salvage Greece and Turkey than to go with the stream. In November 1946 the Republicans, many of them playing on the fear and hatred of Communism, had won control of both Houses. In essence these elections were like those of November 1918:[164] both at once expressed and fired a conservative backlash against social reform and liberal internationalism in the form of aggressive anti-Communism, racism, and diplomatic unilateralism. Swayed by the Red Scare, Woodrow Wilson had sanctioned the Palmer raids in 1919–20. In that same spirit, immediately following his address to Congress, on March 23, 1947, Truman issued an executive order establishing a loyalty program for all federal civil servants, thereby intensifying and legitimating the Red Scare of his day.[165] Of course, the president spoke as much to the Kremlin as to Capitol Hill and Main Street. To make sure that Stalin should get his drift, on March 17 he reiterated some of this declaration's major themes in a message to Congress, with special emphasis on Soviet Russia's violation of the Yalta and Potsdam agreements as well as its "designs to subjugate the free community of Europe." Two days later, equating the Soviets and National Socialists, Secretary of State Marshall declared that "never before in history has the world situation been more threatening to our ideals and interests than at the present time."[166]

All this time throughout the emergent Western orbit, but especially in the United States, distrust and hatred of the Soviet Union intensified. Incongruously, the Kremlin was expected to support the democratization of Eastern Europe, and its failure to do so was construed as the first move of a careful plan to export the Soviet system the world over by means foul and fair. The perception took hold that the regimes in Moscow's sphere were, uniformly and above all, vassal states. Gainsaying the strength and authenticity of local Communist and left-democratic (including agrarian) parties, the censors perceived the drive for socioeconomic reform and diplomatic concord with Russia as an insidious Soviet stratagem. Even Czechoslovakia, which had the most open and vigorous united front, and undertook to serve as a bridge between East and West, was seen and treated as a Soviet satellite. In this tendentious vision the old elites, including the clergy, rather than the embattled popular-front leaders, were the paragons of political virtue. In turn, the Soviets seized upon this hypercriticism to reconsider and curtail their calculated, if awkward, support of non-Communists in the provisional governments of the People's Democracies. The lopsided impasse over the vital nuclear and German questions not only furthered their suspicion of the Western powers but also prompted them to tighten their control on Eastern Europe.

In the West, meanwhile, economic recovery had made major strides until the wretched harvest and winter of 1946–47 exposed the Continent's continuing infirmity. Nature dislocated the national economies, threatening a return of yesterday's distress, hunger, and impoverishment, favoring the treacherous soil on which "domestic and foreign policies meet."[167] Washington feared, above all, the political consequences of this economic relapse: the radicalization of the laboring classes, especially in France and Italy, in favor of Communist parties and their affiliated trade unions, whose leaders risked being outflanked on the left. Although Stalin pressed these leaders to continue collaborating with the governments of national reconstruction, after Truman's address Washington urged Paris and Rome to break with what remained of the popular front. In early May the Communist ministers were dismissed from the French and Italian coalition cabinets, another milestone on the way to the Second Cold War.

Such was the situation and atmosphere when Secretary of State Marshall delivered his carefully vetted and crafted commencement address at Harvard University on June 5, 1947, three months after Truman's address to Congress.[168] He declared Washington's primary purpose to be the conquest of "hunger, poverty, desperation, and chaos," which throughout Europe were causing a grave "economic, social, and political deterioration" with serious consequences for the American economy. Marshall stressed that the United States proposed a policy designed to revive "a working economy in the world so as to permit the emergence of political and social conditions in which free institutions can exist." Having extended assistance "on a piecemeal basis" in response to "various crises" since the end of the war, the American government now proffered an aid program intended as "a cure rather than a mere palliative." But Marshall insisted that in what would have to be a "joint" undertaking, it would be up to the European countries to spell out their needs and "the part they themselves will take."

Certainly Marshall's address had a different tonality from Truman's. The invitation to the European countries to join in a vast program of reconstruction and stabilization was open to the Soviet Union and People's Democracies. Indeed, Marshall emphasized that American policy was "directed not against any country or doctrine." But he also served notice that "governments, political parties, or groups which seek to perpetuate human misery in order to profit therefrom politically or otherwise will encounter the opposition of the United States." Indeed, it is most doubtful that Marshall expected or wanted the Soviets to cooperate.

Seen from Moscow, Marshall's address was as much a defiance as an invitation. Especially in the wake of the dismissal of the Communist ministers in France and Italy, Stalin is likely to have read it as aiming to forge an economic instrument with which to implement the anti-Russian and anti-Communist intention of the Churchill-Truman policy, not to say doctrine, now fixed on the heart rather than periphery of Europe. With distrust running as high among Soviet as Western leaders, Stalin and Molotov were predisposed against exploring the American overture. They were vexed at Moscow having been excluded from the preliminary negotiations between Washington, London, and Paris. They were no less irked that Germany should qualify for aid on the same terms as the countries it had ravaged, and this before German reparations were agreed upon. But above all, Stalin demurred at the likely, nay inevitable interference in the internal affairs of both Soviet

Russia and the People's Democracies. America would demand access to vital statistics at a time when Stalin still sought to hide the full extent of Russia's weakness and handicap. Equally disturbing, by virtue of its demand for an open-ended *right of oversight*, Washington would seek to sway the allocation of resources for Russia's planned economy and Eastern Europe's mixed economies. All in all, Molotov's counterproposal for economic aid without intrusions and strings was as unreal as Marshall's invitation. With hard-liners in the ascendant in both camps, there was little if any room or will for negotiation.

But obviously Washington had the upper hand. Even if unintentionally, it had maneuvered Moscow into turning down a seemingly generous and innocent proposal, reinforcing the perception and charge that the Soviets, incorrigibly intractable, were responsible for the polarization of the world, the more so now that they tightened their grip on the People's Democracies. Desperate for financial aid, but for other weighty reasons as well, most of them were tempted by the American proposal, and Poland and Czechoslovakia actually notified their acceptance, only to be pressured to rescind it.

＊ ＊ ＊

In February 1948 the local Communists seized power, without bloodshed, in Prague: the most democratic and popular of the provisional governments was the first to fall, along with the last bridge between East and West. This takeover symbolized the willful, not to say vengeful turn in the second half of 1947, from the inconstant support of improvised and formless popular-front governments to the peremptory establishment of essentially undifferentiated satellite regimes. Under rigid Soviet control these regimes were also forged into a single diplomatic, military, and economic bloc—Warsaw Pact and Comecon—reinforced by a formidable cultural and ideological carapace. Reenacting Stalin's Great Turn, all the regimes of the Soviet security sphere rushed into forced-draft industrialization and collectivization within the framework of planned economies, for which there was some measure of popular support. Controlled by hard-line Communists loyal to Moscow, the local Communist parties were purged of yesterday's coalitionists; democratic leaders and parties were driven out; and churchmen were prosecuted. Presently, with the secret police firmly in place, there were mass arrests of real and imagined resistants or subversives, and what remained of personal and intellectual freedom was snuffed out.

In Eastern and Balkan Europe—except in Yugoslavia, where Tito stood his ground—Stalin hardened the Communist parties to serve as undisguised instruments of Soviet power, sworn to uphold, above all, Russian hegemony. In the rest of Europe, the role of the Communist parties shifted from supporting to impeding reconstruction and restabilization. Indeed, as Kennan, Truman, and Marshall had forewarned, "as malignant parasites" Communists henceforth would feed on Europe's "diseased tissue," "evil soil of poverty and strife," and "human misery." In keeping with the logic of the situation the Comintern, dissolved during the Grand Alliance, was revived and renamed Cominform in September 1947, signaling this shift in policy as well as the battening down of the Iron Curtain, in keeping with the point of no return on both sides of the unbridgeable divide. Andrei Zhdanov, speaking for the Cominform, proclaimed the world to be divided in two: "the imperialist and anti-democratic camp," chiefly driven by America, whose cardinal purpose is "to strengthen imperialism, hatch a new imperialist war, combat socialism and democracy, and support reactionary and antidemocratic profascist regimes and movements everywhere; . . . the anti-imperialist and democratic camp . . . based in the USSR and the new democracies [whose] purpose is to resist the threat of new wars and imperialist expansion, strengthen democracy, and extirpate the vestiges of fascism." In reverse image of the charge out of Washington, the Kremlin denounced the Marshall Plan as a "carefully veiled attempt to carry through . . . the 'Truman Doctrine's' expansionist policy," beginning with American credits designed to rob the European countries of their "economic and then political independence."[169]

Obviously, the coming of the Second Cold War was an intensely interactive process, to be reconstructed by careful attention to dates. Perhaps the fact that the Western side, starting with Churchill's first move at Fulton, was on the offensive was less important than that it was, in addition, infinitely stronger, except, perhaps, in ideological terms.

The relentless hostility of the major non-Communist powers had contributed significantly to the steeling of the Soviet regime since its creation in 1917: in 1918–20; during the 1930s; and in 1945–48.

Certainly by and large the outside world made few concerted efforts to relax and normalize relations. After 1945 Washington dismissed or ignored Stalin's security concerns on his western borders. Likewise the West, especially the United States, recognized neither the legitimacy nor the complexity of Moscow's resolve to foster the establishment of non-hostile regimes along Russia's vulnerable European frontiers. This same insensitivity, if not hostility, informed President Truman's refusal to extend financial and moral aid to Soviet Russia and the People's Democracies until mid-1947, when it was caught up in the escalating tensions of the Second Cold War. To boot, Washington rattled the nuclear saber, until the Soviets exploded their first atomic bomb in July 1949. All in all, early in the Second Cold War the West, led by the United States, unwarily and confidently played on Russia's weakness and fed the Kremlin's chronic but not entirely groundless siege mentality.

Of course, when making their early probes in Iran and the Dardanelles, the Soviets, just as unwisely, fired Western suspicions and fears, rather than allay them. Especially in America, anti-Sovietism and anti-Communism crystallized too rapidly for Washington to take into account that the "Soviet Union was the successor to the Russian Empire and that Stalin was not only the heir of Marx and Lenin but of Peter the Great and the Tsars of all the Russias."[170] Nor were Washington and London disposed to seriously consider that unlike Hitler's Germany, Stalin's Russia had no "fixed plans" and took no "unnecessary risks,"[171] making its leaders "infinitely more flexible, . . . capable of readjusting, . . . and confident that time was on their side."[172] With Churchill and Truman sounding the alarm, respectively, about the danger of appeasement and the perils of falling dominoes, the Soviet back-down in Iran and Turkey was hailed as a victory over an ideologically driven expansionist regime at once bent and dependent on achieving world ascendancy by a combination of ideological deceit, political subversion, and military brawn. Washington misread or ignored the political and psychological impact on Moscow of turning limited confrontations into "prestige-engaging showdowns." The Kremlin, for its part, was unversed and ingenuous about the "sources" of the "conduct" of American foreign policy and diplomacy, conducive to the projection of its own wishes, phantasms, and fears.

In fact, until 1947–48 Stalin and his advisors practiced, in the main, realpolitik. In addition to being diplomatically cautious but vigilant, they made every effort to bridle and moderate the Communist parties near—throughout Eastern and Balkan Europe—and far—Greece, France, Italy, and China. They did so as part of a self-interested Soviet Russian drive to transform the Second World War's grand but uneasy military, diplomatic, and political alliance into a concert of powers looking to build a new international order respecting the legitimacy and composing the conflicting interests of the major players.

✺ ✺ ✺

It may be helpful to compare France in 1815 and Russia in 1945. Though defeated, France emerged from a quarter century of war essentially unscathed. The fighting had taken place far across the borders, so that the country suffered no material damage. Furthermore, French casualties were not inordinate, the economy was intact, and the victors recognized the loser's prewar borders. France remained the Continent's most advanced, powerful, and influential nation, though England now stood forth as the sole world or global power. As a matter of course, the defeat of Napoleon brought an Allied-sponsored restoration of the monarchy. But this restoration was neither dictated nor absolute, and it validated some of the major achievements of the French Revolution. Reassured by a far-flung *retour à l'ordre*, the great powers recognized the legitimacy of the old-new regime and welcomed France back into the Concert of Powers. All in all, the French Revolution was spared the agonies of protracted quarantine by the outside world, even after its armies convulsed the international system and wrought havoc on not a few provinces of Europe's old order, with more benefits than costs to France.

By contrast, in 1945, even though victorious, Russia was ravaged and spent. At home, twenty-eight years after 1917, the Revolution and regime were strengthened for having weathered a monstrous but also glorious ordeal by fire. Even so, except for China, Soviet Russia was still the most backward of the great powers, determined to resume its prewar drive to catch up to the West. Abroad, throughout liberated Europe, the military defeat of the Axis entailed the political defeat of Fascism along with its conservative and reactionary collaborators and sympathizers. This conservative reflux disproportionately redounded to the benefit of the popular or united fronts which, renewed and galvanized in the resistance, (re)surfaced at the end of the war. As champions of a far-reaching socioeconomic new deal, these coalitions, in which Communists played a major but not paramount role, and which were as discordant as during the 1930s, hearkened to the social promise of the Russian Revolution whose party-state had courted disaster. Upon liberation, Europe witnessed a groundswell for radical reform and renewal, the very opposite of a *retour à l'ordre*, and the attendant revival of the specter of revolution deeply impacted on the diplomacy of the Western governments in the early dawn of the Second Cold War.

Stalin sought to bank rather than fan these flames of social upheaval in the interest of the Kremlin's realpolitik. Like most tsars since Peter the Great, he conceived Russia to be part of Europe, and his projected division of the world into spheres of influence was bound to be Europe-centered. In any case, Stalin looked for the (re)establishment of a concert of great powers which, besides preventing the rebirth of an aggressive and expansionist Germany, would recognize and maintain the postwar territorial settlement and distribution of power. Premised on the mutual recognition of its members, such a concert could resort to the usual balance-of-power mechanisms, such as buffer zones, to attenuate the conflicts of interest inherent to the division of spheres between Soviet Russia and the three Western powers.

Needless to say, immediately after World War Two the situation was much more fluid and contentious than at the conclusion of the Napoleonic Wars. In 1814–15 the victors had been sufficiently united to agree not only on a peace settlement with the defeated enemy (the Treaty of Paris of 1815) but also on a concert of powers to enforce it, along with all European borders. In 1945 the victors were too divided to come to an agreement on the paramount and urgent German question. By virtue of the conflictual political conditions in large parts of Europe, the states also had to confront the difficulty of reconciling the drawing of new territorial lines and spheres with the unresolved constitutional conflicts behind the lines and within the spheres.

Even in 1815, despite the return of normalcy throughout the Continent, the great powers had set up the Holy Alliance to look after, in particular, the maintenance of the European states' internal status quo. As "members of one and the same Christian nation," Europe's sovereigns claimed to share a moral consensus in defense of monarchic legitimacy and social order. Having endorsed the principle of intervention in the internal affairs of sovereign states, in 1820, with the approval of the Holy Alliance, Austria sent troops to help suppress revolts in Naples and Piedmont, and in 1823 France intervened militarily to squash a newly installed constitutional regime in Spain.

At war's end Stalin made every effort to bring about a concert of great powers that would not be coupled with a holy alliance, for which the necessary consensus was in any case wanting: he meant the right of intervention to be reserved to the power exercising hegemony within its sphere. Comforted by his agreement with Churchill, which licensed Moscow's intervention in Eastern Europe in exchange for London's in the eastern Mediterranean, he probably realized that Europe, nay the world, was on the threshold of an era of unprecedented external intervention in the internal affairs of other countries. The instruments of intervention being less military than economic, financial, and cultural, the Kremlin was bound to be at a disadvantage beyond the western lands liberated by the Red Army. As noted before, the United States, without counting the potential of its advanced Western European allies, had many times Soviet Russia's power resources. The Soviet leaders must have been perplexed by the ease and speed with which Washington made huge politically freighted foreign loans and grants-in-aid. Henry Cabot Lodge, Republican senator from Massachusetts, confirmed their worst suspicions, not to say fears, when he declared, in words that could have been their own, that the Marshall Plan would be "the biggest damned interference in internal affairs that there has ever been in history," with the United States assuming responsibility "for the people who stay in power as a result of our efforts."[173] Stalin realized that the United States vastly outstripped Russia in its capacity to project its influence far and wide by not only naval and air power but financial and economic power as well.

Ultimately the Soviets were outclassed on every major score, except ideology. Especially in historical epochs, ideology is a formidable instrument of power at home and abroad. In international politics it serves to justify objectives and actions while at the same time representing them as just and disinterested. Coming out of the war the

Soviet leaders were unshaken, if not fortified, in their belief in progress, socialist construction, economic planning, forced-pace industrialization, and the universal destiny of socialism, with their project serving as universal model and inspiration. But above all, and despite all historical handicaps and war ravages, as well as international obstacles, they continued to be confident that history was on their side. At all events, ideology was the Kremlin's only hope and its only edge for intervention beyond the rimland, in Central and Western Europe.

Ironically, Stalin was neither suited nor disposed to wield the ideological weapon. He never considered ideology separate from the party, which was the spinal cord of the Soviet regime and government and functioned as a military-religious order not only at home but to a large degree abroad as well. With Soviet Russia's national interest his absolute and urgent priority, and obsessed by its multiple deficits, Stalin was as careful not to challenge or provoke the Allies, especially the United States, in Western Europe as he was determined to shield his own sphere of influence from their intrusion. Accordingly, instead of urging the military-religious orders in France and Italy to feed, by word and deed, on the hardships and dislocations of their societies, Stalin directed them to cool their revolutionary ardor and collaborate, in the spirit of the popular front, in postwar governments embarked on reconstruction and reform. Until early spring of 1947 Moscow hoped against hope that its help in moderating the radical political and syndical left during the critical post-liberation moment would pave the way for a mutual desistance of hostile intervention in each other's sphere.

Such was not to be the case. Even assuming the Western governments were aware of Stalin's reason, they were not about to meet him on his ground. They suspected that ultimately Moscow was the command center of all movements for radical or revolutionary change, and assumed that its self-restraint was a short-term expedient, dictated by temporary weakness. In any case, starting with Churchill's Iron Curtain speech in early March 1946, the Western powers, led or pressed by the United States, unceasingly questioned the legitimacy of the invasive primacy of Soviet Russia in Eastern Europe at the same time that they stepped up their charge that everywhere Moscow was infiltrating and subverting free or established governments as part of a design to forcibly expand its totalitarian system to the four corners of the earth. The Kremlin perceived the Truman-Marshall doctrine and plan of action as designed to lock in the Soviet Union and deny it economic aid on acceptable terms while at the same time questioning its probity and ascendance in Eastern Europe.

This renewed isolation, proscription, and boycott unwittingly played into the hands of the hardliners and, above all, of Stalin. If after 1945 there were any historical possibilities for the relaxation of the regime, they were now foreclosed. Once again vindicated and fired by the self-fulfilling prophecy of encirclement by a hostile capitalist world, the Soviet leaders braced the party-state, military-religious order, and planned economy to tackle reconstruction and resume industrialization without foreign aid, in the mode of the 1930s, with outsized attention and allocation of scarce resources to military requirements. The renewed international beleaguerment, at once real and imagined, prepared the ground for the intensification of the politics and culture of fear and suspicion, fueled by the manipulation of the specter of foreign conspiracy. All in all, Soviet Russia turned into a politically run garrison state geared to defense and security rather than foreign aggression and expansion. Of course, Stalin conceived the western periphery to be shielded by this garrison state to include Eastern Europe and the Balkans.

The Kremlin adopted this posture in the face of and in interaction with the adoption of the containment policy by the American-led Western powers. This policy was at once anti-Russian and anti-Communist. In the "Mr. X" article in *Foreign Affairs*, which the Soviet leaders must have read, Kennan merely articulated and structured the ideas that had made their way in American policy-making circles. To be sure, the policy of containment would "confront the Russians with unalterable counter-force" wherever they showed signs of pushing beyond their far-flung perimeter. But the unspoken premise underlying this policy was that the "men in the Kremlin," who were directing Russia's destiny, had never "completed . . . the process of consolidation" started with their seizure of power in November 1917. In more ways than one Russia was "by far the weaker party." Indeed, the United States had the "power to increase enormously the strains under which Soviet policy must operate . . . and in this way promote tendencies which must eventually find their outlet in either the breakup or the gradual mellowing of Soviet power."[174] And so it turned out, for the better or for the worse, and at enormous expense on both sides, as well as in the world at large.

❋ ❋ ❋

NOTES

1. E. H. Carr, *What Is History?* (New York: Knopf, 1962), ch. 2.

2. Ibid., p. 68.

3. Cited in Carr, *Socialism in One Country, 1924–1926* (New York: Macmillan, 1960), p. 278.

4. Ronald Suny, "Stalin and His Stalinism: Power and Authority in the Soviet Union, 1930–53," in Ian Kershaw and Moshe Lewin, eds., *Stalinism and Nazism: Dictatorships in Comparison* (Cambridge: Cambridge University Press, 1997), pp. 26–52, esp. p. 32.

5. Suny, "Stalin and His Stalinism," p. 31.

6. Sheila Fitzpatrick, *The Russian Revolution, 1917–1932* (New York: Oxford University Press, 1982/1994), pp. 100–1.

7. Ibid., p. 104.

8. Alexander Erlich, *The Soviet Industrialization Debate, 1924–1928* (Cambridge, Mass.: Harvard University Press, 1962); Moshe Lewin, *Russian Peasants and Soviet Power: A Study of Collectivization* (London: Allen and Unwin, 1968); James R. Millar and Alec Nove, "A Debate on Collectivization: Was Stalin Really Necessary?" in *Problems of Communism* 25 (July–August 1976): pp. 49–62.

9. Millar in Millar and Nove, "A Debate," p. 56 and p. 60.

10. Suny, "Stalin and His Stalinism," p. 44. Cf. Robert C. Tucker, *Stalin in Power: The Revolution from Above, 1928–1941* (New York: Norton, 1990), ch. 3, esp. pp. 44–45.

11. Suny, "Stalin and His Stalinism," p. 38.

12. Fitzpatrick, *Russian Revolution*, p. 110. See also Tucker, *Stalin*, p. 93 and p. 178.

13. In this paragraph and the next I follow Tucker, *Stalin*, passim, esp. pp. 50–65 and 114–18; Maureen Perrie, "The Tsar, the Emperor, the Leader: Ivan the Terrible, Peter the Great, Anatoli Rybakov's Stalin," in Nick Lampert and Gábor T. Rittersporn, eds., *Stalinism: Its Nature and Aftermath—Essays in Honour of Moshe Lewin* (London: Macmillan, 1992), pp. 77–100; Alec Nove, "Stalin and Stalinism," in Nove, ed., *The Stalin Phenomenon* (London: Weidenfeld and Nicolson, 1993), esp. pp. 6–7. See also chapter 8 above.

14. Cited by Perrie, "The Tsar," p. 81.

15. Tucker, *Stalin*, pp. 328–29.

16. See Nove in Nove, ed., *Stalin Phenomenon*, p. 26.

17. Nove in ibid., pp. 200–201 and p. 20.

18. Tsipko, writing in *Nauka I Zhizn* (no. 12, 1988), cited by Nove in ibid., p. 15.

19. See Moshe Lewin, *Lenin's Last Struggle* (New York: Vintage, 1970).

20. Nove, in Nove, ed., *Stalin Phenomenon*, p. 28 and p. 201.

21. R. W. Davies, *The Soviet Economy in Turmoil, 1929–1930* (Cambridge, Mass.: Harvard University Press, 1989), p. 458.

22. Ibid., p. 460.

23. Cited in ibid., p. 458.

24. Churchill cited in Thomas C. Fiddick, *Russia's Retreat from Poland, 1920: From Permanent Revolution to Peaceful Coexistence* (London: Macmillan, 1990), p. 4.

25. See chapter 8 and chapter 10 above.

26. Fiddick, *Russia's Retreat*, pp. 255–56.

27. Ibid., p. 272.

28. Cited in ibid., p. 273.

29. See John P. Sontag, "The Soviet War Scare of 1926–27," in *The Russian Review* 34:1 (January 1975): pp. 66–77.

30. Cited in Davies, *Turmoil*, p. 442.

31. Ibid., p. 443.

32. Jacques Sapir, "The Economics of War in the Soviet Union during World War II," in Kershaw and Lewin, eds., *Stalinism and Nazism*, pp. 208–36, esp. pp. 211–12, 227.

33. Cited in Davies, *Turmoil*, p. 444 and p. 449. See also John Erickson, *The Soviet High Command: A Military-Political History, 1918–1941* (London: Macmillan, 1962), pt. 4.

34. Davies, *Turmoil*, pp. 453–54.

35. Ibid., pp. 454–55.

36. Cited in ibid., p. 446.

37. Ibid., pp. 446–47.

38. J. V. Stalin, *Works*, vols. 12 and 13 (Moscow: Foreign Language Publishing House, 1955), vol. 12, pp. 242–44.

39. Eugen Varga, *Die Krise des Kapitalismus und ihre politischen Folgen* (Frankfurt: Europäische Verlagsanstalt, 1969).

40. Stalin, *Works*, vol. 12, pp. 261–62.

41. Stalin, *Works*, vol. 13, pp. 40–41.

42. Davies, *Turmoil*, p. 467.

43. Stephen Kotkin, *Magnetic Mountain: Stalinism as a Civilization* (Berkeley: University of California Press, 1995); and Anne D. Rassweiler, *The Generation of Power: A History of Dneprostroi* (New York: Oxford University Press, 1988).

44. Fitzpatrick, *Russian Revolution*, p. 119.

45. Roberta T. Manning, "The Soviet Economic Crisis of 1936–1940 and the Great Purges," in J. Arch Getty and Roberta T. Manning, eds., *Stalinist Terror: New Perspectives* (Cambridge: Cambridge University Press, 1993), pp. 116–41, esp. pp. 132–35.

46. Davies, *The Socialist Offensive: The Collectivization of Soviet Agriculture, 1929–1930* (Cambridge, Mass.: Harvard University Press, 1980), p. 6.

47. Ibid., p. 399.

48. Ibid., p. 399. See also Stephen F. Cohen, *Bukharin and the Bolshevik Revolution: A Political Biography, 1888–1938* (New York: Knopf, 1973), ch. 9.

49. Fitzpatrick, *Russian Revolution*, p. 117.

50. J. Arch Getty, "The Politics of Stalinism," in Nove, ed., *Stalin Phenomenon*, pp. 132–33.

51. Lewin, *Russian Peasants*, pp. 516–19.

52. Stalin, *Works*, vol. 12, esp. p. 183.

53. Nove, in Nove, ed., *Stalin Phenomenon*, p. 36.

54. See Lynne Viola, *The Best Sons of the Fatherland: Workers in the Vanguard of Soviet Collectivization* (New York: Oxford University Press, 1987).

55. Davies, *Socialist Offensive*, p. 411.

56. Ibid., p. 414.

57. Ibid., p. 412.

58. Fitzpatrick, *Russian Revolution*, p. 127. See also Fitzpatrick, *Stalin's Peasants: Resistance and Survival in the Russian Village after Collectivization* (New York: Oxford University Press, 1994).

59. Fitzpatrick, *Russian Revolution*, p. 127.

60. Ibid., pp. 128–29.

61. Viola, "The Second Coming: Class Enemies in the Soviet Countryside, 1927–1935," in Getty and Manning, eds., *Stalinist Terror*, pp. 65–98, esp. p. 96.

62. Manfred Hildermeier, *Geschichte der Sowjetunion, 1917–1991: Entstehung und Niedergang des ersten sozialistischen Staates* (Munich: Beck, 1998), pp. 392–98; and Ronald Suny, *The Soviet Experiment: Russia, the USSR, and the Successor States* (New York: Oxford University Press, 1998), p. 226.

63. Viola, "The Second Coming," pp. 70–75 and 95–96.

64. Davies, *Socialist Offensive*, p. 413.

65. Ralf Stettner, *"Archipel GULag": Stalins Zwangslager—Terrorinstrument und Wirtschaftsgigant: Entstehung, Organisation und Funktion des sowjetischen Lagersystems, 1928–1956* (Munich: Ferdinand Schöningh, 1996), p. 13 and p. 323.

66. See chapter 8 above.

67. Stettner, *"Archipel GULag,"* p. 42 and p. 364.

68. Ibid., p. 365.

69. See chapter 8 above.

70. Stettner, *"Archipel GULag,"* p. 45.

71. Ibid., p. 49.

72. Ibid., pp. 112–13.

73. Ibid., pp. 117–22.

74. Ibid., pp. 168–69.

75. Robert W. Thurston, *Life and Terror in Stalin's Russia, 1934–1941* (New Haven: Yale University Press, 1996), p. 106.

76. Stettner, *"Archipel GULag,"* pp. 173–74.

77. See Appendix 2 in ibid., pp. 376–98.

78. Ibid., pp. 188–89.

79. See Jean-Michel Chaumont, *La concurrence des victimes: Génocide, identité, reconnaissance* (Paris: Découverte, 1997).

80. Carl J. Friedrich and Zbigniew K. Brzezinski, *Totalitarian Dictatorship and Autocracy*, 2nd ed. (Cambridge, Mass.: Harvard University Press, 1965), p. 189.

81. Getty, *Origins of the Great Purges: The Soviet Communist Party Reconsidered, 1933–1938* (Cambridge: Cambridge University Press, 1985), p. 38.

82. Friedrich and Brzezinski, *Totalitarian Dictatorship*, p. 89.

83. Getty, *Great Purges*, pp. 48–56.

84. Thurston, *Life and Terror*, pp. 29–33.

85. Roy A. Medvedev, *Let History Judge: The Origins and Consequences of Stalinism* (New York: Knopf, 1972), p. 137.

86. Robert Sharlet, "Soviet Legal Culture," in Robert C. Tucker, ed., *Stalinism: Essays in Historical Interpretation* (New York: Norton, 1977), pp. 155–79, esp. p. 164.

87. Getty, "The Politics of Repression Revisited," in Getty and Manning, eds., *Stalinist Terror*, pp. 40–62, esp. pp. 41–42. See also Moshe Lewin, "Stalin in the Mirror of the Other," in Kershaw and Lewin, eds., *Stalinism and Nazism*, pp. 107–34.

88. Getty, "Politics of Repression," p. 62.

89. See Tucker, *Stalin*, pp. 120–21, 211–15; and Vadim Z. Rogovin, *1937: Stalin's Year of Terror* (Oak Park, Mich.: Mehring Books, 1998).

90. Cited in Thurston, *Life and Terror*, pp. 16–17.

91. Ibid., pp. 21–22. See also Getty, "Politics of Repression," pp. 44–47.

92. Thurston, *Life and Terror*, pp. 9–15. See also Getty, "Politics of Repression," pp. 50–51.

93. Manning, "The Soviet Economic Crisis," pp. 117–18, 138.

94. Ibid., pp. 140–41, 137–38.

95. William Evans Scott, *Alliance against Hitler: The Origins of the Franco-Soviet Pact* (Durham, N.C.: Duke University Press, 1962); Jiri Hochman, *The Soviet Union and the Failure of Collective Security, 1934–1938* (Ithaca, N.Y.: Cornell University Press, 1984), ch. 2; Piotr S. Wandycz, *The Twilight of French Eastern Alliances, 1926–1936* (Princeton: Princeton University Press, 1988), chs. 11–13.

96. Jonathan Haslam, "Political Opposition to Stalin and the Origins of the Terror in Russia, 1932–1936," in *The Historical Journal* 29:3 (1986): pp. 395–418, esp. p. 413.

97. This and the following two paragraphs give the essence of Isaac Deutscher's insightful if telescoped comparison of the defining circumstances of the Great Terror in the French and Russian revolutions. Deutscher, *Stalin: A Political Biography* (New York: Oxford University Press, 1967), pp. 345–48.

98. Stalin cited in Deutscher, *Stalin*, p. 347.

99. See Sharlet, "Soviet Legal Culture," p. 164.

100. Fred E. Schrader, *Der Moskauer Prozess, 1936: Zur Sozialgeschichte eines politischen Feindbildes* (Frankfurt: Campus, 1995); and Rogovin, *1937*, passim.

101. Ezhov cited by Boris A. Starkov, "Narkom Ezhov," in Getty and Manning, eds., *Stalinist Terror*, pp. 21–39, esp. pp. 25–26.

102. Cited by Starkov, "Narkom Ezhov ," p. 27.

103. Thurston, *Life and Terror*, pp. 36–42, esp. p. 39 and p. 41.

104. Cited in ibid., p. 43.

105. Cited in Medvedev, *Let History Judge*, p. 174. At this very time, Bukharin was writing a two-volume treatise on "The Crisis of Capitalist Culture and Socialism" whose central concern is the total antithesis or opposition of Soviet Socialism and Fascism. Only the second volume, written in jail in March–April 1937, has been recovered. Bukharin, *Gefängnisschriften 1: Der Sozialismus und seine Kultur* (Berlin: BasisDruck, 1996).

106. Cited in Getty, *Great Purges*, p. 138.

107. Cited in ibid., p. 139.

108. Deutscher, *Stalin*, p. 379.

109. Thurston, *Life and Terror*, p. 54. See also Fiddick, *Russia's Retreat*, p. 276. Cf. Rogovin, *1937*, chs. 46–54.

110. Thurston, *Life and Terror*, p. 56.

111. Deutscher, *Stalin*, p. 379.

112. Thurston, *Life and Terror*, pp. 121–23.

113. Roger R. Reese, "The Red Army and the Great Purges," in Getty and Manning, eds., *Stalinist Terror*, pp. 198–214, esp. p. 199; and Erickson, *Soviet High Command*, pt. 5.

114. Getty, *Great Purges*, p. 167.

115. Hildermeier, *Geschichte*, p. 451.

116. Thurston, *Life and Terror*, pp. 61–62.

117. Ibid., pp. 59–61, 63; and J. Arch Getty, Gábor T. Rittersporn, and Viktor N. Zemskov, "Victims of the Soviet Penal System in the Pre-War Years: A First Approach on the Basis of Archival Evidence," in *American Historical Review* 98:4 (October 1993): p. 1023.

118. Thurston, *Life and Terror*, pp. 59–61, 63, 68.

119. See Lewin, *Lenin's Last Struggle*, passim.

120. Thurston, *Life and Terror*, p. 42.

121. Friedrich and Brzezinski, *Totalitarian Dictatorship*, p. 189.

122. Stalin, *Works*, vol. 14 (London: Red Star Press, 1978), p. 421.

123. Deutscher, *Stalin*, p. 380. See also Rogovin, *1937*.

124. Hannah Arendt, *The Origins of Totalitarianism*, 2nd enlarged ed. (New York: Meridian, 1958), pp. 321–22; and Arendt in Carl J. Friedrich, ed., *Totalitarianism* (New York: Grosset and Dunlap, 1964), p. 79.

125. Medvedev, *Let History Judge*, p. 306 and p. 308.

126. Gábor T. Rittersporn, *Simplifications staliniennes et complications soviétiques: Tensions sociales et conflits politiques en URSS, 1933–1953* (Paris: Editions des Archives Contemporaines, 1988), p. 32 and p. 140.

127. Thurston, *Life and Terror*, p. 90.

128. Ibid., p. 159 and p. xx. See Ian Kershaw, *The 'Hitler Myth': Image and Reality in the Third Reich* (New York: Oxford University Press, 1987).

129. Fitzpatrick, *Russian Revolution*, p. 157.

130. Rittersporn, "The Omnipresent Conspiracy: On Soviet Imagery of Politics and Social Relations in the 1930s," in Getty and Manning, eds., *Stalinist Terror*, pp. 99–115.

131. Medvedev, *Let History Judge*, p. 372.

132. Cited in ibid., p. 374.

133. Donald Cameron Watt, *How War Came: The Immediate Origins of the Second World War, 1938–1939* (New York: Pantheon, 1989); and Geoffrey Roberts, *The Soviet Union and the Origins of the Second World War: Russo-German Relations and the Road to War, 1933–1941* (New York: St. Martin's, 1995).

134. Arendt, *Origins*, p. 392 and pp. 414–15.

135. Joachim Hoffmann, *Stalins Vernichtungskrieg, 1941–1945* (Munich: Verlag für Wehrwissenschaften, 1995), chs. 1–2; and François Furet, *Le passé d'une illusion: Essai sur l'idée communiste au XX siècle* (Paris: Laffont/Calmann, 1995), ch. 9.

136. Winston S. Churchill, *The Gathering Storm* (Boston: Houghton Mifflin, 1948), p. 393.

137. Suny, *The Soviet Experiment*, p. 303. See also Hugh Seton-Watson, *Neither War nor Peace: The Struggle for Power in the Postwar World* (New York: Praeger, 1960), p. 24.

138. Medvedev, *Let History Judge*, p. 441.

139. Churchill, *Gathering Storm*, pp. 393–94.

140. Arno J. Mayer, *Why Did the Heavens Not Darken? The "Final Solution" in History* (New York: Pantheon, 1988), ch. VII.

141. Nikita Khrushchev, cited in Richard Overy, *Russia's War: Blood upon the Snow* (New York: TV Books/Penguin Putnam, 1997), pp. 93–97, esp. p. 97.

142. Hoffmann, *Stalins Vernichtungskrieg*, p. 61 and p. 298.

143. Jan T. Gross, *Revolution from Abroad: The Soviet Conquest of Poland's Western Ukraine and Western Belorussia* (Princeton: Princeton University Press, 1988); and Dov Levin, *The Lesser of Two Evils: Eastern Jewry under Soviet Rule, 1939–41* (Philadelphia: Jewish Publication Society, 1995).

144. Gross, *Revolution from Abroad*, p. 230.

145. "From this moment until that in which our enemies shall have been driven from the territory of the Republic, all Frenchmen are permanently requisitioned for service in the armies.

"The young men shall fight; the married men shall forge weapons and transport supplies; the women will make tents and clothes and will serve in the hospitals; the children will make up old linen into lint; the old men will have themselves carried into the public squares to rouse the courage of fighting men, to preach the unity of the Republic and hatred of Kings.

"The public buildings shall be turned into barracks, the public squares into munitions factories, the earthen floors shall be treated with lye to extract saltpetre [for the manufacture of gunpowder].

"All firearms of suitable calibre shall be turned over to the troops; the interior shall be policed with shotguns and with cold steel.

"All saddle horses shall be seized for the cavalry; all draft horses not employed in cultivation will draw the artillery and supply-wagons." Cited in T.C.W. Blanning, *The French Revolutionary Wars, 1787–1802* (London: Arnold, 1996), pp. 100–1.

146. For the text of this radio broadcast, see Marshal Stalin, *On the Great Patriotic War of the Soviet Union* (London: Hutchinson, n.d.), pp. 5–9.

147. Alexander Solzhenitsyn, *The Gulag Archipelago, 1918–1956*, vol. 1 (London: Collins/Fontana, 1974), p. 272.

148. Robert Rhodes James, ed., *Winston S. Churchill: His Complete Speeches, 1897–1963*, vols. VI and VII (New York: Chelsea House, 1974), vol. VI, pp. 6427–31.

149. Naval Intelligence memorandum, January 12, 1946, cited in Joyce and Gabriel Kolko, *The Limits of Power: The World and United States Foreign Policy, 1945–1954* (New York: Harper, 1972), p. 33.

150. George F. Kennan, " 'Long Telegram' " (February 22, 1946) in Kenneth M. Jensen, ed. *Origins of the Cold War: The Novikov, Kennan, and Roberts 'Long Telegrams' of 1946* (Washington, D.C.: United States Institute of Peace, 1991), p. 29.

151. Roberts telegram (March 17, 1946), in Jensen, ed., *Cold War*, p. 54.

152. Cited in Kolko, *Limits of Power*, p. 33.

153. Nikolai Novikov telegram on "U.S. Foreign Policy in the Postwar Period" (September 27, 1946), in Jensen, ed., *Cold War*, pp. 3–16.

154. Kennan, "Long Telegram," pp. 20–21.

155. Cited in John Lewis Gaddis, *Russia, the Soviet Union and the United States: An Interpretive History*, 2nd ed. (New York: McGraw-Hill, 1990), p. 164.

156. Cited in Thomas G. Paterson, *On Every Front: The Making of the Cold War* (New York: Norton, 1979), pp. 150–51.

157. For the sense in which I use the term *old regime*, see my *The Persistence of the Old Regime: Europe to the Great War* (New York: Pantheon, 1981).

158. Cited in Paterson, *On Every Front*, p. 40.

159. Cited in Richard J. Walton, *Henry Wallace, Harry Truman, and the Cold War* (New York: Viking, 1976), pp. 103–5.

160. Cited in ibid., p. 90.

161. See Churchill's broadcast of October 1, 1939, cited in James, ed., *Winston Churchill*, pp. 6160–64. This is the radio talk in which Churchill spoke of Russia as "a riddle wrapped in a mystery inside an enigma," to which Russia's "national interest" might provide "a key."

162. Cited in James, ed., *Churchill*, vol. VII, pp. 7285–93.

163. For the text of President Truman's address, see Joseph M. Jones, *The Fifteen Weeks: February 21 to June 5, 1947* (New York: Viking, 1955), pp. 269–74.

164. For the congressional elections of November 1918, see Mayer, *Politics and Diplomacy of Peacemaking: Containment and Counterrevolution at Versailles, 1918–1919* (New York: Knopf, 1967), ch. 4.

165. Richard M. Freeland, *The Truman Doctrine and the Origin of McCarthyism: Foreign Policy, Domestic Politics, and Internal Security, 1946–1948* (New York: Knopf, 1972), ch. III; and David Caute, *The Great Fear: The Anti-Communist Purge under Truman and Eisenhower* (New York: Harper, 1979), pt. 1.

166. Cited in John C. Campbell, ed., *The United States in World Affairs, 1947–1948* (New York: Harper, 1948), p. 507.

167. Kennan, "Long Telegram," p. 31.

168. For the text of Marshall's speech, see Jones, *Fifteen Weeks*, pp. 281–84.

169. Andrei Zhdanov in *For a Lasting Peace, For a People's Democracy*, No. 1 (September 1947), cited in Gales Stokes, ed., *From Stalinism to Pluralism: A Documentary History of Eastern Europe Since 1945*, 2nd ed. (New York: Oxford University Press, 1996), pp. 40–41.

170. Walter Lippmann, *The Cold War: A Study in U. S. Foreign Policy* (New York: Harper, 1947), p. 30.

171. Kennan, "Long Telegram," p. 29.

172. Roberts, telegram, in Jensen, ed., *Cold War*, p. 53.

173. Cited in Paterson, *On Every Front*, p. 61.

174. Cited in George F. Kennan, *American Diplomacy, 1900–1950* (Chicago: University of Chicago Press, 1951), p. 111 and pp. 126–27.

INDEX

* * *

Abbaye prison, 182, 192
Act of Tolerance for Protestants (France), 433
Adeo nota (Pius VI), 432
Alexander I (Tsar of Russia), 236, 581, 588
Alexander III (Tsar of Russia), 236
Alexeev, Mikhail, 251, 252
"Allocution on the Death of Louis XVI" (Pius VI), 434–35
American Revolution (1776), 26–27, 114–15. *See also* United States
Anglo-Russian Trade Treaty (1921), 621
anti-Jewish pogroms (Russia), 290, 311, 383, 505, 513–25. *See also* Jews
anti-philosphes. *See* counterrevolution
anti-Protestantism: conspiracy myths and, 485–86; counterrevolutionaries and, 490–91. *See also* Protestants
anti-revolution, 7, 58–59. *See also* counter-revolution
anti-Semitism: Bolshevik silence on, 523–25; during Ukraine rebellion, 515–26; Lenin's criticism of, 512, 524; religious dimension of, 486–87; Russian, 63, 65, 290, 311, 383, 464, 485, 502–8. *See also* Jews
Anti-Soviet Trotskyite Center, 654–55
Antonov, Alexander, 389, 390
Antonov-Ovseenko, Vladimir, 252, 393
Arendt, Hannah, 3, 4, 9, 16, 23, 24, 31, 37, 40–41, 73, 83–84, 98, 112–15
Aristotle, 130
d'Artois, Comte, 48, 187, 549, 553, 591, 593, 596. *See also* Charles X (France)
Aulard, Alphonse, 154–55, 156, 157, 438
Auschwitz, 346–48. *See also* anti-Semitism
Austria: battle of Leipzig and, 580; French victories over, 574; war between France and, 197, 553–54, 564
authority: force element of, 74–75; Weber's construction of, 80. *See also* sovereignty
Avignon prison massacre (1791), 502

Bacon, Francis, 132
Barère de Vieuzac, Bertrand, 197, 333–34, 354
Barruel, Abbé Augustin, 61

Bastille (1789), 48, 85, 94
Becker, Carl, 145
Beilis affair (1911–13), 65, 483, 485, 507
Benedict XIV, Pope, 435
Berdyaev, Nicolas, 145, 162
Bernis, Cardinal François-Joachim de Pierre de, 426, 433
Berry, Duc de, 592
Bertier de Sauvigny, L.-B.-F., 85
Bibliothèque Nationale (Paris), 45
Bignon commission (Vendée rebellion), 344–45
Billaud-Varenne, Jean Nicolas, 105, 107–8, 198, 338
Blanc, Louis, 183, 218
Bloch, Ernst, 135
Bloch, Marc, 25
Blücher, Gebhard Lehrecht von, 580, 586
Blue Terror. *See* Red Terror (France)
Bodin, Jean, 99
Boky, Gleb, 281
Bolsheviks: Brest-Litovsk pressed by, 270; civil war legacy to, 405–6; collaboration/break with Makhnovites, 382, 385, 386; compared to Jacobins, 231; comparison of French terror to, 651–53; foreign intervention fought by, 11, 263–64; international isolation of, 12–13, 32, 34, 66, 613–14; Jews among, 509–13; Kronstadt revolt and, 398–403; Orthodox Church relations with, 461–78; peasantry and the, 58–59, 374, 375–76, 404; politics religionized by, 144–45; provisional government set up by, 245–47; resistance to, 49, 50; response to attempt on Lenin's life, 278–82; response to sovereignty collapse by, 282–84; revolutionary goals of the, 29; Russia's prison/exile literature and, 239; Samara government challenge to, 265; silence regarding anti-Semitism, 523–25; social base during 1917 election of, 247–48; sovereignty breakdown and rise of, 36, 49; split between Socialist Revolutionaries and, 270–72; Stalin purges of, 645–46; torn between domestic/international affairs, 302–4;